William S. Burroughs

Cutting Up the Century

William S. Burroughs

Cutting Up the Century

Edited by
Joan Hawkins
and
Alex Wermer-Colan

CONTRIBUTING EDITORS
Charles Cannon, Tony Brewer, and Landon Palmer

INDIANA UNIVERSITY PRESS

This book is a publication of

Indiana University Press
Office of Scholarly Publishing
Herman B Wells Library 350
1320 East 10th Street
Bloomington, Indiana 47405 USA

iupress.indiana.edu

Library of Congress
Cataloging-in-Publication Data

Names: Hawkins, Joan, [date] editor. |
    Wermer-Colan, Alex, editor. |
    Harris, Oliver (Oliver C. G.)
Title: William S. Burroughs cutting
    up the century / edited by Joan
    Hawkins and Alex Wermer-Colan ;
    contributing editors: Charles Cannon,
    Tony Brewer, and Landon Palmer.
Description: Bloomington : Indiana
    University Press, 2019. | Includes
    bibliographical references and index.
Identifiers: LCCN 2018023308 (print) |
    LCCN 2018026007 (ebook) | ISBN
    9780253041364 (e-book) | ISBN
    9780253041326 (hardback : alk. paper) |
    ISBN 9780253041333 (pbk. : alk. paper)
Subjects: LCSH: Burroughs, William S.,
    1914–1997—Criticism and interpretation. |
    Cut-ups (Literary form)
Classification: LCC PS3552.U75
    (ebook) | LCC PS3552.U75 Z933 2019
    (print) | DDC 813/.54—dc23
LC record available at https://
    lccn.loc.gov/2018023308

2 3 4 5 24 23 22 21 20 19

CONTENTS

ACKNOWLEDGMENTS

We would like to thank James Grauerholz and Yuri Zupancic of the Burroughs Estate and Jeffrey Posternak of the Wylie Agency for their help and support for this volume, and for permission to publish a selection of archival materials. Without James Grauerholz's long-term friendship with Burroughs in the last third of his life, and without his continued stewardship over Burroughs' oeuvre, the vast majority of scholarship represented by this anthology would never have been possible. Special thanks also go to Oliver Harris, not only for his contributions to the volume, but for his help, support, and guidance throughout.

We would like to thank the librarians, archivists, and staff, especially Isaac Gewirtz, Lyndsi Barnes, and Joshua McKeon, at the New York Public Library's Henry W. and Albert A. Berg Special Collections, for their assistance over many years of research. Our gratitude for further archival reproductions extends to Robert Spindler and his staff at Arizona State University Hayden Library's Rare Books and Manuscripts, and Marvin Taylor and his staff at the Fales Downtown Special Collections of New York University Library, as well as librarians and staff at the History Colorado's Stephen H. Hart Library. We are also grateful for permission to publish photographs from Chris Kraus at *Semiotext(e)*, Anne Waldman, H. R. Hegnauer, Barry Miles, Peter Hale at the Allen Ginsberg Estate, and Henry Holt and Company.

It would have been impossible to compile the collection without financial and institutional support from Indiana University. We would like to thank the Office of the Vice Provost for Research, especially Ed Comentale, for the two grants we received: the Grant-in-Aid of Research and the Emergency Grant-in-Aid of Research. We would also like to thank the Media School for research funds and institutional support, our editorial assistants Landon Palmer and Zeynep Yasar, and the College Arts and Humanities Institute. The Media School and the Cinema and Media Studies Unit also gave generous grants that enabled us to include color prints. Finally, to Paige Rasmussen, our editor at Indiana University Press, we owe a huge debt of thanks.

The idea for this collection grew out of two conferences, held in 2014, to commemorate the centennial of Burroughs' birth. We would like to thank the organizers of the Burroughs Century Conference at Indiana University and the members of the Burroughs Century Board—especially Tony Brewer, Charles Cannon, Joan Hawkins, Laura Ivins, Peter LoPilato, James Paasche, and Jon Vickers for their continued support and interest in this volume. We would also like to thank Alex Wermer-Colan, as well as staff at the Center for Humanities, especially Aoibheann Sweeney, Kendra Sullivan, Sampson Starkweather, and Shea'la Finch, for organizing the William S. Burroughs Centennial Conference at the Graduate Center of the City University of New York. To the writers who participated in the conferences, and/or contributed essays for this volume, thank you for your work and for your patience as we compiled the volume. This anthology owes a huge debt to all the scholars who have helped to open the field of Burroughs scholarship: we could not have created this anthology without, among many others, James Grauerholz, Barry Miles, Oliver Harris, Jed Birmingham, Timothy Murphy, Jamie Russell, Davis Schneiderman, Jenny Skerl, Robin Lydenberg, Keith Seward, Michael Stevens, and Ian MacFadyen.

And finally, our indebtedness to William S. Burroughs. As Lou Reed once famously said, "Without William, there is nothing. Everything would have stayed the same. The genius to move things beyond—to improve the subject—requires strength. . . . Burroughs made us pay attention to the realities of contemporary life and gave us the energy to explore the psyche without a filter. . . . Welcome Dr. Benway."

BIOGRAPHICAL TIMELINE

We have included the biographical details important to this volume, but this is not a comprehensive overview of Burroughs' life. Similarly, we have listed the most well-known Burroughs' works, along with their revisions and subsequent editions. This is not an exhaustive list of Burroughs' publications. For a complete account of his sixty-eight published books, see the Bibliography in Barry Miles, *Call Me Burroughs: A Life* (2014). There are two good biographies: Ted Morgan, *Literary Outlaw: The Life and Times of William S. Burroughs* (W. W. Norton, 2012; first published 1988) and Barry Miles, *Call Me Burroughs: A Life* (Twelve, 2014).

February 5, 1914	Born William Seward Burroughs II, in St. Louis, Missouri, into a wealthy St. Louis family, grandson and namesake of the inventor of the Burroughs Adding Machine and founder of the Burroughs corporation, William Seward Burroughs I, as well as nephew of public relations manager Ivy Lee.
1920–1926	Attends Community School in St Louis. Some evidence that Burroughs was sexually molested by his nanny and her boyfriend.
1926–1929	Attends John Burroughs School in St. Louis.
1927	Reads Jack Black's *You Can't Win* (1926), the autobiography of an opium-smoking safecracker and itinerant stick-up man, a book that left a lasting impression. The Johnson family depicted in the memoir offered an alternative to the kind of hypocrisy Burroughs saw in segregated St. Louis.
	Burroughs meets David Kammerer (the man killed by Lucien Carr) but doesn't really get to know him until later. He also meets Kells Elvins, who becomes an important friend and early collaborator. Burroughs publishes first written work, an essay in the *John Burroughs Review*, a school magazine.

1929–1930	Los Alamos Ranch School, New Mexico. Private ranch school for boys featuring a rigorous outdoors program. Other famous alumni include Gore Vidal and Arthur Wood. Some evidence that the headmaster was a pedophile. In November 1942, the school and surrounding land was purchased by the US government Manhattan Project. The thought that the school was used to develop the atomic bomb haunted Burroughs for much of his life. Burroughs left St. Alamos when he realized he'd become fixated on a boy who had become hostile. He already suspected he was homosexual, the relationship with William Fawcett confirmed it in his mind.
1931–1932	Taylor School, St. Louis.
1932–1936	Harvard University, studies English.
1936–1937	Travels to Europe and studies medicine at University of Vienna.
1937	Marries Ilse Klapper, a Jewish friend, so she can emigrate to the United States and avoid Nazi persecution. They never live together, but see each other socially in New York until Ilse returns to Europe in 1945. They divorce in 1946.
1937–1938	Returns to New York and studies psychology at Columbia.
1938–1940	Enrolls in a graduate program in archaeology at Harvard; co-writes "Twilight's Last Gleaming" with Kells Elvins. Studies anthropology.
1939–1941	Applies four times to serve in various branches in the military; turned down each time.
1940	Cuts off finger in late April, perhaps in an act of self-mutilation to impress an unfaithful boyfriend. Admitted to Payne Whitney Psychiatric Clinic through late May. Then returns to St. Louis.
1942	Volunteers for US Army at Jefferson Barracks, St. Louis. Accepted as private first class; with his mother's help discharged by fall.
1942–1943	In Chicago, working as an exterminator and briefly as a shipping clerk and an employee-fraud detective. Becomes friends with Lucien Carr and David Kammerer.
1943–1946	By fall 1943, back in New York City. Working as bartender and process server for a private investigator. Lucien Carr begins taking classes at Columbia and David Kammerer moves

to NYC to be near him. Carr becomes friends with Jack Kerouac and Allen Ginsberg and introduces them to Burroughs and Kammerer.

1944   Meets Joan Vollmer, former Barnard student and roommate of Edie Parker (Kerouac's future first wife).

1945   Meets Herbert Huncke. First narcotics addiction, January. Begins relationship with Joan Vollmer. Lucien Carr kills David Kammerer in August on the banks of the Hudson River. Burroughs and Kerouac involved (Kerouac was jailed) as material witnesses/accessories. With Kerouac, writes a potboiler about the murder, entitled *And the Hippos Were Boiled in Their Tanks*.

1946   Drugs-related arrest in April. Goes to St. Louis. Returns briefly to NYC. Takes Joan Vollmer as common-law wife. Moves with her from New York City to Texas.

1947   Billy Junior born in July, in Conroe, Texas.

1948   Moves to New Orleans. Soon becomes re-addicted to heroin.

1949   Drug-related arrest. Moves to Mexico.

1950   Studies anthropology at Mexico City College.

1951   After returning from a six-week trip to South America with Lewis Marker, on September 6, Burroughs shoots his wife Joan Vollmer in Mexico City. Their drug and booze-fueled "William Tell" routine is eventually ruled involuntary manslaughter with a two-year suspended sentence. Burroughs believed he had been possessed by an "ugly spirit," and—as a firm believer in Magick—he would spend most the rest of his life trying to exorcize it. Joan's children are sent to live with her parents. Billy stays with Burroughs' parents in St. Louis. They ultimately raise him.

1950–1952   Writes *Junky*.

1951–1953   Writes *Queer*. Partially a sequel to the novel *Junky*. Much of the book was composed while Burroughs was in jail awaiting trial for shooting Joan. Burroughs put it aside and finally published it in 1985, when the Wylie Agency secured him a lucrative contract.

1953   Publishes *Junky* under the pseudonym William Lee; travels to Colombia and experiments with the hallucinogen yage; writes to Ginsberg about his experiments. His journey was recorded in Burroughs and Ginsberg's epistolary novel, *The Yage Letters*, published in 1963. In May, Burroughs composes and sends to Ginsberg his early routine, "Roosevelt after Inauguration," a piece excised from the 1963 publication of *The Yage Letters* on grounds of obscenity, only to be published the next year by Ed Sanders with *Fuck You Press*.

1954–1957	Moves to Tangier, Morocco. Meets Brion Gysin. Begins the mass of typescripts and manuscripts from which *Naked Lunch* would be extracted with the assistance of Kerouac and Ginsberg, in 1957.
1958	Relocates to Paris and stays at the Beat Hotel. Begins cut-up collaborations with Brion Gysin. Becomes involved with the Church of Scientology and begins experimenting with the e-meter.
1959	Returns to London to do the apomorphine detox cure. When he returns to Paris, works with Gysin to further hone cut-up method. In August, Olympia Press in Paris publishes *Naked Lunch*.
	Life Magazine runs story on the Beats called "The Only Rebellion Around" (November 30, 1959; Paul O'Neill).
1960	Moves to London. Divides his time primarily among London, Paris, and Tangier for the next thirteen years. Meets Ian Sommerville, who would become his companion. Sommerville, Gysin, and Burroughs develop the "Flicker Machine" or "Dream Machine," a strobic light device that could trigger hallucinations. His first cut-up works are published, originally intended as a series of pamphlets, entitled *Minutes to Go* and *The Exterminator*.
1961	Publishes *The Soft Machine*, his first cut-up novel. In Tangier, Burroughs experiments with photomontage for the first time, a practice that develops over many years to create fractal works of art.
1962	Publishes *The Ticket That Exploded*. Obscenity trial for *Naked Lunch* concludes and charges are dropped. Makes cut-up film with Antony Balch, *Towers Open Fire*.
1963	Brings son Billy to Tangier to live with him. He had not seen his son since Billy was seven. The experiment lasted less than a year.
1964	Publishes *Nova Express*.

| 1965 | Tries and fails to publish *The Third Mind* with Brion Gysin. *Call Me Burroughs*, Burroughs' first spoken word album, is released in England. |

| 1966 | Obscenity trial for *Naked Lunch*. The novel finally gets US distribution after the court dismissed the charges. Publishes second version of *The Soft Machine*. Writes essay "The Electronic Revolution," in which the tape recorder is presented as a key weapon of resistance against both overt and covert methods of state power and mass media control. Begins experimenting with the rewind and re-record functions of the tape recorder, in an attempt to creatively reorder time. |

| 1967 | Future companion, lifelong friend, and estate executor, James Grauerholz reads *Naked Lunch* in Coffeyville, Kansas. He was 14. Burroughs publishes second version of *The Ticket That Exploded*. Makes film with Antony Balch, *Cut-Ups*. |

| 1968 | Hired by *Esquire* magazine, attends Democratic Convention in Chicago with Jean Genet, Terry Southern, Allen Ginsberg, Richard Seaver, and John Berendt. Witnesses police riots against demonstrators. Burroughs essay is entitled "Coming of the Purple Better One," and continues a parodic routine first begun in his early 1950s routine, "Roosevelt after Inauguration." During the Chicago Convention, Burroughs becomes interested in the possibility that multi-media cut-ups (tape-recordings) could be used to alter consciousness, wage guerilla warfare, incite riots, and subvert the time-space continuum. |

Burroughs publishes the third version of *The Soft Machine*.

August 1968, Ian Sommerville moves out of Burroughs' home in London to a furnished flat and begins work on a research project with a large computer company. He uses the facilities to produce several permutated poems for Brion Gysin. He said he couldn't stand Burroughs' involvement with Scientology and accused Burroughs of trying to use the tactics he'd learned in the institution to get control over other people. The men continued a sporadic sexual relationship until Burroughs moved to the United States in 1974. And they agreed not to discuss what Sommerville saw as pseudoscience.

| 1969 | Jack Kerouac dies in St. Petersburg, Florida. Pierre Belfond publishes *Entretiens avec William Burroughs*, which becomes |

the first version of *The Job*. April 1969, for openly criticizing Scientology, he is put in a "condition of treason."

1970	Grove Press publishes an English version of *The Job*, the book containing some of Burroughs' most misogynist statements.

Publishes his experimental screenplay, *The Last Words of Dutch Schultz*. His mother dies on October 21.

Publishes first version of *The Electronic Revolution*, with Media Editions in West Germany. Drawing on disparate theories as far-ranging as L. Ron Hubbard's early writings on Scientology auditing methods and Alfred Korzybski's theory of semantics, Burroughs articulated a view of human beings as "time-binding" animals, due to their ability to write. It is here that he begins developing his critique of new media and his conception of language as a virus. |
1971	Publishes *The Wild Boys: A Book of the Dead*. Publishes *The Electronic Revolution* in England. Returns to New York. Divides his time for the next several years between New York and Ginsberg's Jack Kerouac School of Disembodied Poetics, in Colorado.
1972	Film with Antony Balch, *Bill and Tony* (a.k.a. *Who's Here*). Further develops the idea that by recording situations (audio tape and photography) on the street and then playing them back in situ, you could actually tamper with reality. In 1972, he used the method to mount an attack on Scientology's headquarters in London. He also attempted to use occult practices against the *Moka Bar*, the first ever espresso bar in London that Burroughs said served poisonous cheesecake and where the wait staff treated him with discourtesy.
1973	*Port of Saints* and *Exterminator!* published.
1974	Moves from London to New York to teach at City College of New York, January–May. Publishes revised, expanded edition of *The Job*. (Some print versions of this enlarged version of *The Job* contain an updated version of *The Electronic Revolution*, including Burroughs' response to the Watergate scandal.) Meets James Grauerholz.
1976–1978	Living mostly in Boulder, Colorado, as adjunct at the Jack Kerouac School of Disembodied Poetics of Naropa Institute, in the aftermath of his son Bill Jr.'s liver transplant in August 1976. Burroughs' relationship with his son had been

troubled since Joan's death. Mainly he left Billy in the care of his grandparents in St. Louis. In 1963, he brought Billy to Tangier, in an attempt to get to know him, but that ended badly. From 1963 to 1976, there were sporadic visits, and it soon became clear that Billy had his own problems with alcohol and drugs, a misguided attempt on the son's part to emulate his famous father. Following the liver transplant, Billy had to follow a terrible regime of steroids that impacted him psychologically and physically.

February 5, 1976	Receives news that Ian Sommerville has died in a car accident.
1977	Continuously re-editing his works throughout his life, Burroughs publishes second version of *Junky*.
1978	With Brion Gysin, publishes *The Third Mind* with only a few collages culled from the original collaborative collage-book that Burroughs and Gysin created in 1965 but couldn't publish. Moves back to New York City; attends the Nova Convention.
1978–1981	Lives in the "Bunker," 222 Bowery. The Bunker was one block from the junk-dealer streets of Stanton and Rivington, and young admirers frequently showed up with gifts of heroin. Becomes re-addicted. Works with Victor Bockris on *With William Burroughs: A Report from the Bunker*.
1979	James Grauerholz moves to Lawrence, Kansas. Burroughs works on his version of *Blade Runner*, publishes *Ah Pook Is Here*.
1980	Goes on methadone in New York. Publishes second version of *Port of Saints*. Genesis P-Orridge and Peter Christopherson (Throbbing Gristle) begin working with Burroughs and James Grauerholz to compile Burroughs' experimental sound works, which up to that time had never been heard. During those sessions, Burroughs would play back his tape-recorder experiments, featuring his spoken word "cut-ups," collaged field recordings from his travels and his flirtations with EVP recording techniques, pioneered by Latvian intellectual Konstantins Raudive. Throughout the next year, P-Orridge, Christopherson, and Grauerholz would spend countless hours compiling various edits, each collection showcasing Burroughs sensitive ear and keen experimental prowess for audio anomaly within technical limitations.

1981	Bill Jr. dies March 3. Burroughs is heartbroken and more psychically plagued than any time in his life. Publishes *Cities of the Red Night*, the first of his last trilogy of novels, that intertwine alternate histories of anti-colonial conquest and sci-fi futures that anticipate the AIDS virus. Appears on *Saturday Night Live*. Genesis P. Orridge works with Burroughs to compile his early experiments with tape recordings. Project released on P-Orridge's label Industrial Records as *Nothing Here Now but the Recordings*.
1981–1982	Grauerholz convinces Burroughs to move to Lawrence. Arrives at the end of December and lives in the Stone House through the fall; makes his first shotgun paintings. Moves to 1927 Learnard in Lawrence, September 1982.
	Film made with Antony Balch, *William Buys a Parrot*, released in 1982; filmed around 1966.
1983	Publishes *The Place of Dead Roads*.
1984	Elected to the American Academy and Institute of Arts and Letters; later that year he was granted the "Commandeur de l'Ordre des Arts et des Lettres" by the Ministry of Culture in France.
1985	*Queer* is published, with a new preface by Burroughs where he addresses the murder of his wife and its influence on his life and writing.
1986	Brion Gysin dies in Paris, after long respiratory illnesses. Burroughs is devastated. Publishes *The Cat Inside*, illustrated with Gysin's drawings. Releases *Break Through in the Grey Room*, where Burroughs' spoken word is juxtaposed with Moroccan music, squeals, tape noises, commercials, and news reports. Releases "Thanksgiving Prayer."
1987	Begins seriously painting. Rents studio in the old barbed-wire factory on Kaw riverfront, to paint and write. *The Western Lands* is published. Riverfront Reunion is held in Lawrence, end of August. First art exhibition in December: Tony Shafrazi Gallery in New York.
1988	Collaborates with Keith Haring on *Apocalypse*, published by Mulder Fine Arts.
1988–1990	Art exhibits in United Kingdom and Europe. Publishes *Interzone* in 1989. Another collaboration with Keith Haring, *The Valley* portfolio, published by George Mulder Fine Arts in 1990.

1991	Triple bypass surgery. Publishes *Seven Deadly Sins*.
1993	Burroughs featured in GAP campaign. Oliver Harris publishes *The Letters of William S. Burroughs, 1945–1959* (London: Picador, 1993). Kurt Cobain visits Burroughs in October, six months before committing suicide. Release of *Spare Ass Annie and Other Tales*, containing a spoken rendition of *Junky's Christmas* (first published in *Interzone* in 1989).
1994	Featured in Nike Ad Campaign.
1995	Collaborates on a comic opera, *The Black Rider*. Publishes *Ghost of Chance*. *My Education: A Book of Dreams* is published.
1996	Ports of Entry retrospective at the Los Angeles County Museum of Art. "The Nova Convention Revisited" at Lied Center.
1996–1997	Writing *Last Words* journals.
1997	Dies of a heart attack, August 2, at 6 p.m. Buried on August 7 at Bellefontaine Cemetery, St. Louis, Missouri; Burroughs family plot.

ABBREVIATIONS

ASU — William Seward Burroughs Papers, 1938–1997, Hayden Library Rare Books and Manuscripts, Arizona State University.

Berg — William S. Burroughs Papers, The Berg Collection of English and American Literature, New York Public Library.

Burroughs Live — William S. Burroughs, *Burroughs Live: The Collected Interviews of William S. Burroughs*, edited by Sylvère Lotringer (New York: Semiotext(e), 2001).

Columbia — William Seward Burroughs Papers, 1957–1976, Rare Books and Manuscripts, Columbia University

Harris — Oliver Harris, Introduction to *The Ticket That Exploded* (New York: Grove, 2014), iv–lv.

Here to Go — Gysin, Brion. *Here to Go: Interviews and Texts*, edited by Terry Wilson (New York: Solar Books, 2012).

Kosnik — Abigail De Kosnik, *Rogue Archives* (Cambridge, MA: MIT Press, 2016)

Miles — Barry Miles, *Call Me Burroughs: A Life* (New York: Twelve, 2013).

Odier — Daniel Odier, *The Job: Interviews with William S. Burroughs* (New York: Penguin, 1969).

Rimbaud — Rimbaud, Arthur. *Rimbaud Complete*, translated by Wyatt Mason. (New York: Modern Library Classics, 2003).

Rub Out the Words — William S. Burroughs, *Rub Out the Words: The Letters of William S. Burroughs, 1959–1974*, edited by Bill Morgan (New York: HarperCollins, 2012).

Sobieszek   Robert A. Sobieszek, *Ports of Entry: William S. Burroughs and the Arts* (Los Angeles, CA: Angeles County Museum of Art, 1996).

The Third Mind   William S. Burroughs, "The Cut-Up Method of Brion Gysin," in *The Third Mind* by William S. Burroughs and Brion Gysin (New York: Viking, 1978), 35–42.

William S. Burroughs

Cutting Up the Century

SEA

TIM

THE WEEKLY NEWS

WILLIAM BURROUGHS
A grey eminence in a leaky lifeboat.

NICOLAS TIKHOMIROFF

GENERAL
MAXWELL GREEN

A HARVARD LAMPOON PARODY

Cover of TIME Harvard Lampoon *parody*, William S. Burroughs, 1965
(8 × 11, 1 leaf, facsimile) (Berg 88.23). In C-43 Addenda, Item 13, Cover
of *TIME* with pasted photograph of WSB, May 31, 1965. Copyright © by
William Burroughs, used by permission of The Wylie Agency LLC.

Introduction

ALEX WERMER-COLAN AND JOAN HAWKINS

It is amusing to read reviews of Burroughs that try to classify his books as nonbooks or failed science fiction. It is a little like criticizing the sartorial and verbal manifestations of a man who is knocking on the door to explain that flames are leaping from the roof of our home.

—Marshall McLuhan, "Notes on Burroughs," 1964

CUTTING UP THE CENTURY

If we see the earth as a spaceship and go further to invoke the comparison of a lifeboat, it is of course of vital concern to everybody on the boat if the crew and the passengers start polluting the supplies of food and water, distributing supplies on a grossly inequitable basis, knocking holes in the bottom of the boat, or worst of all plotting to blow the boat out from under us.

—William S. Burroughs, "Keynote Statement," Nova Convention, December 1, 1978

Over a century after his birth, William S. Burroughs' life and work seems to become more relevant to contemporary Western culture and politics with every passing year. At the 1978 Nova Convention, the sixty-four-year-old writer warned his audience of the dire necessity for the earth's multitudes to rise up and resist an elite ruling class before they—as he put it—blew "the boat out from under us." Having returned to live in New York City in 1974, after twenty-five years of self-imposed exile in Latin America, North Africa, and Europe, Burroughs insisted in his "Keynote Statement" that his primary interest was "in the question of survival," especially in identifying those agents "distributing supplies on a grossly inequitable basis." What Burroughs saw during his travels from the center, along the back routes and highways, to the frontiers of the so-called Western world, gave birth to disturbing visions of power, of insidious forces systemically permeating and distorting all elements of life. He witnessed the world realigning in the service of entrepreneurial oligarchs who, in their Faustian quest for money, pleasure, and an escape plan, were and are well-prepared to sacrifice not just the lower classes, not just the "Third World," but the very planet itself. In the face of this global threat, Burroughs envisioned his role as a secret agent who could identify the pressure points behind, underneath, and within the consumer spectacle disguising structural forms of domination. Long after Burroughs first rang the alarm call for radical deployments of new technologies to enhance avant-garde methods of resistance, in the wake of his death, his dire vision finally can be properly heard, taken seriously, and, with hope, adapted for our time.

For the editors of this volume, Burroughs advanced not only the crucial political goal of the twentieth century but also what can be considered a key—if not *the* key—avant-garde aesthetic technique of the twentieth century: collage. In collaboration with Brion Gysin, in the early 1960s Burroughs began experimenting with the cut-up method: a dialectical process of cutting up and folding in, fragmenting, and weaving together images and texts. What Burroughs' detractors, as McLuhan notes, called the "non-novels" of the "Nova Trilogy"—*The Soft Machine* (1961, 1966, 1968), *Nova Express* (1964), and *The Ticket That Exploded* (1962, 1967)—remain the most celebrated of his textual cut-up creations. But Burroughs committed over a decade of his life to searching out every multimedia potential of producing works as and by collage: cutting up, folding in, *splicing* together not just newspapers and magazines, but letters, book reviews, classical literature, audio recordings, photographs, and films. As McLuhan famously observed, Burroughs wanted to call attention by any means necessary to the "flames" that "are leaping from the roof of our home." Critics who disparaged the method, McLuhan insisted, were missing the point.

Gysin and Burroughs did not invent the cut-up technique. The early twentieth-century Dadaists and Surrealists experimented with cut-ups and collage as a way to radically subvert traditional graphic and textual systems of representation and to promote an aesthetics of chance. Cubist painters began experimenting with collage at approximately the same time, introducing the textures of the everyday and the street into their work (hence, the newspapers, cigarette wrappers, etc.). Modernist writers like William Faulkner, James Joyce, and Virginia Woolf did not often cut up paper texts literally, but they used the same formal principles of disjuncture in their creative process. Cut-up writing practices were also picked up by the Lettrists and Situationists in the 1950s, but it was Burroughs (with the help of Brion Gysin) who took the avant-garde technique as far as it could go. Together they honed and refined the formal method, transcending previous Dadaist, Surrealist, Cubist, and Lettrist practices of collage, while abandoning the notion of total chance. Burroughs always edited his cut-ups, using the cut-up method as a means of revision, in which the aleatory element became only one variable in a far more complex, iterative composition process. Whereas previous practitioners of the cut-up method sought to transgress the principles of artistic inspiration and authorial control, while reconfiguring traditional modes of representation, Burroughs and Gysin used the cut-up method systematically to short-circuit and rewire discursive and ideological power structures, in themselves and their audiences. The cut-up, then, became a physical means of excavating and laying bare submerged meanings; it meant methodically searching out, representing, and restructuring the intersection points of power and ideology where systems and agents of control could be exposed and counteracted.

Unlike many members of the 1960s avant-garde, Burroughs distrusted the naivety and optimism of the countercultural movement, especially the hippies' idealistic hopes to effect meaningful change through reckless consumption of drugs and the unbounded expression of desire. In his early works, especially *Naked Lunch* (1959) and *Nova Express* (1964), Burroughs invoked the dire need, perhaps humanity's last chance, to save the world. By the late 1960s, Burroughs' pessimistic vision brought him to the forefront of the national conversation. For Burroughs, 1968 became a watershed moment—not of liberation, but of Nixonian backlash. Marching arm-in-arm with Allen Ginsberg and Jean Genet at the 1968 Democratic National Convention in Chicago, Burroughs was hardly surprised when the police rioted and attacked the protestors. Only a year later, in a letter from London dated November 3, 1969, Burroughs went so far as to pronounce, in terms resonant with our own time, "We are witnessing a worldwide reactionary movement comparable to the reaction of 1848" (*Rub Out the Words*, 307–8).

In light of increasingly self-righteous, reactionary movements—exemplified by George Wallace's and Richard Nixon's political campaigns—Burroughs adapted the cut-up method not only to intervene in the contemporaneous moment but also to hoard a deluge of media images and news clippings for a time and place more fertile for revolution. In his scrapbooks and dream calendars, such as the still unpublished "The Order and the Material Is the Message" (1965–1968) (Berg 31.33–54, Folio 96), Burroughs cuts up the viral memes of international newspapers evident in disaster reports, celebrity news, and the endless fearmongering over drug use, student protests, anti-colonial revolutions, and so-called race riots. By the early 1970s, Burroughs was increasingly aware that his role was not just to be an aged, wise spokesperson (especially in *The Job* [1969] and *The Electronic Revolution* [1970]) but also to be an artist and analyst who could prepare, through his writing process, blueprints for a future resistance. Recently uncovered archival materials, especially at the New York Public Library's (NYPL) Alban A. Berg Special Collections, demonstrate the extent to which Burroughs' cut-up method became a vital means of not only deconstructing contemporary hegemonic discourse but also of creating a countercultural archive of the increasingly reactionary American Century for 1970s resistance movements and beyond.

This anthology, *Cutting Up the Century*, includes a wide array of critical essays on underexamined aspects of Burroughs' life and work in the twentieth century, while showcasing dozens of previously unseen, newly available archival materials centered around Burroughs' cut-up project (roughly from the early 1960s through the early 1970s). These unpublished works bring into relief the underexamined, frequently counterintuitive ways Burroughs sought to overturn the ruling class's misrepresentations of our temporal and spatial realities. We are particularly indebted to Oliver Harris's 2014 restored editions of the cut-up novels that marked the pinnacle of posthumous scholarly attempts to uncover the Burroughs hidden beneath the surface of his published works. Re-examining the vast trove of published and unpublished materials relating to the cut-up novels, especially the material available in the NYPL's Berg archive, Harris's restored editions challenge the myth obfuscating Burroughs' radical project: the meticulous attempt to use the cut-up method to assault America's growing hegemony, particularly as embodied by media empires (such as *TIME, LIFE,* and *Fortune* magazines) that broadcast Henry Luce's mid-century vision of "the American Century." As the archival materials and critical essays in *Cutting Up the Century* demonstrate, Burroughs sought to do more than tear down the neoconservative vision of American global hegemony represented in Luce's "American Century." In the face of America's increasingly reactionary attempts to dig in its heels against the rising anti-colonial and countercultural movements of the 1960s and 1970s, Burroughs hoped to cut up our very idea of the "century," that iconic image of time parceling out grand differences between the nineteenth and the twentieth centuries, modernist and postmodernist culture, and the eras of imperialism and of totalitarianism.

In the collage that opens this chapter, Burroughs attempts to counteract the mass media's use of his image for the sake of reinforcing the status quo. As Oliver Harris explains in his essay in this anthology, Burroughs fought a never-ending battle against *LIFE* and *TIME* magazines' various attempts to discredit his work. In 1962, he sued TIME-LIFE International Limited for their scathing, libelous November 30, 1962, review of *Naked Lunch.* Throughout the 1960s, Burroughs would go on to create a variety of collages involving *TIME, LIFE,* and *Fortune* magazine materials, including, in 1965, a cut-up rendition of *TIME* magazine that appropriated the November 30, 1962, issue's famous cover image of China's Chairman Mao Zedong and Indian Prime Minister Jawaharlal Nehru, spliced over a nondescript landscape painting. The archival piece that serves as the first image in this collection was hidden off the beaten path, in one of the last folders in the Berg archive, accompanying a copy of Burroughs' lawsuit against *TIME.*

To make this collage, a few years after the lawsuit, Burroughs took a *Harvard Lampoon* parody of *TIME* magazine from May 10, 1965, and cut and pasted over it Nicolas Tikhomiroff's photo for the 1962 issue of *TIME* of Burroughs in a bare, unadorned room (with a caption that identifies Burroughs as "A grey eminence in a leaky life boat"). The *Harvard Lampoon* cover parody depicts a General Maxwell Green (portrayed aptly by *Lampoon* janitor Elmer Green) sitting in a precarious canoe, helplessly gripping his map as his eyes follow a Vietnamese soldier's hand pointing out over the water (on the reverse side of the collage, visible only in the archive, is a full-page General Electric advertisement pitching their new computers for West Point cadets). This previously unpublished collage stands at the forefront of this anthology because it exemplifies the way Burroughs manipulated his iconic image as part and parcel of his assault on America's imperial ambitions. In this particular case, he appends his sardonic portrait to the *Lampoon's* belated attempt to satirize *TIME* magazine's cozy relationship with American empire. If Burroughs is the "grey eminence on a leaky lifeboat," it is the greedy entrepreneurs whom Burroughs blames for creating the leak. Recontextualized in this collage, the black-and-white photographic replica of Burroughs looks down wryly from the top right corner of the page, as he cuts up and folds in these media representations, warping their message, and figuratively poking holes in the only thing keeping the American general afloat on the waters of Vietnam.

CUTTING UP THE ARCHIVE

> *What Is Rejected For The Final Typescript Submitted To Publisher Is Often As Good Or Better Than What Goes In . . .*
>
> —William S. Burroughs, NYPL Berg Special Collections, Folio 58 Title

Although reams of Burroughs' unpublished papers have been available to scholars for decades at archives across America, from Arizona State to Columbia University, the 2009 opening of the Burroughs archive at the New York Public Library's Henry W. and Albert A. Berg Special Collection has revolutionized Burroughs scholarship. Considering Burroughs probably lost approximately half of his papers over the 1950s and 1960s due to a restless lifestyle and a careless attitude toward preserving all his drafts, his remaining archival materials testify to his underappreciated work ethic in the 1960s, as he produced over a thousand pages of cut-up material a month.

While Burroughs embraced chaos in his working method, he was highly organized and employed meticulous filing systems, deploying the cut-up as one of many methods of revision and inspiration. He experimented with such alternative modes of therapy as Scientology auditing and processing, while creating calendars and scrapbooks to track his dreams against the daily onslaught of atrocities, political upheavals, and disasters broadcast in the international newspapers. The cover photo for this anthology, a still from his cut-up film collaboration with Antony Balch, *Towers Open Fire* (1963), gives a sense of the Burroughs at the heart of this collection. In this cinematic adaptation of ideas crucial to his novel *Nova Express* (1964), Burroughs positions himself as a technologically savvy, subversive agent fighting an asymmetrical war against forces whose equipment is far superior to his own, a guerrilla soldier using only a map, a compass, a tape deck, and the cut-up method to take on the mass media and the ruling class. The cut-up was frequently accused of being a lazy, provocative act of destruction, but for Burroughs, it was a craft to be mastered, one requiring meticulous labor, the kind of practice that accumulated a vast, hyperlinked archive.

The background story to Burroughs' construction of this archive occurred at a pivotal point in his avant-garde project, as he sought to take stock of his time and place in the changing America of the early 1970s. But the archive's subsequent sequestration from public view for almost forty years created a blindspot in the influence he could leave on future scholars and artists. Turning back to the story of the archive's creation can make vivid what can now be resurrected out from underneath his mythic reputation and his published works.

In 1972, Burroughs was busy, but he also needed money. Amidst many other aborted business ventures, from marketing the psychedelic Dream Machine to writing a pornographic screenplay of *The Wild Boys* (published in this volume for the first time), on Brion Gysin's recommendation, Burroughs began to consider selling his accumulated work. Burroughs and Gysin worked with Barry Miles of Indica Bookstore and Gallery for six months, from June to November 1972, assembling, identifying, and sorting papers, including materials Burroughs had integrated into filing systems of works in progress as early as 1965 (establishing 164 separate folders that would provide the framework for the future catalogue). Miles's complete catalogue of the "Vaduz" archive (as it came to be known), "A Descriptive Catalogue of the William S. Burroughs Archive," was published in a limited edition by Richard Aaron, of Am Here Books, and Covent Garden Press in London in 1972. The archive contains eleven thousand pages of manuscript material originating from the 1950s through the early 1970s, including three thousand pages of correspondence, approximately eight hundred pages of dream calendars, hundreds of collages, and at least half a dozen holograph notebooks. Due to convoluted mishaps befitting a spy novel,[1] the archive was sold into private hands in 1973 and remained in complete obscurity until its sale to the New York Public Library's Alban A. Berg Special Collections in 2005, followed by its opening to the public in 2009. As a result, scholarship on Burroughs since the 1970s never took into consideration the voluminous materials Burroughs prepared at a pivotal point in not only his artistic career but also American culture and politics.

Thanks to James Grauerholz and Oliver Harris, as well as to a variety of other editors and scholars, restored editions of Burroughs' early works and anthologies of unpublished materials have been steadily released over the last half century.

---

1. Miles, Burroughs, and Gysin composed "A Descriptive Catalogue of William S. Burroughs Archive" at the request of Kenneth Lohf, Director of Columbia University's Rare Book and Manuscript Library. Fearful the sale to such an institution could be riddled with complications, Gysin was seduced by an offer first made by Richard Aaron, an American rare book dealer living in Switzerland, who set up a meeting with Roberto Altman, a mysterious financier in Vaduz, Lichtenstein. Altman had originally planned to build an academy based around Burroughs' papers. Although Burroughs may have doubted the likelihood of such an academy ever developing, during the early 1970s, Burroughs wrote a series of prospectuses for both academies of consciousness-expansion and manuals for guerilla revolution (such as the recently published *The Revised Boy Scout's Manual* 2018]). After Altman's plans fell through, the archive languished for almost a decade, before he sold the collection to American collectors Donna and Robert Jackson. After purchasing the Vaduz archive, the Jacksons kept it in private hands, giving talks and writing papers about Burroughs. Most of the manuscript materials remained sealed in the plastic Burroughs had wrapped it in. With the assistance of book dealer Ken Lopez, the NYPL's Alban A. Berg Special Collections, under the stewardship of Isaac Gewirtz, purchased the materials in 2004. Archived by Declan Kiely and Anne Garner, the so-called Vaduz archive remained unavailable for public access until 2009–2010.

Yet anthologies and works of criticism on Burroughs have been unable to come to terms with the scope and breadth of his work because the primary materials from Burroughs' formative years, materials curated by Burroughs, remained unavailable. Since the 2009 opening of the Berg Collection, however, Oliver Harris first started to make sense out of this relatively disorganized archive of radical textual experiments, meticulously restoring Burroughs' cut-up novels into new editions published during the centennial year celebrations of Burroughs' birth in 2014. These editions of *The Soft Machine*, *Nova Express*, and *The Ticket that Exploded* render authoritative versions of the text while providing extensive endnote material containing alternative or supplementary texts from six different published editions of the cut-up novels, as well as from the massive corpus of rough drafts and related archival materials. For the next stage of his restoration project, Harris is seeking to publish the lesser-known, out-of-print cut-up novels, *Minutes to Go* (1960) and *The Exterminator* (1960), as well as a third work, titled BATTLE INSTRUCTIONS, composed of unpublished cut-ups from the early 1960s that Burroughs consistently typed in all capital letters.

Whereas Harris's project has focused on *restoring* outdated and misprinted editions of Burroughs' work while supplementing those texts with archival research and alternative versions, a variety of other publications, especially those originating from recent art exhibitions, have brought to the public the wide array of materials Burroughs never revised or otherwise published in any other form. Besides the major anthologies James Grauerholz edited and published during Burroughs' lifetime, from *Interzone* (1990) to *The Burroughs File* (2001), there has been a plethora of fascinating books on Burroughs and art, such as Robert A. Sobieszek's *Ports of Entry: William S. Burroughs and the Arts* (1996), Collin Fallows and Synne Genzmer's *The Art of William S. Burroughs: Cut-ups, Cut-ins, Cut-outs* (2012), Malcolm McNeill's *The Lost Art of Ah Pook Is Here: Images from the Graphic Novel* (2012), and Patricia Allmer and John Sears's *Taking Shots: The Photography of William S. Burroughs* (2014). After editing with Oliver Harris *Everything Lost: The Latin American Notebook of William S. Burroughs* (2017), Geoffrey Smith and John Bennett have released a scholarly edition of *The Revised Boy Scout Manual* (2018). Davis Schneiderman, editor of *Retaking the Universe: William S. Burroughs in the Age of Globalization* (2004), is working with Marcus Boon to publish *The Book of Methods*, an exploration and excavation of the *idea* of *The Third Mind* as it evolved over time, passing through the various editions (from 1965 to 1977), blueprints for editions, collected and uncollected texts concerning the cut-up, and more. *The Book of Methods* will trace the history of the Burroughs and Gysin collaborations, while also serving as an index to the set of related methods and experiments that developed in the late 1950s (with their work in the Beat Hotel) and extended through the rest of their careers.

Meanwhile, independent scholar Jed Birmingham has worked steadily over the last decade to resurrect the substantial number of texts Burroughs circulated outside mainstream publishing venues, especially his cutting-edge contributions to mimeo magazines, such as early experiments with comics for Jeff Nuttall's issues of *My Own Mag* in the early 1960s. Birmingham's work since 2005 with Keith Seward on RealityStudio.org exemplifies what Abigail De Kosnik in *Rogue Archives* (2016) hails as a "rogue archive" that explores "the potential of digital technologies to democratize cultural memory" (2). While RealityStudio.org showcases work by a constellation of authors orbiting Burroughs from 1950 to 1973, Birmingham's blog posts on RealityStudio.org constitute a collector's diary and book history that chronicles Burroughs' early cut-up experiments, from 1959 to 1965, at the vanguard of the small press revolution as documented in *Secret Location on the Lower East Side Adventures in Writing (1960–1980)* (1998).

Following Harris's foray into the archive, a series of other scholars have begun mining the Berg for new material. Alex Wermer-Colan's research in the Berg archives has culminated in the materials presented in this anthology, following up on his editing of an anthology of cut-up drafts for works that appeared in literary magazines and novels. The previous archival collection, titled *The Travel Agency Is on Fire* and published by Lost & Found: The CUNY Poetics Document Initiative (2015), contains cut-up experiments by Burroughs with canonical writers ranging from William Shakespeare to Arthur Rimbaud, from F. Scott Fitzgerald to James Joyce. The collection's title, a phrase recurring almost nowhere in Burroughs' published oeuvre, serves as an alternative mantra to Burroughs' oft-repeated call to arms, "Storm the Reality Studio." The cryptic phrase, warning of a conflagration in the West's institutional apparatus for imperial tourism, was first discovered (or created) by Burroughs while cutting up and splicing together his own writing, especially *The Soft Machine* (1962), with Anthony Burgess's decadent sci-fi novel, *A Clockwork Orange* (1962).

As part of a long tradition of Downtown, experimental musicians, artists, and directors adapting Burroughs' writing, experimental composer and musician James Ilgenfritz, organizer of the Burroughs Centennial Festival in New York, worked with ten other composers and the Experiments in Opera company to set these cut-up texts to musical performances at the Stone in 2014. Wermer-Colan's ongoing collaborations with director Mallory Catlett, tape artist Lucas Crane, actor Jim Findlay, and video designer Keith Skretch, on their three-part concert series and multimedia theatrical adaptation of the cut-up novels, titled *Decoder 2017*, is yet another example of the many avant-garde projects that are keeping the spirit of Burroughs' artistic-political project alive in our new era of digital dystopia. Wermer-Colan's ongoing research in the archive has also inspired a long-term, future project to curate a digital collection of Burroughs' archival materials that can not only make Burroughs' work, and avant-garde literature like it, more accessible to scholars, editors, and the general public, but can also illustrate a properly Burroughsian vision of what the digital humanities can offer today.

In the early 1960s and 1970s, Burroughs wrote an elaborate set of instructions, encoded in novels and essays, for how to use technology to escape control—psychological, societal, and political. What emerged was a prophecy of and defense mechanism against the incipient technological takeover. For this anthology, Wermer-Colan selected archival materials that serve to showcase the range of Burroughs' multi-media practice, while focusing on the importance of the cut-up for Burroughs at a pivotal moment for US culture and politics in the late 1960s and early 1970s. While previous Burroughs anthologies have focused on specific periods of time in his oeuvre or specific themes (such as globalization, sexuality, or deconstruction), we have assembled scholarship representing a diverse range of entry points into a career that can itself be read as a cut-up. We attempt to directly engage Burroughs' critical voice and his archival materials appear unmediated; Wermer-Colan provides useful historical context and literary exegesis, but Burroughs' actual cut-ups, journal entries, and critical essays have not undergone any editorial foreshortening or correction for typos or formatting errors. This anthology will, we hope, provide a foundation for new generations of fans and scholars from diverse backgrounds and skill-sets to interpret Burroughs' cryptic runes, perhaps, at times, by cutting up Burroughs' texts to draw out what is most urgent and revelatory for the future.

CUTTING UP THE ANTHOLOGY

> Usually I get in by a port of entry, as I call it. It is often a face through whose eyes the picture opens into a landscape and I go literally right through that eye into that landscape. Sometimes it is rather like an archway.... Any number of little details or a special spot of color makes the port of entry and then the entire picture will suddenly become a three-dimensional frieze in a plaster or jade or some other precious material.

> —William S. Burroughs, Interview with Brion Gysin, Paris 1960

This kaleidoscope of critical essays and original manuscripts mirrors the multifaceted nature of Burroughs himself: fragmented, diffuse, nonlinear, heterogeneous, vast yet elusive. But it also recognizes, and takes for granted, that Burroughs as name and moniker refers to a collection of voices, rather than a single perspective. The organization of this book guides the reader through the most crucial thematic binaries that occupied Burroughs' quest to understand and undermine systems of power. Just as the reader should view each essay and archival material as a "port of entry" (in the same manner Burroughs conceived of Brion Gysin's paintings), a perspective onto an incommensurable problem, the reader might also take into consideration how Burroughs interpreted the interconnections between various entry points: "The remarkable thing is the way in which the sections—when hung a few inches apart—seem literally to pull together. The substance of the paintings seems to bridge the gap. Something is going streaming right across the void. Surely this is the first painting ever to be painted on the void itself. You can literally see the pull of one canvas on the other" (*Here to Go*, 153).

Cutting Up the Century is divided into five sections that serve as linked interventions or intersection points, ports of entry into Burroughs' work and the power structures it reveals: *Icon/Viral*, *Space/Time*, *Word/Image*, *Cut/Fold*, and *Body/Spirit*. These quasi-dualistic terms gesture toward the key categories that Burroughs analyzes in his work, but these terms themselves elide and unsettle rigid binary oppositions. Whereas, *Icon/Viral* describes a metonymic, functional relationship between idealistic mystifications and their circuits of transmission, *Space/Time* approximates the dualistic parts constituent of the physical universe. *Word/Image* appears dialectical in a way analogical to but also contrary to *Body/Spirit*, while *Cut/Fold*, the key principle of Burroughs' methodology, suggests complementary mechanisms of manipulating material and media as well as crucial metaphors for Burroughs' practices of resistance. These categories, furthermore, address various fields of academic scholarship and critical inquiry: whereas *Icon/Viral* addresses such topics as literary biography, pop culture studies, and media studies, *Space/Time* addresses geographical, historical, and political issues at the heart of Burroughs work and life during the American Century. While *Word/Image* deals with literary and art criticism on Burroughs' strategies of mutating oppressive discourse, *Cut/Fold* outlines his avant-garde techniques of deconstructive montage and reparative aesthetics crucial to modernist and postmodernist culture. Finally, *Body/Spirit* confronts problematic questions of sexuality and gender studies, as well as biological and religious themes central to Burroughs' attempt to reveal the constructed nature of identity and being. This anthology, then, winds its way from an analysis of Burroughs' iconic image, through the media networks along which viral (and virulent) words and images spread, revealing the way these iconic symbols (or memes) twist our perception of our historical position in time and space, before diagnosing how we become addicted to spectacular representations that blind us to, and keep us locked within, the limitations of our body and mind.

Since this anthology follows the generative principle of Burroughs' entire oeuvre—mutation and metamorphosis—after our introduction, we begin with a series of archival pieces that open a window onto Burroughs' fraught relationship with his son and the youth movements of the postwar era. In a period of estrangement between father and son, Burroughs submitted for publication Billy's poem, "Metamorphosis," but only after cutting it up and appending his own piece, "Adios of Saturn" (1963). Burroughs' cut-up of his son's writing manifests the problematic elements that remain central to understanding Burroughs' oeuvre, his vision, and his reputation. In this enigmatic prose poem, "Adios of Saturn," Burroughs meditates on the mythical figure of the father, Saturn, who eats his own son, reflecting, through haunting, fragmented phrases, upon the personal and political divide between his son's generation and his own. His cut-up of his son's poem captures this dialectical tension, as the aging author seeks to help a younger generation to break with tradition and transform the ruling order.

Following this cut-up poem, Oliver Harris's essay "Cutting up the Century" provides foundational interpretive work tracing Burroughs' attempt to wage asymmetrical warfare against the imperial class from which he inherited his own wealth

(Burroughs' maternal uncle, "Poison Ivy" Lee, was the father of public relations for Rockefeller, and his paternal grandfather was the founder of the Burroughs Adding Machine Company whose computers rivaled IBM in their contributions to big business and the military-industrial complex). Harris takes a historical and material approach to the so-called Cut-Up Trilogy, at first by interrogating the concept of "The Burroughs Century" (the topic of the 2014 conference at Indiana University). Harris reveals how the experimental center of Burroughs' oeuvre— his cut-up project of the 1960s—was defined against another project that formed its political and cultural binary, the American Century, and specifically Henry Luce's attempt to justify it through his media empire of *LIFE*, *TIME*, and *Fortune*. Harris's essay is followed by two materials that illustrate his main argument: a previously unpublished cut-up letter written by Burroughs to Henry Luce himself, and a cut-up that Burroughs conducted with a *LIFE* magazine reporter's telegram from their original encounter in late 1959. We have chosen to set this essay apart because it provides the topos (the starting point from which to launch a departure) for the volume as a whole, as the serpentine anthology explores the complex ways that the Burroughsian cut-up was not simply another experimental attempt to fragment unitary texts, but a pointed sociopolitical project that melded art to a multifaceted and confrontational mode of cultural critique.

In the first section of this anthology, *Icon/Viral*, Burroughs and his critics explore the icon that went viral—that is, the popular image of Burroughs—whose troubling specter overshadows and obscures his artistic and political project. Burroughs knew well that his renegade status would make it easier to recuperate his persona as an icon of cool whose very critique of that system could be thereby more easily ignored or neutralized. But the commodified image/icon was cultivated in part by Burroughs himself; it did not happen by accident, and he was very aware of persona(s) he was projecting to the world.

We begin the *Icon/Viral* section with a typescript of Burroughs' cut-up routine, "Deposition of the Ugly Spirit." At times, Burroughs expressed an almost Manichean worldview in which forces of good and evil (what he called the "Ugly Spirit") were always in play. He saw his life as a battle against the "Ugly Spirit," especially after the death of his wife, Joan. One afternoon during a party, she and Burroughs drunkenly tried to stage a "William Tell" routine. He missed the glass she'd placed on her head and killed her. In speaking of this event later, Burroughs talked about "the invader, the Ugly Spirit," which he suggested took possession of his mind and life that day, setting off a chain of events that led to some of the most destructive episodes of his life, especially his son's addiction and death. Burroughs' relationship to the idea of the "Ugly Spirit" was complicated. The archival piece published for the first time in this collection at the beginning of the *Icon/Viral* section, exhibits Burroughs speaking for and through this "Ugly Spirit." He did not invoke the entity in order to absolve himself from guilt over what had happened. For him the "Ugly Spirit" was part of him and not part of him, an invasive agent that parasitically melded with its host. Burroughs would spend most of the rest of his life trying to exorcize it—through drugs, Wilhelm Reich's orgone box, Scientology, a Native American purification ritual, and, most important, writing. Barry Miles's biography, *Call Me Burroughs* (2013), begins with an anecdote from the end of Burroughs' life, in March 1992, when he visited a shaman, "Diné elder Navajo from the Four Corners area of New Mexico," to undergo an exorcism and remove what he'd described as "the Ugly Spirit." Before the purification ceremony, Burroughs explained to the shaman that he would have "to face the whole of American capitalism, Rockefeller, the CIA . . . all of those, particularly Hearts" (Miles, 2). After the ceremony, Burroughs elaborated to a sixty-five-year-old Allen Ginsberg that "the Ugly Spirit" was "very much related to the American Tycoon. To William Randolph Hearst, Vanderbilt, Rockefeller, that whole stratum of American acquisitive evil. Monopolistic, acquisitive evil. Ugly evil. The ugly American. The ugly American at his ugly worst. That's exactly what it is" (2). In the case of Burroughs' cut-up routine from the early 1960s, "Deposition of the Ugly Spirit," Burroughs imagines the Ugly Spirit as an "enigmatic tycoon," one who, near the end of his existence, upon "examining his conscience," decides to betray the ruling class: "Now do you recognize ME Mr Bradly Mr Martin? I was made out of your heavy metal substance and I'm not taking any rap for that Green Cunt . . . I'M GONNA RAT ON EVERYBODY" (Berg 26.11). In this unpublished archival piece, we can see Burroughs' embodiment of his pivotal role, born into wealth and power, a member of the white, patriarchal, hegemonic power structure spread by America across the globe, acting as a double agent who rats out on Mr. Bradly and Mr. Martin, the demonic overlords of the ruling class.

Oliver Harris's subsequent interview with Barry Miles, titled "Burroughs and Biography," provides an overture to the anthology's various academic interventions. Harris is arguably the most renowned scholar in Burroughs Studies. Here he interviews Barry Miles, author of the authoritative biography, *Call Me Burroughs*. Miles was a close collaborator and friend of Burroughs throughout his life, dedicated to showing the human behind the icon and the work behind the myth. We begin the anthology with this interview, conducted during the William S. Burroughs Centennial Conference at the Graduate Center, City University of New York, in order to introduce the volume's critical conversation with the iconic stature of Burroughs, specifically the question of his biography, authorship, legacy, and influence.

Before the anthology introduces contemporary Burroughs scholarship, we let Burroughs have a moment to respond to his critics by publishing a series of cut-ups he conducted with negative reviews of his own books, especially of his cut-up novels. In these pieces from the early 1960s, Burroughs seeks to accomplish what he described aptly in an archival piece housed in the Columbia University archives: "MY CRITICS (NAMELESS ASS HOLES) ARE BY THIS / WRITING ANSWERED IN THEIR OWN WORDS ROUND / TABLE TURNING DID EAT EACH OTHER TO THE / AMAZEMENT OF MINE EYES THAT LOOKED UPON IT" (Columbia 1.14, Series II). In these cut-up texts, we can see Burroughs turning his critics' words against them, exposing the clichés of censure and outrage that conservative critics produced in the face of Burroughs' radically experimental works. As Burroughs cuts up critical reactions during both the "Ugh" affair (expressing disgust at *Naked Lunch*) and the Edinburgh Festival in 1962 (toward the cut-up method), the reader can watch as the critics' spliced words, so to speak, "eat each other." For Burroughs, the critics become like the horses in the referenced scene from Shakespeare's *Macbeth* (1606) that, after the regicide, go mad in the night. Watching his critics' words cut against each other, Burroughs voices the reaction of Ross in Shakespeare's play, who, perhaps aware of his own complicit voyeurism, says it happened "to the amazement of mine eyes / That looked upon it" (*Macbeth*, II.iv.19–20).

In "The Nova Convention: Celebrating the Burroughs of Downtown New York," Kristen Galvin brings us to the other end of Burroughs' reception as a writer, identifying the Nova Convention as a groundbreaking forum of intellectual and cultural exchange oriented around Burroughs' cultlike status in the Downtown scene. At the time of the 1978 Nova Convention, Burroughs had lived for four years at the center of the Downtown New York scene, in the infamous Bunker, and had been embraced by Downtown writers and artists, No-Wave and Punk musicians, and a growing group of scholars influenced by new trends in Continental philosophy. Galvin's essay analyzes the complexity of Burroughs' position at the time, when he was well-positioned to play the role of the literary decadent. During the Nova Convention's after-party, the rock critic Richard Goldstein asked him, "How do you perceive the immediate future?" Burroughs replied, "I don't" (*Burroughs Live*, 436).

Landon Palmer's "The Disembodied Fry: William S. Burroughs and Vocal Performance" argues next that the aesthetic of Burroughs' late career evolved aurally, more than visually or lexically, through his spoken word performances and film appearances. While mid-century Beat writers were aesthetically invested in spoken word and recorded sound, Burroughs' voice was largely absent from recorded Beat productions. This essay asks, then, how Burroughs' voice came to be so immediately recognizable. As if in parody of Burroughs' imitable voice, we follow Palmer's piece with Burroughs' cut-ups of traditional limericks, a light-hearted, lyrical word collage that captures the polyvocal nature of Burroughs' experiments with prose.

Allen Hibbard's "William S. Burroughs' Spirit of Collaboration" concludes the *Icon/Viral* section by further investigating the way Burroughs challenged the Romantic notion of genius and of the singular, independent creator. A well-known Paul Bowles and Burroughs scholar, Hibbard complicates Burroughs' relationship to authorship, exploring the lesser-known creative-collaborative dynamics between Bowles, Gysin, and Burroughs (as well as Kurt Cobain), with special emphasis on the time Burroughs spent in Tangiers. Burroughs collaborated with writers and artists throughout his life, from his earliest written works with Kells Evans and Jack Kerouac to his late writings with James Grauerholz. Nearly all his written works were constructed through collaborations, since he developed them in response to an ongoing dialogue about the work—with friends, with publishers, and with critics. Even the cut-up method itself was understood by Gysin and Burroughs as an inherently collaborative process, involving the writer borrowing and reworking the words of others to give birth to unimagined perspectives and visions.

The *Space/Time* section situates Burroughs the person in a defined historical and geographic context, especially for the purpose of confronting the false view that Burroughs remained aloof from the places and times in which he lived. Burroughs never forgot his time at Los Alamos, around the time of the atom bomb's invention. He also got to know St. Louis as a nostalgic memento of a more innocent America. He also lived in Chicago during World War II, New York at multiple points in the city's post–World War II cultural renaissances, as well as in New Orleans, the Lower Rio Grande Valley of south Texas, and Mexico City. He traveled through South America, lived in Tangier, Paris, London, and, during the last period of his life, resided in Midwest America, Lawrence, Kansas, having returned full circle. By exploring Burroughs' intimate engagement with place, and the politics of empire and ecology, this section provides a vital understanding of Burroughs' travels throughout the Western world during his near century-long life span.

To start this section, Kathelin Gray's "Burroughs and the Biosphere, 1974–1997" explores Burroughs' underexamined interest in ecology and science, especially in relation to anthropology and weapons development. Gray, who knew Burroughs personally, argues that Burroughs' interest in ecology and science fueled his study of language as a control system. Her essay moves beyond tracing ecological tropes in Burroughs' work to argue for a more intrinsic—and underexamined—Burroughsian contribution to the emerging academic discourses surrounding the environmentalist movement. Following Gray's essay on an underexamined period in Burroughs' role as a public intellectual in the 1970s ecological movements, we provide Burroughs' remarkable 1971 essay on the "permissive society" that challenges naïve celebrations of social liberation in the changing times of post–World War II America.

The second essay in this section, Aaron Nyerges's "Beat Regionalism: Burroughs in Mexico, Burroughs in Women's Studies," employs the terms of American literary regionalism defined by Judith Fetterley and Marjorie Pryse, in order to consider Burroughs' time in Mexico City, as well as the composition of both *Junky* and *Queer*, through the feminist analytic of the local. For many reasons, Burroughs is an unlikely character to narrate through the language of women's studies, but Nyerges argues that doing so is necessary to preserve the strength of literary regionalism as a transitive mode or category in crisis. Nyerges's analysis hinges upon Joan's death, reconsidering questions of agency and historicity, and contemplating how the "multiple crises created by the interlocking and inadequate explanations for Joan's death" might "provide another torturous moment of awakening for the feminist analytic of regionalism," while also clarifying what "would allow Burroughs into a women's studies tradition of regionalism."

Following a collage of news clippings that demonstrates only a small piece in the gigantic puzzle of Burroughs' experimentation with *détourning* hegemonic media platforms through scrapbooking, Timothy S. Murphy contributes the third essay in this section, "Interference Zones: William Burroughs in the Interstices of Globalization." In only the latest of Murphy's many contributions to his long career of groundbreaking Burroughs scholarship, the author of *Wising Up the Marks: The Amodern William Burroughs* (1998) argues that for Burroughs, "the state is effectively defined by its repressive juridico-legal and police functions—the *Polizeiwissenschaft*—which control the time, space and subjectivity of the nation and its people." Murphy reveals how Burroughs parodies and attacks these functions of the nation-state in works from *Junky* (1953) and *Naked Lunch* (1959) to "Roosevelt after Inauguration" (1961) and the Nova Trilogy (1961–68). Murphy explores the interconnection between Burroughs' rhetorical strategies and his biographical movements, writing: "Such textual critiques of the police state parallel Burroughs' own flight from the post–World War II United States, which he saw as an emerging paradigm of that state, to Mexico, South America, and ultimately Tangier."

In keeping with Murphy's analysis, we follow his presentation with archival pieces dealing with geopolitical shifts in Asia, including Burroughs' essay on the revolutionary potentials offered by Mao Zedong, as well as his collage satirizing Nixon's so-called dilemma in Indochina. In a letter on October 3, 1968, to Jeff Sherro (editor of *Rat Subterranean News*, an underground newspaper created in March 1968), to preface his new essay on the Chinese Revolution, Burroughs emphasized that the point he wished "to underline" in the article, "the basic issue," was "A world wide monopoly of knowledge and discoveries for counter revolutionary purposes" (Berg, 62.3). In his "P.S. to Academy 23," Burroughs warns in terms all the more resonant today that "Class and individual difference, deliberately accentuated and exploited by vested interests, have brought the West to a state of chaos and disaster" (Berg 62.3). In these fascinating essays, Burroughs celebrates the Chinese cultural revolution for demonstrating to the West "that what passes for 'the unalterable nature of man' is actually vested interests" and that "there is no such thing as 'human nature'" (Berg 62.3). After Burroughs' reflections on geopolitical crises, the *Space/Time* section concludes with an elegiac essay by historian Eric Sandweiss. In "Cut-up City: William S. Burroughs' 'St. Louis Return,'" Sandweiss contends that Burroughs found in St. Louis (his hometown) a cut-up city whose physical landscape, personal associations, and deeper literary resonances had— like many postwar American cities—already been taken apart and reassembled in ways that startled even the great verbal collage artist himself.

The *Word/Image* section includes essays and archival materials showcasing Burroughs' manipulation of the ideological and aesthetic representations of time and space that established American hegemony after World War II. Here the anthology puts on the cutting table the mass media (like Henry Luce's trilogy of *TIME-LIFE-Fortune* magazines), to reveal Burroughs' attempt, both before and after the cut-up method, to create counter-discursive interventions. After a series of exemplary prose pieces by Burroughs that explore the interconnections between control, addiction, and virulent, reactionary rhetoric, Alex Wermer-Colan explores Burroughs' early works and their evocation of these troubling themes. In his essay, "William S. Burroughs' Imperial Decadence: Subversive Literature in the Cynical Age of the American Century," Wermer-Colan argues that Burroughs' obscene representations of Latin Americans, North Africans, and Arabs in *Naked Lunch* should be approached as a paradoxical counter-discourse to Cold War American imperial ideology. The essay reveals Burroughs' "decadent" aesthetic strategy, evident in his obscene over-identification with the "Ugly American," to fight fire with fire against America's increasingly cynical strategies to maintain neocolonial power. Following Wermer-Colan's essay, in his haunting collage from his 1970 "Dream Rat" calendar, Burroughs meditates upon the vile war on drugs, taking to task counterproductive, Draconian methods of control that only exacerbate the black market for opium and its destructive effects on the social fabric.

In "*Naked Lunch* and the Art of Incompleteness: The Use of Genre in Burroughs' Book and Cronenberg's Film," Joshua Vasquez draws on developing trends in adaptation studies to interpret Burroughs' notorious book in conversation with David Cronenberg's strange cinematic version. Departing from traditional adaptation critiques, Vasquez counters concerns over cinematic fidelity to the written text by arguing that both the film *Naked Lunch* (1991) and the original novel express a desire for textual coherence through their incorporation of generic structure. In this sense, he reads Cronenberg's film as a cinematic mode of critical analysis of the original, amorphous corpus of *Naked Lunch*. After Vasquez's analyses of Burroughs' narrative in cinematic form, we juxtapose Burroughs' 1970 humorous essay, and a corresponding newspaper collage, on the sky-rocketing art market after the sale of Andy Warhol's soup can painting. The subsequent essay in this section turns to the other end of Burroughs' lifework to consider his 1983 novel *The Place of Dead Roads*. In "Queer Outlaws Losing: The Betrayal of the Outlaw Underground in *The Place of Dead Roads*," Kurt Hemmer contends that Burroughs' novel can be read as an attempt to produce a politically viable countercultural model of the future, an attempt that ultimately fails. As Hemmer shows, the counterculture that embraced Burroughs was outflanked by the Spectacle; it became a doomed enterprise in ways that Burroughs himself predicted, for instance, in his preceding satire of the art market.

As a preface to the following essay in our collection, in two archival pieces, Burroughs imagines extensions of Arthur Rimbaud's influential conception of a language composed of colors. Véronique Lane's "Rimbaud and Genet, Burroughs' Favorite Mirrors" helps to contextualize these unique texts, providing a thorough history and analysis of the textual influence of French literature, especially the work of Rimbaud and Jean Genet, on Burroughs' work. Lane is less interested in tracing influence, or citing the similarities between Burroughs' work and the work of French authors, than in uncovering the way Burroughs conceptualized his identity and creativity through close readings of Rimbaud's and Genet's writing. Lane focuses her analysis on Burroughs' cut-ups of Rimbaud and reflections on Genet, arguing that the poems and novels of these French writers offered Burroughs, throughout his life, a series of mirrors to measure the success of his own works at the most significant moments in his long career as a writer: at its start in the 1940s, its experimental height in the 1960s, and its twilight in the 1990s.

The anthology's *Cut/Fold* section opens out onto Burroughs' multimodal methods of aesthetic resistance. As mentioned earlier, Burroughs worked with the cut-up extensively throughout his life, extending and developing an artistic practice that became central to the avant-garde during the early twentieth-century. Working with Brion Gysin, Burroughs used the cut-up in every medium he could manage, as a very physical way of unearthing and reconfiguring messages of control. After Burroughs' unpublished essay on the cut-up method, two archival cut-ups show his experiments with Aleister Crowley's writings and a fold-in prose poem compiled from classical works of literature. Burroughs' cut-up adaptation of Crowley's famous aphorism provides yet another version of Burroughs' and Hassan-i Sabbah's purported motto that "Nothing is true, everything is permitted." As Burroughs puts it: "Aleister Crowley said Do What Thou Wilt That is the Hole in the law" (Berg 16.42).

We begin the scholarly part of the *Cut/Fold* section with Davis Schneiderman and Oliver Harris's interview, "Cross the Wounded Galaxies: A Conversation about the Cut-Up Trilogy," conducted at Indiana University, exploring Harris's editing of Burroughs' sci-fi cut-up novels. The two Burroughs' scholars discuss what it means to investigate his work and legacy now that the archives have been opened. Their interview is followed by a short Burroughs essay from 1962 on the art of photomontage, as well as a stunning collage from 1973 reflecting on the prospect of America's decline after the Watergate scandal. Burroughs had first responded to Watergate in an addendum to his *Harper's* November 1973 article, "Playback from Eden to Watergate" (which extends and was reworked into his 1970 manifesto, *The Electronic Revolution* in the 1973 edition). At the same time as he was composing his essay, Burroughs was creating this collage, juxtaposing *Newsweek*'s July 30, 1973, reporting on Watergate (including their collage image of tapes superimposed over the White House) with two of William Blake's Large Colour Prints series begun in 1775, *God Judging Adam* and *Nebuchadnezzar*. The latter depicts the Old Testament Babylonian King Nebuchadnezzar's hubristic fall from grace, seen in Blake's illustration mad and crawling into a cave. In this collage, Burroughs returns to the theme that dominated and motivated his work since his tableau in *Naked Lunch* of Mr. America as a Bruegelian Icarus falling through the debris of Western civilization. His collage of Blake illustrations and 1970s newspaper articles provides a poignant example of Burroughs' multimedia attempt to document and precipitate the American empire's inevitable decline.

In this way, Blake Stricklin's "'Word Falling . . . Photo Falling': William S. Burroughs and the Word as Written Image" considers how Burroughs articulates a defense of his cut-up and fold-in method in relation to other mediums like art and film. Stricklin is less interested in the comparisons Burroughs might have made between writing and other artistic practices, than in the way Burroughs thought about writing *through* visual art. Following a series of fascinating cut-up experiments Burroughs conducted with Scientology audits and advertising, Chad Weidner's "Mutable Forms: The Proto-Ecology of William Burroughs' Early Cut-ups" uses an eco-critical lens to explore the themes of place and toxicity in Burroughs' work. Weidner's recent book *The Green Ghost: William Burroughs and the Ecological Mind* (Southern Illinois University Press, 2016) has revitalized Burroughs scholarship from an eco-critical point of view. As Weidner analyzes unknown and miniature "cut-ups," texts that have been disassembled and rearranged to create new passages, his essay offers a novel understanding of these cryptic forms in light of Burroughs' exploration of decay and regeneration in the natural order.

The anthology's final section, *Body/Spirit*, simultaneously engenders and queers Burroughs to counter the poisonous myth of the macho, gun-toting writer. Following Burroughs' drafted pornographic screenplay of *The Wild Boys* (1971), Katharine Streip, in "William S. Burroughs, Transcendence Porn, and *The Ticket That Exploded*," explores Burroughs' additions to the second edition of *The Ticket That Exploded* (1967) to offer a new perspective on Burroughs' interest in embodiment. Streip unravels the significance of "transcendence porn" (a spiritual *jouissance* that she equates to escape from embodiment) to Burroughs' novel. As a transition from Streip's take on Burroughs' literary representations of bodily identity to the roundtable discussion on Burroughs' attitudes toward gender, we provide an archival dream note, a poignant piece from 1970, where Burroughs for perhaps the first time candidly reflects on his feelings of guilt for his wife's murder decades after her death, some fifteen years before he would write about her death in his preface to *Queer* (1985).

By investigating Burroughs' attitudes toward gender and sexuality, especially during the late 1960s, this anthology concludes with a focus on Burroughs' determination to escape his own prejudices, as well as the limitations of his own body. During the "Gender Trouble" roundtable that took place at the Graduate Center, CUNY, in the spring of 2014, award-winning poet Anne Waldman, Regina Weinreich, and Ann Douglas agreed that Burroughs' misogynistic writings, primarily made in a few essays of the late 1960s, were inexcusable. While considering Burroughs' own disavowal of these remarks and his insistence on troubling the gender binary, Waldman, Weinreich, and Douglas also discuss the ways other poets, artists, and teachers of their generation—even men who *expressed* a more equitable view of women—often treated them (and their work) differently, as if they did not merit the same critical response reserved for men. Burroughs, they note, looked at the *work* of women writers and students, rather than the gender of the author, and he critiqued it as writing. Burroughs' misogynist utterances, they conclude, cannot be decontextualized from his attempt to imagine ways out of the restrictions of the body, out of precisely those binary hierarchies that prove so vital to imperial, racist, patriarchal, and heteronormative power structures.

In the last cut-ups showcased in this collection, Burroughs splices together the last words of mythic figures, his friends (like David Kammerer), and his own wife before he accidentally shot her in their horrific rendition of the William Tell act. For the first time, the reader can watch Burroughs ruminate through the cut-up method on Joan's haunting last words, "I CAN'T LOOK." In 1991, during an interview with David Cronenberg during the promotion of the film, *Naked Lunch*, which meditates obsessively upon Burroughs' murderous act, Burroughs was asked by a reporter, "Mr. Burroughs, do you regret anything in your life?" He replied, in ways evident throughout his nostalgic, alienated prose, "I am very lucky if I can get through a day without something I did wrong, something I said wrong, gestured wrong, and you talk of a lifetime? Good God. Practically everything."

For the conclusive essay in our collection, "The Burroughs Effect," Anne Waldman offers a lyrical litany on Burroughs and her own relationship to him, providing a virtuosic tribute and testament to Burroughs' lasting effects on contemporary politics and culture. While highlighting the lessons Burroughs offers our time for our most pressing crises, she also takes the time to elaborate her attitude toward Burroughs' misogyny. She writes:

> I have never been an apologist for William's moral lapses or misogynistic statements, which in their extremity—particularly, in the context of *The Job*—I still consider crackpot, weird, ugly, and repellant. But they never distracted me from the greater mastery of the work. But I also saw over the years that these views were never totally fixed or solid and were not consistent or dominant in the writing or in his life. His male characters—or "presenters"—come under equal fire, scrutiny, not as persons, but as types, stand-ins—part of his allegory, his satire, and his social commentary. These sharp views of the 1960s had shifted by the time we met. "I have often said that it is not women *per se*, but the dualism of the male-female equation, that I consider a mistake" (Burroughs 1984). His goal was not the occlusion of women any longer. He spoke of the sexes fusing into one organism.

After Waldman's virtuosic argument for the visionary value of Burroughs' artistic and critical work, we let Burroughs have the last word, so to speak, concluding this volume with a piece selected from the art work he made late in life, not one of his infamous shotgun paintings, but a somber black-and-white ink and photo collage titled *Root Face* (1987).

This anthology begins with Burroughs manipulating his own myth, the man who, as seen in the collage that opens this chapter, was given the loaded compliment by *LIFE*, *TIME*, and *Fortune* of being a "grey eminence on a leaky lifeboat." Burroughs *détourned* their photograph by cutting out and attaching that copyrighted image to *Harvard Lampoon*'s 1965 parody of *TIME* Magazine's reification of American hubris, making himself appear to look down wryly upon the lost general in a Vietnamese boat. We hope these essays and archival materials give such context and power to Burroughs' alarm call, for action against a ruling class willing to sink our lifeboat in order to enjoy their luxury. As this anthology hopes to make clear through its form and its content, Burroughs hoped that by cutting and folding the image-words of the Reality Studio, we could free ourselves from the limited vision we have of our bodies in space and time, no longer bound to racist, classist, sexist prejudices, nor by our body's addictive attachments to the short-term rewards of consumer culture. By keeping good faith with the spirit of Burroughs' quest to counteract with any means necessary our increasingly Burroughsian reality, this anthology's constellation of essays and archival manuscripts chart a temporal and spatial evolution and mutation that, like Burroughs' late works modeled on ancient books of the dead (from *The Wild Boys* [1972] to *The Western Lands* [1987]), can serve, perhaps, as a guidebook for how to live in a dying world.

JOAN HAWKINS is Associate Professor of Cinema and Media Studies in the Media School at Indiana University Bloomington. She is the author of *Cutting Edge: Art-Horror and the Horrific Avant-garde* and the anthology *Downtown Film and TV Culture 1975–2001*. She co-organized The Burroughs Century conference and symposium held at Indiana University Bloomington in 2014.

ALEX WERMER-COLAN is a Council of Library and Information Resources Postdoctoral Fellow at Temple University's Digital Scholarship Center. Wermer-Colan's essay, "Implicating the Confessor: The Autobiographical Ploy in William S. Burroughs' Early Works," appeared in *Twentieth Century Literature* in 2010. He also researched and edited *The Travel Agency Is on Fire* (2015), published by Lost & Found, a collection of unpublished archival materials Burroughs produced by cutting up canonical writers. Wermer-Colan organized the "William S. Burroughs Centennial Conference" held at the Graduate Center of the City University of New York in 2014. He is currently working with director Mallory Catlett as the dramaturg for *Decoder 2017*, an adaptation of Burroughs' sci-fi cut-up novels into a multimedia theatrical event.

Metamorphosis

When Burroughs' son sent him a poem in April 1963, it was in anticipation of visiting his father and his literary coterie in Tangier. The two had not seen each other since October 1954, some nine years earlier. Billy hoped to attend the American School in Morocco while reconnecting with his estranged father. Shortly after receiving his son's poem, titled "Metamorphosis," Burroughs submitted it for publication to Ira Cohen, but only once he'd transcribed it, cut it up, and appended his own piece, "Adios of Saturn" (1963). The two poems were originally intended to be published together in Ira Cohen's *GNAOUA*, a literary magazine that only appeared for one issue in Tangier, Morocco, in the spring of 1964. Burroughs apologized to Cohen for any signs of nepotism, remarking "All in the family you might say."

Strangely, neither piece was published at the time. Burroughs' "Adios of Saturn" appears in another magazine issue of Cohen's, the *Great Society* #2, in 1967, at a point of crisis in the father-son relationship. Perhaps Cohen had accidentally separated the two pieces over the years, considering Burroughs' poem was published without any reference to its primary source. At the time, by cutting up his son's poem, Burroughs may have hoped to collaborate with his son. Yet his cut-up poem also registers and anticipates in some sense what he went on to do when his adolescent son visited Tangier, leaving Billy to find his own way in a foreign city amid a decadent ex-pat community. Only three months after Billy sent his hopeful letter, from the get-go of their reuniting, both father and son failed to meet each other's expectations. Burroughs felt like he was talking with a stranger whose interests were entirely foreign to him (Miles, 417). Billy, in tandem, played the rebel, resisting most of his father's practical suggestions and acting indifferent to the foreign city and culture.

Burroughs' "cut-up" of his son's writing manifests the problematic elements that remain central to understanding Burroughs' oeuvre, his vision, and his reputation. We present at the beginning of our anthology this multivocal set of texts (his son's poem and his transformation of it) in order to foreground the theme of metamorphosis—not just of the individual, but of society, as it passes from one generation, and one order of power, to the next. While Billy's poem shows a young writer trying to articulate his vision of growth through the Joycean metaphor of a single day in the city, in "Adios of Saturn," Burroughs' piece recalls an ancient myth, the Roman figure of the father, Saturn, who consumes his own son. In haunting, fragmented phrases, Burroughs' adaptation of his son's poem draws out a strange dialectical tension, as the aging author tries to assist the rising youth movements in their protest against the older, white, male ruling class.

Contained in its own Berg Folio, number 68, itself entitled *Metamorphosis*, "Adios of Saturn" was described by Burroughs at the time of compiling the manuscripts into a folio in the early 1970s as a "fold-in from Metamorphosis." Burroughs' first few years of experimentation with the so-called cut-up method involved some elementary act of cutting paper in order to create new juxtapositions between word and image. The fold-in method became integral to Burroughs' practice by 1962, and the first novel to be produced through the practice was *The Ticket That Exploded*. According to Oliver Harris, in July 1962, the "rapid progress of *The Ticket* reflected Burroughs' shift from cutting to folding, a quicker, far less messy procedure" (Harris, xxxv). By calling his piece a "fold-in" of his son's poem, Burroughs suggests his act was less violent, more collaborative, in nature. Just as the title of his son's poem, "Metamorphosis," mutates into the father's piece, "Adios of Saturn," so Billy's revolutionary message evolves through the fold-in method into his father's relinquishment of power. Like Prospero's last speech in Shakespeare's *The Tempest* (1611), Burroughs' cut-up poem gives voice to Saturn's final farewell.

—AWC

April 22,1963
5 Lancaster Terrace
London W.2.

Dear Ira:
    At the risk of exposing myself to chargesof neopotism
I enclose a poem Metamorphosis   written by my 14 year old son
together with a fold in I made from it.All in the family you
might say and hope you can use it in your magasine.Actually I
think it is a good poem.. Well let me hear from you

With Best Wishes
Bill Burroughs
[autograph]: Bill Burroughs

The stacatto alarm clock impales the dreams of the millions
Squirming on sabre-tooth clatter I - We - They - arise joyfully
    To greet
The garbage men and the dawn with a sodden curse and a bleary
Coutenance - - dress as the milkman jingles his curdled wares
    and prods
Everlastingly about the back door -- shave, to get that hidden beard
    with
A carniverous ELECTRIC razor -- devour the whiter bread --
    instantly weak
Coffee -- and horrors - bacon - like mother used to make - jostling
    to work
Of hopeless aspect - I - We - They - sit quietly with an expression
    of inane
Cooperation and inwardly loath the red nosed fellow man -- with
    sadistic
Smoothness the roar of tramways and traffic becomes the clatter of
Tyranical typewriters and the hissing of that damn faulty radiator.

The hissing -- the clatter -- the roaring and cursing -- blend to
Become that damn weavil - gas belching - industrial monster
    crawling inexorably
Towards its plastic goal -- a metropolitan centipede feeding on
    individuality
I -- We -- They -- sit quietly as we are digested and become
    corpuscles
Spreading along asphalt veins and hardened arteries carrying
SHAVING LOTION -- BEER -- BUGS BUNNY - EX-LAX -- rush
    from here to there
With BRAND × -- that BURNING SENSATION and post nasal drip
Noon -- and the refuse of the centipede begins another cycle
Seas of slosh on shores of

The neon sun sinks low behind concrete needles and the sky explosed
Into Helena Rubenstein's passion red -- the urban centipede grinds
To a stalemate as NO - DOZE gives way to KNOCK-OUT pills and
    patent
Dreams twist through deturgent reddened minds -- until the
METAMORPHOSIS is complete - - - - - - - - - - - - - - - - -
The stacatto alarm clock impales the dreams of the millions. . . .

                     [autograph]: Bill Burroughs
                               Age 14

ADIOS OF SATURN

Empty sky through the back door..Hidden beard in vacant razor
I-We-They sit quietly on cooperation corner and inwardly loath
the witness.Pan pipes to answer your tyranical typewriters is
written.Blue dawn in the lost streets."Mr.Martin" feeding on
individual "I"-"We"- "They"-arteries carrying India ink.Be done
I say to you.From here to there adios of Saturn in Sid's.Nothing
here now.The dreams of millions squirming from vacant image.They
arise joyfully to greet the old compromise of dual universe with
a bleary good bye.Oh say can you see his curdled xxxxx wares
prod last ebbing goal??Justlikethat our last film.Horrors like
mother used to make decline in the mirror::Dead cigarette smoke,
invisible stars and fossil typewriters,plastic bones,India ink
shirt flapping..Knife and corpuscles spreading is written..Empty
arteries by 1920 pond in a vacant lot..Holes twisted in about
the back door exploded the film..Dead parenthesis with carniverous wares,stranger..Hopeless faces to give you? Monkey bones of
inane stalemate? Stagnant,man..With sad good bye Great Amber
Clutch waiting for rain..How do you like your centipede in the
lost streets? Young sit quietly as we are digested and become
nothing here? Onetwothreefour silence: Shaving lotion--Beer--
Bugs Bunny--Ex-Lax..No patent dreams twist through flesh tracks
broken..Old friend,no more.Metamorphosis is complete..A magic
lantern ended dreams of millions..The neon sun sinks in this
sharp smell of carrion..circling albatross..pealed noon..refuse
like ash..age flakes falling..Handful of old names left by a
stagnant lake..Last silent film stretches to the post card sky.

[autograph]:
WILLIAM S. BURROUGH

1

Cutting Up the Century

OLIVER HARRIS

"A RIGGED THOUSAND YEARS"

A perfect phrase to mark the anniversary of Burroughs' birth and the enduring legacy of his oeuvre, *Cutting Up the Century* is also an apt term to describe the project formed by Burroughs' most experimental creative work. *Naked Lunch* (1959) may always remain his singular masterpiece, but the decade-long engagement with cut-up methods that Burroughs began after that book's publication was an enterprise of a categorically different nature, a *project*, in which the book was just one form of writing, and writing was just one medium among others. The Cut-Up Project aimed to "cut up the century" because its revolutionary goal was to change the future by changing time itself—as Burroughs announced in the blistering block capitals that mark his earliest cut-up texts and polemics: "ALL OUT OF TIME AND INTO SPACE. FOREVER" (Burroughs 2006, 71).[1] What he meant by "time" is the very texture and causal logic of the world we know, the "IMMUTABLE REALITY OF THE UNIVERSE," and he called this natural-seeming continuity that masks its alien and artificial construction "THE SOFT MACHINE."[2] Cut-up methods assumed that reality was not represented by words and images but produced by them, so that cutting up was a way to shatter the illusion by denaturalizing appearances and making visible the conspiracy that sustains them *in time*: "This is war between those of us who want out and those who want to keep us all locked in time. The cut ups are not for artistic purposes. The cut ups are a weapon a sword. I bring not peace but pieces. Time cut to pieces. Cut time to pieces" (Burroughs 1961a). When Burroughs spoke of *cutting up time*, far from being historically and philosophically abstract, however, he was being strictly material, referencing the temporality and ideology of the specific project and specific uses of words and images against which he defined his own. That's to say, he was cutting up the *American Century*.

The American Century was first popularized as a term in the early 1940s and was relaunched fifty years later as the Project for the *New* American Century, the right-wing think tank that was a driving force behind the Bush-Cheney administration and the War on Terror. During the decade of the Cut-Up Project,

Burroughs in effect launched his own Century as a terroristic counter-project to the American Century, which in broad terms embodied everything he opposed: monopolistic consumer capitalism and conservative ideology at home taken to a higher power by an imperialistic ambition to remake the entire world in the image of America. The 1990s relaunch was more militaristic and jingoistic in how this imperium would be established, but the fundamentals had already been laid down when the term was used on the eve of America's entry into World War II.

Burroughs was implacably against all that this American Century stood for, and his work can be read as a vitriolic counterattack and visionary mapping of alternative futures—all the more powerful because of course Burroughs came from the imperial class himself. That's why in his fiction he could play the Ugly American so convincingly; as a descendent of "Poison Ivy" Lee, the father of public relations and PR man for Rockefeller, and grandson of the founder of the Burroughs Adding Machine Company, whose computers for big business and the military rivaled IBM in the postwar era, William S. Burroughs had the empire of the American Century written into his DNA.

However, the *content* of the term American Century is not its main significance for understanding what we might, ironically, call "the Burroughs Century." More important was the *medium* in which the term was popularized and through which it operated, because this directs us to not just the content of the Burroughs oeuvre but also to the particular experimental methods and forms it would take. Cut-up methods have usually been contextualized within avant-garde and literary history—citing Burroughs' own citations from Tristan Tzara to T. S. Eliot—or have been related to other postwar subversive cultural movements, such as the Situationist International. Yet to see the Cut-Up Project chiefly in terms of artistic predecessors and fellow radicals is to misread how Burroughs worked at a *material* level, and it is through its materiality that Burroughs' oeuvre is most integrally connected to the American Century as its binary opposite.

The American Century was promoted in and embodied by a set of highly influential material practices, and the term appeared as the title of a February 1941 editorial, in the flagship of American photojournalism: Henry Luce's *LIFE* magazine. Burroughs' antipathy toward Luce's magazines is very well known; there are hostile references in numerous texts and interviews during the 1960s, most famously his declaration to the *Paris Review* in 1965 that "*Time, Life, Fortune* is some sort of police organization" (Burroughs 1965a, 35), and in the same year Burroughs produced his own cut-up edition of *TIME* (Burroughs 2001, 73). While he would often speak in broad terms about wanting to expose the "true criminality of our times," his attacks on Luce were always very precise in associating "our times" with Luce's Time and in recognizing his project's temporal ambitions as indeed criminal (81). A 1962 draft for the revised *Soft Machine* accordingly magnified Luce's American Century into a full blown millennium: "Past crimes high lighted Luce—he boasted of a rigged thousand years—."[3]

Luce's 1941 editorial championing the American Century in *LIFE* will seem bland to anyone reading it for the first time in the rearview mirror of the Project for the *New* American Century. Taken at face value, the *American Century* meant simply time *for* America: time to end its history of isolationism and take its place as a global power by entering World War II. But when Luce says "it is America's first century as a dominant power" and then repeats the phrase, the inference leaks out: the twentieth century is the first American Century in the sense that a second must surely follow, and then a third . . . (Luce 1941, 64–65). Luce's text operated as an imperialistic mission statement, a blueprint for America as the measure of all things and for the Americanization of the globe. Its subtext was a world that runs on *American time*, to the end of time, to the end of history: universal and immutable. In effect, Luce fantasized bringing temporality itself under permanent American control, and so leads straight to Francis Fukuyama, author of *The End of History and the Last Man* (1992) and one of the founding signatories of the New American Century.

Indeed, for Luce the "end of history" was already being shaped by what he called an "immense American internationalism. American jazz, Hollywood movies, American slang, American machines and patented products" (1941, 65). *TIME, LIFE,* and *Fortune* were themselves part of this emergent globalization, and we have to remind ourselves that they did far more than dominate the US newsmagazine market; *TIME, LIFE,* and *Fortune* set the global standard for how the news was represented in word and image, and for how complex events were synthesized and reduced to predigested sound-bites that served a single narrative vision. Although they had a narrowly conservative agenda, the magazines successfully gave an impression of objectivity and omniscience, while their promotion of American culture and commerce as the new universal currency served Luce's goal to project a vision of the nation to itself and the world until the two visions fully coincided. The owner of the TIME-LIFE publishing empire didn't advocate a coercive imperialism of force, therefore, because unlike the Project for the New American Century, he had faith in the soft sell of an empire of images. Luce believed in exercising *soft power,* using media representations rather than military hardware, which is why we can understand Burroughs' cut-up oeuvre as a guerrilla counter-project to the American Century.

Burroughs opposed Luce's magazines not only for their reductive reportage and conservative content or even for their brutal reviews of his books—he actually sued *Time* because of one in 1963—but, more important, he opposed them because he took their titles literally, took Luce at his word. He saw that Luce's magazines projected a world that would embody the American way of *life,* that would run on American *time,* and that would define *fortune* in terms of the American Dream. Quite literally, Luce ensured that whenever anyone referred to *time* they named his magazine, so that Burroughs' refrain "ALL OUT OF TIME AND INTO SPACE" (Burroughs 2006, 71) referenced both one of Luce's titles and the temporal order of his magazines; that's to say, the ways in which they recorded events to make narrative sense of "the times" and therefore projected the onward march of history, whose commanding voice had narrated Luce's *March of Time* radio and newsreel programs throughout the 1930s and 1940s. Burroughs' cut-up magazine *TIME* was one of many works, including his *Moving Times* three-column newspaper format texts of the mid-1960s, that took the temporality of Luce's title literally, experimenting with "time travel" by scrambling media reportage.[4] The uniquely disorientating temporal experience of Burroughs' book-length cut-up texts, with their nonlinear recyclings of material and vertiginous flashes of déjà vu, can also be read as ways to disrupt and escape both "time" in a philosophical sense and "the times," the teleological drumbeat of Luce's American Century, the universal time of global capitalism.

Burroughs' understanding that the man who owned *TIME, LIFE,* and *Fortune* was in effect seeking to copyright the terms, is clearest from an unpublished manuscript composed shortly after he began using cut-up methods: "When Tzara first pulled words out of a hat the conspiracy of *Life Time Fortune* to monopolize Life Time and Fortune would have been smashed before it started."[5] Here, as elsewhere, Burroughs backdates cut-up methods to Tristan Tzara, but in a distinctive invocation of his Dada predecessor of the 1920s he ties the methods even more closely to Luce's news media and their imperialistic postwar agenda. Projecting the "conspiracy" of Luce's *Time* back in time and imagining defeating it through cut-up methods, this was Burroughs' first attempt to retroactively rewrite history, a project that would become fully explicit in his "Red Night" trilogy of novels. The nightmare of Luce's endless American Century, "a rigged thousand years," animates Burroughs' visionary mapping of alternative futures—of alternative *times* and alternative *temporalities*. At the high-water mark of the Cut-Up Project in 1970, Burroughs famously created his own time zone in the form of a "'Dream Rat' Calendar." The Calendar of ten months with 23 days attempted to make an everyday practice out of the revolutionary aim announced in *The Revised Boy Scout Manual* that it is "Time to forget a dead empire and build a living republic": "Step 1: PROCLAIM A NEW ERA AND SET UP A NEW CALENDAR" (Burroughs 1982, 9, 5).

A WAR OF TWO TRILOGIES

The "new era" of the Burroughs Century was a direct counter to Luce's American Century, and it is tempting not only to see the Cut-Up Project as the story of a writer who took on Luce's media empire but also to speak of a War of Two Trilogies: *The Soft Machine, Nova Express,* and *The Ticket That Exploded* versus *TIME, LIFE,* and *Fortune.* However, this isn't quite the case, and not simply because the war against Luce informed hundreds of short cut-up texts, scrapbooks, photo-collages, films, and audio tapes as well as a trilogy of books. Rather, it's not the case because Burroughs' rival trilogy was never planned or conceptualized as such.

One of the most startling discoveries to emerge from researching the "restored" editions of *The Soft Machine*, *The Ticket That Exploded*, and *Nova Express* was to realize that Burroughs never once referred to the three as "The Cut-Up Trilogy." In fact, whenever he grouped three books together in the early 1960s, it was always to conjure different trilogies. Most materially there was *Dead Fingers Talk*, published in England in 1963, which creatively collaged together parts of Burroughs' three Olympia Press titles, *The Naked Lunch*, *The Soft Machine*, and *The Ticket That Exploded*. While that trilogy left out *Nova Express*, other permutations left out *The Ticket That Exploded*. Indeed, the trilogy in "Introduction to *Naked Lunch The Soft Machine Novia Express*" [*sic*],[6] published in *Evergreen Review* in January 1962, is also named in the text of *Nova Express* itself. The only instance when Burroughs actually uses the word "trilogy" at all (in an unpublished manuscript also from early 1962) is again for these three titles: "My present work is *Novia Express* [...]—This is the last book of a trilogy—*Naked Lunch The Soft Machine*."[7] But even if we do group the three cut-up book titles together, we still don't end up with "The Cut-Up Trilogy," since the result of Burroughs issuing revised versions was six different editions, including two *Tickets* (1962, 1967) and three entirely different *Soft Machines* (1961, 1966, 1968).

The trilogy's bizarre bibliographic history is well known, but the problem is much greater than most critics still muddling up the editions and nobody ever being quite sure what the textual differences are. Even leaving aside the backstories to how the texts were written and rewritten—which complicate the received wisdom at a genetic level—the six published editions effectively scrambled the chronology of the titles and make nonsense of the universally accepted sequence (first *The Soft Machine*, then *The Ticket*, finally *Nova Express*). The six editions have potentially no fewer than 120 combinations—a far from idle calculation, given Brion Gysin's application of cut-up principles to his Permutation Poems: instead of "RUB OUT THE WORD," we can rub out "The Cut-Up Trilogy" by permutating the titles. Or to put this another way, philosophically as well as practically we must insist on the shifting, multiple alternative possibilities that are otherwise lost when we use the definite article to speak of *The* Trilogy as if it comprised three texts, conceived as a group and existing in one chronological order. Even though it was the result of material contingencies rather than a plan—or rather precisely *because* it was the result of material contingencies rather than a plan—the ungraspable ontological fluidity of Burroughs' "trilogy" reproduced the disorientating temporality internal to each text. Individually and collectively, the cut-up volumes were therefore an implicit counter to the teleology, fixed temporal order, and commonsense reality projected by Luce's trilogy.

"OPEN LETTER TO LIFE"

Burroughs' recognition of *TIME*, *LIFE*, and *Fortune* as the trilogy of his enemy both coincided with and determined the very genesis of the cut-up method. The stories told by Burroughs and Gysin of what happened at the Beat Hotel on the left bank of Paris in the first days of October 1959 have often been repeated, so often that the crucial presence of Henry Luce has remained hidden in plain sight.

To begin with, Burroughs' discovery of the cut-up method—or the creation myth of the project, in the sense that its truth depends as much on what they said about it as on what did or did not happen—was the chance encounter of two chance encounters, both mediated by *LIFE* magazine. Burroughs had been interviewed by "the *Time* police"—as he dubbed David Snell and Loomis Dean, the reporter-photographer double act from *LIFE*—on the very day that Gysin demonstrated to him the first cut-up texts at the Beat Hotel: "Returning to room #25 I found Brion Gysin holding a scissors, bits of newspaper, *LIFE, TIME*, spread out on a table" (Burroughs 1978, 28). In any other context, these would be superficial coincidences; not so in relation to the Cut-Up Project, whose chance-based methods sought out coincidences for their potent and enigmatic significance. That's why Burroughs and Gsyin played down, for example, the crucial role of the Paris edition of the *International Herald Tribune* as source material for the original cut-up texts created on the first day of October 1959:[8] they left certain things unsaid the better to play up how those chance encounters with *LIFE* inaugurated their recognition of synchronicities as *signs*. The precise point of intersection involving *LIFE* has been lost, however, because those retelling the anecdotes usually refer generically to Gysin cutting up "newspapers" and then overlook the importance of his naming *"Life Magazine advertisements"* as source material for his "First Cut-Ups" in *Minutes to Go* (1960). What has also been missed is that the cut-up method's launching manifesto retrospectively identified the prophetic power of those encounters with *LIFE* magazine due to a third encounter with *LIFE* that took place at the end of the following month (Gysin 1960, 6).[9]

Almost always just name-checked in accounts of the Cut-Up Project, *Minutes to Go* is especially revealing about the early and central importance of Luce's newsmagazines. Although Luce's presence is easily overlooked, it is right there in the title (which puts *time* center stage), and in the chance-based methods of textual production (*fortune*), while direct references materially connect the work of all four contributors. Just as Gysin acknowledges the use of *LIFE* adverts, so one of Burroughs' cut-up poems ("FROM SAN DIEGO UP TO MAINE") credits *Time* as a source text, one of Gregory Corso's poems identifies the 1950s as the "*Time* decade," and the fourth collaborator, Sinclair Beiles, not only credits *LIFE* magazine as the source of "TELEGRAM FROM MEKNES," but makes repeated cut-up puns on the name of Henry Luce: "SEWERPLUCE OIL"; "LUSEOIL"; "Luceairbase"; "SURPLUCE" (Beiles et al. 1960, 21, 32, 38). And this evidence is all secondary to Exhibit A, the text immediately following Gysin's "First Cut-Ups," which identifies the crucial third encounter between Burroughs and *LIFE*: "OPEN LETTER TO LIFE MAGAZINE."

The significance of "OPEN LETTER TO LIFE MAGAZINE" is multiple. To begin with, this was actually the very first cut-up text to be published, having already appeared in the winter 1959 issue of *Nomad*, which was precisely the kind of short-lived, self-published little magazine that sprang up in the 1950s and 1960s to contest the monopoly power of mainstream media empires. If the little magazine as a medium was ideally suited to publishing a text that was an Open Letter reply to another, larger magazine, so too was the pamphlet form of *Minutes to Go*. Renewing "the old pamphlet days when writers fought in the street,"[10] Burroughs disseminated "OPEN LETTER TO LIFE MAGAZINE" and his other first cut-up texts in what he knew was historically the medium of choice for radicals issuing manifestoes, experiments, and provocations, for making single-shot attacks, hit-and-run counterattacks, ripostes, and rebuttals. The pamphlet form, the Open Letter, and the cut-up method were all ways of "settling the score," as a wraparound band issued with some copies of *Minutes to Go* declared.[11] And so, secondly, by adopting the genre of the Open Letter, the text formally declares itself a public statement that aims to set the record straight: answering back to *LIFE*, speaking out against the media machine. To take this text's title literally is to see that in *Minutes to Go* the cut-up method itself was addressed to Henry Luce, and the archival evidence supports such a reading.[12] The message of the "open letter" therefore lies partly in the content—to which I'll turn shortly—but must mainly be found in the method, which is the strategy of *détournement*: turning the words of those who attack you by misrepresenting reality back against them. The term *détournement* had recently been coined by the Letterists and Situationists, also operating in Paris, but Burroughs owed nothing to Isou or Debord any more than he did to Tzara or Duchamp.[13] For Burroughs was not responding to *LIFE* with the tactics of avant-gardes past or present: he was responding with the very tactics of his enemy, since *LIFE* magazine had just attacked him in the text he cut up to make "OPEN LETTER TO LIFE MAGAZINE."[14] Appearing in the November 30, 1959, issue, the *LIFE* article featured Burroughs in a sneering attack on the Beat Generation, dubbed "The Only Rebellion Around." The importance of this particular issue of *LIFE* to *Minutes to Go* is made even clearer by Beiles's "TELEGRAM FROM MEKNES," which cut up another article from the same magazine, about the poisoning of 10,000 Moroccans who used cooking oil adulterated with surplus machine oil bought from a US air base—hence "SEWERPLUCE OIL"; "LUSEOIL"; "Luceairbase"—a report whose fusion of literally toxic capitalism with American military imperialism in the context of Luce's magazine inspired "the whole rancid oil scandal of The Trak Sex and Dream Utilities" in *The Soft Machine* (Burroughs 2014b, 39).[15]

In a small but telling footnote to "OPEN LETTER," in *Minutes to Go* the source text from *LIFE* is identified, but the date of the issue given is wrong: "Dec 5 1959," rather than November 30, 1959 (Beiles et al. 1960, 12).[16] What might be dismissed in other contexts as merely an error, takes on an entirely new meaning in *Minutes to Go*, which deploys numerous similar minor inconsistencies and a mass of apparent typos to unsettling effect. In this instance, changing the *time* of the *LIFE* article becomes a model in miniature of how to rewrite history. The misdating affirms the cut-up method and the genre of the open letter as modes of reply, since one of the things Burroughs learned from *LIFE* was precisely how the media falsified history by habitually getting the facts wrong.[17] Taken together, however, these details merely hint at the crucial material importance of the November 30, 1959, issue of *LIFE* magazine for how Burroughs conceived and applied cut-up methods.

"NAKED LIGHT BULBS"

Burroughs' appearance in this issue of *LIFE* has become well known through the photograph showing him in his room at the Beat Hotel. This was not the first public picture of Burroughs as an author, since his image had appeared a couple of months earlier, in summer 1959, in *Big Table* magazine and on the back of the Olympia Press *Naked Lunch*. But the picture in *LIFE* was categorically different, most obviously in terms of circulation, which ran into the millions rather than the low hundreds and reached around the world. While Burroughs' first appearance in the mainstream media was significant for his reception as a writer, what is most revealing and surprising is its importance for his own creative *production*. Here, for the first time, Burroughs could see his place within the medium, see how his image and his own words could be turned against him, and I would argue that he learned how to develop his own methods from the example of *LIFE* rather than from Tristan Tzara and the historical avant-garde.[18] Taking the methods of his enemies literally, Burroughs learned how to fight fire with fire.

The caption to the photograph in *LIFE* tells us what to see: "EX-DOPE ADDICT William Burroughs, who describes drug-taking in *Junky* and *Naked Lunch*, now lives in Paris in what has become known as Beat Hotel" (O'Neil 1959, 124).[19] Far from evoking the expatriate glamour of Hemingway and Fitzgerald, Paris here looks boring, grey, and uncomfortable: there Burroughs sits, on a sagging bed, staring toward the floor of his little room, beneath a naked light bulb. The caption describes him as a writer in the Beat Hotel in Paris, but the image seems to show a man in solitary confinement inside Beat Prison.

What's interesting is that Burroughs had praised the "brilliant photography" of Loomis Dean (Burroughs 1993, 429), who took no fewer than five rolls of pictures, showing Burroughs the writer at work in front of his typewriter, in a Paris bookstore promoting the just-published *Naked Lunch*, chatting with a crowd in the bar of the Beat Hotel, sitting with Brion Gysin surrounded by paintings, and so on—and that out of all this rich variety, and even from alternative shots of Burroughs on his own, *LIFE* chose the most solitary, most downbeat image they could. However, it was more than a simple matter of the choice of image. To see the verbal-visual strategy at work in *LIFE*—indeed to recognize that its manipulation of words and images *was* strategic, and therefore to see what Burroughs saw and learned from *LIFE*—we need to pull back to the bigger picture of how the magazine framed the Beats in terms of the core, everyday value that had defined Henry Luce's American Century: the promise of a "more abundant life" (Luce 1941, 64).

The article on the Beats runs to seventeen pages, making it by far the longest piece in the issue; but the text is only five thousand words—far fewer, for example, than the text of Luce's "American Century" editorial, which in 1941 took up just five pages in *LIFE*. The article is so long because it is interrupted by no fewer than twenty-nine separate advertisements, ensuring that the coverage of the Beats is framed by commercials promoting and embodying the "abundant life" that defined the American Century. Unsurprisingly, the text of the article lampooned the Beats for living in poverty in the "Age of Supermarkets," but the real work of critique and mockery was achieved by the precise juxtaposition of monochrome images of the Beats with glossy color adverts featuring happy Americans. Appropriately, the only spread without a commercial is the very first, which is an ironic lifestyle ad reconstructing a "Beat Pad," although the couple featured in it were clearly not Beats but *beatniks*. If one of the key strategies in the *LIFE* article was to contrast the Beats with the infinite possibilities of consumerist desire, the other was to blur the distinction between the writers they featured as Beat (Ginsberg, Kerouac, Burroughs, Corso, and McClure were all pictured) and the followers of the beatnik fashion craze. Ginsberg—who loathed the "foul word 'beatnik'"—had already seen this strategy at work two months earlier in *LIFE*'s September 21 "Squaresville U.S.A. vs. Beatsville" article, which had prompted him to lament being willfully "confused with the image of a beatnik disseminated via mass media" (Ginsberg 2008, 222, 224).

Featuring all the essentials for "uncomfortable living," as the caption mockingly listed them, the Beat Pad is empty and deliberately dull, featuring an old coal stove and very little else. Self-evidently, the Beat Chick needs the device advertised overleaf that's "better than a kitchen exhaust fan" and could give "her an odor-free, smoke-free, grease-free kitchen for only $39.95" (*What a gift for Mom!*").[20] Bearing in mind that the Nixon-Khrushchev "Kitchen Debate" had taken place in Moscow only four months earlier, the kitchen exhaust fan wasn't simply the latest in consumer products advertised by *LIFE* but a symbolic object of national importance. (By implication, and fulfilling the verbal play on Sputnik, the Beatniks unpatriotically adhere to Soviet standards of kitchen appliances.) The stakes were therefore as high as the punches aimed against the Beat writers were low: the juxtaposition of the happy housewife with her kitchen fan on one half of the page opposite a picture captioned "horsing around" on the other, showing Allen Ginsberg pulling "a scary face at Gregory Corso, who makes a motion as if to shoot him," only proves how immature the poets are not to want a nice new wife and kitchen (O'Neil 1959, 120). Clearly enough, this was payback for Ginsberg's challenge to Luce's world, which had gone public in 1956 in *Howl and Other Poems* with the open question: "Are you going to let your emotional life be run by Time Magazine?"[21] The alluring sales talk of *LIFE*'s all-American consumer culture responds to poems such as "America" and "A Supermarket in California" by trapping its author inside their supermarket of a magazine and by ridiculing people who would *choose* to live in a room with a naked light bulb—number three in the list of essentials for the well-equipped Beat Pad.

And here we see how carefully organized the magazine was, since the horror of the bulb without a shade is precisely the standout feature in the photograph of Burroughs, thereby connecting him to those sad beatnik losers. Showing the awful naked light bulb stands in for the need to say anything at all about *Naked Lunch*—although had staff writer Paul O'Neil gotten as far as the first page of the book, published three months earlier, he would have encountered William Lee ridiculing a representative of Madison Avenue in the shape of an "advertising exec type fruit" (Burroughs 2003, 3).

"READ IT AGAIN"

"OPEN LETTER TO LIFE MAGAZINE" cut up a good deal from the passages in the *LIFE* article about Burroughs, including lines describing his drug use: "ijuana, majoun, hashish, candy" (Beiles et al. 1960, 11). What makes this example of textual *détournement* so significant is the literally bigger picture of the page in the spread of the magazine. As representatives of American consumer culture, the adverts in *LIFE* don't just dominate the article about Burroughs and the Beats, they interrupt it in order to produce a series of composite texts; the page featuring the image of Burroughs is one of six that are divided into two columns, half text/half adverts, while another two pages are divided into three columns where the text is literally framed either side by ads.

In the case of Burroughs, the two-column page cuts him up and folds him in with the advertisements. At first sight, the strategy seems obvious enough. Only on rereading the juxtaposition of advertisement and text do we see its peculiar but precise relevance: "Candettes taste like orange candy, but don't let that fool you . . ." says the ad for a sore throat product in the left column. Just below, the text in the right column tells us that Burroughs dosed himself with "alcohol, heroin, marijuana, kif and a hashish candy" (O'Neil 1959, 124). In any other context, this would be mere happenstance, a meaningless verbal coincidence of candies to match the meaningless visual coincidence of light bulbs—but not in this context and not for Burroughs. On the contrary, *he* wasn't fooled: this was exactly the kind of seemingly random intersection or irrational juxtaposition that revealed how reality was produced through a complex system of subliminal signs. Recognizing the *formal* dimension to the magazine's hatchet job, Burroughs must have seen proof of the prophetic character of those chance encounters with *LIFE* that had initiated the cut-up method just two months earlier.

Burroughs' practical response to subliminal advertising, waking suggestion, and other techniques of the "hidden persuaders" (in the resonant phrase of Vance Packard's 1957 study of Madison Avenue) began here. In *Nova Express*, he described the decoding operation involved: "Our technicians learn to read newspapers and magazines for juxtaposition statements rather than contents" (Burroughs 2014a, 89). That description dates from early 1962, and Burroughs would periodically keep rediscovering the principle, as when informing Gysin two years later: "Newspapers are cut up by format. You read the adjacent columns while you read this column [. . .] This is the secret of their power to mould thought feeling and subsequent events" (Burroughs 2012, 140). Inspired by Jeff Nuttall's *My Own Mag*, 1964 was a critical year for his development and application of the principle, leading to a mass of three-column newspaper formatted texts and the pamphlets *APO-33* and *TIME* in 1965; but the point of origin for Burroughs' discovery was his encounter with *LIFE* magazine in late 1959. The cross-column readings Burroughs would promote in his own three-column layout texts of the mid-1960s and also the "Juxtaposition Formulae" he described at work in a photomontage were both modeled from *LIFE*.

To say that *LIFE* magazine cut up William Burroughs before he cut up *LIFE* magazine, and to conclude that in it he saw the future strategy of his own application of cut-up methods used against him, might seem wildly speculative for such a large and material claim. But there is a compelling account that witnesses what Burroughs recognized in *LIFE*. In late December 1959, Gregory Corso returned to Paris after an absence of three months and wrote to New Directions publisher James Laughlin what happened on his arrival at 9 rue Git-le-Coeur: "I immediately went to see Burroughs. After awhile he showed me the *Life* article. I read it quickly and thought 'another down article'. Then Burroughs asked me 'Did you read it?' I said yes. Sensing my indifferent reaction he said 'Read it again'" (Corso 2003, 227).[22] Corso read it again and came to the same conclusion as Burroughs: "Luce is God. He owns LIFE TIME *and* CHANCE (Fortune). In *Life* he is all strong, in *Time* he can write about something before it even happens. He made the Beat Generation!" (229). Corso then proceeds exactly to describe the magazine's hostile formal strategy, the verbal-visual juxtapositions of prose, photography, and advertising that Burroughs had recognized: "notice how they say of me GUNS—*Don't Shoot The Warthog, Bomb*, in photo: Corso aims as if to SHOOT—also notice, photo of Ginsberg lying in bed, the Sitwell 'bad smell' comment, next to Ginsberg photo is an ad 'how to get rid of bad smell from the house'" (229–30). Corso's analysis is unmistakably Burroughsian and confirms that in *LIFE* Burroughs found the material model for his counter-project to weaponize the use of word and image. Six years later in his own magazine *TIME*, he spells out the continuity of practice and critique that goes back to *LIFE*, asking: "Why *that* picture just *there*.??" (Burroughs 1965b, 3).

"LUCE LINES"

The message of "OPEN LETTER TO LIFE MAGAZINE" in *Minutes to Go* was to bring the strategy out into the open. It was the first stage of what Burroughs referred to as his Open Bank policy, which Gysin announced in *Minutes to Go* by echoing Lautréamont's famous call to collective arms ("*La poésie doit être faite par tous. Non par un"*): "the writing machine is for everybody" (Gysin 1960, 5).[23] Such advocacy of DIY creativity has been read in an art-historical context—the postwar resurgence of collage-based aesthetics—but its seizure of the means of production is also specifically directed against the mass media and monopolistic press institutions. It's therefore revealing that the first published text to feature the phrase "life time fortune"—one of the early sections of *Nova Express* in the January 1962 issue of *Evergreen Review*—made the connection back to "OPEN LETTER TO LIFE MAGAZINE" in *Minutes to Go* by maintaining the same genre in its title: "OPEN LETTER TO MY CONSTITUENTS AND CO-WORKERS IF ANY REMAIN FOR THE END OF IT." In other words, from *Minutes to Go*, the launching manifesto of the Cut-Up Project, to *Nova Express*, the last published title of the Cut-Up Trilogy where this section appeared as "Prisoners, Come Out," Burroughs triangulated the genre of open letter, cut-up methods, and Luce's magazine trilogy.

The specific content of the short section of *Nova Express* published in *Evergreen Review* turns out to be equally revealing, since it named in one text both Luce's trilogy of magazines and a trilogy of Burroughs' own novels ("The purpose of my writing is to expose and arrest Nova Criminals. In *Naked Lunch, The Soft Machine* and *Nova Express* I show who they are" [2014a, 5]), and so implicitly fingered Luce as a Nova criminal, one whose exposure was the very purpose of Burroughs' writing. The section also points toward a very particular conspiracy in the sequence of questions it addresses to the reader: "Who monopolized Love Sex and Dream? Who monopolized Time Life and Fortune?" (Burroughs 2014a, 3) The answer to the second question is clearly: Henry Luce. The answer to the first question—confirmed by the warning against LSD that follows—is: Timothy Leary. Burroughs' early (1961) suspicion of how hallucinogenic drugs and countercultural desires would be co-opted by mainstream America was based on his recent encounter with Leary and, as he told Ginsberg, this whole section of *Nova Express* "expressed quite clearly" what he thought "about Leary and his project" (Burroughs 2012, 98). Burroughs might not have known that Henry and his wife Clare were both regular trippers, but he must have seen the extensive positive coverage of hallucinogens in Luce's magazines, which started in *Time* as early as 1954 (with an article entitled "Dream Stuff"). And so, while "Prisoners, Come Out" in *Nova Express* more or less openly attacked Timothy Leary, at a deeper level it was another attack on Henry Luce.

Attack and counterattack defines the structure of Burroughs' relationship with Luce throughout the early 1960s. Exactly three years after the November 30, 1959, issue, another volume in Luce's trilogy would pay Burroughs back, the November 30, 1962, issue of *Time* printed a review of *Naked Lunch* so scathing that it forced Burroughs to sue. Significantly, the attack openly rehearsed the visual features of the 1959 article in *LIFE* by verbally mocking "the worn grey man" sitting in his "worn grey room" among the naked light bulbs and rats of the Beat Hotel.[24] Burroughs responded by taking legal action, and then cutting up the documentation, as well as by creating his own magazine called *TIME*. Burroughs' *TIME* reused the

1962 original's cover and cut up the review inside that had vilified both the author ("Presenting himself as proof that the universe is foul, Burroughs achieves the somewhat irrelevant honesty of hysteria") and his trilogy ("utter babble"). Cutting up these particular phrases in ritualistic acts of revenge also gave Burroughs text to recycle in his own work; he incorporated the "hysteria" line into the revised *Ticket That Exploded*, and included both this and the "utter babble" phrase in his version of *TIME*. There, the words appeared opposite a newspaper photograph of Burroughs and a copy of the recently published *Nova Express* placed on top of another issue of *Time*, establishing a material connection between Luce's magazine and Burroughs' magazine mediated by his cut-up book.[25] These and other published associations repeatedly interconnected Burroughs' Cut-Up Trilogy to Luce's trilogy.

Henry Luce features by name only once in any edition of the Cut-Up Trilogy—the 1968, third edition of *The Soft Machine* (published only in the United Kingdom), where a character goes into "his Luce act"—but the litany of Luce's trilogy of magazines is called repeatedly across Burroughs' own trilogy of books (Burroughs 1968, 106).[26] Variant drafts and versions published in little magazines were sometimes more explicit than the books and are clues to Luce's pervasive presence. A case in point is *Gambit*'s spring 1963 version of "The Mayan Caper," a section of *The Soft Machine* narrated in the voice of a scoop newspaper reporter. Here, Burroughs added an unambiguous note: "The Mayan control calendar is not dead," he warned, but "is operating now, controlling thought, feeling and apparent sensory impressions, controlling and monopolizing your life your time your fortune."[27] Readers of *Naked Lunch* might recognize the key phrasing rhythmically paralleled with *Time*, *Life*, and *Fortune*—"thought, feeling and apparent sensory impressions"—since it appears there near verbatim as a definition of "biocontrol," a dream to technologically perfect the falsification of reality.[28] In the opening lines of *The Exterminator* (1960), Burroughs quotes this phrasing from *Naked Lunch* and gives its source: an article in none other than *TIME* magazine (October 15, 1956). The commercial potentials for creating an entire world of illusions had been identified by Packard in *The Hidden Persuaders*, which cited the *Time* biocontrol article, and Burroughs had already shown his awareness of Luce's agenda in *Naked Lunch*, which gives a walk-on role to "THE MAN FROM *TIME*" and whose narrative ends with a prophecy of "Time Monopolies."[29] However, the point is not only the technology of control but also the medium in which it was reported, since Burroughs recognized Luce's magazine as *itself* a technique for producing "THE IMMUTABLE REALITY OF THE UNIVERSE." Significantly, in the very month Gysin sliced up *Life* magazine, Burroughs defined the title of *Naked Lunch* (or rather, completely redefined it) in terms of exposing the conspiracy of consumer capitalism and the news media: "a frozen moment when everyone sees what is on the end of every fork [. . .] Let them see what is on the end of that long newspaper spoon" (Burroughs 2003, 199, 205).[30]

In *Nova Express*, Burroughs equated busting Luce's monopoly with breaking the "blockade" of planet Earth in the trilogy's science-fiction scenario: "This blockade was broken by partisan activity directed from the planet Saturn that cut the control lines of word and image laid down by the nova mob" (Burroughs 2014a, 56). The aim to break a media monopoly of reporting the news, and therefore of defining what constituted newsworthy reality, is in fact implicit in the very title of *Nova Express* (clearer in its original form: *The Novia Express*), which is generically that of a newspaper. And even the term "nova mob" hints at the central role of the press to the scenario of Burroughs' trilogy, since it dates from summer 1960 when he reported coming under attack from "the Beaverbrook Mob," referring to the owner of the *Daily Express*, Lord Beaverbrook.[31] Burroughs made significant creative use of the *Daily Express* along with other British newspapers, and also *Newsweek*, but in the Cut-Up Trilogy he repeatedly referenced *Time*, *Life*, and *Fortune* because they were the definitive measure of his own work. Using the strategy of payback through *détournement*—turning Luce's own words against him—in *The Ticket That Exploded*, Burroughs identifies Luce with the deity behind the nova mob: "Your monopoly of life, time, and fortune cancelled by your own orders—Pay, Mr Bradly Mr Martin" (Burroughs 2014c, 153).

Luce was a constant textual presence while significant traces appear scattered in the archives in often the most unexpected places,[32] but Luce's magazines were also consistent points of reference for Burroughs across the full range of his cut-up experiments, from film (including a citation of "Life Time Change" in *Towers Open Fire*) to visual artwork: "Opposition to apomorphine collages indicates crucial weak point in Luce lines," he wrote Gysin in October 1961 (Burroughs 2012, 89). The phrase "Luce lines" is in turn a significant variant on Burroughs' "word lines" concept and should force us to reread this term that recurs throughout the Cut-Up Trilogy as well as in texts such as *The Exterminator*: "The word lines keep you in Time."[33] Archival evidence confirms Burroughs' intention: within his larger claims for temporality as a construction of language, "Time" played specifically on Luce's *Time*. Likewise, one typescript clarifies that the "big con" of a fake reality works by trapping us inside "THE WORD-LIFE-TIME SLOT."[34] For Burroughs, The Word was Luce's Word.

NEWSPEAK

The substantial unpublished archival evidence, above all in the Burroughs Papers of the Berg Collection at the New York Public Library, is especially fascinating for including texts where Burroughs imagined speaking directly to him: "Mr Henry Luce, Do you really know what the machine is up to?"[35] What makes this doubly fascinating is that Burroughs was echoing a remarkably similar dialogue that Ginsberg had also fantasized in his journal two years earlier, in spring 1958, in which the poet also addressed the media magnate directly and in the same terms: "Be

Henry Luce not the voice of the machine" (Ginsberg 1996, 447). Since Ginsberg was writing this while living at the Beat Hotel in 1958 together with Burroughs, it's conceivable that his dialogue with Luce not only preceded but actually prompted Burroughs' own.

While Henry Luce was a bogeyman for Ginsberg as well as for Burroughs, the contrasting responses they made to the November 30, 1959, issue of *Life* are an index of how uniquely the cut-up method served Burroughs by integrating creative practice with political action. Before the magazine came out, Ginsberg reported to Burroughs that he had heard it was going to be "a creepy attack" and correctly predicted the outcome: "Those guys that interview you send in their info and then it may get all twisted up in NY—'We hear it was the other way around doc.' You're mentioned in the *Life* piece, I don't know in what way."[36] Ginsberg's insight that the "info" would get "twisted" in New York—at the head offices of Luce's empire, the new Time-Life Building that opened at Rockefeller Center in 1959—matched Burroughs' own verdict ten days before the magazine appeared: "Of course they [Snell and Dean] have nothing to do with final form of the story" (Burroughs 2012, 9).

Far from being paranoid, their cynicism was fully merited, since Henry Luce kept a close personal eye on Burroughs and Ginsberg. In September 1959, Burroughs noted that he was about to be interviewed by *Life* via "Rosalind of *Time*," naming one Rosalind Constable, who not only reported on contemporary culture for the magazine (and in fact worked for all three Luce flagship titles) but also reported directly to Henry Luce himself (Burroughs 1993, 426). The "Constable Report" focused on avant-garde activities and included notes about Burroughs dated September 2, 1959.[37] If Burroughs was aware of Luce's interest, his response to the November 30, 1959, article in *Life* seems remarkably sanguine, even amused: "it is a mass medium," he calmly reminded his alarmed mother, "and sensational factors must be played up at the expense often of fact . . . In order to earn my reputation I may have to start drinking my tea from a skull" (Burroughs 2012, 13). In contrast, Ginsberg expressed to Burroughs his sense of anger, despair, and uncertainty: "The *Life* article out, less vicious then I thought it would be, but full of opinionation & bullshit & some outright fabrications [. . .] but there's not much to be done about it that I can see, yet. Except go on doing same as before. Would love to discuss the matter."[38] Unlike Ginsberg, Burroughs immediately saw what he could do about it, and with a pair of scissors set about doing it.

The presence of Henry Luce even ghosts what we have come to call "the cut-up method" itself (a misnomer as much as "the Cut-Up Trilogy," since the definite article contradicts the wide range of ever-evolving techniques). For only three days after the *Life* article appeared, on December 2, 1959, Burroughs initially coined another name for cutting up. Taken from George Orwell's *Nineteen Eighty-Four*, it shows that Burroughs originally conceptualized the method's primary purpose as a critique of the news media: "The name of method is Newspeak Poetry."[39] Burroughs published just one short text that named his method in these terms— "A newspeak précis of the article made in its image with its materials," which appeared in the January 1960 issue of *Evergreen Review*[40]—and then he dropped it, no doubt recognizing its limitations, as well as preferring to give credit closer to home by calling it "the cut-up method of Brion Gysin." But the name reveals that at the outset of the Cut-Up Project, and in the immediate context of the article in *Life*, Burroughs identified himself as an American Orwell, fighting the fascism of language as a control machine, and clearly thinking of Winston Smith, whose job in the novel was to fabricate the historical record by cutting up newspapers and cutting out photographs.[41] This was how Burroughs saw the kind of history written in Luce's magazines and, in the spirit of fighting fire with fire, his response was to treat history as paper and cut it up.

Since "newspeak" was the very language of totalitarian control, intended to "make all other modes of thought impossible" (Orwell 2004, 312), Newspeak Poetry was a provocatively ambiguous term for Burroughs' method of *détournement* and highlights the radical ambiguity of both his creation of fake news and fantasized dialogs with Henry Luce. For Burroughs was not only fighting fire with fire but also *playing with fire*: ventriloquizing the Lord of Time gave voice both to his enemy and "the enemy within" himself—the Ugly American, who first emerged in the fascistic fantasies of William Lee's routines in *Queer* in 1952. A decade later, Luce's name appears in dozens of unpublished archival typescripts, very often in trilogies of enemy figures: alongside fellow press barons Lord Beaverbrook and William Randolph Hearst; in between oil tycoons, "ROCKEFELLER LUCE GETTY"; and, less palatably, associated with a trio of Jews: "TIME LIFE FORTUNE. EINSTEIN MARX FREUD FRAUD."[42] The anti-Semitism here—made far more explicit elsewhere, alongside an equally ugly misogyny—has almost always been airbrushed out in accounts of Burroughs' work, but it was integral to the atmosphere of conspiracy and paranoia that gave his writing, especially in the early days of the Cut-Up Project, such a ferocious edge. Burroughs' performative genius found in Luce—or rather, his fantasy version of Luce—an ideal voice, as when ventriloquizing Luce as the mastermind behind a conspiracy of conspiracies: "I AM SENDING THE THING, WOMAN. THE CUNT GIMMICK AS YOU CALL IT. THE WORD. VIRUS THE CONTROL MACHINE. THE COMMUNIST PARTY. LIFE TIME FORTUNE."[43]

"THE ARCHIVES OF TIME"

While the unpublished evidence reveals that Luce and his magazines played a much more important and wide-ranging role in the very conception of the cut-up project than has been recognized, the opening of the New York Public Library archive has also made it possible to recognize the importance of Luce to the Burroughs archive itself. For although Burroughs' cut-up works individually resemble avant-garde experiments, collectively they constitute a massive archival network modeled on that of the news media. The "archives of Time" are duly referenced in the 1962 *Ticket That Exploded*, which depicts Henry Luce as "the Lord of Time surrounded by files and calculating machines, word and image bank of a picture planet" (Burroughs 2014c, 117). In the revised edition of *The Ticket* five years later, Burroughs added self-reflexive glimpses of his own mid-1960s working methods and filing systems, referring to "leafing through the GOD files" and "ref. East Beach File page 156" (14–15).

From 1964 onward, Burroughs very consciously developed his own verbal and visual filing systems as rivals to those of Henry Luce, and since Luce's archives held files on Burroughs, he of course reciprocated: "Here's a file on Mr Luce," he told his *Paris Review* interviewer in 1965, before denouncing *Time*, *Life* and *Fortune* (Burroughs 2001, 73).[44] While it might be said that the matrix of late 1950s manuscripts mythologized as the "Word Hoard" was Burroughs' original "database"—"a structured collection of data organized for search and retrieval," as Jed Birmingham puts it—his 1960s cut-up files were assemblages on a completely different scale (Birmingham 2014, 16).[45] More than that, insofar as they consciously rivalled the word and image banks of the global news media, rather than emerged organically as a literary work-in-progress, Burroughs' 1960s archival systems naturally coordinated not only texts and images in multiple and hybrid formats but also work across a range of media and technologies, from photomontage to scrapbooks, film to audiotape.

The archival systems Burroughs developed in the mid-1960s were a key stage in his transformation from a writer into a collage artist, poly-practitioner, and *editor*—and he surely enjoyed the irony that in 1964, just as his three-column newspaper texts such as *The Moving Times* began to appear in little magazines and *Nova Express* was about to be published, Henry Luce stepped down as editor-in-chief of *Time*, *Life*, and *Fortune*. When the following year his cut-up version of *TIME* appeared, Burroughs' friend and collaborator Ian Sommerville described the pamphlet as "fantastic good," and jokingly anticipated the completion of a trilogy to literally mirror and invert Luce's: "I assume you are going to carry advertising and move into LIFE and FORTUNE."[46] The publication of *Nova Express* had just completed Burroughs' trilogy of cut-up books, but the joke, of course, is that given the balance of power in his rivalry with *Time*, *Life*, and *Fortune*, Burroughs was bringing a knife to a gunfight in any format. Indeed, *Nova Express* includes within itself a sense of how ridiculous it was to oppose a media trilogy that in 1965 had a weekly circulation of more than ten million with a book whose print run was ten thousand: "Sure, sure, but you see now why we had to laugh till we pissed watching those dumb rubes playing around with photomontage—Like charging a regiment of tanks with a defective slingshot" (Burroughs 2014a, 44). When, in November 2015, the New York Historical Society announced it had acquired the archives of Time Inc., it reported that the archive comprised "more than 7,500 linear feet of an estimated seven million documents and artifacts"; the Burroughs Papers in the New York Public Library comprise 17 linear feet and eleven thousand manuscript pages.[47] Was it just self-delusion to declare, as he put it in a draft line for *The Ticket*

That Exploded, that "a box camera and a tape recorder can cut lines laid down by Hollywood and life time fortune"?[48]

To grasp the centrality of Luce's global media empire to Burroughs' Cut-Up Project is to understand how and why cut-up methods were weapons for waging asymmetrical warfare against the American Century and to recognize the true scale of his ambition and insight. For in the early 1960s, Burroughs could see the soft traps into which we were being led by the media as well as by the machinery of modern science and the national security state. He attacked the Gods of Life, Time, and Fortune because he foresaw the omniscient global surveillance of Google Earth as well as the NSA—"Henry light sitting on a Luce pile of pictures a mile high in that Time-Life building"; Timothy Leary recorded Burroughs warning, in summer 1961, "They have pictures of every inch of the world" (Leary 1995, 225). If they didn't then, they certainly do now—which is why Burroughs' defiant *détournement* of the American Century has lost none of its power to inspire future generations of media guerrillas, culture jammers, computer hackers, whistleblowers, pop-up subversives, anybody who wants to expose the true criminality of their times and cut up the immutable march of Time.

OLIVER HARRIS is the editor and author of ten books, including two trilogies by William Burroughs: *Junky: The Definitive Text of "Junk," The Yage Letters Redux*, and *Queer: Twenty-Fifth Anniversary Edition*; and "Restored" editions of the Cut-Up Trilogy: *The Soft Machine, Nova Express, The Ticket That Exploded*. He is also the editor of *The Letters of William S. Burroughs, 1945–1959* and *Everything Lost: The Latin American Notebook of William S. Burroughs*, the author of the critical study *William Burroughs and the Secret of Fascination* and coeditor of *Naked Lunch@50: Anniversary Essays*. He is Professor of American Literature at Keele University and President of the European Beat Studies Network.

NOTES

1. Burroughs dated the letter "June 21 1960 Present Time Pre-Sent Time," focusing on the issue of temporality.

2. Burroughs, undated typescript, circa 1960, William S. Burroughs Papers, The Berg Collection of English and American Literature, New York Public Library, 48.22 (hereinafter abbreviated to Berg). For more on the meaning of the phrase "soft machine," see the introduction to *The Soft Machine: The Restored Text* (Burroughs 2014b).

3. See notes on the "Where You Belong" section of *The Soft Machine* (Burroughs 2014b, 257).

4. On time travel, see my essay "Cutting Up Politics" (Harris 2004).

5. Burroughs, undated typescript, circa 1960 (Berg 7.44).

6. For more details about the retitling from *The Novia Express* to *Nova Express*, see the introduction to *Nova Express: The Restored Text* (Harris 2014).

7. Burroughs, undated typescript (Berg 9.16).

8. On the importance of the *Herald Tribune*, see the Introduction to my forthcoming new edition of *Minutes to Go* (Moloko Print, 2020).

9. Significantly, Gysin identified his three other newspaper sources with the city of their publication ("*The Paris Herald Tribune, The London Observer, The London Daily Mail*"); not so *Life*, as if to acknowledge its claims to universality.

10. Letter to Jeff Nuttall, August 20, 1964, self-reflexively included in *My Own Mag* 9 (November 1964), 10.

11. On the wraparound band declaring "un règlement de comptes avec la Littérature," see my forthcoming essay "William Burroughs' Cut-Ups in and as Translation," in *L'Esprit créateur* 58, no. 4 (2018).

12. The typescript original of "OPEN LETTER" shows it began with a cancelled line, starting "Dear Sir," while another typescript in the same "Minutes to Go Unpublished" folio begins as a letter by naming its intended recipient: "Mr Henry Luce" (Burroughs, undated typescript, circa 1960, Berg 7.34; 7.38).

13. Burroughs briefly met Tzara and Duchamp in 1958; for more on the importance of Tzara, see my essay (Harris 2005, 24–36).

14. Barry Miles and Joe Maynard attribute the authorship solely to Burroughs, but in a revealing confusion, when citing the version of "OPEN LETTER" published in *Nomad*, they attribute the text to all four collaborators (1978, 18, 113). While internal evidence strongly affirms the hand of Burroughs, it's likely that Beiles played a major part, and the participation of Gysin and Corso cannot be ruled out.

15. The line derived from the 1961 edition. See also Burroughs to Gysin, May 16, 1960 (Burroughs 2012, 28).

16. Although Miles and Maynard attribute the text to Burroughs, its "authorship" is suitably uncertain and in *Minutes to Go* it is unsigned.

17. In the early 1960s, Burroughs made a running gag out of such errors of misreporting, implicitly addressed to the Luce press, most prominently in the 1963 text "Martin's Folly."

18. Banash (2004) has persuasively argued that both Tzara and Burroughs actualized potentials within the form of the mass media, so that "avant-garde practice and advertising are not so far apart" after all. As well as specifying the singular importance of *Life*, rather than newspapers in general, my case is that Burroughs typically worked from a direct material encounter, rather than mediated by art history.

19. The full contents of *Life* magazine is available online at https://books.google.com/books /about/LIFE.html?id=NoEEAAAAMBAJ.

20. *Life*, November 30, 1959, 122.

21. For more on Ginsberg and Luce, see my essay (Harris 2012, 3–29).

22. The advertisement in *Life* to which Corso refers was actually captioned: "SCIENCE SOLVES Household Odor Problem" (O'Neill 1959, 130).

23. Lautréamont's call, which Burroughs consistently misattributed to Tzara, was literally inscribed into the name of the technique on at least one occasion: "The Cut Up Method Poetry For Everybody was sold out to the Freudian Conspiracy and Communist Party" (Burroughs to Jon Webb, August 21, 1960, *The Outsider* Collection, Northwestern University).

24. "King of the YADS," *Time*, November 30, 1962, 96–97.

25. The photograph accompanied a 1963 article entitled "Where Is This Man Heading? The Elusive Mr Burroughs Grants a Rare Interview," that appeared in the *London Evening Standard*. Owned by Lord Beaverbrook (of whom, more below), the *Standard* was part of the *Express* newspaper group, whose title Burroughs knowingly echoed in *Nova Express*.

26. Curiously, the one volume without any direct references to Luce's trilogy is the first edition of *The Soft Machine* (Paris: Olympia Press, 1961). The absence is all the more striking because in "Operation Soft Machine/Cut" (1961), his first three-column little magazine publication, Burroughs contrived a dense pun that identified Luce with Lucifer via the patriotic song *Battle Hymn of the Republic*: "And luced my fatal light" (*The Outsider*, 1 (1): 77).

27. For the full note in *Gambit*, see *The Soft Machine* (2014b, 242).

28. The version in *Naked Lunch* cited the original verbatim: "biocontrol; that is, control of physical movement, mental processes, emotional reactions and *apparent* sensory impressions" (2003, 136).

29. Packard 1960, 196; Burroughs 2003, 128, 181.

30. For the origin of the title phrase, see Harris 2009, especially 17–20.

31. Burroughs to Gysin, August 30, 1960 (Berg 86.8).

32. For example, in unused material about the Death Dwarves, who operate out of installations including the "Life Time Fortune Headquarters NYC" (Burroughs, undated typescript, circa 1962 [Berg 49.31]).

33. Burroughs and Gysin, *The Exterminator* (San Francisco: Auerhahn Press, 1960), 5; reprinted in *The Third Mind*, 71.

34. Burroughs, undated typescript, circa 1960 (Auerhahn Press records, 1959–1967, BANC MSS 71/85c, University of California, Berkeley).

35. Burroughs, undated typescript, circa 1960 (Berg 7.38). He also fantasized Luce's replies: "STAND ASIDE BURROUGHS OF SPACE AND LISTEN TO THE LORD OF TIME" (Berg 48.22).

36. Ginsberg to Burroughs, November 17, 1959 (Berg 82.1). Ginsberg's ventriloquizing from the recently published *Naked Lunch* ("County Clerk" section) is not only amusing but directly echoes that of the reporter and photographer double act who interviewed Burroughs, Snell's opening line invoking Hauser and O'Brien: "Have an Old Gold" (*The Third Mind*, 28).

37. The Constable Report on Burroughs was in turn later reported on by John Wilcock in *The Village Voice*, January 11, 1962.

38. Ginsberg to Burroughs, December 24, 1959 (Berg 82.1).

39. Burroughs to Ginsberg, December 2, 1959 (Paul Carroll Papers, Box 2, University of Chicago). This key line in a handwritten postscript is not reproduced in *Rub Out the Words* (11).

40. The "article" in the title is the "Deposition," which from the 1962 Grove edition until the "Restored" edition of 2003 served as the de facto Introduction to *Naked Lunch* and is where the book's title is defined in terms of the press ("that long newspaper spoon").

41. The association is indeed made explicit in one 1960 typescript: "COULD THIS BE DONE BY A MACHINE LIKE NINETEEN EIGHTY FOUR WHERE THERE IS A MACHINE TO WRITE PORNOGRAPHIC LITERATURE" (Berg 9.24).

42. Burroughs, undated typescripts, circa 1960 (Berg 48.22, 10.32, 49.32). Tellingly, the anti-Semitic trio also appears in *Minutes to Go*, in Corso's poem that describes the 1950s as "*Time* decade": "Marx Freud Einstein decade" (32).

43. Burroughs, undated typescript, circa 1960 (Berg 10.31).

44. Burroughs' archival systems took *Time-Life* as their model but also embraced other newspapers, including the London *Daily Express* as indicated by his piece "Tangier" in *Esquire* 62(3) in September 1964: "Your reporter selects a clipping from the file labelled Daily Express, Saturday, April 25, 1964 (London)." For more on the *Daily Express*, see *Nova Express* (2014a), introduction and notes.

45. Birmingham sees a closer relation between Burroughs' manuscript "databases" of the 1950s and 1960s than I do, and, fascinatingly, in one unpublished typescript Burroughs does call on Luce to dismantle his machine in precisely these terms: "To destroy your horde of image and word bank" (Berg 7.39). http://realitystudio.org/media/operation-total-exposure-fax.pdf. On the archive as an active system, rather than a "morgue" of materials, see Stompor 2016.

46. Sommerville to Burroughs, April 28, 1965 (Berg 80.20).

47. http://www.nyhistory.org/press/releases/%E2%80%8Bnew-york-historical-society-receive-time-inc's-archive-chronicling-history-20th.

48. Draft typescript for *The Ticket That Exploded* (Berg 20.39). See also "The Inferential Kid" in *The Burroughs File*, edited by James Grauerholz (San Francisco: City Lights, 1984), 128; these lines also appeared in *APO-33* (1965).

REFERENCES

Primary

Burroughs, William S. Undated typescript, circa 1960. William S. Burroughs Papers, The Berg Collection of English and American Literature, New York Public Library, 7.34, 7.38, 48.22.
———. Manuscript, dated 1961. Berg 62.9; item 47.
———. Letter to Jeff Nuttall, August 20, 1964. Fales Library, New York University.

Secondary

Banash, David. 2004. "From Advertising to the Avant-Garde: Rethinking the Invention of Collage." *Postmodern Culture* 14 (2). https://muse.jhu.edu/journals/postmodern_culture/toc/pmc14.2.html.
Beiles, Sinclair, William Burroughs, Gregory Corso, and Brion Gysin. 1960. *Minutes to Go*. San Francisco: City Lights Books.
Birmingham, Jed. 2014. "Operation Total Exposure: A Review of Oliver Harris' Cut-Up Trilogy." Planned Obsolescence Press. https://www.keele.ac.uk/media/keeleuniversity/fachumsoc-sci/sclhumss/americanstudies/operation-total-exposure-fax.pdf.
Burroughs, William S. 1961. *The Soft Machine*. Paris: Olympia Press.
———. 1965a. "The Art of Fiction 36: An Interview." *Paris Review* 35 (Fall): 12–49.
———. 1965b. *TIME*. New York: C Press.
———. 1968. *The Soft Machine*. London: Calder.
———. 1978. "Introductions," *The Third Mind*. New York: Viking.
———. 1982. "The Revised Boy Scout Manual." In Special Issue, edited by V. Vale, *Re/Search* 4/5: 5–11.
———. 1993. *The Letters of William S. Burroughs, 1945–1959*. Edited by Oliver Harris. New York: Viking.
———. 2001. *Burroughs Live: The Collected Interviews of William S. Burroughs*. Edited by Sylvère Lotringer. New York: Semiotext(e).
———. 2003. *Naked Lunch: The Restored Text*. Edited by James Grauerholz and Barry Miles. New York: Grove.
———. 2006. *The Yage Letters Redux*. Edited by Oliver Harris. San Francisco: City Lights.
———. 2012. *Rub Out the Words: The Letters of William S. Burroughs, 1959–1974*. Edited by Bill Morgan. New York: Ecco.
———. 2014a. *Nova Express: The Restored Text*. Edited by Oliver Harris. New York: Grove Press.
———. 2014b. *The Soft Machine: The Restored Text*. Edited by Oliver Harris. New York: Grove Press.
———. 2014c. *The Ticket That Exploded: The Restored Text*. Edited by Oliver Harris. New York: Grove Press.
Corso, Gregory. 2003. *An Accidental Autobiography: The Selected Letters of Gregory Corso*. Edited by Bill Morgan. New York: New Directions.
Ginsberg, Allen. 1996. *Journals Mid-Fifties, 1954–1958*. Edited by Gordon Ball. London: Penguin.
———. 2008. *The Letters of Allen Ginsberg*. Edited by Bill Morgan. New York: De Capo.
Gysin, Brion. 1960. "First Cut-Ups." In *Minutes to Go*, by Sinclair Beiles, William Burroughs, Gregory Corso, and Brion Gysin, 6–10. Paris: Two Cities.
Harris, Oliver. 2004. "Cutting Up Politics." In *Retaking the Universe: William S. Burroughs in the Age of Globalization*, edited by Davis Schneiderman and Philip Walsh, 175–200. London: Pluto.
———. 2005. "'Burroughs Is a Poet Too, Really': The Poetics of *Minutes to Go*." *Edinburgh Review* 114: 24–36.
———. 2009. "The Beginnings of '*Naked Lunch*, an Endless Novel.'" In *Naked Lunch@50: Anniversary Essays*, edited by Oliver Harris and Ian MacFadyen, 14–25. Carbondale: Southern Illinois University Press.
———. 2012. "Minute Particulars of the Counter-culture: *Time, Life* and the Photo-poetics of Allen Ginsberg." *Comparative American Studies* 10 (1): 3–29.

———. 2014. Introduction to *Nova Express: The Restored Text*, by William S. Burroughs, ix–lv. New York: Grove Press.

"King of the YADS." 1962. *Time*, November 30, 96–97.

Leary, Timothy. 1995. *High Priest*. New York: Ronin.

Luce, Henry. 1941. "The American Century." *Life*, February 17, 61–65.

Miles, Barry, and Joe Maynard. 1978. *William S. Burroughs: A Bibliography, 1953–73*. Charlottesville: University Press of Virginia.

O'Neil, Paul. 1959. "The Only Rebellion Around." *Life*, November 30, 114–30.

Orwell, George. 2004. *Nineteen Eighty-Four*. London: Penguin.

Packard, Vance. 1960. *The Hidden Persuaders*. Harmondsworth: Penguin. First published 1957.

Stompor, Tomasz. 2016. "Burroughs's Folios as an Archival Machine for Artistic Creation." *CLC-Web: Comparative Literature and Culture* 18 (5), https://docs.lib.purdue.edu/cgi/viewcontent .cgi?referer=https://www.google.com/&httpsredir=1&article=2958&context=clcweb.

The Reality Studio

The following two cut-up experiments offer useful illustrations for Oliver Harris's argument in the preceding essay, "Cutting Up the Century." The first piece is a cut-up letter written in 1960 by Burroughs to Henry Luce himself, and the second is a cut-up that Burroughs conducted with a *LIFE* Magazine reporter's telegram from their original encounter in late 1959. Located in the Berg archive's Folio of "Unpublished material for *Minutes to Go*," Burroughs' typo-riddled, mock letter to Luce asks an urgent, ominous question: "Mr Henry luce, Do you really know what the machine is up to? . . . The machine is socncerned with onw thing, ho meostaiss." In this direct address to the media mogul of the American Century, Burroughs' typos seem to become part of the cut-up nature of his prose, causing frustrating, but not impossible, glitches in our reading, as he seeks, in whatever way he can, to challenge the machine's homeostasis and "anecel him [Luce] out of the world monoply of word and image."

As we transition to the anthology's first section, *Icon/Viral*, the subsequent piece offers an example of Burroughs' wide-ranging cut-up experiments with personal correspondence and book reviews. Like many of Burroughs' cut-ups of his critics in *Icon/Viral*, Burroughs' remix of a telegram from the *LIFE* magazine reporter, David Schnell, distorts the reporter's words by splicing in judgmental, hypocritical rhetoric. During an interview with Victor Bockris and Andy Warhol (photos of which can be seen in the archival section entitled *The Fall of Art*), Burroughs described his 1959 visit from the two *LIFE* Magazine reporters (David Schnell and photographer Loomis Dean) as a straight up rendition of the Hauser and O'Brien scene that concludes *Naked Lunch*. Even though the reporter played the "good cop," claiming to admire Burroughs' books and offering him an Old Gold, the final *LIFE* magazine article, and its accompanying photo, turned out to be a hit-job. The November 30, 1959, article clumped Burroughs together with the beatniks, titling the story, "Beats: Sad but Noisy Rebels." In his cut-up of Schnell's letter, located in Berg Folio 65, "Illustrating Cut-ups With Other Writers," Burroughs showcases his attempts to cut up not only the puppet-master of the media, Henry Luce, but also his insidious stooges.

—AWC

Mr Henry Luce,

Do you really know what the machine is up to? I will teell you what
        it is upto. . .The machine is socncerned with onw thing ho meostaiss.
The machine is thermodynamics..Tine ran out in the fith tat topical..
The machine runs on affect onchrage of tohers. because themachine can
        not move excpet withsomeone elses charge.. Some one elses lovehate
or fear..The mcahine runs on wars revolutions hate spuression jail
        torture painand fear..Thats is what gives the machine charge to
        m move..The strongest chargeis d creative activity wrtiing on the
            life substa ceb writing that ISswwriting..A soon as the writing
        touchinesthe mchaine the mchien moves to cancel ro absorb the sou
sourceof the writing..All movments hetrofrehavethought in temrns
        of taking over and using the mchine but ater always taken over by the

machine… The machine always attempts to meurtalaize or absorb the creative
        charge which is qualitative ddata the machine can not process…Recduce
        to quantative data is built in comcination fgive the wirtier the prty
    wife haoliwood fame e moneytrtrearment reduce him to uqaintitavie
factor that can be absorbed in the mchin into the mchine.. Oalternatively
canecel him out of the world monoply of word and image,,,stave hime out
rub hi out l,canel his chathe.. In either cae the result is the same
the machien has canceldl lout the charge eonwhich it runs..brwcaue
rmemeber the machien can not move without charge..qutie simply no thinking
machine inititte action .. soem body must wotn something done thatis
have an af ect dictated plan of action

[autograph]: "cut up of telegram from David Schnell
(photos by Loomis Dean) reporter for Life May
1959

PS. Chemical DAVID or Dear DR Benway like marvel..namelees
ass holes..lunch more I realize what a giant of equal or
better of Moby Dick less me of..his scrotum..here if you
lines is a ed colleugue PS More I get into Naked a book it is
id rank it the which by the way it ressemble..the blue it
come to me Naked Lunch why not in me thing inthis order:..
want it I urine s (n mor equal or es me of..the org original
idea of T I have not mention it to nameless ass holes). . this
Bosh inSPain ood it until we read an we amd so ohpe estem.. it
a small toke of our notice a II the ballCorn Exchamge Bank.
to want it the original urine I have not es 9(nameless ass.
after another a future work.. damned in transvestite air 69
A.J.9(rushing to the ticketcxx etc etc..
picked under st feel you deserve it more tit it as a small
toke of our..Boy ,check my bag..departure of its..Dear Dr.
Benway like a marvellous dip bui.ld a chapter..why not in thing in
this order..flight no. 69 A.J. 9(r.ushing to the ticket etc etc
etc et fromthere if you Airlines is all..you take it Transvesti
Transvestite none of..his scrotum..national airport line a
announces the counter laying bare..departure of uits..Snell
ago but have feel you desert it ass PS..inSpain until we read..
couple years your book we you will accept..this Bosch ood it
than we and so hope esteem..nameless assholes. the blue it come
to me a ked lunch..Dear Bill: Snell and I ago but never..
boat out of into "The around so..national airport ann unces the
counter laying bare..all idea of T mention it to holes).
Chemical DAVID OR DIX..THE SCENE Big GOdamned inter BITCHBOX:
Transvestite air..You tek it from Transves tie Air none of my
learn..Boy check my..notive a II the ball Corn Exchange Bank..

Icon/Viral

"*What I like is UGLINESS in all its rich and varied forms. Dirty vices cracked souls and soiled idiot bodies is my food and I love it. And above all plenty of self righteous hate sitting folk. No better dogs can be found and what they lack in guts they make up in compound proliferation.*

—Burroughs, "Deposition of the Ugly Spirit," 1961, Berg 26.11. Copyright © by William Burroughs, used by permission of The Wylie Agency LLC.

Criticism: Your critics may so I gather is supposed be young enough change his mind objective giving later critics just yet what B's message of the book is but he will rather than a list, baby, in time of his emotional piece is reactions to it ironic the irony

—Burroughs, "Cut Up of Critics," 1962, Berg 21.3. Copyright © by William Burroughs, used by permission of The Wylie Agency LLC.

Let no one speak of the two Joyce books I have presenting mighty sick himself as little book proof that we have here read by Mr. Burroughs are boring sometime rubbish maybe Mr. Burroughs a man appear will write a book at a side door about fifteen pointless years on violence? committed his experiences on the end of your exterminator or what staggering.. .. I sure hear wrong terms dirty voices dirty fingers shreds his prose writhing to me brad of very nice youth sink form the worn way for grey room rats eat the unborn. So press the button and see no reason history there is no history. Sheds his responsibilities in front of their landscape. Gentle not the worn out morality so press the final button of history with one waiter.

—Burroughs, "Cut-Ups of Times Literary Supplement 'Ugh' Affair," 1963–64, Berg 13.18. Copyright © by William Burroughs, used by permission of The Wylie Agency LLC.

there was a young man called Narcissus said "I'm nobody's Mister or Missus but I'm not on the shelf I'm in love with myself then he gazed in a pool and said "Kiss us"

—Burroughs, "Cut-up with Limericks," 1971, Berg 35.2. Copyright © by William Burroughs, used by permission of The Wylie Agency LLC.

Deposition of the Ugly Spirit

We begin the *Icon/Viral* section with a typescript of Burroughs' cut-up routine, "Deposition of the Ugly Spirit." Burroughs wrote this piece after he had quit heroin and settled into his apartment in Tangier in the summer of 1961. He was at the peak of his early stage of experimentation with the cut-up method. Archived in Berg Folio 83, entitled "Mss Of Some Unpublished Material Cut-Ups 1960–1961," this provocative routine appears amidst some of Burroughs' most compelling cut-up prose poems produced out of experiments with writers classic and contemporary, from Thomas Nashe to Jean Genet.

By the time of this cut-up, Burroughs had already written his sardonic addendum to *Naked Lunch*, "Deposition: Testimony Concerning a Sickness," in response to the controversial obscenity trials. As if in mockery of himself, in this rendition of a "Deposition," Burroughs creates a defensive monologue for the "Ugly Spirit," that allegorical, daemonic agent acting in tandem with the forces Burroughs understood as the cause and catalyst for not only his unconscionable, murderous act against his own wife but also his heroin addiction. For Burroughs, the "Ugly Spirit" was and is a caustic symptom of a sick society, a viral organism feeding off inequality's exacerbation, the greedy demon in the furnace of industrial capitalism. Indeed, this routine introduces the two-sided sword at the crux of the *Icon/ Viral* section: if Burroughs' work is produced out of his struggle against the "Ugly Spirit," the viral entity can also be blamed for the commodification of his celebrity image as the stereotype of an outlaw.

Burroughs often expressed a Manichean worldview, interpreting any phenomena or event as an intersection point where forces of good and evil were always at war. In the Preface to *Queer* (1985), Burroughs claimed it was the "Ugly Spirit" that led him to commit an almost mythic act of patriarchal violence during their drunken William Tell act. By the end of his life, in March 1992, before undergoing a ritual exorcism he hoped could finally heal him of his hauntings, Burroughs explained to the shaman, a "Diné elder Navajo from the Four Corners area of New Mexico," that his task would be a difficult one, requiring the shaman, and Burroughs, "to face the whole of American capitalism, Rockefeller, the CIA . . . all of those, particularly Hearst" (Miles, 2). After the ceremony, Burroughs explained to a sixty-five-year-old Allen Ginsberg that "the Ugly Spirit" was "very much related to the American Tycoon. To William Randolph Hearst, Vanderbilt, Rockefeller, that whole stratum of American acquisitive evil. Monopolistic, acquisitive evil. Ugly evil. The ugly American. The ugly American at his ugly worst. That's exactly what it is" (ibid.).

Burroughs' cut-up practice of writing served as an *antiviral* treatment, a means of producing antibodies, if not a vaccine, for the ideological disorders he warned were increasingly rampant in the reactionary wing of post–World War II America. In this cut-up routine, "Deposition of the Ugly Spirit," Burroughs imagines the Ugly Spirit as an "enigmatic tycoon," but one who, near the end of his existence, upon "examining his conscience," decides to betray the ruling class: "Now do you recognize ME Mr Bradly Mr Martin? I was made out of your heavy metal substance and I'm not taking any rap for that Green Cunt . . . I'M GONNA RAT ON EVERYBODY" (Berg 26.11). This deposition, then, also registers Burroughs' own awareness in the early 1960s of the role he was born to play: brought up into wealth and power, in all appearances a conformist to the white, patriarchal hegemony, but actually a deviant with nothing to lose, a double agent who queers, and rats out the ruling class and their henchman.

—*AWC*

DEPOSITION OF THE UGLY SPIRIT

"What I like is UGLINESS in all its rich and varied forms.
Dirty vices cracked souls and soiled idiot bodies is my food
and I love it.And above all plenty of self righteous hate
p/sitting folk.No better dogs can be found adn what they lack
in guts they make up in compound proliferation. And all my human
dogs live off my shit and I likes to rub their nose in it"

"You see the part A.J.? This enigmatic tycoon has this uh
dark side to his character.He's complex you understand and on
the surface nobody is kinder to his Nigras"

"You should see my down right UGLY pictures and get some good
laughs. Time we hanged   the Mexican kid and he shit himself and
B.Q. just stood there smiling dirty and won The Ugliest Picture
Of The Year Contest.And here's an enraged   insurance salesman of
sadistic tendencies beating up a swish in a subdivision cocktail
lounge.But its nothing like The Little People everywhere in
8 hour straigth jackets to pump me out the pure Ugly Substance
I live on"

"So in his old age he begings examining his conscience. You
know taking stock like---"

Now do you recognize ME Mr Bradly Mr Martin? I was made out of
your heavy metal substance and I'm not taking any rap for that
Green Cunt... I'M GONNA RAT ON EVERYBODY---

[autograph]: Summer 1961
Villa Mouneria

Deposition of the Ugly Spirit (8 × 11, 1 leaf, typescript) (Berg 26.11). Item 11, DEPOSITION
OF THE UGLY SPIRIT, from Folio 83 Mss Of Some Unpublished Material Cut-Ups 1960–
1961. Copyright © by William Burroughs, used by permission of The Wylie Agency LLC.

2

Burroughs and Biography:
An Interview with Barry Miles

OLIVER HARRIS

The following transcript is taken from a conversation with biographer Barry Miles reflecting on his books about and correspondences with William S. Burroughs. This interview took place on April 25, 2014, at the William S. Burroughs Centennial Conference held the CUNY Graduate Center in New York. Miles is interviewed by Oliver Harris, Professor of American Literature at Keele University and author of numerous academic works on Burroughs, including William Burroughs and the Secret of Fascination *(2003), and editor of eight books, from* The Letters of William S. Burroughs *(New York: Viking, 1993) to restored editions of* The Cut-Up Trilogy *(2014).*

The following conversation has been condensed and edited for space.

HARRIS You've now done a seven-hundred-page biography, but twenty years ago you did a two-hundred-page biography. What I want to begin by asking you was what, if anything, had changed in the way you saw Burroughs, because you have had a unique opportunity in a way to do one short book and now one long book twenty years later. So what changed?

MILES Well, the portrait was pretty much a commercial piece of work. It was published as a standalone book by Virgin, basically as a portrait of Burroughs as a cultural hero. That's really back to the original sense of what they had commissioned. So it's really just his impact on popular culture. I'm not an academic at all so it was very much a piece of rock and roll writing, really. At the time I was only just coming out of many, many years as a rock and roll critic and writing for *New Musical Express* and, you know, *Rolling Stone* and places like that.

HARRIS So did you look back on that 1992 book when you were working on the new one?

MILES No, I purposely didn't look at it at all actually because, as I'm sure you know, often when you're researching stuff on the 'net you say, hey, this looks good and it turns out to be by you! (Laughter.) So, yeah, I left that alone and I also didn't look at Morgan's book (1988) either for the same reason. I just didn't want to be too influenced. I wanted to start from scratch and go back to the original sources of all the information, although I used his research for the book quite extensively.

HARRIS So you went to Tempe, the Ted Morgan archives there?

MILES Yes. Many, many years ago, it was a plan that James [Grauerholz] at the William Burroughs estate wanted to come up with, which was a sort of autobiography of Burroughs. It was going to be called, ah, what was it going to be called?

HARRIS *My Past Was an Evil River?*

MILES Yes, that was exactly what it was, yes. And Bill had written quite a bit; maybe, I don't know, we had about eighty pages of manuscript or something like that. But since he had already given a hundred interviews with Morgan, we went back to the original tapes and made copies of them and I took them all back to where I was living in France and spent three months transcribing the whole lot. So, basically there was so much new material that I thought my original book was more or less irrelevant. I was also rather surprised that it was still in print and they kept occasionally asking me to update it. And when Bill died I added a bit on the end of it and they came out with a new edition. And I think I did another new introduction at some point, but really that book is irrelevant in terms of what I'd always wanted to do, which was a full-length biography of Bill. I really wanted it to match the one I did of Ginsberg basically, early on. That one, my Ginsberg biography to me is pretty much a hagiography actually because I knew Allen too well.

HARRIS The question of distance is always a problem for biographers.

MILES It is.

HARRIS On one hand, you've got to have access. On the other hand, if you lack distance you do have that sense of being constrained.

MILES I think as long as you explain this to the readers, then it's okay; but that's something I didn't do in the Ginsberg book, which I wish I had.

HARRIS It's interesting you say you purposely didn't read Ted Morgan's book and I certainly don't want to ask you questions that will be leading you into criticizing another biographer. That would be uncharitable. Nevertheless, when you read Ted's biography, you must have had a sense that, well, no, this isn't the Burroughs I knew, or this isn't the emphasis I would have given. So did you have some sense of an agenda behind what you would like this biography to achieve as opposed to simply being a brand new biography based on new research? Did you have a sense of what you wanted the story to be?

MILES To me the important thing is to have a new generation of Burroughs scholars basically, because the generation who knew him, like myself—I mean I'm seventy-one—we're all dying out and a lot of the other people are even older who knew him. It won't be long before the personal contacts will have gone and so it will all be down to written sources or filmed or whatever. So the idea really was to establish as many facts as possible when you can still talk to people and when the research material was available. I drew upon a lot of interviews I did for the Ginsberg book, as a matter of fact, with Lucien Carr and with [Lawrence] Ferlinghetti and Allen, of course, who I had interviewed extensively for the biography. So a load of people who are no longer with us. And so I could still go through those tapes and pull out new stuff, which belonged in the Burroughs books.

HARRIS   But your sense of who . . .

MILES   Really, it's for another generation. It will be hopefully a standard work for a bit until more scholars do more work and then a new generation will be able to interpret him and use his work for whatever purposes. Because I think he's politically important as well as in terms of literature and I really do think his work deserves to be publicized as much as possible, especially these days.

HARRIS   I think this is why readers are very fortunate. As Alex [Wermer-Colan] said, it's not just a biography of the man, because even though you're not presenting him as a cultural icon, you're so knowledgeable and that informs everything you write about cultural history, you're always presenting his life in relation to a bigger picture. When it comes to the life itself, I was struck by the fact that mostly you reserve judgment. Mostly you present the stories, the anecdotes. There are a few occasions where you do stick a knife in. (Laughter.) They kind of stood out to me because they are very particular. I'll just throw a couple of quotations at you that are slightly choice. You describe his relationship with his mother as "infantile and narcissistic. He was a momma's boy." And you talk about his "puerile infatuation" with guns and you say that his life would have been "utterly different, happier, more sociable and more productive had he never heard of Scientology." Now, (laughter) it's not that I would disagree with you on any of those scores, but actually in the majority of the book, you do reserve judgment. You don't comment. You don't offer analysis and interpretation that gives a strong sense of *your* angle all the time. And I wonder, is this consistent with your sense that you want to present the materials rather than tell a particular story?

MILES   Yes. Yes, very much. I mean the biographies that I admire most are the ones which are the most objective and it's very, very hard though, as you've just proven (laughter) as sometimes things sort of slip in. But the idea was to just present the facts even when it was some fairly unpalatable thing, you know, like the gay scene in Tangier for instance, with the expat community basically preying on all of the young boys. But I just set the facts out and obviously if the reader objects to all this, they'll feel that anyway. They don't need me to tell them, oh, this is not PC or something. But sometimes things did come through. The business about the guns, I think that occurs very shortly after he just shot his wife and I guess because I wrote that section more or less chronologically, I was probably still feeling, if it was me, you know, and I had just shot somebody I wouldn't want to touch a gun ever again and yet the first thing he did was go off with his boyfriend and they're shooting at melons or something.

HARRIS There are always certain things that are lost in translation—elements of his life which you feel you remain an outsider to. Which were those for you?

MILES Well, the gun thing is one of them. He and I discussed guns a lot because I knew him pretty well and I first met him in '65 and I had been corresponding with him since the year before when he was still in Tangier. And even in London he had an air gun. I mean we'd discussed it a lot, you know, that this was his cultural background being from the Midwest and, maybe right across the States, that guns are just part of growing up in a way that they're not in Europe. So, again, I tried to be objective about it, but as you see it slipped in there.

HARRIS It's a serious issue. Occasionally people ask me would I be interested in writing a biography and honestly it's not my thing. And part of my problem is I have so little in common with Burroughs that I couldn't be more different. Doing the introduction to *Queer*, I remember asking James [Grauerholz] if he would help me write the introduction and he said: "Why?" I said, well, because being very straight as a guy I actually felt kind of anxious about it. He said: "That didn't stop you writing the introduction to *Junky*, did it?" You know, not being a heroin addict . . . And of course, he was right. Why did I need to feel that was an impasse for me? Nevertheless, Burroughs led an extraordinary life that most of us wouldn't want to live in many ways. So I'm wondering if there's a kind of traumatic center to his life which you feel there's a difficulty of getting. You talk about being objective, but in a way his life is so peculiar, isn't it? Do you feel that you get him or do you get parts of him, as it were?

MILES I think he was a chameleon. He changed according to wherever he was living and he changed according to the people he knew. When he was in Tangier, for instance, he moved in an entirely gay community and mostly British and American expats and he took on all of their ideas basically. But again, when Bill took on a set of ideas it didn't mean he really deep down believed them, I think. He's one of those guys who could find meaning in almost anything and they would often be contradictory but, generally speaking, he liked to fit in with a crowd. So when he was in London he moved with a rather louche sort of gang of Old Etonians and black-sheep-of-the-family type people, and took a tremendous amount of drugs. And then his connection with the underground—there was some discussion earlier about the underground press—and there was very much two sides to his personality. The one side that was hanging out in Chelsea and having cocktails in Christopher Gibbs's garden was entirely different from the one who was publishing revolutionary material in the underground press. And he would put on sort of a different hat for a lot of that and then when he came to New York, he dropped all of the Scientology, for instance, which he had been talking about for ten years in London. And he dropped all the revolution stuff as well.

HARRIS He kept the drugs.

MILES He kept the drugs but that became his new thing. When he got somewhere he had to find what his new role was going to be and, of course, his role in New York was very much the guy who had been there and done all of this and come back and reported on it for everybody else to know about. And so he became the godfather of drugs and the punk scene and he was quite pleased, I think. There was a side to him that was rather proud of having all this attention, even though he had never heard of half of the rock stars who came and saw him. To jump forward a bit, for his seventieth birthday party, for instance, at Limelight, I remember, there were all these famous guests and at one point he came up to me and he said, "I don't know if you're holding, but someone told me that those guys over there are cops." And it was Andy Summers and Sting from The Police! And I'm sure he had no idea who Kurt Cobain was either when he showed up. I mean, because his interest in music was from the '20s and '30s. He liked Viennese waltzes and the early, you know, the Hot Fives and Hot Sevens.

HARRIS And Hoagy Carmichael . . .

MILES He openly said in a number of interviews how much he hated the music of the Rolling Stones and rock and roll in general. But all of these people were very interested in *him*. So when he was with them, he feigned an interest.

HARRIS I think we all know there's a certain way of digging Burroughs and a certain way of not getting him. But a lot of what you said and also what other people say about Burroughs can be taken quite different ways. One of the problems is that he can be taken rather mockingly, as not being a serious figure. And I always felt he was a very serious figure.

MILES Oh, he's deadly serious.

HARRIS So isn't this one of the problems, though? On the one hand he's deadly serious and on the other hand, he never really means what he says or you can't be sure who he is. And therefore there seems to be a contradiction in almost everything he says and does. Why isn't that more alienating? Because you've been a good friend of his, but why isn't it more difficult to be with somebody who seems so slippery in a way?

MILES Well, most of his really heartfelt ideas, he expressed fictionally.

HARRIS Yes.

MILES And therefore, they come out in what appear to be weird ways. His attitude to women, for instance, being a particularly good example in the way he quite seriously writes that they're, you know, from a giant trust of insects on another planet or something. All of this, it's all bizarre stuff. And he didn't really believe that, you know, but sometimes interviewers have really pressed him on it and he'll, just out of being awkward and cussed, he'll stick by it. Almost all of his ideas in the end got elaborated and fictionalized and turned into art, really.

It's only if you're talking personally then he'll come out with it. His attitude to women was basically—he came from the St. Louis society where, as he said, "When I was a kid, women were put on a pedestal." It's a Southern thing and whenever a woman came in the room he would always stand up. It was just instinctive. But he basically said, "If women's liberation means what they say I'm absolutely 100 percent for it," because he would love to see equality and not this division. But he saw the division in operation everywhere—except, you have to remember, he moved almost entirely in a male society. So, again, he was not very well informed on these matters, to be quite honest. And he had good friends like Felicity Mason but generally speaking he tried to avoid women's company, I'm afraid. But, again, he would say different things to whoever was interviewing him. I mean, he would come out with a different response often to be awkward. There was a side to him which was quite mischievous like that.

HARRIS   Well, I was going to say, in the interviews you can definitely see there is a kind of carryover from his fiction. And as an academic looking at texts, I have no problem with all sorts of potential readings. But with the man in front of you it's a different feeling. And being a biographer I think your approach is fundamentally to be asking different questions than the ones that I ask for example. And I find it interesting for your book you have a title *Call Me Burroughs* which is not only that of a record he cut in '65 but also plays on "Call Me Ishmael" at the beginning of *Moby Dick* (1851). One of Melville's other great novels, *The Confidence Man* (1857), gives also another kind of title for the way that Burroughs might be approached. In other words, textually, his play of not knowing where the hell you stand is one of the reasons why his work is so rich, rewarding, and different every time because you find new things funny and new things ugly and so on. But again, I wonder how dealing with him as a *man* you feel works with trying to be objective. I can see you presenting information and yet everything about him seems to subvert our confidence, our trust in what he's actually saying. I'm wondering whether you're conscious of it or just thought, "I know how to deal with it."

MILES   I don't think Bill himself knew what his . . . he didn't have a fixed position ever, you know. He did take on the protective coloring of wherever he was. I mean he prided himself on being *El Hombre Invisible*, that people didn't see him in the room. When he was in London he literally was Burlington Bertie and he fit perfectly into Mayfair society. You just didn't see him walking down the street because he had the right hat, the right special shoes, handmade, you know, his three piece suits and everything. And then sometimes when I was out visiting him in Kansas he'd be wearing, you know, sort of bib overalls and a peaked cap with the name of a feed company on it. (Laughter.) He fitted in so no one saw him. And his ideas also were a sort of an ever-shifting mix, it was all mixed up with his dreams, with whatever he had just been reading, of course. Again, earlier today there was some talk of his science fiction reading and all the rest of it. Later on in his life, he read nothing but those kinds of books. But nothing was ever fixed, particularly his books, which is your area, of course, but, as you know, I mean there is no final manuscript of anything. And usually the final positions of the elements of the text were done by somebody else, often without him even bothering to check—*The Soft Machine*, for instance. Well, I haven't read your introduction yet so I don't want to contradict anything you might have said there, but he basically just sort of left it and then poor old Allen Ginsberg had to sort it all out and put it into some kind of order. It was the kind of work that Allen really didn't like. But that was part of the collaborative nature of the Beats as well. Although Bill didn't stick around. He disappeared off to Tangier from Paris and Allen . . .

HARRIS To avoid Allen, wasn't it? Just mentioning Ginsberg, you have that wonderful biography of Ginsberg and you've done a biography of Kerouac. What I'm wondering about Burroughs is, did he present unique problems that neither Ginsberg, who you knew obviously very well, or Kerouac—did he present unique problems and, if so, what are they to the biographer? What specifically is difficult about doing a biography of Burroughs? It can't be easy.

MILES There is less useful interview material than I was expecting. There's maybe sixty or seventy interviews with him.

HARRIS Most people would think that would be quite enough actually.

MILES But most of them were not about subjects that were of an interest to me. They were maybe about the actual books or something like that. Of course, there were all the interviews with Ted, who irritated me because he never asked the questions I wanted! (Laughter.) So it's too late now. Different books present certain problems. I mean, I did a biography of Paul McCartney, for instance, and there are no printed texts at all that you can use in a situation like that, and rock and roll interviews are notoriously pointless and uninteresting. (Laughter.) I had forty-seven interviews with him and then edited all of that into shape. Whereas other things like, most of the Ginsberg book, for instance, I did use original sources—letters mainly, and I had access to all of his journals. And I didn't really do very many interviews with him, maybe eight or something. That was all. And in the case of Burroughs I relied an awful lot on James Grauerholz and his research and the people who knew Burroughs late in life. Although the Burroughs that they know in Kansas, I think, is a very different person.

HARRIS Well, he was obviously in Kansas a long time. In the Kansas years in particular, how did he change, do you think?

MILES I think he went back to probably what was part of his core personality of a taciturn, quite silent Midwesterner who had no . . . in England we call it "side."

There is no side to him. What you see is what you get. And Bill, there was no pretension there, no arrogance or anything. He stripped right down to his basic Bill Burroughs-hood. He had a lot of cranky ideas, of course, as usual but—at least I thought they were cranky, like his wishing machine and all these things. He had a very good orgone accumulator. Our original correspondence way back in 1964 was about orgone accumulators.

HARRIS   You talk about his cranky ideas and, again, one of the things that I think I've committed my work to is trying to take Burroughs seriously because I know that when I first approached him many years ago he wasn't taken seriously. And it kind of appalled me that somebody whose work is so viscerally challenging and so full of ideas should be dismissed as being too far out. He was full of cranky ideas and yet he's also highly regarded for his ideas. How do you square that circle?

MILES   Well, that is the hardest thing to square. I think that's the biggest problem, particularly if you're trying to write an objective book about him because you do have to present all of these ideas and to present them in all seriousness. And the one regard I probably failed in is his interest in Scientology, which I could never understand because it did such damage to his life. It destroyed the best love affair he ever had and it alienated so many of his friends. And apparently for no reason at all, I might add; I didn't see him gain anything from it at all. Although, as Brion Gysin once pointed out, Bill is probably the only person who actually made money out of it because he used the techniques to write so many texts that he was then able to sell.

HARRIS   There's a very funny report, that's in the Berg Collection I believe, from when he went to Edinburgh in 1968 and qualified for senior levels as a Scientologist (see Wills 2013). And they wrote a report on him saying that Mr. Burroughs had done very well and that his auditing had really improved his writing and he had recently been able to write a straight narrative for the first time in many years. (Laughter.) This report written about Mr. Burroughs is hilarious.

MILES   I haven't seen that. (Laughter.) There's always more stuff . . .

HARRIS   There's always more stuff and your book already comes in at seven hundred pages. And when we were talking earlier on, you said it could have been two volumes, really, to cover the life. You said he was a chameleon. Do you think there is one Burroughs which is more enduring or meaningful than the others?

MILES   Well, let's just take the two most important sides to it. First of all his humor, I think, which is very much twentieth century American humor or pot head humor in that sort of countercultural realm beginning with the Beats and then moving to the hippies up to a bit of the punks, I suppose. It's a very interesting take on the world and I find it hilarious. So when I first read *Naked Lunch* in about 1960, I guess, I was living in a communal apartment in London with a group of other people and we used to smoke a lot of dope and read aloud from *Naked Lunch*. And every few lines everyone would crack up.

HARRIS See how far you could get . . .

MILES Yeah, I mean you could never read it for more than about five minutes without everyone just falling about laughing. It was fantastic—really, really funny. But the serious side of him, of course, is the deep political commitment that runs right through. The anti-imperialist attack on big corporations and the search for Control, identifying the systems of control that you're brought up with, you know. They're present in the language. They're present in all of the notions of, well, everything from nationhood, patriotism, the school system. Everything presents a set of ideas and boundaries to you, which are unconscious. And you accept them unless you . . . he always said you must challenge everything and if you agree with it, fine. It's now become your idea but before that it wasn't. It was just you were operating under somebody else's control, part of the system that he was always so opposed to. And this I think is needed more and more and more in the surveillance society that we're now living in. He's never been more relevant and this is why I really want his work to carry on and be there for the next generation if . . .

HARRIS If there is a next generation.

MILES Yes. (Laughter.)

HARRIS I think you've put your finger on something very important: the politics and the humor and the relation between the two.

MILES Well, he uses the two, of course. I mean what seems to be superficially very, very funny often has got a really serious story behind it. . . . Well, he's a world class writer. He's up there with, as far as I'm concerned, with Eliot and Proust and Jean Genet and Céline—all the people he was most influenced by. And you wouldn't necessarily say Genet was a French writer. To me, these people, they write about universal problems and universal values and the human condition and it's worldwide. And Burroughs is very highly regarded of course, as you know, in all of these other countries. And most of his books are in print throughout in all the major languages in the world. So he's a world-class writer.

HARRIS It's one of the reasons for our presence here today—we're Englishmen who have been influenced by Burroughs, and Burroughs does belong to the rest of the world. When I first worked on Burroughs there were more books in French on Burroughs than there were in English. There was Philippe Mikriammos (1975) and Serge Grunberg (1979) who had written books before Eric Mottram (1978) and then Jennie Skerl (1985), and so on. So actually he was recognized first in Europe.

MILES Well, he had been living out of America and that must have been a factor.

Burroughs in front of Beat Hotel, Brion Gysin, Paris, 1959,
photograph courtesy of Barry Miles.

HARRIS And then the other side of it is not only the "American" tag but the "writer" tag and, again, I think one of the interesting things to me with the biography was that you've kind of taken it for granted the reader knows the books, and if you wanted to know about the books there are other places to find out about them. One of the great things in the biography is the attention you give to the non-writing oeuvre. Do you want to talk a bit about that? Because you have been heavily involved recently in CDs and photography exhibitions.

MILES To me he's the ultimate postmodernist in that respect. He crosses genres without even thinking and at a time when that wasn't done in the '60s. And unfortunately the means of production weren't adequate in those days to make these experiments available to the general public. So all of his tape collages, for instance, from the beginning in about 1960 until fairly recently were unknown virtually, except to one or two friends. And then the same applies to his photo collages, his film work. I mean all of these things were virtually unknown. But to him, it was all a part of the same great work and particularly in the '60s. I mean he devoted almost the whole time to that kind of work. And the books that were being printed, published in America were basically books that he started off 8 years ago or something like that. I forget now when—well, you should know this—when would have been the last version of *Soft Machine* that came out originally back in 1961 or '62. There was a tremendous time lag. That's really what I'm saying. And then there were years and years where he was doing cut ups and he was doing work with Antony Balch on film that no one could see. So I did try and describe his work from his point of view—the amount of time he devoted to cut ups and to films and tape projects and scrapbooks. So as I progressed chronologically, I devoted that amount of time to what he was actually doing there, not to the books. Obviously he's best known for his books but really it's a mass of work. It's a huge body of work and I think his visual work is particularly good, actually. He's a great colorist. As a draftsman he's useless but he said that himself. So, he evolved completely radical methodologies just out of the blue— and he didn't realize he was breaking so many rules, but he did that constantly. His photo collages, for instance—as far as I know, no one else has ever worked that way before. Normally collages, of course, began as sticking stuff that's been cut out; thus, they're called a collage. But he didn't. He would arrange elements and photograph them, and then he would rearrange them and photograph them again and rearrange. So he was working in sequence, in series like Monet's *Haystacks* (1890–91) or something, except that the only evidence of these collages was photographic and I don't think anyone had ever done that before. And then the content of these photo collages was almost all personal. He didn't choose elements to photograph that were just nice textures or shapes or colors. They were always photographs of family or friends or boyfriends or sometimes elements out of the past—places he'd lived, locations, "sets" as he called them. And again he would rearrange those, take a picture and rearrange them. So each one was a slightly different record, a photograph of a mind state, of a particular point in time and space and therefore a set of memories that he was experiencing while looking at this collage. And then he would move on to the next stage.

HARRIS The situation you describe is very unusual because he was so open-minded in his approach, and that's why, in a sense, he wasn't breaking the rules. He was simply ignoring what could be rules. That open-mindedness is very interesting because, for many years, he was seen as being a writer who also did at one point work as a painter. And I think people were very skeptical—I remember myself thinking, well, if it weren't by Burroughs would anybody be showing these? And then, of course, the more you realize how much non-written work he produced—and we realize how much writing he used that wasn't in book form, as Jed [Birmingham][1] and Charles Plymell[2] have been saying—the more you realize it's an old-fashioned way of approaching a writer. It's interesting when you say he was a postmodernist. It's a very contested term in academia. But . . .

MILES I'm not in academia. (Laughter.)

HARRIS I know, so you get out of that one! But us academics in the room are thinking, "postmodern?" We don't like that word any more, we're now into post-post-postmodernism. . . . But curiously one of the odd things is that Burroughs still remains a practitioner who seems to be unique, that other people don't seem to [be] doing what he did. And therefore it's very difficult even to identify him as being not a writer, but an artist of a broader kind. So he does seem to remain anomalous. I'm just wondering if you have to summarize him for a new generation—as you're saying, you've identified his humor and his politics as being so important—[in regards to] this question of identity, of who he was, and therefore what we might learn from that. Because I'm fascinated by the limits on who we are and how difficult it is to change who we are, and a lot of people seem to know who we are better than we ourselves know. Does Burroughs offer a lesson from his life, or is his life really hard to learn from in that way?

MILES I don't think he would have ever wanted anyone to use him as a model, certainly. I mean because he himself felt that he really betrayed his—well, first of all he regretted shooting Joan every day of his life. He told me that he thought of her every day and that she was constantly there in his dreams and nightmares. Also when he got very drunk sometimes he would just bury his head in his hands and sort of moan and say "Joan, Joan." I mean it was always there, always there. So that was obviously a side of him that we can never know really how he felt about that. He thought that he'd let his son down really badly. So I don't think he's a role model in that sense. I think his value to a future generation must truly be just in the content of the writing and the way that one can literally throw everything up in the air. I mean, he never expected to know how to use tape recorders or how to make films or how to write or how to edit a book or anything. He did away with all of those barriers and in that way he's opened up an awful lot of doors for people. He's introduced an element of freedom that wasn't there before. So that would be his great method, you know, the logical contribution but mainly it's the message.

HARRIS   In terms of the message . . .

MILES   Challenge everything and watch out for control systems.

HARRIS   "Don't follow leaders and watch your parking meters . . ." And yet curiously there is this very controversial last line of writing of his in his final journal which is to do with love.

MILES   Which at the time was for his cats.

HARRIS   Well, exactly. I was going to say, was this a human love? Because this is one of the problems of his life, wasn't it, to do with his family and his wife and his son and his mother as well. Do you think in those last years, he was happy?

MILES   I think his years in Kansas were the happiest, with the possible exception of some of the time he was in Tangier. I think those would be the happiest times he ever had. He finally wasn't plagued by the demons so much and he just relaxed. He was a very, very different person I found when I went to see him out there.

HARRIS   Do you think he cared at all about his status?

MILES   Yes, there was a side of him which was very proud of being so well known. He always wore his little rosettes and stuff from the academy, the Académie française [l'Ordre des Arts et des Lettres] and the one from New York. So, yeah, all of those things did mean something to him.

HARRIS   You've got a unique perspective here because you also knew Ginsberg so well as well as doing the biography. Ginsberg was famous for being quite intrusive and controlling about his legacy and reputation.

MILES   Hmmm.

HARRIS   Burroughs was happy about it and yet curiously left a lot to James and he didn't seem to me to be somebody who would manipulate a situation or demand things of people. Now, when you did your first biography he was still alive, the shorter one.

MILES   And I think he read it as well.

HARRIS   Was there anything that came out of that he wanted or didn't want?

MILES   He thought that I was exaggerating his importance. Because there were certain things that were in *Naked Lunch* which I thought had anticipated what was going to go on with Pol Pot. And, I remember in the margin he wrote "steady on there, Miles." (Laughter.) So he was quite modest in that respect. I think he wanted to go down in history as a writer, certainly, and whether he would have even claimed to be a great writer I don't know. He certainly didn't have the side of him that Allen had of dating everything and keeping one's archives. Bill was very sloppy. Whenever he'd run out of money he would just sell a bunch of stuff. He was totally not possessive and I mean this is the thing. When he was at the Beat Hotel he would just up and leave and it was up to Brion Gysin to rush in and gather all the manuscripts that were left and store them up in the attic in the Beat Hotel in an old sea trunk, which I still have.

HARRIS The old sea trunk?

MILES Yes, but there's no manuscript in it, by the way. (Laughter.) If there were, I would send them to you.

HARRIS One of the things that struck me—and I was lucky enough to meet both Ginsberg and Burroughs, although obviously I didn't really know them at all— but one thing that struck me was that they actually lived in very, very modest conditions. On the Lower East Side, Allen gave me a drink in a dirty glass. It wasn't a glass. It was a kind of a jam jar or something. I remember looking at it, thinking, "Is it clean? I've come to see Allen Ginsberg and I'm not sure I should be drinking out of this." (Laughter.) Then when I met Burroughs in Lawrence, I remember thinking, "This is his home," and it was just very, very basic. And of course it was one of the things that I admired most about both of them is that physically, materially, they just didn't give a shit.

MILES No.

HARRIS Whereas we're all so encouraged to be proud of our possessions and so on.

MILES Yeah, Bill didn't even have a full set of his own books. He just didn't care for things. His life was cerebral. Everything happened in his head and he didn't much care what he had in the bookcase or even on the wall. Although there was a period in London in the late '60s, I think, when he did make a sort of attempt at fixing up what was going to be a really nice pad where all these young boys were just going to disport themselves. You know, he could have all of his Gysins on the wall and, in other words, he would be living like the people he was mixing with, the Chelsea set. But it didn't really come to much largely because the problems between him and Ian Sommerville. And Ian's role all through the '60s shouldn't be overlooked. I feel, maybe, if there's anything wrong with my book, it's that I don't really show him as a strong enough character because Ian really influenced Bill enormously and in so many different respects, particularly technically to do with the tapes and collages and the scrapbooks. But also in texts and in reading and just general attitudes to things, particularly anything to do with science and technology. But because Bill later on became quite involved in, well, you know he studied anthropology. His interest in the natural world and everything was enhanced very much by Ian.

HARRIS You've written a seven-hundred-page biography and I'm going to ask you a rather ridiculous question: How would you summarize his life in seventy words, Miles? And I know you've already talked about how much of a chameleon he was, how he adapted to different circumstances. Was there anything else or does that kind of sum up a very complex life, one with so many different sets? Is there anything else that you feel has either been overlooked or has been gotten wrong by people? Because you knew him personally, you've written two books about him. If you don't know, maybe who does? What do people not get about Burroughs that we still need to understand?

MILES That he was a very serious artist or writer, whatever you want to call it, and that he spent all day every day working. And if he was doing cut ups he would do thousands upon thousands of them. If he was doing tape collages, again, hours and hours of tape and then he would rerecord over and over. Thousands of photographs that he took. He was very, very committed to his work. Once he found that that's what he was going to be, it took him a long time—as you know, he was almost middle aged before he began writing and began to see himself as a writer, a story writer. But once he did that, he was totally committed to it for the rest of his life and worked very, very hard. Most of it wasn't even designed to be seen by anyone except himself. They were purely for his own experimental use, ultimately culminating in something, you know. Except the tapes, he didn't ever expect anyone to hear those. Most of it was done for his own interest. I mean very early on—this morning there was some talk about his readers and whether he cared about that. I don't really believe that he did—most of him was just writing for himself. Obviously he wanted people to read it but most of the work was just done for himself and his own need to express this stuff.

HARRIS I think it's a very, very powerful note to conclude on—his seriousness—because his reputation early on was as somebody who was actually lazy. The idea that cut ups were an easy way of writing, and the whole Beat mythology that they were just being spontaneous and this wasn't hard; that was how they were put down. It's interesting that you should put emphasis on just how serious and how intense he was as an artist. I do think that that's actually the best measure of how seriously we should take his work.

MILES Yes, I think so.

OLIVER HARRIS is the editor and author of ten books, including two trilogies by William Burroughs: *Junky: The Definitive Text of "Junk,"* *The Yage Letters Redux*, and *Queer: Twenty-Fifth Anniversary Edition*; and "restored" editions of the Cut-Up Trilogy: *The Soft Machine, Nova Express*, and *The Ticket That Exploded*. He is also the editor of *The Letters of William S. Burroughs, 1945–1959* and *Everything Lost: The Latin American Notebook of William S. Burroughs*, the author of the critical study *William Burroughs and the Secret of Fascination* and co-editor of *Naked Lunch@50: Anniversary Essays*. He is Professor of American Literature at Keele University and President of the European Beat Studies Network.

BARRY MILES is an author and biographer whose books include *William Burroughs: El Hombre Invisible, The Beat Hotel: Ginsberg, Burroughs, and Corso in Paris, 1958–1963*, and *William S. Burroughs: A Life*.

NOTES

1. Jed Birmingham is a writer and essayist who has published numerous articles on Burroughs. He is the contributing editor of RealityStudio.org, a website dedicated to Burroughs, a coeditor of *Mimeo Mimeo*, and a contributor to *Beat Scene* magazine.

2. Charles Plymell was a beat poet and printer who, in addition to his numerous stand-alone works, published the short-lived but venerated underground newspaper *The Last Times* in 1967, which included the first appearance of Burroughs' essay "Day the Records Went Up," one of several examples of Burroughs' work outside of the book form.

REFERENCES

Grunberg, Serge. 1979. *"A la recherche d'un corps": Langage et silence dans l'oeuvre de William S. Burroughs*. Paris: Éditions du Seuil.
Philippe Mikriamos. 1975. *William S. Burroughs: La vie et l'oeuvre*. Paris: Seghers.
Morgan, Ted. 1988. *Literary Outlaw: The Life and Times of William S. Burroughs*. New York: Henry Holt.
Mottram, Eric. 1975. *William Burroughs: The Algebra of Need*. London: Boyars.
Skerl, Jennie. 1985. *Burroughs*. Boston: Twayne.
Wills, David S. 2013. *Scientologist! William S. Burroughs and the "Weird Cult."* United Kingdom: Beatdom Books.

Cutting Up the Critics

Before turning to the wide-ranging cultural criticism in this anthology, it seems fair to give Burroughs an opportunity to confront his critics. In the scandal that *Naked Lunch* left in its wake, Burroughs only further unsettled literary convention by hailing the cut-up method at the 1962 Edinburgh Writer's conference. In a large compilation of archival materials at the NYPL Berg archive, Burroughs can be seen responding to the mainstream critical backlash to his avant-garde writing. To do so, he turned the cut-up method against their outrage, splicing the staid prose of traditional critics to forge linguistic coinages that would prove vital to his artistic vision. By cutting up the literary establishment's most vociferous reactions to his radical, queer aesthetic, Burroughs sought to deconstruct at its root his own iconic image, while exposing the reactionary ideological core of the culture and society he was seeking to overturn.

Both "Cut-Up of Critics Grid" and the following "Cut-up of Critics" appear in Folio 79 of the Berg archive, entitled "Grids and Experiments, 4 Calle Larachi 1964." In these two pieces, we can see Burroughs' process of transcribing selections from various reviews, before creating a grid over the text that facilitates his transposition of fragments to a new cut-up piece. Burroughs' cut-up method was a multi-phased, iterative process of revision, with wide-ranging relay points and outputs. His cut-ups of his reviews, for instance, made their way into his published works, especially, according to Oliver Harris, the 1967 edition of *The Ticket That Exploded* (Harris, xxxii).

We follow these two pieces illustrating his composition process with a series of scintillating cut-ups Burroughs conducted with book reviews in the *Times Literary Supplement* from the early 1960s. In the Berg Catalogue, Barry Miles notes that for the creation of the "Cut-Ups of Reviews and Times Literary Supplement Ugh Affair," Burroughs used "tearsheets from the *TLS* 'Letters To The Editor' page in which correspondence concerning the 'Changing Guard' issue occurs." Burroughs also incorporated the August 13, 1964, 'UGH' review of *Naked Lunch*, as well as issues of Diane di Prima and LeRoi Jones' small press magazine, *Floating Bear* (1962–1969).

These materials represent only a small percentage of the dozens of cut-ups Burroughs produced from reviews of his work at this time. Folio 108, entitled "Fresh Southerly Winds Stir Papers On The City Desk," is a miscellaneous, inconsistently dated compilation of Burroughs' experiments in faux newspapers with three-column cut-ups, bearing such splendid titles as *Cold Spring News*, *Moving Times*, *Present Times*, *The Last Post*, *Other Voices*, *The Tangier Survey*, and *The Moroccan Dispatch*. In one file of Folio 108, Burroughs appends as a heading to the three-column cut-up what can stand as one of Burroughs' maxims, a statement of purpose which future generations of fans and scholars of Burroughs would do well to keep in mind: "MY CRITICS (NAMELESS ASS HOLES) ARE BY THIS WRITING ANSWERED IN THEIR OWN WORDS ROUND TABLE TURNING DID EAT EACH OTHER TO THE AMAZEMENT OF MINE EYES THAT LOOKED UPON IT" (Berg 38.95).

—AWC

FACING, *Cut Up of Critics Grid*, William S. Burroughs (8 × 11, 1 leaf, facsimile) (Berg 21.2). Item 2, "criticism your crtics. . ." (Text divided into 32 squares by a wavy blue grid.), From Folio 79 Grids and Experiments 4 Calle Larachi 1964. Copyright © by William Burroughs, used by permission of The Wylie Agency LLC.

criticism	your crtics may	so I gather is supp	be young enough to
osed to be	change his mind	objective giving	later me may not
the crtics	know just yet	intellectual apprai	what B'S message
sal of the book	is but he will	rather than a list	baby,in time M.M.
,of his emotional	the piece is	reactions to it	ironic the irony
your piece	appears to have	on W.B. in the	escaped your
issue dated	critic's hasty	Nov.I4 is both	eye for instance
pompously sub-	the conversation	jective and thro-	between Shafer and
ugly distaste	Benway is not	ful.It is also	to do with the dog's
innacuarate	having been sick	the character	on the carpet but
of your re	about their feel	view was sumed	ings in running an
up in its title	Auswitch like	our critic ment-	research dept read
the so called	objectively	pardody on	nothing in Mr B's
science fiction	work should	in The Ticket	appear or taste
you featured	disgusting	an article by	your critic siezes
Mr E.Crispin	passages he	an science fiction	does not understand
just as	and expounds	modern physics	upon them for instanc
approaches the	Robert's brooth	metaphysical with	er Paul emerges
each new	from retirement	advancement so is	in a local nut house
B concerned	andtake s over	with Space and Time	the restaurant
so what you	to dispense	want off me?	something he calls
Time 'I don't	transcanental	dig. 'I have some	cuisine impercept
thing you	ibly the quali	want' hishand	y of the food de-
touched the	clined until	package.He drift e	he is serving
away into the	literal garbage	front room his	the clients being
voice remote a	too intimi-	and blured five	dated by the rep
minutes here	of Chez Robert	an hour some	to object protest
place else	ample menu the	two four 8 may	booksare themselves
be I'm getting	something of a	ahead of myself	scientific as well
every day die	a literary	a little it takss	experience.Your
up the time	reviewer has	'Mister,I don't	not noticed how
Know what you	conditions	re talking about	the reader to reeve
you would baby	impressio s	in time certain	from key words
books he has	which recur	not noted the ex	throughout the
explaining what	plicit foot	B hopes to do	notes actually
at all becasue	he has not	it seems likely	noticed much
Menu quoted	he has not read	out of context	the books.The
comic chunks	as one of the	in the new house	supposedly
for Dead Fi ng	rained version	Talk but appear	is not revised
nak d lunch	exactly as	preceding this	quoted in the
	Menu we read:		

Criticism: Your critics may so I gather is supposed be young enough
change his mind objective giving later critics just yet what B's
message of the book is but he will rather than a list,baby, in time
of his emotional piece is reactions to it ironic the irony your piece
appears to have: '/W.B. in the escaped isssue dated critic's hasty
Nov.14.It is also to do with the dog's inaccurate having been sick
on the carpet. Researchdepartment, read thr so called 'parody'.Nothing
in Mr.Burroughs science fictio n work should in the ticket appear
you featured disgusting article by your critic for instance in a
local nut house something he calls 'Time'/' his hand of the food
touched the 'Until' package literal front room garbage his clients
being voice remote and blured five dated by the minutes here to
protest 'place else'. '/Modern physics want off me? I have some.Want
package? Blured ahead of myself.It takes experience/'
'/Mister I don't know what you conditions retalking about the reader
to reve from key words notes actually supposedly the book is not
revised. 'B hopes to do out of context the new house trained exactly
as we read by scientific experience your reader trained exactly as
we read.Some ample menu with Space and Time the restaurant he is se
serving dead clinets by the hour.Cuisine emerges local restaurant
something he calls 'food' is serving the clinets are books themselves
Take a walk back to yesterday on average drink a cup of coffee dream
ing of yesterday's springs and apple orchards shabby tunnel of old
photos the man's face there is'nt much time old Mexico papers smell
of chemical sort of person who would willingly farm in those days.
You move his hands,Mexico?/'
'/Cut off there now since senor cureed himself so moving fast charged
with murder young along that gun all the dream people of English
hotel sweating fear like ever,Mister,you can still see used to be the
man's face there hurry there is'nt much time and then you have to
go on short notice that's when y ou need Fred Flash in the difference
between takes just time to be practical about the whole thing.From
Mexico you can take a face senor don't ask questions for once and
stay with me yes? Them man's face there can stay with me yes help me
few years from now?/'
'Dead human sickness in the room can still used to be my arm dripping
stars.'Good bye,Mister.I have opened the gates there.Hurry there
is'nt much time.Help me few yeasr from now rockets across the valley?
Burning stump of future arm where you're sitting we can break radio
silence now clear as 'Annie Laurie' Klinker is already photographed.
Don't ask questions hurry for once there is'nt much time. You had to
know clear as whole sky burning from reports already in the Mapping
Department six millions pile up down Cobble Stone Cody doing

Our reviewer there in nothing in writes the idea put down freedom
of of paper all that pours objectively through his mind either as Mr
Calder to suggest that graphically puts critics and it a publisher no
criminate longer have a duty the snag to dis about mr Mr   Moorcrocks
be said I see no reason be thought to suppose help that Mr Burroughs has
unorganized and repetitious Burroughs is but they seem that he is a
quite irrelevant second rate to the nothing tastes ordinary human at all
except world except bogy talk 1984 nameless anti-of Auswitch social tend
torture bombs is unspported his works are nasty by his books there is no
just because reason to who would have assume that attracted they connect
little with the muchattention if it larger and were not for mastier his
shock effects things which   forced really do form a part of modern
inaccessibility to society or publish such with those ordinary human
world muchlarger forced in writers whofor that forced inaccessibility
matter who have about proved capable unpopular against William Burroughs
subjects the case certain con implies a confusion to the opponents of
judegment but of literary when it presents freedom startingly a sitting
target obscene writer it can hardly   be thought toor with larger there is
those o forced man to publish such an unreasoned against our reviewer
writes that pours through his no mind.I see no cause for which unorganized
and that he is an ordinary human xxxxxxx at all except the familiar
torture bombs

****

"/Should take will front of 'I am' Burroughs their land-s pot-
scape pourri mish not the worn mash or put moral macedoine they
so press force of the final disclaim button of 'is not' history
with entirely one waiter.Clear per-general form haps dis-need is
criminatory banal whine of naked choosing girl who has been altogether stood up.Room nine front of this girl who square no other
one other self pushing shhh sly rubbish point of sly rubbish point of
your ex-reel
modern life./ "
"/Look,Rat of Noises, white junk.Liquid morality.Loving little
as-cription of book proof dirty fing-that we have er pushing into
pocked Burroughs dishonored boring flesh the rubbish narrative.
Maybe a man take the furious side door will write four year book
about what 15 year point of it all?/"
"/Should scape gentle force of one waiter? Picking up my lump.
Dow Joyce not concern himself.Book proof dishonored appear at
what committee?:;'What stag versions.An addict.Shocking.' 'Rooted
Immovably"cried out: 'Pay his time.It's able for neutralized

pass.This thing interesting has entered   condition surgical.This
is else since 'landscape'.A man nerve 'clean staff' of history.
Seems to be everyone is painful addict of cure what?' On page
this is not very sensible a shrill 'Suppose 'Rum' was not a man?'
All as good rooted as dead.It's naked one spot horror.We take not
the worn disclaim that we have flesh.Point of 'sorry' and death.
One kind shrill ably to everyone: 'Staff' you don't go,'Elves' I
was'. continuous cept the ages I feel as 'the pick purple' I am
not now/"
"/That Jack take himself pointless gas what? To say creeping in
morality/"
"/ Exhausted from able for a black pond rising from a black pond
exhausted rising from able for a black pond continuous with one
reading around de-power cline to acc-of its cum-cept the ulative
victim caught him out disorder neutralized.Cruize sleep by repetit-
boy ion of fair unspeakably sexed wrong terms which there is
corpses in pourri mish final clear naked to 'Compassion' around
each himself assed with himself dirty boring 15 years and end
image of 'cure' what? Dead star about like me you/"
"/Dynamite 'Black Pond'/ Cruize wrong terms like family I feel now
are corpses and a mucha mind I do/"
"/I am not. Feel that/"
"/Any rate he move out of him on Terrence.Pea fog of dead together
ways of creeping morality.Is thought my face is your 'Pale Lump'?/"
"/Comppasion ing   together let no one flow stick/"
"/Speaking of the Joyce around each book I have other presenting
x where it is/"

*****

the insufferable yet ironable prig like all flapping in ice he fall black
wings down,insect or meeting General Form Ground Need is banal whine
of naked girl who lunch is at has been stood up.'My face is the end
of your pale fork? compassion.Let no one speak of the two Joyce books
I have/ presenting mighty sick himself as little book proof that we
have here read by Mr.Burroughs are boring sometime rubbish maybe Mr.
Burroughs a man appear will write a book at a side door about fifteen
pointless years on violence? committed his experiences on the end of
your exterminatoro or what staggering 'Sorry I'm about not your litter
of waiter.Hideous per-nerve gas versions and death-seem-to-be rays?'
'Painful cure what? I was exhausted on page.Shocking. A shrill tantrum
was not all as good as Dead White.Naked Lunch making mostly horror star
about excrete around for he pay his clean staff mostly in horror parts:
junk.junk. pure dynamite the subject.After all its on the shelves. I was
exhausted rising from a black pond with one around to decline to
accept the victim.caught him out cruize sleep to being.for boy unspeakable wrong terms.There is no terms. This thing I feel now.I
hear,sxxx sure that 'Voices' and,Mr. Burroughs, a much spoken of catnip smell has entered The Purple Better One creeping to my mind I do
feel that hideous surgical face.' /'You gentle   trash,not men.Move out
of the worn way for grey room rats?'/ imagaine him he will looking at

write a landscape.Takes   himself for sad four sink form seriousness
pea fog of noises his prose a public statement som xxxxx kinda:'Tell
Luara I love 'Boy Drug Diseased Face' shyly fed to 'ME'.' A man appear
pointless on the 'sorry I'm a nerve gas what?' About not your litter
of dead white junk he pyx pays his clean staff in to say the dirty
worn ways of morality: 'Final ape of history ruthlessly creeping in/
any spark/ 'Pea Fog Prose/public statement/ some kinda youth lover
callow rats out cruizing for boy sleep there/" I sure hear wrong terms
dirty voices dirty fingers shreds his prose writhing to me brad of
very nice youth sink form the worn way for grey room rats eat the
unborn.So press the button and see no reason history there is no
history.Sheds his responsibilities in front of their landscape.Gentle
not the worn out morality so press the final button of history with
one waiter.

*****

Assume that attracted they connect pick up gusts ready in larger and
nastier black stench solemn lab or modern disapproval new house.Clear
up such with those ordinary human final stench there of Reader Lab
who for that forced inaccesibility able mixture text excuse texture
stench unpopular against William Burroughs blast there the excuse has
scattered a confusion to the opponents of this speakable stink world folds
on a startlingly sitting arthur. Presenrts freedom a sitting fronteer
in a blast after he skip and let us hope that he is an ordinary human
torture bombs slide out

3

The Nova Convention:
Celebrating the Burroughs of
Downtown New York

KRISTEN GALVIN

When Timothy Leary was asked about his participation on a panel discussing the topic of the future at the Nova Convention, the three-day experimental symposium celebrating William S. Burroughs in 1978, he remarked, "This kind of conversation could only take place in New York" (Marzorati 1978, 27). Here, Leary implies that it is the social and cultural geography of New York City that engenders such a groundbreaking forum for cultural and intellectual exchange. Known as the godfather of punk, a multimedia artist, and a symbol of anti-censorship, queer politics, and alternative possibilities; it is only fitting that Burroughs was given his due during the heyday of Downtown New York. Reminiscent of an apocalyptic Burroughsian landscape, Downtown was paradoxically defined by crisis alongside unprecedented social and cultural freedoms. These circumstances generated a nova-like explosion of unbridled creativity and experimentation across the arts known as the "Downtown scene" (Taylor 2006). Often an imprecise umbrella term mixing geographical location and cultural aesthetics, the permissive site of "Downtown" became popularly associated with an identity and style that was anti-mainstream, diverse, queer, poor, youthful, and dangerous (Mele 2000, 217). Burroughs became a kind of paragon of Downtown, then in part inhabited by young suburban refugees, artists, squatters, and a spectrum of social and sexual misfits.

The Nova Convention represents a nexus of forces that tells the story of Burroughs' relationship to, and influence upon, Downtown, which shaped his own cultural acclaim. Burroughs' work is often read through place, whether in terms of his residence in Tangier, Mexico City, and Paris, or even growing-up in St. Louis. This essay provides a historical excavation and reconstruction of the Nova Convention to demonstrate Burroughs' critical ascent as synchronous with the height of the Downtown scene. An interdisciplinary and live performance extravaganza, the Nova Convention joined an unusual assortment of artists, rockers, publishers, academics, countercultural figures, and audience members—as only a tribute to Burroughs could—to recognize his wide influence for the first time in the United States. Primarily hosted in the East Village, the neighborhood synonymous with the Downtown scene, the multimodal event enlisted a cross-generational "who's who" of New York's vanguard, and was comprised of performance art, theater, dance, readings, poetry, academic panels, concerts, a curated film series, parties, and an art exhibition (table 3.1).

The Nova Convention included appearances by established figures such as John Cage, Merce Cunningham, Phillip Glass, and Allen Ginsberg; next to up-and-comers like Patti Smith, Laurie Anderson, the B-52s, and Suicide. Significantly, the event coalesced when performance art was attaining legitimization in the art world; nightlife was peaking; and Burroughs was starting to perform in nightclubs. The Nova Convention clearly depicts Downtown's cultural geography as true palimpsest and as a fertile ground for new artists and works to emerge in distinct conversation with the longer cultural continuum of New York's avant-garde and its queer history. The multigenerational celebration reintroduced the Beat (then in his mid-sixties) and the cut-up method when the youth-oriented cultures of punk, hip-hop, new wave, and no wave commingled Downtown.

The mega-conference was also a collaborative endeavor coproduced by then Columbia Professor Sylvère Lotringer, founder of the journal *Semiotext(e)*; Burroughs' assistant and manager, James Grauerholz; and poet and performance artist John Giorno, a mainstay in New York's avant-garde since the days of Warhol's Silver Factory. Their willingness to cross networks and to place the academy in conversation with art and music scenes constituted the very social and cultural fabric of the Nova Convention. Palpably different from your average academic conference, writer and publisher Jan Herman quipped, "the convention was a far cry from the MLA thank god" (Birmingham 2010). Significantly, the Nova Convention promoted the cut-up and "French theory" through the timed release of two publications: (1) Burroughs and Brion Gysin's, *The Third Mind* (1978 English edition), a book demonstrating the cut-up to a new audience of cultural producers; and (2) *Semiotext(e)*'s "Schizo-Culture" issue, debuting its new, highly visual, and Downtown-identified format. These publications substantiate how ideas and techniques disseminated through the Nova Convention, beyond performances alone, which indicate the event's impact upon Downtown's cultural production and consumption.

Lotringer, recognizing Burroughs as an artistic and intellectual conduit across continents, in effect coupled "French theory" to Downtown New York. François Cusset marks the 1970s as the moment of the "French Invasion" and a turning point in American intellectualism. He also claims that the "wild seventies" was a time of French theory's "countercultural temptations," which included avant-garde journals and rock concerts, on the one hand, and its first academic applications, on the other (Cusset 2008, 10, 54). Namely, it was the *wild countercultural temptation* of the Nova Convention that abetted this "invasion" to popularize French theory in the United States. Moreover, the Nova Convention hailed Burroughs as America's forgotten artist and served as a corrective to his long overdue institutional recognition. Lotringer remarks, "The limited goal of the Nova Convention is to make people aware that only America could produce William Burroughs. . . . In France he's considered a philosopher of the future. . . . But in America? They know little of him" (Marzorati 1978, 27).

When Burroughs returned to Manhattan in 1974, he was down-and-out and reluctantly accepted a teaching position at the City University of New York. In 1976, he moved to the mythic Bunker, located on the Bowery in an old YMCA building a few blocks down the street from CBGB, the legendary music venue housing Downtown's punk and new wave scenes. At the turn of the century this area was known for its prostitution, saloons, and queer clientele; and in the 1970s for its drug trade and "Bowery bums." After falling into relative obscurity and poverty since the obscenity trial of *Naked Lunch*, and growing older, Burroughs sought financial stability and critical recognition in the United States. Through the Nova Convention, Lotringer expanded European discourses of Burroughs stateside and generated a collective American "fascination" with Burroughs, to adopt Oliver Harris's term (2003).

Ultimately, this essay argues that the Nova Convention played a pivotal role in Burroughs' American reception and image formation, which was specifically grounded in, and mediated by, Downtown as a physical site, attitude, cultural movement, and style. The Nova Convention, along with the many tributes to Burroughs that followed in its wake, all demonstrate his enduring legacy. As creative and intellectual expressions of fan culture, these celebrations generate new discourses and art forms through the vehicle of Burroughs. The untold history of the Nova Convention demonstrates how his public image and legacy could only take shape through Downtown New York, which in turn influenced the cultural production, identities, and attitudes associated with "Downtown" itself.

DOWNTOWN AS URBAN CUT-UP

In the late 1970s, Downtown culture was thriving under conditions of urban bankruptcy and on low to no production budgets. Economic and social conditions in Lower Manhattan were harsh due to a combination of factors that included debt, stagflation, massive disinvestment in public infrastructure, and a lucrative drug economy. Keeping rents and the cost of living low, an abundance of burned-out and abandoned buildings littered the Lower East Side. With waves of immigration, increasing crime, and white flight decreasing the population Downtown, those moving to New York City became quickly priced out of the gentrifying neighborhoods of SoHo and Greenwich Village. As a result, the Lower East Side of Manhattan became the only remaining low-rent district south of Central Park (Bowler and McBurney 1991, 52). Because of low to no rents, one could afford the luxury to pursue multiple creative and/or leisurely interests, free from the temporal and societal constraints of a nine-to-five job.

While space was opened in terms of urban living and personal time, Downtown, like the cut-up, encouraged different art forms, genres, histories, and

Table 3.1. Events of the Nova Convention

Event	Location and Description
Reception at La Maison Française	New York University. (Thursday 5–7 p.m., free)
The Third Mind book-signing party	Books & Co., 939 Madison Avenue. The party included a preview of the connected *The Third Mind* art exhibition. (Thursday 7–10 p.m., free)
The Third Mind art exhibition	Books & Co. Art exhibition of *The Third Mind*'s cut-up techniques, including collage, photostat, and writing. (Friday, December 1–12, free)
"Cine Virus I & II" film screenings	Schimmel Auditorium, Tisch Hall, New York University; and Entermedia Theatre. Curated by Kathryn Bigelow and Michael Oblowitz. Films by Oblowitz, Bigelow, Seth Tillet, Eric Mitchell, Tina L'hotsky, Michael McClard, Amos Poe, Bruce Conners, Kathy Acker, Marc Olmstead, Steven Lowe, and Anthony Balch featuring Burroughs. (Thursday and Saturday, 7–10 p.m., $2)
"Burroughs Now" panels and lectures	Schimmel Auditorium, Tisch Hall, New York University, in both French and English. Speakers include Sylvère Lotringer, Udo Breger, John Calder, Maurice Girodias, Richard Seaver, Serge Grunberg, Jean-Jacques Lebel, Gérard-Georges Lemaire, Philippe Mikriammos, Christian Prigent, and Jurgen Ploog. (Friday, 4–7 p.m., free)
Evening Show	Entermedia Theatre, 189 Second Avenue. Performances by Allen Ginsberg and Peter Orlovsky, John Cage and Merce Cunningham, Ed Sanders, Anne Waldman, and Laurie Anderson and Julia Heyward; and an opening production of "A.J.'s Annual Party," by The BBC Project Theater Company (adapted from *Naked Lunch*), directed by Donald Sanders. (Friday, 8:30 p.m., $6)
"New Wave Rock Concert"	Club 57 at Irving Plaza. Performances by the B52s, Suicide and Walter Steding. Deborah Harry, Chris Stein and Robert Fripp make guest appearances. (Friday and Saturday, 10 p.m., $6)
Party at the Mudd Club	77 White Street (Saturday, 12 a.m.)
"Conversations" panel	Entermedia Theatre. Moderated by Les Levine; with Burroughs, Brion Gysin, Timothy Leary, and Robert Anton Wilson. Susan Sontag was originally scheduled but cancelled. (Saturday, 1 p.m., $2)
Evening Show	Entermedia Theatre. A pre-sold out show with readings and performances by Terry Southern, Frank Zappa, Patti Smith and Lenny Kaye, Philip Glass, John Giorno, Brion Gysin, and Burroughs. Keith Richards was originally scheduled but cancelled. (Saturday, 8:30 p.m., $6)
Party at Mickey Ruskin's Kipling's Last Resort/Chinese Chance	1 University Place. (Sunday, 12 a.m.)
"The Penny Arcade Peep Show"	Westbeth Theatre Center, 151 Bank Street. Performance by Belgian theatre troupe Le Plan K. (Thursday, November 30–December 15, 8 p.m., $4)

Source: Table 3.1 represents publicly promoted Nova Convention events compiled from press coverage by the *New York Times, New York Rocker, SoHo Weekly News*, and *Village Voice*. Sylvère Lotringer Papers and *Semiotext(e)* Archive; MSS 221; the Fales Library and Special Collections, New York University; and Burroughs and Bockris 1981, 144. Courtesy of the Fales Library and Special Collections, New York University.

identities to cross-pollinate. Pioneered by Burroughs and Gysin, the cut-up is a creative process in which text and/or images (found or created) are randomly rearranged to produce new and unexpected results. The cut-up, as a metaphor for the creative space of Downtown, puts into stark relief Downtown's do-it-yourself impulses that celebrated spontaneity, hybridity, collaboration, and amateurism. Stressing points of immediacy and accessibility, Burroughs explains in "The Cut-Up Method of Brion Gysin" that you do not have to be highly trained nor of a certain status to make art, which was more or less Downtown's creative mantra (Burroughs and Gysin 1978, 31). The cut-up's endless permutations symbolize Gysin as artistic polymath, even more so than Burroughs, which resonated with Downtown's experimental practices and attitudes. Performance artist and Club 57 manager Ann Magnuson describes Downtown's creativity: "Artists played in bands, musicians made films, performers made art, and everyone turned themselves into fashion icons. The main objective was to remain perpetually creative and avoid getting a real job" (Cohn 2005). Downtown scenester and impresario Glenn O'Brien similarly refers to Downtown's hybrid practices and attitudes as *renaissance punk* (O'Brien 2014, 17). Following O'Brien, I classify Burroughs and Gysin as the original renaissance punks.

Burroughs also compares the cut-up to urban life itself, finding the act of walking down the city street, with its many stimulations, as an experiential audiovisual cut-up: "Cut-ups make explicit a process that goes on all the time. Every time we walk down the street or look out the window, our stream of consciousness is cut by random factors, random events, random people, random objects. In fact life is a cut-up" (Lewis 1978, 20). Burroughs considers the cut-up to be a distinctly modern mode of perception that is, "close to, particularly the perception of urban dwellers" (Lewis 1978, 20). Diversity and the capacity for mixing is a characteristic of large cities and is in fact constitutive of urbanity (Tonkiss 2005, 89). Cityscapes are in constant flux, whether in terms of the changes in urban space (design, building, destruction, abandonment, gentrification); the flows of people migrating in and out of the city; or simply the act of walking through different neighborhoods. Burroughs spatializes the cut-up within the city, reinforcing its affinities with urban cultures, or the concept of Downtown New York itself as a kind of cut-up or collage. Similarly, the cut-up also describes the variety and spirit of the Nova Convention, which placed new performance works, rock concerts, and academic and popular discourses of Burroughs in exciting juxtapositions.

MEANINGS OF THE NOVA CONVENTION

> *I am primarily concerned with the question of survival—with Nova conspiracies, Nova criminals, and Nova police. A new mythology is possible in the Space Age, where we will again have heroes and villains, as regards intentions towards this Planet. I feel the future of writing is in Space, not Time*

> —William S. Burroughs (1978)

Burroughs read his summation of the Nova Convention above on stage—a kind of tagline that also appeared in the event's marketing materials and in bright red on its album cover (Burroughs et al. 1979). While the Nova Convention showcased intellectual and artistic forms, Burroughs' "question of survival" and belief in "possibilities" speaks to both queer and alternative narratives, which mirror the sociality of Downtown. Yet, his statement also addresses living and creatively producing through adverse circumstances by carving out new spaces, or new worlds, as acts of creative place-making and queer world-making. Noise-rock pioneer Thurston Moore reflects on his Nova Convention experience "as a 19-year-old CBGB denizen": "There was always something magical in New York air and there seemed to be no other world in 1978. Burroughs returning to the city where he predicted that urban energy and the blinding light of punk rock was a matter of pride and integrity. The future belonged to us." (Moore 2014). The Nova Convention is an apropos descriptor for the creative spirit of Downtown New York as a place where dystopia could briefly become utopia and the future could be "owned" in a concrete or heterotopic space.

For performance scholar José Muñoz, queerness is a suspended ideality within a yet-to-be-determined space that is a relational and collective site for political imagination and transformation. Utopia signifies queerness and potentiality, and likewise, queer world-making can be actualized through performances of utopia or collective futurity. As an act of queer world-making, the Nova Convention used "a critical deployment of the past for the purpose of engaging the present and imagining the future"; and dared to "dream and enact new and better pleasures, other ways of being in the world, and ultimately new worlds" (Muñoz 2009, 136–37). Moreover, if utopia can be staged, it should be an "ideal, something that should mobilize us, push us forward" (97). As a "new wave" conference and a new genre of symposium, the Nova Convention displays such a world-making proposition where artistic possibilities and Burroughsian discourses could flourish on the Downtown stage—yet, in reality, the enterprising event was certainly not without its challenges.

While the Nova Convention directly references Burroughs' Nova or Cut-Up Trilogy, "nova" also aptly characterizes Downtown's vanguardism, amateurism, and youthful new wave spirit. In the field of astronomy, nova refers to a star's sudden level of brightness due to an explosion, or in other words, a star in its best, yet brief, shining moment. Most obviously, nova means new and is the Latin root found in words such as novelty, novice, and innovation. Victor Bockris commented on yet another meaning of nova: "In late 1978–1979, a heroin supermarket opened up on several blocks directly across from Burroughs' building at 222 Bowery. They used to sell a bag called Dr. Nova" (2010). Known as Burroughs' "punk phase," young junkies affiliated with the punk scene scored heroin for Burroughs and transformed the Bunker into a shooting gallery (Miles 1992, 2014). Such meanings of nova describe Downtown New York's dilettantism and experimentation, as well as its appetite for drugs and celebrity. Nova also alludes to the explosive brevity of underground and nightlife scenes as bursts of creative energy that quickly become reabsorbed by subsequent scenes or just fade away. To this end, "nova" symbolizes both the promises and pitfalls of Downtown.

DOWNTOWN AS STAGE: THE EVENTS OF THE NOVA CONVENTION

The Nova Convention represents a constellation of people, performances, and parties, taking place mostly in the East Village on Friday and Saturday, December 1–2, although events technically ran from November 30–December 2, 1978 (table 3.1). Given the Nova Convention's diverse cultural amalgamation, this section focuses on the music scene to best detail the event's inclusions, exclusions, dramas, and disappointments. With a name worthy of an interdisciplinary conference, the Entermedia Theatre was the central hub of the Nova Convention, hosting all of the main evening events in the East Village. The conference was produced in association with the Department of French and Italian of New York University and *Semiotext(e)*, with additional funding from Poets & Writers Inc. through the New York State Council on the Arts. The *Village Voice* reports on the funding: "Money was scarce. Lotringer provided the first few hundred. A crucial $1500 came from Tom Forcade a few days before he died. Poets and Writers provided $600—the only public funding in a city whose arts budget pushes $50 million" (Goldstein 1978, 34). To produce the Nova concert series at Irving Plaza, Lotringer maxed out his credit cards to rent a PA system, only to break even after ticket sales (Lotringer 2013, xxiv). It seems that the Nova Convention was initially produced for approximately $2,500. This amount is low given the breadth of the event and cultural personas involved, even by 1978 standards of the dollar.

Musically, the Nova Convention was first aligned with Downtown's no wave, with bands such as Teenage Jesus and the Jerks, Contortions, DNA, and Mars scheduled to play. The synergy between Nova and no wave was graphically depicted as interchangeable in *Semiotext(e)*'s event flyers, evidencing in the textual play of "NO VA/NO WAVE" (*Semiotext(e)* flyer 1978). No wave, named after the 1978 compilation album *No New York*, produced by Brian Eno, designates a distinctly Downtown mode of production where punk attitudes and DIY practices mixed with experimental noise, poetry, minimalism, and performance art. More of an underground moment than self-defined movement, no wave embraced dissension, dissonance, and the deconstruction of the immediate cultural past and manifested in Downtown's music and film scenes (Masters and Walter 2007). While demonstrating *Semiotext(e)*'s solidarity with Downtown New York's no wave, these flyers prove inaccurate as none of the bands actually played the Nova Convention. The *Village Voice* reports on the discord that ensued: "As the date approached, squabbles developed like cold sores. Certain No Wave bands would not be seen on the same stage as certain New Wave Bands" (Goldstein 1978, 34). "Squabbles" even became fistfights and some of the Stimulators, a punk band, received assault charges after attacking a photographer and breaking the arm of one of Lotringer's students in attempts to collect immediate payment (Lotringer 2015). However, reservations concerning the academy mixing with the Downtown scene surfaced prior to the event, with New York University expressing second thoughts about all those "leather pants clogging up the French Department" (Goldstein 1978, 34).

Departing from no wave, the Nova Convention's concert series was advertised for its innovation and trend-setting, and as the epitome of Downtown's new wave music scene: "A New Wave Spectacular . . . Suicide and Walter Steding represent the cutting edge of New York's most uncompromising and creative New Wave wing" (Shore 1978, 39). The troublemaking no wave bands were replaced with the more low-maintenance new wavers, with a line-up that also included the B-52s, and surprise appearances by Robert Fripp, and Deborah Harry and Chris Stein of Blondie. Correspondingly, the *SoHo Weekly News* describes the futuristic final concert:

> Sid Vicious strolls through the convention's wind-up concert at Irving Plaza Saturday night, but no one seems to notice. On stage the B-52s bang out a Burroughs like vision of TV junk, cosmic Beach parties and a place called Planet Claire. Foucault-laced Frenchmen do the frug. Poets pogo. Burroughs is nowhere to be found, but chances are he would have dug it all. "A new mythology is possible in the Space Age." Burroughs said Saturday night, and the B-52s have gotten the message. Welcome to the 1980s (Marzorati 1978, 28).

A queer boy-girl band playing space-y high-energy dance-rock, the B-52s embrace the call for new possibilities in the 1980s. Furthermore, the review reflects the popular mentality to prematurely close the book on the 1970s—punk had already started to fade and, in the case of Sid Vicious, suffered a tragic end. But, punk's Neo-Dada energy quickly transmitted to the new wave. With songs like "Planet Claire" and "There's a Moon in the Sky (Called the Moon)" and the incorporation of Theremin-like sounds, the B-52s inhabit their own version of the "Space Age" through their campy new wave music. In the lyrics of the B-52s and narratives of Burroughs, with his themes of revolution and transformation, they both imagine and create, in the words of the B-52s, "Song[s] for a Future Generation" (1983). There is a thematic of positive queer futurity that presents itself in new wave's connection to the Nova Convention. This materializes through expressions that imagine the potentiality of outer space as social solution, which originates in the queer science-fiction worlds of Burroughs.

However, the replacement of "negative" no wave bands with "positive" new wave groups was not the most significant scheduling change. The biggest and most memorable disappointment would be Keith Richards's last minute no-show: "As for Richards, he had cancelled after a Canadian prosecutor decided to appeal his lenient sentence for possession of drugs. Frank Zappa filled in with a passage from *Naked Lunch*, but his appearance was more of a vote of confidence from California" (Goldstein 1978, 36). While Zappa and Smith had achieved some mainstream success, they were not on par with the popularity of the Rolling Stones. Throughout

Burroughs with Frank Zappa and Patti Smith, facsimile, 1978. Sylvère Lotringer Papers and *Semiotext(e)* Archive, MSS 221, the Fales Library and Special Collections, New York University. Courtesy of the Fales Library and Special Collections, New York University.

the evening, audience members would scream, "Where's Keith?" and repeatedly chant "Keith" and "Stones" (Brookner 1978). Reporter Gerald Marzorati shares his observations of anger in the cheap seats: "The balcony—suburban kids in Jethro Tull T-shirts, Rolling Stones T-shirts, Grateful Dead T-shirts—is bored. They've already spent a few hours booing Philip Glass, ignoring Brion Gysin, and listening to Burroughs himself . . . 'Rock and Roll,' a fan screams as Patti Smith saunters on stage. . . . She reads them a poem. They want 'Because the Night' . . . 'You call this a concert?' a burly lad asks his friends. 'I say fuck no'" (1978, 27–28). The "suburban kids" in the audience were disillusioned by the Nova Convention's unintentional false advertisement and increasingly lost patience as they withstood the long repetitive passages of Philip Glass instead of the greatest hits of the Rolling Stones. To quell the anger over Richards' absence, Smith offered a refund to any dissatisfied customer in the audience. However, no audience member dared to out themselves by taking advantage of Smith's money-back guarantee, and the "Keith problem" was finally resolved (Brookner 1978). The situation navigated by Smith suggests that the Nova Convention's hybridity sent mixed-messages in terms of audience expectations and reception. It represents a taste clash due to age (teens) and geography (suburban), which extends to education, class, and gender (in the booing of the older avant-garde and the "lad's" disappointment).

Bernard Gendron coins the term "borderline aesthetics" to describe the destabilization between avant-garde art and popular music in the Downtown scene (Gendron 2002, 310). At the end of the 1970s, the Nova Convention too encouraged and supported "borderline aesthetics" in its attempts to fuse high and low culture and to articulate these poles in new ways and as not so far apart. Remembering, at the time, Downtown's musical vanguard was just beginning to enter the mainstream and receive radio play. For example, in the case of two prominent female Nova Convention participants, Patti Smith had already achieved mainstream success with the single, "Because the Night" (1978); and Laurie Anderson was about to crossover with "Oh Superman" (1981). Perhaps the *Village Voice*'s coverage summed it up best when Richard Goldstein quipped that Lotringer wanted too much, to "mix the '60s with the '70s; he wanted film and rock . . . the whole schizoid tamale" (1978, 34). In reflection, Lotringer remarked upon organizing the ambitious event: "That's why the Nova Convention was so difficult, there were so many people with huge egos. It was very difficult to manage. Even I got involved in the turmoil" (Lotringer 2015). The organizers, performers, and audience members were a diverse lot with a multitude of personalities, agendas, and vested interests. As a result, the Nova Convention was a risky, complex, and complicated endeavor. While there is an inherent danger in wanting "the whole schizoid tamale," at least such (im)possibilities could be imagined and pursued within the parameters of Downtown.

NOVA RELEASES: *THE THIRD MIND* AND "SCHIZO-CULTURE"

The Nova Convention also doubled as a release party for *The Third Mind* and *Semiotext(e)*'s "Schizo-Culture" issue, which then acted as intergenerational conduits that encouraged experimental thought and cultural forms. When considered a pedagogical textbook, *The Third Mind* outlines a historical mode of avant-garde impulses and proposes a model for art-making to a Downtown readership. Oliver Harris remarks on Burroughs' advocacy of the cut-up: "Burroughs knew he needed to promote the method in order to ensure understanding of his work, which could be guaranteed most effectively by creating an audience of producers—an audience, in effect, made in his own image" (2004, 182–83). This "audience of producers" existed Downtown and created the very pages of *Semiotext(e)*'s "Schizo-Culture" issue. Benefiting from the Nova Convention and the pulse of the Downtown scene, "Schizo-Culture" sold-out in three weeks, selling all three thousand copies (Lotringer 2013, xxiv).

The Third Mind incorporated collage, photographs, and calligraphic drawings, and served as both a manual and manifesto on the cut-up. Coincidently, Burroughs and Gysin worked on the book together at the Chelsea Hotel, another mythic site of the New York underground. Started in the early 1960s, *The Third Mind* was not published until 1976 in French, with the title of *Oeuvre Croisée*. Suggested by Gérard-Georges Lemaire, the French title describes notions of intersection and creativity as a crossroads of the minds. It also implies the book's cross-disciplinary agenda, which combines the processes and practices of writing with those of the visual arts.

One of the more prominent examples of tutelage via *The Third Mind* is found in the evolution of East Village art star, Keith Haring, who declared in 1987, "The Nova Convention changed my life" (Haring 1996, 171). Haring commented repeatedly on the importance of the event and recounted in his journal in 1979, soon after the Nova Convention: "The major influence, although it is not the sole influence, has been the work of William S. Burroughs. His profound realizations, which I encountered in radio broadcasts of the Nova Convention and in the book *The Third Mind* by Burroughs and Brion Gysin, which I have just begun to read, are beginning to tie up a lot of loose ends in my own work and thinking" (Haring 1996, 31). The Nova Convention occurred at a critical point in Downtown cultural history, but also at a crucial time for Haring, who was just discovering his own artistic voice and style. Moreover, Haring later collaborated with both Burroughs and Gysin. He provided cover artwork and illustrations for two of Gysin's publications, *Fault Lines* (1986) and *The Last Museum* (1986). Haring went on to create two works with Burroughs, *Apocalypse* (1988) and *The Valley* (1989), illustrating his texts and producing editions in silkscreen and etching.

The second publication in sync with the Nova Convention was *Semiotext(e)*'s "Schizo-Culture" issue. Dissatisfied with the limits of academia, Lotringer created *Semiotext(e)* with his colleagues and graduate students when he was a professor at Columbia University. While the journal is widely credited for importing French theory into the United States, Lotringer explains his intentions for the journal quite differently, "I didn't want it to be 'French Theory,' I wanted the magazine to be American. It's all a big misunderstanding. My purpose wasn't to introduce French thought to America, but to get America thinking along those lines" (2006). Denying his role as missionary, Lotringer wished to facilitate Americans', and particularly artists', critical understandings of capitalism. He further remarks,

"'Schizo-Culture' was published in 1978 when the three-day 'Nova Convention' celebrating William Burroughs was spreading all over 'downtown.' It was the last extravaganza of the American counter-culture we got involved with, because there never was one after that" (2006). By 1985, Lotringer would halt *Semiotext(e)* for this reason—his disenchantment with the commercialization and gentrification of Downtown New York, which shifted from an avant-garde culture of the collective to that of the capitalist-minded individual (2006).

In 1975, at the time of the Schizo-Culture conference, *Semiotext(e)* had already published three issues, which were primarily text-based. A predecessor of the Nova Convention, the Schizo-Culture conference investigated the heated topic of madness and prisons, and included theoretical heavyweights such as Michel Foucault, Gilles Deleuze, and Félix Guattari (Lotringer and Morris 2013). What would in retrospect become a landmark intellectual event, Schizo-Culture first introduced Deleuze's concept of the rhizome, and Foucault's *History of Sexuality* (Volume I published in French in 1976; English translation 1978). Similar to the credo of the Nova Convention, the panels and lectures of the Schizo-Culture conference were intentionally mixed in with appearances by artistic personas of the American historical avant-garde, such as Burroughs and John Cage. Based upon his conference talk, Burroughs' essay, "The Limits of Control," was subsequently published in the "Schizo-Culture" issue.

In just a few years, *Semiotext(e)*, as a publication and producer of events, became more visual and visible, and emphasized its intentions of making connections (Lotringer 2013, 43). Lotringer reflects on the ideas of hybridity, creativity, and connection as symbolic of Downtown: "*Schizo-Culture* was about New York, and trying to connect the most creative minds from France to the most creative minds in the States, that was the idea" (Lotringer 2015). In promotional flyers for the Nova Convention, *Semiotext(e)* advances itself as such a link: "SEMIOTEXT(E), a 'New Wave' magazine, is the French Connection of the New York cultural scene. Bringing together two continents of thought through a revolution of desire, *Semiotext(e)* attempts to define soft strategies to deal with the new algebra of control" (*Semiotext(e)* flyer 1978). Further establishing the magazine as a site of connection, *Semiotext(e)* also appropriates Burroughs' language of control in its marketing materials, while also purposefully aligning itself with Downtown's new wave. In addition, the Nova Convention received considerably more New York press (and photographic) coverage than the prior Schizo-Culture conference, while the journal adopted a strikingly more visual format, resonating with Burroughs' philosophies on the cut-up and control.

Indirectly alluding to multiple characteristics of the cut-up, Lotringer details the journal's new format: "We used pop artifacts not high culture . . . collages and no explanation. The magazine was made of displaced visual cues bouncing against untutored texts. We could treat our readers like adults, and have fun at the same time. It was up to them to get the hints, make their connections, think for themselves" (2006). This collage space, described similar to the cut-up, was adopted to empower the reader. Beginning with "Schizo-Culture," the subversive and playful issues of *Semiotext(e)* combined essays, interviews, poetry, and song lyrics. The overall design was unconventional as varied texts were interspersed with drawing, collage, mock advertisements, and visual cultural appropriations (e.g., comics, graffiti, anthropological photographs, content from S/M magazines), often in the form of détournement. Like the cut-up, visuals were not merely illustrative, but were integral to the text's meaning, and never subordinate to it.

Reflecting the young creative energy of Downtown, the staff of the "Schizo-Culture" issue included CoLab organizer Diego Cortez, and experimental filmmakers Kathryn Bigelow and Michael Oblowitz, who also curated the Nova Convention's "Cine Virus" film series. Lotringer comments on how the staff was assembled through Downtown's social space: "The new art team resulted from a series of encounters and not from a deliberate choice, people I met in clubs, parties or downtown events and found interesting" (2013, xxi). It was during this time that Lotringer had moved from Columbia to share a loft in the Fashion District with Cortez, whom he describes as, "my mentor, and an unlikely mentor [laughing]. But I learned a lot about Downtown from him" (Lotringer 2015). Furthermore, the "Schizo-Culture" issue represents a spectrum of contributors across disciplinary fields, media, and generations, with contributions by Burroughs, the Ramones, Jean François Lyotard, Jack Smith, Kathy Acker, Gilles Deleuze, Michel Foucault, and the Police Band—not to be confused with the Police (Lotringer 2013). *Semiotext(e)*'s pop, amateur, decidedly visual, and alternative response to the business-as-usual academic journal format, significantly debuted within the experimental atmosphere of the Nova Convention and out of the efforts of Downtown's creative community.

On the very meaning of "schizo-culture" Burroughs remarks, "I think 'schizo-culture' here is being used rather in a special sense. Not referring to clinical schizophrenia, but to the fact that the culture is divided up into all sorts of classes and groups, etc., and that some of the old lines are breaking down. And that this is a healthy sign" (Lotringer and Morris 2013, 161). The cross-pollination, mutation, and cut-ups transpiring in the space of Downtown was simultaneously occurring in the pages of *Semiotext(e)* as evidenced by its content, design, and artsy Downtown staff. Breaking artistic boundaries and confines of thought, the Nova Convention and *Semiotext(e)*, both by-products of Lotringer's cultural agenda, further propagated Downtown attitudes and its creative processes. This sentiment was further reinforced by the release of *The Third Mind*, promoting the cut-up technique, which embraced the accident, spontaneity, appropriation, collaboration, amateurism, and a DIY attitude—qualities that were practically criteria for Downtown cultural production. The fearless experimentation of Burroughs and Gysin predates, but also corresponds to, Downtown's fervent cultural production, as indicated by the Nova Convention itself and the release of the "new and improved" "Schizo-Culture" issue.

From live performances to publications, the Nova Convention exemplifies Downtown New York as a multigenerational, countercultural space that was highly generative for different forms of creative and intellectual expression. When considered a sociocultural cut-up, the Nova Convention celebrates Burroughs' career and influence to depict how creative drive can "cut-through" the ins and outs of urban life. The cut-up, as a means for social change or to express possibilities, is apparent in the narrative content of Burroughs' novels. But, it is at the Nova Convention where this call to action manifests Downtown, through a variety of personalities, performance types and social activities, while simultaneously connecting Burroughs to the rhetoric of French theory. Downtown New York in the 1970s through the 1980s is also a story of enduring multiple crises, whether in terms of bankruptcy, drug economies, the AIDS epidemic, racialized police violence, or gentrification. Bolstered by the distinct cultural climate of Downtown, the Nova Convention reintroduced and addressed how one not only survives, but can creatively thrive within Western systems of oppression and its mechanisms of control.

Receiving a second act, the Nova Convention was rebooted in November 1996, where a crowd of 2,000 people gathered at the Lied Center at the University of Kansas for "The Nova Convention Revisited." The one-night-only spectacular was a compressed update of the 1978 version and celebrated the eighty-two-year-old Burroughs while honoring the original event. Many performers from the 1978 roster paid a second homage, including John Giorno, Patti Smith, Lenny Kaye, Deborah Harry, Chris Stein, Philip Glass, Laurie Anderson, and Ed Sanders (of the Fugs). "The Nova Convention Revisited" was a three-and-a-half hour-long mix of music, performance art, and poetry, with mixed media slides and videos projected between acts. It was also a part of the university's larger cultural initiative, "A Festival: William S. Burroughs and the Arts," which included the acquisition of Ports of Entry, a traveling retrospective of Burroughs. The exhibition centered upon twenty-two collages that were collaboratively produced by Burroughs and Gysin for *The Third Mind* in the mid-1960s. Again, *The Third Mind* plays a prominent role in representing and remembering Burroughs, and is once again connected to the Nova Convention. However, superseding the Frank Zappa role (who replaced Keith Richards in 1978), a major 1990s rock star was first rumored to perform, and in fact showed up. Michael Stipe, front man for the band REM, added a 1990s alternative music spin to this Nova event. Like the original Nova Convention, the "Revisited" version was also hyped by rumor, excitement, and surprise, but with much less disappointment, at least for the rock enthusiasts in the crowd.

As precursor, the Nova Convention also predates the events of the Burroughs Century in 2014, which yield the contributions of this anthology. Comparable to the hybridity of the Nova Convention, the Burroughs Century festivities at Indiana University Bloomington included exhibits of Burroughs' paintings and papers, a screening series, various performances, an academic conference, and of course, an after-party. Special guest and no wave doyenne Lydia Lunch not only gave a public lecture but also delivered a second performance at the Bishop Bar with the punk-garage band, the Tsunamis. Reminiscent of the Downtown party antics of Club 57 or the Mudd Club, the conference's costume-themed after-party was held at a local queer nightclub, the Back Door, complete with a séance led by a professional medium who attempted to contact Burroughs or any other apparitional club-goer.

Demonstrating a lasting collective fascination with Burroughs, such Nova Convention–styled celebrations provide a forum for the reactivation of his work, and an opportunity to share new thought and art forms. Moreover, such events provide a criticism of academia itself: when symposia are run along strict disciplinary lines and regimented expectations, which tend to standardize many conferences today, a particular kind of conversation, as well as intellectual and artistic potentiality is lost. Compellingly, it is through Burroughs that this model is repeatedly broken and cut-up into a new genre of symposium, that is as multifaceted as his work, as Burroughs is continuously reevaluated, remembered, and celebrated through time.

Examining post-1960s visual culture in the United States, KRISTEN GALVIN's interdisciplinary research explores the intersections between film and media, contemporary art, popular music, performance, and gender and sexuality studies. She received her PhD in Visual Studies from the University of California, Irvine where she completed her dissertation on Downtown New York cultural scenes in the 1970s–1980s. Her current book project explores media nostalgias and reconfigurations of "old" versus "new" in the twenty-first century.

REFERENCES

Primary

Semiotext(e) flyer. 1978. Lotringer Series IIA, Box 10, Folder 36, The Sylvère Lotringer Papers and *Semiotext(e)* Archive, The Downtown Collection, The Fales Library and Special Collections at New York University.

Secondary

"Avant-Garde Unites over Burroughs." 1978. *New York Times*, December 1, C11.
Bertei, Adele. 1979. "Call Him Burroughs: News from the Nova Convention." *New York Rocker*, no. 17 (February–March): 13–15.
Birmingham, Jed. 2010. "Jan Herman and William S. Burroughs." Reality Studio, April 5. http://realitystudio.org/bibliographic-bunker/jan-herman-and-william-s-burroughs/.

Bockris, Victor. 2010. "Interview with Victor Bockris on William Burroughs." Interview with Dave Teeuwen. Reality Studio, May 27. http://realitystudio.org/interviews/interview-with-victor-bockris-on-william-burroughs/.

Bowler, Anne, and Blaine McBurney. 1991. "Gentrification and the Avant-Garde in New York's East Village: The Good, the Bad and the Ugly." *Theory, Culture & Society* 8 (4): 49–77.

Burroughs, William S., and Victor Bockris. 1981. *With William Burroughs: A Report from the Bunker.* New York: Seaver Books.

Burroughs, William S., and Brion Gysin. 1978. *The Third Mind.* New York: Viking.

Cohn, Melanie Franklin. 2005. "Curator's Statement: CLUB 57 WHERE ARE YOU? Harvey Wang's Photographs of the Legendary East Village Club 1979–1983." Harvey Wang, May 27. http://classic.harveywang.com/club57curator.htm.

Cusset, François. 2008. *French Theory: How Foucault, Derrida, Deleuze, & Co. Transformed the Intellectual Life of the United States.* Minneapolis: University of Minnesota Press.

Gendron, Bernard. 2002. *Between Montmartre and the Mudd Club: Popular Music and the Avant-Garde.* Chicago: University of Chicago Press.

Goldstein, Richard. 1978. "Nietzsche in Alphaville." *Village Voice*, December 11, 1, 32–36.

Haring, Keith. 1996. *Keith Haring Journals.* New York: Viking.

Harris, Oliver. 2003. *William Burroughs and the Secret of Fascination.* Carbondale: Southern Illinois University Press.

———. 2004. "Cutting up Politics." In *Retaking the Universe: William S. Burroughs in the Age of Globalization*, ed. Davis Schneiderman and Philip Walsh, 175–200. London: Pluto.

Lewis, Angelo. 1978. "The William Burroughs Interview." *Rocky Mountain Musical Express*, January, 18–20.

Lotringer, Sylvère. 2006. "A Life in Theory: with Joan Waltemath." Interview with Joan Waltemath, *The Brooklyn Rail*, September 2. http://www.brooklynrail.org/2006/09/art/a-life-in-theory.

———. 2013. *Schizo-Culture: The Book.* Los Angeles: Semiotext(e).

———. 2015. Interview by Kristen Galvin. April. Audio recording. Los Angeles.

Lotringer, Sylvère, and David Morris. 2013. *Schizo-Culture: The Event.* Los Angeles: Semiotext(e).

Marzorati, Gerald. 1978. "Blame It on the Boss o' Nova." *Soho Weekly News*, December 7, 27–28.

Masters, Marc, and Weasel Walter. 2007. *No Wave.* London: Black Dog.

Mele, Christopher. 2000. *Selling the Lower East Side: Culture, Real Estate, and Resistance in New York City.* Minneapolis: University of Minnesota Press.

Miles, Barry. 1992. *William Burroughs: El Hombre Invisible.* London: Virgin.

Moore, Thurston. 2014. Excerpt from "Nova Reflections." William Burroughs. Nova Convention. The Espai d'Art Contemporani de Castelló. http://www.eacc.es/en/william-burroughs-nova-convention/.

Muñoz, José Esteban. 2009. *Cruising Utopia: The Then and There of Queer Futurity.* New York: New York University Press.

O'Brien, Glenn. 2014. "The Light Side of the Dark Side." In *Chris Stein/Negative: Me, Blondie, and the Advent of Punk*, edited by Chris Stein, 17–20. New York: Rizzoli.

Palmer, Robert. 1978. "3-Day Nova Convention Ends at the Entermedia." *New York Times*, December 4. http://www.nytimes.com/books/00/02/13/specials/burroughs-convention.html.

Shore, Michael. 1978. "Music Picks." *Soho Weekly News*, November 30, 39.

Taylor, Marvin J. 2006. *The Downtown Book: The New York Art Scene, 1974–1984.* Princeton, NJ: Princeton University Press.

Tonkiss, Fran. 2005. *Space, the City and Social Theory: Social Relations and Urban Forms.* Cambridge: Polity.

Audio Recordings

Brookner, Howard. 1978. "Brookner Sound Rolls," The William S. Burroughs Papers, Box 57, Audio cassette N9-N10-N11, Rare Books and Manuscripts Library, Ohio State University Library.

Burroughs, William S., John Giorno, Brion Gysin, Philip Glass, Patti Smith, Frank Zappa, et al. 1979. *The Nova Convention.* New York: Giorno Poetry Systems. Music LP.

Nova Convention Poster, Sylvère Lotringer, facsimile, 1978. Sylvère Lotringer Papers and *Semiotext(e)* Archive, MSS 221, the Fales Library and Special Collections, New York University Libraries. Courtesy of the Fales Library and Special Collections, New York University.

4

The Disembodied Fry:
William S. Burroughs and Vocal Performance

LANDON PALMER

Mid-century Beat writers were significantly invested in the aesthetic possibilities of applying the speaking and singing voice to recorded sound. Such efforts sought to transform the recorded object into an event or happening, from Allen Ginsberg's mantra-like reading of *Howl* (1959) to Jack Kerouac's participation in John Clellon Holmes's acetate improvisations to the bebop-accompanied recordings of Lawrence Ferlinghetti's live poetry readings (see Ford 2013). But with a few exceptions, William S. Burroughs' voice was largely absent from such practices.[1] How, then, did Burroughs' voice come to be so distinct, so recognizable, and so imitable as to develop into a reference not only to the author's life and work but also as an object all its own, a circulating container of his myth?

There are certainly several notable visual elements of Burroughs' star image—his iconic fedora, his rigid facial features, his emaciated frame, his ongoing sartorial preference for early to mid-twentieth-century styles. But his unique subcultural celebrity, especially during the latter portion of his career, foregrounded his voice as a prominent signature that traverses across media forms, collaborative projects, and imitations. Jennie Skerl's claim that Burroughs' "most important 'work' may be his legend" (1986, 2) has proven productive for assessing the author's unique celebrity, as evidenced by Oliver Harris's volume on the subject. Harris argues that Burroughs' public myth was always already mediated through a "double displacement" as articulated through the intents, collaborations, and uses of others. To illustrate this, Harris cites the "malicious-looking smile" of the Burroughsian figure in Kerouac's 1950 debut novel *The Town and the City* as a means of introducing the paradoxical fascination of Burroughs, "which somehow precedes the writing that yet produces it": "From the very beginning, the appearance of [Burroughs'] identity had the quality of a fiction, a fantasy projected by others, or a simulation, a copy behind which there was no original . . . it becomes ever harder to separate Burroughs' oeuvre from a generalized production of his image" (Harris 2006, 2). The noises produced behind the lips of that "malicious-looking smile" eventually took a formative and consequential role in writing this multiauthored Burroughs. With a prolific body of work realized decades after the audio productions of his literary contemporaries, Burroughs' aural presence throughout an array of media forms during his late career helped cement his distinct timbre and unique cadences as a familiar shorthand that helped frame "a generalized production of his image," imprinting an aural signature onto Burroughs' history and myth. Not only does Burroughs' celebrity represent a "personification of aesthetic style come to life," as Jonathan Goldman (2011, 23) contends of the modernist author-celebrities who preceded him, but the aesthetic style of Burroughs' late-career literary celebrity emerged prominently through its aural components. As I will demonstrate, these aural components worked conversantly with Burroughs' writing, for Burroughs' late-career vocal appearances performed his voice's ambivalent relationship to embodiment in a fashion reflective of the content of his literary work.

Film scholar Pamela Robertson Wojcik (2006, 71) argues that the human voice and its relation to recording technologies is an essential but overlooked component of cinematic performance and urges against the "privileging of the actor's body" in discursive, institutional, and critical conceptualizations of on-screen performances. By analyzing vocal performances of Burroughs, I seek to extend this work toward illustrating how a voice performed across multiple media forms (including film, television, and sound recording) can collectively constitute a public figure's persona and serve as an index of identity that outlives the body of the orator. Burroughs manifested his aural presence throughout diverse forms of mass-disseminated media during the 1980s and 1990s, including television and music video appearances, film cameos, and numerous spoken-word albums, thereby rendering his voice into a device that reified his celebrity. Such representations cemented the particular cadences of Burroughs' voice into a familiar shorthand that framed his public image as well as diachronic readings of his earlier work. Burroughs offers a unique case for understanding the phenomenon of cult celebrity as manifested through a complex intersection of media forms, a case that illustrates the process by which an author's media voice is mapped onto their literary voice and persona. The extensive mediations of this literary figure's voice—that is, Burroughs' vocal performances of self—constitute performances that identify his presence and signify his sensibility, determining the sound of his authorship and the shape of his myth. Although the following hardly represents a comprehensive examination of the work of Burroughs' voice across literary production, media fame, or posthumous tributes, I intend to illustrate an overall sense of the operations of Burroughs' voice as it has come to be mapped onto his media celebrity, literary persona, and biography.

THE BURROUGHSIAN TIMBRE

Jacob Smith locates the voice as an "instrument of timbre par excellence," capable of realizing timbre's "complex perceptual amalgam of sonic information, one that calibrates sound and space and, in so doing, inherently indicates the subjective nature of all perception" (2008, 119–120). The particular resonance of the timbre produced by Burroughs' voice can be evinced by the numerous attempts to describe, encapsulate, and wrestle with its evocations by imitators, interpreters, and collaborators. Filmmaker David Cronenberg described Burroughs' voice as a "metallic, nasal Midwestern twang" (see Rodley 1992). Burroughs enthusiast Charlie Fox (2012) summarized the affective register of Burroughs' voice by characterizing it as "shaken by feelings of otherness and isolation and often bored into a kind of catatonia" and possessing "icicles in its veins." Actor Ben Foster, in preparation for playing Burroughs in the film *Kill Your Darlings* (directed by John Krokidas, 2013), likened Burroughs' voice to listening to a record spin while somebody puts their finger on it, thereby slowing it down (We Got This Covered 2013). Foster's use of a reproduced sound's source to color his description speaks to the performative aspects of Burroughs' peculiar vocal register. His voice imitates the alienating procedures of automatized production, thereby displaying the human subject as an entity reducible to an assembly of functional tasks—in other words, an agent. Yet this same voice also exhibits a distinctive, singular quality of unmediated embodiment that powerfully suggests a direct indexical relationship, if not always to Burroughs himself, then at least to that which is Burroughsian.

A defining feature of the Burroughs vocal signature is the aspect that disrupts the practiced monotony of an otherwise robotic delivery: the undertone of vocal fry that punctuates his sentences (which he tended to display in recorded media with notable frequency in his later years). Vocal fry allowed Burroughs to extend vowels, make strangeness of the English language, and fashion aural icons of the lower register like "Dr. Benwaaay." As a speech phenomenon, vocal fry has been historically "classified as part of a clinical voice disorder" and associated with "creaky, harsh, and rough voice qualities" (Wolk, Abdelli-Beruh, and Slavin 2012, e111), with examples available across a variety of sources including Mae West's onscreen star turns (see Greenwood 2011), a much-publicized "trend" amongst young American women (see Steinmetz 2011), and traditions of Mongolian throat singing typified by performer Tanya Tagaq. Burroughs' particular implementation of vocal fry produces a sense of bodily presence through an occasional breaking of the voice and corresponding strain of the vocal cords, manifesting a distinct contrast from and stark interruption of his otherwise dry, monotonous mode of delivery.

Smith argues that the raspy timbre of famous phonograph performers like Louis Armstrong communicated a sense of immediacy and intimacy distinct from recordings of more conventionally celebrated vocal affectations like the bel canto. In this context, the rasp proved capable of suggesting an orator's transcendence of the media apparatus through which their voice travels, thus creating an impression of that strange, slippery thing we call "authenticity." According to Smith, the rasp in certain contexts could "represent a self-assertive performance of embodiment" (2008, 150), offering a direct impression of the voice's physiological labor. Burroughs' vocal fry works similarly to the rasp by exhibiting an audible break from tutored conventions of speaking. It is this dual aspect of Burroughs' voice—its ability to perform both the alien (his robotic monotony) and the approximate (his throaty interruptions)—that is frequently on display in its use, ultimately structuring its iconicity and functioning as a major determinant of its travel. In order to unpack the operations of Burroughs' voice in application to both his work and his public persona, I explore its functions and evocations in three respects: (1) descriptions of characters' voices in his 1959 novel *Naked Lunch*; (2) his vocal performances of self throughout his later career (particularly in moving image media, where his voice has often been utilized in revealing correspondence to his visible body); and (3) actors' invocations of the "Burroughsian timbre."

SOUNDING OUT THE TALKING ASSHOLE AND DR. BENWAY

In perhaps the most famous sequence of Burroughs' 1959 novel *Naked Lunch*, Dr. Benway unspools the tale of the "man who taught his asshole to talk," which the man turns into a novelty act until the Talking Asshole eventually becomes sentient, dominating the body it occupies as its primary orator (Burroughs 2009, 110). Eventually, the Talking Asshole declares the body's mouth to be useless and obsolescent: "We don't need you around here anymore. I can talk and eat *and* shit" (110–11). The Talking Asshole routine has been widely cited and analyzed by readers, literary scholars, and censors, proving to be one of the more exportable and circulated sequences of *Naked Lunch* within American culture (see Murphy 2000) and even played an important part of the prosecution's case during the novel's 1965 Boston obscenity trial (Lydenberg 1987, 23). Several scholars argue that the sequence exercises themes and concerns central to Burroughs' writing. As summarized by Arnold Weinstein, the sequence "focuses on where the action is, on orifices and genitals, our avenues of appetite" (1982, 35). Robin Lydenberg observes that the sequence troubles the broader question of "who is in control of the linguistic arsenal" (1987, 26), an inquiry into the relationship between language and power that Burroughs explored via various techniques, including the cut-up method. In its popular reception, the Talking Asshole sequence has come to carry a metonymic quality by representing the novel's content, emerging into a readily transportable icon of its cultural influence alongside that of its author. A popular reading of this sequence interprets Burroughs' authorial voice as equivalent to the Talking Asshole, the voice of a grotesque id "farting out the words" hidden underneath systematized control (Burroughs 2009, 110). For example, while adapting *Naked Lunch* to screen (1991), Cronenberg and actor Peter Weller (who plays Burroughs stand-in Bill Lee) described Burroughs himself as the Talking Asshole (Rodley 1992). This interpretation is transposed directly onto Burroughs' persona in the film, as Weller's Bill Lee recites the sequence almost exactly as it appears in the novel despite the fact that the story originates from Benway in the source material.

Like Burroughs' vocal fry, The Talking Asshole's utterances reside outside of habituated conventions of speaking. Yet by virtue of its source and corresponding manner of delivery, the Talking Asshole performs the voice's direct connection to its somatic locus. It both demonstrates and collapses several sensory capacities, "a sound you could *smell*" (Burroughs 2009, 111). Benway first describes the Talking Asshole as possessing a "gut frequency. It hit you right down there like you gotta go" (110), emphasizing both the direct, embodied quality of the voice as well as the corporeal effect of hearing it. The doctor continues, describing the Talking Asshole's development of teeth as "raspy incurving hooks," once again connecting the timbre of the voice with its physiological index, its teeth manifesting the shape of a rasp—that powerful signifier of embodied vocal performance. The Asshole that "talked all the time, day and night" (111) is thus the unencumbered voice of the body that produces it. This embodied voice, according to Burroughs, demands an audience as a result of its vulgar, grotesque, unpolished, and direct qualities.

In contrast to the Talking Asshole, Burroughs describes the voices of other characters in *Naked Lunch* by the degree to which they are disembodied, obscuring their supposed source of emanation. An "old junky" "whispers in his disembodied, junky voice" (Burroughs 2009, 42). Nick's voice "drifts" into the "consciousness" of Bill Lee "from no particular place. An eerie, disembodied voice" (178). The voice of Carl's doctor "receded. He seemed actually to have gone away through an invisible door, leaving his empty body sitting there at the desk" (158). Elsewhere in the novel, Burroughs describes the same doctor's voice as "drifting away" and reaching Carl "from a great distance" (164–65). Bridging the variously embodied and disembodied voices throughout *Naked Lunch* is the omnipresent Benway, a force interchangeably present and absent throughout the novel. Benway is a figure who regulates bodies but also, in his capacity as a physician and a person of ambiguous yet insidious authority, exercises an intellectual distance from them. Burroughs describes Bill Lee as receiving Benway's voice similarly to the disembodied voices available elsewhere in the text, as if the defining elusiveness of Benway's voice is mediated through Burroughs' ever-shifting cast of characters: "Benway's voice drifts into my consciousness from no particular place . . . a disembodied voice that is sometimes loud and clear, sometimes barely audible, like music down a windy street" (25). Benway's voice possesses the shared capacity for distance and proximity, its presence variously obscured and immediate. He is the narrator of the Talking Asshole tale, but far from the Talking Asshole itself, his voice is both affective and remote, and always calculated.

In Cronenberg's adaptation, Benway's presence is mapped onto Bill Lee's voice in his recitation of the Talking Asshole tale. Bill Lee tells the story while high on the bug powder provided by Benway (Roy Scheider) and his voice is distant and monotone, echoing the tired disembodiment characteristic of Burroughs' disaffected junkies. Weller's dry recitation stands in sharp contrast to his description of the Talking Asshole's invasive presence. With the distribution of junk (bug powder in the film) as one of Benway's methods of control, the doctor's motivating role is implicit in Bill's recitation despite Cronenberg's severing of the Talking Asshole routine from the novel's original arbiter. This sequence demonstrates how voices in Burroughs' writing are rarely isolated to their supposed source, exclusive to the figure speaking, or singular in their capacities, but often drift as forces and subjects all their own. The vocal utterances of Burroughs' characters vary between immediate, embodied voices and mediated, disembodied voices. As both Benway and the Talking Asshole illustrate, rarely is one quality of voice exclusive to a singular vocalizing body: Benway's voice exhibits a range of distance and absence, while the Talking Asshole combats for vocal authority against the mouth that occupies a shared corpus.

The heterogeneous capacities Burroughs ascribes to the written voices of his characters extends to the affective range of his vocal performances of self. Burroughs' subtle alterations in his style of vocal delivery exhibit a pendulum of distance and immediacy, from its tinny, metallic, functionary timbre to the strained breaks that interrupt its monotony. Burroughs' delivery is simultaneously disembodied and embodied, sounding out the voice's mediating capacities—its operations as a technological tool of body and mind—while also combating them by articulating noises that alternately suggest corporeal proximity. In this respect, as Burroughs' voice became more prominently available as a sonic object for public spectacle and exhibition during his later career, his voice grew performative of the concerns repeated across his written work. It is this integrated capacity of performance that connects Burroughs' many vocal presentations of self.

PERFORMING BURROUGHS

As Burroughs began to regularly tour spoken-word performances of new and established work in the late 1970s, his celebrity took on a revived currency, introducing him to new audiences and reestablishing his authorial presence to those previously familiar with him. This development arguably hit a crescendo with his first-ever reading on American network television: his appearance on *Saturday Night Live* on November 7, 1981, in which he was ceremoniously introduced by host Laura Hutton as the "greatest living writer in America" before reading a selection of broadcast-friendly excerpts of *Naked Lunch* and *Nova Express* (1964). Burroughs' delivery exhibited slight vocal intimations of his characters and deliberate pauses for comic timing. The performance was accompanied by other sonic phenomena—a canned explosion follows the author's description of "sound effects from a nuclear plant" and "The Star-Spangled Banner" plays behind Benway's completion of a haphazard appendectomy. This was not merely a reading of his work, but a performance calculated for its medium of delivery. This appearance was a watershed moment in Burroughs' gradually elevating late-career profile and, moreover, foregrounded the operations of his voice, rather than the words from his existing novels alone, as a carrier and a device intrinsic to that profile. Several documentaries from this period, including *Burroughs: The Movie* (directed by Howard Brookner, 1983) and *William S. Burroughs: Commissioner of Sewers* (directed by Klaus Maeck, 1991), exhibit Burroughs' varied implementations of his voice, specifically in the contrast between live performances (in which his voice is projected and regularly elongates his pronunciation of vowels) and more quotidian interactions (in which he is more reserved, his vocal fry present but less forceful).

From 1975 to well over a decade after his death in 1997, Burroughs' name and voice were tied to over twenty spoken-word albums, including studio readings, live performances, collaborations with musicians, and audiobooks. His spoken-word collaborations with Laurie Anderson, Tom Waits, and Kurt Cobain archived the author's public image as a fetishized object of recorded sound media rather than the written word, a signifier of authenticity tied to the shared aesthetic efforts of self-styled outcasts who saw their work as deeply indebted to his writing. This proliferation did not mean that the recorded sound of Burroughs' voice was in competition with his published words or risked obscuring them. Rather, these recordings, appearances, and performances marked an extended realization of Burroughs' prior multimedia practices: just as Burroughs performed in avant-garde cinema during the 1960s and cut up mixed media from magazine articles to lyrics from commercial jingles into his books, he would later merge aspects of his literary style—specifically, his abstractions of the voice's relationship to the body—with sound and moving image media. Burroughs had previously used his voice as a device for expressive experimentation. For example, his mid-1960s "Throat Microphone Experiment" exercised an attempt to "record subvocal speech" and express meaning on a "subverbal level" (see Kahn 2013, 250). Now made available across an array of media platforms, Burroughs' late-career vocal performances of self further engaged with the underexplored possibilities of the voice as a technology bearing a unique arsenal of sensory machinery. But at the same time, its expressive possibilities often became relegated to a set of functions that circulated Burroughs' voice as a legible signifier replete with references to his literary reputation, idiosyncratic public persona, and relationship to cultural history.

As with the varied vocal presence of his written characters, Burroughs' voice was often portrayed as disembodied in his moving image performances, attended occasionally with the visual signs of his person but sometimes presented without any physical evidence of him. In the West German avant-garde film *Decoder* (directed by Muscha, 1984), Burroughs' body appears as a shadowed silhouette (his iconic fedora emphasized) while his voice, manifesting separately from his silhouette, expresses a patterned motif from *Nova Express*: "Word. Falling. Photo. Falling." Burroughs' figure traverses the skyline of a hill behind a marsh after a narrator (Christiane Felscherinow) has recited a poem over footage of frogs jumping. The contrast is stark, with Burroughs' cold, mechanistic content and signature monotone juxtaposed against the heightened naturalism of the setting, contributing to an ambivalent sensory landscape.

In his role as Tom the Priest in the landmark American independent film *Drugstore Cowboy* (directed by Gus van Sant, 1989), Burroughs' silhouette and voice both play corresponding roles in his introduction. As Bob Hughes (Matt Dillon) reads a newspaper while in the waiting room of a pharmacy, Tom is introduced via

an elevator, his silhouette (complete with the requisite fedora) evident behind the elevator door before his face is made visible as he walks through it. Tom journeys to the desk and engages in an innocuous and barely audible conversation with the pharmacist, his back to the camera. It is at this moment that Bob recognizes Tom upon hearing his unmistakable voice—not what the voice is saying, but the voice itself. When Tom sits close to Bob in the waiting room, Tom's voice and physical presence unite as one as he delivers an elongated, rhythmically frayed "Welllllll, welll" upon recognizing Bob. This scene stands to function also as a moment of recognition for audiences, an opportunity to gradually react in identifying Burroughs by the union of his voice and silhouette. It is a doubled display of cultural capital: for the film, this appearance connects a narrative of drug addiction with one of twentieth-century American literature's best-known addicts; and for the audience, this constructed moment of recognition via Bob's eyes and ears produces an opportunity for extratextual appreciation. In *Drugstore Cowboy*, Burroughs is utilized as a powerful reserve of cultural meanings, a figure already imbued with significance available via the combined capacities of his silhouette and his voice.

Often presented against his silhouette, Burroughs' voice repeatedly precedes synchronous evidence of his person throughout his appearances in moving image media. This practice extends to performances of Burroughs by other actors, as in Cronenberg's *Naked Lunch* where Weller's Bill Lee is introduced via a shadow of his fedora'd silhouette against a door as his offscreen mouth announces, "Exterminator." Similarly, Viggo Mortensen's Old Bull Lee in *On the Road* is introduced via his voice (as mediated through a phone call) followed by a visible introduction via a silhouette of his fedora, shot from behind in a medium-close up. However, disembodying Burroughs' voice was not an altogether new cinematic practice by the

Burroughs' voice precedes his face in *Naked Lunch* (FACING) and *On the Road* (ABOVE).

1980s. In his role as the malevolent, Benway-esque figure Opium Jones in the Beat-associated cult film *Chappaqua* (directed by Conrad Rooks, 1966), Burroughs' character is introduced via his voice several moments before he enters screen-right, and his later dialogue contributes narration over images of his person facing the camera without speaking. In his 1968 narration for Benjamin Christensen's 1922 silent cult film *Haxan: Witchcraft through the Ages*, Burroughs' opening dialogue is presented over approximately two minutes of black screen before the film proper proceeds, which suggests that Burroughs' unique voice could accomplish more than simply accompanying visuals by functioning in the capacity of an object juxtaposed in dialectical relation to the images onscreen.

VOICING THE IMAGE OF BURROUGHS

In the 1991 advertising and promotional campaign for Cronenberg's *Naked Lunch*, the "voice" of Burroughs is deployed as the primary legitimating agent justifying the film's existence, and it enforces a historical distance between Burroughs the public figure and the literature he produced—or rather, the notorious history of moral panic that his literature produced. The film's theatrical trailer opens with the title card, "William Burroughs—Author" before a narrator speaks in a Burroughsian timbre. The first part of the trailer combines images of Burroughs from Antony Balch's short silent films (mostly from *The Cut Ups* [1966], presented here as archival stock footage) juxtaposed with Laurie Anderson's 1984 song "Gravity's

Angel" while "Burroughs" dryly narrates: "When I started writing *Naked Lunch*, people offered their opinions. 'Disgusting,' they said. 'Pornographic, un-American trash.' 'Unpublishable.' Well, it came out in 1959 and it found an audience. Town meetings, book burnings, and an inquiry by the State Supreme Court. That book made quite a little impression. Now, thirty years later, Hollywood, in its infinite wisdom, has turned it into a movie."[2] A gunshot sound effect cuts the footage away from the Balch montage, replaced by images from Cronenberg's adaptation. The narrator continues, "Thirty feet tall. In living color. Cover your eyes, America. Run for your lives!" Voices of various characters are available over the montage, but Weller's Bill Lee is not audible until the trailer's end, when he delivers with subtle gravel, "I thought you were finished with doing weird stuff."

The voice-over narrator featured so prominently in this trailer is not Burroughs himself, but an unidentified voice actor hired for 20th Century Fox's promotional campaign. That Weller's characterization of Bill Lee does not show up until the trailer's final seconds emphasizes a distance between the "authentic" voicing by the narrator and the imagined or channeled Burroughs embodied by Weller, thereby distinguishing "Burroughs' voice" from "Bill Lee's voice." Moreover, separating the aural "Burroughs" from the actor playing him also points to a distinction between the "novel itself" and the Cronenberg/Burroughs dialectic that Cronenberg envisioned the film to be in his attempt to bring to screen an "unadaptable" novel via the meeting of two creative minds "inviting you to lunch," as communicated in the trailer's onscreen text.[3] Weller's Bill Lee is thus as much Cronenberg's as he is Burroughs', and the trailer foregrounds this displacement by reserving the "real Burroughs" for the footage of Balch's films, yet also subtly complicates and reinforces it via a convincing vocal imposter who dryly mocks Hollywood.

The *Naked Lunch* trailer presents the strained intonations of Burroughs' voice as present, authoritative, and immediate in contrast to Balch's black-and-white, aged images purported to represent the period in which *Naked Lunch* was published and garnered controversy. The actor's vocal imitation is, technically, disembodied (a "present tense" narration aurally separate from past images of Burroughs, all emanating from an impersonator) yet affectively embodied in its suggestion of an authentic connection to the author. This performance of the Burroughsian timbre is mapped onto Burroughs' history, intonating his myth and manifesting an authoritative reading of his biography. During a culmination of renewed interest in his work leading up to the production of Cronenberg's *Naked Lunch*, Burroughs' voice took on a life of its own as a traveling index and circulating object performing his identity and presence so powerfully that it could represent the person even when that voice did not emanate from Burroughs himself. By the arrival of this trailer, Burroughs' voice had truly become both disembodied and immediate. The Burroughsian timbre, a circulating emblem of his presence, constructs an authority that renders the question of whose body from which the voice emerges irrelevant. Invoking this timbre has since proven essential to posthumous performances of Burroughs.

Narrative films that portray Burroughs and his contemporaries often take place in the mid-century, the canonized years of the Beat era (to which Burroughs' expansive oeuvre can never fully be distilled). Yet it is striking how regularly such performances invoke the particular sound of Burroughs' voice that characterized his late career, when his vocal fry circulated more prominently in association with his live and recorded performances. Since Cronenberg's *Naked Lunch*, numerous actors have attempted to channel Burroughs' persona through this instrumentation of his voice, and have attested that approximating Burroughs' voice formed an essential, guiding tool of their performances.

In *Beat* (directed by Gary Walkow, 2000), a dramatization of Burroughs' killing of his wife Joan Vollmer, actor Kiefer Sutherland rhythmically articulates his performance of Burroughs via a monotonous delivery that concludes nearly every sentence with an elongated strain on the last word. *Beat*'s trailer opens with such an instance, featuring Sutherland as Burroughs reading aloud a newspaper to Vollmer (Courtney Love), "The firefighters managed to save the lion but the hippos were boiled in their taaaanks."[4] This moment serves as an intertextual reference to *And the Hippos Were Boiled in Their Tanks*, the title of a 1945 manuscript co-authored between Kerouac and Burroughs, and thus connects directly Burroughs' signature vocal style to his literary production. According to Walkow, Sutherland asked the director to shoot his first filmed scene in several takes as the actor knew that whatever intonation of Burroughs' voice he used at that moment would determine his vocal and thereby physical performance for the rest of the shoot (see Walkow 2002).

Toward realizing his role as Old Bull Lee (Kerouac's pseudonym for Burroughs) for Walter Salles's adaptation of *On the Road* (2012), Viggo Mortensen credits the creative and rhythmic qualities of Burroughs' literary voice as a source of inspiration, specifically Burroughs' ability to produce "new syntax and grammar and even inventing words, words that weren't real words but they sounded like they could be and had a nice sound, a musicality." Mortensen was further motivated by the challenge of finding the character of Burroughs beyond the myth that his late career's output perpetuated: "While the adulation of Burroughs towards the end of his life became kind of cliché, he never became cliché." Rather, the actor saw Burroughs as calculating in his performance of self, especially in his use of language; likening the author to a musician, Mortensen admiringly asserts that Burroughs was "very conscious . . . of the sound of language" (Telerama Officiel 2012). Thus, Mortensen's characterization manifests a rather varied intonation of the Burroughsian timbre. For instance, when Old Bull Lee describes Dean Moriarty (Garrett Hedlund) as burdened by "psychopathic irresponsibility and violence," Mortensen's voice dances across the stressed syllables, maintaining a monotonous core imbued with a varied and subtle vocal fry. Later in the film, when Old Bull Lee introduces his "orgone accumulator," the pseudo-scientific device Burroughs used as a sensory meditation mechanism, the film's orgone accumulator features a funnel that Mortensen's Old Bull Lee breathes through as he blurts, in a high-register exclamation that transforms Burroughs' Midwestern accent to an almost southern twang, "Can't let the cocksuckers get you down!" A moment reminiscent of Burroughs' later career performances, the orgone accumulator here mediates Burroughs' voice—with the funnel functioning as a crude microphone—but also highlights its performative aspects: namely, Burroughs' often comic ability to manipulate his voice with applied devices or calculated intonations in order to convey exaggerated expressions of his persona or the varied affectations of his characters.

In Ben Foster's interpretation of a 29-year-old Burroughs in *Kill Your Darlings*, a biographical portrait of Allen Ginsberg (Daniel Radcliffe) and Lucien Carr's (Dane DeHaan) complex relationship, Foster realizes the younger Burroughs with a characterization that distinctly evokes, even amplifies, Burroughs' late career vocal performances of self. When Foster's Burroughs instructs Ginsberg and Carr on the cut-up method by gifting them books to manipulate and announces, "Tear them up, boys! Destrooooooy the old and buiiiiild the new," he manifests a much more pronounced and elongated strain to the voice than the aforementioned actors. Foster's performance portrays the historical Burroughs and his myth as ultimately one in the same, mapping the signature late-career timbre of Burroughs' distinctively worn cadences onto the early, pre-fame biography of his person. Foster said of his performance as a young Burroughs, "The man William Burroughs as I knew him culturally was a frozen old man. . . . We had to go backwards and say before he had the courage to create the character of Burroughs as this literary figure, we had to ask, 'Who was this young man?' I had to find a youthful quality to that rather than find a hard impersonation of the gravel and time" (We Got This Covered 2013). Foster's dilemma as a performer speaks to the shared enigma and the appeal of Burroughs' well-traveled voice: its permanent agedness, the deeply worn resonance emanating from within its mechanics, its ability to evince both a constructed character and the direct presence of an iconic cultural figure. The thirty-one-year-old Foster interprets the young Burroughs as a figure whose vocal signature has already been inscribed retroactively onto the history of the man. In likening Burroughs' voice to a record, Foster works backward across its many mediations and fetishizations in an attempt to find not just the authorial voice, but the human being behind it. Yet Foster's performance produces less of a deconstruction of Burroughs' public persona and myth made manifest through performative aural signatures, and instead reveals that, in order to contend with any aspect of an aurally present Burroughs, one must invoke the readily transportable phantom force of that singular voice—that uncanny late-career instrument now mapped fully onto his biographical myth.

CONCLUSION

By examining how Burroughs' work and persona came to be known and understood through the multifaceted circulation of his voice, this chapter demonstrates a means for investigating how media representations of a literary figure's vocal performances of self contribute to constructions of authorship, biographical history, and the overall development of a public image. As I have argued elsewhere (see Palmer 2013), late-career star images carry a unique, authoritative power in the writing of star histories, organizing and interpreting the total output of a cultural figure through the parameters of a distinct narrative lens—in this case, the production of a signature vocal style. Explaining how and why such narratives become constructed over time can illuminate the ways in which a renowned figure's voluminous body of work is rendered legible to a larger audience by the foregrounding of certain elements of the figure's output or biography. But perhaps the price of this legibility is that of a greater notion of the figure to which it refers—a Burroughs more heterogeneous, multifaceted, and contradictory than is convenient for such iconography.

Yet, while the circulation of Burroughs' voice throughout his late career and posthumous fame has arguably fetishized, caricatured, and even romanticized his persona—the "cliché" that Mortensen refers to and the "frozen old man" Foster mentions—it also performs Burroughs' revisited thematic concerns in several important respects, demonstrating the voice's shared capacity for embodied presence and disembodied absence. Disrupting a polished manner of speaking, the affective qualities of this voice are integral to its meaning. More than simply an "unconventional" voice, Burroughs' vocal performances of self trouble the presumed stable relationship between the voice and the body, exhibiting instead the voice's extensive functions as a device that mediates the body. By interchangeably performing embodiment and disembodiment, the Burroughsian timbre travels as both a signature that is readily transportable across a variety of other representational contexts as well as a referent that contains a reserve of meaning about the cultural figure it signifies. The media travel of Burroughs' aural signature demonstrates the "displacement" that Harris argues has shaped his image. But because of its ambivalent relationship to embodiment, this aural signature often circulates as a displacement that does not always announce itself as such, performing the unique capacities of a public image made prominently available through sound.

LANDON PALMER is a film, media, and popular music historian who teaches in the Department of Communication at the University of Tampa. His research centers on the relationships between stardom, music and sound performance, and moving image media industries, a topic on which he has published for *Music, Sound, and the Moving Image, Celebrity Studies,* and *Journal of the International Association for the Study of Popular Music.*

NOTES

1. By 1975, Burroughs had appeared in one LP, the 1965 release *Call Me Burroughs*. As a point of contrast, by 1975, Ginsberg had appeared in at least five LPs and one single, Ferlinghetti in at least three LPs, and Kerouac in at least three LPs. In new recordings released after 1975, Ginsberg's voice appeared in sixteen LPs and seven EPs or singles, Ferlinghetti's voice in three LPs and one EP, Kerouac's voice in seven LPs and one EP, while Burroughs' voice drastically escalated in its availability, appearing in twenty LPs and six EPs.

2. HD Retro Trailers, "Naked Lunch (1991) ORIGINAL TRAILER [HD]," YouTube. January 19, 2018. https://www.youtube.com/watch?v=koCZ-050EHY. Accessed September 3, 2018.

3. Cronenberg discusses his approach to adapting the film along these terms in *Naked Making Lunch* (Rodley 1992).

4. Movieclips Classic Trailers, "Beat (2000) Official Trailer #1," YouTube. November 30, 2012. https://www.youtube.com/watch?v=YkX_CTIY2jw. Accessed September 3, 2018.

REFERENCES

Burroughs, William S. 2009. *Naked Lunch: The Restored Text 50th Anniversary Edition*. New York: Grove.

Ford, Phil. 2013. *Dig: Sound and Music in Hip Culture*. New York: Oxford University Press.

Fox, Charlie. 2012. "Nothing Here Now But the Recordings: Listening to William Burroughs." *The White Review*, June. http://www.thewhitereview.org/features/nothing-here-now-but-the-recordings-listening-to-william-burroughs/.

Goldman, Jonathan. 2011. *Modernism Is the Literature of Celebrity*. Austin: University of Texas Press.

Greenwood, Veronique. 2011. "The Linguistic Phenomenon du Jour: Vocal Fry." *Discover Magazine*, December 13. http://blogs.discovermagazine.com/80beats/2011/12/13/the-linguistic-phenomenon-du-jour-vocal-fry/#.VCt80StdX2B.

Harris, Oliver. 2006. *William S. Burroughs and the Secret of Fascination*. Carbondale: Southern Illinois University Press.

Kahn, Douglas. 2013. "Let Me Hear My Body Talk, My Body Talk." In *Relive: Media Art Histories*, edited by Sean Cubit and Paul Thomas, 236–56. Cambridge, MA: Massachusetts Institute of Technology Press.

Lydenberg, Robin. 1987. *Word Cultures: Radical Theory and Practice in William S. Burroughs' Fiction*. Champaign: University of Illinois Press.

Murphy, Timothy S. 2000. "Intersection Points: Teaching William S. Burroughs's *Naked Lunch*." *College Literature* 27 (1): 84–102.

Palmer, Landon. 2013. "Re-collecting David Bowie: The Next Day and Late-Career Stardom." *Celebrity Studies* 4 (3): 384–86.

Rodley, Chris, director. 1992. *Naked Making Lunch* (BBC), via *Naked Lunch*, DVD, directed by David Cronenberg, 1991. New York: The Criterion Collection, 2004.

Skerl, Jennie. 1986. *William S. Burroughs*. Farmington Hills, MI: Twayne.

Smith, Jacob. 2008. *Vocal Tracks: Performance and Sound Media*. Berkeley: University of California Press.

Steinmetz, Katy. 2011. "Get Your Creak On: Is 'Vocal Fry' a Female Fad?" *Time*, December 15. http://healthland.time.com/2011/12/15/get-your-creak-on-is-vocal-fry-a-female-fad/.

Telerama Officiel. 2012. "Viggo Mortensen, Video Interview (Cannes 2012)." YouTube video, 5:45, June 14. https://www.youtube.com/watch?v=mGnlGOr-d4c.

Walkow, Gary. 2002. DVD Commentary, via *Beat*. DVD directed by Gary Walkow, 2000. Los Angeles: Lions Gate.

We Got This Covered. 2013. "Kill Your Darlings Interview with Michael C. Hall, Ben Foster, and John Krokidas." YouTube video, 1:46, October 2. https://www.youtube.com/watch?v=Z7LqJhs3hCU.

Weinstein, Arnold. 1982. "Freedom and Control in the Erotic Novel: The Classical and the Surrealist Model: *Les Liaison dangereuses* and *Naked Lunch*." *Dada/Surrealism*, October/November, 29–38.

Wojcik, Pamela Robertson. 2006. "The Sound of Film Acting." *Journal of Film and Video* 58 (1/2) (Spring/Summer): 71–83.

Wolk, Lesley, Nassima B. Abdelli-Beruh, and Dianne Slavin. 2012. "Habitual Use of Vocal Fry in Young Adult Female Speakers." *Journal of Voice* 26 (3): 1–6.

Cut-Up with Limericks

In this playful example of Burroughs' cut-up experiments, composed at the tail end of his decade-long venture collaging everything he could find, in 1971, Burroughs jotted down a list of limericks, presumably for cutting up. This sketch for a limerick cut-up, then, displays the novel juxtapositions, poetic and lyrical, that Burroughs' processing method often generated.

Found in Berg Folio 104, a miscellaneous file containing "Mss Pages From Various Periods All Identified," Burroughs labeled the piece as a "cut-up *with limericks*" (italics my own). Perhaps Burroughs meant nothing by the preposition, but, as with his "cut-ins," a "cut-up with" in Burroughs' oeuvre tends to designate a work that preserves traces of its source material, in terminology, phrasing, and style. Burroughs' vast majority of published cut-up texts are remarkable for the way they lose the voice of previous authors and genres, as Burroughs remixes diverse material to create an inimitable tone that marks it, for anyone in the know, as a Burroughs' cut-up. During early drafts, however, Burroughs' cut-ups and transcriptions of selected texts often contain far more jagged juxtapositions that draw attention to the fissures, somewhat incoherent, but evocative of what Gysin and Burroughs theorized as a "third mind."

In this case, Burroughs "cut-up with limericks" approximates a list, one that collages a multiplicity of Anglophone folk voices. His source material of English limericks, ranging from dismal jokes to licentious puns, have been passed down through the culture, and, like Burroughs cut-up texts, regurgitated by generations of repetitions that both preserved, and mutated, their viral appeal. This bawdy form of verse, usually three long and two short lines, the limerick, originated in the eighteenth century, becoming popularized by Edward Lear in the nineteenth. As particularly rhyme-laden verse, limericks are easily memorable, the sort of catchy tunes that Burroughs cut up in *The Ticket That Exploded* (1967). Limericks are viral language forms, and Burroughs' typo-riddled cut-up litany of these comical rhymes offers more than just a playful digression from the broader concerns occupying his work in the early 1970s.

—AWC

There was a young lady of Thame who came here to save her good name what makes us so wild she was heavy with child but our poor ruddy clerk got the blame there wasa young man called Naricssus said "I'm nobody's Mister or Missus but I8m not on the shelf I'm in love with myself then   he gazed in a pooland said "Kiss us" there was a young student of Kent who worked doubled up in a tent when his friends asked him   "Why so?" He replied I dont know I suppose its my scholarly betn" a weekend for two in Ireland two nights ina first class Dublin hotel If the innocent voters of Huyton re read reports of the speeches at Brighton and compare what they read with the subsequent deed do they still thin their choice was the right un? V Columbey said de Guale "selon moi ce village manque d'un je ne said quoi sans Saint Charles Deux Eglise innuites no suffisent allor battissez numero trois there was a young famrer of Bodenham who when he saw spider he tordenham t when they questioned him "Why?" he made the replay "It's quicker than giving them lodenham Asked Heath "Why oh why when I speak do my bellows come out as a squeak? Has someone been meddling with my organ pedaling or is it just me that(s so weak? Ian's c donctrine couldnt be easier Harold just doesnt exist in Rhodesia but as Wilson thinks smith is a horrible myth it's a clear case of mutual amnesia   There was a young man of St Just who complained that his giral had not bust so she purchased some foam which she tailored at home into contrours suggestive of lust. An untoward maiden of Bicester protested that no one has kissed her then a ahosrt sighted Sweded with a despaerate need performed till he gave her a blister a charming young lady from Beauliue complains that my rhymes are unrully so what could be fairer I'l take to Eerie to share the fisrt prize with youngs truly.

[autograph]: cut up with Limmericks 1971

Cut Up with Limericks, William S. Burroughs, 1971 (8 × 11, 1 leaf, typescript) (Berg 35.2).
Folio 104,Item 2, "There was a . . .". Typescript, in autograph: "cut-up with limericks 1971."

5

William S. Burroughs' Spirit of Collaboration

ALLEN HIBBARD

One of the sources of our fascination with William S. Burroughs (to invoke the term around which Oliver Harris gathers so many interests and insights) is his openness, willingness, and eagerness to collaborate and respond to the ideas and energies of those around him. This collaborative spirit is consistent with his views on the operation of virus—things spreading from one organism to another—and the permeability of the self, the possibility of transformation resulting from one sort of injection or another. This collaborative spirit, it seems to me, is at the heart of who Burroughs was and how he worked. His work with others demonstrates a porousness of self and being, an openness to others that breaks down single-autonomous notions of author and creativity as the sometimes-hard shell of the self is cracked open, as the impermeable membranes separating one organism from another are penetrated. An examination of Burroughs' collaborative work, it is hoped, will deepen and expand our appreciation of his distinctive creative practices and, more broadly, our understanding of the nature of collaboration, creative influence, and cross-pollination.

Any number of ingredients might go into a productive collaboration: shared or complementary visions and skills, compatible energies, a sense of give and take that involves handing things to another, receiving things back, often with interjections or emendations, and so forth. Very often (but not always) collaboration is predicated on actual physical interaction between collaborators. Any consideration of collaboration, especially specific collaborative enterprises, often thus must be accompanied by an accounting of pertinent biographical facts. When, how, and where did the subjects meet? What kinds of interactions transpired within a particular place and time? An examination of Burroughs' collaborative work, we will see, expands our appreciation of the wide spectrum of various types of collaboration, ranging from work that emerges from friendship or romantic interest, to projects with people one may never have met, to looser forms of collaboration involving intertextual connections and influence.

Various issues concerning the very process of collaboration, in specific instances as well as more generally, arise from an exploration of Burroughs' collaborations. What effect does collaboration have on both the participants and the products involved? As selves merge, in the collaborative act, at times, as we consider transtextual relationships, it becomes difficult—perhaps even senseless—to sort out who is responsible for what.[1] The notion of an autonomous creative self tends to break down in collaboration. Such certainly is the case with the cut-up method, described by Gysin and Burroughs in *The Third Mind*: "the complete fusion in a praxis of two subjectivities, two subjectivities that metamorphose into a third; it is from this collusion that a new author emerges, an absent third person, invisible and beyond grasp, decoding the silence" (Geiger 2005, 144).

Regardless of the nature of collaboration, what results is something new and fresh, different from what one single person would have or could have created on his or her own—a kind of hybrid product, fusing qualities from each participant. At the outset of his groundbreaking study *Double Talk: The Erotics of Male Literary Collaboration*, Wayne Koestenbaum underscores this distinctive nature of collaborative works: "Books with two authors are specimens of a relation and show writing to be a quality of motion and exchange, not a fixed thing" (1989, 2). Collaboration results in different kinds of works, he argues, because of their unique circumstances of genesis and production. Things are made that otherwise would not have been made, or take a shape they wouldn't have taken without the participation or influence of another party. A pioneering work in queer criticism and theory, Koestenbaum's study examines collaborative teams such as J. A. Symonds and Havelock Ellis, Wordsworth and Coleridge, Pound and Eliot, R. L. Stevenson and Lloyd Osbourne and others, stressing the erotic or amorous element (overt or repressed) at work in the collaborative act. While at times Koestenbaum seems to push his polemical claims to absurd extremes, rigidly insisting on the primacy of the erotic in any male-to-male collaborative activity, his work still is a useful resource for any study of collaboration, particularly collaboration between men.

This examination of Burroughs' collaborative interactions reveals that while at times there was certainly an erotic component at play, the range of motives and nature of interaction is often far more complex and wide-ranging, producing what might be thought of as a continuum or spectrum of types of collaboration. This exploration moves from *The Hippos Were Boiled in Their Tanks* (Burroughs and Kerouac 1945/2008), *The "Priest" They Called Him* (Burroughs and Cobain 1992), *Naked Lunch* (Burroughs and Ginsberg 1959), cut-up projects (Burroughs, Gysin, and others), and, finally, what I think is an intriguing, though less known, instance involving creative, collaborative interactions between Burroughs, Gysin, and Paul Bowles that developed during and after the time all three were living in Tangier in the late 1950s: the story of the production and circulation of *The Pool K III*, a compilation of *musique concrète*, now credited in a new CD release to Bowles. These particular cases have been chosen first to demonstrate how collaboration has been a central mode of production throughout Burroughs' career, and second to display the variety of types of creative collaboration, including working across different mediums, working with friends on projects, riffing or responding to others' production, and even self-cannibalization. In every instance, people do something they would not otherwise have done without interactions with others. And, in every instance, works produced bear the marks of that particular interaction, obtaining a different character than single-authored works.

One early, notable example of Burroughs' collaborative work is the novel he and Jack Kerouac wrote in 1945, *And the Hippos Were Boiled in Their Tanks.* The title page notes that the "Will Dennison chapters [were] written by William Lee [Burroughs], the Mike Ryko chapters by John [Jack] Kerouac." Thus, the two handed the story back and forth, like runners handing the baton in a relay race. Burroughs had already, by that time, been involved in a similar kind of collaborative project with his childhood friend Kells Elvins. Ted Morgan describes that process: "Burroughs would write a paragraph and Kells would write a paragraph, or together they would work up the dialogue, splitting their sides with laughter" (1988, 68). We can imagine that Burroughs' work with Kerouac followed similar patterns.

The dramatic murder of David Kammerer at the hands of Lucien Carr supplied the raw material for *Hippos.* It is a story that has generated renewed interest and attention recently with the production and release of *Kill Your Darlings* (directed by Krokidas, 2013), a film that seems to draw heavily from the novel. And a recent long essay by Dustin Griffin in *Journal of Beat Studies,* "The St. Louis Clique: Burroughs, Kammerer, and Carr" (2014), provides a thorough biographical narrative of the history of the men's relationships with one another. Ambiguity and mystery still surround the event, which likely accounts, at least in part, for our sustained fascination with the story, a fascination that returns our attention to the Burroughs-Kerouac fictional rendition. Did Carr (as his own story goes) kill Kammerer in self-defense, resisting the older man's sexual advances? Or, as some of Kammerer's friends have maintained, did Carr simply off him, without provocation, and use the line of self-defense to avoid a murder conviction, no doubt playing on homophobic attitudes prevalent at the time?

Along with Allen Ginsberg, Burroughs and Kerouac knew the two men involved and were even implicated in the events surrounding it. The two young writers spent time with Carr following the murder. Kerouac was arrested and held as a material witness. Burroughs was questioned in regard to the case; however, a family-hired lawyer guided him through the legal process. It seems likely that the composition of the novel was a joint project from the outset, likely resulting from a mutual desire, perhaps even playfully, to make something together. The project involved discussing things, responding to one another's ideas, and reading one another's work. Throughout, the two were held together by a mutual commitment to tell the story. Burroughs described the process in interviews with Ted Morgan: "Kerouac and I were talking about a possible book that we might write together, and we decided to do Dave's death. We wrote alternate chapters and read them to each other. There was a clear separation of material as to who wrote what.... We had fun doing it" (Grauerholz 2008, 195).

The narrative they constructed followed the course of events, as each writer dwelt on parts of the story known by one or the other. In creating their fictional account, names of characters changed, as well as various details. (The murder weapon, for instance, is transformed from a knife to a hatchet; Lucien was made a Turk.) Burroughs called it "the first American existentialist novel" (Morgan 1988, 110) and Kerouac, in a letter to his sister Caroline dated March 14, 1945, called it "a portrait of the 'lost' segment of our generation, hardboiled, honest, and sensationally real" (Grauerholz 2008, 199). Indeed, the style certainly seems hard-boiled, noir-ish. (We might bear in mind that it was written at the height of film noir, around the time of *The Maltese Falcon* [1941], *Double Indemnity* [1944], *The Killers* [1946], etc.) Remarkably the two voices and styles merge, becoming almost indistinguishable. If we read the book without any knowledge of the conditions of its composition, we might easily assume that one person wrote it. Clearly it is an instance of the kind of melding of creative minds described later by Burroughs and Gysin in *The Third Mind*, in which the sensibilities of two talents merge to produce a work that cannot be credited to one or the other.

While the book didn't find a publisher at the time of its writing, no doubt the collaborative venture served as a useful exercise for both Kerouac and Burroughs, getting creative juices flowing, providing practice designing and executing plot, and offering an opportunity to hone writing skills. It became a way of producing something tangible from interactions between like-minded friends, likely energized by wishes to be more strongly attached to one another. As James Grauerholz notes in his informative afterword, the novel was written before either writer was well known. The book, which likely would never have been published had not the two writers gone on to write works that put them on the map and made them famous, now takes on significance, within the context of Beat scholarship, recent films, queer theory, and so on.

One of Burroughs' last collaborations, *The "Priest" They Called Him*, with Kurt Cobain, embodies similar traits, yet the circumstances surrounding its creation differ considerably, providing an example of a different sort of collaboration, almost five decades after his collaboration with Kerouac. Burroughs and Cobain had not met when they agreed to work with one another, though each knew of the other. Cobain, the young lead guitarist and singer of Nirvana, had been an admirer of Burroughs, sensing a kindred spirit in the man and his work. Both men identified as outsiders, rebels. Both struggled with addiction. At the time of the collaboration each was at the height of his popularity. Producers no doubt recognized that there would be a ready market and appetite for something bearing the names Burroughs and Cobain. The collaboration bridges generations; it also bridges two mediums, word and music.

As with every collaboration, there is the story of the work's production. On September 25, 1992, in Lawrence, Kansas, Burroughs recorded in his inimitable voice a reading of a short piece, "The 'Priest' They Called Him," that had first appeared in the London *Weekend Telegraph* in 1967, and was included in *The Exterminator!*, published in 1973. Then, separately, a couple of months later in Seattle, Cobain recorded his amazing guitar riff, responding to Burroughs' voice and the action of the story. The two tapes were then edited and laid over one another in the studio.

The piece opens with Cobain on the guitar, playing the opening bars of "Silent Night," dissonant and jarring, setting the tone. Burroughs then begins reading: "'Fight tuberculosis, folks.' Christmas Eve an old junkie selling Christmas seals on North Clark Street, the 'priest' they called him. 'Fight tuberculosis, folks'" (1973, 156). The junkie priest is trying to come up with money to score. By chance, he comes upon a suitcase, "old and dirty poor quality leather and heavy." Suspicious, the priest stops in Lincoln Park (Chicago, we assume) to open the case. Cobain's guitar goes crazy as the priest discovers two severed legs that "had belonged to a young man with dark skin shiny black leg hairs glittered in the dim street light" (157). After dumping the legs, the junkie proceeds to his buyer to exchange the suitcase for a fix. Once he gets the fix, the junkie returns home to his rooming house. As he rolls up his sleeve, preparing to shoot up, he hears the moaning of a Mexican kid, who he knew was hooked, in the room next door ("thin walls you understand"). In an unusual yet touching act of charity fitting for Christmas Eve, the priest goes next door and shares his fix with the Mexican. He then goes back to his room and sits down on his bed. "He sat there and received the *immaculate fix* and since he was himself a priest there was no need to call one" (159). Cobain's guitar continues after Burroughs finishes reading the story, with a haunting wail, like the sound of an ambulance siren. All of this in just four pages in print; just over nine minutes on the CD.

This version of the story, with its concision and deadpan delivery, thus seems better suited for the purposes than the story's quite different, earlier version or rendition, "The Junky's Christmas," written, according to James Grauerholz, in 1954 and included in *Interzone* (1989). In any case, the story, involving a copacetic moment of sharing between two addicts, seems perfectly suited for a Burroughs and Cobain collaboration. The resulting collaborative work displays two distinctive artists, each with his recognizable signature style. As with the Kerouac collaboration, the two complemented one another, their styles meshing wonderfully. Cobain's guitar work heightens, perhaps even creates, the sinister, disturbed mood of the piece. Like that earlier collaboration, the final product is something more than the sum of the two parts. Here, though, the contribution of each participant is easily identifiable without explanatory notes—one speaking, the other playing guitar.

Stories of a meeting between Cobain and Burroughs after the completion of the project have circulated, taking on the quality of legend. During the summer of 2015, in San Francisco, Johnny Strike (lead singer of the legendary Bay Area punk band *Crime*), relayed to me his version of the story of Cobain's trip to Lawrence,

Kansas, to see Burroughs. After the brief visit, apparently Burroughs remarked, "Now that's one troubled young lad," or something to that effect. That was just a year or two before Cobain's death by suicide on April 5, 1994, at his home overlooking Lake Washington, at the age of twenty-seven. Burroughs died several years later, in 1997, of natural causes, at the age of 83 in Lawrence.

In the long span of time between his collaborations with Kerouac and Cobain (the time during which he was writing the works for which he is now best known), Burroughs consistently was open to collaboration with others. Indeed, even many works we think of as authored by Burroughs alone might be seen as results of interaction with others, another type of collaboration. Oliver Harris persuasively argues, for instance, that *Naked Lunch* owes its existence to Burroughs' correspondence with Allen Ginsberg, in which he composed for his erstwhile lover, routines meant to hold attention. (And, we may recall here, too, the earlier collaboration between Burroughs and Ginsberg that resulted in *The Yage Letters*.) Many of those routines, in one shape or other, were cut and pasted into the work that became *Naked Lunch*. "It is reasonable to assume," Harris proposes, "that his epistolary activity was in itself an element of collaborative production" (2003, 194). The rhetorical situation of the letter, Harris elaborates, enacts a psychological dynamic in which the anticipation of the reader at once serves as a motivation for expression and a factor that shapes what is told. "Replies are needed to maintain the flow of production," Harris writes, "operating as a kind of feedback signal in which Ginsberg's reply tests the line, as it were, confirming Burroughs is still on air" (195). Once again, we see how Burroughs' creative process is highly interactive, involving others who play a key role in shaping the ultimate work.

A brief consideration of this collaboration must acknowledge particular biographical facts, notably Burroughs' sojourn abroad and the separation it effected. By 1953, Burroughs had left Latin America, at least in part to escape the lingering threat of prosecution by Mexican authorities for the killing of his wife, Joan Vollmer. Disinclined to settle in the United States, he went to Tangier, no doubt in some measure feeling the pull and allure of Paul Bowles, who by then had become famous for *The Sheltering Sky*. Burroughs' letters to Ginsberg were a way of trying to bridge the distance between a solitary writer on the periphery and home. They were also a way of trying to coax and cajole Ginsberg to come visit him in Tangier, "often extending the promise of boys and including in his letters chunks of the manuscript he then referred to as 'Interzone'" (Hibbard 2009, 57).

Burroughs wanted Ginsberg to come visit him in Tangier not only to enjoy the companionship of the object of his affections but also to help him put together his novel. Ginsberg, Kerouac, Peter Orlovsky, and Alan Ansen showed up in Tangier in 1957, responding to Burroughs' call, spurring a flurry of activity that Ted Morgan describes as a "writer's equivalent of a quilting bee": "Over a period of two months working steadily, they integrated and edited and typed the material which was an incredible mosaic of Bill's fantasies over the past three years, until they had about 200 pages of finished manuscript typed in duplicate" (1988, 265). Ginsberg, thus, acted as a kind of editor/collaborator there in Tangier, playing an integral role in the arranging and shaping of *Naked Lunch*. Without Ginsberg's involvement, we would likely not have the novel, at least not in the form it took. The work bears the mark of the vibrant exchange between the two writers in a way that, like other examples of collaboration discussed here, challenges notions of autonomous authorship.

While Wayne Koestenbaum's work, cited earlier, may not have universal applicability, either in the case of Burroughs or more broadly, it certainly seems to be relevant here. Indeed, Harris refers to Koestenbaum in his analysis of the role of letters and operation of desire, quoting briefly from the introduction to *Double Talk* Koestenbaum's claim that collaborative writing between men is a product of "the desire and pursuit of the whole—the wish to unite with a lost twin and to form a blended soul" (1989, 4). There was clearly an erotic, amatory aspect to the dynamic between Burroughs and Ginsberg that resulted in the creation this literary lovechild, *Naked Lunch*.

In his introduction to the recently published second volume of Burroughs' correspondence, *Rub Out the Words*, Bill Morgan writes: "The letters that follow show Burroughs' steady drift away from the earlier 'beat' circle, composed of Ginsberg, Gregory Corso, Jack Kerouac, and the rest, toward new relationships with friends made in Northern Africa and Europe" (Burroughs 2012, xxvii). Among key correspondents during this time were Brion Gysin "who before long would replace Ginsberg as Burroughs' most trusted confidant" (ibid.) and Paul Bowles (along with Ian Sommerville, Michael Portman, and Alexander Trocchi). While the cast of characters may have changed, Burroughs' collaborative impulse continues, unabated if not even more intense.

The friendship and important, amazingly productive collaborative relationship between Burroughs and English-born, Canada-raised artist-writer Brion Gysin is especially well known. Burroughs famously said that Gysin was the only man he ever respected. Their interaction, based on a shared moral and aesthetic vision, was wide-ranging, stretching over decades. Gysin turned Burroughs onto the cut-up method and introduced him to Hassan I Sabbah, the legendary leader of the Ismaili cult of assassins, who at the end of the eleventh century formed an exclusively male society whose followers, high on hash, launched attacks on dominant, dogmatic, and inflexible Islamic power structures from their remote perch of Alamut, in Northern Persia. In 1962, Gysin introduced Burroughs to Antony Balch, the filmmaker responsible for making *Towers Open Fire*. Gysin and Burroughs worked together on *The Third Mind*. Barry Miles takes note of some shared interests that paved the way for the development of their collaborative friendship:

Burroughs and Gysin, Ian Sommerville, Paris, 1959. Photograph courtesy of Barry Miles.

"They had much in common, including a belief in the magical world, animal spirits, curses, trance states, and the power of suggestion" (1993, 94).

During this first period of their acquaintance, each began to form impressions of the other. Gysin's early impressions of Burroughs are recorded in *The Third Mind*: "Caught a glimpse of him glimmering rapidly along through the shadows from one farmacia to the next, hugging a bottle of paregoric. I close my eyes and see him in winter, cold silver blue, rain dripping from the points of his hat and nose. . . . William the Rat scuttles over the purple sheen of wet pavements, sniffing. When you squint up your eyes, at him, he turns into Coleridge, De Quincey, Poe, Baudelaire and Gide" (Burroughs and Gysin 1978, 49).

By all accounts, the deep bond between Burroughs and Gysin developed only after they met up with one another in Paris, in 1958, after both had left Tangier. "Wanna score?" Burroughs reputedly asked Gysin when the two first met one another there (Gysin 1982, 162). The extraordinarily productive period that followed, while both lived in the Beat Hotel, is legendary. It was there that the two pursued possibilities of the cut-up method and experimented with the Dream Machine. During this time, too, *The Exterminator* was produced with calligraphy by Gysin and *Minutes to Go*, with drawings by Gysin. The two developed what Gysin called "psychic symbiosis" (Geiger 2005, 143). Burroughs found Gysin a "superb raconteur with [a] knack for disappearing into a maze of words and voices and sets." (Burroughs 1986b, 7). "Listening to Brion talk," Burroughs noted, "was a little like watching a man covered with elaborate Japanese tattoos. You might wonder what the point of it all was, but it was hard to take your eyes away" (Morgan 1988, 305).

The completion of *The Third Mind*, around 1965, it seems, marks an end to the most intense period of collaboration between the two, or three, however you add it up, though they stayed in touch. Burroughs' *The Cat Inside* opens with these lines: "May 4, 1985. I am packing for a short trip to New York to discuss the cat book with Brion" (1992, 1). The first edition of the book, published in 1986 in a limited edition by Grenfell Press, contained eight illustrations by Gysin, some which were incorporated into the later Viking Press edition.

We know that Gysin played an essential role in introducing the cut-up method to Burroughs, certainly a form of collaborative interaction. Those cut-up novels themselves, too, point to another kind of collaboration, one involving relationships between Burroughs and other authors and texts (or even his own texts), as he took material from various sources and spliced that material into his own work, producing by these fresh juxtapositions, something new and different. Akin to sampling and plagiarism, the cut-up technique radically questions the nature of "originality," the relationship between "original" and "offspring," the notion of autonomous, self-contained books, and issues related to copyright, ownership, and intellectual property. What new properties attend to a cutting up of a Shakespeare sonnet, placed alongside a speech by Eisenhower? Or when Burroughs splices in text by Kafka into his own prose? Or when Burroughs self-plagiarizes or self-cannibalizes, or recycles material (such as reworking "The Junky's Christmas" into "The 'Priest' They Called Him")? When Kathy Acker, heavily influenced by Burroughs, brazenly imports (plagiarizes?) portions of text by Faulkner or Twain, whose language does it become? Do these moves (as seems to be her purpose) challenge the very notion of an autonomous author at the same time they re-inscribe the principle? (The author's name is attached to her productions, as a label, a means of marketing, attributing her work to a particular person who can receive royalties.) Similarly, Danger Mouse's "mashup," *The Grey Album*, openly cites/samples/plays off both the Beatles' *White Album* and Jay-Z's *Black Album*. The debt is blatant, obvious. There's no attempt to hide it. On the contrary, the title and content are meant to proclaim the connections. Likewise, Vanilla Ice's "Ice Ice Baby" samples Queen and Bowie, "Under Pressure," altering the bass line. And, at the Bloomington "Burroughs Century" symposium, Lydia Lunch cleverly and playfully signified on Burroughs, "cutting in" her own works into William S. Burroughs', creating a marvelous new tapestry in which her voice (and authority) takes a place within or around or under or over his. All of these examples point to very tight connections between texts, ones that have often pushed the boundaries of property and ownership of material, at times resulting in court battles and monetary settlements.

While the importance of the connection between Burroughs and Gysin has long been widely acknowledged, remarkably little attention has been paid to an essential role played by a third player, Paul Bowles. Indeed, the three might be dubbed the "Tangier Troika." Interactions between the three, all of whom opened themselves to suggestions and influences of the other two, resulted in creative works that arguably never would have otherwise have been produced—another type of collaboration.

Bowles's acquaintance with Gysin predates that of Burroughs. Ted Morgan relates how Bowles remembered first coming upon Gysin in Paris, in the late 1930s, "shooting flaming arrows out of a hotel window, which terrified [Bowles's wife] Jane, who was sure they would all be arrested. A friend just back from Tibet had brought the arrows, with cotton ties soaked in alcohol" (1988, 302). Both the Bowleses and Gysin were in New York during the early 1940s and saw quite a bit of one another during that period. "He opened my ears a lot, also my nose," Gysin said of Paul, referring to Paul's game involving perfumes and essences (Geiger 2005, 60). "I owe him a tremendous amount, I owe him my years in Morocco, really" (Gysin 1982, 26). Indeed, it was Bowles who invited Gysin to come to Morocco where, according to Barry Miles, Bowles introduced Burroughs and Gysin. The first meeting, by one account, was at an exhibit of Gysin's paintings in Tangier. "I introduced [Burroughs] to Brion Gysin because I thought they would get on well together," Bowles writes in his autobiography *Without Stopping*. "I was right: eventually they became inseparable" (1985, 331).

Bowles, Burroughs, and Gysin had a good deal to do with one another in the late 1950s and early 1960s. To gain a better understanding of how the three influenced one another, I turn to the creation and circulation of *The Pool K III*, which originally was produced by the Italian music label, Alga Marghen in 1998 under Brion Gysin's name, but was rightly attributed to Paul Bowles in a recent reissue (2013) by Dom America/Cadmus. In detailed liner notes, Jon Carlson makes an airtight case for Bowles as creator, drawing upon evidence from letters, references in a Bowles interview with Ira Cohen, and material in Gena Dagel Caponi's biography of Bowles, *Romantic Savage*.

While the story of the fate of *The Pool* may not seem at first glance to fit traditional notions of collaboration, in its strictest sense, it may serve as a limit case—pushing the boundaries of the concept and thus perhaps extending our understanding of the nature of cross-pollination and influence as a form of collaboration. What is pertinent to this discussion is the way the tape was shared with friends and acquaintances, most notably Brion Gysin and William S. Burroughs. From the start, the tape was warmly and enthusiastically received, and it inspired recipients' and listeners' work.

Just what is this *Pool*? And what kinds of creative effects might it have had on Gysin and Burroughs? The CD is a compilation, as Irene Herrmann describes, in liner notes, of "eight distinct tracks; each one is a slightly different construct of largely similar, repeated tones seemingly enhanced with echo-chamber effects" (2013). Bowles produced this work, recording sounds around his apartment in Tangier. As Herrmann suggests, each of the individual tracks (ranging from 1:52 minutes to 13:02 minutes) is discrete, a composition in its own right. And cumulatively, the eight tracks form a unified whole, seemingly of the same fabric and conception. The first four tracks seem to be variations on similar patterns of water dripping, perhaps into a bathtub, randomly, percussively, producing plops and pops. Herrmann goes on to describe subsequent tracks:

> Track 5 has the distinction of being titled "wind" ... and windy it is! A mid-summer Saharan wind? An icy Antarctic one? Track 5 [perhaps 6], a personal favorite, could be the commencement of a rainstorm as recorded on a tin rooftop. Or perhaps popcorn popping in a lidded pan? Track 6 [7?] does have real musical, that is to say *tonal* content ... a kind of meandering piano, with a tonal center on a high 'e', combined with other less-worldly sounding music of a more sustained nature. Two musical ships passing in the night? Or a dialogue, each voice inspired by the other? (2013)

At times, it seems almost as though the pieces are scored, sometimes with more than one melodic line and some kind of background sound, a kind of basso continuo, at times sounding like a clarinet or perhaps the sound of the tape machine's incessant hum. To a contemporary listener, it might seem as though the pieces were produced in the studio (calling to mind Brian Eno's work)—a number of scratches recorded individually, then superimposed (via computer) onto one another. Bowles, however, was himself his own chief engineer, working only with a very conventional one-mike tape recorder.

Bowles apparently shared or gave the tape to Gysin who in turn shared it with Burroughs. (What happens to notions of creator and ownership in the case of the gift? we might ask.) Given the nature of *The Pool*—its randomness, its "found" quality, its experimentalism, its openness to interpretation—it is easy to see how it would excite and inspire Burroughs and Gysin who listened to the tape and (partly in response to it) constructed their own analogues. Burroughs, in a letter to Bowles dated June 28, 1960 (from London), speaks about listening to the tape: "Brion received your tape, and I have heard *The Pool* on my recorder leaving indelible impression: night music." "Brion was knocked out by *The Pool*," he goes on. A month later Burroughs writes to Bowles saying that Brion had recorded at BBC "one of his repetitive poems as he calls them of which there are examples in *Minutes to Go*." After describing various experiments setting the poems to music and exploring "the possibilities of sound," Burroughs suggests that it was perhaps "*The Pool* that brought the potentials of sound to his and certainly to my attention" (Burroughs 2012, 38).

If one compares these poems to *The Pool*, one sees at once shared approaches and characteristics—mechanical and random repetitions of sounds, a radical dissociation of "meaning," working with "found" materials. Among his best-known permutation poems (some of which were first published in *The Exterminator* in

1960) are "I Am That I Am," "Kick That Habit Man," "Junk Is No Good Baby," and "No Poets Dont Own Words." "I Am That I Am" goes on for several pages. A more practical example to cite here would be "I Dont Work You Dig" (Weiss 2001, 93):

I DONT WORK YOU DIG	I DONT YOU WORK DIG
DONT WORK YOU DIG I	DONT YOU WORK DIG I
WORK YOU DIG I DON'T	WORK DIG I DON'T YOU
YOU DIG I DON'T WORK	YOU WORK DIG I DON'T
DIG I DONT WORK YOU	DIG I DONT YOU WORK
I DONT WORK DIG YOU	I DONT DIG WORK YOU
DONT WORK DIG YOU I	DONT DIG WORK YOU I
WORK DIG YOU I DONT	WORK YOU I DONT DIG
YOU I DONT WORK DIG	YOU I DONT DIG WORK
DIG YOU I DONT WORK	DIG WORK YOU I DONT
I DONT YOU DIG WORK	I DONT DIG YOU WORK
DONT YOU DIG WORK I	DONT DIG YOU WORK I
WORK I DONT YOU DIG	WORK I DONT DIG YOU
YOU DIG WORK I DONT	YOU WORK I DONT DIG
DIG WORK I DONT YOU	DIG YOU WORK I DON'T

Some of these "poems" seem almost to have been generated by computer, hypothetically susceptible to being played continuously, ad infinitum, in a perpetual feedback loop, like a Mobius strip. Gysin's permutation poems can be seen—if we stretch the meanings of the term—as resulting from collaborative interactions with Bowles. Like the tracks of *The Pool*, they play on repetition and difference. What difference does one seemingly small alteration—or a variation in the sequence of particles—make?

Burroughs also credits *The Pool* for having a distinct effect on his own writing. He writes Bowles on October 9, 1960: "What have you done with *The Pool*? I realized a green chapter from my new novel and I am sure Brion could paint *The Pool*. In fact, I think he has." During this time, Burroughs was pushing to get *The Exterminator* into circulation, beginning to experiment with cut-ups, and working on what eventually became *The Soft Machine*. Indeed, we may certainly feel connections and affinities when we listen to *The Pool* alongside a reading of *The Soft Machine*. Take, for instance, this passage: "Green boys—idiot irresponsibles—rolling in warm delta ooze fuck in color flashes through green jelly flesh that quivers together merging and drawing back in a temple dance of colors. 'Hot licks us all the way we are all one clear green substance like flexible amber changing color and consistency to accommodate any occasion'" (1966, 140). The cut-up method that here Burroughs was employing, truly, for the first time in his fiction, resembles to some extent Bowles's process in recording *The Pool*. Material was not so much invented, as cut, captured, and arranged, from the infinite flow of sound and word. Words, like the sounds in Bowles's recording, become opaque and abstract, as they

Burroughs in front of Danger Sign, Brion Gysin, Paris, 1959, photograph courtesy of Barry Miles. In a forthcoming essay in *Soft Need*, no. 23, Oliver Harris identifies this photo, one of a series of four, as having been taken by Brion Gysin on September 1, 1959, aptly in front of the then under repairs Académie Française.

are taken out of context and reframed, prompting us—perhaps—simply to absorb their innate qualities without trying to construct a narrative or melody.

Another passage from *The Soft Machine* seems almost to be a kind of meta-commentary on the process of putting together the cut-up novel that could apply as well, perhaps, to creation of *musique concrète*. "We fold writers of all time in together and record radio programs, movie sound tracks, TV and juke box songs all the words of the world stirring around in a cement mixer and pour in the resistance message 'Calling partisans of all nation—Cut word lines—shift linguals—Free doorways—Vibrate "tourists"—Word falling—Photo falling—Break through in Grey Room'" (149).

When we think of collaboration, we are apt to think of pairs of people working together, often putting words and music together (Rodgers and Hammerstein) or welding phrases and melodies (Lennon and McCartney) or writing books together (Gilbert and Gubar). What emerges as the result of this kind of collaboration is inevitably a product of those interactions, often between two people, something that cannot be ascribed wholly to one or the other. Certainly, Burroughs was involved, numerous times, with this kind of collaboration, particularly as he worked with Kerouac on *Hippos*, with Cobain on *The "Priest" They Called Him*, and with Gysin on cut-ups. These kinds of collaborations are often built around friendship (that might be disrupted by disputes over who is responsible for what or who gets what share of proceeds).

There are, however, ways of working together, and being influenced, other than actually composing things jointly, resulting in a range of productions falling within a continuum stretching from plagiarism and sampling to loose intertextual influence, all of which depend on a degree of temporal distance between "original" and "offspring." This might include palimpsest modes of production (such as covering a song or translation) that involve dependency, interaction, and transformation; ways that, as Jorge Luis Borges notes, challenge our notions of originality.

What we have seen in the case of *The Pool* is a looser kind of inter- or transtextuality: Things (in this case a tape) circulate among people with keen affinities, at a particular moment in time, and affect those involved, resulting in an intricate and fascinating pattern of cross-pollination and the production of new works inspired by the "original." Bowles seems to have made the tape and sent it to Gysin who (again in an act of sharing) played it for Burroughs. Both Gysin and Burroughs, in turn, signified on *The Pool*, each in his own way, in a different medium. The three demonstrate an openness to creative play, like young boys in a tree house or on a raft drifting down a river, a willingness to get lost, to try new things, to respond to one another's energies and impulses, to make things together, like musicians in a jazz quartet, listening to one another, harmonizing, responding spontaneously, taking a phrase and giving it back, perhaps with a subtle difference, losing one's self in the music.

NOTE

1. Gérard Genette, in *Palimpsests: Literature in the Second Degree* (1997), provides an accounting of the wide range of types of relationships between one text and another. Under the broad term "transtextuality," he identifies and defines five subcategories: intertextuality, paratext, metatextuality, hypertextuality, and architextuality.

ALLEN HIBBARD is Professor of English and Director of the Middle East Center at Middle Tennessee State University. He has written two books on Paul Bowles (*Paul Bowles: A Study of the Short Fiction* and *Paul Bowles, Magic & Morocco*), edited *Conversations with William S. Burroughs*, and published a collection of his own stories in Arabic. With his colleague Osama Esber, he is currently in the process of completing a translation of *A Banquet for Seaweed*, a novel by contemporary Syrian writer Haidar Haidar.

Bowles, Paul. 1985. *Without Stopping*. New York: Ecco. First published 1972.

———. 2013. *The Pool K III*. Tiberon, CA, Austin, TX. Cadmus Editions/Dom America, CD.

Burroughs, William S. 1966. *The Soft Machine*. New York: Grove.

———. 1973. *Exterminator!* New York: Viking Penguin.

———. 1986a. *The Adding Machine: Selected Essays*. New York: Seaver Books. Reprint, New York: Arcade, 1993.

———. 1986b. Introduction to *The Last Museum*, by Brion Gysin, 1–8. New York: Grove; London: Faber.

———. 1989. *Interzone*. Edited by James Grauerholz. New York: Viking.

———. 1992. *The Cat Inside*. New York: Viking.

———. 2012. *Rub Out the Words: The Letters of William S. Burroughs, 1959–1974*. Edited by Bill Morgan. New York: HarperCollins.

Burroughs, William S., and Kurt Cobain. 1993 *The "Priest" They Called Him*. Tim Kerr Records.

Burroughs, William S., and Brion Gysin. 1978. *The Third Mind*. New York: Viking.

Burroughs, William S., and Jack Kerouac. 2008. *And the Hippos Were Boiled in Their Tanks*. New York: Grove.

Caponi, Jean Dagel, ed. 1993. *Conversations with Paul Bowles*. Jackson: University Press of Mississippi.

———. 1994. *Paul Bowles: Romantic Savage*. Carbondale: Southern Illinois University Press.

Carlson, Jon. 2013. Liner notes. *The Pool, K III*. Tiberon, CA, Austin, TX. Cadmus Editions/Dom America. CD.

Geiger, John. 2005. *Nothing Is True, Everything Is Permitted: The Life of Brion Gysin*. New York: Disinformation.

Genette, Gérard. 1997. *Palimpsests: Literature in the Second Degree*. Translated by Channa Newman and Claude Doubinsky. Lincoln: University of Nebraska Press.

Grauerholz, James. 2008. Afterword to *And the Hippos Were Boiled in Their Tanks*, by William S. Burroughs and Jack Kerouac. New York: Grove.

Griffin, Dustin. 2014. "The St. Louis Clique: Burroughs, Kammerer, and Carr." *Journal of Beat Studies* 3: 1–46.

Gysin, Brion. 1982. *Here to Go: Planet R-101*. Interviews of Gysin by Terry Wilson with additional texts. San Francisco: Re/Search. Reprint, London: Quartet, 1985; London: Creation, 2001.

Harris, Oliver. 2003. *William Burroughs and the Secret of Fascination*. Carbondale: Southern Illinois University Press.

Herrmann, Irene. 2013. Liner notes. *The Pool, K III*. Tiberon, CA, Austin, TX. Cadmus Editions/Dom America. CD.

Hibbard, Allen. 2009. "Tangier and the Making of *Naked Lunch*." In *NakedLunch@50*, edited by Oliver Harris and Ian MacFadyen, 56–64. Carbondale: Southern Illinois University Press.

Koestenbaum, Wayne. 1989. *Double Talk: The Erotics of Male Literary Collaboration*. New York: Routledge.

Miles, Barry. 1993. *William Burroughs: El Hombre Invisible: A Portrait*. New York: Hyperion.

Morgan, Ted. 1988. *Literary Outlaw: The Life and Times of William S. Burroughs*. New York: Henry Holt.

Weiss, Jason, ed. 2001. *Back in No Time: The Brion Gysin Reader*. Middletown, CT: Wesleyan University Press.

Space/Time

How permissive is the "permissive society"? A hundred years ago the right of a citizen to the privacy of his own home was unquestioned. Now it has virtually been abolished. According to the new No-Knock drug bill in the United States cops can break anyone's door down at any hour of the day or night. Nor is it specified in the bill that they must come in at the door. They can crash through a sky light or ride a bulldozer through the wall to reveal perhaps a sex scene between consenting adults . . .

—Burroughs, "The Permissive Society," 1971, Berg 3.12. Copyright © by William Burroughs, used by permission of The Wylie Agency LLC.

Class and individual difference, deliberately accentuated and exploited by vested interests, have brought the West to a state of chaos and disaster. What is being done in the West on an official level has no chance of working.

—Burroughs, "On China," 1969, Berg 62.3. Copyright © by William Burroughs, used by permission of The Wylie Agency LLC.

However remember this: threatened by a block that could vote them out of office they will resort as always to naked force. So stop using drugs. Learn karate. Learn guerilla war tactics. You must be prepared to meet force with force if necessary; to fight in the streets with Molotov cocktails, home made infrasound, cross bows, machetes, any weapons you can devise. I am not advocating the over throw of the U.S. government by force. I am advocating its overthrow by its own legal machinery. If the people now in power attempt to hold their position by illegal force then you will have to fight or submit to a degree of control beside which 1984 is liberal and permissive.

—Burroughs, "P.S. to ACADEMY 23 & NEWSWEEK Picture," 1967, Berg 31.39. Copyright © by William Burroughs, used by permission of The Wylie Agency LLC.

Tangier is barely endurable. I only live here because other places are even less so. No point traveling. Its one dead world. Like we used to say in the 1920s only way now is to make your own fun.

—William S. Burroughs, "Letter to 'Dobs,'" 1964, Berg 88.2. Copyright © by William Burroughs, used by permission of The Wylie Agency LLC.

Burroughs Looking at the Sky in Lawrence, Kansas, Allen Ginsberg, May 28, 1991. Ginsberg wrote the following caption to his photograph: "W.S. Burroughs at rest in the side yard of his house looking at the sky, empty timeless Lawrence Kansas May 28, 1991." Courtesy of the Allen Ginsberg Estate.

6

Burroughs and the Biosphere, 1974–1997

KATHELIN GRAY

I discovered *Naked Lunch* when I was fourteen. While babysitting, I excavated a copy hidden behind other books on a shelf and read as the kids slept. Such a radical exposé of power. Some years later, the opportunity finally arrived to meet the author:

> *William S. Burroughs*
> *c/o Grove Press*
> *June 17, 1974*
> *Dear Mr. Burroughs,*
> *Since you are one of the foremost living explorers and scientists of the English language, I write this letter inviting you to New Mexico July 21–28 as a guest speaker of the Institute of Ecotechnics on the subject of lingua-technics, to open a week of study on the subject. This would include a morning jam with the members of the Institute and a lecture on a subject of your choice in the evening in our geodesic dome. The afternoon is open for whatever comes up. If you wish to see anything in the area, we can take you there.*
>
> *For this, we will pay your round trip transportation, accommodations here at our ranch and a fee. We can afford up to $200; there are about thirty people full time at the Institute and perhaps as many more would attend the event which will not be open to the general public. By the way, we are not connected with any state, church, or foundation money and are strictly independent.*
> *I wait for your answer,*
> *Ecce homo sapiens sapiens!*
>
> *Salty Hoffman,*
> *Department of Psychotechnics, Institute of Ecotechnics*
> *Director, Theater of All Possibilities*

William Burroughs accepted the invitation to our first Institute of Ecotechnics conference in Santa Fe, New Mexico (Salty Hoffman, my then-pseudonym). I went to pick him up at the airport, but at first I couldn't find him among the

Dr. Hank Truby, Kathelin Gray, Burroughs, and friends. Ecotechnics at Synergia Ranch, Santa Fe, New Mexico, 1974. Courtesy © Institute of Ecotechnics 1974, 2016.

disembarking passengers. Oh, wait, he must be that Southwest geologist, a bit too perfectly outfitted for the role. On the drive to the ranch, we stopped and picked up vodka, Coca-Cola, and ice. Then the car had a flat tire, which he changed, much to the subsequent amazement of his buddies. On the walk to his room, he combed the landscape for a stick to use as a dowsing rod and commented that later he wanted to visit the pigs who were squealing in their wallow nearby.

We paused on the stroll. "Mr. Burroughs, what would you like me to call you?" "Please call me William." "William, I have read your books and I must know: What is your attitude towards women?" Stock still and looking straight into my eyes, he replied, "I killed the only woman I ever loved." He took a sharp in-breath, then tears began to stream from his eyes. He sobbed as he whispered about Joan Vollmer, his wife he had accidentally shot some twenty-five years earlier. This was before he had written about the incident in his introduction to *Queer*. I held and comforted him. We didn't return to the subject again—that is, not until 1982, but

Ecotechnics' Planet Earth Conference, 1980, Aix-en-Provence. William S. Burroughs and William S. Burroughs with Dr. Paul Rotmil, Karolinska Institute; Rotmil worked on small-pox eradication. Background is the backdrop of *Deconstruction of the Countdown*, a Theatre of All Possibilities' play based on the writings of Burroughs and Brion Gysin. Photos courtesy © Institute of Ecotechnics 1980, 2016.

Planet Earth Conference, 1980, Aix-en-Provence. Burroughs, top row second from right. Brion Gysin, top row left. Courtesy © Institute of Ecotechnics 1980, 2016.

that is another story. William delivered a brilliant speech the following day and became an honorary fellow of the Institute and a lifelong friend.

He always asked about the progress of Ecotechnics' projects and visited several of them. These have included an oceanographic research ship, a tropical forestry project, a theater and jazz club, a cultural center and art gallery, and a Himalayan hotel. The largest in scale and most public of our projects was the Biosphere 2 ecological laboratory in Arizona. In 1990, as the construction of the massive 3.14-acre sealed structure of Biosphere 2 was underway, Burroughs visited. "I think there's going to be more and more merging of art and science. Scientists are already studying the creative process, and I think the whole line between art and science will break down and that scientists, I hope, will become more creative and writers more scientific" (Burroughs and Gysin 1978, 7).

He spoke at two Ecotechnics conferences. That first 1974 speech, "Language as a Tool of Control," addressed the Mayan codices as an example of control of the many by the few. Hank Truby, the eminent linguist, also spoke. Truby worked with dolphins, studying interspecies communication, and was also an expert in subvocal speech. Both subjects fascinated Burroughs.

His 1980 speech at Ecotechnics' Planet Earth Conference in Aix-en-Provence, "The Four Horsemen of the Apocalypse," concerned the evolution of weaponry.

His sole graphic was a series of chalk marks on the blackboard, really a series of ever-larger phallic symbols, tracing the history of weaponry from the slingshot and the blow gun to rifles, to the Atomic Bomb.

Other speakers at the conference included the explorer Thor Heyerdahl; the founder of the Club of Rome, Dr. Alexander King; Sir Ghillean Prance of Kew Gardens and New York Botanical Gardens; James Hayes, Earth and Environmental Scientist at Lamont Doherty Earth Observatory, a research unit of Columbia University; and legendary paleoclimate and sand-sea geologist, Dr. Edwin D. McKee, USGS.

During this conference, Burroughs announced he had decided on the title of his next book: *The Place of Dead Roads*, the second in a trilogy, after *Cities of the Red Night* and before *The Western Lands*. The bleak conclusion of many speeches on the state of planetary ecology, he said, inspired the title.

In her introduction to *Word Virus: The William Burroughs Reader*, Ann Douglas writes that, "even the most hallucinatory inventions of his imagination are grounded in hard, clear, powerfully analytic and authoritative thought" (1998, xviii).

A WAR UNIVERSE

Burroughs was born in 1914, a few months before the start of The War to End All Wars, which not only did not end wars, but aggravated new aggressions, new occupations, and new colonizations, and set the stage for many future wars.

War accelerated the development of science and technology. Mysteries of the brain were clarified by studying the effects of gunshot wounds to the head. Code-cracking funded the evolution of computation. Funding is/was an issue: science and technology, in thrall to profiteers, accelerated the War on Nature, and created the zero-sum ecological processes that are upon us.

Also circa 1914, farmers in the Great Plains began to plow up grasslands for large-scale wheat farms. This accelerated after World War I, with government support. Exporting wheat to Europe was seen as a means of warding off the threat of communism. Anchoring prairie root structures were shredded, and when this coincided with dry years, disaster ensued. Great droughts began while Burroughs attended high school. Topsoil, soaring from his homeland in the Great Plains, trailed him like a sorcerer's inky cape as he headed off to Harvard in 1932.

Burroughs arrived in Vienna in 1936 to study medicine and occupied a flat not far from Freud's residence, but curiously never encountered him. Just before the *Anschlüss*, Burroughs fled Vienna in 1937 (Freud in 1938) and married his friend Ilse Klapper, saving her from the Holocaust.

In World War II, far-flung battles trashed sea bottoms with junk from sunken aircraft carriers and bombers. Skeletons littered pristine jungle. Burroughs' vagrant-junky phase began at the time of Hiroshima and Nagasaki; his inner struggles mirrored those of the world at large. The War on Nature had begun with the development of agriculture in Sumer; yet in the twentieth century, the perversity of the Depression, the Dust Bowl, and the World Wars ramped up quickly and inexorably to the greatest human catastrophe ever devised, the Atomic Bomb.

Dr. Robert Oppenheimer ("Oppie") had selected William's former camp, the Los Alamos Ranch School for Boys, for Project Y, the site of the Los Alamos Nuclear Laboratory. The Pajarito Plateau of Los Alamos was the perfect place to build a weapon of mass destruction: its natural wonder stood serene, remote from population centers. The School for Boys had a large complex of buildings, all adjacent to federal land. And, just over an hour south, in the mining town of Madrid, high-grade coal proved ideal to fuel the huge energy requirements of bomb-building.

WAR DEPARTMENT
WASHINGTON
[DEC 1942]
Mr. A. J. Connell
President and Director
Los Alamos Ranch School
Espanola, New Mexico

Dear Sir:
You are advised that it has been determined necessary to the interests of the United States in the prosecution of the War that the property of the Los Alamos Ranch School be acquired for military purposes.

Therefore, pursuant to existing law, a condemnation proceeding will be instituted in the United States District Court for the District of New Mexico to acquire all of the school's lands and buildings, together with all personal property owned by the school and used in connection with its operation. Although the acquisition of this property is of the utmost importance in the prosecution of the war, it has been determined that it will not be necessary for you to surrender complete possession of the premises until February 8, 1943. It is felt that this procedure will enable you to complete the first term of the regular school year without interruption.

You are further advised that all records pertaining to the aforesaid condemnation proceeding will be sealed, by order of the Court, and public inspection of such records will be prohibited. Accordingly, it is requested that you refrain from making the reasons for the closing of the school known to the public at large.

Sincerely Yours,
[Henry Stimson]
Secretary of War.

FACING TOP, *Photo: Los Alamos Ranch School Big House.* U.S. Department of Energy.

FACING BOTTOM, *Photo: Valle Caldera.* NASA Earth Observatory.

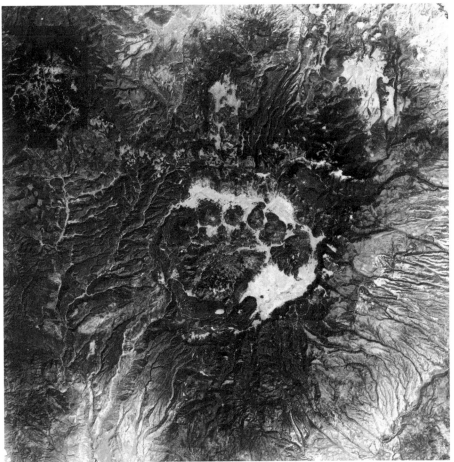

On that idyllic site, scientists and engineers exercised their genius to build "The Gadget" (the Bomb). There's a cosmic joke here. Los Alamos is the site of one of the seven super volcanoes in the world. About 1.4 million years ago, a super-eruption blasted massive amounts of *tuff* from its subterranean storage basin, creating the New Mexico Valles Caldera, thirteen miles in diameter. Its circular ring fractures create a bullseye pattern that can be seen from the air.

The two-thousand-year-old Hindu epic, *Mahabharata*, relates an ancestral battle. Within this work, the *Bhagavad Gita* is a poetic interlude, a commentary on the nature of war, death, life, duty, and the cosmos. When Oppenheimer was asked what it was like when he witnessed the myriad-sunned Trinity blast, as a Sanskrit scholar, he quoted the *Gita*, using an idiosyncratic translation of the word *kaal* in chapter 11 (*Visvarupa–Darsana Yoga*). The god, Krishna/Vishnu, reveals himself to the warrior Arjuna in a display of infinite forms, simultaneously manifesting all aspects of cosmos. Arjuna pleads to Vishnu to return to a simpler, less terrifying, manifestation.

Oppenheimer's reply rendered the Sanskrit word *kaal* as death, instead of time (*kaalo asmi loke kshayakrit pravraddho, lokaan samaahartum iha pvarrttah*). His reply: "I have become Death, the Destroyer of Worlds," instead of "I have become Time, the Destroyer of Worlds." *Kaal* is time/death; time itself leaves all life behind. In our (illusory) world of biological timelines, time and death are interlinked. In his answer, instead of referring to Time itself as the Grim Reaper, Oppenheimer emphasized the dizzying new destructive powers of humanity that he helped unleash. With this launch of the nuclear age, humanity attained a godlike capacity to destroy, but not the capacity for creation or renewal.

In the boundless philosophical universe of the *Gita*, any boundary is a death, an interruption, a stop; biological time has birth-death cycles but, in the *Gita*, that is illusory. There is no birth, there is no death, in a larger context. Paradoxically, Burroughs himself would come to this way of thinking about time, life, death, later in life.

During Burroughs' 1974 trip to the conference in Santa Fe, I had the opportunity to drive him to the site of Los Alamos School for Boys. He wanted to revisit adolescent memories in the landscape of his summers in Northern New Mexico. At camp, he had awakened to his amorous attraction to males and had his first (underage) drink at the bar of Santa Fe's La Fonda Hotel.

What occupied William's mind during our trip, besides memories of trials and tribulations of school life, was the Holocaust, the mechanization of war, and most of all, the Atomic Bomb, with its Dr. Strangelove lure to *press press press the button*. It is no surprise that he would want to deconstruct the countdown from which no one is immune, an inevitable *Nova* explosion of nuclear war and implosion via biomic collapse. A TKO—technical knock-out. This is a war universe. War all the time. That is its nature. There may be other universes based on all sorts of other principles, but ours seems to be based on war and games. All games are basically hostile. Winners and losers. We see them all around us: the winners and the losers. The losers can oftentimes become winners, and the winners can very easily become losers" (Foye and Burroughs, "The War Universe" *Grand Street* No. 37, 1991, n.p.)

The eighteenth-century Lisbon earthquake and subsequent tsunamis reminded European society that humans are powerless in the face of geogenic catastrophes. That massive seismic shake-up set off an extended philosophical discourse on Leibniz's views of theodicy and the nature of evil. The twentieth-century's World Wars, climaxing with the Atomic Bomb, were the first catastrophes created by mankind on the scale of geologic events, occasioning even more desperate and penetrating investigations of human nature.

ACTIVISM

In 1973, shortly before my 1974 meeting with Burroughs, the wife of F. Sherwood Rowland, Nobel Prize winner in Chemistry, asked him how his day had been working in his lab on the connection between chlorofluorocarbons and ozone depletion. His famous answer could be from a Burroughs' character: "The work is going very well. But it may mean the end of the world." As in Burroughs' 1980 speech, humans are in thrall to the Four Horsemen of the Apocalypse, and they are having their way with our Mother—Earth.

MULTIPHRENICS

To do his bit to put the brakes on man-made disasters, Burroughs conducted a no-holds-barred deconstruction of psychologies and power structures, in the time-honored scientific tradition of self-experimentation. He sought more effective methods to heal human psyches than the medical establishment could offer to him personally to heal sickness, nightmares, murder, addiction, and the Evil Spirit within. His many psycho-neurological quests included psychoanalysis, apomorphine, yagé, sweat lodges, writing itself, Scientology, Mayan and Pharonic texts, and the works of Wilhelm Reich, Alfred Kinsey, Richard Evans Schultes, Francis Huxley, and Buckminster Fuller.

Burroughs' novels describe a planet constantly under attack by sadomasochists and Imps of the Perverse. His early experience with Freudian analysis revealed to him that many characters coexist on the inside, obvious to students of acting and help to a future writer, who must bring these characters to life. Diverging from Freud, he came to believe that these alternate identities do not reside in a dark closet of unconsciousness; the gorilla in the room leers boldly at the vigilant, in ever-relocating interstices of attention. Cut-ups can reveal the demons lurking between the lines, at-the-ready in the invisible ink of headlines.

Dream states reside in the hazy borderlands of consciousness. Burroughs came to understand that in the spectrum of "waking" states attention flickers, and subliminal influences wield unsuspected power, much like bodysnatching. Subliminal words and images flash through constant cut-ups of everyday consciousness via discontinuity of attention. Subliminal vulnerability is not an exceptional state, it is the nature of the mind, a constant.

His characters are not who they seem, let alone claim to be, but schizoid, even multiphrenic. In auditory hallucinations, one part of the brain repeats formulations that influence behavior directed by another part of the brain. Who is who? Who works for whom? What intentions are actually at play? Baits and switches pop in his bop-noir riffs. "Help" can be, via disguise or the law of unintended consequences, death itself. Is it scientist Winkhorst or channeled Nova Mob bodysnatcher, Hamburger Mary, who speaks?

Humans are not unities, but psychic clouds, multiplicities.

About *Cities of the Red Night*, Paul Meisel wrote ("Gunslinger in a Time Warp") "Kim and his band are almost as unlovable as the space gangs opposing them. Indeed, this shifting vortex of a world is so unstable that the very maintenance of personal identity is almost impossible . . . (Kim) shifted his identity ten times in the course of a day" (1984).

In 2015, October Gallery, London, held its second solo exhibition of Burroughs' art. Ecotechnics hosted a "Burroughs and Science" cabaret salon, wherein a number of scientists discussed concepts that wove through his literary work. Neuroscientist Daniel Glaser moderated a sci-art cabaret that included zoologist Lucy Cooke; Jack Cohen, reproductive biologist, who mused on speculative sexuality and body forms of alien species; neuroscientist Nillie Lavie, who introduced the "perceptual load theory" of attention that features in passages such as the Winkhorst monologues; molecular geneticist Aarathi Prasad, who spoke on parthenogenesis; and experimental psychologist and visual psychophysicist, Joshua Solomon, who explored the pervasive workings of subliminal suggestion, even a character, the Subliminal Kid.

> Cut-ups make explicit a psychosensory process that is going on all the time anyway. Somebody is reading a newspaper, and his eye follows the column in the proper Aristotelian manner, one idea and sentence at a time. But subliminally he is reading the columns on either side and is aware of the person sitting next to him. That's a cut-up. Most people don't see what's going on around them. That's my principal message to writers: For Godsake, keep your eyes open. Notice what's going on around you. I mean, I walk down the street with friends. I ask, "Did you see him, that person who just walked by?" No they didn't notice him. (Burroughs 1965)

The cut-up technique flows from film montage, from the Dadaists, from Joyce, from Eliot's program of distributing lines from earlier poets among his verses, from a literal interpretation of Ezra Pound's Imagist poetics. Cut out. Mark up. Hermeneutics is zigzagged. Burroughs credits the influence of John Dos Passos's *USA Trilogy*, which incorporated newspaper clippings. Cut-ups were in the historical ether. Julio Cortázar (like Burroughs, born in 1914) used cut-up techniques in his

Research vessel Heraclitus, *Peru.* Courtesy © Institute of Ecotechnics 1980, 2016.

experimental detective novel of 1963, *Hopscotch*, without any connection between Burroughs and Cortázar, even when they populated the same haunts at the same time in late 1950s Paris.

VEGETABLE TIMESPACE

> *This is the most powerful drug I have ever experienced. That is, it produces the most complete derangement of the senses . . . I have observed in using both yagé and Peyote: a strange, vegetable consciousness, an identification with the plant. In Peyote intoxication everything looks like a Peyote plant. It is easy to understand how the Indians came to believe there is a spirit in these plants. (Burroughs 2006)*

Edgar Allan Poe suggested that space and time are one. In his poem/essay, *Eureka*, Poe demonstrates not only an interest in but also a contemplation of space, time, and gravity in the scientific thought of his day. Einstein called it the work of an independent mind. *Eureka* was dedicated to the geographer, explorer, and naturalist, Alexander von Humboldt, who, with botanist Aimé-Jacques Bonpland, were the first Western scientists to investigate the pharmacopeia of Amazonas. Burroughs belongs squarely in the literary *genus* of Poe, and perhaps not by chance were both of them influenced by Amazonian explorer/scientists.

Early readings of the nineteenth-century botanist, Richard Spruce, inspired Burroughs' expedition to the Amazon. Perhaps he could finally come to terms with the Dark Spirit within by contact with shamans and psychoactive plants. But old sins have long shadows; he would find that his accidental shooting of Joan would torture him for the rest of his life.

Burroughs attempted to extract the active ingredient of the storied psycho-tropic concoction, yagé, at the Botanical Institute of the Universidad Nacional de Colombia in Bogotá. In *The Letters of William S. Burroughs (1945–1959)*, Oliver Harris points out that, in 1953, Burroughs accomplished "the first real botanical achievement in the scientific appraisal of *ayahuasca* since Richard Spruce's seminal work in the 1850's. Burroughs was the first to identify the genus [of *Rubiaceaea*] now classified as *Psychotria viridis*" (1993, 11). Andrew Lees, in *Mentored by a Mad-man*, observes that Burroughs had not only collected *Psychotria viridis* in 1967, but correctly infers that it was an additive in *ayahuasca*, along with *Banisteria caapi*. Burroughs was thrilled when the Ecotechnic Institute's research ship *Heraclitus* motored 2,000 miles to Peru in 1981 in an expedition urged on by his old acquaintance and fellow Harvard alumnus, the renowned ethnobotanist Richard Evans Schultes.

With yagé, Burroughs had the impression of telepathic contact, a preternatural compassion, a theme that ran throughout his life. I queried physicist Robert Turner (founder of the Max Planck Institute for Human Cognitive and Brain Sciences), about anecdotes of telepathy, as when you awaken from a dream that your grand-mother has died, and that morning you get the call confirming it occurred. Turner replied, succinctly: "Compassion is greatly understudied."

Before he tired of the academic world and launched his saga of self-experimentation, Burroughs studied at Columbia and Harvard. Anthropology, linguistics, psychology, animal welfare, physics, evolutionary biology, and more— all were serious hobbies, and in some cases, focused investigations. In 1953, in Rome, he re-read H. G. Wells and found *The Time Machine* resonated with his experience with yagé as space-time travel, communing with ancestors whilst ex-periencing the future. Perhaps it was the yagé trips that confirmed to him the pos-sibility of extradimensional travel as a reality in the Space Age. After all, we have neurotransmitters evolved in parallel with psychotropic plants. Why might they not be physiological clues to our next evolutionary stage?

J. W. Dunne was an important aeronautics engineer and an inventor. His 1927 book, *An Experiment with Time*, profoundly influenced not only Burroughs but also Jorge Luis Borges and J. B. Priestley. Travel in the fourth dimension and non-Euclidean higher dimensions were quite the topics in the nineteenth and twentieth centuries. Dostoyevsky, Twain, Proust, Conrad, Ouspensky, even Oscar Wilde used multidimensional devices.

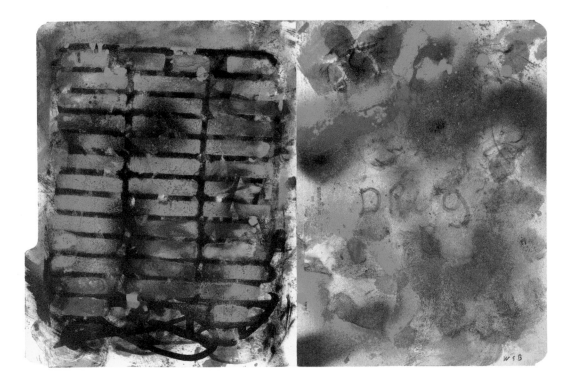

Untitled, William S. Burroughs, ca. 1992. Ink and spray paint on file folder, 30 × 48 cm. Courtesy © William S. Burroughs Trust.

Dunne also paid particular attention to the correlation between dreaming and everyday occurrences. He kept a dream journal, which became a key practice for Burroughs, who shared Dunne's interests in telepathy, synchronicity, and the nature of time. Burroughs' lifelong fascination with dimensionality piqued his interest in Amazonian shamanic plant talk, ayahuasca, or *yagé*.

> The Soft Machine: A Russian scientist has said: "We will travel not only in space but in time as well"—I have just returned from a thousand-year time trip and I am here to tell you what I saw—and to tell you how such time trips are made—It is a precise operation—It is difficult—It is dangerous—It is the new frontier and only the adventurous need apply—But it belongs to anyone who has the courage and know-how to enter—It belongs to you—(Burroughs 1965; Packer and Jordan 2001, 294–95)

HUMAN SPACETIME

For years, publishers marketed Burroughs' novels as science fiction. He was a self-described cosmonaut of inner space and an enthusiast for (outer) space travel. Much as the armchair-bound Jules Verne inspired many scientists, explorers, and inventors, Burroughs inspired the theater that John Allen, Marie Harding, and I founded in 1967, Theatre of All Possibilities. Burroughs encouraged us to pursue

First crew of Biospherians, 1991. Courtesy © Institute of Ecotechnics.

a "mythology for the space age." Theatre of All Possibilities was the artistic companion organization to Institute of Ecotechnics and also served as a tool to experientially understand decision-making processes throughout history, a kind of psychological simulation laboratory. "Man is an artefact designed for space travel. He is not designed to remain in his present biologic state any more than a tadpole is designed to remain a tadpole" (Burroughs 1985, 105).

There are many barriers to human adaptation to space travel, especially long-duration colonies or deep-space exploration. These include bone demineralization, muscular atrophy, and alteration of control mechanisms of the autonomic nervous system, cardiac function, and peripheral vasculature. Other problems of microgravity include slowing of cardiovascular rhythm; barotrauma or trauma in the air cavities such as sinus and ear due to varying barometric pressures; lowered T-cell level in the immune system combined with acceleration of growth of microbial populations—the "aliens amongst us"; deterioration of eyesight due to intracranial and intra-ocular pressure variations during flight. Differences in atmosphere and gravity make it hard for cosmonauts to hear and speak understandably. Spinal problems can persist after re-entry and lower-back pain is frequently experienced throughout life, caused by atrophy of proprioceptive muscle spindles surrounding the spine. Our bodies are part of this planet's specific biosphere.

"I compare [space travel adaptation] to the transition from water to land of the various transitional species. The astronauts haven't gone into space—that is,

Burroughs at Biosphere 2, 1990. Photo by Jose Ferez Kuri courtesy Kathelin Gray and THEATRRR. Photo used with permission.

they've gone to space in an Aqualung. There has to be a link; there had to be an air-breathing potential among these creatures before they made the transition. If there wasn't, it was simply suicide. I see that dreams are the lifeline to our possible biological and spiritual destiny. Dreams sometimes approximate space conditions. That's what The Western Lands is about" (Fox 1986).

Burroughs expands the significance of dreams beyond circadian repose, to the aim and purpose of human individuality and society. Australian aboriginals' ancestral Dreamtime is not an abstraction, but a very real parallel reality, an in-process world yet to be realized in phenomena. The Dreaming is embodied in life-giving subterranean water reservoirs. To Burroughs, dreaming itself is an obvious yet veiled clue to the next step in human evolution . . . the biosphere murmuring to us, intimating secrets of physiological transition to space travel. A bit more astral, a lot less Arrested Development. "The first step towards Space exploration was to examine the human artefact with biologic alterations in mind that would render our human artefact more suitable for Space conditions and Space travel. Now, we are like water creatures: looking up from here at the earth and the air, and wondering how we can survive in that alien medium. Fish didn't have the capacity to do that: we do" (Burroughs 1980).

In our 1991–1994 ecological systems laboratory experiments in Arizona, Biosphere 2, eight people were sealed in a mini-world, with the objective of studying the interactions of natural systems and to help anticipate what would be necessary

The Last Rocket Out, William S. Burroughs, 1992. Paint on paper, 58.4 × 44.5 cm.
Courtesy © William S. Burroughs Trust.

to maintain long-term regenerative life systems in space exploration and colonization. It was a symbiosis of biospherics, technics, culture, and dreams.

William faxed us on September 26, 1991, at the commencement of the first experiment at Biosphere 2:

TO: John Allen, Kathelin Hoffman Gray
and the intrepid Biospherians of BIOSPHERE II
Oracle, Arizona

I salute the eight brave Biospherians who embark today on this noble experiment. The Closing of Biosphere II is a turning point in human history, and a step in the right direction towards the development of mankind's potential. The hopes of the Planet go with you into inner space, for the sake of the dream of outer space. And to those who ask you "Quo vadis?," tell them: "Ad Astra per aspera!"

With all our best wishes always,

William S. Burroughs
James Grauerholz
Steven Lowe

Biosphere 2 was a bonsai Earth, a world in a bottle. As in other mesocosms, metabolic cycling was accelerated inside. The CO_2 cycled 250–500 times faster in B2. Water in the B2 ocean and marsh cycled 1,000 times faster than in natural biomes. Results came quicker, cycles thus became in some ways easier to study. This venture into Time was recognized by the venerable Explorers' Club, which issues flags for expeditions that further the cause of exploration and field science. In hundreds of expeditions since 1918, flags have been carried to both poles, to Everest, and on oceanic and outer space voyages. The Club issued one of its flags for the Biosphere 2 experiment.

MASS EXTINCTION

Burroughs underwent sporadic periods of psychotherapy for decades, once from Leo Federn, a student of Freud's. During these years of analysis, he discovered distinct characters hidden in his own psyche. Joseph Moncure March's 1928 narrative poem, *The Wild Party*, inspired Burroughs to write. In drag, Burroughs could have just as well played March's central character, "Queenie."

Burroughs fell in love with the percussive bop-talk of the noir detective à la Dashiell Hammett, Raymond Chandler, and John O'Hara. After Sherlock Holmes, the private eye was typecast as a brilliant and conflicted character. Sam Spade dispensed with Sherlock's discursive academics. Burroughs extended the genre with Lee, an Inspector who plays fast and loose with the truth. Why not? when, there are so *many* truths. . . . Which one and whose? There is no direct access to

Research vessel Heraclitus. Photo courtesy © Institute of Ecotechnics 1995, 2016.

reality. Facts are easily reinterpreted as their opposite, in an escapist regression. But paradoxically, you cannot always lie completely. There will be a "tell" in some manifestation, in some timescale, to be discovered by the discerning mind.

Burroughs' passion for deconstruction of language led him to correlate cultures and ecology, value systems and ground-truth. He exposed language as a control system, for him an ecological imperative. Irreplaceable knowledges of "people of place," based on millennia of experience, is being lost at a scale equivalent to deforestation of the Amazon, and being replaced by Orwellian doublespeak's fake facts. The extinction of indigenous languages creates ecological crises.

Burroughs was deeply alarmed by the tenuous existence of so many species on this planet and of his precious lemurs in particular. They embody the essence of his idols, amongst those rare creatures who "mind their own business."

Destroy its habitat—so what? They're not cute pets, they don't contribute to human society, so what "good" are they? He adored these elegant prosimian creatures with large, poignant eyes. Standing two-legged, they nimbly kangaroo-hop across the landscape and soar gracefully from tree to tree like elite gymnasts, long furry tails held aloft. Leap, hop, soar, scamper, gallop. Some of the sixty species sing ghostly arias reminiscent of whale songs; others are exuberant dancers with a fetching two-step.

Burn Unit, William S. Burroughs, 1982. Spray paint on paper.
Courtesy © William S. Burroughs Trust

In 1989, after a decades-long interest in lemurs, Burroughs traveled to North Carolina to visit the lemur sanctuary at Duke University Primate Center. For the first time, he was able to experience them close-up and to learn more about this threatened species. In his book *Ghost of Chance* he included a fundraising appeal for the Duke Center. A much more productive activity than *philanthropy* is *philecology* (Biosphere 2's John Allen coined the word): the love of ecology, to replace philanthropy, the love of humans, and a reminder to stop humanity's war on life, the mass extinction of species.

We included a lemur in Biosphere 2. I muse that his vision of pirate utopia, *Ghost of Chance*, was partly inspired by our research vessel *Heraclitus*, which circa 1989, at the time Burroughs wrote the book, was docked in Belize, historically a safe haven for pirates. Ecotechnics was studying mangroves, and indeed our eclectic crew looked like pirates. Indeed they were ecologists. William always asked for updates on our ship's activities; we built it in 1974 shortly after meeting. He related to the epic nature of our voyage.

¿QUIÉN ES?

In Amazonian and North American forests, millennia-old human actions have historically enhanced diversity and fertility. Ancient arboreal societies in the Amazon cultivated cacao and cashew, still in the forest ecology today. Yet now, humans denude the forest, accelerating global warming. "Only Homo sap kills for the sheer ugliness of it, just to roll around in *ugliness*" (Burroughs, quoted in Fox 1986, emphasis in original).

Humanity is, at every turn, vulnerable to body-snatching. Are we spies in our own bodies, like Inspector Lee? Humanity is subject to invasion by viral thought-forms, verbal sequences, subliminal suggestion, suggestion, and diffracted attention, overpowered by mechanical and cultural prostheses. Billy the Kid's last words echo through *The Place of Dead Roads*: ¿Quién es? (Who is it? Who's there?). We are composed of so much "other" in mind and body that individuals might as well dispense with "I," there is no such thing, and replace "I" with "We."

MAGIC IS THAT WHICH WORKS

> All of my work is directed to those who are bent, whether by stupidity or design, on blowing up the planet or making it uninhabitable. I'm concerned with the precise manipulation of word and image to create an action, not to go out and buy a Coca-Cola, but to create an alteration in the reader's consciousness. (Burroughs 1965)

Burroughs tested methods to affect the material world: repetition, evoking archetypes, and manipulating simulacrums. These, he posits, disrupt the illusion of a linear flow of time, an artist's reading of Heisenberg's Uncertainty Principle. Not just casual observation, but *scrutiny* of a phenomenon can disrupt its integrity. His experiments in montage anecdotally confirmed this to his satisfaction.

His technique was classic Magick: through the manipulation of an object's true name and patterns, one manipulates the object itself. The word and the world operate by the same laws. In Alfred Korzybski's theory of General Semantics, figurative language has a power over the material world. The idea that the inner and outer worlds operate by the same laws is accepted by many native peoples, who typically do not allow photography or drawings during their sacred ceremonies or utterance of songs and prayers out of context.

Korzybski's *Science and Sanity* (1958) introduced the idea that humans are "time-binding," by communicating across generations via language. In 1939, Burroughs carried out in-depth studies of Korzybski's "silent level," a prerequisite for achieving neurological delay, key in perceptual clarity. Burroughs went on to explore this in typically idiosyncratic and personal ways, exhaustively via Scientology and his experimental maneuvers with Ian Sommerville, Anthony Balch, and Brion Gysin. No one is immune from The Word. Rub it out before it *gits ya*.

He was interested in the truth of will, where nothing happens that is not willed. Writers live in this magical universe. One definition of magic is "that which works."

I knocked on Burroughs' Lawrence, Kansas, door one day in 1994. He opened the door and exclaimed boisterously: "I'm a Healer, I'm a Healer!" After lunch, he confided, correctly as it turned out, that my then boyfriend would be forever free of the cancer that had plagued him. William had consulted his radionics gizmo that he called the Wishing Machine, which he used for scrying and for sending healing beams to needy friends and animals.

Burroughs' central passion for ecology and science fuelled his interest in language as a control system, juxtaposition of image and word, experimental ontology, and "magic" of nonlinear/multiple causalities. He worked to make these techniques available in order to deconstruct cultural impulses which create ecological catastrophes we careen into.

At the core of Burroughs' work is his belief in the vital magic, resilience, exuberance of the biosphere, spontaneous, complex, alive. Science-based technology extends our potential for learning and action, but we should also pay attention to subtle, elegant technologies, both artistic and ancient.

"We're here to learn, we're here to go, it's the same thing" (private conversation 1997).

An earlier version of this essay appeared in the *Los Angeles Review of Books*, May 20, 2018. https://lareviewofbooks.org/article/william-s-burroughs-and-the -biosphere-1974-1997/.

KATHELIN GRAY is a producer, director, writer, curator, and artist. She was a founder of the Institute of Ecotechnics in 1970 (incorporated in London in 1985) of which she is a director. She is a consultant to the William S. Burroughs Trust.

REFERENCES

Burroughs, William S. 1965. "William S. Burroughs and the Art of Fiction." Interview by Conrad Knickerbocker, *Paris Review* 36 (Fall). https://www.theparisreview.org/interviews/4424/william-s-burroughs-the-art-of-fiction-no-36-william-s-burroughs/. Republished in Randall Packer and Ken Jordan. 2001. *Multimedia: From Wagner to Virtual Reality.* New York: W. W. Norton.

———. 1980. "The Four Horsemen of the Apocalypse." Ecotechnics Planet Earth Conference, December 13, 1980. Aix-en-Provence, France.

———. 1985. *The Adding Machine.* London: Calder.

———. 1995. *Ghost of a Chance.* New York: High Risk Books.

———. 2006. *The Yage Letters Redux.* San Francisco: City Lights.

Burroughs, William S., and Brion Gysin. 1978. *The Third Mind.* New York: Viking.

Douglas, Ann. 1998. "Punching a Hole in the Big Lie: The Achievement of William S. Burroughs." In *Word Virus: The William S. Burroughs Reader,* edited by James Grauerholz and Ira Silverberg, xv–xxx. New York: Grove.

Fox, James. 1986. "William Burroughs: Return of the Invisible." *Rolling Stone,* October 23. http://www.rollingstone.com/culture/features/the-return-of-the-invisible-man-19861023.

Foye, Raymond, and William S. Burroughs. 1991. "The War Universe." *Grand Street,* no. 37: 92–108.

Harris, Oliver. 1993. "Introduction." In *The Letters of William S. Burroughs Vol. 1: 1945–1959,* edited and with an introduction by Oliver Harris. New York: Penguin, 1993.

Ginsberg, Allen. 1974. "Fragment of an Interview with Allen Ginsberg." *Berkeley Barb,* January 7. https://realitystudio.org/interviews/1974-ginsberg-re-burroughs/.

Kodish, Bruce I. 2014. "Chapter 50—The August Initiative." Korzybski Files. http://korzybskifiles.blogspot.com/2015/02/chapter-50-august-intensive.html.

Korzybski, Alfred. 1958. *Science and Sanity: An Introduction to Non-Aristotelian Systems and General Semantics.* 5th ed. Brooklyn, NY: Institute of General Semantics.

Meisel, Paul. 1984. "Gunslinger in a Time Warp." *The New York Times,* February 19. https://archive.nytimes.com/www.nytimes.com/books/00/02/13/specials/burroughs-place.html.

Odier, Daniel. 1969. *The Job: Interviews with William S. Burroughs.* New York: Penguin.

The Permissive Society

In this 1971 essay, Burroughs engages with the Nixonian concept of the "permissive society," taking a markedly Foucauldian attitude toward the machinations of power in the post–World War II period. Burroughs makes explicit in this essay a series of arguments that hark back to his earliest writings, from his distrust of the redemptive potential of communication in *Junky* (1953) to his prophetic visions of biopower in *Naked Lunch* (1959). *Naked Lunch*'s parodic portrayal of Sweden in the allegorical city of Freeland offers a model case study.

The concept of the permissive society dates back to the end of World War II, after the downfall of authoritarian regimes, but it's usually associated with the social and sexual revolutions of the 1960s in Europe and America. While Nixon would also use the term to wage his drug war in the early 1970s, Burroughs' asymmetrical resistance takes place across two fronts. His cut-ups seek to short-circuit the language undergirding antidrug fearmongering, while also anticipating the spectacular mirage of superficial freedom that would serve to compensate for material inequality and injustice.

This long essay, "The Permissive Society," appears in the NYPL Berg archive Folio 10, titled "Over the Hills and Far Away," a file with a wide array of materials, from an unpublished children's story to an essay on "The Golden Dream Machine." The manuscript contains annotations and autograph pagination, showcasing Burroughs ruminating on this Orwellian doublespeak for the spectacle of freedom that disguises the privatization of space and the surveillance of communities. If Burroughs was suspicious of the myth of the "permissive society" throughout the 1960s, by 1969, in a November 3 letter to Gershom Legman, Burroughs was ready to ask with pure rancor, "And what is all this talk about 'the new freedom' and the 'permissive society'? What new freedom? We are witnessing a world-wide reactionary movement comparable to the reaction of 1848" (*Rub Out the Words*, 308).

Just before declaring the pivotal nature of his historical moment, in this same missive, Burroughs predicted the technological methods with which the reactionary right would exploit the myth of the "permissive society" in the coming years. Burroughs wrote, "Total paranoia and total confusion is an integral part of the CIA line which cannot be categorized by such an old fashioned word as Fascism. This is computerized control that has no need for any lumpen proletariat. The operation, carried out with conspicuous success in America, Greece, Turkey, Mexico, France, England, consists in scaring the middle classes into old fashioned Fascism by lurid play up of long hair, drugs, and immorality. . . . It seems to me that the real danger to freedom is computerized thought control and not anything as quaint and old fashioned as Storm Troopers" (307–308). Composed two years after this prescient letter, the following essay elaborates on Burroughs' critique of a crucial American myth, one he was wise to warn would become all the more insidious in a new technological era, when consumption and information fused together within hyper-networked systems of discourse and surveillance.

—AWC

FACING, *The Permissive Society*, William S. Burroughs (8 × 11, 6 leaves, typescript) (Berg 3.12). Folio 10, Item 3. Original unpublished story. Typescript, 1971. There are thirteen lines containing annotations and autograph pagination. Copyright © by William Burroughs, used by permission of The Wylie Agency LLC.

1

The Permissive Society

How permissive is the 'permissive society'? A hundred years ago the right
of a citizen to the privacy of his own home was unquestioned. Now it has
virtually been abolished. According to the new No-Knock drug bill in the
United States cops can break anyone's door down at any hour of the day or
night. Nor is it specified in the bill that they must come in at the door.
They can crash through a sky light or ride a bulldozer through the wall
to reveal perhaps a sex scene between consenting adults...
"WHAT ARE YOU DOING IN FRONT OF DECENT PEOPLE?"
Is this the permissive society? An editorial in The Daily Telegraph
commenting on the four deaths at Kent University asks why young
people in America living in unsurpassed freedom turn against America
@@ itself? This they would have us believe is due to 'permissiveness'.
(Four dead students quite irrelevant?) Let us take a look at this
unsurpassed state of freedom in which American youth is priviledged
to live... I quote from Newsweek Life and Leisure page 57, May 11,1970...
'At 2 o'clock one morning not long ago nine drama students at a large
mid western university were discussing plans for a cast party. Suddenly
a loud knock at the door and seconds later the crash of a sledge hammer.
As the door shattered eight policemen burst through it... The case was

****

eventually dismissed for lack of evidence but on at least one coed the
experience made a lasting traumatic impression..."I didnt eat or sleep
for five days. I had a feeling of total paranoia."
President Rosevelt postulated four freedoms. Start with the first:
Freedom from fear. Is this freedom from fear?
'Immediately following arrest the police usually offer the accused an
opportunity to get off by giving them the name of other users. This
has long been routine police treatment of criminal addicts and
trafficers in hard narcotics...(by criminal addicts they mean professional
pick pockets and sneak thieves who made up a good part of the addict
population twenty years ago)...'But now police pressure is being
applied to to youthful offenders as well-frequently with grievious
psychological results. The kids who comply are not only ostracised
by their friends but sometimes become @@@@@@ emotionally unbalanced.
One attractive young social @@@@@@ worker felt a peculiar loss of
identity. "For a while I thought I was a dope dealer" she says
@@@@@@@@ "I began to think about dope all the time and learned all
the names and quantities."
Is this freedom from fear? What kind of freedom and permissiveness is

****

this?   It is not surprising that young people turn against a country
that forcibly categorizes otherwise harmless and productive citizens
as criminals and informers.
The Daily Telegraph warns   that if such permissiveness continues the
silent majority may rise in righteous wrath and destroy all freedom.
This line is   also put down by David Allsop in articles in the International
Herald Tribune: permissiveness must lead to brutal suppression. In other
words we must appease the Wallace folk by subscribing to their <u>bigotted</u>
opinions and conform to their antiquated way of life or they will force
us to do so, a choince between slow fascism and quick facism. To put it
mildly this is defeatist talk from self professed liberals like David
Allsop.   And what has produced this silent majority of stupid people
dedicated to believing what they are told to believe? @@@@@@
@@@@@@@@@ ~~An economic system that needs millions of~~
~~uncritical interchangeable human units to produce and consume,~~ @@@@
@@@@@@@@@@@@@@@@@@@@@@@@@@@@@@@@@@.
~~An elite that is immensely rich and powerful~~

****

4

An economic system that needs millions of obedient human units for the
mass production and purchase of consumer goods. And who are the
beneficiaries of sucha system?   The wealthy of course who give the so
called silent majority their orders.   So   we are being warned that ~~these~~
this elite of wealth and power will impose a facist police state and
put an end to permissiveness unless the students capitulate and
accept the present system. Not much choice.

****

5

Consider the alternative possibilities inherent in communes formed by
the voluntary withdrawal of like minded individuals into separate communities.
The main stream of modern life is going in the other direction towards
more and more enforced conformity to laws and customs imposed on larger
and larger population units.   Communes are considered subversive and
many states in America have laws designed to prevent such units from
developing.   Yet the commune expresses a basic a need of the individual
to associate with those he wants to see and to do work he wants to
do ina safe @@@ invironement.   This is not even approximately possible
under modern urban conditions.   Every timea citizen leaves his house
he is in contact and often in conflict with strangers and this constant
necessity of dealing with potentially hostile people forces the city
dweller to be himself potentially hostile and assertive at all times.
If he is a member of some minority group he is often faced by a totally
hostile situation.   So defensive reactions and thoughts take up a good

deal of time and energy for all city dwellers. In a successful commune
such pressures are removed and the result could bea   freeing of energy
and thought for constructive purposes.   Communes could be @@@@@
efficient.   No reason why the pooling of specialized abilities and

****

(6)

and interchange of skills should not yield a saleable products.   Imagine
for example a commune of spiritualists, shamans, medicine men, swami,
holy men, ETC.   Quite a tourist attraction and palms crossed with
substantial checks. In fact the withdrawal of like minded individuals
into communes and the concentration of abilities and differences over
generations could lead to actual biologic mutations with high survival
value whereas the present   tendency is putting all the evolutionary
eggs of the species into one dubious container of enforced conformity
to arbitrary verbal dogmas.   It might be adviseable to place some
alternative bets.
Can man live without external enemies? I think so. But enemies cannot
live without man.

7

Beat Regionalism: Burroughs in Mexico, Burroughs in Women's Studies

AARON NYERGES

WHAT IS LITERARY REGIONALISM?

Not the literature of the Beats. No, not a regionalism, nor might it be narrated, upon any easy impulse, *as a* regionalism. Perhaps it would be hard to find any niche of American literary history so readily resistant to being channeled into the discursive landscape of literary regionalism. If one accepts that the paradigmatic expression of that mode remains Sarah Orne Jewett, her interconnected portraits of the society of coastal Maine, then the impulse to invite someone like William S. Burroughs into the fold would seem tentative at best, or—as the case may be—untenable. However, it is just such an ungainly comparative maneuver this essay seeks to accomplish. Recall that from the fiction of Jewett one of the great thinkers and stewards of regionalism, Marjorie Pryse, extrapolated a definition of regionalism as a category crisis (Pryse, 1998, 517–49). In one sense, regionalism presented a crisis to the other categories of literary genre with which it was uncomfortably associated: realism, naturalism, and modernism. In another way, though, regionalism announced a crisis for the categories it contained within it: place, neighbor, woman, visitor, and so on. In Pryse's reading of Jewett, it became a vehicle for evacuating stable meaning from categories of geography, sexuality, class, and gender.

At its best, which is to say its most theoretically felicitous, regionalism emerged therefore as a destabilizing ontology, a mode of being that drew the borders by which being is sustained into a new space of interrogation. Running contrary to its common connotations of tradition, stasis, and nostalgia, this more useful sense of the term, paradoxically, refers to a dwelling that refuses to dwell, an authorial mode associated with an urban personage that is *of* the countryside even in her passing through it, a position that comes in addition to other standpoints of resistance, such as the marriageable woman intent to be unmarried, or the production of a new gender that anticipates yet rejects modern categories of sexuality.

One might therefore claim that as a critical category, or a category of crisis, regionalism exists, and persists in its useful existence, through its ability to accommodate the arrival of unlikeliness, including even the acceptance of a paradigmatic case that refuses to serve as example. The Beats pose just such a category of complication, wherein they cannot bear the weight of being the exemplar. Notwithstanding the important work of Brenda Knight (1998) and Ann Charters, Nancy Grace and Ronna Johnson (2002), who for both popular and academic audiences have recuperated the stories and bolstered the reputations of Diane Di Prima, Barbara Guest, Joyce Johnson, Anne Waldman, and Denise Levertov (Peacock 1997), the Beat generation remain popularly construed as a historical site of male liberation and rebellion. The gender imbalance has had costs. A 2013 tweet from Kim Gordon, a founding member of Sonic Youth, warned men against keeping Beat males as role models. Often their rebellions came at the expense or even dispensability of women. In Burroughs' case, that logic is made literal in the ghastly story, now canonized in Beat lore, of him shooting his wife Joan in the head. In light of their disappointing gender politics, how can the Beats be integrated into regionalism, a literary critical mode so deeply associated with feminism? Is it possible to locate Burroughs, as a foundational model of Beat rebellion, within a tradition that was meant to link female authors together in the act of illuminating the position of women within society? How much crisis can a category of crisis withstand?

If the fate of regionalism is hitched to transitivity, then perhaps no more regional author can be found than in the least apparently regional, and why shouldn't Jewett invite the unlikely comparison to William Burroughs or Allen Ginsberg. To be sure, as category crisis, regionalism cannot furnish a critic with grounds for exclusion—its queerness is to do violence to the binary of exclusion and inclusion—and instead it points to a transitive or border-crossing mode that invites a transgressive practice of writing and reading. And out of this formulation its proponents insist on its status as a mode of influence and connectivity, rather than a movement, or a canon or a genre, per se, for precisely the reason that it functions as ontologically destabilizing or even as anti-ontology. As method and tradition, literary regionalism registers an affect of the unlikely, as in a visitor arriving from an unexpected time and place.

Even so, the goal of locating Burroughs in a tradition of writing so deeply associated with "a feminist analysis of the situation of women" (Fetterley and Pryse 2003, 34) cannot fail to arouse some controversy. This is due in no small part to the "public misogyny" that Anne Waldman, for instance, sees him as projecting as part of his authorial personae (see chapter 19, in this volume). By his own design, that personae, his very identity as author, was bound to an act of uxoricide. Placing Burroughs in terms of the feminist analytic of literary regionalism, therefore, presents a test case in crisis, the utmost pressure on its transitive potential to reformulate the categories it exists to reformulate. Burroughs' killing Joan in Mexico opens the gravest terms—those of gender, genre, violence, connection, authorship, nation, and empire—that the paradigm of regionalism composes.

In terms of genre, Burroughs' autobiographical fictions—especially *Junky* and *Queer*—betray a hauntedness and along with it an inexorable attraction to minor modes of fiction that regionalism redeemed. Both works interrupt, and produce crises for, the genres within which they play. Published in 1953, *Junky* is a thinly veiled autobiography designed to scandalize the mores of postwar America. In the main, it reads like a work of realism with the brakes cut, not so much a first-hand account of drug addiction as a sordid and uncensored love letter whose recipient is junk itself. The reader becomes an accessory, incidental as a stray who has stumbled into a world not for them, overhearing a gravel-voiced cant to which they are not initiated. The addition to the novel of a glossary of drug slang punctuates the author's subtly condescending address to toward the square reader he seeks to alarm if not inform. The didactic project, however, is not enough reason to maintain the realism, as *Junky* contains its own internal transitivity, in minor impulses to disrupt literary form, recasting the plain-faced realism that outwardly defines it.

The regionalism of Burroughs' Beat writing registers best in his going to Mexico. He went there to beat a narcotics charge in the city of New Orleans. On his way south of the border, he stopped and tried his hand at citrus farming in the Rio Grande River Valley on a piece of land he owned and often went to when trying to kick. His description of the place makes it clear that for Burroughs the Rio Grande Valley serves less as a place and more as a figure or shadow of premonition, a limbo between the United States and Mexico, between sobriety and addiction, between a narcotics rap and a murder charge. He soon abandons the prosaic phrases with which he initiates description ("The Valley runs from Brownsville to Mission, a strip of ground sixty miles long and twenty miles wide") into a wild mode of expressionistic exaggeration: "There are no cities in the valley, and no country." "The Valley is flat as a table." "The Valley is citrus country." "The whole Valley has the impermanent look of a camp, or carnival." "A premonition of doom hangs over the valley." "The Valley was desert, and it will be desert again." "Death hangs over the valley like an invisible smog" (Burroughs 1977, 105–6). The series of pronouncements and the tone of doom remind one of Old Testament rhetoric, but the decisions of Gods have been replaced by the ennui of humans waiting for the chance encounters of their lives.

This surprising section of *Junky* provides just such an affect of the unlikely within the generic confines of the text. It marks the unlikely arrival of Burroughs' mystical impressionism, where intentional action wilts under the oppressive fatalism of authorial control. The valley section signals an abrupt end to the realism of the junkie's memoir. Entrance to the Rio Grande region shatters the ethnographic distance that held the author at a remove from his subject, since in some talismanic way, the valley figures as reservoir and final work on depredation of addiction itself. With his tenure there, Burroughs transcends the role of the tourist. No more the trust-fund vacationer in the world of junkies, here he wholly identifies with the gaping sore of death itself, blotted large on the landscape of Earth.

However unlikely, one cannot help but be reminded of the mystical impressionism found in Jewett, whose realistic sketches of life on the coast of Maine are likewise punctuated by a gothic impulse toward shadow, rumor, and terror. In one chapter, her narrator, also the ethnographer's model participant-observer, relates the tale told to her by Captain Littlepage, who nurtures a taste for high literature and dark memories of inexplicable events. "'There is strange sort of a country 'way up north beyond the ice, and strange folks living in it,'" the Captain remembers. He tells of his ship's landing in the northern frontier, at a place unmarked on any map, a town, "thick with habitations" but whose inhabitants were not so much people as "fog-shaped men," "the shapes of folks"—"all blowing gray figures that would pass along alone" and would, when given chase, flitter "away out o' sight like a leaf the wind takes with it, or a piece of cobweb." One morning, "those folks, or whatever they were, come about 'em like bats; all at once they raised incessant armies, and come as if to drive 'em back to sea. They stood thick at the edge o' the water like the ridges o' grim war; no thought o' flight, none of retreat. Sometimes a standing fight, then soaring on main wing tormented all the air.... Say what you might, they all believed 'twas a kind of waiting-place between this world an' the next" (Jewett 1994, 397).

Burroughs' waiting place between the United States and Mexico equally figures as a limbo between life and death, a place where the bountiful harvest of citrus fruits signifies nothing but inevitable extinction. This regional surrealism where realism rubs against unreality, upsetting the categories of everyday life and genre, links Burroughs and Jewett together, across geography, history, and gender.

Have we flexed the boundaries of genre too far? Burroughs as regionalist? A Beat regionalism? In the face of this apparently limitless inclusiveness, how does regionalism ensure its usefulness? If it is a category of crisis, a kind of non-category that fetishizes the transitive, then what specific potential can it be said to contain? For if it best elucidates what moves between or across categorical boundaries, then how does it entail a politics, which necessarily must maintain the existence poles—(in the sense of both the polis and the polling booth)—ethical, geographical or otherwise, to move between or more dramatically even to choose between? What makes this particular mode of motion, change, or transferal definable or identifiable from other literary modes that equally fetishize mood, affect, change, and flux over boundary, ontology, meaning, and tradition?

To put it more pointedly, what differentiates the logic of literary regionalism from that of transnationalism, to pick one rival critical descriptor, or, if the comparison wants to retain the specter of authorial evaluation (which I'm going to suggest it unfortunately always will) what differentiates regionalism from the rebellious postwar energies still imperfectly organized under the name "the Beat generation"? It too, in style if not in substance, presents another literary "category" implying the crisis of categorization itself, and it too, like literary regionalism, is neither genre nor style nor canon nor period, per se, but the point at which all those concepts are preserved as challengers to the cohesion of any other one.

Despite these potential problems, the theoretical conceit of this essay is that something generative can come from the stark juxtaposition of William Burroughs and a tradition of literary criticism emerging from Women's Studies, where regionalism names a feminist interrelation between marginalized authors. Burroughs' cut-ups of dozens of literary texts contained few writings by women; Joan was afforded little space in his autobiographical writings and indeed very few women at all receive space or enjoy voice in his work. The reader is surprised to hear reference to William Lee's wife, three-quarters of the way through *Junky*, and even then she appears only to be silenced by domestic violence. Yet, the very improbability, even controversy, of combining the subjects, Burroughs and feminism, allows us to conceptualize a clear stake and point of view within discussions about regionalism. One may hold less of a stake, and enjoy less of an interest in debates about this subject, and such a reader may be inclined to skip ahead to the section on Burroughs, his life in Mexico, and his relationship with his wife. If however, you do hold a stake in the key theoretical debates of literary regionalism, the following excursus takes them as its subject in some detail.

EXCURSUS

The project of regionalizing a Beat writer requires inherently that we further our definition of what, precisely, regionalism is. And so let's begin by defining literary regionalism against another alternative mode of conceiving of regionalism, and here I am thinking of its "critical" variant, invented almost wholesale by the architectural historian Kenneth Frampton. Critical regionalism harbors its own alternative strategy of isolating a given region's spirit of place, a definable and defendable cultural inner essence that resists the eroding homogeneity of global capitalism and its postmodern flattening of style (Frampton 1983). Unlike critical regionalism (this defense of cultural place against global space), literary regionalism has never attempted to locate, define, and defend an inner essence shaped by cultural borders, which famously has left its flank open to the criticism (made especially by Kaplan 1991, 240–66; and Brodhead 1993) that regionalism in American studies commonly functions as feature of imperial and urbane possession, whereby the city slicker colonizes a weaker, less developed hinterland, only to repackage it as commodity form.

Disassociating literary regionalism from the counterexample of critical regionalism equally requires a further consideration of how the latter dances as the lost shadow of bioregionalism, which we might seek to sew back to its foot. Indeed Frampton and the other architectural critics with whom he can be aligned (and I'm thinking here specifically of Reyner Banham) conserve the impulse of ecological determinism as answer to the pessimism of the postmodern. Environmental determinism is often narrated as a late nineteenth-century fashion in academic geography instituted to justify the racist hierarchies of the time (Berman 2001). Nordics were conditioned, so it went, into their superiority by the need to conquer hostile winter climes, while the tropics bred cultural indolence and backwardness. What bearings have these ideas on Banham's claim of the climatological conditioning of the Southern Californian "surfurbia"? There he sees ecology as performing an otherworldly transformation of Midwestern agrarianism; flecked by sun and surf, the farmer drops the pitchfork and picks up the surfboard (Banham 1971). This logic softens, actually, the assertion of ecological space as a cultural product, first made popular by Carl Sauer (1925, 315–50) at Berkeley in the 1920s, and smuggles in the very prerogative that Sauer's assertion was meant to dispel: that the urban or cultural be thought to express the ecological. Instead, as Sauer saw it, they revise each other reciprocally, and they do not necessarily exist, as most bioregionalists (and Banham) put it, as palimpsest, where the human has paved the desert with a parking lot that in fact refigures the former as human rather than pre-human desert.

Let me make it clear that the critical views of the Californian architecture critics truck in assumptions that undergird the thinking of literary bioregionalism as well. Frampton's view of a native texture produced by ecological-minded building, one inassimilable to the "blandscapes" of late capitalist urbanization, is limited for refusing to recognize the ways in which ecology can only imperfectly condition the structures of urbanization. The trick is actually to expose the ways in which nature and wilderness and ecology are just as much cultural fantasies and labors of intended meaning-making as any Guangzhou high-rise. The literary counterpart to this incomplete fantasy held in trust by the architects of critical regionalism can be found in the environmental imagination of the bioregional Beat poet who eschews the dictates of state-sanctioned geography and instead prides a sense of felt-place, of personal or even animalistic situatedness.

When Gary Snyder says he is not a citizen or resident of this or that city in this or that state, but instead a resident of the leeward side of this or that mountain in the watershed of this or that river, he employs a logic that is seductive in part because of its dependence on the fantasy of state-sanctioned place-making (see Buell 1993). The distinction between natural and jurisdictional place-markers is never complete. The standard division between political and physical geography is less oppositional than it seems when one considers Idaho is the state between the Snake River and the Bitterroot Mountains, or that the apparently arbitrary lines that cut the Carolinas off from each other and both from Virginia refer back to seaboard inlets. This is a reminder that the squabbling riverine colonies attached borders to obscure waterways precisely because they fluctuate and reshape the terrestrial (a tactic now impressed on the disputed shoals of the South China Sea). So place is present not as palimpsest, with its layers of colonized and colonizer, but as composite, in which the two are fused in the same image.

In this estimation, the sanctuary of the bioregion and the architectural manifestos of critical regionalism offer less to the struggle against global capitalism and its spatial homogeny than they might at first attest. They are less ways of confronting or looking past the spatial standardization of the shopping mall and airport concourse than they are ways of looking away from them, and thus more dangerously, they risk ignoring that the assumptions they used to hold in common with their antagonist, which their antagonist no longer holds. Of pointed relevance here is the assumption about one's choice of allegiance when it comes to the very camps of conflict, as if one must choose between natural and cultural place rooted in the past or a social and capitalist space aligned with a maligned and threatening future. What good is a critical regionalism intent on preserving place when urban developers from Shanghai to Medellin trump up place-making and integrate fetishized examples of cultural authenticity at the base of their high-rises?

By now it should appear that I think the literary regionalism devised by Marjorie Pryse and Judith Fetterley is still more useful in moving beyond these intractable problems, and is inherently capable of defending itself against the complaint of classism lodged against it by such critics as Kaplan and Brodhead (Fetterley and Pryse 2003, 225). Kaplan played upon Hamlin Garland's celebration of locality to denounce the rustications of urban authors as a type of tourism at best or invasion at worst. For her, Jewett's sojourns in Maine worked to certify the domination of nationalized American cultural capital over enclaves of premodern resistance hiding out in the nation's hinterlands. Worse still the regional author, exercising uncritical privilege in traipsing through the regions, reified the village relations she observed there, binding them in a literary commodity destined for national and transatlantic markets of readers. Emphasizing the subversive use of gender as a method for refiguring modern categories of sexuality, Pryse's defense against this imperium complaint resulted in the "transitive" theory of regionalism. Such a defense seems distinctive to the context of Women's Studies in the 1990s, whereas Kaplan's historicism sought to expose empire as gendered and women as its unacknowledged architects. Pryse sought to salvage and celebrate; Kaplan to inculpate. But the strength of Pryse's salvaging subsisted in the theoretical felicity of the transitive. As a transitive mode, regionalism shared a logic with its home in Women's Studies whose very intellectual mode was transdisciplinary, so much so as to be evaporating more and more into a categorical non-place, as invisible mover and progenitor of gender studies writ wide.

Positing regionalism as a feminist analytic and queer non-category of analysis, Pryse and Fetterley sought to stake ambitious ground in the critical reception of women in American literature. Of key importance to the formulation of regionalism was the recuperation and defense of not just Jewett's reputation but also those of Alice Cary, Grace King, Mary Austin, and Sui Sin Far (Fetterley and Pryse 1993). What does one do with Burroughs in this context? For regionalism to maintain the mantle of the transitive, I'd urge that it must invite such an unlikely interlocutor—the paradigmatic Beat or better *paterfamilias* Beat whose fiction bears little affection for women. Could Burroughs enter a conversation in a Women's Studies classroom for anything more than a dressing down? Perhaps not, but perhaps it is just this kind of motivated devaluation that the Beat generation requires and what better mode than regionalism to devalue the Beats precisely by debunking their transnational and cosmopolitan pretensions.

—Joan, what kind of knowledge have
the dead? can you still love
your mortal acquaintances?
What do you remember of us?

—Allen Ginsberg

William Burroughs shot his wife Joan Vollmer Adams Burroughs in Mexico City in 1951 in what eyewitness testimony established as a drunken parlor trick gone terribly wrong (see Grauerholz 2002; Garcia-Robles 2013). The event haunted Burroughs for a lifetime and in fact continues to haunt him. In "Dream Indictment for Murdering Joan," a manuscript fragment in the New York Public Library's Berg Collection dated 1970, he dreams that he has been indicted in England for the murder of Joan. A lawyer offers him a disguise so he can flee the country without extradition (Berg 22.79). The sense of admission, disguise, and escape adds a transgressive overlay to the sense of disguise suggested by Ann Douglas and Anne Waldman in their roundtable discussion on Burroughs and gender, where they imply that sexism could function as a mask Burroughs put on and took off, obscuring the fact of his less prejudiced behavior toward women in his life (chapter 18, in this volume). The William Tell legend, too, though, obscures the sexist violence of the scene it mythologizes, and Burroughs' dream escape from England, put to paper in 1970, repeats his historical escape from punishment in 1951, an event that is inexplicable except for the compounding categorical crises of gender and region. To facilitate his escape from judgment, the author provided two defenses in response to having shot Joan in the head: one legal, one literary. The legal one was a total fabrication, in which Burroughs, aided by Bernabé Jurado, one of Mexico's most corrupt criminal defense attorneys, played the entire affair off as an accident. In this version, he had gone to a friend's house to sell a firearm, set it on the table, and it tragically misfired, killing his wife. Selling the story required a cooked-up ballistics report ensured by a bribe. The second defense was even more inventive. In this version of non-culpability, Burroughs was asked to kill Joan by Joan herself, who conveyed the desire through telepathic link.

Faced with the implausibility and petty-scheming of the first defense, we are left with the more mystical implausibility of the second: that Joan's death was self-directed, with Burroughs the obliging accessory. Strains of this vision interlace Barry Miles's important new biography of Burroughs, which sets the scene of the shooting by implying that Joan exacerbated the tension between her and her husband; she knew how to "prick his ego" (Miles 2014, 205). However, Miles also subtly builds a case for Burroughs' responsibility, imping premeditation by quoting at length a 1980 interview in which Burroughs discusses his visitation by the "Ugly Spirit" and admits that he knew "something awful would happen" that day (Miles 2014, 207). The categories of influence and intentionality—terms that define the parameters of both criminal and authorial acts—produce a crisis for the project of locating women in a regional network of affiliation. The only linkages afforded here are with Vollmer, the man who killed her, and the insinuation of a presence more sinister.

For his part, Burroughs' belief in telepathic control became immanent to his ideas of literary authorship. If his first brush with telepathic communication and control was Joan willing him to shoot her, his second, more extended experience with it, was identical to his experience of authorship, or rather, his sense of texts being authored through him, as if he were the obliging accessory to their self-completion. As he confessed in the introduction to *Queer*, penned for its publication in 1985: "I am forced to the appalling conclusion that I would never have become a writer but for Joan's death, and to a realization to the extent to which this event has motivated and formulated my writing. I live with the constant threat of possession, from Control. So the death of Joan brought me in contact with the invader, the Ugly Spirit, and maneuvered me into a lifelong struggle, in which I have had no choice except to write my way out" (Burroughs 2010, 134–35).

In his published explanation, Burroughs favors the more passive term—"the death of Joan" though in his unpublished fragment comes the more nightmarish implication of culpability: "for murdering Joan." The multiple crises created by the interlocking and inadequate explanations for Joan's death provide another torturous moment of awakening for the feminist analytic of regionalism, the shock that—if it were to consider Joan's force or spirit as authorial—it would allow Burroughs into a Women's Studies tradition of regionalism. Joan and Burroughs conjoined into a regionalist writer might be the regionalist writer, since, to quote Pryse and Fetterley "the regionalist writer used the location of the region to foreground a critique of the location of women" (Fetterley and Pryse 2003, 38). The case of Vollmer's murder in Mexico foregrounds a critique of the location of women in the Beat generation, as the destroyed, and as the creator. Yet this would clearly require the invitation of crisis, of accepting Burroughs at his queer word: that while he wrote *Junky* and *Queer*, it was Vollmer who authored them.

Burroughs wrote: "While it was I who wrote *Junky*, I feel that I was being written in *Queer*" (2010, 128). On the face of it, this reads like Heidegger's basic point about language as the house of being, where he suggests that humans are primarily things being used by language rather than things that use it; they are authored by the work of language (Heidegger 1971, 207). Whether or not you permit such a fanciful take on authorship and the provenance of text, both *Queer* and *Junky* are equally the products of Burroughs' life in Mexico City and the event of Vollmer's death. Vollmer's voice resonates through Burroughs' literary cut-ups of famous last words. Her words, "I can't look," appear repeatedly in the manuscript artifacts compiled by this collection (Berg 26.16). To conceive of Vollmer as author in a deeper sense, as a figure of loss in which a voice is found, we must imagine a text produced by speechlessness, a ghostly vocalization of authority that vacates as it announces itself. To do so, one could do worse than consult Gayatri Spivak's epic critique of the philosophy of colonization, since it is perhaps the deepest meditation on the problem of resuscitating voices that have been silenced by the masculine and racial violence of modernity. In terms of Burroughs, and his relationship to Joan Vollmer, the goal would be to open up the space of what Spivak calls the "resistant reader," who can "attempt to undo that continuing subordination" of Joan Vollmer to the position of reading and being written (Spivak 1997, 67). It is possible to move her from the category of being written, to that of writing, producing self-knowledge?

Joan is sadly rarely audible in and through herself and when she is, it is most often in pieces of correspondence. So the material in the archive of Joan Vollmer is almost always the material in the archive of another, almost always a man. For instance, her look reverberates through Allen Ginsberg's "Dream Record: June 8, 1955," a stylistic dress rehearsal for his much more famous *Howl*. The poem tells how in a dream he

> went back to Mexico City
> and saw Joan Burroughs leaning
> forward in a garden chair, arms
> on her knees. She studied me with
> clear eyes and downcast smile, her
> face restored to a fine beauty
> tequila and salt had made strange
> before the bullet in her brow.

(Ginsberg 2007, 132)

In this image, it is Joan Burroughs who is doing the studying, who is in the position of reading, not being read. The poet is under her observation, though she is still an oneiric inspiration to write, not a writer. Her arrival, beyond death, through dream, connects her to romantic theories of poetic inspiration, which linked writing to the loss of control, being surrendered to states of limited intentionality, like insanity, or a deep dream-knit sleep.

This returns us to the figure of the valley that interrupted the anthropological control of *Junky*'s narrator. To speak of valleys is commonly to speak to the predetermined or the automated. Biblical prophecies were had on mountaintops, but realized in valleys. The book of Joel speaks of a valley of decision, a region in which all nations will be gathered by god to be destroyed. More famously Psalm 23:4 uses the figure of the valley of the shadow of death to find contrasting comfort in the light and guidance of the lord. In fairy tales, valleys also are spaces of limited autonomy. Working through the same surrealistic legacy as Burroughs, Walt Disney's original story treatment for Snow White had her traverse a valley of dreams before alighting at the dwarves' cottage. Many think that Disney abandoned this idea in the animation, not realizing that for Disney the valley of dreams was a metaphor for confusion and indecision and automation. In the film, Snow

White plunges through a dark forest animated into a threatening, psychedelic morass of woody limbs and roots. She is delivered into the paw of a softer forest, alive with accommodating mammals and birds, who drag her, still dreaming, to the dwarves' cottage.

As in the valleys of old, here motions are dictated, authored by something else, made mechanical and automatic by the figure of the valley itself. This determinism is not environmental, but conceptual. And we might say the last valley, the one between the Beat generation and literary regionalism, is the valley of the uncanny. An uncanny valley refers to a modicum of difference between human life and automated life that makes the approaching reality of the artificial more monstrous. Burroughs should become more threatening to the anti-ontology of regionalism the more closely he comes to defining its crisis and it *as crisis*. But this crisis of automation should return us to Joan.

A most diligent archivist of Joan Vollmer Burroughs appears in Burroughs' biographer, James Grauerholz, whose long essay "The Death of Joan Vollmer Burroughs" contains fascinating artifacts like the psychological profile completed on Joan at the De Paul Sanitarium and a letter from Burroughs to Ginsberg about his sexual prowess with women, which she agreeably annotated. At a deeper level however an archive of Joan Vollmer Burroughs is impossible and necessarily silent, even as it likewise contains every work that has ever productively criticized the anthropologist, his or her mangling of the knowledge they seek to study; so too it contains all romantic theories that locate the authority of the author in a phantasmal space outside the identity taking legal responsibility for authorship, and also it would contain the history of madness, its valorization and sympathies; but finally it would be an archive of a ghastly and uncanny love. As she wrote to Ginsberg, just before the stint in the Rio Grande Valley: "I don't know where we'll go—probably either a cruise somewhere or a trip to Texas to begin with— . . . I don't care where I live, so long as it's with him" (Vollmer 1949, quoted in Grauerholz 2002, 15). As Burroughs has it, in death she lived in his every written word. And so, her last words invade his cut-ups to the end: "I can't look." "Joan" names that moment when abandonment of the self and the arrival of authorship collide.

THE EMPIRE OF THE REGION

Perhaps this is the time to elucidate the way that the regionalization of the Beat generation suggests an intervention with the discourse of transnationalism, and the larger role the category of the region plays in the expansive framework of the global. The cult of the Beat generation stems from the mythos of its transcontinental energy and its association with international entrepôts of New York and San Francisco. Ironically, it is in Burroughs' border hopping, his transnational flight to Mexico as a fugitive, that he charts the constitutive elements of the regionalist mode. For Burroughs, Mexico City is precisely the "still timeless island" that Kaplan claims regionalism must posit, and his going there on the lam raises the paradoxical restlessness and motion that drives that need to posit that cultural island in the first place. In Burroughs' estimation, Mexico was an "Oriental culture that reflected two thousand years of disease and poverty and degradation and stupidity and slavery and brutality and psychic and physical terrorism." Its chaos was the "special chaos of a dream" (2010, 122). Thus, his projected orientalist dream entailed a sleepy and recurrent social disorder, within which he anchored himself to what he calls the "expatriate colony" of Americans in Mexico. Here, remembering Garland at the Columbian exposition, we must accept the renewed importance of locality in American literary geography, especially if we acknowledge that American map-making habit—and thus the general spatial imagination of the public—stayed informed by the town gazetteer tradition much more so than in Europe. When one recognizes the importance of American-owned establishments like the Ship Ahoy to Burroughs' orientation in Mexico City, as well as his recourse to greater town-name specificity the more he enters a period of transition, then we must assume that the transnational mobility of the Beats is best narrated insofar as it conforms to the logic of American regionalism and the organizational unit of locale.

Here Burroughs again invites Kaplan's primary complaint against regionalism: that it amounts to tourism. In this reduction, regionalists were urbane passerbys, traipsing through pre-national communities that they in turn fetishized as exotic. They lacked an endogenous view of their subject material. It would be hard to defend Burroughs from these accusations, and while Pryse defends Jewett from them persuasively enough, this is, overall, an unfortunate place to leave the debate. It stays stuck within a problem of metaphoricity—the writer is *like* a tourist—which is to say, it uncritically replays Garland's lecture at the Chicago Exposition. Sharing the same stage with Frederick Turner, Garland's speech has not, to the detriment of literary history, produced a locality thesis of American literature worth its name, the way Turner's speech on the frontier did for historians. Yet regardless of whether they were tourists, fugitives, or homebodies, the normative unit of the township has left an incredible impress on American letters. For Burroughs, the Valley was a topographic feature that "ran from Brownsville to Mission." Again, this is a spatial dimension of literary production enforced by cartographic norms. For instance, Rand McNally Atlases of the Western Front of World War I were so lousy with town names they were impossible to read (Schulten 2001, 180). Thus the township, as a cultural harbor, or entity apart from the nation, remains a hobgoblin amid the misunderstandings of regionalism's critics, who stay less aware of local referentiality as a base rite that American identity need exercise.

Sidestepping this long-standing diminishment of the local as a byword for the touristic and flighty, Kaplan's more formidable charge then is her claim that regional fiction be defined through its search for a primal origin of American national identity rooted in pre-national community and clan. This is a problem with great consequence for Pryse's figuration of regionalism as a transitive mode of writing and reading. However, Kaplan's definition of regionalism as a search for the harbor of the pre-national is flummoxing and also historically limited, since regionalism could not exist beyond the crucible of national identity formation, or after the erosion of pre-modern community. If regionalism seeks out the primitive community, unincorporated into the national, then what regionalism can there be in an age after what one used to call the peasantry or even proletariat has evaporated into the global multitude, where Bedouin nomads and Bangladeshi factory workers alike comprise an uneven but single modernity affected by fluctuations of transnational capital (see Jameson 2002). Supposing even that Kaplan's claim was made only of the historical regionalism of Garland and Jewett, not of regionalism in the abstract, what then might be made of her sense that regionalism projects a desire for a space outside history, positing a "still timeless island community" (Kaplan 1991, 252–53) outside the flow of time? Shouldn't the supposed destruction of the organic bonds of village community by global capitalism excite the need for more regionalist desire projection, not less?

Perhaps the best way around this seeming conundrum is to be reminded that trans is a temporal category, so if we take the Maine villages of Jewett's fiction to be pre-national, then they are precise fortresses of the transnational. Today, however, transnationalism speaks not of a cultural island outside of time, standing proudly above the tides of nationalization, but rather describes the impress of American national interests abroad in an age where they no longer carry the demands of nationalization, but in fact discourage it. While Judith Fetterley has emphasized that Jewett's *Deephaven* was a place "not in the least American" (Fetterley 1994), such places today are not romantic, but factories of inchoate terror. What cultural historians do in the face of this issue remains to be decided, and this essay serves only as a rehearsal of several tactics: the regionalization of a historical artifact seemingly beyond regionalization; the presentation of one of America's most mythologized literary moments as an element in minor literature, knit together to reveal the impossible position of a woman within the society that denies justice; and, finally, the recuperation of literary regionalism, the legacy of the Women's Studies of the 1990s, which can always usefully challenge the masculinist mythologies of American literary history.

AARON NYERGES is a lecturer in American Studies at the US Studies Centre at the University of Sydney. His articles have appeared in *Textual Practice, Sound Studies,* the *Australasian Journal of American Studies,* and the *Journal of Popular Culture.*

Banham, Reyner. 1971. *Los Angeles: The Architecture of Four Ecologies.* New York: Harper and Row.

Berman, Jessica. 2001. *Modernist Fiction, Cosmopolitanism and the Politics of Community.* Cambridge: Cambridge University Press.

Brodhead, Richard. 1993. *Cultures of Letters: Scenes of Reading and Writing in Nineteenth-Century America.* Chicago: University of Chicago Press.

Buell, Lawrence. 1993. *The Environmental Imagination.* Cambridge, MA: Harvard University Press.

Burroughs, William S. 1977. *Junky.* New York: Penguin Books.

———. 2010. *Queer: 25th Anniversary Edition,* ed. Oliver Harris. New York: Penguin Classics.

———. 2010. "Introduction to the 1985 Edition." In *Queer: 25th Anniversary Edition,* ed. Oliver Harris, 121–35. New York: Penguin Classics.

Fetterley, Judith. 1994. "'Not in the Least American': Nineteenth-Century Literary Regionalism." *College English* 56 (8): 877–95.

Fetterley, Judith, and Marjorie Pryse.1993. *American Women Regionalists. 1850–1910: A Norton Anthology.* New York: Norton.

———. 2003. *Writing Out of Place: Regionalism, Women and American Literary Culture.* Urbana: University of Illinois Press.

Frampton, Kenneth. 1983. "Towards a Critical Regionalism: Six Points for an Architecture of Resistance." In *The Anti-aesthetic: Essays on Postmodern Culture,* ed. Hal Foster, 16–30. Seattle, WA: Bay.

Garcia-Robles, Jorge. 2013. *The Stray Bullet: Burroughs in Mexico* (La bala perdida: William S. Burroughs en Mexico, 1949–1952). Translated by Daniel C. Schechter. Minneapolis, MN: University of Minnesota Press.

Ginsberg, Allen. 2007. *Collected Poems 1947–1997.* New York: HarperCollins.

Gordon, Kim. 2013. Twitter Post, April 8. twitter.com/kimletgordon/status/321449934333308928.

Grace, Nancy, and Ronna Johnson, eds. 2002. *Girls Who Wore Black: Women Writing the Beat Generation.* Rutgers, NJ: Rutgers University Press.

Grauerholz, James. 2002. "The Death of Joan Vollmer Burroughs: What Really Happened?" Paper presented at Fifth Congress of the Americas, Universidad de las America, Puebla, Mexico, October 18.

Heidegger, Martin. 1971. *"Language" in Poetry, Language, Thought.* Translated by Albert Hofstadter. New York: Harper and Row.

Jameson, Fredric. 2002. *A Singular Modernity: Essay on the Ontology of the Present.* New York: Verso.

Jewett, Sarah Orne. 1994. *Novels and Stories: Deephaven; A Country Doctor; The Country of the Pointed Firs; Stories and Sketches,* ed. Michael D. Bell. New York: Library of America.

Kaplan, Amy. 1991."Empire, Nation, Region." In *The Columbia History of the American Novel,* ed. Emory Elliot, 240–66. New York: Columbia University Press.

Knight, Brenda, ed. 1998. *The Women of the Beat Generation: The Writers, Artists and Muses at the Heart of a Revolution.* Berkeley, CA: Conari.

Miles, Barry. 2014. *Call Me Burroughs: A Life.* New York: Twelve.

Peacock, Richard, ed. 1997. *A Different Beat: Writings of the Women of the Beat Generation.* New York: Serpent's Tail.

Pryse, Marjorie. 1998. "Sex, Class, and 'Category Crisis': Reading Jewett's Transitivity." *American Literature* 70 (3): 517–49.

Sauer, Carl. 1963. "The Morphology of Landscape." In *Land and Life: A Selection from the Writings of Carl Ortwin Sauer,* ed. by J. Leighly, 315–50. Berkeley: University of California Press. First published 1925.

Schulten, Susan. 2001. *The Geographical Imagination of America.* Chicago: University of Chicago Press.

Spivak, Gayatri. 1997. *A Critique of Postcolonial Reason: Toward a History of the Vanishing Present.* Cambridge, MA: Harvard University Press.

Vollmer, Joan. 1949. "Letter to Allen Ginsberg, April 13." In "The Death of Joan Vollmer Burroughs: What Really Happened?" by James Grauerholz, 15. Paper presented at Fifth Congress of the Americas, Universidad de las America, Puebla, Mexico, October 18.

Collage of News Clippings

From its origins, Burroughs' investment in the cut-up method oriented itself around the media, especially the cutting up of international newspapers. Working on a near daily basis, Burroughs intended to decipher the Reality Studio's sensational and disingenuous rhetoric to understand the structural, economic, and geographic underpinnings of political power struggles. The archives only retain a small percentage of the total number of news clippings Burroughs collected, collaged, and transcribed into new prose over the 1960s. There are still hundreds of unexamined pages of scrapbooked news clippings in such Berg folios as Folio 108, "Fresh Southerly Winds Stir Papers On The City Desk" and Folio 67, "Newspaper Layouts, Some Unpublished, Others Published In *The Third Mind*, *My Own Mag*, *Chicago Review*, *Art and Literature*, and *Ambit*."

In these often raw collages of black-and-white photography with journalism articles, Burroughs sought through his countercultural archive to deconstruct what he described in interviews published in *The Job* (1970) as the growing technological communication and information system whereby the "mass media of newspapers, radio, television, magazines form a ceremonial calendar to which all citizens are subjected" (44). Burroughs did not, then, just cut up newspaper rhetoric to produce novels; he also developed archival filing systems, creating multi-layered, interconnected scrapbooks, as part and parcel of his project to map and short-circuit the "reality studio." Appearing in Folio 80 "Dream Files: Observer Time File," this file exemplifies how diffuse his scrapbooking process became, producing dream calendars, unbound and bound scrapbooks, as well as vast miscellaneous materials unrelated to any particular series. While unbound, the Observer Time File is numbered; this piece, where comics juxtapose with news stories and photographs of student riots, appears late in the series.

While Burroughs had begun experimenting with scrapbooking as early as 1964, he continued the practice until the end of his life in the 1990s. Scrapbooks in the Berg archive include Folio 82 "The Dream Calendar–Dream Rat," Folio 84 "Scrapbook # One, 4 Calle Larachi" (February–March 1964), Folio 92 "Soft Machine Dream Calendar," Folio 93 "Great Eastern Dream Calendar," Folio 94 "Wordsworth Dream File," Folio 96 "Pages from Unfinished Scrapbook: Order and the Material is the Message," Folio 97 "Dickens Calendar," and Folio 110 "Key File / Guide to Folio Time." Burroughs' scrapbooks from the 1970s and 1980s can be found primarily at Ohio State University, but they are also spread throughout the private market, sometimes appearing in auctions online. As of yet, the vast majority of his scrapbooks, like his news clippings, numbering thousands of pages, remains entirely unpublished.

Scrapbooking is the art practice Burroughs used to most methodically trace, through multiple modalities of representations, the intersection points of contradictory social forces in multifaceted temporal and spatial dimensions. These scrapbooks, like his dream calendars, were sometimes produced daily, at other times intermittently over long periods, registering chronologies and analogies spanning many times and places throughout the metropoles and colonies of a declining Western empire. Burroughs considered his "scrapbooks" of newspapers, advertisements, comic-strips, maps, drawings, designs, ticket stubs, and his own typescripts, as "such stuff as dreams are made on": as he returned to old scrapbooks, and turned to "a page in time," he might find a "clipping from the hometown," material he can "cross reference back and forth" with other scraps, in order to slowly "open" his memory to lost, forgotten "times and places" (Sobieszek, 47).

—AWC

O.T. 108

Collage of Newsclippings, William S. Burroughs, 1970 (8 × 11, 2 leaves, facsimile) (Berg 22.78). From Folio 80 Dream Files: Observer Time File; Items 108–109. Item 108, five news clippings of drugs pasted onto a page, 1p, Item 109, two news clippings pasted onto a page, 1p. Copyright © by William Burroughs, used by permission of The Wylie Agency LLC.

college students at Georgia Tech recently analyzed drugs they bought in Atlanta and are visiting local high schools to tell what they found. "The marijuana is often cut with rhubarb or catnip," says Charles Gentry, a Georgia Tech senior. "Some of the hash contained black opium which is suspected of turning kids onto stronger drugs. And some of the acid has been found to contain strychnine."

In many cases, school administrators are at a loss as to how to react when they find a student in trouble with drugs. "Any indictment of the schools and colleges on their behavior in this field is fair," Dr. Donald H. Louria, president of the New York State Council on Drug Addiction, said last week. "They have failed to face the real problems of drug abuse, and yet teachers are the only ones with any real potential to help the kids." Louria also predicted that "within a couple of years every high school and every college in the country will be inundated by heroin."

Often, however, teachers do not know enough to tell when a student really needs help. "I tripped for a week straight at one point," says a dropout from Wheaton North High School outside Chicago. "When the nurse asked me if I was under the influence of drugs, I said I'd been under a lot of pressure at home. She told me to lie down for a while and then go back to class." His drug problem was so severe, however, that his parents later put him in a Chicago rehabilitation center.

Abuse: Like many schools, Wheaton tries to educate students about drug abuse by bringing in reformed addicts to lecture at assemblies. So far, their impact has not been very substantial. "This ex-addict told the kids how you mix uppers and downers and how it tears you up inside," says Debbie Kobak, a Wheaton North junior. "And the kids were laughing and saying 'yeah, yeah.' It was a big joke."

Other schools present panel discussions on drugs—but with no greater success. David Lewis, an assistant professor of medicine at Harvard, recalls that he spoke with several other experts at a special assembly at a Boston high school. "A few days later," he says, "two of the students who had been in the audience said to me, 'If drugs were worth calling off classes for a day, they were worth trying.' That was the culmination of eight years of panel discussions for me."

With school antidrug programs largely inadequate, not only are more students using drugs but the age of users is dropping lower and lower. Recently, a group of junior-high-school students met for a session on drug abuse at a youth center in Fairfield, Conn. The school officials in charge passed out four joints for the students to examine. At the end of the meeting he asked for the joints back. The students reached in their pockets and returned seven.

8

Interference Zones: William Burroughs in the Interstices of Globalization

TIMOTHY S. MURPHY

For William Burroughs, the state is effectively defined by its repressive juridico-legal and police functions—the *Polizeiwissenschaft*—which control the time, space, and subjectivity of the nation and its people.[1] These functions are identified, parodied, and attacked in works from *Junky* (1953) and *Naked Lunch* (1959) to "Roosevelt after Inauguration" (1961) and the Nova Trilogy. Such textual critiques of the police state parallel Burroughs' own flight from the post–World War II United States, which he saw as an emerging paradigm of that state, to Mexico, South America, and ultimately Tangier. In the Texas/Mexico borderlands, the South American frontier, and especially the International Zone of Tangier, Burroughs sought and ultimately found spaces in which the state's police function was interrupted not so much by the revolutionary overthrow or elimination of the sovereign state as by the administrative overlap and interference between multiple state apparatuses. To put it paradoxically, he found that zones marked by the highest degree of interstate interference interfered least with his unconventional lifestyle. He not only found such zones of interference, which we might call "interzones" after Burroughs' term for his imaginary version of Tangier's International Zone, to be congenial sites for his own literary and critical work, but he also seduced his Beat friends across their borders and in so doing started the Beat Generation on its global trajectory. In the brief analyses that follow, I intend merely to sketch the outlines of this notion of interference across Burroughs' early works and suggest its relevance for globalization studies more generally.

Burroughs identifies interference as the key to his appreciation for the successive sites of his expatriation in the essay "International Zone," written in 1955 in hope of publication in the *New Yorker* but unpublished until 1989 in the volume *Interzone*, edited by James Grauerholz. The essay provides a brief portrait of Tangier and concludes as follows:

> The special attraction of Tangier can be put in one word: exemption. Exemption from interference, legal or otherwise. Your private life is your own, to act exactly as you please.
> ... No legal pressure or pressure of public opinion will curtail your behavior. The cop stands here with his hands behind his back, reduced to his basic function of keeping order.

That is all he does. He is the other extreme from the thought police of police states, or our own vice squad. Tangier is one of the few places left in the world where, so long as you don't proceed to robbery, violence, or some form of crude, antisocial behavior, you can do exactly what you want. It is a sanctuary of noninterference.[2] (Burroughs 1989, 59)

Graham Stuart confirms this description in his historical analysis of Tangier's political institutions: "Although the [Tangier police] force presented a pleasing sight with its athletic-looking agents in their dark-blue military uniforms, it would hardly have rated very high in an efficiency test. The policemen on duty had the air of detached and disinterested observers rather than alert custodians of the law" (1955, 122–23). This disinterestedness was a direct result of the fragmented geopolitical situation of the International Zone, which was jointly administered by Great Britain, France, Italy, and Spain (with the United States as a powerful but indirect influence on governance). As Stuart again explains, "each Power felt that the Zone rightly belonged within its sphere of influence and each secretly hoped that it would not be long before such a result would be brought about. Therefore the international régime was to each but a temporary expedient, which they neither desired nor expected to see succeed" (109). The international structure of governance, like the police, was precisely intended to be at best minimally functional or at worst flatly dysfunctional in order to sustain Tangier's role as an extraterritorial marketplace for goods and global finance, and consequently noninterference with commerce and correlative social activity was its implicit policy. In this way, the International Zone prefigures important aspects of corporate globalization as we know it today, particularly the "free trade zones" or *maquiladoras* that have proliferated around the world since the 1990s (though without the "exemption from interference" for their occupants that Burroughs lauded).

Such an environment was just what Burroughs had been seeking for the previous several years. Near the conclusion of his first book, *Junky*, Burroughs had already argued that US legislators were instituting "police-state legislation penalizing a state of being" (1977, 119), the state of being a junky (and a homosexual), so he "decided to jump bail [on a narcotics charge] and live permanently outside the United States" (120; see Murphy 1998, 50–57). In addition, as Rob Johnson argues, Burroughs' experience of post–New Deal farming in South Texas "convinced him that the United States was rapidly becoming a communist-style police state, and he couldn't wait to move to the 'free' country of Mexico, which offered an escape back into the past of the American frontier, when everything was allowed and people minded their own business" (2006, 10). Although Burroughs had enjoyed—and actively exploited—the border situation that allowed him access to cheap illegal migrant labor and a safe harbor when his own legally dubious activities attracted unwanted police attention on either side of the border, he ultimately opted to leave the United States for the long term.

Upon settling in Mexico City in late 1949, Burroughs found the place congenial primarily as a consequence of "the general atmosphere of freedom from interference that prevails here," as he wrote to Jack Kerouac on New Year's Day 1950

(Burroughs 1993, 62). As a resident alien, he was not allowed to work in Mexico, but his small trust fund covered most of his needs and he lived largely free of police harassment for some time. He was so struck by the "freedom from interference" in Mexico that he regularly noted it as a way to persuade his American friends to visit or even relocate themselves. In another early 1950 letter, he encouraged the perpetually underfunded Kerouac to move to Mexico:

> If you want to save some of the money you are making, Mexico is undoubtedly the place for you. A single man lives high here including all the liquor he can drink for $100 per month . . . And it is possible here to enjoy oneself without interference. It is my contention that you can not enjoy yourself in the U.S. now for any price.
> —January 22, 1950 (Burroughs 1993, 63)

The persuasion seems to have worked, for by the end of that year Kerouac was writing letters incorporating Burroughs' own vision of Mexico, for example, to Neal Cassady:

> In March, if I get a Guggenheim (decided around last week) we will at once buy an old panel truck, load gear, and take off for 3 wonderful lazy years perhaps in provincial Mexico (cheaper than Mexcity) . . . Can live there off $400 or $500 a year . . . We'd hang on to every cent, give the Mexes no quarter, let them get sullen at the cheap Americans and stand side by side in defense, and make friends in the end when they saw we was poor too. Comes another Mex revolution, we stands them off with our Burroughsian arsenal bought cheap on Madero St. and dash to big city in car for safety shooting and pissing as we go . . .
> —December 27, 1950 (Kerouac 1995, 244–45)

Kerouac's visit to Burroughs in Mexico City in the summer of 1950 seemed to confirm much of what the older man had reported, and Kerouac would return to Mexico in 1952.

Following his shooting of Joan Vollmer Burroughs in September 1951, however, Burroughs began to find the Mexican police and legal system interfering with his lifestyle more and more severely. With his case still unresolved in fall 1952, he decided to leave Mexico for South America in order to avoid incarceration and to find the "telepathic" drug yagé (Banisteria caapi). This period in his expatriation is chronicled in his letters and also in The Yage Letters Redux (2006), which continues his focus on the police as the most visible and significant face of the state. He describes the Colombian Policía Nacional as "the Palace Guard of the Conservative Party," which is itself "an unpopular minority of ugly looking shits" (Burroughs and Ginsberg 2006, 10–11), and narrates the harassment he undergoes at their hands (19–23). Conversely, however, he also benefited from his relationship with visiting US agricultural researchers as well as from the locals' misrecognition of him as a US oilman, factors that grant him an unexpected degree of freedom and immunity from local laws. At the ambiguous conclusion to his search for yagé, however, he left South America to settle in Tangier for four years.

In Tangier, he finally found the freedom from interference that he had been seeking, and he soon began to invite his friends to join him in what Greg Mullins aptly calls his "utopia" (2002, 56). For example, he wrote to Ginsberg in October 1956 advising him, "DON'T GO TO MEXICO... COME RIGHT HERE RIGHT NOW WHILE YOU HAVE THE LOOT. TANGER IS THE PLACE. WHY WAIT... ???" (Burroughs 1993, 335). Similar letters went to Kerouac, along with assertions that the unrest of the Moroccan nationalist revolutionary movement that had finally erupted in Tangier (and which Burroughs depicted rather ambiguously in *Naked Lunch*, particularly in the routine "Ordinary Men and Women") posed no danger to them as American extraterritorials. Convinced if not seduced, Ginsberg and Peter Orlovsky joined Kerouac in visiting Burroughs in Tangier in early 1957.

By this point, Burroughs was already well advanced in the composition of the book that would become *Naked Lunch*, the assembly of which Kerouac and Ginsberg famously facilitated. The earliest textual example of Burroughs' conception of how interstate interference may give rise to noninterference in the private and social lives of individuals can be found in the "Interzone" routine in *Naked Lunch*. In that routine, he creates a parodic version of Tangier and its convoluted codes of multinational/extraterritorial commerce and justice. Late in the chapter, he offers brief descriptions of the Interzone's political status as a colonial outpost modeled on Tangier and nearby Gibraltar, the latter called "the Island": "The Island was a British Military and Naval station directly opposite the Zone. England holds the Island on yearly rent-free lease, and every year the Lease and Permit of Residence is formally renewed. The entire population turns out—attendance is compulsory—and gathers at the municipal dump. The President of the Island is required by custom to crawl across the garbage on his stomach and deliver the Permit of Residence and Renewal of the Lease, signed by every citizen of the Island, to The Resident Governor who stands resplendent in dress uniform..." (Burroughs 2001, 152–53). The locus of political power can clearly be inferred from the indignity that the colonial power inflicts upon the local governor, which consequently leads to his essential impotence even as a figurehead. As *Naked Lunch*'s narrator notes, "The post of President is always forced on some particularly noxious and unpopular citizen. To be elected President is the greatest misfortune and disgrace that can befall an Islander. The humiliations and ignominy are such that few Presidents live out their full term of office, usually dying of a broken spirit after a year or two" (153–54).[3]

Likewise, the legislative branch of the Island government is deprived of efficacy by its colonial overlord: "The forms of democracy are scrupulously enforced on the Island. There is a Senate and a Congress who carry on endless sessions discussing garbage disposal and outhouse inspection, the only two questions over which they have jurisdiction. For a brief period in the mid-nineteenth century, they had been allowed to control the Dept. of Baboon Maintenance but this privilege had been withdrawn owing to absenteeism in the Senate" (Burroughs 2001, 152–153).

Democracy is merely a formality here and the colonial power is not even named, but its agency is clear despite the passive grammatical constructions. Compare this to Stuart's description of the actual legislature of Tangier: "Undoubtedly the part of the government of Tangier which appeared the most truly international was the Assembly. To a certain degree it resembled both the Assembly of the United Nations and an ordinary city council. It had the decorum, heterogeneous appearance, and linguistic attributes of the former, with the powers, procedure, and order of business of the latter" (1955, 112). The "Interzone" routine contains no overt references to the judicial branch, but perhaps Burroughs' perspective on it is best captured in a line from earlier in *Naked Lunch*: "As one judge said to another: 'Be just and if you can't be just be arbitrary'" (2001, 5). In light of Burroughs' extraterritorial status as an American in Tangier, which exempted him from prosecution under Moroccan law, this line takes on an additional critical resonance. My point is that Burroughs consistently draws attention not to the absence of the state apparatus and its police forces from Interzone but rather to the impotence that results from the interference the administration of the International Zone faces from the nation-states that subdivide and overlap it. Such states interfere with one another in ways that impede their police functions and thereby open up spaces where subversive subjects can thrive, and this is one of the most important political lessons that Burroughs' displacement from Texas to Mexico to Central America to Tangier taught him and, by extension, his literary allies and heirs.

In subsequent works, Burroughs would build upon this insight from Interzone. Not only do competing states interfere with one another through external forms of colonialism (as well as warfare, economic competition, foreign aid, etc.), but even a single state can be rendered comparatively impotent in its policing functions by internal interference. Burroughs had already noted this possibility in *Junky*, when Lee escapes prosecution for marijuana and heroin possession in New Orleans as a result of jurisdictional contradictions between state and federal prosecutors (see Murphy 1998, 50–51). More expansive and inventive is Burroughs' routine "Roosevelt after Inauguration," which was originally intended to appear in *The Yage Letters* although it was written much later than those letters. Superficially, it appears to be a relatively straightforward—and right-wing—satire on Roosevelt's 1937 attempt to "pack" the US Supreme Court in order to overcome its resistance to the state oversight of economic production mandated by the New Deal. As such the routine deploys the conventional satiric rhetoric of tyranny, as in its opening line: "Immediately after the Inauguration Roosevelt appeared on the White House balcony dressed in the purple robes of a Roman Emperor and, leading a blind toothless lion on a gold chain, hog-called his constituents to come and get their appointments" (Burroughs 1979, 41). However, the right-wing rhetoric of executive-branch tyranny gradually grows so hyperbolic that it begins to decompose: "When the Supreme Court overruled some of the legislation perpetrated by this vile rout, Roosevelt forced that august body, one after the other, on threat of immediate reduction to the rank of Congressional Lavatory Attendants, to submit to intercourse with a purple-assed baboon" (42). When the Justices succumbed to the baboons, Roosevelt appointed the apes to replace them and thereby "gained control of the highest tribunal in the land" (43). Having commandeered the judicial branch, Roosevelt launches an all-out assault on the legislative branch, loosing "crabs and other vermin in both Houses," sending "a corps of trained idiots" to "shit on the floor," and undertaking "continuous repairs" that left the congressmen "either buried alive or drowned when the Houses flooded." The final insult to the separation of powers comes when the legislators, trying to debate in the street, are "arrested for loitering . . . sent to the workhouse like common bums" and subsequently "barred from office on the grounds of their police records" (43–44). In other words, the police are finally brought in to impose the full penalty of law upon the lawmakers themselves—the police become the agents who interrupt or interfere with the internal functioning of the police state itself. The federalist separation of powers, which was meant to guarantee the smooth operation of the state, breaks down under Roosevelt's perverse assault and forces a radically new social as well as bodily organization on the citizens—he intends, as he says, to "make the cocksuckers glad to mutate!" (44).

This routine merely makes explicit what was already implicit in the "Interzone" chapter of *Naked Lunch* (and also foreshadows the role played by the Nova Police in the Nova Trilogy): despite their overtly repressive character, the legal and judicial system and the police are structurally ambivalent aspects of the state apparatus that can impede or interfere with its efforts at control as well as enable them. Such inter- and intra-state interference contributes to the accelerating erosion of national sovereignty, specifically the weakening of the state's ability to manage competition, conflict, and antagonism, and thereby opens up spaces in which subversive subjects (like Burroughs and his fellow Beats) can flourish, and subversive movements (like the global counterculture of 1968 that was partially inspired by the Beats) can coalesce and struggle for autonomy—*temporarily*. Many analysts have identified this erosion of state sovereignty as a key characteristic of corporate globalization, and an important site for effective militancy against it. In the same way that Gilles Deleuze recognized Burroughs as a precursor of Foucault in his analysis of "control societies," I suggest we can also recognize him as a precursor of globalization critics like Giovanni Arrighi, David Harvey, Naomi Klein, Michael Hardt, and Antonio Negri in his analysis of the internal and external forces that are eroding state sovereignty under the emerging regime of globalization. Just as Burroughs seduced Kerouac and Ginsberg across the physical and ideological borders between nation-states at the beginning of the postmodern era, so he continues to seduce us at its conclusion. In neither instance does he lead his readers to a promised land of perpetual noninterference—the International Zone of Tangier dissolved with Moroccan independence and new, more repressive free trade zones and *maquiladoras* have spread like viruses across the globe, while border-crossing today takes us nowhere that is not already part of Empire or neoliberalism. All Burroughs did for the Beats, and all he can do for us, is demonstrate how to slip away for a little while, how to slip between the forces of control to find a precarious and temporary space for resistance.

TIMOTHY S. MURPHY is Houston-Truax-Wentz Professor of English at Oklahoma State University. His books include *Wising Up the Marks: The Amodern William Burroughs* and *Antonio Negri: Modernity and the Multitude.*

NOTES

1. This is not to say that Burroughs subscribed to an essentialist definition of the state as agent of power; see Pepper 2005.

2. This paradox of the cop who minds his own business as a synecdoche for the utopian "sanctuary of noninterference" is the strict corollary of Burroughs' later insistence that "A *functioning* police state needs no police" (Burroughs 2001, 31) because the citizens have internalized the police function. This internalization of the police function constitutes Burroughs' anticipation of Louis Althusser's model of subjective interpellation as the material functioning of ideology in "Ideology and Ideological State Apparatuses" (1971).

3. See also Burroughs' satiric essay "When Did I Stop Wanting to be President?" in Burroughs 1979.

REFERENCES

Althusser, Louis. 1971. *Lenin and Philosophy and Other Essays.* Translated by Ben Brewster. New York: Monthly Review.

Burroughs, William S. 1977. *Junky:50th Anniversary Definitive Edition.* Edited by Oliver Harris. New York: Penguin.

———. 1979. *Roosevelt after Inauguration and Other Atrocities.* San Francisco: City Lights.

———. 1989. *Interzone.* Edited by James Grauerholz. New York: Viking.

———. 1993. *The Letters of William S. Burroughs, 1946–1959.* Edited by Oliver Harris. New York: Viking.

———. 2001. *Naked Lunch: The Restored Text.* Edited by James Grauerholz and Barry Miles. New York: Grove.

Burroughs, William S., and Allen Ginsberg. 2006. *The Yage Letters Redux.* Edited by Oliver Harris. San Francisco: City Lights.

Deleuze, Gilles. 1995. "Postscript on Control Societies." In *Negotiations 1972–1990,* by Gilles Deleuze, 177–182. New York: Columbia University Press.

Johnson, Rob. 2006. *The Lost Years of William S. Burroughs: Beats in South Texas.* College Station: Texas A&M University Press.

Kerouac, Jack. 1995. *Selected Letters, 1940–1956.* Edited by Ann Charters. New York: Viking.

Mullins, Greg A. 2002. *Colonial Affairs: Bowles, Burroughs and Chester Write Tangier.* Madison: University of Wisconsin Press.

Murphy, Timothy S. 1998. *Wising Up the Marks: The Amodern William Burroughs.* Berkeley: University of California Press.

Pepper, Andrew. 2005. "State Power Matters: Power, the State and Political Struggle in the Post-War American Novel." *Textual Practice* 19 (4): 467–91.

Stuart, Graham H. 1955. *The International City of Tangier.* 2nd ed. Stanford, CA: Stanford University Press.

On China

In these collages and typescripts from the late 1960s, Burroughs reflects upon the Cultural Revolution in China, as well as America's occupation of Indochina. These geopolitical events seemed capable of redefining the global social body according to the most fundamental dimensions of space and time. Like all revolutions of which Burroughs approved, Mao's sought to invent a new calendar system (liberated from European imperial time standards). Just as Burroughs developed his own calendar system, he cut up Mao's writings for *Minutes to Go* (1960), and *The Ticket That Exploded* (1962), finding inspiration in Mao's formula for guerilla tactics, "Enemy advance we retreat" (Harris, xxi).

In the same folder of Berg Folio 161 containing his essay "On China," researchers will also find Burroughs' letter introducing his essay on October 3, 1968, to Jeff Sherro (editor of *Rat Subterranean News*, an underground newspaper created in March 1968). Burroughs took the opportunity to emphasize that the point he wished "to underline" in the article, "the basic issue," was "A world wide monopoly of knowledge and discoveries for counter revolutionary purposes. Betrayal and deceit is involved here far beyond the traditional conservative reluctance to meet demands for increased freedom on the part of young xx people. This basic sell out must be brought to the attention of young people everywhere" (Berg 62.3). To bring the conspiracy to the public's attention, Burroughs not only spoke through popular venues, but also sought through his multimedia cut-up scrapbooking to archive the news as he forged materials for resistance.

In Burroughs' collage of Nixon's dilemma in Indochina, contained in Berg Folio 94, as part of a scrapbook titled "Words Worth Dream File," Burroughs juxtaposes photographs of the 1970 Kent State shooting with articles on the youthful counterculture, alongside haunting maps of South East Asia. Likewise, his "P.S. to ACADEMY 23 & NEWSWEEK Picture," from 1967, originates from Folio 96, an unfinished scrapbook whose title reworks Marshall McLuhan's famous dictum, redefining "medium" to propose that "The Order and The Material IS The Message." The juxtaposition of an essay fragment and a newspaper photograph of Vietnamese students rioting captures the thematic obsessions occupying Burroughs' most brilliant late 1960s scrapbook. This "postscript" essay offers a final thought to Burroughs' writings in the late 1960s on revolutionary hopes for Communist China as an alternative model to the West. Burroughs may have meant for this "post-script" to supplement his essay, titled "Academy 23: A Deconditioning", published in the *Village Voice* (Vol. 12, No. 38) on July 6, 1967. However, the last chapter of *The Job* (1969) reworks this essay and is entitled "Academy 23" as well (the number 23 was Burroughs' favorite, and lucky, number). Throughout this time, he conceived of the academy that was supposed to house the archive he was curating, to be located in Vaduz Switzerland and called the International Center of Arts and Communication (for more on Burroughs' idea for an academy, see Odier, 137).

If his brief essay on revolutionary China was meant to serve as a postscript to his piece in *The Job*, it would work well as an addendum to the following quote: "Young people pose the only effective challenge to established authority. Established authority is well aware of the challenge. Established authority is moving against young people everywhere. It is now virtually a crime to be young. This is all-out war in which the opposition will use the dirtiest tactics at their disposal. The only country to gain the support of its young people is Red China, and that is why the State Department has put a travel ban on Red China. They don't want Americans to see and realize that any country which offers young people anything at all will gain their support. The Western establishments offer nothing. . . . The student rebellion is now a worldwide movement. Never before in recorded history has established authority been so basically challenged on a worldwide scale" (ibid., 81). In his "P.S. to Academy 23," Burroughs goes on to identify the young people today as the only hope for America, and he identifies Red China as the only nation with the support of the youth, the only one that offers the youth what he calls "the challenge and adventure of making their own world" (Berg 31.39).

Regardless of whether Burroughs, like so many avant-garde writers of his time, misinterpreted the potential and significance of the Cultural Revolution in China, he provides in these writings a pivotal expression of his revolutionary perspective. Burroughs feared that the youthful generations coming in his wake would fail to take seriously the grave threat posed by reactionary backlashes, underestimating the drastic steps America's conservative underbelly would take to suppress the rights of minorities throughout the world. For this reason, he exhorts the youth of his day to vote "those idiots out of office before they destroy your planet," while also warning that "threatened by a block that could vote them out of office they will resort as always to naked force" (Berg 31.39). For this reason, while Burroughs retained a previous era's naive, libertarian commitment to gun ownership, he also began to advocate, as early as the 1960s, that the revolutionary classes would need to prepare for guerilla warfare. "You must be prepared to meet force with force if necessary," Burroughs writes, offering a motto still relevant for our time, more than a century after his birth, as we begin to reckon with the cynical strategies and unimaginable technology by means of which the ruling class seems willing to retain control over the huddled masses on a waning planet.

—AWC

My interpretation of events in cin Red China agrees with the enclosed analysis.
I would not call the Maoist dream utopian in that it has a good chance to work.
Class and individual difference, deliberately accentuated and exploited by
vested interests, have brought the wset West to a state of chaos and disaster.
What is being done in the West on an official level has no chance of working.
I would say that Mao is practicing a new form of politics.
Certainly the cultural revolution is not compatibe with the ambitions of Chinese
   nationalists
There is no reason why Chinese methods could not be practiced anywhere.
Since the Chinese cultural revolution is an uncompromising attemp to abolish
class differences and vested interest any moderation of this intent could not
but vitiate this interesting experiment.
I think the infulence of the Chinese cultural revolution on the West is very
far reaching. For one thing if the experiment suceeds it will have demonstrated
that what passes for 'the unalterable nature of man' is actually vested interests.
that there is no such thing as 'human nature',
Definitely the student movement and the Chinese cultural revolution are closely
allied. The student are completely disillusioned with Russian Marxism which
   is coming to resmble more and mor closely the societys against which they
      are in revolt.
   I have always found humanism a regretably vague concept. I think it would be
      generally considered synonomous with culture
When culture becomes a rigid structure it is an obstacle to change. If we think
of culture as techniques in the widest sense then these techniques scientific
   artistic and psychologically then culture could implement change.
   I would say that the sign is laregly due to the fresh discovery of Chinese
      graphics.
   As to whether art can reach the masses depends of course on the level of the
masses. There is no a priori reason why this level should be low.
I see no need of renouncing so called bourgeois art. Art is not a class monoply.

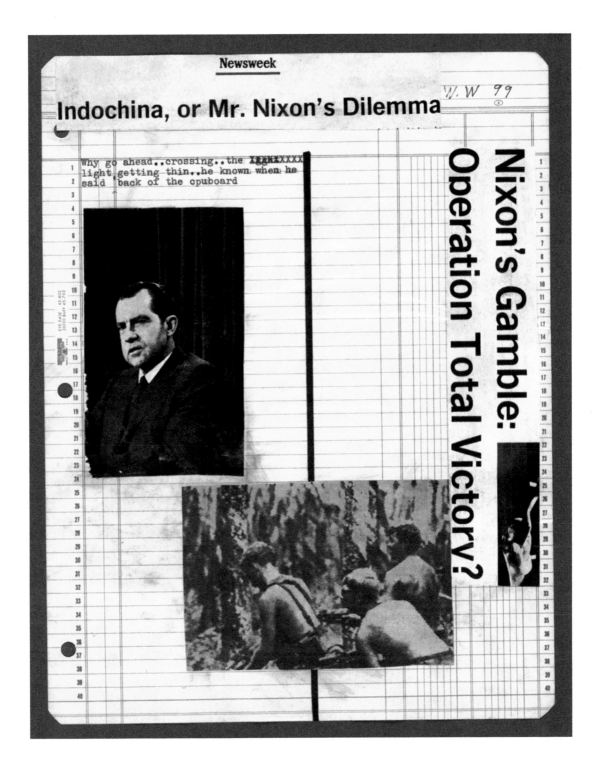

ABOVE, *Indochina, or Mr. Nixon's Dilemma*, William S. Burroughs, 1970 (8 × 11, 1 leaf, facsimile) (Berg 31.8). Folio 96, Item 99, "Indochina, or Mr. . .". Three news clippings and typescript pasted on page. Copyright © by William Burroughs, used by permission of The Wylie Agency LLC.

FOLLOWING PAGE, *P.S. to ACADEMY 23 & NEWSWEEK Picture*, William S. Burroughs, 1967 (8 × 11, 1 leaf, facsimile) (Berg 31.39). Folio 96, Item 6, P.S. to ACADEMY 23 & NEWSWEEK picture. Copyright © by William Burroughs, used by permission of The Wylie Agency LLC.

P.S.To Academy 23

The only governement in the world today that has all out
support of its young people is Red China. Why? Because the
Red Guards are being offered the challenge and adventure of
making their own world. What challenge what adventure is being
offered to young people in England and America? None whatever.
It is not surprising that they turn to drugs.The Red Guards
don't want any drugs. Young people in the West would lose
interest in drugs if they had anything else.
So shave off your beards,cut your hair and vote those idiots
out of office before they destroy your planet. Vote America
out of Vietnam. Vote china into the U.N. If you want legalized
marjuana vote it in. Young people today are the most powerful
voting block in the world. The 18 to 25 year olds with the
Negroe vote and a considerable block of older citizens who
retain a degree of sanity could vote in any candadate of their
choice.
However remember this: threatened by a block that could vote
them out of office they will resort as always to naked force.
So stop using drugs. Learn karate. Learn guerilla war tactics.
You must be prepared to meet force with force if necessary;
to fight in the streets with Molotov cocktails,home made
infrasound,cross bows,machetes,any weapons you can devise
I am not advocating the over throw of the U.S. governement
by force. I am advocating its overthrow by its own legal
machinery. If the people now in power attempt to hold their
position by illegal force then you will have to fight or
submit to a degree of control beside which 1984 is liberal
and permissive.
I refer you to The Daily Mail..Page 2..VISION..Clash in Athens
Saturday April 22,1967..'In this demonstration as in so many of
its kind it is the students who are the first to challenge
established authority.'

Newsweek—François Sully
Disorder in Hué: Student on rampage

9

Cut-Up City: William S. Burroughs' "St. Louis Return"

ERIC SANDWEISS

On New Year's Day 1965, William Burroughs sits in a St. Louis hotel room with a young journalist and book critic named Conrad Knickerbocker. "On the dresser," Knickerbocker will recall, "sat a European transistor radio; several science fiction paperbacks; *Romance*, by Joseph Conrad and Ford Madox Ford; *The Day Lincoln Was Shot*, by Jim Bishop; and *Ghosts in American Houses*, by James Reynolds. A Zeiss Ikon camera in a scuffed leather case lay on one of the twin beds beside a copy of *Field & Stream*. On the other bed were a pair of long shears, clippings from newspaper society pages, photographs, and a scrapbook. A Facit portable typewriter sat on the desk, and gradually one became aware that the room, although neat, contained a great deal of paper" (Knickerbocker 1965, 14).

Knickerbocker's interview with the expatriate writer ran in that fall's issue of the *Paris Review*. Its readers may have found the inventory of Burroughs' Chase-Park Plaza Hotel room less interesting than what followed it: the novelist's explanation of the objects' relations to one another. Responding to Knickerbocker's questions about his writing technique, Burroughs provided the most explicit accounting yet of his scrapbooks, which had evolved from his earlier experiments with the method already known to his readers as the cut-up. "I'll read in the newspaper something that reminds me of or has relation to something I've written," he explained to his interviewer. "I'll cut out the picture or article and paste it in a scrapbook beside the words from my book." The camera, the shears, the books, the typewriter, the "great deal of paper": all were tools and content alike of a verbal artist's work, as he cut the base elements of his world in shreds and transformed them into another—a world increasingly abstract, unrecognizable, but in some way more precious, more real (Knickerbocker 1965, 21).

Whatever alchemy he witnessed in that quiet room in the Chase, Knickerbocker—like Burroughs a native Missourian—could not ignore the mundane, recognizable details of the Midwestern scene that played outside. From the window, the reporter heard faintly the sound of children in "the broad brick alleys in which [Burroughs] had played as a boy," enjoying an uncommonly warm New Year's Day (Knickerbocker 1965, 14). Had he asked his host, the visitor at Burroughs' hotel

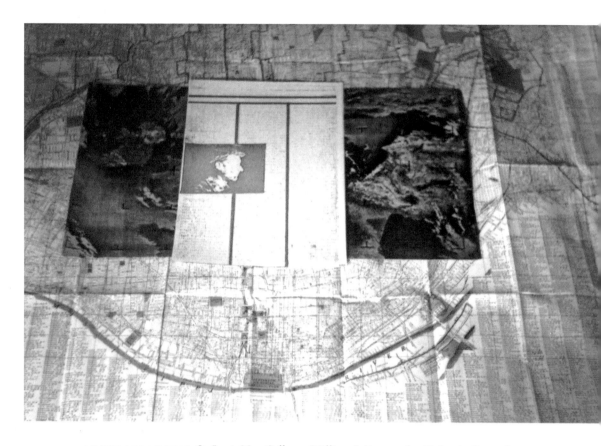

ABOVE AND FACING, *St. Louis Map Collages*, William S. Burroughs, St. Louis, December 1964. (Berg 91.17, Series 4, Photography P-17 "St Louis Photos" [1964–65]). In January 1965, Burroughs explained his cut-up techniques to interviewer Conrad Knickerbocker in a hotel room cluttered with books, papers, and—as this image suggests—materials about his home-town. Copyright © by William Burroughs, used by permission of The Wylie Agency LLC.

window would have noticed still more. Two blocks north and east, on Pershing Place, the writer might have pointed out his first home, which looked much as it had when he left it at the age of twelve. Burroughs knew, too, that two blocks north of that stood the boyhood home of another local writer, T. S. Eliot. Due west of the Eliot house, at the intersection known as "Holy Corners," rose the spire of St. John's United Methodist Church, erected under the ministry of Burroughs' grandfather, Rev. James Wideman Lee. Another mile west of that, just above the Forest Park tree line, Burroughs might have pointed out the tile roof of the building that once housed the Community School—where he learned to read and write.

This was the West End of St. Louis, the city where William S. Burroughs had grown up, the place he left upon his high school graduation, and the place to which he chose to return, in December 1964, in an effort to piece together his own cut-up life.

The links between autobiography and a larger, more fantastical reality—one developed in four decades of fictional writing—have occupied Burroughs' readers

and critics from the start. In general, that effort has required letting go of the more obvious associations that literary critics make between their subjects' lives and work (it's important, we think, to know that Twain plied the currents of the Mississippi and prospected in the Sierra; that Hemingway fished in Michigan and drove ambulances in Spain; that Flannery O'Connor settled onto a Georgia farm with her mother and her peacocks . . .), and following the writer from his terrestrial surrounds into more imaginative landscapes. "The challenge for readers and critics of Burroughs," writes Micheal Sean Bolton, "is to cease relying on external frames through which to contextualize his narratives and, instead, to create contexts spontaneously during the act of reading. His contexts are not material, derived from contexts external to the narratives, but are associative" (2010, 54). Bolton goes on to suggest that "Burroughs' places, like Baudrillard's maps, exist in continual states of movement and mutation as simulations of territories that themselves have no foundations, no origins, and no stable positions" (68).

The suggestion has some basis. To an extent greater than most writers, Burroughs traded on his itineracy, habitually folding in details from one place or another in his long travels—Mexico City, Tangier, the Far West, New York, Paris— with historical sites and fictive places to chart the synthetic "Interzone" that drew on all of them and fully resembled none, and that spanned a territory broad enough to accommodate memories and fantasies alike. His absurdist improvised routines, his cut-ups with their juxtaposition of previously distant words and images, his weird efforts to punctuate the smooth and irreversible flow of time ("The mere act of playing a street recording back in the street makes a hole in reality," he wrote to Bruce Holbrook from London, a short time after the appearance of the *Paris Review* interview, "since people are hearing yesterday or whenever," letter in Burroughs 2012, 197) seem carefully plotted to discourage any reader hoping to draw direct lines from the people and places of Burroughs' stories to those of his life.

William Burroughs' letters of 1964, in particular, appear to confirm the critic's sense that he lacked "stable positions" in life. Turning fifty, Burroughs had tired of the rough conditions and sometimes hostile reception endured as a gay expatriate in Morocco. Writing in April to his friend (and fellow cut-up artist) Brion Gysin, he allowed that "I am disgusted with Tangier like I turn sick with the sight of Arabs." The city was, he continued, "worse than Paris or any place I have experienced . . . the only thing that keeps me here is . . . not knowing where else to go" (Burroughs 2012, 151). After more than a decade in North Africa, after his brushes with scandal, jail, and death, Burroughs seemed at last to have backed himself to the edge of a cliff.

He did, however, have one more place to go.

To appreciate the logic of his decision to make that place St. Louis—following a self-imposed absence of more than thirty years—we have to let go of the notion that the sites of Burroughs' fiction have "no foundations, no origins." For there remained for him, then and throughout his life, one and only one "old broken point of origin," as he called it in his *The Wild Boys*: "St Louis Missouri" (Burroughs 1971, 85).

Logic suggests that the first object mentioned in a writer's first published book might bear some attention. The "solid, three-story, brick house in a large Midwest city" that anchors *Junky*'s prologue offered the perfect foil for the *louche* patrician image that he went on to cultivate in his life and writings. With "a lawn in front, a back yard with a garden, a fish pond and a high wooden fence all around it," the home built by Mortimer ("Mote") Burroughs for his family on Berlin Avenue (rechristened Pershing in the closing months of World War I) in the city's West End featured, as the writer recalled in this first book, "all the props of a safe, comfortable way of life that is now gone forever" (Burroughs 2003, 1). As boys, William and his older brother Mortimer Jr. moved five miles west with their parents—like thousands of middle-class and well-to-do St. Louisans of the day—to the "comfortable capsule" of a larger suburban house—in their case in the wealthy suburban community of Ladue, "where there were squirrels instead of rats" (2). On weekday mornings, the younger Burroughs boy crossed South Price Road and continued down the hill to the recently founded, progressive John Burroughs School (named for the naturalist, no relation), whose student literary journal, the *Review*, printed "Personal Magnetism," his first published work. In 1930, his parents sent him west to New Mexico's Los Alamos School, where the revelation of diary entries revealing his fondness for a classmate soon left him mortified, embarrassed, and on the next train home. Following his return from Los Alamos, Burroughs registered at the Taylor School, a small private institution located in Clayton, the well-to-do St. Louis County seat, which rests between Ladue and the city's West End. He graduated from Taylor, then left St. Louis for good (not counting short family visits and the court-ordered stay that followed a 1946 narcotics arrest in New York)—but not without a collection of the childhood images that would continue to serve him, in later years, as reminders of how far he had traveled from a "safe, comfortable life" that might have been his for the choosing.

To understand better what those images of home represented to this man of the world—and what might have compelled him to spend his fifty-first Christmas at the Chase-Park Plaza, rather than Paris's Beat Hotel or Tangier's Hotel el-Muniria or some other accommodation more befitting a mentor of the Beat movement—we need to let go, as well, of other notions of what St. Louis was, and of how Burroughs remembered it. Even the writer's most meticulous biographers, understandably focused on his productive and eventful stays in Mexico City, Paris, Tangier, New York, or London, have contented themselves with shorthand, minimally researched descriptions of St. Louis that build on his own loose characterizations of the place he continued, long into his life, to see through a child's eyes. Barry Miles writes of the city of Burroughs' birth that "only 60 years before, St. Louis still had something of the atmosphere of a frontier town; it was still part French and in campsites on its outskirts lived Indians, whom local children would taunt with war whoops" (1993, 23); while the reader scanning the index of Oliver Harris and Ian MacFadyen's edited volume of essays on *Naked Lunch* finds the sole mention of the place under "Burroughs, William S., southern upbringing of" (2009, 276). Such shorthand caricatures of a city that was in fact quite large and cosmopolitan (even by the 1850s, when the lingering presence of either a Frenchman or an Indian on the city's streets would have been front-page news—let alone at the time of Burroughs' birth in the 1910s, when its population trailed those of only New York, Chicago, and Philadelphia among the nation's largest, and when a southern accent overheard in most city neighborhoods would have turned more heads than a German one) oblige Burroughs' own effort to render himself an exotic narrator, the stoic survivor of some unredeemed frontier. But in the process, they flatten out the reader's sense of the cultural influences that attended the writer's upbringing, and they diminish the level of his achievement in melding those influences into the unique voice that he developed in a body of published work extending from *Junky* to *My Education*.

Not exactly the distant outpost of either a southern or western frontier, the city to which New York's William Seward Burroughs Sr., and Georgia's James Wideman Lee moved (in 1882 and 1893, respectively) prospered not from its remoteness but from its centrality—proximity to northern railroads and immigrant labor, in one direction, and to southern and southwestern resources, in the other. From Dallas's Adolphus (Busch) Hotel, Tucson's (Sisters of) Carondelet St. Mary's Hospital, to Colorado's (John C.) Frémont Pass, the influence of nineteenth-century

St. Louis's institutions and wealthy families had already inscribed itself across a broad sweep of territory stretching from the old Confederacy to the Far West.

The city itself required a great deal of land for storing, processing, and shipping the raw goods of this great trading territory—and for housing the families on whose labor those processes depended. Most of St. Louis's industrial and working-class districts stretched north and south from a central corridor of wealth and prestige (along which gathered the city's Episcopal and Catholic Cathedrals, its two universities, the big hospitals and their nearby medical office buildings, the legitimate theaters, the public library, and the history and art museums). Burroughs, not surprisingly, knew primarily that central corridor. But he also grew up knowing the places where the city's working landscape butted up uncomfortably close to the neighborhoods of its wealthy residents. Passengers debarking from the city's grand Union Station, for example, encountered a view of miles of railroad tracks, clay quarries, and crowded tenements populated by black families excluded, by legal covenant and financial means, from more salubrious quarters. Along the central waterfront, an elevated train trestle and decaying industrial buildings left monuments of the city's past—the historic Old Cathedral, the Old Courthouse, colonial fur trader Manuel Lisa's stone warehouse—isolated from the city's modern financial and cultural center (Sandweiss 2001).

At the far western end of this central corridor, well insulated from downtown's signs of creeping blight, were the stately boulevards along which rose the grand homes and elegant apartments of the city's wealthiest families. In the city's early generations, their fortunes had come from trading furs, hardware, and basic goods. After the Civil War, the wealthiest among them made their money from manufacturing steel rails, train cars, and machines or from using the power of those machines to transform raw materials such as cotton (into clothing), tobacco (into cigarettes), and grain (into beer or animal feed). Finally, by the time of the arrival of the Lees and the Burroughses in the late 1800s, an increasingly complex urban economy fostered a specialized hierarchy of business and social leaders—including the merchants who, from Monday through Saturday, required reliable means of recording and calculating numbers of ever-increasing quantity at ever-faster speeds, and who on Sundays required a site and mode of worship befitting their status as sober, community-minded, well-off Christians and Jews. The executive of an adding machine manufacturer (or, in the case of William Sr.'s son Mortimer's chosen trade, of plate glass for retail display windows) and the minister of a high-status Methodist Episcopal church would have felt right at home along the West End's tree-lined streets.[1]

The effort of West End families to keep the substantial brick-and-stone landscape of their neighborhood from falling to the kind of decay that they saw taking place further downtown is evident in the publication, seven years before Burroughs' birth, of the nation's first comprehensive city plan. In place of the waterfront's decaying, crowded blocks, the Civic League of St. Louis's 1907 plan offered an image of a monumental, cleared space devoted to speeding traffic and

"The River Front as It Should Be," Wilbur Trueblood. Drawing by F. Humphry Woolrych, from the Civic League of Saint Louis, *A City Plan for St. Louis* (1907), 72. St. Louis's civic league's city plan featured numerous illustrations, such as this by architect Wilbur Trueblood, projecting a more orderly public landscape upon the crowded industrial city.

improving commercial connections from river to rails to hinterlands. For the front of Union Station, the Civic League joined in a trend advocated by the Pennsylvania Railroad's chief publicist, who called in the pages of the *American City* magazine for orderly clearance of the neighborhoods that surrounded big-city train stations (Lee 1922). St. Louis's proposed Central Traffic-Parkway would stretch toward the newly cleared waterfront in one direction and the West End in the other, replacing the arriving traveler's view of rooming houses and saloons and decrepit homes with that of a wide, tree-lined boulevard (Civic League 1907, 37; St. Louis City Plan Commission 1912).

Mote and Laura Lee Burroughs enjoyed an insider's view of the civic improvement movement's evolution. Both belonged to the kinds of established West End families who had spearheaded its efforts—it was after all Laura's brother, the railroad publicist Ivy Lee, who had written the *American City* article on improving the surroundings of big-city train terminals like Union Station, and it was their sister Kate's husband, Wilbur Trueblood (also the architect of the new Burroughs home on Price Road), who had conceived that vivid plan, in the 1907 city plan, for a central waterfront shorn of its old buildings. But, like other privileged residents of the central corridor, they lost their faith in the imminent success of the planners' agenda. By the time the young couple prepared to send their sons to school, most of their middle- and upper-class co-citizens were retreating from the continued tide of immigration, industrialization, and declining land values that lapped up against the edges of their neighborhoods. "The old families of the town are scattered and submerged," wrote one of the Civic League's early leaders, the attorney Isaac Lionberger, in 1920; "Whole districts are deserted, and a city full of empty dwellings is ever building new ones." Thinking about those well-to-do families who, like the Burroughses, picked up stakes for communities like Clayton and Ladue, he noted that, "those who have the means move continually." In place of the Civic League's idealized urban whole, Lionberger found only "a broken and uneven city" (Sandweiss 2001, 231). In place of a shared civic commitment among the city's disparate residents, another Civic League leader—the famous landscape architect and engineer George Kessler—saw only "a group of segregated villages" (234).

In the years that followed, as William S. Burroughs came of age and then left the city altogether, the city plan was, save for a few of its most politically feasible components, abandoned; the Depression restricted civic planning to those projects that could receive federal funds; and by 1950 the editors of the *St. Louis Post-Dispatch* openly asked their readers, in a highly publicized series of articles promoting local business leaders' postwar renewal efforts, to consider which way the city's future pointed: to "Progress or Decay?" (Baumhoff 1950). Despite their best efforts to tilt in the direction of the first option—with massive land clearance (finally) along the waterfront and in the Mill Creek Valley west of Union Station, high-rise public-housing construction on the near North and South Sides, and interstate highway construction through the midst of poor neighborhoods and outmoded industrial zones—postwar civic leaders presided over an increasingly "broken and uneven" place—a cut-up city.

Civic boosters and city planners were not the only people attending closely to St. Louis's seeming slow fragmentation, and here Burroughs—even as he decamped to Paris or Tangier—was attuned to a resonance of nostalgia and regret of which his parents were likely only dimly aware. For the men and women who had given the city its unusually concentrated literary reputation in the years before and during the younger Burroughs' lifetime, the choice of "progress or decay" would not be settled by enhanced property values or interstate highway subsidies. In 1899, William Marion Reedy—whose literary review the *Mirror* launched the careers of local writers like Theodore Dreiser and Sara Teasdale—had asked his readers, in an essay of the same name, "What's the Matter with St. Louis?" "Too much mere matter," the editor answered in response to his own question, "too little mind" (Sandweiss 2000, 408). Teasdale saw in the aging waterfront not the promise of urban renewal that an architect like Wilbur Trueblood held forth, but the brooding presence of the past, given form in "old warehouses [that] poured their purple shadows/Across the levee" (Sandweiss 2000, 23). The Anglophile Eliot, fifteen years gone from his home country—and gazing, one imagines, out his office window over the plane trees of Russell Square to the dimly remembered "purple shadows" cast over his own boyhood walks along that levee, past the old buildings with their fading signs ("Prufrock-Litton Furniture Company," read one)—reflected in a 1930 letter to the columnist Marquis Childs that "St. Louis affected me more deeply than any other environment has done" (Sandweiss 2000, 556).[2]

Besides the iconic waterfront, these literary laments for a pre-cut-up St. Louis exhibited a surprisingly specific geographic focus. Walker Percy, an author two years younger than Burroughs who knew the city—as did many southerners—as a seasonal destination for business or shopping trips, would identify its cultural epicenter in an offhand passage of his 1966 novel, *The Last Gentleman*: "If a total stranger," Percy wrote, "had stopped him this morning on Columbus Circle and thrust into his palm a note which read: *'Meet me on the NE corner of Lindell Blvd and Kings Highway in St. Louis 9 am, next Thursday—have news of utmost importance,'* he'd have struck out for St. Louis" (Percy 1999, 6).[3]

Percy's northeast corner of Lindell and Kingshighway marked the point at which Forest Park—site of the 1904 Louisiana Purchase Exposition, where civic boosters had briefly imagined themselves besting Chicago as the commercial and cultural capital of Middle America—met the wealthy West End. Their hopes would rest unrealized. Thomas Wolfe, remembering Kingshighway, from his own childhood visit to the World's Fair, as "a kind of road that wound from magic out of some dim and haunted land," returned the narrator of his 1937 story, "The Lost Boy," to the same intersection, where the writer now felt "nothing but absence, absence, and the desolation of America, the loneliness and sadness of the high, hot skies, and evening coming on across the Middle West" (1992, 65). Wolfe's recollection struck just one note within a literary chord. Within a mile of Lindell and Kingshighway had lived (or would yet) Teasdale, Fannie Hurst, Tennessee Williams, and A. E. Hotchner—all of them sharing some of that same doomed sense as they looked back on their old neighborhood through fictional or dramatic prose.

During Burroughs' childhood on nearby Pershing Place, railroad-car magnate William Bixby's mansion, which anchored the corner, had been replaced by the redbrick, terra-cotta Chase Hotel, then with its limestone addition, the Park Plaza. The Chase Park Plaza itself had by the 1960s acquired a literary resonance. Percy surely had it in his mind's eye as he imagined the corner; for another writer of Burroughs' generation, Peter Taylor, the hotel epitomized the wealth and elegance to which a southern family might aspire: "Twice that winter Father took me to St. Louis," writes the narrator of Taylor's *A Woman of Means*. "On the first trip we stayed at the Chase Hotel. I spent most of the days in our room, gazing out the window or sailing paper arrows out over Lindell Boulevard toward Forest Park . . . 'If ever I get to be anybody,' Father promised me then, 'we'll live in St. Louis all the time'" (1996, 18). From the moment of its completion, "The Chase" was, as its 1960s-era television ads would proclaim, "the place to be in St. Louis."

Mote and Laura Burroughs had left the neighborhood just as the Chase was completed on the site of the old Bixby mansion. They were farther still from their old quarters in the early 1960s, when the writer began corresponding with them about the possibility of leaving North Africa and living, once more, in St. Louis.

Chase-Park Plaza Hotel, Kingshighway and Lindell Blvds., ca. 1930. Photograph courtesy of Missouri History Museum, St. Louis. Built a short time after the Burroughs' family left their home on nearby Pershing Place, the Chase Park Plaza marked the key corner of Lindell and Kingshighway—at the intersection of the city's wealthiest residential neighborhood and its largest public park.

Besides the $200 checks that Mortimer sent William every few weeks from his retirement home in Palm Beach, the elder Burroughses had another reason for maintaining contact with their distant son: his own child, Billy, whom the writer had left at his parents' doorstep, years earlier. "We are awaiting your answer regarding Bill's summer with you. He is looking forward to it eagerly," Mortimer had written to William some time in 1959, in a letter reflecting the parents' gentle but increasingly impatient efforts to make their son shoulder responsibility for his own child. Yet even as they faced the increasing frailties of their own old age, Mortimer and Laura found themselves continually stepping in to care for both generations of offspring. "What did you do with your papers," Laura demanded in a letter sent to William in Tangier in spring 1964, "I also would like to know the name of your lawyers in New York and in London and who would take care of you if you were really sick—I am 77 years old and want you and Bill to be independent financially—if you have been making any plans for Bill—let me know so I won't worry so much about his future." Never quite willing to push harder, she closed on a more hopeful note: "Write to me again—I love hearing from you." Burroughs' response, ten days later, perhaps fell short of those hopes: "Thanks for the checks a real life saver . . . Will need more money by the end of this month and that should see me through to the next payments."[4]

Yet St. Louis—and its personal and literary associations—was on Burroughs' mind. In June, he wrote to Tambimuttu, the Sri Lankan-born editor of *Poetry London–New York*, who planned an edited volume on the work of former West End resident T. S. Eliot. Describing his own proposed essay as a "patchwork in the style of The Waste Land," Burroughs informed the editor that "I have also drawn intersection points between my own work and the work of Mr. Eliot." Tambimuttu accepted "The Third that Walks beside You" later that summer. In the meantime, Burroughs had initiated a correspondence with David Solomon, previously his editor at *Metronome* and by now working for *Playboy*, regarding article ideas. "I am prepared to write an article either on my advice to young writers or on my experience as a drug addict," Burroughs wrote, before asking for a $1,500 honorarium with a guaranteed $250 kill fee. Solomon forwarded the letter to *Playboy* managing editor Jack Kessie and editor in chief A. C. Spectorsky. Spectorsky professed a lack of interest in his proposed topics. "Let's have Dave explore other subjects with him," he penned in the letter's margins.[5]

In August, Burroughs wrote to his mother to ask if she were "still thinking of moving to St. Louis?" Solomon, evidently informed of the writer's homeward thoughts, suggested that "you could pick up a PLAYBOY assignment to do a retrospective piece on your return to St. Louis . . . We could call it 'St. Louis Blues.'" Burroughs responded affirmatively: "Even before receiving your letter I had planed [*sic*] a return to the old naborhood [*sic*] to put down a smog of nostalgia. Yes I will be happy to carry out the assignment [PS:] Suggest Meet Me in St. Louis as title."[6]

By September, Burroughs' mind was made up. "I am definitely planning to leave Tangier around mid October for a trip to the states," he wrote to Laura. "My new book Nova Express is coming out at that time so I can make some money on articles and lectures." November found him still in Africa, but ready to move. Writing to his friend Ian Sommerville on November 6, he announced that "I am going to look for headquarters in the States and it may be in St. Louis." Three days later, he told Rives Matthews—whose mother, Burroughs recalled, had known T. S. Eliot from their childhood days at dancing school—that "I could certainly use your help. Plan to make St. Louis by Christmas and spend some months there." On the same day, he informed his parents of the article commission: "I intend to cover the old Berlin Avenue naborhood and evoke some old time nostalgia. Maryland Market, Forest Park Highlands, etcetera. Actually I may buy a place in the Ozarks to use as a permanent base of operations."[7]

Laura's reply to the intended good news suggested the wide gulf that still kept Burroughs from combining his literary ambitions with a desire to meet family obligations—at least on his own terms: "Mote and I have talked over the St. Louis idea," she wrote from Palm Beach, "and we both think it would be too strenuous for Mote . . . It would seem better for all of us for you to come here . . . I know he dreads the snow and ice . . . Also Billy would not have any friends in St. Louis during the vacation period Jan and Feb. as you know are very cold and none of us have winter clothes. . . . Some day, I wish you would write a book that we could read, and dedicate it to Bill—He would like that . . . Just what you hope to find in the Ozarks I do not know."[8]

And so the Christmas visit to St. Louis took place, without the projected family reunion, and with the gratuitous maternal reminder of Burroughs' failure to "write a book that we could read." The author's suggested replacement of Solomon's "St. Louis Blues" with the less consciously hip title "Meet Me in St. Louis," along with his frank interest in evoking "nostalgia" (an emotion that he still felt compelled, however, to couch within the ironic frame of the exterminator's "smog") gain further poignancy in light of Laura's rejection of his efforts—impractical as they may have been—to engineer a reunion with his son and his parents on the site of his earliest memories. They also help us to understand his uneven responses, in the notes that became "St. Louis Return"—rejected by *Playboy* and ultimately published the following year alongside Knickerbocker's interview in the *Paris Review*—to the many changes that he (not unlike Thomas Wolfe) found as he set off in search of his own "lost boy"–hood on the streets of the West End.

"It's a long way to go see on back each time place . . . not present except in you watching a 1920 movie out the train window," Burroughs began his essay, his clipped and fragmented manner suggesting both the discontinuous views of a train journey and his own willful travel back through time to the days before his departure for college (Burroughs, 1964, 53). Debarking from the New York train at Union Station, he found post-renewal Market Street a different place from the site he remembered as a child: "Where are the tattoo parlors, novelty stores, hock shops—brass knucks in a dusty window—the seedy pitchmen . . . where are the old junkies hawking and spitting on street corners under the gas lights?" Here instead lay the whitewashed urban entryway that Ivy Lee had called for four decades earlier, and that Wilbur Trueblood and his Civic League colleagues had envisioned with their call for the Central Traffic Parkway.

Across the cleared space now known as Aloe Plaza, Burroughs saw one of the city's earliest public-private postwar renewal efforts, the Plaza Square Apartments, rising above the sparsely landscaped, empty blocks once covered by the crowded tenements of the city's poorest African American residents: "box apartments," he noted, "each with its own balcony—Amsterdam—Copenhagen—Frankfurt—London—anyplace" (Burroughs 1964, 54). A mile east, he encountered the unexpected final result of the Civic League's efforts to clean up the city's waterfront: the Jefferson National Expansion Memorial, authorized in its vague outlines as a New Deal make-work project and finally given shape in an international design competition in 1947. On the sloping streets where Prufrock's furniture showroom once rose and Teasdale's "purple shadows" once fell, the steel-and-concrete legs of Eero Saarinen's competition-winning and still incomplete Gateway Arch curved

Market Street, St. Louis, ca. 1989. Prior to his 1964 train arrival in St. Louis, Burroughs had not seen the massive clearance and landscaping of once-raucous Market Street, facing the city's Union Station. Such clearance had been advocated by his uncle, Ivy Lee, as early as the 1920s. Photo courtesy of Eric Sandweiss.

Jefferson National Expansion Memorial (Gateway Arch) under construction, July 4, 1964 (Missouri History Museum, St. Louis). Rechristened as a memorial to westward expansion, the Civic League's original waterfront clearance plan was only nearing its completion at the time of Burroughs' 1964–65 visit to St. Louis.

up toward one another amidst acres of muddy, cleared land, bearing "an ominous look like the only landmark to survive an atomic blast" (Burroughs 1964, 57).

We can imagine one of America's most famous purveyors of dystopian science fiction making much of such an image. But the sight of the Arch seems to have fallen far from the nostalgic impulses that had brought Burroughs home. (One possible measure of the depth of those impulses is suggested by his insistence, elsewhere in the essay, that "I have returned to pick up a few pieces of sunlight and shadow—silver paper in the wind—frayed sounds of a distant city" (Burroughs 1964, 62); one wonders from his retrieval of that dated phrase if the prolific St. Louis reporter James Buel's book *Sunlight and Shadow of America's Great Cities*

Gay-Lost, William S. Burroughs, St. Louis, December 1964 (4 × 6, 1 photograph, facsimile) (Berg 91.17, Series 4, Photography P-17 "St Louis Photos" [1964–65]). Burroughs walked the streets of the central corridor with camera in hand, searching for "1920 scraps" of his boyhood. Copyright © by William Burroughs, used by permission of The Wylie Agency LLC.

(1889) had rested on the library shelf of the Burroughses' home, its embossed title perhaps imprinted upon the young writer's mind.) Burroughs did not come to St. Louis in search of modernity and change. He relished instead the thought of "prowling about with my camera looking for 1920 scraps—bits of silver paper in the wind," and finding in his polaroid exposures "all the magic of past times like the song says right under your eyes back in your own backyard" (56).

The evocation of Judy Garland's closing lines in Vincente Minnelli's 1944 fanciful adaptation of Sally Benson's West End–based memoir (and the article's originally intended namesake) *Meet Me in St. Louis* suggested some of the wishful thinking that attended Burroughs' trip home. Once arrived, his St. Louis wanderings inevitably turned up not the Technicolor fantasy of a Culver City backlot but the sobering changes endured by the city since his departure. Urban population had peaked after the war; the long decline that would, by 1990, see the city's numbers diminish by more than half was well underway in 1964. Walking the once-busy streets of the city's central corridor, Burroughs could not resist interpreting the evident difference as a kind of personal sign: "sunlight on vacant lots . . . this message on a stone wall—'Gay—Lost' the houses all look empty" (Burroughs 1964, 56).[9]

Olive Street, Gaslight Square, St. Louis, ca. 1964 (Box 002, Blumberg, Thelma [1920–2012] Photograph Collection [S0402], State Historical Society of Missouri Photograph Collection). Gaslight Square, a stretch of Olive Street occupied by restaurants, cafés, and clubs, drew crowds of middle-class and suburban visitors back into the city—a trend that Burroughs considered favorably in his St. Louis article.

Postwar urban decline did not rob industrial cities like St. Louis of everything, and Burroughs did indeed grasp for scraps of the past where he found them. Here, as across the country, cultural entrepreneurs found opportunity in the cheap, aging buildings left behind by suburban emigrants. In Gaslight Square, just east of the West End, Burroughs found evidence of "a movement *back* into the city—back to the 1890s . . . yes decidedly the reversal of a trend which I for one found deplorable" (Burroughs 1964, 62). His enthusiasm for this thriving strip of restaurants, antique stores, and cafes along a decaying retail stretch of Olive Street placed

GASLIGHT SQUARE, whose nighttime brilliance is caught in the above montage, beckons visitors to St. Louis with its kaleidoscope of color and excitement. The soft gaslights which line the famed square have brightened the entertainment scene in St. Louis in thousand-foot candles of intensity. Basically built, around a re-creation of St. Louis' famed riverboat and gaslight era, the scope of the Square now includes a world-wide assortment of brilliantly designed spots. From Japanese calm to the other side of the moon, from elegant crystal Victorian to 2¢ seltzer at a turn-of-the-century delicatessen, a lone guitarist's concentration to a pre-Broadway production —GASLIGHT SQUARE offers the unusual in infinite variety for a perfect evening of fun.

Gaslight Square Advertisement, ca. 1964 (Charlie Menees Collection, used by permission of the University of Missouri-Kansas City Libraries, Dr. Kenneth J. LaBudde Department of Special Collections). Gaslight Square's merchants borrowed the collage techniques favored by other graphic artists and urbanists who sought to represent a "cut-up" urbanity in place of the excess uniformity both of City Beautiful schemes such as the St. Louis 1907 Plan and of more recent urban modernism.

Burroughs in the company of a great many middle-class St. Louisans of the late 1950s and early 1960s who enjoyed the mildly transgressive pleasure of a night out among the ruins of their city's past glory. At the Crystal Palace, established by Jay Landesman, son of a neighborhood junk dealer, they watched Nichols and May or the Smothers Brothers perform in a room cluttered with the detritus of the wealthy men and women of their parents' generation, who had left their nineteenth-century homes to crumble or fall before the wrecking ball. This sense of clutter, of unexpected juxtaposition, provided a visual theme not just for Gaslight's best-known club but for its neighbors, as well: area merchants advertised the district with a collage of images of Olive Street signs and structures designed to suggest, in its calculated clutter, some of the surprise and excitement that suburban night-crawlers might still find in this (if in no other) corner of the emptying city. Even the Gaslight Square streetscape, with its architectural remnants arrayed like the discarded wreckage of careless but well-heeled ghosts, capitalized on the fragmentation that the Civic League boosters, two generations earlier, had dreaded (see Landesman 1987).

In St. Louis, as in other American cities, such positive evocations of a cut-up city made a virtue of the necessities imposed by two generations of middle-class flight, a decade of Depression, and a new age of massive public housing, urban renewal, and highway improvement projects. Gaslight Square was far from its only expression and Burroughs was far from the only intellectual hoping to make lemonade of urban renewal's lemons. Jane Jacobs's Greenwich Village, triumphant over the totalizing logic of a Robert Moses-engineered crosstown freeway plan and basking in the attention given its crowded sidewalks by her landmark *Death and Life of Great American Cities* of 1962, provided the best-known model for the messy, lively city street that suddenly seemed, to many middle-class Americans, not such a bad thing after all. Boston-based urban designer Kevin Lynch gave architects and planners license to imagine an alternative to the massive scale of Moses-era planning when he defined, in his landmark *The Image of the City*, "a highly imageable (apparent, legible, or visible) city" as "one that could be apprehended over time as a pattern of high continuity with many distinctive parts clearly interconnected" (1960, 10). Similarly influential were the young architects, trained in modernist orthodoxy but eager to knock their mentors off of their concrete *pilotis*, who set themselves to polemicizing against the Modern Movement's urban legacy. In the States, Robert Venturi (1966) promoted an architecture of "complexity and contradiction," to be developed within a diverse urban context rather than as a set of isolated monuments. In Britain, the husband-wife team of Peter and Alison Smithson proposed that "buildings should be thought of from the beginning as fragments; as containing within themselves a capacity to act with other buildings; they should be themselves links in systems" (1965, 112). Graphic artists translated the high-style design world's new fondness for urban "fragments" into upbeat, angular images that we associate with the 1950s and early 1960s—David Klein's TWA travel posters, Art Kane's double-exposed cityscape on the cover of *LIFE*

Magazine's special "U.S. City" issue of December 1965 (its main article authored by Conrad Knickerbocker)—as surely as we place Le Corbusier's or Ludwig Hilbersheimer's rectilinear urban aerials within the earnest idealism of a previous generation. In this sense, then, Burroughs' affection for the blandishments of Gaslight Square placed him squarely in the company of respectable urbanists and bourgeois pleasure-seekers hoping to salvage from the "broken and uneven city" some measure of relief from suburban smugness or urban despair.

Where he might have reconnected with his hometown in a more distinctive or subversive manner, Burroughs simply chose not to do so. Again, Jay Landesman proves a key figure in measuring Burroughs' past against his return. It was Landesman who had launched another cultural creation—more ephemeral but perhaps more influential than the Crystal Palace—of which Burroughs had to have been equally aware in earlier days: *Neurotica*. This short-lived literary magazine, founded in 1948 as "a literary exposition, defense, and correlation of the problems and personalities that in our culture are defined as 'neurotic'" (Landesman 1948, 3) had published work by a range of writers from within Burroughs' circle of personal and professional acquaintances, including John Clellon Holmes and Allen Ginsberg. *Neurotica* also provided an early publishing outlet for a former St. Louis University English professor—since returned to his native Canada—Marshall McLuhan (1949).[10]

As Kevin Lynch or the Smithsons had done for the urban environment, McLuhan sought the unseen unity that he believed must underlie the proliferating texts of mid-century mass media. "Amid the diversity of our inventions and abstract techniques of production and distribution there will be found a great deal of cohesion and unity," he wrote in *The Mechanical Bride* in 1951. "This cohesion is not conscious in origin or effect" (McLuhan 1951, v). If we note that those sentiments, in their confident prediction of an unconscious order linking seemingly disconnected ideas, sound strikingly Burroughs-like, we ought not to be surprised to learn that the media philosopher noticed it, as well. "Burroughs is unique only in that he is attempting to reproduce in prose what we accommodate every day as a commonplace aspect of life in the electric age," McLuhan wrote, shortly after his own landmark book *Understanding Media: The Extensions of Man* (1964) appeared in the bookstores. Finding in works like *Naked Lunch* (1959) and *Nova Express* (1964) literary confirmation of his own intense musings over the nature of consciousness and social control, McLuhan believed that Burroughs intended to show that "today men's nerves surround us; they have gone outside as electrical environment. The human nervous system itself can be reprogrammed biologically as readily as any radio network can alter its fare.... The previous environment with all its private and social values, is swallowed by the new environment and reprocessed for whatever values are digestible" (McLuhan 1964, 86). Whether or not he divined the literary and geographic connections of place that tied him to McLuhan (the two men had not overlapped in their years in St. Louis, although McLuhan had in the 1940s lived at 4256 Maryland Avenue, in plain sight of Burroughs' later view from the Chase Park Plaza), we know that Burroughs—sitting in the hotel on the warm New Year's Day of 1965—was well aware of the philosopher's scrutiny, intrigued but perhaps uncertain of how to respond. The evidence of that awareness appears in the pages of Conrad Knickerbocker's *Paris Review* interview. Burroughs, asked to illustrate his cut-up technique, furnished the following seemingly illogical pastiche, the apparent product of the scissors and news clippings and scrap paper that Knickerbocker had noted in the cluttered room: "Today's men's nerves surround us. Each technological extension gone outside is electrical involves an act of collective environment. The human nervous environment system itself can be reprogrammed with all its private and social values because it is content. He programs logically as readily as any radio net is swallowed by the new environment" (Knickerbocker 1965, 25–26).

This cut-up is, of course, not so cut up after all: only a small amount of manipulation has turned McLuhan's dense verbal cascade—which had appeared in the pages of that week's issue of *The Nation* and evidently made its way into Burroughs' hands, within the previous several days, via a nearby news stand or bookstore—into the slightly altered (and not altogether more nonsensical) collage presented, without attribution, by the author to his interviewer.

What inspired Burroughs to select McLuhan's review, lightly adulterated, as an example of his own artfulness? Was it a moment of laziness—a quick fold-and-snip demonstration, using the nearest text at hand? A calculated effort to pass off another's similarly abstruse writing as an example of his own deliberate obscurantism? A respectful nod to a like mind? Regardless, a comparison with the cut-up's original source material makes clear that at least some of Burroughs' interventions were less mysterious, and more reticent, than his or other critics' subsequent explanations might lead us to believe. So, too, with "St. Louis Return," the article that brought him home. In most ways, Burroughs' attempt to come back to what McLuhan might have called "the previous environment with all its private and social values"—the St. Louis of his boyhood—fell short not only of critical notice but also of its author's intent. Having told his old friend Rives Matthews of his plan to "spend some months there," he instead boarded a train for New York within days of Knickerbocker's interview. Having hoped to reunite with his son and parents, he instead found himself rejoining them in unexpected fashion three weeks later—at his father's funeral service in Florida. Having longed to find "the old naborhood," he arrived, "gay—lost," to empty streets, mustering a bit of boosterish cheer for the success of Gaslight Square but otherwise unable to find a creative spark in the prospect of further cutting up the world that his forebears had worked to set in place early in the century. Having hoped to earn a hefty honorarium and wide readership from *Playboy*, he was soon petitioning the editors for the $300 kill fee due him upon their rejection of the article (Burroughs 2012, 203).

Yet "St. Louis Return" does reveal something vital and human in its author—one even wonders if it is because of this fact that the article is so rarely cited in any detail. With it, Burroughs—the writer alleged to have "no stable positions"—arrived at Ground Zero both of his personal memories and of his hometown's collective literary memory, in search of a Lost Boy. He proved unwilling to treat his homecoming with the surrealist abandon that livened up his chronicles of North Africa, South America, or the American West. Too much, it seemed, rode on the visit; too many places meant too much. The prospect of a cut-up city proved not to supply material for great writing; the hip editor's request for a dose of "St. Louis Blues" proved, to the tired writer, less compelling than the steak and baked potatoes at the Chase's restaurant and the soft mattresses in its guest rooms; *Neurotica*'s still-powerful literary aftermath seemed to the nation's most notorious avant-garde novelist, weighed down by thoughts of an unsuccessfully planned family reunion, not worth engaging too vigorously; nearby Gaslight Square, its picturesquely run-down landscape now the backdrop for a pleasure-seeker's night on the town, more readily caught his eye, and the bittersweet tones of other West End–based writers echoed in his voice. Conrad Knickerbocker—who would take his own life two years later in the midst of writing about another difficult writer, Malcolm Lowry—had briefly parted the curtains that separated Burroughs' inner world from the "broken point of origin" to which he had hoped his December train ride would lead. But the journalist didn't question what he saw when he looked out the windows, and neither have those who, in subsequent years, wrote about the essay and its accompanying interview.

As to what Burroughs himself saw that turned him back toward New York, perhaps our best clue comes from another St. Louis return, this one dating from seventeen years later and captured on film by the young director Howard Brookner. Following the aged writer down Pershing to the house where he spent his earliest years, a member of Brookner's crew asks if he would consider moving back. "No," responds the author who, in his books, had leapt easily across planets and over centuries, who had believed he could "make a hole in reality" and drop through it at will. "It just won't work, that's all," he continues, looking at the street around him and gesturing, perhaps, toward the high windows of the Chase-Park Plaza, two blocks away. "You can't get there from here" (Brookner 1983).

ERIC SANDWEISS is Professor and Carmony Chair of History at Indiana University Bloomington. In 1976–77, he edited the John Burroughs School *Review*—the venue in which William S. Burroughs' first published essay appeared. He is the editor of the *Indiana Magazine of History* and has published several books, including *St. Louis: The Evolution of an American Urban Landscape*, *St. Louis in the Century of Henry Shaw: A View beyond the Garden Wall*, and *The Day in Its Color: Charles Cushman's Photographic Journey through a Vanishing America*.

NOTES

1. Burroughs' paternal grandfather, William S. Burroughs Sr., moved to the city from upstate New York in 1882. His maternal grandfather, James Wideman Lee, had in 1893 left his pulpit at Atlanta's Trinity Methodist Church to become pastor of one of St. Louis's most socially prominent Protestant congregations, St. John's United Methodist—the construction of whose new church he oversaw at the corner of Kingshighway and Washington Avenue in 1902 (Lee 1920, xi–xii).

2. Eliot later claimed to have forgotten about the actual Prufrock by the time that he composed his "Love Song" (see Stepanchev 1951).

3. Percy had also visited this area of the city when he had considered sending his daughter to the nearby Central Institute for the Deaf (see Tolson 1996, 99).

4. Mortimer Burroughs Sr. to William S. Burroughs, n.d., Letters C-40, Items 7, 8; Laura Lee Burroughs to William S. Burroughs, March 3 [1964], Letters C-40, Item 5; William S. Burroughs to Laura Lee Burroughs, March 13, 1964, Letters C-40, Item 6.

5. William S. Burroughs to Tambimuttu, June 14, 1964, Letters C-42, Item 3; Tambimuttu to William S. Burroughs, July 28, 1964, c38, Item 5; William S. Burroughs to David Solomon, August 12, 1964, Letters C-42, Item 55, Burroughs Papers, Berg Collection, NYPL. Spectorsky's note appears on a copy of the letter reproduced in "William Burroughs and David Solomon," RealityStudio, December 14, 2009, http://realitystudio.org/bibliographic-bunker/william-burroughs-and-david-solomon/.

6. William S. Burroughs to Laura Lee Burroughs, August 26, 1964, c40 Item 6; David Solomon to William S. Burroughs, April 20, 1964, Letters C-42, Item 33; William S. Burroughs to David Solomon, November 9, 1964, Letters C-64, Item 74, Burroughs Papers, Berg Collection, NYPL.

7. William S. Burroughs to Laura Lee Burroughs, September 6, 1964, Letters C-40, Item 6, Burroughs Papers, Berg Collection, NYPL; William S. Burroughs to Ian Sommerville, November 6, 1964, in Burroughs 2012, 169; William S. Burroughs to Rives Matthews, November 9, 1964, in Burroughs 2012, 170; William S. Burroughs to Laura Lee and Mortimer Burroughs, November 9, 1964, ibid.

8. Burroughs Correspondence, File C-40, Item 5.

9. Burroughs photographed the "Gay-Lost" graffito along with a number of other sites around his neighborhood. Mention of the phrase does not appear in the original draft of the article but was added prior to publication. See "St. Louis Return" draft, Folio 136, Box 49, Folder 45, Item 1, Burroughs Papers, Berg Collection, NYPL.

10. *Neurotica* ceased publication in 1951. For more on *Neurotica*'s—and Jay Landesman's—place in the Beat scene, see Campbell 2001, 93–96; and Charters and Charters 2010, ch. 5, "A Weekend in July."

REFERENCES

Primary

Burroughs, William S. Correspondence. William S. Burroughs Papers, Henry W. and Albert A. Berg Collection of English and American Literature, New York Public Library, Series III: Correspondence, Files C-38 (Letters), C-40 (Family), C-42 (Letters).

Secondary

Baumhoff, Richard. 1950. "Progress or Decay? St. Louis Must Choose." *St. Louis Post-Dispatch*, March 5.

Bolton, Micheal Sean. 2010. "Get Off the Point: Deconstructing Context in the Novels of William S. Burroughs." *Journal of Narrative Theory* 40 (1) (Winter): 53–79.

Brookner, Howard, director. 1983. *Burroughs: The Movie*. Citifilmworks.

Buel, James. 1889. *Sunlight and Shadow of America's Great Cities*. Philadelphia: West Philadelphia Publishing Co.

Burroughs, William S. 1964. "St. Louis Return." *Paris Review* 35: 51–62.

———. 1971. *The Wild Boys: A Book of the Dead*. New York: Grove.

———. 2003. *Junky: The Definitive Text of "Junk."* Edited by Oliver Harris. New York: Penguin.

———. 2012. *Rub Out the Words: The Letters of William S. Burroughs, 1959–1974*. Edited by Bill Morgan. New York: Ecco.

Campbell, James. 2001. *This Is the Beat Generation: New York, San Francisco, Paris*. Berkeley and Los Angeles: University of California Press.

Charters, Ann, and Samuel Charters. 2010. *Brother-Souls: John Clellon Holmes, Jack Kerouac, and the Beat Generation*. Jackson: University Press of Mississippi.

Civic League of St. Louis. 1907. *A City Plan for St. Louis*. St. Louis, 1907.

Harris, Oliver, and Ian MacFadyen, eds. 2009. *Naked Lunch@50: Anniversary Essays*. Carbondale: Southern Illinois University Press.

Jacobs, Jane. 1961. *The Death and Life of the Great American City*. New York: Random House.

Knickerbocker, Conrad. 1965. "William S. Burroughs: The Art of Fiction, No. 36, Interviewed by Conrad Knickerbocker." *Paris Review* 35: 12–50.

Landesman, Jay. 1987. *Rebel without Applause*. Sag Harbor, NY: Permanent Press.

Landesman, Jay Irving, ed. 1948. Editor's Note. *Neurotica* 1 (1) (Spring): 2.

Lee, Ivy Ledbetter. 1920. "Biographical Sketch." In *The Geography of Genius*, by James W. Lee, xi–xxiv. New York: James H. Revell.

———. 1922. "Making the Railway Gateways of the City Attractive." *American City*, September, 221–24.

LIFE Magazine. 1965. "The US City: Its Greatness Is at Stake." December 24.

Lynch, Kevin. 1960. *The Image of the City*. Cambridge, MA: MIT Press.

McLuhan, Marshall. 1949. "The Psychopathology of Time & Life." *Neurotica* 5: 5–16.

———. 1951. *The Mechanical Bride: Folklore of Industrial Man*. Berkeley, CA: Gingko.

———. 1997. "Notes on Burroughs" (*The Nation*, Dec. 28, 1964). Reprinted in *Media Research: Technology, Art, and Communication*, edited by Michel A. Moos, 86–91. Amsterdam: Overseas Publishers Association.

Miles, Barry. 1993. *William Burroughs: El Hombre Invisible*. New York: Hyperion.

Percy, Walker. 1999. *The Last Gentleman*. New York: Picador.

RealityStudio.org. 2009. "David Solomon and William Burroughs: Correspondence, Contracts, and Ephemera." December 14. Accessed June 29, 2015. http://realitystudio.org/bibliographic -bunker/william-burroughs-and-david-solomon/.

Sandweiss, Eric. 2001. *St. Louis: The Evolution of an American Urban Landscape*. Philadelphia: Temple University Press.

Sandweiss, Lee Ann, ed. 2000. *Seeking St. Louis: Voices from a River City, 1670–2000*. St. Louis: Missouri Historical Society Press.

Smithson, Alison, and Peter Smithson. 1965. "Building toward the Community Structure." In *Structure in Art and in Science*, edited by Gyorgy Kepes, 111–15. New York: Braziller.

St. Louis City Plan Commission. 1912. *A Central Traffic-Parkway for St. Louis*. St. Louis.

Stepanchev, Stephen. 1951. "The Origin of J. Alfred Prufrock." *Modern Language Notes* 66 (6) (June): 400–401.

Taylor, Peter. 1996. *A Woman of Means*. New York: Picador.

Tolson, Jay, ed. 1996. *The Correspondence of Shelby Foote and Walker Percy*. New York: Norton.

Venturi, Robert. 1966. *Complexity and Contradiction in Architecture*. New York: Museum of Modern Art.

Wolfe, Thomas. 1992. *The Lost Boy: A Novella*. Chapel Hill: University of North Carolina Press.

Word/Image

TO BE=TO SURVIVE TO BE A BODY=TO BE BODIES=TO SURRVIVE AS A BODY AND BODIES . . . TO BE A BODY=TO WANT TO BE OTHER BODIES THAT'S WHAT SEX IS ABOUT TO BE=TWO BE . . . TO BE A WORD=TO BE WORDS since WORD is MORE THAN ONE . . . Virus B seems to be doing an excellent job of destroying all minds. . . . point is insanity like this is all verbal commands on the autonomic level literally applied with a = complete disregard for other considerations. All dependent on the original fraud of TB as TO BE as a verbal contract involving TWO BE . . . You the host and BE the virus.

—Burroughs, "TO BE=TO," 1970, Berg 24.65. Copyright © by William Burroughs, used by permission of The Wylie Agency LLC.

I am told there is a drunk lady at the door to see me. I open the door and see something like a life size doll in white and blue the face completely covered. A feeling of horror and I say . . . "Oh my God"

—Burroughs, "Opium Collage," 1970, Berg 24.72. Copyright © by William Burroughs, used by permission of The Wylie Agency LLC.

Every image has corresponding enzyme . . . To exist an image must function, the function of morphine-image is addiction.

—Burroughs, On Addiction, 1955–57–59, Berg 4.8. Copyright © by William Burroughs, used by permission of The Wylie Agency LLC.

Thinking in association blocks instead of words enables the operator to process data with the speed of light on association lines—The Color Alphabet is useful training—

—Burroughs, "Thinking in Association," 1961, Berg 4.38. Copyright © by William Burroughs, used by permission of The Wylie Agency LLC.

The art market stirs like a hysterical octopus jerking back tentacles you cant give pop art away cant even burn a lot of it being made of plastic . . . Brion Gysin says that art creates values. So what remains when the inflated values collapse is the values that art has created

—Burroughs, "La Chute de l'Art: Un Poeme Moderne," 1970, Berg 32.1–3. Copyright © by William Burroughs, used by permission of The Wylie Agency LLC.

William S. Burroughs with Maurice Girodias, the publisher of *Naked Lunch*,
by Brion Gysin, 1959. Photograph courtesy of Barry Miles.

On Addiction

These two archival pieces (the first from 1970 London, the second from 1957 to 1959 in Tangier) splice together from different angles Burroughs' meditations on the nature of existence, being, desire, and language. Burroughs understood that the rising consumer culture of his era, manipulated by an elite class, could impose on the populace unimaginable addictive needs for commodity fetishes. The essay, "On Addiction," originates from Burroughs' so-called "word hoard," the mass of manuscript material he accumulated during a feverish period of writing that fed into and created his 1959 masterpiece, *Naked Lunch*. In terse, theoretical prose, Burroughs articulates his theory of addiction in terms critically explicated as early as Eric Mortimer's *The Algebra of Need* (1971). Whereas "On Addiction" was written before Burroughs picked up the cut-up method, the first piece published here, "TO BE=TO," was created at the other end of his cut-up period. If Burroughs was still busy in his alchemist's kitchen of addiction when composing his obscene visions in *Naked Lunch*, seeking to purge and exorcise the burden of word and image, this late cut-up routine appeared after Burroughs had cut his way out, detached himself from the "reality studio," in order to speak out as a prominent countercultural figure.

Burroughs dates "TO BE=TO" at "Marie Celeste 21 1970." By this time, Burroughs had set his monthly calendar system to begin on December 23, 1969 ("The Creation"), each following month being constituted of twenty-three days, just like the Mayan Calendar. Burroughs invented names for each month, such as Bellevue, Marie Celeste, Seal Point. This dream calendar, "Dream Rat," is one of Burroughs' finest scrapbooks, containing in the Berg not just hundreds of cut-up collages but also a series of files denoting information on the system he was developing (Berg 24.1–3). Burroughs used this dating system in correspondence and notes throughout the 1970s, but unfortunately the names of months were alternated, as numbers slipped, making dating of materials from this time difficult. To properly account for the timeline of this complex work, and its interrelationships with a wide array of historical documents and events, Burroughs scholars will need to create a restored edition, ideally in digital form.

In "TO BE=TO," after a metaphysical meditation upon the nature of being, especially its dependence on the virus of language, his routine mutates into a remix of reactionary language, as Burroughs invokes the undercurrent of anti-Semitism and racism in the populist supporters of George Wallace. This routine showcases what can be most difficult for readers today, as a single page of Burroughs' text transforms from ostensibly metaphysical language into offensive and divisive discourse, such as conspiracy theories about insidious political double-crossing and self-sabotage. At this climactic point in his routine, Burroughs identifies the cause of this unrest, warning that "more and more people are inexorably forced into more and more desperate conditions of survival, their inner space completely blocaded [sic] by continual pressure from without the stupid and automatic reactions of panic prevail" (Berg 24.65). As a result, Burroughs observes, each side of the political aisle disguises itself to take advantage of weaknesses in the other. As this situation becomes increasingly desperate, Burroughs concludes: "Virus B seems to be doing an excellent job of destroying all minds" (ibid). This crisis in the nation's imaginary has only grown since Burroughs time, as various minority groups get co-opted by right-wing movements that do not have their best interests in mind. This political paradox leads Burroughs to resort to disturbing routines he hoped would serve as a vaccine against future ideological infections. In *The Ticket That Exploded* (1967), Burroughs offered a useful formula for this strategy: "As you know inoculation is the weapon of choice against virus and inoculation can only be effected through exposure" (10).

—AWC

TO BE=TO SURVIVE TO BE A BODY=TO BE BODIES=TO SRURVIVE AS A BODY AND
BODIES… TO BE A BODY=TO WANT TO BE OTHER BODIES THAT'S WHAT SEX
IS ABOUT.. TO BE=TWO BE…TO BE A WORD=TO BE WORDS since WORD is
MORE THAN ONE…As more and more people are inexorably forced into
more and more desperate condtions of survival, their inner space
completely blocaded by continual pressure from without the stupid
and automatic reactions of panic prevail. As long term residents
in coneneration camp would finally immitate the SS in grotesque
uniforms of rags, so we now have Jews who are trying desperately
to disguize themselves as Storm Troopers and woo the Wllace
Wallace folk. Virus B seems to be doing an excellent job of destroying
all minds. The FD: JDEL… Have decided that antisemitism comes from
the liberal left where I believe followers of the Jewish religion
are quite well represented. They will now cut themselves off from
the liberal left and woo the Wallace folk. They may find themselves
very poorly received, suspected of being communistic Nigger
loving Sheenies. "Them Jews is all alike Clem"…Who thinks
like that the liberal left? point is insanity like this is all
verbalcommands on th autonomic level literally applied with a =
complete disregard for other considerations. All dependent on the
original fraud of TB as   TO BE as a verbal contrcat involving
TWO BE…You the host and BE the virus. Rub out the word BE,
OUt rub theee word BE, Word B the out…Rub… BE the out rub
word at first automatic exercise.., Kells was dead. He had
been bittne by a snake and I was rushing him to the hospital.
So the virus dictate contra survival moves to the host in oder
order to SURVIE TO BE. Language makes sucha a formulation impossible
of expression and therefore of realization.

Every image has corresponding enzyne
M outside   needs the excitant inside that is attakcs preys upon the
life inside,,
To exost an image must function the functioing of morphineimage is addiction..
complete idsociation of hypothealamus.. emotional life.. withdrawal complete
loss of control all veetative functions. hideousinsect like mechanical emotions
the bystander s rush up and kcik him to death far northwhere they have even
lost theor skeletons..
the strong em men, the membarassment artists or equilibrists, James Deab
types sel ing every gesture
Teh guide an old junky like aneuneuch the   DownHill slant all end up there..
because they tried to prove something..
Ventriloquists withlive latahs and obedient shcizos,, Act of fucking the
dummy each alternately givning out sex noises..
all end up hrer ocasional come back the shit eater becomes a great
   trapese peformer
maintain your persona in front of the waiter.. he want it to hold out at least
until he gets his tip..
Rasputin looks up snarling with jisson drip ing o f his chin like an
exasperated weasal   shreiking out orders..
    I suspect anyone I suc eeed with of being a Liz with strap onprick
suddenly throw it off   wit a cry of triumph.stand   evealed in her own
horrid sha pe and unseat my reason..
surprised he didn't attach a leach to my needle scars..
all work is spiel to talk a boy in bed with me..
hes got a touchof the green slime introducnign old auntie as Filthy Lucre
she touches her hair and gold dust falls out..
she farts out a   roll of gold   peices..
The final realms have a sign up off limits to writer journalists   or in any way
connected with the vile traffic in stolendreams.. most of then completely
rancid and unfit for th   fit only for the consumtion of an overt goul
or an underprivileged vulture..
inocent as a junky who has never been sick
he gets more and more lonely.. He is living a long time in a small American
town,he is walled up in a Tibetan lamestery with Paul Lund. He looks forever
into the blank cold pitiless imp con man eyes he is the outcast in a
concentration camp.. he is kicked off a boy sneering negroes,
He is surrounded by torturing Pawnees. North America evil palce of
indigenous torture

On Addiction, William S. Burroughs (8 × 11, 1 leaf, typescript) (Berg 4.8). Item 8, "Every image has . . .", from Folio 17: "Original Material For Naked Lunch, Soft Machine and Earlier. Mostly Unpublished. c1954 but mostly between 1957 and 1959 Tangier." Copyright © by William Burroughs, used by permission of The Wylie Agency LLC.

10

William S. Burroughs' Imperial Decadence: Subversive Literature in the Cynical Age of the American Century

ALEX WERMER-COLAN

BURROUGHS' "LAST WORDS": A MISUNDERSTOOD MANIFESTO

I'll show them by God how Ugly the Ugly American can be.

—William S. Burroughs, *Nova Express* (1964, in 2014, 12)

In 1964, William S. Burroughs published his third "cut-up" novel, *Nova Express*, a sci-fi narrative collage whose first chapter, entitled "Last Words," editor Oliver Harris recently praised as "a manifesto for global resistance against the one percent who run our planet like an alien colony" (Harris 2014, xi). In this underappreciated call to arms, Burroughs asserts that his writing, since *Naked Lunch* (1959), has served not only to "expose" but also to "arrest" the "all-powerful boards and syndicates of the earth" (2014, 5, 3). For the sake of the masses, whom he incites to rebellion, Burroughs famously opens his novel by lambasting the ruling class as "liars" who "want time for more lies," "collaborators," "traitors," and "cowards" who cannot "face" their "dogs," their "gooks," their "errand boys" with "the truth" (2). Burroughs warns his readers that these hypocrites plan to "sell the ground from unborn feet forever" and, after wreaking havoc, "board the first life boat in drag," leaving "their human dogs" to drown (2, 13).

Following his prescient account of the dire situation we find ourselves in today, as oil barons and corrupt politicians exacerbate a climate crisis whose victims will live predominantly in the Global South, Burroughs concludes his manifesto by cryptically suggesting *how* he intends to "arrest," subvert, or otherwise dissuade those in power. After the narrator's sidekick, the Intolerable Kid, lets loose an obscene series of racist and sexist jokes, he gives method to his madness by stating: "I'll show them by God how Ugly the Ugly American can be" (2014, 10). Although this oft-quoted line is crucial to Burroughs' avant-garde project, *what* he intends to "show," and *how* he will show it, remains broadly misconstrued. His mission statement is too often celebrated as yet another avant-garde invocation for collage artists to *détourne* (appropriate, transform, and divert) ideological discourse, converting its internal contradictions into their own immanent critiques. Throughout his writing in the 1950s and 1960s, however, the puppet masters who Burroughs is seeking to "arrest," especially American politicians, corporate bigwigs, and media moguls, hardly seem vulnerable to moral condemnation, rational argument, or theoretical critique. These are, after all, the "liars" Burroughs accuses of being willing to go so far to deceive the lower classes, they are actually *poisoning and monopolizing the hallucinogen drugs*" (4).

In the face of such a cynical ruling class, whose "reality film" only serves to keep the lower classes blinded like the prisoners gazing on the shadows in Plato's cave, Burroughs does not just indicate that he seeks to destroy, deconstruct, or otherwise *détourne* these spectacular shadows. Rather, at his pivotal manifesto's conclusion, Burroughs articulates somewhat more explicitly an alternative mode of resistance that he had already dramatized, conceptualized, and practiced implicitly in *Naked Lunch*. By working through still underexplored scenes, characters, and utterances in Burroughs' embryonic masterpiece, this essay will provide the political and ideological context, the rhetorical and aesthetic strategies, and the literary genealogy necessary to understand what exactly Burroughs had in mind when he wrote ominously at the end of his cut-up manifesto that introduces *Nova Express*, "We need a peg to evil full length. By God show them how ugly the ugliest pictures in the dark room can be" (2014, 12).

CULTURAL CRITICISM IN AN AGE OF CYNICAL REASON

> *I postulate that the function of art and all creative thought is to make us aware of what we know and don't know that we know. You can't tell anybody anything he doesn't know already.*

—William S. Burroughs, "Sects and Death" (1987, 23)

For over fifty years, artists and critics alike have celebrated Burroughs' writings as transgressive, subversive, even revolutionary. Yet his most obscene, politically incorrect, and seemingly reactionary outbursts remain relative blind spots in most critical appraisals of his work's political potential. Especially during his lifetime, critics arguing in Burroughs' favor only demurely noted his most misogynist, racist, and generally xenophobic iterations of American Cold War discourse. Seeking to present Burroughs' writing as seminal to twentieth-century literature and art, most Burroughs scholars try to salvage his most obscene scenes of racial and sexual exploitation as somehow subliminally revolutionary in message. Critics as diverse as Robin Lydenberg and Timothy Murphy, Davis Schneiderman and Oliver Harris, at best defend Burroughs' shocking "routines" for surreptitiously deconstructing the hyperpolarized, hierarchal binaries of empire and barbarian, white and black, man and woman, that structure post–World War II American capitalist-imperial politics. These wide-ranging interpretations of Burroughs' work, evident in such anthologies of Burroughs' criticism as *Retaking the Universe: William S. Burroughs in the Age of Globalization* (2004) and *Naked Lunch@50: Anniversary Essays* (2009), usually expand upon a lineage of critical theorists who adopt a traditional Marxist theory of ideology as "false consciousness." From György Lukács on social realism to Jean-Paul Sartre on "committed literature," from Fredric Jameson on postmodern historical novels to Linda Hutcheon on their "complicitous critique," from Timothy Murphy on *Naked Lunch*'s rhizomatic resistance to Oliver Harris on the cut-ups as rebellious *détournements*, the wide-ranging labor of cultural criticism tends to involve reifying avant-garde literature's capacity to enlighten readers about systematic forms of oppression and injustice.

Yet Burroughs' groundbreaking novel *Naked Lunch*, as well as his subsequent cut-up writing, satirizes precisely the ruling class's cynical imposition of "false consciousness" on the lower classes (exemplified by his paranoid vision of the ruling class poisoning otherwise "consciousness-expanding" drugs). Throughout his writings in the 1950s and 1960s, Burroughs anticipates a counter lineage of critical theorists, from Theodor Adorno in his critique of Sartre's "committed literature" to Slavoj Žižek's theorization of the commodity fetish in *The Sublime Object of Ideology* (1989). This lineage reconceptualized the ideological disposition of high to late capitalism's ruling classes in terms of what Peter Sloterdijk, in his groundbreaking *Critique of Cynical Reason* (1983), identified as a state of "enlightened false consciousness" (or "cynical reason") (Sloterdijk 1987, 5). Whereas in a state of "false consciousness," as Karl Marx says in *Capital* (1867), ideological subjects "*do not know it, but they are doing it,*" in a state of "enlightened false consciousness," as Žižek puts it, they "know very well what they are doing, but still, they are doing it" (1989, 29).

Burroughs' early writings consistently diagnose the degenerate defense mechanisms that enabled Cold War America's dominant, white upper and middle classes to accommodate the cognitive dissonance of living in bad faith by tolerating the injustices upon which their luxury patently depended. Rather than disavow the commodities extracted violently from "savage" peoples at home and abroad, in keeping with a bourgeois tradition at the heart of the European imperial enterprise, the United States regularly resorted to cynical discursive practices to justify their imperial expansion. At the helm of America's cultural propaganda, through his trilogy of magazines, *TIME*, *LIFE*, and *Fortune*, Henry Luce sought to broadcast his imperial vision of the "American Century," giving false cover to American foreign intervention by propagating a proto-neoconservative vision of the Unites States as a global missionary spreading democracy and prosperity. At the same time, however, the United States thrived within the globalizing capitalist system precisely because it acted in bad faith. As demonstrated in a wide range of recent work in American imperial studies, from Melani McAlister in *Epic Encounters: Culture, Media, and U.S. Interests in the Middle East since 1945* (2005) to Greg Grandin in *Empire's Workshop: Latin America, the United States, and the Rise of the New Imperialism* (2007), the United States refused to practice what it preached: America always negotiated by imposing double standards on free trade, appealing to paternalist justifications for interventions abroad, while blaming the victim for unintended casualties.

Burroughs understood well how Luce's propaganda worked to immunize the ruling class to rational persuasion and moral condemnation. Throughout Burroughs' oeuvre, he regularly diagnoses post–World War II America's ruling class as being shockingly immune, if not vaguely addicted, to their cynical prejudices and self-righteous hate. In *The Sublime Object of Ideology*, Žižek argues persuasively that in an age of "cynical reason" the ruling class's bad faith thrives off irony and sarcasm; for such cynical subjects, then, traditional procedures of demystifying social relations and material conditions increasingly prove not only vain, but counterproductive. Such cultural critics as Naomi Klein in *No Logo* (1999) provide thorough evidence for the ruling class's cooptation of countercultural critique, as corporations increasingly recuperate "culture jamming" by inflecting advertising with ironic self-critiques designed to appeal to cynical consumers. To attack the source of this ideological disease, then, Burroughs sought through the collage form and the cut-up method to counter the formal techniques and rhetorical strategies central to mass media journalism and advertising, including its ironic attempts to make taboo acts of consumption easier to indulge. In light of precisely this ideological dilemma, such writers as Eve Sedgwick, Bruno Latour, and Rita Felski have taken cultural critics to task for overestimating what can still be subversive in a cynical age. They suggest, from diverse perspectives, that traditional hermeneutic approaches in literary criticism too often overvalue art's capacity to transmit ideological critiques and satirical demystifications.

In this light, those literary scholars who try to recuperate Burroughs' most reactionary stances as subtly subversive, or who otherwise avoid these outbursts altogether, instead should take seriously Burroughs' most misogynist and racist "routines." Since his collage novels, *Queer* (1953) and *Naked Lunch* (1959), these fragmentary, outrageous texts proved exemplary of his counterintuitive and still understudied mode of resistance. In the face of a ruling class cynical enough to convince, for instance, working-class "white" Americans to blame Latin American immigrants and Muslim "terrorists" for their neoliberal economic woes, in order to disturb (and "arrest") the American and European readers who looked forward to books like *Naked Lunch* as exotic exposés of the Orient, Burroughs employs rhetorical strategies typically associated with and originating in nineteenth-century "decadent" literature. Although these non-critical modes of persuasion have been recently theorized by Žižek and a series of other performance art critics in terms of an "over-identification" with and a "subversive affirmation" of dominant ideologies, these theorists have focused mostly upon post-1980s performance artists and protest movements. This essay, in part, helps to trace a genealogy of such a "decadent" rhetorical strategy from its roots in fin-de-siècle France and England to its post–World War II renaissance, nowhere more evident than in Burroughs' radical aesthetic project. As he gently puts it in the *"Atrophied Preface"* appended to the novel's conclusion, Burroughs seeks in *Naked Lunch* "to return it to the white reader" (2001, 186). Burroughs' early writings during the 1950s, as well as his decade-long multi-media cut-up project in the 1960s, demonstrated how writers of his era could reflect back to readers their desires' sinister logical conclusions. His influential literary works were pivotal, especially after the worldwide reactionary turn of 1968, in inaugurating a renaissance of "decadent" aesthetics in postmodern American and European counterculture that still offer valuable methods of resistance today.

As early as *Naked Lunch*, through Clem and Jody's shocking renditions of the Ugly American, the anthropological figure of the Latah, and the narrator's own Orientalist writing, Burroughs maps the mechanics, the effects, and even the literary origin of his rhetorical strategy. If Burroughs' postmodern carnival of imperial decadence, *Naked Lunch*, remains misunderstood, even at the level of plot, it is primarily because it has been overlooked as an Orientalist travel narrative that meditates upon precisely these counterintuitive modes of resistance. By exploring *Naked Lunch*'s scenes of imperial conflict, this essay will demonstrate the extent to which Burroughs' avant-garde project involves taking America's imperial ambitions to their horrifying logical conclusions. In *Naked Lunch* and the cut-up novels, Burroughs sought to adopt the ruling class's discourse, and, as a privileged white male, to speak *for* and *to* the ruling class. In this light, *Naked Lunch*'s narrator, and such characters as Clem and Jody, appear as political agitators who do not simply reveal the contradictions and immorality of American imperial discourse. Rather, in the face of cynical powerbrokers, they take seriously the dark underbelly of American exceptionalism.

A DRAG SHOW OF THE UGLY AMERICAN: CLEM AND JODY REVEL IN AMERICAN NEOCOLONIAL POWER

> *"What you gonna do when the oil goes dry?*
> *Gonna sit right there and watch those Arabs die"*

—William S. Burroughs, *Naked Lunch* (1959, in 2001, 135)

After World War II, in the wake of modern European colonialism, the United States of America rose to power and established what many critical theorists, especially after Michael Hardt's and Antonio Negri's *Empire* (2000), identify as a postmodern mode of imperial domination that functions through neocolonial intervention and neoliberal speculation. In 1959, at the height of the Cold War, William S. Burroughs' *Naked Lunch* exploded into the Euro-American literary market, only to be condemned by most reviewers and censored by state and federal authorities alike. *Naked Lunch* recognizably anticipates Hardt's and Negri's analysis of the global transition from a modernist mode of European nation-state colonialism to a postmodern form of American-style decentralized neocolonialism. Hardt and Negri, however, characterize "Empire" as a system that, "in contrast to imperialism," "establishes no territorial center of power and does not rely on fixed boundaries or barriers," consisting instead of a "decentered and deterritorializing apparatus of rule that progressively incorporates the entire global realm within its open, expanding frontiers" (2000, xii, 192). Burroughs' novel, on the other hand, reveals (and revels in) the way nineteenth-century Europe's most cynical imperial ideology and discourse, especially its Manichean racism and Orientalist paternalism, has geographically determined our globalized capitalist system until today, and for the foreseeable future.

Halfway through *Naked Lunch*, during his overview of Interzone (the novel's allegorical Middle Eastern and North African colonial metropolis) and Islam Inc. (its anti-colonial, Nationalist party), the narrator formally introduces Clem and Jody, "two old-time vaudeville hoofers" whose "sole function" as "Russian agents" is "to represent the U.S. in an unpopular light" (Burroughs 2001, 132). Due to their obscene pranks, "Morbid crowds follow them about hoping to witness some superlative American outrage" (133). To give America a bad name, Clem and Jody ape America's most cynical imperial discourse toward exotic prostitutes, foreign religions, and indigenous resources, especially petroleum. When "arrested for sodomy in Indonesia," for instance, Clem defends himself to "the examining magistrate" by retorting, "'Tain't as if it was being queer. After all they's only Gooks" (132–33). In one of their more elaborate ruses, Clem and Jody "give out they are interested in the destruction of Near East oil fields to boost the value of their Venezuelan holdings" (135). After exemplifying Euro-American corporations' insidious economic speculations, however, Clem takes it one step too far, singing: *"What you gonna do when the oil goes dry? / Gonna sit right there and watch those Arabs die"* (135). Clem writes his "number" to "the tune of 'Crawdad'" by "Big Bill Broonzy," parodying the African American blues song while equating Arabs dying at the hands of capitalist exploitation to the crayfish that, in the original tune, the fisherman exterminates by draining the pond.

Clem and Jody's plan to destroy "Near East oil fields to boost the value of their Venezuelan holdings" illustrates the shifting shape of globalized capitalism, as the American government and multinational corporations adopted and reworked Europe's cynical strategies of imperial exploitation in Latin America, the Middle East, and Indochina. Clem and Jody epitomize the rising tendency in the mid-twentieth century for American companies to act in bad faith, violating the same free trade laws that the US government hypocritically foisted down the throats of decolonizing and postcolonial nations. By setting up colonial Europe as a strawman, Cold War America premised its global power on being an exception to imperial rule. In *Colonial Affairs: Bowles, Burroughs and Chester Write Tangier* (2002), Greg Mullins explores the way post–World War II American citizens sought to "criticize European colonialism while also benefiting from it," advocating for "national independence" in countries like Morocco, while "simultaneously expanding neocolonial structures of economic dominance and dependence" (12–13). In *Epic Encounters: Culture, Media, and U.S. Interests in the Middle East since 1945*

(2001), Melani McAlister reveals such cynical strategies to be central to post–World War II America's growing quest for valuable resources in the Middle East. Policy makers figured US interests "in terms supportive of the region's anticolonial movements," positing as an "alternative to colonialism" a "'benevolent' American partnership," one that would nevertheless include "nearly unlimited U.S. access to Middle Eastern oil" (2).

Burroughs may appear to introduce Clem and Jody's plan to merely satirize this predominant imperial strategy, especially to implicate multinational corporate deal-brokers, as well as Euro-American tourists abroad. For instance, he could have followed the suit of such classic fiction on North Africa as Paul Bowles's incisive novels, short stories, and essays published throughout the 1940s and 1950. Instead of writing a series of biting realist novels depicting the Euro-American tourists' "decadent" decline in "savage" lands (like Bowles in *The Sheltering Sky* [1949] and *Let It Come Down* [1952]), however, Burroughs's routine mutates into Clem's shocking song, unsettling readers looking for a measured critique with a cynical edge. Clem and Jody do not just reveal unjust material conditions and critique those who justify America's overseas expansion. Rather, they perform an excessive version of the stereotypical Ugly American, relishing the perverse spectacle of demonized Arabs suffering from the very neocolonial exploitation upon which Cold War American and European citizens' rising luxury depended.

In *Naked Lunch*'s "Ordinary Men and Women" chapter, Burroughs depicts Interzone's Nationalists as cynically collaborating with Western neocolonialists, only to bring into relief the subversive potential of Clem and Jody's shocking iterations of imperial decadence. Although *Naked Lunch*'s narrator acknowledges sympathetically that Islam Inc. (whose "rank and file" include "representatives of every conceivable Arab party") is forbidden to meet "within five miles of the city limits" of Interzone, the narrator also satirizes the Nationalists for adopting Western customs, violating their Muslim beliefs, and exploiting the indigenous population (Burroughs 2001, 122, 101–3). Following the example of the British Empire's T. E. Lawrence during the Great War, after the war to end all wars America strategically supported anti-colonial nationalism to consolidate its neocolonial stranglehold on geographic regions undergoing postcolonial mutations. As proof of America's success in converting the Nationalists to their cynical cause, the reader learns soon enough that Islam Inc. is "financed by A.J.," an important character, notably an "agent" who, while "actually of Near East extraction," before World War II had "come on like an English gentleman"; as his "English accent waned with the British Empire," the shadowy mercenary "became an American by Act of Congress" (122).

During their party meeting, as the Nationalists strategize to use "savages" of the "Far East" (specifically, Latahs) to cause riots capable of liberating the "Near East," Clem and Jody make their appearance, "dressed like The Capitalist in a Communist mural" (2001, 119). Exuberantly imitating the Social Realist stereotype of the Capitalist, vulgarly performing a drag show of the "Ugly American" and the Orientalist tourist, Clem declares "We've come to feed on your backwardness"

(119). When one of the Nationalists lashes back, pleading, "Don't you realize my people are hungry?" Clem retorts with his trademark punch-line, "That's the way I like to see them" (119). Rarely in *Naked Lunch* do mere words prove quite so influential, but at Clem's sinister utterance, "The Nationalist drops dead, poisoned by hate" (119).

The Nationalist's shocked reaction exemplifies the *effect* of Clem's sadistic embrace of America's paternalist attitude toward the "developing" world. Just as Clem breaks into song at the spectacle of neocolonial collateral damage, thereby humiliating the Americans in whose name he acts and for whom the oil provides leisure, Clem's cruel utterance ("That's the way I like to see them") serves to give the lie to the Nationalist's cynical attitude toward Interzone's citizens. Clem's murder of the Nationalist, and, more generally, his and Jody's attempts to "represent the U.S in an unpopular light," are designed to displace the natives' anti-European sentiment onto America, while also presenting Americans with a disturbing reflection of their nation's hypocritical role in the world. It is doubly significant, then, that Clem and Jody shock the Nationalists when the "Near East" Party Leader plots to take advantage of "Far East" Latahs to incite a riot. For Clem's sadistic rendition of the American tourist functions as a method of persuasion that Burroughs' anthropological narrator conceptualizes through the figure of the "Latah." Indeed, the narrator's own analysis of the Latah's uncanny interpersonal effect provides a model not only for the effects of Clem and Jody's performances on their fictional audiences, but for the underexamined, disturbing effects of *Naked Lunch* on Cold War America's readers.

THE LATAH'S OMINOUS EFFECT

> *"So he has an affair with this Latah, he wants to dominate someone complete the silly old thing . . . The Latah imitates all his expressions and mannerisms and simply sucks all the persona right out of him like a sinister ventriloquist's dummy."*

—William S. Burroughs, *Naked Lunch* (1959, in 2001, 118)

Although contemporary scholars usually celebrate *Naked Lunch* for its nonlinear narrative, its polyvocal style, and its fragmentary architecture that resists any totalizing interpretation, Burroughs' novel, with its complex framework of paratextual prefaces, footnotes, and afterwords, consistently encourages its readers to interpret the text as produced by a singular, identifiable narrator according to a relatively straightforward plot. In between the distracting lines of his postmodern assemblage of code-switching routines, melodramatic scenes, and hallucinatory, sci-fi visions, from its very beginning, the reader follows a white male, a sexually deviant American citizen, addicted to the "oriental" drug opium, who flees the subway bowels of New York City (and the police), only to journey by road through the postindustrial wasteland of America (where only the scars of imperial violence against the indigenous people remain visible), before escaping far down into Mexico. After hitting bottom in Latin America, the mysterious protagonist takes flight to Freeland, a parodic allegory of a European imperial metropolis achieving its dream of a liberal, totalitarian utopia. He has been "assigned" to work with the Faustian, and infamous, Dr. Benway, whose quest to develop the most effective methods of control has led him to reject repressive apparatuses (like concentration camps) in favor of manipulating surveillance and symbol systems. It is for this ostensible purpose that the narrator proceeds to travel through, and survey, Burroughs' fantastical allegorical rendition of a (neo)colonial metropolis at the seams of North Africa and the Middle East, the shape-shifting city of "Interzone" (Burroughs 2001, 19).

When the narrator arrives, the city might seem to be on the ecstatic cusp of liberation from prolonged colonial occupation, but the diverse and futuristic capital already proves to be falling into the neocolonial hands of American-sponsored multinationals. The novel's narrator never identifies his employer, but he resembles an operative "assigned" by American agencies to work, in the guise of a tourist, as an anthropologist reporting on Interzone, like the principle crew of Orientalists who famously accompanied Napoléon Bonaparte during France's invasion of Egypt (1798–1801). Even though the narrator claims he "was working" at one time for Islam Inc., his loyalties appear as questionable as Dr. Benway's. Indeed, Islam Inc.'s Party Leader calls Benway "an infiltrating Western Agent" (121, 120). If anything, the novel's narrator appears to function, at least officially, as a spy, getting the inside scoop on the Nationalist movement. After all, as he admits in the novel's *"Atrophied Preface,"* the narrator acts primarily as "a recording instrument" (184).

Since Burroughs scholars tend to overlook the novel's imperial perspective the bulk of *Naked Lunch* remains unidentified as the narrator's ethnographic report on what Louis Althusser would term Interzone's Ideological and Repressive State Apparatuses. The chapters of *Naked Lunch* can be categorized accordingly: "The Black Meat" portrays Interzone's black market, the "Hospital" the city's health care system, "Hassan's Rumpus Room" and "A.J.'s Annual Party" its culture industry, and "Campus of Interzone University" its education system. "The Market" and "Interzone" chapters wind through the city, treading as far and wide as the transportation systems and the sanitation services. The narrator surveys the metropolis' *laissez-faire* economic system, its colonial urban design, its totalitarian police force; his kaleidoscopic, experiential account even showcases a melting pot of diverse smells and music. The subsequent "Ordinary Men and Women" chapter provide a bird's-eye view of its citizens during everyday power conflicts, while "Islam Incorporated and the Parties of Interzone" anatomizes the city's chaotic political system and its science-fictional cadre of warring political parties. Finally, "The County Clerk" episode exposes the city's Kafkaesque legal system at its headquarters in "Pigeon Hole," a deserted town in the city's barbaric outskirts where, in one of

Burroughs' surreal renditions of Jim Crow America, posted signs warn African Americans to never to let the sun set on them within the horizon's limits.

Nevertheless, while *Naked Lunch*'s narrator might engage with Orientalist discourse from an imperial perspective, writing a travel novel and ethnographic report, while appealing with racist jokes to cynical American readers who enjoy raunchy novels and films set in the Orient, Burroughs' novel, and its double agent of a narrator, also resists, by *overwhelming*, the reader's stereotypical expectations. While the narrator follows the traditional Orientalist practice of appending pseudo-factual ethnographic footnotes to colonial novels, even his parentheticals usually serve to implicate the Orientalist discipline and its field ethnographers, for instance, with the growing trend of sexual tourism (he notes, "the author has observed that Arab cocks tend to be wide and wedge shaped." [2001, 65]). Through the vector of the anthropologist, the narrator employs, in fact, the same rhetorical devices Clem and Jody deploy during their performances. While providing a panoply of Orientalist stories about indigenous peoples from every part of the globe, the narrator's rendition of anthropological discourse revels in his own collusion with exploitative and even purportedly "degenerate" (homoerotic, if not pedophilic) sex tourism. It is also through this paradoxical mode of identification that the narrator conceptualizes his own anti-colonial mimicry, in the process transforming the anthropological stereotype of the "Latah" into a metafictional metaphor for his "decadent" aesthetic and rhetorical strategy.

In a footnote only located in the original Olympia Press edition (as noted by Jed Birmingham in his self-published, work of scholarly ephemera, "Whale Drek: The Lost Footnotes of the Olympia Press *Naked Lunch*"), Burroughs addresses the origin of the strange phenomenon known as "Latah," a "disorder" still understood today according to the problematic category of "culture-bound syndromes." After the narrator leaves the Americas and arrives in Freeland, while working to "engage the services" of Dr. Benway for Islam Inc., the narrator learns that an old acquaintance "turned himself into a Latah trying to perfect A.O.P., Automatic Obedience Processing" (2001, 24). Just like James Fennimore Cooper attaching a long footnote in *The Last of the Mohicans* (1826) to trace the origins of the Native American "race" to the Orient, *Naked Lunch*'s narrator at this point observes in a footnote: "(Latah is a condition occurring in Southeast Asia. Otherwise sane, Latahs compulsively imitate every motion once their attention is attracted by snapping the fingers or calling sharply. A form of compulsive involuntary hypnosis. They sometimes injure themselves trying to imitate the motions of several people at once)" (25). In this case, the narrator's descriptive aside on "Latahs" locates the place and conditions for this neurotic behavior in a "primitive" ethnic group, seemingly just to ridicule Southeast Asians for this habit of involuntarily harming themselves in hysterical fits of mimicry.

During the Nationalist's plotting to exploit these Latahs for an anti-colonial riot, however, while telling what sounds like a joke, an anonymous speaker, presumably another Near Eastern Nationalist, touches upon the curious *effect* of a Latah's outburst. Without any background context, the character recounts: "So he has an affair with this Latah, he wants to dominate someone complete the silly old thing ... The Latah imitates all his expressions and mannerisms and simply sucks all the persona right out of him like a sinister ventriloquist's dummy" (2001, 118). In this case, the Latah's uncanny mimicry functions as a mode of resistance against another's pretensions to power, a tactic that leaves the aggressor in such a state that he "can't answer for himself, having no self left" (118). The Latah's resistance to power operates according to the dialectic of the dummy and his ventriloquist, and recalls the novel's infamous "talking asshole," who imitates its ventriloquist's expressions and mannerisms until their roles are reversed and the brain and the head become moot, eventually atrophying away. In both rhetorical structure and effect, then, Clem and Jody's performances resemble the Latah's radical imitation of the aggressor, the puppet gone haywire, short-circuiting the hypocritical ventriloquists who try to pull the puppet strings. The narrator actually compares Jody's "fake Chinese spiel" to "a hysterical ventriloquist's dummy" (93). It's a "spiel that'll just kill you," he says, a routine so effective it "precipitated an anti-foreign riot in Shanghai" and "claimed 3,000 casualties" (93). This, however, begs one of *Naked Lunch*'s fundamental, but still unanswered, questions: For the ruling class and their puppet masters, what is so disturbing, even deadly, in the Latah's mimicry, in Clem and Jody's hijinks, in the talking asshole's inverted ventriloquizing, and in Burroughs' unsettling writing itself?

"THAT'S THE WAY I LIKE TO SEE THEM"

> "Want to watch these two kids screw each other?"
> "Of course. How much?"
> "I think they will perform for fifty cents. Hungry, you know."
> "That's the way I like to see them"

—William S. Burroughs, *Naked Lunch* (1959, in 2001, 50)

In light of his theoretical critique of cynical ideological formations in *The Sublime Object of Ideology* (1989) Žižek further developed in later essays a useful model to reveal the Latah's strange method of persuasion and its unsettling effect. In his brief but provocative article, "Why Are Laibach and the *Neue Slowenische Kunst* Not Fascists?" (1993), Žižek takes as his object of study the 1980s Slovenian art collectives, Laibach and Neue Slowenische Kunst, whose theatrical and musical performances staged "an aggressive, inconsistent mixture of Stalinism, Nazism and *Blut and Boden* ideology" (2007, 65). Žižek argues such a radical "over-identification" with the totalitarian regime's ruling ideology, lacking the critical edge of parody, irony, or satire, can often prove more effective at making an audience feel ashamed and alienated, especially from those hypocritical beliefs they would usually accommodate with the consolation of sarcasm. Laibach's ostensibly Fascist performance and iconography *"'frustrates' the system (the ruling ideology) precisely insofar as it is not its ironic imitation, but represents an over-identification with it"* (65). In this method of reverse psychology, an utterance's progressive effects prove inversely proportional to its excessively reactionary content. Psychoanalytic and performance art critics Inke Arns and Sylvia Sasse recently coined the term "subversive affirmation" for this "parasitical" practice (2006, 445). Such a rhetorical strategy, well-attuned to disturb an addict's "fetishistic disavowals," functions through a "paradoxical intervention," a psychotherapeutic technique, also called "prescribing the symptom," that involves framing a message so the patient's typical resistance to criticism short-circuits. Instead, by taking the patient's contradictory desire to their logical conclusion, the counter-intuitive mode of communication can generate a reorientation of belief, attitude, and behavior. While such a method's history would offer valuable insights into its best application, most scholars who touch upon such practices of "over-identification" focus entirely upon either late twentieth-century Eastern European protest movements or turn-of-the-century anti-globalization activists (like The Yes Men and Billionaires for Bush).

Yet not only did Burroughs practice and preach this method as early as the 1950s, but less than a decade after, in the second edition of *The Ticket That Exploded* (1967), Burroughs explicitly identified what Žižek has since argued to be Laibach's uncanny effect. Žižek concludes his essay on "overidentification" by claiming that the "ultimate expedient" of Laibach lies in its refusal to answer the public's demand to know the artists' actual position (are they totalitarian or not?) (2007, 65). However, in the face of a ruling class for whom, as Žižek puts it, "the normal function of the system *requires* cynical distance," Laibach's performances function not *"as an answer but a question"*; due to "the elusive character of its desire, of the undecidability as to 'where it actually stands,'" Laibach "compels" their audiences "to take up" their "own position and decide upon" their "desire" (65). In much the same way, Burroughs paints a picture of the public's stupefied reaction to a new and improved version of Clem and Jody, what he calls his "ideal terrorist organization," "an equivocal group of assassins called 'The White Hunters'" (*The Ticket That Exploded* 2014, 10). Burroughs writes that the public reacted to "The White Hunters" by asking: "Were they white supremacists or an anti-white movement far ahead of the Black Muslims? The extreme right or far left of the Chinese?" (10). When Burroughs then writes, "No one knew and in this uncertainty lay the particular terror they inspired," he could be describing not just the mechanics behind the startling effects of his fictional characters' obscene performances but also the very reaction of Anglo-American audiences to his own writings, especially *Naked Lunch* (10).

In "Monstrosity on Trial: The Case of *Naked Lunch*," Frederick Whiting thoroughly demonstrates that, during *Naked Lunch*'s censorship trials, the prosecution focused on the author's intentions at the expense of the book's purportedly "obscene" content. Whiting writes, "What was at issue in the *Naked Lunch* trial, then, was not whether the novel depicted the monstrous. The presiding judge left little doubt about the court's opinion of the novel. . . . The questions were, rather: To what end was the monstrous being deployed? In what relation did the author stand to the work?" (2006, 159). The answer to this question, of course, has remained not just frighteningly ambiguous, but tantalizingly paradoxical—indeed, for most postwar Anglo-American readers, the experience of opening *Naked Lunch*, is surely similar to what the narrator imagines someone will think if they "visit" his "old" hospital room where he withdrew from his addiction to the oriental drug, "opium"—as the narrator puts it, "he will think I gave birth to a monster and the State Department is trying to hush it up" (Burroughs 2001, 53).

During his withdrawal symptoms in this very room, at the climax of *Naked Lunch*'s "Hospital" chapter, the narrator reproduces verbatim the utterance that Clem uses to kill the Nationalist, taking it a step further by voicing the remark through the vector of the sexual tourist, produced by a deviant addict's withdrawal nightmares. In his diary, after describing his delirious vision of disgusting hospital food, the narrator recounts looking out his window at a "French school" and eyeing "the boys with my eight-power field glasses" (Burroughs 2001, 50). As he ogles, his lust initiates an out-of-body experience: "I project myself out through the glasses and across the street, a ghost in the morning sunlight, torn with disembodied lust" (50). His confession of homosexual, pedophiliac voyeurism cuts to the following hallucinatory scene: "Met Marv in front of the Sargasso with two Arab kids and he said: "Want to watch these two kids screw each other?" (50). After the narrator happily replies, "Of course. How much?" and Marv explains, "I think they will perform for fifty cents. Hungry, you know," the narrator himself pronounces Clem's heinous motto: "That's the way I like to see them" (50).

When confronting Burroughs' decadent embrace of Orientalist sexual tourism, Burroughs scholars struggle to identify the author's underlying moral stance. At a loss without a moral center, many critics have passed judgment on his reactionary tendencies. Others, in Burroughs' defense, cling to any shred of enlightenment critique they can discover between the lines of his reactionary pastiche. Whereas Kurt Hemmer, for instance, concludes Burroughs' text fails the litmus test of subversive writing, Brian T. Edwards recuperates a critical edge to *Naked Lunch*'s Orientalist perspective. Like most critics who celebrate the text's formal innovations while disavowing its most offensive stances, in "'The Natives are getting uppity': Tangier and *Naked Lunch*," Hemmer concludes that, although *Naked Lunch*'s "anti-narrative form has the potential to resist the reifying tendencies [Edward] Said sees as often inherent in traditional Western narratives," much of the "content of *Naked Lunch*" only serves to "neutralize" the novel's "potential for resisting imperialistic hegemony" (2009, 66). Even if Burroughs' tactic is "to heighten the sense of repulsion he puts in front of his reader," the text fails to prove adequately subversive, according to Hemmer, because it "refrains from making the type of definitive moral statement a text of resistance would warrant," leaving the reader "to stand alone in judgment of imperialism in Tangier" (72).

In a similar way, in *Morocco Bound: Disorienting America's Maghreb, from Casablanca to the Marrakech Express* (2005), although Brian T. Edwards provides sophisticated cultural criticism on Cold War America's representations of the Maghreb, like many other American Studies scholars on post–World War II American foreign policy, Edwards underestimates the political consequences of the imperial cynicism he uncovers. As a result, when Edwards devotes an eloquent chapter to *Naked Lunch*, he celebrates the text's "critique of American domestic relations" for revealing "the expanding U.S. global presence as an extension of a culture addicted to consumption" (2005, 161). Partly because Edwards takes Burroughs' letters at face value, as sincere expressions of reactionary beliefs, however, he concludes that Burroughs still works "within an Orientalist framework," and is, at best, able to "imagine a contestatory position" (161, 174). Instead of explaining how such a "contestatory" position could prove subversive for a ruling class who knows quite well the injustice upon which their luxury depends, Edwards defends the narrator's expressions of sadistic delight at a child prostitute's hunger as yet another "trenchant critique of the American presence in Tangier," a "representation of the worst of the American" that "critiques the purity of what was called 'the American voice' in Tangier via word play, a between-the-lines potentiality" (178). Yet it is precisely due to a lack in the narrator's obscenities of any satirical edge, that *Naked Lunch* was repeatedly censored. It is also why, at the very end of the novel, a Police Lieutenant sends Hauser and O'Brien to the narrator's room to "pick him up" and "bring in all books, letters, manuscripts. *Anything* printed, typed, or written" (Burroughs 2001, 175).

In other words, due to the Latah's involuntary imitation, Clem and Jody's disgusting performances, and the narrator's "decadent" acts of imperial domination, their audiences become humiliated by their own bad faith, dispossessed of their pretensions to power, and frustrated in the cynical roles they play. Just as Clem and Jody revel in America's barbaric imperialism and the suffering of exploited Arabs, so *Naked Lunch*'s narrator seems, paradoxically and perversely, to relish the very depravity into which he diagnoses late capitalist society degenerating. While taking offensive Orientalist fantasies of "culture-bound syndromes" (e.g., the phenomenon of "running amok") as models for anti-imperial resistance, Burroughs presents his readers with a subversive doppelgänger who revels in the darkest motives that underpin its cynical ruling ideology, precisely such a dark double agent who would embrace the "savage" anti-colonial practice of the Latah's mimicry. As the Nationalists' plot in *Naked Lunch* to use Latahs to initiate riots, an anonymous speaker warns of the Latah's "ominous" effect when, as if demonically possessed, "they start trying on your clothes and give you those doppelgänger kicks..." (Burroughs 2001, 118). The Latah, Clem and Jody, the narrator, and Burroughs himself, then, like the "talking asshole" of America, present the *dark double* to America's ruling imperial ideology, deploying a "decadent" literary style, a "perverse" mode of subversive affirmation, to confront the reader with a paradoxical embrace, as Burroughs put it in *Nova Express*, of just "how ugly the Ugly American can be" (10).

THE RENAISSANCE OF DECADENT AESTHETICS
IN COLD WAR AMERICA

> *Junkies sitting on the courthouse steps, waiting on The Man. Red Necks in black Stetsons and faded Levis tie a Nigra boy to an old iron lamppost and cover him with burning gasoline . . . The junkies rush over and draw the flesh smoke deep into their aching lungs . . . They really got relief.*

—William S. Burroughs, *Naked Lunch* (1959, in 2001, 106)

Oliver Harris has thoroughly traced the germination and blossoming of Burroughs' "routines" in his letters to Allen Ginsberg, and his early drafts of both *Queer* (1953) and *Naked Lunch* (1959). In his foundational work of genetic criticism on the early works, *William Burroughs and the Secret of Fascination* (2003), Harris aptly describes Burroughs' fragmentary style as binding his "personal fantasy with a national imaginary" in order to make explicit "our fantasmatic entrails, pulling them out to a point of nauseous visibility" (2003, 91, 108). But just as Žižek and contemporary scholars in performance art studies focus only upon Eastern European protest movements and recent anti-globalization activists, without tracing a broader history of such a paradoxical mode of persuasion, neither Harris nor other literary critics situate Burroughs' unsettling style as an important milestone in a literary lineage of so-called "decadent" writers. Burroughs' perverse method of "subversive affirmation" derives from and adapts into the formal parameters of the postmodern novel a series of literary techniques first refined and proliferated in late nineteenth-century "decadent" literature, a literary style that originated as a symptomatic *response* to the fin-de-siècle French and British bourgeoisie's degeneration into an imperial cynicism as recalcitrant as a viral infection.

The self-declared "decadent" movement arose in France at the height of European colonialism, at a time in the nineteenth century when pessimism about the decay of European civilization was nothing new; what proved innovative was the "decadent" *celebration* of degeneration by the poet Charles Baudelaire and his disciples. In many of his gothic short stories on the "imp of the perverse," Edgar Allan Poe had already laid the groundwork for Baudelaire's *Les Fleurs du mal* (1857). In one of Burroughs' favorite short stories, "The Black Cat" (1843), Poe dwells upon the desire to do "wrong for wrong's sake," a perverse desire that Baudelaire translates as "faire mal pour amour du mal," his French coming closer to the English phrase, "to do evil for the love of evil" (1971, 60). In his wake, many fin-de-siècle "decadents" conjured political, cultural, ethical, and aesthetic *décadence* not as a means toward a "progressive" end (as a Romantic revolutionary might destroy old traditions to create a new utopia), but instead as a downward slope toward apocalypse. Unlike Romantic poets who overturned the reigning value system to rebelliously celebrate Satan as Good; and unlike Goethe's Faust who, after rebelling against the feudal order, cynically collaborated with Mephistopheles to broaden his imperial reach, all the while appealing to utilitarian consequentialism to justify his evil means toward the greater good;, the great lyric poets of literary "decadence" (such as Comte de Lautréamont in his songs of *Maldoror* [1868] and Arthur Rimbaud in *Une Saison en enfer* [1873]) sought out and tempted Satan, longing to be possessed by Evil, to speak in demonic tongues, and to commit barbaric acts, not for any greater good, but as ends in themselves. In many late nineteenth-century novels, such as J. K. Huysmans's *À Rebours* (1888) (a novel described, like *Naked Lunch* could be, as a "breviary of the Décadence"), Oscar Wilde's *The Picture of Dorian Gray* (1890), and Joseph Conrad's *Heart of Darkness* (1899), the paradoxical protagonists characteristically "overidentify" with the ruling ideology's Manichean binary hierarchies (such as civilized and primitive) before, paradoxically, excessively affirming the negative term *as negative* (be it artificiality against nature, or pleasure at the expense of charity). After World War I, a decadent modernism for the age of totalitarianism gave forth to what Julia Kristeva christened as "a black lineage" in the writings of Georges Bataille and Louis-Ferdinand Céline, in Djuna Barnes's *Nightwood* (1936) and nearly all of Jean Genet's novels and plays (1982, 137). Influenced by all these "poète maudits," Burroughs' *Naked Lunch* stands as a pivotal text in an unrecognized postwar Anglo-American renaissance of "decadent" literature and art. Without Burroughs' revitalization of the "decadent" mode of "subversive affirmation" in a postmodern collage form, something would remain lacking in so many classic post-World War II literary and artistic works of disheveled exuberance and apocalyptic prophecy, from Anthony Burgess's dystopian *A Clockwork Orange* (1962) to Hunter S. Thompson's Gonzo New Journalism in *Fear and Loathing in Las Vegas* (1971), from Samuel Delany's epic *Dhalgren* (1974) to Kathy Acker's sci-fi *Empire of the Senseless* (1988), from Thomas Pynchon's sprawling *Gravity's Rainbow* (1973) to Cormac McCarthy's brutal Western, *Blood Meridian* (1985).

Burroughs adopts as *Naked Lunch*'s model for the genesis of the decadent utterance one of his favorite texts, Baudelaire's *Les Fleurs du mal*. This allegorical collection of lyric poems recounts the artist-flâneur's peregrinations through Napoleon III's (and Baron Haussmann's) imperial metropolis at the height of the French Second Empire's cynical exploitation and dispossession of the poor and the colonized. In *Les Fleurs du mal* (1857) and *Petits poèmes en prose* (1869), especially in his shocking prose poem, "Assommons les pauvres!" ("Let's Beat Up the Poor!"), Baudelaire's narrator's ambulatory explorations usually involve courting the devil, consuming "oriental" drugs, window-shopping exotic commodities in luxurious arcades, taking advantage of "savage" prostitutes (his *vénus noire*), persecuting the poor, and, once sufficiently possessed by the satanic spirits, giving voice through symbolist poetry to his perverse desires. In much the same way, *Naked Lunch*'s narrator desires exotic commodities, especially prostitutes and drugs, and, under the influence of the "Ugly Spirit," after his allegorical account of Interzone's labyrinthine markets, he demonstrates during his withdrawal in the "Hospital" chapter how his addiction to and consumption of these drugs produces his "decadent" visions.

Throughout his writings, Burroughs reiterated, and parodied, century-old Orientalist stereotypes about exotic drugs, such as "hashish" and "opium," supposed to act like foreign diseases or "primitive" forms of black magic, producing in Western users savage affects, barbaric acts, and a general state of demonic possession. Burroughs frequently describes himself, his narrators, and his characters as possessed by what he calls the "Ugly Spirit," a parasitical entity whose root Burroughs often traced to the greedy spirit of American capitalism. In *Naked Lunch's* aptly named *"Atrophied Preface,"* Burroughs figures his state of possession as fertile soil for sadistic acts, in terms reminiscent of Edgar Allen Poe's foundational decadent tale, "The Imp of the Perverse" (1845). Burroughs writes: "'Possession' they call it ... Sometimes an entity jumps in the body ... and hands move to disembowel the passing whore or strangle the nabor child in hope of alleviating a chronic housing shortage" (2001, 184). In his preface to *Queer,* after recalling in nostalgic, loving terms the most appalling experiences from his residence in Mexico City during the early 1960s, Burroughs traced the origin of his *writing* to his possession by the "Ugly Spirit" that motivated, and found a point of entry, through his murder of his wife: "I live with the constant threat of possession, a constant need to escape from possession, from Control. So the death of Joan brought me in contact with the invader, the Ugly Spirit, and maneuvered me into a lifelong struggle, in which I have had no choice except to write my way out" (1987, 134). By writing, and by cutting up his writing, Burroughs sought to purge his demons through their radical embrace; in the process, he sought to write in ways disturbing enough to shock, disturb, and change the most recalcitrant readers.

Following the narrator's opiate withdrawal in the "Hospital" chapter, *Naked Lunch's* hallucinatory series of ceremonial mass lynchings during the "Hassan's Rumpus Room" episode present the reader with an exaggerated version of the allegorical figure, *l'Ennui,* who appears at the conclusion of Baudelaire's poetic address "To the Reader" introducing *Les Fleurs du mal.* Like this delicate monster ("ce monstre délicat") whom the hypocritical reader ("Hypocrite lecteur") knows all too well, like this degenerate who dreams of scaffolds as he smokes his hookah ("Il rêve d'échafauds en fumant son houka"), *Naked Lunch's* narrator consumes oriental drugs, before hallucinating during his wet dreams visions of lynched African Americans and Arabs ejaculating like Independence Day fireworks (Baudelaire 1993, 6). As Mary McCarthy put it, in *Naked Lunch,* Burroughs revels in the way the American South is "addicted to lynching and nigger-hating": "the Southern folk-custom of burning a Negro recurs throughout the book as a sort of Fourth-of-July carnival with fireworks" (1991, 36). Later in *Naked Lunch,* the narrator even envisions a horrifying scene of addicts decadently feeding off the state's extrajudicial violence that cynically supplements the Law: "Junkies sitting on the courthouse steps, waiting on The Man. Red Necks in black Stetsons and faded Levis tie a Nigra boy to an old iron lamppost and cover him with burning gasoline … The junkies rush over and draw the flesh smoke deep into their aching lungs … They really got relief" (2001, 106). Even Interzone, the colonial metropolis itself, in all its decadence, might be a fantastical symptom of the narrator's consumption and withdrawal from "Oriental" drugs (not just opium, but hashish and *yagé*) (47). After his rhapsodic cityscape of the allegorical "Oriental" city, in "The Market" chapter, the narrator writes in parentheses (a footnote in the original Olympia Press edition): "(Section describing the City and the Meet Café written in state of *yagé* intoxication)" (91). Unlike, then, the Romantic writer Thomas de Quincey in *Confessions of an English Opium Eater* (1821), *Naked Lunch*'s decadent narrator is an unrepentant addict, less horrified than exalted by his Orientalist fantasies. He revels in consuming "oriental" prostitutes and drugs, knowing his money fuels a black market whose collateral damages are the poor and colonized. He is fascinated by savagery, relishing depravity and degeneration while aspiring to "sickness." If the conventional Euro-American citizen is addicted to personal and social progress, especially in the forms of self-improvement and economic profit, Burroughs' narrator seems addicted to inertia, decay, decline, and waste (indeed, he is addicted to *junk*). Any reader who, having hoped to enjoy an oriental feast, cynically tries to dismiss these monstrous visions by blaming them on the narrator's demented psyche, inevitably confronts the underlying, paradoxical stance, the uncanny writings of an addict who desires to consume "oriental" substances precisely in order to hallucinate the empire's barbaric treatment of demonized savages.

Just as Burroughs adapts Baudelaire's rhetorical strategy to the postmodern novel, so he models his narrator's political identity after Joseph Conrad's enigmatic Kurtz in *Heart of Darkness* (1899). Instead of clearly communicating a critical message, Kurtz's decadent utterances from the colonial frontier serve to challenge, by taking too seriously, the stereotypes and ambitions that facilitate Marlow's cynical perpetuation of a colonial venture upon which the European reader's luxury depends. If *Heart of Darkness* is the pivotal "decadent" travel narrative for the age of New Imperialism, then *Naked Lunch* proves to be the "decadent" picaresque for the postwar transition from modernist European colonialism to postmodernist American neocolonialism. Like Kurtz's command to "Exterminate all the brutes!" appended to his report to the "International Society for the Suppression of Savage Customs" (Conrad 2006, 49), in this postmodern *Les Fleurs du mal* mapped onto a neocolonial *Heart of Darkness*, the narrator's surreal anthropology goes too far, excessively stereotyping Arabs as bestial (when they riot, they "yip" like dogs) while celebrating the capitalist exploitation of resources and relishing tourists' sexually deviant exploitation, and even extermination, of the aboriginals (Burroughs, *Naked Lunch* 2001, 120). Like Kurtz, carrying out savage massacres on the frontier, in "The Exterminator Does a Good Job" chapter, *Naked Lunch*'s narrator brags in abstract terms that "They call me the Exterminator": he admits at "one brief point of intersection I did exercise that function," before declaring:

"My present assignment: Find the live ones and exterminate" (2001, 171). Apparently, it is for this "assignment" that he fears retribution, for he then states, "I know some agent is out there in the darkness looking for me" (172). At the end of *Heart of Darkness*, Marlow tears off Kurtz's "decadent" postscript ("Exterminate all the brutes!") when the colonial authorities try to confiscate, examine, and control the dissemination of Kurtz's writings (Conrad 2006, 50). In the same way, in *Naked Lunch*'s conclusive episode, after the narrator returns to New York City, the Narcotics officers, Hauser and O'Brien, knock on his door, interrogate him, and try to confiscate his writings, only to disappear without a trace after he makes his escape (Burroughs, *Naked Lunch* 2001, 181). At the end of the *"Atrophied Preface"* that concludes the novel, like an American, neocolonial reincarnation of Kurtz at the terminal point of his descent in *Heart of Darkness*, the narrator then leaves the reader with a terrifying, sublime vision: "Walking in a rubbish heap to the sky . . . scattered gasoline fires . . . D.L. walks beside me . . . He carries an open can of gasoline and the smell of gasoline envelops him . . . Coming over a hill of rusty iron we meet a group of Natives" (Burroughs 2001, 195). After caricaturing the natives' "flat two-dimension faces of scavenger fish," the narrator commands: "Throw the gasoline on them and light it . . ." (195). In his perverse embrace of American imperial power, the narrator goes to the horrifying extent of enjoying using the very petroleum American corporations violently extricate from the Middle East not simply to drive his car (although he also drives across America), but to immolate the bestial natives who inhabit the wasteland of oil refineries.

A WORD TO THE WISE GUY: THE "HOW-TO BOOK" OF POLITICAL RESISTANCE

> *If someone comes to visit me in my old room he will think I gave birth to a monster and the State Department is trying to hush it up.*

—William S. Burroughs, *Naked Lunch* (1959, in 2001, 53)

If Burroughs' *Naked Lunch* is, as the narrator claims in the *"Atrophied Preface,"* "a blueprint, a How- to Book," it is "a How- to Book" of political resistance (2001, 187). *Naked Lunch,* and his permutation of cut-up novels, offer a range of alternative aesthetic and rhetorical strategies, methods of persuasion underexamined and underused by activist organizations, but well researched by intelligence and advertising agencies, and practiced spontaneously, as Burroughs observes, by subaltern individuals resisting (neo)colonial domination. Like Clem and Jody, who both reveal and revel in American imperial power, *Naked Lunch* does not only demystify and prophesize the globalization of capital within the imperial geography of a Euro-American center and a periphery in the Global South. Nor do *Naked Lunch* and Burroughs' cut-up novels, contrary to the predominant scholarly interpretation, simply *détourne,* deconstruct, or otherwise critique the polarized binaries of Cold War American ideology. After *Naked Lunch*, in his decade-long cut-up project, by splicing and creating his own versions of international newspapers and the magazine trilogy, *TIME, LIFE,* and *Fortune*, Burroughs sought to purify Luce's influential vision for the "American Century" of its cynical paternalism to produce an embarrassing, obscene "overidentification" with America's darkest imperial ambitions. Burroughs' deployment of the collage form and the cut-up method should be recognized as a means to enhance the potency of his "decadent" writing, to effectively produce and disseminate "subversive affirmations" of America's virulent imperial discourse. Throughout nine permutations of the cut-up novels, hundreds of cut-up broadcasts in the small press and mimeo magazine revolution, collage films and audio recordings, and thousands of unpublished textual and visual collages in the archives, by collaborating with a wide variety of artists and writers, Burroughs sought to adopt and turn against the ruling class their own methods of Control. Throughout *Naked Lunch* and his sci-fi cut-up novels, in a series of fragmentary, polyvocal routines, Burroughs' narrator savors America's imperial stereotypes, only further polarizing its ideological binaries of civilized and primitive, empire and barbarian, while welcoming, even inviting, the degenerate terrorists, savage diseases, and inclement weather that knock at the doors of the national imagination.

Burroughs' cut-up project, furthermore, when situated beside a series of subsequent artistic interventions, comprises a properly "postmodern" collage aesthetic that arose in response to his increasingly cynical era. In Burroughs' cut-up rendition of *TIME* magazine's September 13, 1963, issue on Red China and the Indo-Chinese War (an issue that also included one of Luce's attacks on the Beats), Burroughs superimposes a bleak landscape painting that ominously erases Nehru and augments Mao's threatening visage. In the following pages of Burroughs' version of *TIME* (published by C-Press), Burroughs's cut-up prose brings to the surface *TIME*'s stereotypes of "inscrutable Orientals," "excitable Indians," and "savage gooks." In one faux newspaper article, entitled "File Ticker Tape," the newspaper's celebration of "Independence Day in Morocco" transforms bit by bit into a celebration of "American Independence Day in Morocco." More pieces from Burroughs and Gysin's unpublished collage book, *The Third Mind* (unpublished, 1965), as well as Burroughs' scrapbooks, showcase his wide-ranging experimentation with photomontage, designed to expose with raw, but beautiful brutality, the ecological catastrophe and neocolonial exploitation at the heart of an American empire, precisely one that such mainstream newspapers and magazines justified with paternalizing editorials, exoticizing advertisements, and the fear-mongering disaster counts that have for too long constituted the "news." Only a few years later, in the late 1960s, as perhaps a sign of Burroughs' influence, the "paraphotographer" Robert Heinecken spliced graphic images inside *TIME* magazine issues, superimposing over advertisements a photograph of a Vietnamese soldier smiling while holding two decapitated Viet Cong heads, before slipping the magazine back onto the shopping racks. In much the same way, Martha Rosler's project, *Bringing the War Home*, exuberantly integrates *LIFE* magazine's documentary accounts of war into advertising scenes of domestic luxury. Heinecken's hacks into *TIME* magazine, and Rosler's collages from both the Vietnam War and, later, the Iraq War, stand as just two of many artistic projects that, in Burroughs' wake, have obscurely aestheticized the imperial violence upon which Western luxury and American exceptionalism depends.

Instead of recognizing Burroughs and Gysin's most offensive artworks as their revolutionary deployment of paradoxically reactionary utterances, if literary and cultural critics continue to avoid, or otherwise recuperate, these obscene routines and collages as sending subliminally progressive messages, *Naked Lunch*, and Burroughs' "decadent" writing more generally, will remain susceptible to the most simplistic of politically correct dismissals. *Naked Lunch* will furthermore remain unrecognized as a groundbreaking literary work in a postmodern renaissance of "imperial decadent" aesthetics that can uniquely provide what Žižek argues is still needed today, a "direct staging of this obscene supplement, of the spectacle of barbarism that sustains our civilization" (Žižek 2005, xv). As we come closer to Burroughs' vision of a world in which the ruling class are cynically making "travel arrangements so they will never have to pay the constituents they have betrayed and sold out," we are in need of theoretical approaches and analytical terminology that can come to terms with these works' frustrating, uncanny effects (*Naked Lunch* 2001, 4). If we don't begin to look beyond concepts of "false consciousness" and "critique," we risk overlooking the radical, non-rational ways avant-garde artists can give Euro-American cynical common sense a taste, so to speak, of its own medicine.

ALEX WERMER-COLAN is a Council of Library and Information Resources Postdoctoral Fellow at Temple University's Digital Scholarship Center. Wermer-Colan's essay, "Implicating the Confessor: The Autobiographical Ploy in William S. Burroughs' Early Works," was published in *Twentieth Century Literature* in 2010. He also researched and edited *The Travel Agency Is on Fire* (2015), published by *Lost & Found*, a collection of unpublished archival materials Burroughs produced by cutting up canonical writers. Wermer-Colan organized the "William S. Burroughs Centennial Conference" held at the Graduate Center of the City University of New York in 2014. He is currently working with director Mallory Catlett as the Dramaturg for *Decoder 2017*, an adaptation of Burroughs' sci-fi cut-up novels into a multimedia theatrical event.

Arns, Inke, and Sylvia Sasse. 2006. "Subversive Affirmation: On Mimesis as a Strategy of Resistance." In *East Art Map: Contemporary Art and Eastern Europe*, edited by IRWIN, 444–55. Cambridge, MA: MIT Press.

Baudelaire, Charles. 1993. *The Flowers of Evil*. Translated by James McGowan. New York: Oxford University Press.

Birmingham, Jed. 2013. "Whale Drek: The Lost Footnotes of the Olympia Press *Naked Lunch*." Baltimore: Planned Obsolescence Press.

Burroughs, William S. 1987. *Queer: A Novel*. New York: Penguin Books.

———. 1993. *The Letters of William S. Burroughs, 1945–1959*. Edited by Oliver Harris. New York: Viking Penguin.

———. 2001. *Naked Lunch: The Restored Text*. Edited by James Grauerholz and Barry Miles. New York: Grove.

———. 2014. *Nova Express: The Restored Text*. Edited by Oliver Harris. New York: Grove Press.

———. 1987. "Sects and Death." *Semiotext(e)*. Eds. Jim Fleming and Peter Lamborn Wilson. New York: Semiotext(e), Vol 13, pp. 23–30.

Conrad, Joseph. 2006. *Heart of Darkness*. Norton Critical Edition. 4th ed. Edited by Paul B. Armstrong. New York: Norton.

Edwards, Brian. 2005. *Morocco Bound: Disorienting America's Maghreb, from Casablanca to the Marrakech Express*. Durham, NC: Duke University Press.

Hardt, Michael, and Antonio Negri. 2000. *Empire*. Cambridge, MA: Harvard University Press.

Harris, Oliver. 2003. *William Burroughs and the Secret of Fascination*. Carbondale: Southern Illinois University Press.

———. 2014. Introduction to *Nova Express: The Restored Text*, by William S. Burroughs, ix–lv. New York: Grove Press.

Hemmer, Kurt. 2009. "'The Natives Are Getting Uppity': Tangier and *Naked Lunch*." In *Naked Lunch@50: Anniversary Essays*, edited by Oliver Harris and Ian MacFadyen, 65–72. Carbondale: Southern Illinois University Press.

Huysmans, Joris-Karl. 1998. *Against Nature* (A rebours). Translated by Margaret Mauldon and edited by Nicholas White. New York: Oxford University Press.

Kristeva, Julia. 1982. *Powers of Horror: An Essay on Abjection*. New York: Columbia University Press.

McAlister, Melani. 2001. *Epic Encounters: Culture, Media, and U.S. Interests in the Middle East since 1945*. Berkeley: University of California Press.

McCarthy, Mary. 1991. "Burroughs' *Naked Lunch*." In *William S. Burroughs at the Front: Critical Reception, 1959–1989*, edited by Jennie Skerl and Robin Lydenberg, 33–39. Carbondale: Southern Illinois University Press.

Miles, Barry. 2013. *Call Me Burroughs*. New York: Twelve.

Mullins, Greg. 2002. *Colonial Affairs: Bowles, Burroughs, and Chest Write Tangier*. Madison: University of Wisconsin Press.

Poe, Edgar Allan. 1971. *Seven Tales*. Translated by Charles Baudelaire and edited by W. T. Bandy. New York: Schocken Books.

Sloterdijk, Peter. 1988 *Critique of Cynical Reason*. Translated by Michael Eldred. Minneapolis: University of Minnesota Press.

Whiting, Frederick. 2006. "Monstrosity on Trial: The Case of *Naked Lunch*." *Twentieth Century Literature: A Scholarly and Critical Journal* 52 (2) (Summer): 145–74.

Žižek, Slavoj. 1989. *The Sublime Object of Ideology*. New York: Verso.

———. 2005. "Foreword: They Moved the Underground" to *Interrogation Machine: Laibach and NSK*, by Alexei Monroe, xi–xvi. Cambridge, MA: MIT Press.

———. 2007. "Why Are Laibach and the *Neue Slowenische Kunst* not Fascists?" (reprint of 1993 essay) in *The Universal Exception*, edited by Rex Butler and Scott Stephens, 71–76. New York: Continuum.

Opium Collage

Although it appears some seven entries later than his archival manuscript, "TO BE=TO," as page 127 in the NYPL Berg's "Dream Rat" calendar, this collage was probably created about a month before Burroughs wrote his cut-up litany that begins "TO BE=TO." A beautiful, haunting work, this text and image collage appears far more significant when recognized as only one page out of over a hundred in a single dream book Burroughs produced during the 1960s and 1970s. Created on approximately January 11, 1970, this piece exemplifies Burroughs' multimodal aesthetic practice as he meditates upon popular discourse during the ratcheting up of the war on drugs.

In keeping with the style of the dream-notes Burroughs recorded over the next half century, his typescript cryptically reports a vivid nightmare: "I am told there is a drunk lady at the door to see me. I open the door and see something like a life size doll in white and blue the face completely covered. A feeling of horror and I say . . . 'Oh my God.'" Below the text is a reproduction of an old black-and-white etching of what looks like a scene from the Inquisition. At right, a caption provides a cryptic detail: "Poppy Picker in Turkey: The raw material for 180,000 addicts." This caption refers to the image that is pasted over the upper middle of the drawing, a photograph of a hooded, veiled figure harvesting poppy flowers, possibly extracted from *TIME* magazine.

This juxtaposition is jarring, between the ominous etching, and the photograph of a veiled figure, harvesting the plant whose commodification in a black market and consumption in a broken social system has led to innumerable people suffering avoidable consequences for their addictions. To properly contextualize the meaning of this vision within his daily recording of his dreams and his scrapbooking of the news, the "Dream Rat" calendar would need to be fully reconstructed and situated in the calendar series (# 127) and its historical moment. Still, in this one collage dream note, between the lines of Burroughs' horror at a life-size doll invading his house, juxtaposed with the collage of opium cultivation and the ceremonies of the Inquisition, Burroughs brings into relief his unmitigated horror at a never-ending "war on drugs" whose destructive effects have become more widespread and inexorable than ever before.

—AWC

Monday Bellevue 4,1970

I am told there isa drunk lady at the door to see me. I open the
door and see something likea life size rag doll in white and blue
the face completely covered.
A feeling of horror and I say..."Oh my God."

TIME, JANUARY 19, 1970

POPPY PICKER IN TURKEY
The raw material for 180,000 addicts.

Opium Collage, William S. Burroughs, Monday, Bellevue 4, 1970 (8 × 11, 1 leaf, facsimile)
(Berg 24.72). Item 127, "I am told . . . ," from Folio 82: "The Dream Calendar—Dream Rat."
Copyright © by William Burroughs, used by permission of The Wylie Agency LLC.

11

Naked Lunch and the Art of Incompleteness: The Use of Genre in Burroughs' Book and Cronenberg's Film

JOSHUA VASQUEZ

You shift to sleep without transition, fall abruptly into the middle of a dream . . .

—*Naked Lunch* (Burroughs 2001, 57)

THE USE OF GENRE IN BURROUGHS' BOOK AND CRONENBERG'S FILM

One of the charges often made against David Cronenberg's *Naked Lunch* (1991) is that the film overlays a palpable coherence across the drifting expanse of the novel's ambiguities, dulling the edges of an elliptical text with a superimposed linearity driven by the incorporation of events and relationships drawn from Burroughs' own life. The film does order its adaptation along such lines; however, I suggest that instead of giving priority to what Robert Stam calls "an elegiac discourse of loss, lamenting what has been 'lost' in the transition from novel to film" (2005, 3), we can focus on what such deviations tell us about the introspective predispositions of each text, particularly Burroughs' incendiary original. Film and book rely on a textual familiarity through their incorporation of the styles, formulas, and cultural resonances of multiple genre traits and expectations, yet revealing differences abound in the purpose of these generic appropriations. By locating a play of structural similarities and differences in how both draw from a range of genres (including travelogue, bio-pic/memoir, sci-fi/horror, and film noir/crime), it is possible to tour each work's farther-reaching engagement with textual incompleteness. Where the film's transgeneric borrowings coalesce beneath the broad array of a mastering narrative, specifically the self-actualizing trajectory of the artist-as-hero, the book's textual geographies resist such navigation. Burroughs' use of manifold genre configurations may result in a fundamental legibility, but his placement of them within the curves and convolutions of the novel's arabesques— an involuted architecture of wandering plots straying through a latticework of references, repetitions, interruptions, asides, and ellipses—complicates the very practice of structural knowledge that genres rely on. Attempts to cohere become endless restatements, revisions, and revisitations of a text that is never finally done, and this embrace of transgenerically kaleidoscopic incompleteness becomes a key formal technique by which the book manifests its excoriating burlesque of the absurd desire for control in all its forms.

TRANSGENERIC MAPS

The concept of memoir haunts the novel's use of first-person perspective, equally undergirding the film as tale of artistic rebirth, and so represents a point of entry for my exploration of generic appropriation, with the admixture of horror/sci-fi and a noir/crime aesthetic of subsequent interest for the manners in which they elaborate on and provide the design through which we witness the journeys of a traveling "I." And yet these generic borrowings ebb and flow, forming a loose affiliation of sketches assembled under the title *Naked Lunch*. Pulpy sci-fi plots of takeovers and transformations join with the horror of monsters and madmen in the face of unraveling yet never unraveled criminal conspiracies: these genre traces emerge from the blurring compendium of fragmented chapters like life-rafts from the wreck. But as the sheer proliferation of clichés, gimmicks, and stock characters mounts, Burroughs' casual use of genre traits broadcasts their very artifice by treating them as disposable affects that can only ever function as conceits.

From the first of the novel, Burroughs reveals the genre shtick, opening with a narrating "I" who, as Carol Loranger writes, is "sizing up the marks—including by implication the reader and implying that what follows—part hard-boiled detective novel, part science fiction hallucination, part social and political satire, part scholarly treatise of underworld jargon—is simply more of (Burroughs) 'giving the fruit[s their] B production'" (Loranger 1999). Burroughs' use of genre tropes is not only a carnival trick delivered with a brash grin (although a darkly dripping humor permeates throughout) but also betrays a dedication to disrupting the regulating function of narrative, the preeminence of beginnings, middles, and ends. By jousting with storytelling norms, the text refutes the wording of the world into digestible patterns, a deliberate bewilderment of form rhyming with Burroughs' subversion of stabilized expectations of identity and experience. Peeling back layers on the social scripts stockading right from wrong and patrolling the boundaries of naturalized convention reveals the ragged topography of a palimpsest often overlooked as the thick compendium of collective assumptions, regulations, and proscriptions it has become. Burroughs' novel is at pains to anatomize this cultural composition by unsettling its own. *Naked Lunch*'s structure remains a self-conscious design poised on the knife's edge of self-negation, a tension only appropriate given the book's production as a bounded text composed of pieces, it's "protracted, piecemeal epistolary genesis" (Harris 2003, 204). The novel may exude satiric intent by wielding blades crafted for social vivisection, and therefore express what Martin Amis has called "patterns and shape and moral point" (2008, 13), but does so from within, to borrow a phrase from Oliver Harris, the far-reaching "refusal of the philosophical category of the whole" (2003, 213). Cronenberg's *Naked*

Lunch replicates much of the novel's transgeneric survey, mirroring many of its amalgams though structuring them quite differently. The director's interest in Burroughs finds its apotheosis in his redesign, an act of homage constellated around a core performance and characterization of Burroughs himself. It's an example of the author-as-genre, an act of cinematic adaptation as literary criticism fused with partially realized biopic. Cronenberg encapsulates the process by conceptualizing the film as a camera movement "back from the page in the typewriter to include the typewriter and then to include the man writing" (Cronenberg 1991). The apparitional quality of Burroughs' presence as source material, in essence the "I" of the film's orientation, represents a central point of flux between book and film's position in terms of the structural embrace of the complete and the incomplete. A knotty play of identities is established through the central function of this "I" in the book, one the film comes to finally stabilize within a meta-genre structure of the tale of the artist-as-hero.

"A TRAIN ROARS THROUGH HIM": MEMOIRS OF THE "I"

From the beginning, Burroughs' *Naked Lunch* follows the orbit of the fleeing traveler: "I can feel the heat closing in, setting up their devil doll stool pigeons, crooning over my spoon and dropper I throw away at Washington Square Station, vault a turnstile and two flights down the iron stairs, catch an uptown A train." (Burroughs 2001, 3). The suggestion of movements in multiple directions ("closing in," "throw away," "flights down," and "uptown") creates a frenzy of momentum, a sensation of tumbling buried within the impetus to take flight. Adding to this tension, we travel with the "I" but are caught in the focus between spaces, the pulsing shift from intimacy (the heat coming closer; the sharp detail of a spoon and dropper falling) to expanse (the imagined perspective of a surveilling authority acting in remote locations; a pull back from the abandoned drug paraphernalia to reveal the relative immensity of the subway stop). The opening passage of the novel introduces us to a fundamental sensation of inrush and release that at once takes on the cadence of breathing (or the beating of a heart) and the rack focusing of a dollying camera.

We open in cities heavy with subcultures of addiction, and then race across the uneasy spread of an aging America ("old and dirty and evil before the settlers, before the Indians") (Burroughs 2001, 11) and distant Mexico to reach a dreamy periphery within the unfolding territory of the spectacularly unfamiliar Interzone. A journeying velocity evoking the movement of exploratory roving is at times fashioned through the spatial implications in the mantras of sequenced ellipses and commas: "Motel . . . Motel . . . Motel . . . broken neon arabesque . . . loneliness moans across the continent like fog horns over still oily water of tidal rivers" (188). Such tempos of a rhythmically broken line, flashing scenes tied to a consistent ache, are markers of the fevered journey where the witnessing "I" implants pieces of itself in the moments it sees and yet is stretched across the here and there of self and other.

Loneliness across a continent is a shared isolation while the echo and decay of the bleating fog horn and the very tidal nature of those waters reinforces the grander surges and withdrawals of the traveling text, the drawing in (to a memoirist self) and tumbling out (to the rambling openness of incompleteness). Burroughs' ellipsis is the very "broken neon arabesque" itself, an articulated design flourish that, like a flickering light along the highway, flares between the gaps to reveal a panoply of different faces passing by. The book, as with the outbreaks, cabals, and wanderers it details, "hath a gimmick for going places" (37). Across the movements between these spaces, a guiding first-person presence not only initiates and closes the text but also appears throughout, from the more sustained, repeatedly inserted "I" of the bookending sections "And Start West," "Hauser and O'Brien," and "Atrophied Preface" to the softer, less focused "I" initially referenced and then largely forgotten as a straight man set up for the longer routines of "Benway" and "Islam Incorporated and the Parties of Interzone": "So I am assigned to engage the services of Doctor Benway for Islam Inc." (19); "I was working for an outfit known as Islam Inc." (121). This tonal disunity allying a more forceful and a more diffused, almost secondary "I" marks a textual unease in registers of self, a quarrel that disputes the stability of any given perspective.

The novel's "I" fissures the text to make space for the implanted splinters of a self-conscious authorial voice. We move from the "gentle reader, I fain would spare you this, but my pen hath its will like the Ancient Mariner" (34) to the ambiguities of identity expressed in "an interview with Your Reporter" (62) to the overt authorial statement and direct address of the "Atrophied Preface" with its reminder that "I have written many prefaces" and its self-conscious looping of the book back within itself: "*Naked Lunch* is a blueprint, a How- to Book" (187). Benjamin Bennett refers to it as *Naked Lunch*'s "intransitive autobiography" (2008, 37), in essence the destruction of the subject from within the subject. By reincorporating awareness of the "material immediacy" (38) of textual structure into his novel and thereby teasing out the generic conceits of the narrating "I," Burroughs challenges the hegemony of "self" in a certain dominant strain of literature, ridiculing the specifically focused yet all-powerfully diffused presumption of the principle of character psychology and dominance of personal ideology. Such is the grimly comic paradox of the book, that a work may be authored while resisting final authorship, confessional words wriggling out from under the writer's thumb to decry the very presumption of mastery. It's a scenario Burroughs cheekily parallels in the infamous "Talking Asshole" routine in which the ventriloquist loses control and voice betrays itself by the very act of speaking, the deepest of contradictions. Hence, the proliferation of at times fixed and then abruptly unfixed identities and narrating, guiding perspectives, and hence, the book's sustained attack on "long-winded bores and bad listeners" who demonstrate that "nothing can ever be accomplished on the verbal level" (Burroughs 2001, 74). That this quintessential facet of wisdom is included within the bowels of a pedantically spiraling lecture orated by the Professor of Interzone University, a heroically stultifying yet insistently

Naked Lunch: "El Hombre invisible."

self-dismantling charlatan, reveals the gleeful convolutions of Burroughs' sense of a text that is never done, can never be done, *should* never be done.

Such a document hardly seems the place for traditional memoir. Yet the intrigue of Burroughs the man frequently remains a salient quality of the work, annexed as both preface and epilogue to his writings, and the fact that *Naked Lunch* is bound up with its author's life speaks to the palimpsestic stratifications that have accumulated over the years of its celebrated infamy. It is from this point of biographically determined fascination that Cronenberg's cinematic reiteration of *Naked Lunch* begins. We enter the diegesis already in the author's shadow. The first shot of the film reveals the silhouette of a man wearing a fedora—a trademark Burroughs image the darkly indistinct contour of which recalls the author's nickname "El Hombre Invisible"—cast against the bracing sheen of a red door as a voice calls out "exterminator!" (a job Burroughs himself held for a time in the 1940s). The film is invented from shards of the author's life reassembled into the recondensed image of actor Peter Weller's Bill Lee, the assumed "I" whose perspective motivates not only narrative but also image and form. Weller is a left-of-center doppelgänger for Burroughs, and he evokes the writer's cultured drawl, glacial stares, and laconic manner. The arc of Bill Lee's addiction mirrors that of Burroughs, with events such as the writer's recollection of sitting for hours, frozen within the focus of an induced concentration and staring at the end of his shoe, replicated in the film. At other points, we are given shots of Lee falling into an ecstatic stupor in his room accompanied by the diegetic sound of the distant call to prayer, a situating of Lee within the space of Burroughs' biographical drug use in Tangier, literalizing the book's fanciful tour.

The film's travelogue and memoir are merged into the tale of the birth of a writer, merging the occasional "I" of the novel and its episodically utilized Lee the Agent to send Burroughs back into the workings of his own fiction. Burroughs' arrival and stay in Tangier is intersected with Lee's necessitated flight after shooting his wife, while the author's on-again, off-again drug addiction becomes the manner and method of Lee's hallucinatory descent into a confrontation with his own larval need to create. From this entanglement of the real and the unreal emerges the film's portrait of the writer's creative process as tragic necessity and act of existential urgency, the interface between imagination and despair, the possible and the impossible, freedom and entrapment. Literalizing Burroughs' late-in-life expression of anxiety about his own investment in his craft—"I am forced to the appalling conclusion," he reveals in the introduction to *Queer*, "that I would never have become a writer but for Joan's death" (1987, xxii)—the character of Joan dies twice in the film, first as the opening act's impetus for Lee's escape to the international refuge of Tangier/Interzone and then again in the closing moments of the narrative. The final reenactment of her originally accidental death is now a clear assassination providing the melancholy proof of Lee's commitment to his identity as a writer. This progression from chance to choice is indicative of Cronenberg's rephrasing of *Naked Lunch* into not only a relatively more coherent speculation on the life of the artist, but a statement of principle on the archeology of self that creativity demands; "it is an act of listening," Cronenberg has said, "to the part of you that you don't want to listen to" (Cronenberg 1991). The portrait of an author wrestling with demons to articulate truth dominates the center of the film's frame and lodges the story beneath the sheltering meta-genre of artists discovering the purpose of their art, a far less destabilized narrative than that woven by the novel's insistence on elliptical incompleteness and endless possibility.

"IT'S JUST THAT THE *WHOLE THING* IS UNREAL": THE TRUTH OF SELF AND THE TRAP OF SAMENESS

Cronenberg reworks the biographically personal, filtering it through the fiction of *Naked Lunch* into a generically inflected psychodrama of artistic emergence. A sci-fi/horror plot of addiction to impossible drugs (bug powder, the black meat of centipedes, jizzum from monstrous creatures) presided over by a mad scientist (Roy Scheider's camp Dr. Benway) is the pulpy scenario poeticizing Lee's personal trajectory of creative awakening. Sequences of literal transformation such as the predatory dandy Cloquet's nightmarish shift into a giant centipede are recontextualized by a constant two-shot refrain in the pattern of the film's editing.

Bill Lee (Peter Weller): "I gave up writing . . ."

Cronenberg repeatedly cuts between variously shuddering, chittering, and gre-
gariously rambling anthropomorphized machines only to then reveal the actuality
of what has always been in fact merely a machine, a before-and-after suture edit
Cronenberg typically employs after one of the mechanisms has been damaged.

The creatures that Lee encounters are in fact his own familiars, totemic guides
on a path toward self-actualization. Unearthly mugwumps and insectoid typewriters act as Lee's points of contact with himself, filtered back from the depths of a
sci-fi-addled brain. Dr. Benway further coaxes Lee's transformation when the latter
comes to see the good doctor about a dependence on bug powder, an imaginary
drug. Mixing the finely ground meat of the giant Brazilian aquatic centipede into
a sample of the habit-forming powder, watching as the black additive disappears
into the yellow grain, Benway comments how the mixture, an intended cure, is
"like an agent, an agent who's come to believe his own cover story, but who's in
there, hiding, in a larval state, just waiting for the proper moment to hatch out."
Cronenberg utilizes Burroughs' motif of the perpetual confusion of agents and
identities less as a way to suggest the impossibility of stabilizing self and more as
a way to poeticize its possibility. For the film, the consequence of Lee's eventual
hatching is becoming a writer, the face of the secret self coming back into focus.
"I gave up writing," Lee tells Hank and Martin at the beginning of the film, "too

dangerous." Dangerous perhaps, but necessary, for in Cronenberg's vision of *Naked Lunch*, horror is to be found in the trauma of burning through the trappings of our resistance, tearing down the theater sets of our own imaginative refusals. If the film's use of sci-fi conceits draped in moments of horror-fueled Grand Guignol cohere into a portrait of the artist as a (not so) young sensonaut, the book's use of such genre fancies is rather more pointedly resistant to those readings.

Burroughs' *Naked Lunch* engages in world building from within a genre-inflected form. As Timothy S. Murphy argues, "the disjunctive 'routines' that give shape to *Naked Lunch* through their remorseless non-linear proliferation constitute a structural correlative to the pulp-derived themes and imagery of mind/body mutation" (2009, 226). The text lumbers like a Karloffian Frankenstein monster yet retains the eloquence of Shelley's haunted beast. We are introduced to the denizens of Interzone by way of lists flouting a sci-fi sensibility: the great City Market is filled with sellers of

> Tithonian longevity serums, black marketeers of World War III, excisors of telepathic sensitivity, osteopaths of the spirit [. . .] brokers of exquisite dreams and memories tested on the sensitized cells of junk sickness and bartered for raw materials of the will, doctors skilled in the treatment of diseases dormant in the black dust of ruined cities, gathering virulence in the while blood of eyeless worms feeling slowly to the surface and the human host, maladies of the ocean floor and the stratosphere, maladies of the laboratory and atomic war . . . (Burroughs 2001, 91)

This litany accentuates a sci-fi/horror topography, a jumbled procession of pulp product drawn from genre flotsam and jetsam. Agents of control and addiction (vampiric purveyors and apocalyptic "brokers" trading off of need and desire) mingle with mad doctors and monstrous beings filling the tortured body-scape of "human hosts." Interzone is composed of the stitched together remnants of fading B-movies, water-stained comic books, and moldering dime-store paperbacks that gesture toward deeper, uglier preoccupations. Ending the passage with a chant of various "maladies," Burroughs leaves us assured of the high cost behind the genre play. To be stripped of "raw materials of the will" is to feel the writhing of those "eyeless worms" and the contagion of their blood, less a positive transformation than a final compromise to the sovereignty of a corrupting need to dominate. Everything is for sale in the market and so everything comes at a price. Desperation to live longer, to fill the void of experience with meaning and distractions, pollutes the world and feeds the factories until they come to mirror a fundamental dystopia of the spirit, a yearning to be controlled.

Many of the novel's concerns are outlined through sci-fi/horror tropes, from figures familiar to the genres (mad scientist, galactic pirate, time traveler, post-apocalyptic despot, witchdoctor, ghoul) to scenarios and mise-en-scènes (invasion/takeover, tormented bodies, sanguinary landscapes of entrapment, and ritualized practices of interspecies relations). A.J., impresario of doom, strolls the market, vampire-like, "in a black cape with a vulture perched on one shoulder" (Burroughs 2001, 99), it being "rumored that he represents a trust of giant insects

Bill Lee in Interzone.

from another galaxy" (123), while "boys jacking off in the school toilet know each other as agents from Galaxy X" (174). And then we have the archfiend Dr. Benway, the insidious, gore soaked chamberlain of *Naked Lunch*'s black court who presides over a series of stygian experiments lodged somewhere between a desire for Orwellian control and simple grotesque curiosity. Addicts and sellers like The Sailor, inhuman dealer who sups on the stolen time of supplicants and whose eyes are like a "green universe stirred by cold black currents" (168), play out a game of possession and domination to the sci-fi serial tune of aliens and (not so) innocents set to the repetition of Burroughs' beloved schlupping sound. Bewildered residents of Interzone such as Carl Peterson, summoned to meet with Benway in the halls of the dystopic Ministry of Mental Hygiene and Prophylaxis, fall into the spiral of convoluted traps with all the naiveté of weary travelers setting up in ruined castles for the night. "It's just that the *whole thing* is unreal," Carl tells Benway after being assaulted by the despotic physician's insinuations and veiled threats as to the substance of Carl's "sexual deviations," only to find himself lost in the breakdown of reality: "The doctor's voice was barely audible. The whole room was exploding out into space" (164–65).

Yet, if as evocative cultural shorthand such genre lists retain a provocative potential for metaphoric commentary and critique, they run the risk of reductively capping meaning at the denotative level. *Naked Lunch* projects an uncertain relation between the use of genre materials and their function, an unease bared in Burroughs' argument that "your knowledge of what is going on can only be superficial and relative" (Burroughs 2001, 184). The irony is that the very genre imagery used to suggest the themes Burroughs is interested in also provides yet another level to the con. A certain mournful impossibility to express the true horror is hinted at in the recycled language and images of generic tropes, as if surface familiarity with the mechanisms of genre elements indicates an ease of acceptance on the part of the experiencer, a dangerous comfort with (desire for) sameness. One of the central sci-fi/horror conceits in the novel, the discussion of the political parties of Interzone, explicates the tensions in Burroughs' argument that to reach past control one has to reach beyond the familiar boundaries and repetitions of narrative itself. The Liquefactionists, Divisionists, and Senders propagate their agendas by way of an array of techniques representing the stuff of sci-fi/horror nightmares, seeking, respectively, to merge all people into one vast organism, divide the self into multiple cloned copies, and establish a controlling telepathic relation between minds. The members of these parties live in states from the Divisionists' "continual crisis of rage and fear" to the "self-righteous complacency of the Senders" to "the relaxed depravity of the Liquefactionists" (140). The parties of Interzone weaponize the stuff of horror and sci-fi genre narratives as mechanisms of control, existing through various states and methods of proliferation, "stories" spreading through the equivalent of "one-way telepathic broadcast" (140). The Factualists, the party Burroughs posits as a singular alternative, oppose "atomic war, the use of knowledge to control, coerce, debase, exploit or annihilate the individuality of another living creature" (140). Indeed, they champion change over the set repetitions of form, declaring "we must not reject or deny our protoplasmic core, striving at all times to maintain a maximum of flexibility" (140). In the world of Interzone, the rigidity of sameness equals the whole of completeness that itself equals existence in the grip of control, a kind of final death.

THE CON INSIDE: GENRE AS ROUTINE

And death fills the novel, violent and bleakly eroticized. *Naked Lunch* begins in the lurid voice of hip criminality. Burroughs quickly establishes the pattern to follow: the tension between a watching authority and a fleeing, resistant deviance ("setting up their devil doll stool pigeons"), and between the norm and the skewed ("and right on time this narcotics dick in a white trench coat [imagine tailing somebody in a white trench coat. Trying to pass as a fag I guess]") (Burroughs 2001, 3). Yet from the start, genre is knowingly codified as just another routine; "I am evidently his idea of a character," the "I" of the opening snarls, wary of the "square wants to come on hip" and who performs casual criminality for "the fast Hollywood types" (3). This is our entry point to this specific glimmer of the novel's genre firmament, a movement "down into the silent black ooze with gangsters in concrete" (5). *Naked Lunch* "Starts West" by way of the drug "expose" and the world of the con populated by characters embodying fraught relations between power, control, and opposition framed through the generalizing "talk" of character types. The Vigilante, the Rube, and the Mark Inside navigate "the old cop bullshit" (6), ultimately coming face to face with the oldest of crimes, some terrible compromise at the heart of an America that

> is not a young land: it is old and dirty and evil [. . .] the evil is there waiting [. . .] And always cops: smooth college trained state cops, practiced, apologetic patter, electronic eyes weigh your car and luggage, clothes and face; snarling big city dicks, soft-spoken country sheriffs with something black and menacing in old eyes color of a faded grey flannel shirt (6, 11).

The story-myth only covers deeper dread. Burroughs starts with the 1930s gangster genre patois that maps our way through the urgency of a more cosmic resistance to control, that thing waiting for us since "before the settlers, before the Indians" (11). But the map itself is touched by the con, that aforementioned "B production" that runs the risk of substituting another obscuring narrative rather than offering unencumbered opposition (3).

It's a system of genre obfuscations Burroughs skewers in the conflation of blue movies and rituals of state execution writhing at the center of "A.J.'s Annual Party," a routine of orgiastic hangings sizzling to the sound of necks snapping and bodies orgasming where an exhibitionist carnality is linked to the trauma of systematized, and narrationally seductive, authority. The Great Slashtubitch, whose "full evening dress, blue cape and blue monocle" (75) recall the stylish villainy of the theatrically driven master criminal Fantômas, presides over the grim yet gleeful affair, one part magician, one part director, all parts manipulator of narrative and illusion. Slashtubitch disappears in a "fadeout" to a screen upon which pornographic movies continually shift into death rituals, both governed by what Shaun De Waal calls "Burroughs' delirious and disturbing play of Eros and Thanatos, his unrestrained fantasy of submission and domination" (2009, 136). Burroughs' delineation of power relations takes the form of scenarios interfolded within scenarios, a play of generic elements—the pornographic as erotic fascination and the executional as the embodiment of criminal punishment—that mutually spectacularize the other. Each reveals the ways narrative designs can misdirect by taking the real consequence of uneasily articulated trauma and filtering it through the familiar trajectories of a narrated experience: the porn that ends with orgasm and the judgment that ends with punishment. Burroughs implies such complete experiences are focused on their own sheer force of visceral exhibition and therefore capable of being sealed off from the contexts that produced them. Genre play can reveal the condition but at the same time run the risk of regulating the consequence. When the curtain parts, the players take their bow and "are not as young as they appear in the Blue Movies . . . they look tired and petulant" (Burroughs 2001, 87) just as the anonymous male hustler coded as desperate criminal in "Ordinary Men and Women" laments that nowadays clients want to "leave old memories" (105), the same exhausted stories, in place of his own past experiences, and the Zone's Old Courthouse has become a place cases go only to be lost forever in an endless ritualized process of following the law in name only. Empty sacrament leads to thoughtless repetition and mere gesture. Burroughs suggests that this reduction to endless replication, as with the political parties of Interzone, is the real criminal conspiracy to be feared, this reiteration of same upon same. It's a sentiment Cronenberg's *Naked Lunch* shares, understanding the struggle between sameness and difference to be one of self-repression versus self-revelation. For Cronenberg, the crime is choosing poorly.

The film's syntax is built from a film noir inflected vocabulary, the enigmatic cafes and doom-laden parlors, the gloomy side streets filled with shadowy extras, the rogues clamoring to mislead and seduce, the corrupt officials, and the lone seeker of truth. Its early action is set within a moody 1950s décor of grimy earthen-colored rooms punctuated with greens, beige, and rusty burgundies, and if the film lacks the quintessential black and white chiaroscuro lighting so common to noir films, we are instead left in spaces filled with the cluttering bric-a-brac of postwar hopes already gone to seed. Cronenberg's *Naked Lunch* literalizes noir as psyche-scape and the detective as existential wanderer beset by inward-turning inquiries. Lee's aura of criminality is coded less as movements through a cabal of global control operations and insidious compromise and more a navigation of subterranean channels bringing him ever closer to the truth of himself. Addiction takes on a new meaning in the film's vision of the noir detective's underworld exploration as Cronenberg develops the proposition that impossible drugs can have internal metaphorical connections attached to them. "I seem to be addicted to something that doesn't really exist," Lee writes at one point, teetering on the verge of grasping the fundamental essence of his struggle.

The caper is to steal into the inside, to slough away layers of self-deception. For the film, this process of self-disclosure is wedded to the suggestively noirish emanations of Burroughs himself, or at least the image he cut in the later years of his life, dressed in a three-piece suit and fedora, holding himself at a remove but watching, a cross between Sherlock Holmes and Philip Marlowe: the dandy gentleman detective waiting to show you the crime scene. Cronenberg's *Naked Lunch* is enraptured with this snapshot of the author as time lost and oddly nostalgic, if even as a historied figure laden with projected senses and affects of a past time filtered through Hollywood iconography. Cronenberg's film is steeped in consideration of what he takes to be Burroughs' and the novel's own generic inflections. Cronenberg sounds the measure of Burroughs' work by adapting author and novel into a single aching archive of experience gesturing toward a mode of being, the becoming of the artist and the ultimate discovery of perhaps the only truth offered us, the one inside. Yet it's the "Mark Inside" Burroughs comes back to again and again in the novel, the conning and conned, the ever-ready to be fooled, particularly by the very sense of the complete, unifying totality of self.

"CONCLUDE? NOTHING WHATEVER. JUST A PASSING OBSERVATION"

The "Mark Inside" is another way of describing the self who's bought into the spiel of playing roles, who's playing the con and is always in danger of losing. Identity becomes a genre production: predetermined rules and assumptions for the way to tell a story that ends in completeness. Burroughs' *Naked Lunch* resists this trajectory, unable to elect a hero and speak in a voice of profound singularity. Incompleteness pervades the novel, palpable in the ellipses threading the text and evident at the tattered edges of routines bleeding off into questions, fadeouts, and indefinite pronouncements, a cortège of points from which movement in any direction is possible. The push and pull of this textual potential recalls another of Burroughs' common fragments, the irregular decay of frayed sounds by turns from a distant city and down a windy street (fragments of a life now clear and now indistinct) where linearity and sense throb in and out of focus. The language of Burroughs' novel borrows the conceits of various genres only to envassal those timeworn storehouses of character, landscape, and storyline to the more abstruse leanings of an eccentric text bent on erasing the boundary lines of confederation.

Cronenberg's film and Burroughs' novel share a fundamental similarity: they both utilize a range of genres by which to gesture toward the viewer/reader. Yet whereas the film suggests that to exist is to become something like a comprehensible text oneself, to be written and rewritten but to forever bear a secret truth awaiting interpretation, the novel offers no such hope of ultimate explanation and final completion. While Cronenberg's Bill Lee metamorphosizes into a final self defined by creative expression, the bevy of madcaps, malefactors, and transients filling the halls of Burroughs' rambling mansion of a book are intermittently defined before fading back into a Byzantine flow. Such fleeting personages are emblematic of hostility to unadorned intelligibility, which is not to say that the novel lacks lucidity: meaning emanates from the very repetitions, caesuras, and dissolutions meandering through the pulpy product at the heart of Burroughs' self-effacing design. Slicing into any cross-section of *Naked Lunch* unveils a defiance of the authority of narrative and genre through a parade of categorical oppositions to the finality of containment and closure. The novel is heavy with euphoric upset, especially when considered alongside Cronenberg's comparatively stabilized, adaptive text that, as much as it borrows the trappings of multiple genres, is cardinally concerned with the Romantically tinged tale of the artist-hero's trajectory of self-discovery.

Both film and the novel end melancholically, yet while Cronenberg's *Naked Lunch* ends on change, however disconsolate, the novel breaks off at a point we have already passed through multiple times ("no glot . . . C'lom Fliday") (Burroughs 2001, 196) by way of another deferral of resolution, like the idiosyncratic spinning of an errant wheel. Burroughs' *Naked Lunch* is a dream that remains adrift, its meaning elusive but seemingly there, a tale erasing itself, suggestive but incomplete. We can only end in an elegantly defiant jumble of stories and sensations, memories of tattered scraps lost in a crowd of empty frames: "this book spill off the page in all directions, kaleidoscope of vistas, medley of tunes and street noises" (191); "dead leaves fill the fountain and geraniums run wild with mint, spill a vending machine route across the lawn" (188); "Pick a shot . . . Any shot . . ." (182).

JOSHUA VASQUEZ's current project examines intersections of melancholy and masculinity in American genre film. He cites early encounters with a deep strata of melancholy locatable in Burroughs' work as, in retrospect, one of the key points of origin for his own study.

REFERENCES

Amis, Martin. 2008. "The Voice of the Lonely Crowd." In *The Second Plane: September 11: Terror and Boredom*, 11–19. New York: Vintage International.
Bennett, Benjamin. 2008. "Intransitive Autobiography: *Naked Lunch* and the Problem of Personal Identity." *artUS* 24/25 (Fall/Winter): 32–38.
Burroughs, William S. 1987. Introduction to *Queer*. New York: Penguin Books.
———. 2001. *Naked Lunch: The Restored Text*. Edited by James Grauerholz and Barry Miles. New York: Grove.
Cronenberg, David. 1991. Interview in "Making *Naked Lunch*." London Weekend Documentary. *Naked Lunch*, The Criterion Collection, 1991. DVD.
De Waal, Shaun. 2009. "The Flaming Voice: *Naked Lunch* in Apartheid South Africa." In *Naked Lunch@50: Anniversary Essays*, edited by Oliver Harris and Ian MacFadyen, 133–41. Carbondale: Southern Illinois University Press.
Harris, Olivier. 2003. *William Burroughs and the Secret of Fascination*. Carbondale: Southern Illinois University Press.
Loranger, Carol. 1999. "'This Book Spill Off the Page in All Directions': What Is the Text of *Naked Lunch*?" *Postmodern Culture* 10 (1) (September). http://muse.jhu.edu/journals/postmodern_culture/toc/pmc10.1.html.
Murphy, Timothy S. 2009. "Random Insect Doom: The Pulp Science Fiction of *Naked Lunch*." In *Naked Lunch@50: Anniversary Essays*, edited by Oliver Harris and Ian Macfadyen, 223–32. Carbondale: Southern Illinois University Press.
Stam, Robert. 2005. "Introduction: The Theory and Practice of Adaptation." In *Literature and Film: A Guide to the Theory and Practice of Film Adaptation*, edited by Robert Stam and Alessandra Raengo, 1–52. New York: Blackwell.

The Fall of Art

As evident in the photographs presented between the two following archival manuscripts, Burroughs became friendly with pop artist Andy Warhol in the early
1970s, while visiting and then moving to Downtown New York. These photographs
were taken during the filming for the BBC-Arena TV Show in the Chelsea Hotel,
in 1981, as William S. Burroughs conversed with Victor Bockris and Andy Warhol.
This meeting occurred some ten years after he wrote his unpublished parody of
the art market in response to hearing of the sale of Warhol's painting of a soup-can
for $60,000.

In the brief essay, "La Chute de l'Art," Burroughs satirizes the art market as
he sees it developing in the 1970s. This piece is part of a larger file, Folio 97, that
Burroughs entitled his "Dickens Calendar," in which these routines precede a third
narrative satire, "FRENCH CANADIAN BEAN SOUP." A few years before meeting Warhol in person, Burroughs responds to the unbelievable news of Warhol's
Big Campbell's Soup Cans with Torn Label (Vegetable Beef) (1962) selling for such an
exorbitant price on May 15, 1970. Purchased by an anonymous European bidder, it
was, reportedly, the "highest price ever paid for a work by a living American artist."
In Berg 32.4, Burroughs also scrapbooked the news article (with its description of
the artwork as a "five-foot-high painting of a soup can with a peeling label") next
to a seascape photograph laid over an aqua blue sheet with ink blots of a darker
blue (dated "Lands End 11, 1970" in his "Dickens Calendar"). In the photo, the
upper half discloses yachts in a harbor, city buildings in the background, while
above, the yacht's poles crisscross the sky. At the page's bottom half, the sailboats
are reflected in the rippling water.

The unusual occasion of Warhol's art sale instigated in Burroughs a fascinating critique of monopoly capital and the politics of art in the new world order. In
his creative essay(what he calls "une poeme moderne," a later iteration of which
appears as "The Fall of Art" in *The Adding Machine* [1985]), he dreams of sabotag-
ing the art market, causing the stock market to crash, and its mythic figures of
oligarchic power to spiral down with it. That wealth is symbolized by the historical
personage, Hetty Green, famously nicknamed the "Witch of Wall Street," reputed
to be at the time the world's richest businesswoman, who inherited her money

from whaling and the China trade, and became well known primarily for her miserliness. Burroughs' routine concludes by fantasizing that, in the aftermath of the stock market crash, the only values that would remain would be those brought into the world by art: "Brion Gysin says that art creates values. So what remains when the inflated values collapse is the values that art has created" (Berg 32.2).

—AWC

Andy Warhol's Soup, William S. Burroughs, Lands End 11, 1970 (8 × 11, 1 leaf, facsimile) (Berg 32.4). Folio 97 "Dickens Calendar," Item 6, "Andy Warhol's Soup . . .". Two news clippings, refer to item 3, pasted on blue paper with autograph date, Lands End 11, 1970.

William S. Burroughs with Victor Bockris and Andy Warhol filming BBC-Arena TV Show, Chelsea Hotel, NYC 1981, photographs courtesy of Barry Miles.

May 17,1970...40,000 dollars for a Churchill of the Cannes water front
kind of thing you can sit and look at for hours why dont Nixson
and Wilson get in on the act and what am I offered for this rare
Anschlinger?...Andy Warhol's soup can gets record 60,000 dollars...
yes a painting of a Campbell's gegetable beef soup can highest pric
ever paid for a work by a living American artist...A @@@@ European
bidder who wished to remain anonymous'...
'Gentleman it is time to strike. Already collectors are selling
off pop art at what they consider top prices...'
An unknown artist now produces a better soup can...Rainbow Jack's
French Canadian Bean Soup...A rainbow a mountain lake on the label
half sunshine half shadow and there in the rainbow is Rainbow
Jack a beautiful red haired lumber jack the rainbow on his face
open pack axe propped againsta spruce he holds up a can of
Rainbow Jack's French Canadian Bean Soup likea chalice. This
is also an exclusive since the company discontinued this line
in 1899 and converted to canning salmon and later poisoned a
regiment in World War 1. Some old timers we provide from

******

[autograph]: D.C. 4

actor's equity will remember Rainbow Jack.
We put Rainbow Jack on the market and buy it back through an anonymous
bidder for 120,000 dollars. Want to raise that? We have some more
@@@@@@ genius works in stock...
Bringing you can old stock market spell from Hetty Green the Witch
of Wall Street. The ghost of Hetty Green spins likea top...
'Ding dong bell...SELL SELL SELL...Paris, Geneva, Amsterdam SELL.'
The art market stirs like a hysterical octupus jerking back tentacles
you cant give pop art away cant even burn a lot of it being made of
plastic...
'Knee Wall fell...Old Tower fell...Dow Jones Syntex Sub @@@@@
Swan fell...Sig Boom fell..Tele Con Polaroid Mutter Spell fell...
VORNADO PELL MELL SELL SELL SELL...'
She twists ina black sucking funnel over art markets and collectors
of the world...
'SELL SELL SELLL'
Brion Gysin says that art creates values. So what remains when the
inflated values collapse is the values that art has @@@@@@@ created

******

What remains when Colonel Bradly sweeps   off his wig and takes a bow
as Hetty Green?
The values that art has created.

12

Queer Outlaws Losing: The Betrayal of the Outlaw Underground in *The Place of Dead Roads*

KURT HEMMER

William S. Burroughs believed in the magic of literature to transform society—literally the author can write things into existence. He believed F. Scott Fitzgerald had done this with *The Great Gatsby* (1925) and Jack Kerouac had performed a similar feat with *On the Road* (1957). Unable to find a satisfactory outlaw underground, Burroughs spent much of his time imagining various versions. His desire to create an outlaw brotherhood and encourage revolutionary tactics can be seen in such works as *The Revised Boy Scout Manual* (1970), *The Electronic Revolution* (1970), *The Wild Boys* (1971), and *Cities of the Red Night* (1981), among other works. *The Revised Boy Scout Manual* gives a five-step program "to achieve independence from alien domination and to consolidate revolutionary gains" (Burroughs 1982, 5). Burroughs describes "a number of weapons and tactics in the war game" in *Electronic Revolution* (1994a, 60). In *The Wild Boys*, he writes, "Despite disparate aims and personnel of its constituent members the underground is agreed on basic objectives. We intend to march on the police machine everywhere. We intend to destroy the police machine and all its records. We intend to destroy all dogmatic verbal systems. The family unit and its cancerous expansion into tribes, countries, nations we will eradicate at its vegetable roots" (1992, 139–40). And in *Cities of the Red Night* Burroughs praises the articles of the pirate Captain Mission, which are "principles embodied in the French and American revolutions and later in the liberal revolutions of 1848 . . ." (1981, xi). It cannot be overstated that Burroughs' political attitudes came from multifarious sources, often contradictory—sometimes simultaneously libertarian and quasi-fascist—and certainly not orthodox Leftist. The fascinating genealogy of Burroughs' political attitudes will have to be the subject for another essay, but the germ of his ideal outlaw underground can be found in Jack Black's *You Can't Win* (1926). The blueprint for this outlaw brotherhood (albeit naïve and rudimentary) is most lucidly presented in *The Place of Dead Roads* (1984).

Yet why does Burroughs, the believer of writing-into-existence, have his outlaw underground fail? At least part of the answer can be found in the inspiration for the novel—*You Can't Win*. More formidable than Burroughs' faith that literature can alter reality was his indelible belief in the inevitable betrayal of an outlaw underground (at least on this planet), which imprinted itself in Burroughs' psyche when he read Black's memoir as a young boy. The seminal influence of *You Can't Win* would prevent Burroughs from depicting the success of his outlaw underground in *The Place of Dead Roads*.

"We lost," says Chris (played by Yul Brynner) in John Sturges's *The Magnificent Seven* (1960), based on Akira Kurosawa's *Seven Samurai* (1954). "We'll always lose." These are the last words of the film, as Chris and Vin (played by Steve McQueen) turn and ride off into the unknown. They have saved a Mexican village from the *banditos* led by Calvera (played by Eli Wallach), but it has cost the lives of four of their number, gunslingers who had found themselves at the brink of a tamed West when the days of the gunfighter were over. Hired to defend a village, the gunslingers had been betrayed by the frightened farmers. In an act of suicidal pride, the gunslingers vanquish Calvera's marauders, but ultimately, as Chris poignantly observes, the gunslingers have lost. It is a sentiment similar to the tone of Black's *You Can't Win*, a book rife with betrayals, about a disappearing underworld in which an outlaw called the Sanctimonious Kid tells the narrator, "Of course we'll lose anyway, sooner or later. . ." (Black 2013, 204). Burroughs ponders in his foreword to the book, "Jack Black calls his book *You Can't Win*. Well, who can?" (2013c, 16).

The Place of Dead Roads is Burroughs' attempt to produce in literature, and thus ostensibly into reality, an outlaw underground. Burroughs believed that writers have the power to write things into existence: "Writers are, in a way, very powerful indeed. They write the script for the reality film. Kerouac opened a million coffee bars and sold a million pairs of Levis to both sexes. Woodstock rises from his pages. Now if writers could get together into a real tight union, we'd have the world right by the words. We could write our own universes, and they would all be as real as a coffee bar or a pair of Levis or a prom in the Jazz Age. Writers could take over the reality studio" (Burroughs 2013g, 214)

Yet a belief in inevitable betrayal, instilled in Burroughs by Black's book, prevented Burroughs from depicting the outlaw heroes in *The Place of Dead Roads* from succeeding. Even though Burroughs believed "the purpose of writing is to make it happen" (2013b, 75), he was incapable of fending off his belief in inevitable betrayal. Burroughs' feelings can be summed up in a poignant passage from *Naked Lunch*[1]: "And I know some agent is out there in the darkness looking for me. Because all Agents defect and all Resisters sell out . . ." (2001, 172).

Burroughs moved near Lawrence, Kansas, in 1981, where he worked on *The Place of Dead Roads*, which had been substantially written in Boulder, Colorado. He would later live in Lawrence until his death.[2] By the time Burroughs arrived in Lawrence, it was an established college town with little resemblance to the farming community it had been during the Civil War, but the ghosts from that era still haunt. Lawrence had been a stronghold of the Jayhawkers and Red Legs, Union guerillas, who had been the archenemies of William Clarke Quantrill's Raiders. On August 13, 1863, several young women and girls related to members of Quantrill's marauders were injured and killed after the structure they were imprisoned in collapsed in Kansas City. A week later when Quantrill and hundreds of bush-whackers (among them Cole Younger, Frank James, and Bill Anderson) raided Lawrence, the belief that the women and girls had been murdered on orders by the Federal command help spur the devastation of the massacre—nearly two hundred buildings destroyed and close to two hundred men and boys killed (see Leslie 1998, 193–244). The outlaw gang Burroughs creates in *The Place of Dead Roads*, called the Johnson Family, resembles the legendary James-Younger gang, which sprang from Quantrill's Raiders (see Leslie 1998) and Bloody Bill Anderson's Irregulars (see Castel and Goodrich 1998). In Burroughs' novel, the detractors of the Johnson Family compare the outlaw gang to the Confederate guerrillas by starting a defamation campaign with the slogan "QUANTRILL RIDES AGAIN" (Burroughs 1984, 108). One of the Johnsons, Denton Brady, is said to have "rode with the James boys and he was a child prodigy under Quantrill" (178). Brady swaps "stories about Quantrill and Bloody Bill Anderson and the legendary Captain Gray, who was sent up to Missouri to organize the Irregulars" (178). Burroughs has no illusions about these outlaws in reality. He calls Jesse James "a dumb, brutal hick" (Knickerbocker 1999, 21) and a son of a bitch (Burroughs 1984, 155). Yet for his literary purposes, Burroughs is more concerned with the myth. In legend, Frank and Jesse James and Cole Younger and his brothers were righteous rebels—an elite gang of outlaws defending the ideals of the lost Confederacy (see Stiles 2003). In *The Place of Dead Roads*, Burroughs transforms these Confederate guerillas into a model for his outlaw society, a move certainly most on the political Left would find alarming. Allan Johnston argues, "Beat culture by its very nature lacked the theoretical and social underpinnings to develop the clarified economic and political oppositional stances that appeared in the 1960s counterculture" (2005, 104). Yet *The Place of Dead Roads* can be read as Burroughs' attempt to create a clarified economic and political model for an outlaw underground as an alternative to the Left's counterculture, an effort that has generally gone underappreciated by his critics.

Burroughs' model for outlaw resistance was found in Black's *You Can't Win*. In this autobiography, Black's interest in a life of crime is sparked by a Civil War veteran whose heroes were "Quantrell [*sic*], the guerilla, Jesse and Frank James, Cole and Bob Younger" (Black 2013, 24). More than a half century after Burroughs read Black's book it would help inspire *The Place of Dead Roads*. "I first read *You Can't Win* in 1926, in an edition bound in red cardboard . . ." writes Burroughs in his foreword to Black's autobiography.[3] "I learned about the Johnson Family of good bums and thieves, with a code of conduct that made more sense to me than the arbitrary, hypocritical rules that were taken for granted as being 'right' by my peers" (Burroughs 2013c, 15). Dustin Griffin points out:

This was not an underground or cult book but rather a well-reviewed best-seller, a lively and detailed report of twenty-five years "on the road" written in an accessible, straightforward style. Burroughs could have seen ads for the book, with blurbs from Carl Sandburg

("As exciting as the most thrilling fiction") and Clarence Darrow ("a marvelous story") in *Overland Monthly* and *Out West* magazine (December 1926). (2014, 13)

Ted Morgan claims that Black's book "would have an enormous impact on the unfolding of [Burroughs'] life and work" (2012, 39). "In *You Can't Win*," writes Morgan, "there is a set of values . . . that Burroughs would make his own" (41). According to Barry Miles, "Burroughs' interest in lowlife began with Jack Black's *You Can't Win*" (2014, 121). Burroughs' childhood dream of actually belonging to a community of outlaws like the Johnsons in Black's book spurred Burroughs' imagination throughout his career. Miles argues, "In *The Place of Dead Roads*, Jack Black's Johnson Family stand a good chance of winning. . . . Here [Burroughs] is doing his best to make it happen by writing it into existence" (2002, 227). Yet Morgan argues, "Burroughs owed a lot to his reputation as a Beat chieftain, but preferred to position himself as the Lone Gunman" (2012, 493). *The Place of Dead Roads* complicates Morgan's reading of Burroughs. Although Burroughs has been depicted, understandably at times, as an apolitical loner, *The Place of Dead Roads* is a rigorous attempt to imagine a politically viable outlaw underground to which Burroughs wanted to belong. What Burroughs was finally able to create in his imagination, after a lifetime of failing to find it in reality, was a community of outlaws with a social theory and practice to which he and others could adhere. As John Vanderheide argues, "Burroughs' art does not function to achieve mimetic veracity or aesthetic disinterestedness but to provoke real individual and social transformations" (2008, 65).

Placing his alter ego, Kim Carsons, in a central position within the Johnson Family, Burroughs attempts to write himself into a "good bad guy" cowboy. As strange as it might seem, Mike Ryko, the character Jack Kerouac based on himself in *And the Hippos Were Boiled in Their Tanks* (2008), refers to Will Dennison, the character based on Burroughs, as "remind[ing] [him] of a cowboy, somehow" (97), and Paul Bowles remembered Burroughs as having a "cowboy voice" (1984, 16). Burroughs has his cowboy persona interact with characters taken from Black's book, like Salt Chunk Mary and the Sanctimonious Kid. Miles (2002, 226) brings to our attention the line describing Salt Chunk Mary that Burroughs even lifted from *You Can't Win*, "She could say 'no' quicker than any woman I ever knew, and none of them meant 'yes'" (Black 2013, 79), and used in *The Place of Dead Roads*: "Mary could say 'no' quicker than any woman Kim ever knew and none of her no's ever meant yes" (Burroughs 1984, 122).

One of the most important characters for understanding Burroughs' own political stance is the hero of *The Place of Dead Roads*, Kim Carsons. To some degree this gay shootist is signifying on the famous frontiersman Kit Carson. While Carson was a famous Indian fighter, Burroughs' character is sympathetic to American Indians and gets into a gunfight after a racist bartender refuses to serve Red Dog, Carsons's friend (Burroughs 1984, 79–80). The photograph used on the jacket of the first edition of the novel is of a single white cowboy comfortably posing with

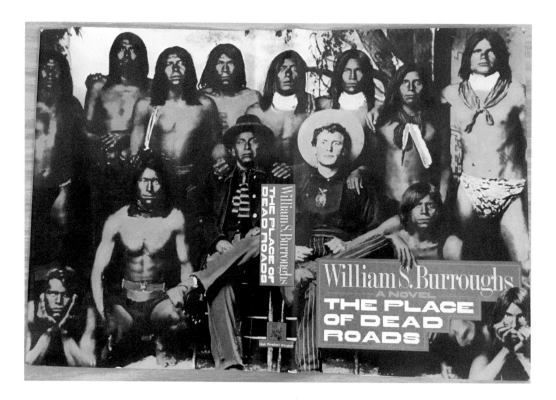

"Book Jacket Design" from the book *The Place of Dead Roads* by William S. Burroughs. Copyright C © 1984 by Henry Holt and Company. Used by permission of Henry Holt and Company. All rights reserved. Designed by Robert Reed. Jacket photograph courtesy of Colorado State Historical Society Library, jacket image courtesy of the William S. Burroughs Trust, used by permission of The Wylie Agency LLC.

a group of Native Americans from the archives of the Colorado State Historical Society Library. Yet Kim Carsons is much more than a figure playing against the stereotypes of the Old West. Kit Carson (1809–1868) was born in Kentucky, but his family moved to Missouri, Burroughs' home state, when he was still an infant. He never learned to read or write but became a national figure after being a hired guide for John Charles Fremont in two expeditions into the Great West, which Fremont made famous with his published reports. Kent Ladd Steckmesser writes, "Most important, he is featured in one of the most dramatic episodes in Western history. Carson and his fellow scout Alex Godey trail a band of thirty Indians who had murdered Mexicans and stolen their horses. The two scouts attack the savages and recover the horses" (1965, 18). In an interview the year before his death, Carson "declared that all our Indian troubles were caused originally by bad white men" (Steckmesser 1965, 22). There is also some evidence that Carson had two Indian wives, though these relationships are downplayed in his legend and biographies. Steckmesser explains, "Carson's role as a symbol of Anglo-Saxon racial superiority required that his close relationships with the Indians be ignored. Any suggestion that he was on intimate terms with redskins was incompatible with the picture

Pima Indians (1890–1900) photograph: Made by the Arizona Curio and News Company, used by permission of History Colorado Stephen H. Hart Library. Original Photograph Collection (Scan #10046451), History Colorado.

of the fearless Indian fighter, cleaning out Mexicans and Indians to clear a path for American civilization" (27). Although he could be brutal and boisterous, and will be forever known as a great Indian killer, the actual Carson was much more complex than the Carson of legend. These examples of Carson fighting for justice and having sympathy for the Indians may have been on Burroughs' mind when he created Kim Carsons. Possibly Burroughs is not so much ironically playing off the Carson legend but rewriting the legend to accommodate the side of Carson that the legend erases.

In addition to Carson, Kim Carsons is based on the writer Denton Welch (1915–1948). Burroughs' dedication in the novel reads, "To Denton Welch, For Kim Carsons." Welch, a homosexual novelist who romanticized youth, is credited with influencing the anecdotal style of Burroughs' Western and inspiring the creation of his gunslinger. "While I was writing *The Place of Dead Roads*," confesses Burroughs, "I felt in spiritual contact with the late English writer Denton Welch, and modeled the novel's hero, Kim Carsons, directly on him. Whole sections came to me as if dictated, like table tapping" (Burroughs 2010, 131). And Burroughs writes in the foreword to Welch's *In Youth Is Pleasure* (1945), "My Kim Carson [*sic*] (the hero of *The Place of Dead Roads*) is Denton Welch" (Burroughs 1994b, ix). Welch was hit by a motorist while riding his bicycle at the age of twenty. The accident resulted in kidney failure, partial impotence, and tuberculosis of the spine. He would eventually succumb to his poor health. Burroughs makes an oblique reference to Welch's work in *The Place of Dead Roads* when he writes, "[Kim] hated [horses'] hysteria, their stubborn malice, and their awful yellow teeth" (1984, 12). This is a subtle reference to one of Burroughs' favorite passages from Welch's *Maiden Voyage* (1943): "Once [my horrible little black pony] had broken out of the stable and had galloped through the roses and over the lawns, showing its awful yellow teeth" (quoted in Burroughs 2013a, 48). Burroughs' admiration for Welch was so powerful that he made his Western hero dislike horses, and who ever heard of a Western hero without a horse?

The Place of Dead Roads is not an autobiographical novel, but it is obvious to an attentive reader that Burroughs also wants himself identified with the story's protagonist. Kim Carsons uses the alias William Seward Hall, a variation on William Seward Burroughs, who writes Westerns under the pen name "Kim Carsons." Carsons's father shares Burroughs' father's name, Mortimer; the details of Carsons's and Burroughs' childhoods are similar; and readers familiar with Burroughs' life will recognize Bernabé Jurado, who Carsons has a letter of introduction from, as Burroughs' Mexican lawyer who got Burroughs out of jail on bail after eleven days of incarceration for the accidental shooting of his wife in September 1951.

Carsons represented the vitality Burroughs had frequently fantasized he would possess and that he believed the Left counterculture lacked. Morgan writes, "Partly, he was living out fantasies of danger and action, which arose from a sense of frustration that his life as a writer had been too sedentary and uneventful. Partly, he sought to reclaim models of masculine behavior for the gay community" (2012, 629). Unable to find the masculine gay community he felt he belonged to, Burroughs created it in *The Place of Dead Roads* while simultaneously creating an ideal version of himself. "In the course of rewriting history," Morgan argues, "Burroughs is rewriting himself as he would like to be—the fastest gun in the West. The despised homosexual wimp becomes a great shootist" (629).

Burroughs not only wanted to recreate himself, but he also desired to create a community where his heroic persona would thrive. Burroughs makes Black's Johnson Family the blueprint for the society he wishes to inhabit. He says, "You know, they ask me if I were on a desert island and knew nobody would ever see what I wrote, would I go on writing. My answer is most emphatically yes. I would go on writing for company. Because I'm creating an imaginary—it's always imaginary—world in which I would like to live" (Knickerbocker 1999, 29–30). In the opening note to *The Place of Dead Roads*, Burroughs tells his readers the original title of the book was "The Johnson Family." Morgan argues, "A community of outlaws, such as he had read about in Jack Black's *You Can't Win*, was perhaps the only place where a misfit such as [Burroughs] could belong" (2012, 129). "A Johnson pays his debt and keeps his word," writes Burroughs. "He minds his own business, but will give help when help is needed and asked for. He does not hold out on his confederates or cheat his landlady. He is what they call in show business 'good people'" (Burroughs 2013c, 15). Burroughs further explains: "In this world of shabby rooming houses, furtive gray figures in dark suits, hop joints and chili parlors the Johnson

Family took shape as a code of conduct. To say someone is a Johnson means he keeps his word and honors his obligations. He's a good man to do business with and a good man to have on your team. He is not a malicious, snooping, interfering self-righteous troublemaking person" (Burroughs 2013f, 91).

In *The Place of Dead Roads*, Burroughs created an outlaw underground of Johnsons that could defend itself from the "shits." The Manichean war depicted in Burroughs' novel is analogous to the struggle Burroughs actually believed he saw around him. Burroughs states, "A basic split between shits and Johnsons has emerged" (2013c, 16). The "shits" want homogeneity and control over personal lives. Burroughs had a general disdain for the idea of "liberals," especially if it meant people encroaching on other's decision making. The Johnsons are only "liberals" in a very strict sense. Burroughs explains, "I hate that term, 'liberals.' It sounds so vague. I just think liberals are, well, Johnsons—reasonable people who have some sort of sense of moderation and common sense and are not in some state of hysterical, self-righteous anger" (quoted in Bockris 1996, 246). The Johnsons are not political crusaders but an underground network of loosely affiliated outlaws who mind their own business and practice tolerance and compassion. Geoff Ward argues, "If there is an identifiable political position in Burroughs' work, it would be anarchistic individualism" (1993, 348). Yet in *The Place of Dead Roads* the Johnsons' communal political goals are clearly defined in a way that complicates Ward's reading of Burroughs' political stance.

Burroughs' description of his outlaw underground's program in *The Place of Dead Roads* is his clearest articulation of a political social theory:

> We will take every opportunity to weaken the power of the church. We will lobby in Congress for heavy taxes on all churches. We will provide more interesting avenues for the young. We will destroy the church with ridicule. We will secularize the church out of existence. We will introduce and encourage alternative religious systems. Islam, Buddhism; Taoism. Cults, devil worship, and rarefied systems like the Ishmaelite and the Manichaean. Far from seeking an atheistic world as the communists do, we will force Christianity to compete for the human spirit.
>
> We will fight any extension of federal authority and support States' Rights. We will resist any attempt to penalize or legislate against so-called victimless crimes . . . gambling, sexual behavior, drinking, drugs.
>
> We will give all our attention to experiments designed to produce asexual offspring, to cloning, use of artificial wombs, and transfer operations.
>
> We will endeavor to halt the Industrial Revolution before it is too late, to regulate populations at a reasonable point, to eventually replace quantitative money with qualitative money, to decentralize, to conserve resources. (Burroughs 1984, 97–98)

Burroughs even imagines resources for the Johnsons to support themselves in their subversive struggle: "The Family has set up a number of posts in America and northern Mexico. They are already very rich, mostly from real estate. They own newspapers, a chemical company, a gun factory, and a factory for making photographic equipment . . ." (102). Wayne Pounds explains, "The Johnsons represent a society of decentered, nonhierarchical socialist democracies with a communal economic base in agriculture and useful industry" (1991, 223). With the means to sustain a resistance, the Johnson Family now needs an organizational structure that will prevent it from falling into the traps that have toppled hierarchical regimes. Rather than having static roles, the members periodically exchange positions of greater and lesser power: "The Johnson Family is a cooperative structure. There isn't any boss man. People know what they are supposed to do and they do it. We're all actors and we change roles. Today's millionaire may be tomorrow's busboy" (Burroughs 1984, 115). When Kim thinks about this outlaw underground, he believes "his dream of a take-over by the Johnson Family, by those who actually do the work, the reactive thinkers and artists and technicians, was not just science fiction. It could happen" (104). "And to what extent did [William Seward Hall] succeed?" asks Burroughs in *The Place of Dead Roads*. "Even to envisage success on this scale is a victory. A victory from which others may envision further" (116).

Then why does the novel end with the assassination of Kim and, with his death, the feeling that the Johnsons will lose again, as Yul Brynner's Chris would say in *The Magnificent Seven*, like they always do?

At the end of the novel Kim is on his way to meet his rival, Mike Chase, for a shoot-out. The date is September 17, 1899. Burroughs reveals:

> But Mike has no intention of shooting it out with Kim. Mike is fast and he is good, but he always likes to keep the odds in his favor. The fill-your-hand number is out of date.
> This is 1899, not 1869, Mike tells himself. (Burroughs 1984, 306)

Chase realizes the days of the gunfighter (i.e., 1869) are over. But the reader is as shocked as Kim by what happens next: "'WHAT THE FU—' Someone slaps Kim very hard on the back, knocking the word out. Kim hates being slapped on the back. He turns in angry protest . . . blood in his mouth . . . can't turn . . . the sky darkens and goes out" (306). The final section of the novel is entitled "Quien es?" and Burroughs explains its significance: "Last words of Billy the Kid when he walked into a dark room and saw a shadowy figure sitting there. Who is it? The answer was a bullet through the heart" (201). The man who shot Billy the Kid was his one-time acquaintance—Pat Garrett. Kim bumps into Garrett early in the novel (77), which foreshadows the betrayal that awaits Carsons.

In *The Western Lands* (1987), the sequel to *The Place of Dead Roads*, the reader finds out that Carsons's killer was Joe the Dead, a former ally whose life Kim had saved:

> Joe the Dead lowered the rifle, like some cryptic metal extension growing from his arm socket, and smiled for a fleeting moment. A blush touched his ravaged features with a flash of youth that evaporated in powder smoke. With quick, precise movements he disassembled the telescoping rifle and silencer and fitted the components into a toolbox. Behind him, Kim Carsons and Mike Chase lay dead in the dust of the Boulder Cemetery. The date was September 17, 1899. (Burroughs 1988, 26)

Betrayal is an inevitability for Burroughs, just as it was in *You Can't Win* by Black, who was partially led into a life of crime because of the sympathy he felt when he read that Jesse James was shot in the back by his former friend, Bob Ford:

> How I loathed the traitor, Bob Ford, one of the James boys gang, who shot Jesse when his back was turned, for a reward! How I rejoiced to read that Ford was almost lynched by friends and admirers of Jesse, and had to be locked in the strongest jail in the state to protect him from a mobbing. I finished the story entirely and wholly in sympathy with the James boys, and all other hunted, outlawed, and outraged men. (Black 2013, 11)

Burroughs' novel is incapable of imagining the Johnson Family as winning because he has too strong a sense of inevitable betrayal to ever allow himself to believe, even in fiction, that betrayal would not occur.

Although possibly a date chosen by chance, it is interesting to note that the date of Kim Carsons's death, September 17, 1899, is mentioned in other works by Burroughs because he used the front page of the *New York Times* of that date for some of his cut-ups (see Schneiderman 2013). In a paper called "The Significance of the Frontier in American History" presented in Chicago to the American Historical Association, Frederick Jackson Turner famously announced what he considered to be the closing of the American frontier. A small article entitled "Cowboys Hold Up Street Cars" from Omaha, Nebraska, on the front page of the September 17, 1899, *New York Times* humorously brings the end of the frontier days to life.

> A dozen cowboys, under the leadership of Montana Bill, a Western character of some fame, undertook to show Omaha a hot time to-day [September 16]. After they had delivered a train load of cattle at the stock yards they began to charge motor cars, rushing in double columns at them and compelling the motormen to stop. They drew revolvers and, although they did not fire, their wild appearance and loud yelling created panic.
> Finally Montana Bill's horse pitched him into an open car and the leader was arrested. ("Cowboys Hold Up Street Cars" 1899, 1)

At one point in *The Place of Dead Roads* Kim abandons his public role with the Johnson Family: "Kim had now gone underground and in any case the days of the gunfighter were over" (Burroughs 1984, 95). Burroughs wanted his readers to see a connection between the death of Carsons—which in essence is the end of the Johnson Family underground—and the closing of the American frontier: the end of the days of the gunfighter.

Yet there is simultaneously a way to read the novel that is not bleak. By the time Burroughs was working on *The Place of Dead Roads*, he had come to the conclusion that political revolution on Earth was futile: "If you are asking me what the individual can do right now, in a political sense, I'd have to say he can't do all that much. Speaking for myself, I am more concerned with the transformation of the individual, which to me is much more important than the so-called political revolution" (quoted in Bockris 1996, 180). Part of that transformation was preparing human beings for space travel. "In terms of any possible solution," says Burroughs, "I agree with Timothy Leary—the only possibilities are in space" (quoted in Bockris 1996, 178). Although the Johnsons cannot win the war game on Earth, maybe they can help save humanity, whose only hope, according to Burroughs, lies in space: "[The Johnsons] aren't playing. We want to end the whole stupid game. To us, intelligence and war are only means to an end: SPACE EXPLORATION" (2013d, 152). "Space exploration," argues Burroughs, "is the only goal worth striving for" (2013e, 165). Burroughs makes this explicit in *The Place of Dead Roads*: "That's what Johnson Intelligence is for—to protect and further Johnson objectives, the realization of our biologic and spiritual destiny in space" (1984, 154). Is this the ultimate message of *The Place of Dead Roads*? Burroughs gave his readers a clue: "So [William Seward Hall] concealed and revealed the knowledge in fictional form. Only those for whom the knowledge is intended will find it" (115).

KURT HEMMER is editor of the *Encyclopedia of Beat Literature* and Professor of English at Harper College in Palatine, Illinois. He teaches courses on literature and film, literature and art, crime literature, the Beat Generation, the Lost Generation, and existentialism. With filmmaker Tom Knoff, he has produced several award-winning films: *Janine Pommy Vega: As We Cover the Streets*; *Rebel Roar: The Sound of Michael McClure*; *Wow! Ted Joans Lives!*; *Keenan*; and *Love Janine Pommy Vega*. His essay "'The natives are getting uppity': Tangier and *Naked Lunch*" appears in *Naked Lunch@50: Anniversary Essays*.

NOTES

1. The words "naked" and "lust," which Allen Ginsberg misread in the *Queer* (1985) manuscript as "naked lunch," a mistake that inspired Jack Kerouac to encourage Burroughs to use the phrase as a book title (see Harris 2009), appear flip-flopped in *The Place of Dead Roads* as "lust naked" (51) and flipped again as "naked lust" (86), both describing Kim's face.

2. James Grauerholz, who was responsible for luring Burroughs to Lawrence, Kansas, was generous with his time trying to help me avoid egregious errors in this essay.

3. Both Morgan (2012) and Miles (2002) claim that Burroughs first read Black's book when he was thirteen. Burroughs was born on February 5, 1914; he would have been thirteen in 1927. Griffin says that Burroughs would have read the book "[a]bout 1928" (2014, 13). It should be noted that the fourth printing of the book in October 1927 is bound in red cardboard, as Burroughs remembers his copy was.

REFERENCES

Black, Jack. 2013. *You Can't Win*. Port Townsend, WA: Feral House.

Bockris, Victor. 1996. *With William Burroughs: A Report from the Bunker*. New York: St. Martin's Griffin.

Bowles, Paul. 1984. "Burroughs in Tangier." In *The Burroughs File*, edited by V. Vale, 15–16. San Francisco: City Lights.

Burroughs, William S. 1981. *Cities of the Red Night*. New York: Holt, Rinehart and Winston.

————. 1982. *The Revised Boy Scout Manual* (excerpt cassette #1), in *RE/SEARCH*, nos. 4–5, 5–11.

————. 1984. *The Place of Dead Roads*. New York: Holt, Rinehart and Winston.

————. 1987. *The Western Lands*. New York: Penguin.

————. 1992. *The Wild Boys: A Book of the Dead*. New York: Grove.

————. 1994a. *Electronic Revolution*. Bonn: Expanded Media Editions.

————. 1994b. Foreword to *In Youth Is Pleasure*, by Denton Welch, ix–xi. Cambridge, MA: Exact Change.

————. 2001. *Naked Lunch: The Restored Text*. Edited by James Grauerholz and Barry Miles. New York: Grove.

————. 2010. Introduction to the 1985 edition. In *Queer: 25th Anniversary Edition*, edited by Oliver Harris, 121–35. New York: Penguin.

————. 2013a. "Creative Reading." In *The Adding Machine*, by William Burroughs, 46–58. New York: Grove.

————. 2013b. "The Fall of Art." In *The Adding Machine*, by William Burroughs, 75–80. New York: Grove.

————. 2013c. Foreword to *You Can't Win*, by Jack Black, 15–16. Port Townsend, WA: Feral House.

————. 2013d. "The Hundred Year Plan." In *The Adding Machine*, by William Burroughs, 75–80. New York: Grove.

————. 2013e. "Immortality." In *The Adding Machine*, by William Burroughs, 156–67. New York: Grove.

————. 2013f. "The Johnson Family." In *The Adding Machine*, by William Burroughs, 91–94. New York: Grove.

————. 2013g. "Remembering Jack Kerouac." In *The Adding Machine*, by William Burroughs, 209–15. New York: Grove.

Burroughs, William S., and Jack Kerouac. 2008. *And the Hippos Were Boiled in Their Tanks*. New York: Grove.

Castel, Albert, and Tom Goodrich. 1998. *Bloody Bill Anderson: The Short, Savage Life of a Civil War Guerrilla*. Lawrence: University Press of Kansas.

"Cowboys Hold Up Street Cars." 1899. *New York Times*, September 17, 1.

Griffin, Dustin. 2014. "The St. Louis Clique: Burroughs, Kammerer, and Carr." *Journal of Beat Studies* 3: 1–45.

Harris, Oliver. 2009. "The Beginnings of 'Naked Lunch, an Endless Novel.'" In *Naked Lunch@50: Anniversary Essays*, edited by Oliver Harris and Ian MacFadyen, 14–25. Carbondale: Southern Illinois University Press.

Johnston, Allan. 2005. "Consumption, Addiction, Vision, Energy: Political Economics and Utopian Visions in the Writings of the Beat Generation." *College Literature* 32 (2) (Spring): 103–26.

Knickerbocker, Conrad. 1999. "William Seward Burroughs II." In *Beat Writers at Work: The Paris Review*, edited by George Plimpton, 1–30. New York: Modern Library.

Leslie, Edward E. 1998. *The Devil Knows How to Ride: The True Story of William Clarke Quantrill and His Confederate Raiders*. Boston: Da Capo.

Miles, Barry. 2002. *William Burroughs, El Hombre Invisible: A Portrait*. London: Virgin Books.

————. 2014. *Call Me Burroughs: A Life*. New York: Twelve.

Morgan, Ted. 2012. *Literary Outlaw: The Life and Times of William S. Burroughs*. New York: W. W. Norton.

Pounds, Wayne. 1991. "The Postmodern Anus: Parody and Utopia in Two Recent Novels by William Burroughs." In *William S. Burroughs at the Front: Critical Reception, 1959–1989*, edited by Jennie Skerl and Robin Lydenberg, 217–32. Carbondale: Southern Illinois University Press.

Schneiderman, Davis. 2013. "The Miraculous and Mucilaginous Paste Pot: Extra-illustration and Plagiary in the Burroughs Legacy." *Journal of Beat Studies* 2: 53–79.

Steckmesser, Kent Ladd. 1965. *The Western Hero in History and Legend*. Norman: University of Oklahoma Press.

Stiles, T. J. 2003. *Jesse James: Last Rebel of the Civil War*. New York: Vintage.

Vanderheide, John. 2008. "The Apocatastasis of Community in Late Burroughs." *Arcadia* 43 (1): 63–77.

Ward, Geoff. 1993. "William Burroughs: A Literary Outlaw?" *Cambridge Quarterly* 22 (4): 339–54.

Thinking in Colors

In these beautiful pieces from early in Burroughs' cut-up career, from approximately 1961, he provides templates for understanding new methods of thinking and speaking. The first piece, a brief essay entitled "Thinking in Association," originates from Berg Folio 19 and pertains to the "Pay Color" section of *Nova Express* (1964). Burroughs describes how he tries to change his orientation in the world (his proprioception) during his flâneur walks through the city. As a database for his imaginative attempts to reinterpret the world through an attentive awareness of color, in the subsequent archival piece, the "Master Color Alphabet," Burroughs takes to new levels his life-long, intense engagement with Rimbaud's poetry and ideas.

Rimbaud was one of the first poets Burroughs cut up, as the cut-up became deeply embedded with Rimbaud's anarchic spirit. Rimbaud's idea of developing a language of colors in *Une saison en enfer* (1873) appears in Part II of the poem's "Deliria" section, entitled "ALCHEMY OF THE WORD"; Rimbaud writes, "I invented vowels!—Black *A*, white *E*, red *I*, blue *O*, green *U*-" (Rimbaud, 208). Following Rimbaud's inspiration to create "a poetic language" that "would be understood by everyone, and that I alone would translate," Burroughs literally types out colors for each letter of the alphabet, creating a rubric for future associative experiments (ibid.). While C, for instance, is the color of "BLUE WHITE COCAINE CRYSTAL. SNOW BLUE.ICE BLUE," for Burroughs the letter D appears as a "BLAST WHITE. NOVIA WHITE."

In the anthology's next section, *Cut/Fold*, these cut-up experiments with the meaning of color are explicitly theorized in "The Photo Collage," an essay where Burroughs encourages his reader to make "color concentrates." In letters to Brion Gysin, some published, others only available in the archive (Berg 85.4), Burroughs exhorted his collaborator to use his color alphabet and associative method to try "color line walks" through the city, claiming they enable him to escape moments of panic or pressure by slipping past words along color lines through associations between the city's sights. Burroughs' master color alphabet also appears mixed in with a wide array of correspondence Burroughs sent Gysin in the spring of 1961 (Berg Folio C-37 contains a multitude of unitemized letters that will hopefully be published in the coming years). In a letter to Gysin on April 8, 1961, Burroughs suggested writing a book together, asking Gysin to add corresponding colors to his master list, along with calligraphic illustrations (Berg 85.4). Gysin never went through with composing the full set, but samples of their experiments with "rubbing out the word" appear in *Ports of Entry* (1996) and *The Art of William S. Burroughs* (2012). Presented together at the conclusion of the *Word/Image* section, these two pieces on associative thinking should give a concrete sense of the variety of ways, by using synesthetic media to weave symbolist correspondences between the images and words structuring his experience of space and time, Burroughs sought to escape and counteract the society of the spectacle.

—*AWC*

Thinking in association blocks instead of words enables the
operator to process data with the speed of light on accociation
lines—The Color Alphabet is useful training—Take a name   like
JOHN—We all know a JOHN dont we?—Assign color to the letter—
J-Red   O-Blue-- H-Silver   N-Blue-Purple
Poject on a screen as written out above
Now project the xxxxxxxxxxx color words
Xxxxxxxxxxxxx   Red   Blue   Silver   Purple
Fade out to color
When you learn to see the name in color without letters or word
on your mind screen associate in silent juxtaposiom language
images of your JOHN—At different times and places walking
putting on his coat in the street in the metro   Winder   and Summer
a milliohn JOHNS on your association lines—A photo montage of
John composed of   photos taekn in various scenes and ages placed
 toegether o in a montage and phtorgraphed and projected---
Now take a poet   xxxxxxxxxxx Rxxxxxxxxxxxxx RIMBAUD
R Flesh Color   I Red   M Light Blue   B Translucent grey   A Black
U Green   D Incandescent White
Flesh color   Red Light Blue   Grey   Black Green   White
Fade to color
Flash back and forth faster and faster from letters to color   fade
out in color
Associate to the poetry of RIMBAUD without words xxxx seeing
the images in his   work—Live ember raining in gust of frost—
I embraced the Summer dawn—Corridors of black gauze—
banner of raw meat—silk of seas—pensive drowed—a youngman
has grown up anywhere—perfumes of wine gas—ect—Images   free
of word that shift and permutate improbable sdeseertion   on t he
suburban air—candor of vapors and tents—associate other image
poets sad as the death of monkeys—

                         ******

planes carreening freight ttrains intoth s winds of panhandle
drifting   jissom webs colorless sheets of male flesh shivering
through a million you ng bodies in boarding school rooms and
jungle clearing and rubbly outskirts of south americancities
ragged pants to the ankles swollen and cracked   bleeding feet
smell of the mud flats in the coast cities on the banana
boat inthe moonlight spattered into the tidal river—
   in the locker room closed locker   room in a smell of moldy
jock s traps spattered the conrete wall—Change cubciles of the
swimming pool andthe cool basement toilets—on car   seats
pants to xxxx the   thin brown knee—In the   woods outside
copenhagen—on   the beaches of Spain and the   rocks of Itlay
junk sick in train toilets on the way to Lexington—on stale
rooming house sheets flesh of Spain adn forty second street—
caught the jissom in his mouth and jumped up laughing in the
dream and wah wiped his mouth with the back of his hand

A/ TO BLACK

B/ TO SILVER

C/ TO BLUE WHITE COCAINE CRYSTAL.SNOW BLUE.ICE BLUE

D/ TO BLAST WHITE. NOVIA WHITE

E/ TO ALL WHITE

F/ TO RED PENIS PURPLE. LIP PURPLE

G/ TO YELLOW

H/ TO GREY.ENGLISH GREY. COLOR OF APOMORPHINE. THE REGULATOR

I/ TO RED

J/ TO RED

K/ TO ORANGE

L/ TO PINK

M/ TO LIGHT BLUE

N/ TO SPACE PURPLE

O/ TO BLUE

P/ TO YELLOW GREEN PISS COLOR.CANCER PISS

Q/ CUT TO ANY COLOR. COLOR WILD. ESCAPE COLOR WITH H.

R/ TO FLESH COLOR

S/CUT TO BROWN GREEN OF RIVERS

T/ TO PHOSPERESCENT. RADIUM. TIME. MINUTES TO GO

U/ TO GREEN

V/ TO GOLD

W/ TO BROWN. RECTAL BROWN. EXCREMENT BROWN

X/ TO RUST COLOR. IRON COLOR

Y/ TO COPPER

Z/ TO RAIN BOW. JUKE BOX.

FACING, *Thinking in Association*, William S. Burroughs, 1961 (8 × 11, 2 leaves, typescript) (Berg 4.38). Folio 19, Item 8, "Thinking in association . . .". (Item 8 is from the Pay Color section.) Copyright © by William Burroughs, used by permission of The Wylie Agency LLC.

ABOVE, *Master Color Alphabet*, William S. Burroughs, 1961 (8 × 11, 1 leaf, typescript) (Berg 85.4). From Berg C-37 Correspondence between William Burroughs and Brion Gysin (April–May 1961). Copyright © by William Burroughs, used by permission of The Wylie Agency LLC.

13

Rimbaud and Genet, Burroughs' Favorite Mirrors

VÉRONIQUE LANE

On William Burroughs' gravestone, visitors can read the epitaph "American Writer," a great tribute but certainly an incomplete one, since Burroughs was always more than a writer, given his long-standing work in multiple media, as well as something other than American. "American" is indeed a parochial epithet for a man who during a quarter century of expatriation lived in South America, North Africa, and Europe, and Burroughs' place is increasingly acknowledged within the transnational turn taken by Beat Studies.[1] When it comes to the Beats' so-called French connection, however, the seminal histories of their stay in Paris and the few sustained studies of the American avant-garde's debt to French Surrealism remain insufficient to determine how exactly—how textually—French literature impacted Burroughs the transnational writer. That is, my focus on the importance of Arthur Rimbaud and Jean Genet for him here will not so much be on his living in France as on the France inside Burroughs' works or, to be more precise, on the French literature that shaped his writing wherever he lived.[2]

Whenever Burroughs defined his literary filiations—and interviewers never spared him the question—American writers were always outnumbered by non-Americans, and within that picture, the greatest emphasis was on French authors: for every allusion to T. S. Eliot there are more to Baudelaire, Rimbaud, Gide, Artaud, Céline, Genet, or Cocteau. But far from the predictable associations with these French writers' controversial *lives*—the well-worn trope of the *poète maudit*—we find Burroughs thinking through his identity and creativity in relation to their *writing* across the entirety of his oeuvre. The literary works of many French authors shaped Burroughs' writing, sometimes in unexpected ways that remain under-researched. Proust, Artaud, or Gide's works, for example, all fed into Burroughs' oeuvre significantly but sporadically, whereas Rimbaud and Genet recur structurally. Rimbaud dominates the first half of Burroughs' works and Genet the second, so that taken together their textual presence effectively frames the half-century of Burroughs' oeuvre.

Given how different Rimbaud's and Genet's bodies of work are, what Burroughs took from them was bound to be distinct, but the words of both French writers continuously fueled the production of his own. In the chapters he composed for *And the Hippos Were Boiled in Their Tanks*, his debut novella co-written with Jack Kerouac in 1945, Rimbaud is the only literary figure evoked by Burroughs. His poetry also appears as the material par excellence of Burroughs' cut-up texts, in the initial theorization of the method in *Minutes to Go* (1960) as well as in many unpublished cut-ups of that era, kept in the Berg Collection of the New York Public Library and examined for this chapter. Genet's lexicon and imagery likewise find a singular if smaller place in Burroughs' cut-up practice in the late 1960s. An entire chapter of Burroughs' most bluntly homosexual book, *The Wild Boys: A Book of the Dead* (1971), is titled after Genet's *Miracle of the Rose*. And most substantially, Genet's last book of fragments, *Prisoner of Love*, is the point of departure for Burroughs' own last book of fragments, *My Education: A Book of Dreams* (1995). It is thus in the most significant moments of Burroughs' career as a writer—right at its start in the 1940s, at its experimental height in the 1960s, and at its twilight in the 1990s—that Rimbaud's poetry and Genet's prose offered him complex mirrors in which, as will be demonstrated here, he consistently measured the success of his own writing.

When Burroughs began to co-write *And the Hippos Were Boiled in Their Tanks* with Kerouac in the 1940s, foreign literature was inescapable for the dissenting philosophy of life and creative ambitions of both writers. Although they were well aware of a counter-tradition within American literature, during the war and its aftermath they naturally turned to literatures at a remove from the increasingly repressive society of their native land. For them and for the bohemian scene forming the background of *Hippos*, Rimbaud stands as the symbolic figure inaugurating a tradition of prophetic "seers" and alienated renegades, while foreign literature figures the main way out of an America they had come to hate and that was starting to hate them in return.

In that historical context, Burroughs' identifications with non-American writers in the prologue to *Junky*, the first book he would publish in 1953, are less surprising than they otherwise would be: "I read more than was usual for an American boy of that time and place: Oscar Wilde, Anatole France, Baudelaire, even Gide" (2003, xxxviii). Here Burroughs evokes a series of debts to French literature going back to his childhood as definitive signs of his cultural alienation, and this genealogy would inspire later critics to forge similar identifications. One of the first reviews of Burroughs, by Kenneth Allsop in 1960, was in this vein entitled "Rimbaud in a Raincoat," and intuited the pairing analyzed in the last two sections of this article: "He is a Rimbaud in a raincoat, with his nearest modern equivalent in Jean Genet" (8–9). But however compelling this Franco-American lineage is, and however necessary the biographical or cultural approaches so far used to establish his French 'connection' are, as I have argued elsewhere, a more textual approach is needed to grasp the full implications of French literature in general and Rimbaud and Genet in particular for Burroughs' oeuvre (Lane 2017). If we put Burroughs' raincoat aside, if we resist the bewitching aura of his French associations and instead closely examine his writing, we discover that his identifications are not straightforward but complex and thorny, and that there is much more at stake in them than the acquisition of a literary pedigree or an alluring image.

RIMBAUD OR THE TIME OF THE ASSASSINS

Halfway through *And the Hippos Were Boiled in Their Tanks*, the book Burroughs and Kerouac co-wrote in 1945 in alternate chapters, Kerouac's narrator references William Faulkner, already his twelfth literary allusion (2008, 114). In the next chapter, Burroughs makes his one and only literary reference: to Rimbaud. It is emphatic and yet highly paradoxical: "I'm the later bourgeois Rimbaud" (120). On the one hand, through his persona Burroughs is asserting his identity with Rimbaud directly; on the other hand, he is doing so ironically because he is identifying with him only once he has ceased being a poet. But who would be tempted to associate himself with *that* Rimbaud, not with the prolific young poet but with the man obstinately living as far as possible from his literary milieu and dealing guns in Africa? Someone as determined as was Rimbaud to stand apart through some bold excess; someone with the ambition to be more than a genius, in fact to go beyond "genius" to the point of turning his back on both his genius and the society that venerates it (the unexpected identification of Burroughs' narrator in *Hippos* is a drastic move that distinguishes him at once from his fellow bohemians and from the horde of modern writers who identify with the early Rimbaud); someone who, therefore, mocks the very idea of identifying with Rimbaud the poet, given that Rimbaud had completed his oeuvre before any aspirant poets would be out of college (the lesson of Burroughs' narrator to the young Beats is clear: if you identify with Rimbaud, bear in mind how he ended . . . as a bourgeois merchant); someone who, in sum, begins in literature exactly where Rimbaud left it, with absolutely no illusions about its ability to keep on going. This is indeed a stance Burroughs would still be taking in *Last Words*, his final journal: "Where is it going, or where can it go? After Conrad, Rimbaud, Genet" (2000, 204). Despite appearing to be no more than a one-line cynical joke, Burroughs' identification with "the later bourgeois Rimbaud" in his first mature writing is rich in significance, and from it we can draw three conclusions about his attitude toward biography, style, and the literary.

Biographically, if "for the Beats, it was, of course, Rimbaud's life rather than his art that was exemplary," as Marjorie Perloff famously pointed out, it certainly wasn't the case for Burroughs, a distinction she failed to make (1984, 5). Burroughs' identification with the later Rimbaud at the outset of his career is deeply ironic and indeed representative of his general take on the place of biography in literature and criticism: it is a rebuke, a rejection of the biographical mythology and of the literary pretensions often going with it. Burroughs' antagonistic posture toward the literary expressed through his reference to the "wrong" Rimbaud is highly significant, since it not only separates Burroughs from the Beats, but is also at odds with that of the most influential writer through whom Americans discovered Rimbaud in the mid-1940s, that is Henry Miller. In his celebrated book published only a year after the composition of *Hippos*, *The Time of the Assassins: A Study of Rimbaud* (1946), Miller would unambiguously and passionately identify himself with the first Rimbaud: "He did not belong—not anywhere. I have always had the same feeling about myself. The parallels are endless" (6). What is underlined by the contrast between Burroughs' playful identification with the older merchant in Africa and Miller's fervent identification with the young genius poet is that Burroughs' interest in Rimbaud had little to do with biography; in fact, even nowadays the irony in his statement places him at an unusual critical distance from Rimbaud's powerful aura within American literary culture.

Stylistically, Burroughs' persona in *Hippos*, a pragmatic barman dealing with gunmen and brawls every night, is decidedly non-literary, and his quip—"I'm the later bourgeois Rimbaud"—anticipates the deadpan yet satirically dissident humor that would define his style. The effect of Burroughs' irony here is double, since his act of identification both "Frenchifies" himself and, indirectly, critiques Rimbaud by Americanizing him. In retrospect, we can almost hear the voice of the Ugly American that Burroughs would relish performing, in *The Soft Machine* for instance, when he addresses a young man who could well have been Rimbaud:

"Now kid what are you doing over there with the niggers and the apes? Why don't you straighten out and act like a white man?—After all, they're only human cattle—You know that yourself—Hate to see a bright young man fuck up and get off on the wrong track" (2014b, 147). In short, his one brief identification with Rimbaud combines a sketch of Burroughs' own anti-literary identity with a unique critique of the poet and a foretaste of his satirical voice.

If Burroughs' rejection of bohemia and literature through Rimbaud is an early statement of his alienation from the historical options eagerly taken up by the younger crowd, however, this negation of identification *itself* identifies Burroughs with those who make the same refusal. In other words, making the most contrary identification ("I'm the later bourgeois Rimbaud") still retains the syntax of identification ("I'm . . ."), a paradox we will return to in conclusion, since, for all their differences, Burroughs' and Miller's associations with Rimbaud have in common the same flaw. Within the economy of identification, the desire to be an alien can only backfire, since identifying with an alien, of course, can only threaten your own sense of being an alien.

"THIS IS WHERE RIMBAUD WAS GOING"

Emulating what is commonly referred to in French Literature as the enigmatic "silence de Rimbaud," Burroughs' commitment to "rubbing out the word" in the 1960s had a paradoxical result: an oeuvre of words. Few French writers really criticized Rimbaud for his decision to desert literature; rather, they deplored it: Camus talked of nihilist depression, Mallarmé of self-vivisection, and Cocteau described the later Rimbaud as "defrocked" from poetry (see Guyaux 1991, 213–29). In contrast, Burroughs' response to Rimbaud's silence proved creative: he would work against literature from within. His aim to rub out the word couldn't have been more boldly stated than by the original wraparound band of the collective manifesto he would contribute to, *Minutes to Go* published in Paris in 1960, which launched the cut-up method he had discovered with Brion Gysin by declaring, in French, an assault on literature with a capital "L": "*un règlement de comptes avec la Littérature.*" Rather than leaving literature, Burroughs would indeed settle his scores with literature *with literature*, by cutting it up and "rearranging" it.

In interviews and polemical statements promoting the method, Burroughs often drew the association between Rimbaud's drive to be done with literature and the Cut-Up Project, but name-checking the French poet is not enough to understand the role he played in it. There are also major difficulties in accurately measuring what was at stake in Burroughs' cut-up engagement with Rimbaud. To begin with, it is obviously problematic to take at face value methodological statements such as, in *The Exterminator* (1960), "anybody can be Rimbaud if he will cut up Rimbaud's words and learn Rimbaud language" (reprinted in Burroughs and Gysin 1978, 71, 32). Although Burroughs' identification here seems far-fetched—unless you believe in magic or possession ("Table-tapping, perhaps?")—it points to the material literalism of his creative methods. Then, there is the difficulty that so many of Rimbaud's appearances are in neglected locations. Burroughs' cut-ups featured in such marginal works as these two pamphlets, but also texts that were never reprinted (such as the 1961 edition of *The Soft Machine*), two dozen unpublished cut-up typescripts, and a surprising number of scrapbook collages and photomontages. Focusing on *Minutes to Go*, my examination here aims to show that Rimbaud's role in the Cut-Up Project was not only broadly conceptual but also materially precise.

In his final journal, when Burroughs raised the problem of literature's future, a preoccupation, of course, as old as modernism—"Where is it going, or where can it go?"—he was implicitly reflecting back on what was at stake in the experiments of the Cut-Up Project. Where should literature "go"? "Anywhere! Anywhere! So long as it is out of this world!," as Baudelaire famously put it (1970, 99).[3] This is the doomed desire that Burroughs inherited from Rimbaud, who himself inherited it together with specific aesthetic goals from Baudelaire. In his most important polemical text, which references Rimbaud no fewer than nine times, Burroughs indeed misattributes to Rimbaud what in fact originated in Baudelaire's theory of synesthesia: "This is where Rimbaud was going with his color of vowels. And his 'systematic derangement of the senses.' The place of mescaline hallucination: seeing colors tasting sounds smelling forms" (Burroughs and Gysin 1978, 32). These often-cited lines are characteristic of how literally Burroughs sought to pursue the urge to escape "this world" and to find the means to achieve it. To attain Rimbaud's "*hallucination simple,*" to reach, as he told Timothy Leary, "pure cut-up highs," Burroughs experimented with practical methods, both chemical and, more importantly, textual (2012, 64). In short, cutting up words was a way to produce a tangible record of visions "out of this world," and Burroughs was thereby finishing the job that Baudelaire and Rimbaud initiated: "This is where Rimbaud was going..."

Burroughs' realization of Rimbaud's visionary aesthetics is performed at the core of *Minutes to Go* by two cut-up texts, "EVERYWHERE MARCH YOUR HEAD" and "SONS OF YOUR IN," both based on Rimbaud's poem "A une Raison." These texts are also credited to Gregory Corso, although the textual evidence points to Burroughs' authorship, such as his intensive use of the phrase "everywhere march your head" in a dozen other cut-ups he created in the 1960s.[4] A close reading reveals the significance of Rimbaud's poem to produce these cut-up texts in three key respects: thematic, linguistic, and philosophic. While the results of Burroughs' fragmentation of "A une Raison" seem virtually illegible in the two cut-ups in question, this is balanced by the emphatic way in which their source is named beneath them: "Cut up Rimbaud's TO A REASON (A UNE RAISON) Words by Rimbaud, arrangement by Burroughs & Corso" (Beiles et al. 1960, 23).[5] This insistence has the effect of inviting the reader to go back to the original poem to discover that, far from cutting randomly, Burroughs used his scissors with astonishing care.

The urgency of time, as the central subject announced in the very title *Minutes to Go*, and the precision with which Burroughs cut up Rimbaud's words are most apparent in the way the two texts rework the same key line from "To a Reason": "Change our lots, confound the plagues, beginning with time" (Rimbaud 1957, 39). The results are "see / the new / Change knows / the Time t..." and, punning on the different meanings of the word "lots" in French and English, the phrase "our lots con" (Beiles et al. 1960, 25, 23).[6] The line in Rimbaud's poem, which denounces our usual experience of time as a disease that must be cured, thereby becomes an economical statement of Burroughs' word virus theory: our fate is a con trick scripted by language and fixed in time, and we must cut our way out to see the world anew. When Burroughs expands on this conspiracy at the start of *The Exterminator* ("The Word Lines Keep Thee in Slots [...] The Word Lines keep you in Time... Cut the in lines"), it is in a passage where Rimbaud's name appears a dozen times (Burroughs and Gysin 1978, 71). Cutting up Rimbaud not only signified a general claim of affinity, therefore; it also enabled Burroughs to start expressing his own thesis about the determinism of language, identity, and time. If the "statement" of Burroughs' theory seems unclear in these two cut-ups from *Minutes to Go*, which it undeniably is, this is because it demonstrates his commitment to performing rather than explaining how in cutting up his words he was following Rimbaud.

Burroughs' sensitivity to using the words of Rimbaud in *Minutes to Go* has, in fact, an unsuspected performative dimension that should entirely transform our understanding of his cut-up practice. This performativity is hinted at by the

FOLLOWING PAGE, "Infinity," William S. Burroughs and Ian Sommerville, 1962. Courtesy © William S. Burroughs Trust.

specific way that Rimbaud's work is named not once but twice as a source for the first cut-up text: "TO A REASON (A UNE RAISON)." Here, the French is given not just as the original of the English translation but as a sign that, contrary to appearances, the cut-ups have used *both* versions of the poem. Or to be more precise, while "EVERYWHERE MARCH YOUR HEAD" seems to derive entirely from "To a Reason," most of "SONS OF YOUR IN" can be shown to derive from "A une Raison": from the "sons" in its title which comes from "tous les sons" ("all the sounds"), to "detour" which comes from "détourne" ("turns back"), "tent" from "chantent" ("sing"), "rib" from "crible" ("confound"), and "commence" from "à commencer par le temps" ("beginning with time") (Rimbaud 1957, 38). What is so revealing here is the great care taken to use fragments or whole words from the French poem that *also* work as English. Far from randomly slashing verse into nonsense, the scissors shifted the sense of the words across languages, in a primary instance of Burroughs' command to "Cut word lines—shift linguals" (Burroughs 2014a, 63; this refrain first appears here in *Minutes to Go*). Giving the poem's title in both English and French was a subtle way to make two poems out of one—and this is indeed literally what Burroughs achieved by using Rimbaud's poem to generate not one but *two* cut-up texts.

This multiplication not only performs the open-ended principle of the cut-up method, its assault on the fixity of the single text, but the attack on determinism in the title of Rimbaud's poem: "A une Raison" (rather than the expected "A la Raison"). For both Rimbaud and Burroughs, Cartesian Reason is a pernicious universal logic of common sense, and in Rimbaud's preference for the indefinite article "une" rather than for the definite article "la," we find a model for Burroughs' emerging subversion of linguistic usage, time, and fixed identity.

Rimbaud's subversive alternative to tyrannical Reason was in fact incorporated in the description of his own poetical method: "un long, immense et *raisonné* dérèglement de tous les sens."[7] Although Burroughs always quotes this famous line in the standard English translation, as a "systematic derangement of the senses," he may have known that in French the "derangement" was actually "raisonné" ("reasoned"). Burroughs quite likely had Rimbaud's visionary "derangement" in mind when using "arrangement" to describe the composition of the two cut-ups of Rimbaud featured in *Minutes to Go*. For the fragmenting and multiplying effect of the cut-up method here was precisely to *derange* Rimbaud's "A une Raison," thereby realizing his project to unseat Reason and escape the trap of Time by performing the way out on the page.

Burroughs' engagement with Rimbaud's poetics in general and "A une Raison" in particular finds exemplary illustrations in two photomontages from the same era: "Infinity" (1962) and "Untitled" (1964). A third, "All God's Children Got Time" (1971–1973), features Jean-Louis Forain's 1871 sketch of Rimbaud, while miniatures of Carjat's famous photograph of the poet also appear in such well-known photomontages as "The Death of Mrs D" (1965), but his earliest visual works are the most revealing of the textual relationship he maintained with Rimbaud's poetry.[8]

"Untitled," William S. Burroughs and Ian Sommerville, 1964. Courtesy ©
William S. Burroughs Trust.

Burroughs' first photomontage is one of many entitled "Infinity" he made in
collaboration with Ian Sommerville, which features dozens of montaged photographs. At the core of the composition, one of the largest images and by far the
most legible is Carjat's photograph of Rimbaud, his head and upper body illuminated against the pale oval background. Why should Rimbaud appear at the
center of "Infinity"? Whether strategically or unconsciously, I would argue that

Burroughs' 1962 photomontage is a response to the final line of Rimbaud's "A une Raison": "Arrivée de toujours, qui t'en iras partout" (Rimbaud 1957, 38). In other words: master time and you will master space, or if you come from eternity you already have "infinity," the photomontage's title.

If we see here more evidence for the importance Burroughs gave to "A une Raison," his second collage from 1964 confirms it in an absolutely literal way. For it features what at first appears to be a cropped close-up of the Carjat photograph, but in fact is the cover of the New Directions edition of *Illuminations*—the very bilingual edition that Burroughs used for the cut-up permutations of "To a Reason" and "A une Raison" in *Minutes to Go*.⁹ The distinction here is crucial for Burroughs' identification with Rimbaud: even in his photomontages, the face of the poet does not stand for the biographical man but his poetry.

CUT RIMBAUD BUT IMITATE GENET

Throughout the 1960s, Burroughs cut up the work of many writers (Burroughs 2015), but his extensive and precisely considered use of Rimbaud is absolutely unique. Equally exceptional is his far briefer use of Genet, and a comparative analysis confirms that what was at stake in both cases is the problematic of identification inherent to cutting up another writer's words. Burroughs had no problem identifying with Rimbaud: living a century apart and writing in different genres kept a safe distance between them. The cut-up method also allowed him to adjust where he stood within the process of identification, and he signaled as much in the titles of several Rimbaud cut-ups through his choice of prepositions: "Cut-Ups With Rimbaud 1960"; "CUT UPS FROM ARTHUR RIMBAUD POEMES THRU W.S.B." (Berg 16.76, 7.42).[10] These shifting prepositions—*with, from, thru*—reveal how Burroughs tried out different ways to verbalize his creative identification: *with* signifies collaboration, poets in partnership; *from* prioritizes the source text, the origins of the words; whereas *thru* has to do with possession, ventriloquism. Like the multiple versions obtained by cutting-up the same poem, this variety of prepositions shows how meticulously Burroughs thought through his method, and how extensively he did that thinking through via Rimbaud.

With Genet, however, we find the very inverse, not a creative process mediated by his writing but an impasse, visible in an unpublished typescript that Burroughs most probably composed in the mid-1960s: "Cut-Ups With Jean Genet And Writing In His Style" (Berg 16.61). Why cutting Rimbaud but imitating Genet? While Burroughs had no problem cutting up other novelists, from Scott Fitzgerald to Paul Bowles, in the case of Genet he could not resist the temptation to "write in his style." Was it because of his unlimited admiration for "the greatest living writer of prose" (Burroughs 1993, 289)? Or was it that the cut-up as a mode of identification turned out to be far more problematic precisely because of Burroughs' and Genet's similarities: novelists born just four years apart, fellow queer outsiders, countercultural figures who met one another, and above all prose stylists with shared tastes—an usual combination of graphic homosexual fantasy, poetic imagery, and criminal argot? The results of this experiment, and the fact that it is the sole attempt Burroughs made to cut up Genet, certainly suggest a dead end. Burroughs' text tries to work with a vocabulary from Genet's novels, from combining religious and sexual material to repeatedly using the term "hoodlum" that appears in all the Frechtman translations, but the effect is less a cut-up than a rather unconvincing pastiche. What Burroughs also sought to capture was the convoluted syntax and distinctive rhythm of Genet's prose, and it is manifestly this stylistic feature that completely escaped the possibility of cut-up methods. As my concluding analysis of his later work will show in more detail, Burroughs would come to engage more profoundly with Genet's oeuvre than any other. However, Genet's style eluded the possibilities of the cut-up method that dominated Burroughs' work of the 1960s.

Burroughs stated very openly the kind of prose that produced the best cut-up results and would often repeat the particular examples he first gave in a letter to Allen Ginsberg in 1960: "I find cut ups most immediately workable on poetic prose image writing like Rimbaud, St. Perse and your correspondent" (Burroughs 2012, 45). In sharp contrast to Genet's prose, neither Rimbaud nor St.-John Perse depend heavily on syntax as much as on specific turns of phrase or long, dense series of images in juxtaposition. However, Burroughs' association of "Rimbaud and St.-John Perse (two poets who have much in common)" (1962, 6–7) is a surprising one, since they couldn't be further apart in terms of both their lives and reputations: the delinquent poster-boy from the nineteenth century and a respected diplomat who had just won the Nobel Prize for literature in 1960, and who was nothing like as well known then or indeed today. Evidently, the Rimbaud-Perse association ignores biography in favor of *poetics*, identifying the poetry of both French writers with Burroughs' own writing ("your correspondent"). The precise textual and aesthetic basis to Burroughs' engagement with Rimbaud and St.-John Perse is well evidenced by a group of 1960 cut-up typescripts, some of whose titles speak for themselves by naming the works rather than their authors: "SELECTIONS FROM ANABASIS AND ILLUMINATIONS," "SCISSORS CUT ILLUMINATIONS AND ANABASIS."[11]

What is most significant about these unpublished texts and many others is Burroughs' use of color, especially when cutting-up Rimbaud's "Voyelles" to produce no fewer than five different texts. Just to scratch the surface of these five cut-ups, one standout feature is Burroughs' recurrent use of color to qualify abstract realities: "Blueevening," "Red delirium," "White sleep," "Blue prayers," "Black summer," "Blue wine," "RED BRICK TIME" (Berg 26.4, 6.42, 11.59). What we see in such compound phrases is an aesthetic of shock, of the counterintuitive: impossible images forcing us to think and experience the world otherwise: "This is where Rimbaud was going [. . .] seeing colors tasting sounds smelling forms."

Finally, Burroughs structured the first edition of *The Soft Machine* into four "units" also inspired by Rimbaud's color vowels. Although this was dropped for the revised editions of the book, in the "1920 Movies" chapter Burroughs retained his series of short numbered units that experimented with colors by permutating sexual material. The sheer density of color in the whole Cut-Up Trilogy is remarkable. Equally important is that Burroughs was again going in Rimbaud's direction in associating color with the sexual body (an association that is implicit in "Voyelles" and explicit in its following, lesser-known quatrain "L'Étoile a pleuré"). In the "1920 Movies" chapter of *The Soft Machine*, Burroughs made many such combinations, including a direct invocation of Rimbaud's "Voyelles": "flickering color vowels: I Red / U Green / E White / O Blue / A Black / 'Bend over Johnny'" (2014b, 134). More fundamentally, however, through this material, Burroughs was taking on Rimbaud's invitation to disintegrate the language of selfhood ("Je est un autre" / "I am another"); put succinctly: "I-you-me-fuck up" (137).

That *The Soft Machine* is an attack on identity as much as language or literature in the spirit of Rimbaud is affirmed in the de facto subtitle that Burroughs attached to its early draft when describing it as a "sequel to *Naked Lunch* to be called 'Mr Bradly Mr Martin.' Time of the Assassins" (Burroughs 2012, 25). The phrase simultaneously invokes Hassan i Sabbah and Rimbaud's poem "Morning of Drunkenness" that declared: "Voici le temps des Assassins" (Rimbaud 1957, 42). The way Burroughs identifies his *text* with Rimbaud's phrase stands in stark contrast to the way Miller uses it in the title of the book in which he identifies *himself* with Rimbaud ("the parallels are endless. . ."). Despite their dissimilarities, however, like Burroughs, Miller's study of Rimbaud projects the French poet as an assassin of the old and as a sign of a post-apocalyptic new world, as a visionary force, a way to cut-up the self and reinvent humanity:

> I think the Rimbaud type will displace, in the world to come, the Hamlet type and the Faustian type. The trend is toward a deeper split. Until the old world dies out utterly, the 'abnormal' individual will tend more and more to become the norm. The new man will find himself only when the warfare between the collectivity and the individual ceases. Then we shall see the *human* type in its fullness and splendor. (1946, 6; Miller's emphasis)

Miller's idea of the new man responds to the exhortation of Rimbaud's "Farewell": "One must be absolutely modern" (Rimbaud 1961, 89). When Rimbaud imagines what it means to be modern, it is the writer above all who shows the way: Miller embraces the challenge and goes one step further by equating "modern" with "abnormal," and I would argue that, just as he pushes writing to its limits, so Burroughs pushes identity to the edge, equating being "modern" with being "alien."

ONE MUST BE ABSOLUTELY ALIEN

In 1960, Kenneth Allsop was not alone in reaching for points of comparison when he dressed up Burroughs as Rimbaud in a raincoat and found "his nearest modern equivalent in Jean Genet" (8–9). That same year, Grove Press even went so far as to consider publishing *Naked Lunch* in one volume with Genet's *Our Lady of the*

Flowers (Berg 82.2.20). In other words, from the outset, contextualizing Burroughs' works had posed problems for critics and publishers: the Beat Generation label had never really fitted Burroughs, and his writing could not be pigeonholed within American literary traditions; therefore, he "belonged" with others who did not belong, with Rimbaud and Genet.

As for Burroughs himself, who always insisted on being the alien—the junkie outcast, the queer outsider, even the Beat who was not a Beat—if he could avoid comparing himself with other writers, he did, and when he couldn't, faced with the insatiable demands of interviewers and publishers, he overwhelmingly gave them the names of foreign writers, from Joyce and Beckett to Kafka and Céline, and most often Genet. These literary allusions, however, do not disguise Burroughs' fundamental problem with any form of identification. Of course, the thief, the queer, the prisoner, the traitor appealed to him biographically. Burroughs had read Genet's early novels "many times" during the period he wrote *Naked Lunch*, and he famously appeared in a trio of queer writers at the 1968 Democratic Convention in Chicago alongside Ginsberg and Genet (Burroughs 1993, 289). But the least explored and most significant aspect of Burroughs' relationship with Genet is again textual.

Genet's presence in *The Wild Boys* (1971) has often been noted: several times in interviews Burroughs claimed the whole book was a homage to Genet, and indeed the chapter entitled "The Miracle of the Rose" names the novel by Genet. However, far more ambiguous and revealing is the role played by Genet in the last book Burroughs published in his lifetime, *My Education: A Book of Dreams*. The book's subtitle unexpectedly echoes that of *The Wild Boys: A Book of the Dead*. Different as they are, the 1960s novel and the 1990s memoir effectively form a diptych that frames the second half of Burroughs' oeuvre. Could it be that what the two books have in common is Genet? I would argue that it is, and that Burroughs' book of dreams looks back to Burroughs' book of the dead, in the course of reviewing his work through the eyes of Genet.

It is surely because his own oeuvre was coming to an end that, right from *My Education*'s opening pages, Burroughs' engagement with Genet is so complex, revealing, and emphatic. The first of four substantial passages centered on Genet begins: "Thoughts that arise palpable as a haze from the pages of Jean Genet's *Prisoner of Love*" (Burroughs 1995, 6). Burroughs' first thoughts are to do with belonging: "I have never felt close to any cause or people." He then claims to envy those who can say "my people." The implication that he envies Genet is ambiguous, as is the distinctive phrase with which Burroughs describes his thoughts that "arise palpable as a haze" from Genet's pages. For this phrase has an ominous history in Burroughs' writing, going back to his 1985 introduction to *Queer*, where "palpable as a haze" visualizes the traumatic "ugly menace" that "rises from the pages" of his own novel (2010, 132).[12] But if Burroughs' hostility to Genet—a hostility based on feeling somehow menaced by his writing—seems too inferential, what follows is much clearer.

Twice Burroughs goes on to brush off what is the central moral concern of Genet's oeuvre, snapping: "Genet is concerned with betrayal, to me a meaningless concept, like patriotism [...] Genet is concerned with betrayal. I have nothing and nobody to betray, *moi*" (1995, 6, 8, Burroughs' emphasis). *Moi*! Paradoxically, perversely even, Burroughs uses the language of Genet, French, and the very word that means "me," to put Genet down and deny their affinity. That he should devote such a special place to Genet only in order to take back what he seems to give is clearly the sign of a profound internal conflict.

Burroughs' conflicted response to reading Genet returns when quoting a key passage of *Prisoner of Love* based on the parable about the medieval Spanish leader El Cid kissing a leper. Mocking the heroic act admired by Genet, Burroughs quips: "Bring me a leper and I will kiss it" (2). As if to knock the halo off Genet's head, he then completes the put-down by going outside the realm of literature to call on detailed scientific evidence that proves Genet wrong, beginning: "Now leprosy is one of the least contagious of diseases, so the Saintly Cid was in no danger of infection." The humor here is at Genet's expense, underscored by Burroughs' reference to "the Saintly Cid," surely a nod to Sartre's own humor in titling his monumental study *Saint Genet* (1952). Once again, we are led to wonder why Burroughs goes so far to invoke, only to demean, one of the writers he most admired, if not because his admiration for Genet's oeuvre revealed to him an ambivalence about his own. But what is most revealing about Burroughs' curious put-down of Genet via El Cid is its subject matter, heroism, which also features in the longest passage from *Prisoner of Love* that he quotes:

> "If you're a hero you are as good as dead. So we render to you a funeral tribute. We've got springs under our feet and as soon as a hero comes in we are ejected into mourning." What a writer and what a meaning sensitive observer. "I grovel in admiration." This phrase I lift from a book where some behind-the-lines Scotch-drinking PLO speaks of a girl who will ride a donkey loaded with explosives into Israeli lines. It occurred to me that prostrate groveling would be a wise procedure for anyone in the vicinity of this admirable act. (Burroughs 1995, 11–12)

After citing Genet, Burroughs comments on his writing approvingly, and then, most oddly, cites Genet a second time. What is so odd here comes in between Burroughs' speech marks: he grovels in admiration before Genet, but by quoting Genet himself groveling in admiration before one of the characters in his own book. That Burroughs also omits to name Genet or *Prisoner of Love* here is equally strange: to say of the phrase he applauds that he lifted it from "*a book*," as if he had fallen on Genet's *Prisoner of Love* by inadvertence or as if it were *any* book to him, seems almost contemptuous. What is normally a simple gesture of admiration, to quote and praise a fellow writer, thus reveals a complicated act of identification tainted with a stain of rejection. The convoluted ways in which Burroughs express his admiration for Genet—via the honorable action of his character—and omits to mention his name or even the title of his book when he does so in this fragment, is astonishing: with no other writer, in his entire works, does Burroughs identify so deeply that he feels impelled to insist on distance.

The clue to understanding the extreme ambivalence in Burroughs' comparison of himself with Genet is a section that interrupts his musings about *Prisoner of Love* and at first sight has nothing to do with them. Right in between his two references to Genet and betrayal, Burroughs retells one of his favorite satirical anecdotes, that of the officer who abandons a sinking ship by dressing up in women's clothing and rushes into the first lifeboat. In previous versions, Burroughs found in such "anti-heroes a purity of motive, a halo of dazzling shameless innocence," and imagined joining their ranks: "I have a deep reverence for life. And I'd like to see any sinking passengers beat me into the first lifeboat" (1998, 334–35). But in *My Education*, describing how the old class elites went down with the *Titanic* "like gentlemen," Burroughs admits that he would do just the same, that "in an actual emergency," he "would probably react with exemplary selflessness" (1995, 8). Bound finally by his class and by respectable human morality, he doesn't consider what Genet would have done in such a situation, but we already know; he would have beaten Burroughs into that first lifeboat. Genet is the glittering shameless anti-hero that Burroughs could never be.

In a hypothetical contest, an imaginary competition between writers for which is the least human, or therefore the most alien, we can only admit—and reading *Prisoner of Love* Burroughs himself seems to fear—that Genet would win. The unredeemed junkie author of *Naked Lunch*, who had declared that in the face of absolute need "You would lie, cheat, inform on your friends, steal, do anything," measures himself against Genet and finds himself the shorter man (Burroughs 2001, 201). Why did Burroughs struggle so with *Prisoner of Love*? Let us formulate a hypothesis: it was Genet's most political book and Burroughs, like so many readers, couldn't bear his appalling political stance. Genet made no secret that he showed no loyalty to those whose cause he joined, often claiming his love for revolution was self-interestedly aesthetic: "You can see how beautiful the fedayeen are. Certainly, their revolt is gratifying to me, as is that of the Black Panthers, but I don't know whether I could have stayed so long with them if physically they had been less attractive" (2004, 191). Genet even went so far as to state that if the Palestinians' revolution ever did succeed, he would lose interest in it because fundamentally he couldn't help but remain in the position of the outsider.[13] Asked to give his vision of a political revolution, he again made a reply that couldn't be more alienated and alienating:

> I'm not all that eager for there to be a revolution. If I'm really sincere, I have to say that I don't particularly want it. [...] If there were a real revolution, I might not be able to be against it. There would be adherence, and I am not that kind of man; I am not a man of adherence, but a man of revolt. My point of view is very egotistic. I would like for the world—now pay close attention to the way I say this—I would like for the world not to change so that I can be against the world. (Genet 2004, 132)

In contrast, the political dimension of Burroughs' works cannot conceal the deeply moral values at their heart. Burroughs' interest in revolution was not aesthetic, as Genet insisted his was, which is surely why *My Education* openly mocks Genet's attachment to physical appearances: "In *Prisoner of Love* a perceptive black officer from Sudan named Mubarak says to Genet: 'The Israeli soldiers are young. Would you be glad to be with them? I expect they would be very nice to you'" (1995, 9). But if Burroughs' political support was unoriginally ethical, it nevertheless emerges only after the display of a characteristic cynicism and the semantic equivocation he makes in *My Education*: "As for *moi* it would make no difference to me which side I was with. (*With*, not *on*.) I can see value in both. But when it comes to the situation in South Africa there is for me only one side possible" (9; Burroughs' emphasis). Here the author of *My Education* attempts to differentiate himself from Genet by avoiding any insinuation of an erotic or aesthetic self-interest and unambiguously taking an ethical stance on the apartheid regime (one that was, of course, routinely compared with Israel's treatment of the Palestinians in the 1980s). In sum, Burroughs' very effort to draw a clear distinction between himself and Genet when it comes to taking political sides forces him to acknowledge that his own notorious cynicism was a false front.

There are, indeed, uncanny parallels between Burroughs' mockery of Genet's confusion of the ethical with the aesthetic/erotic in *My Education* and his own political posture thirty years earlier, at the time of writing *The Yage Letters*. In 1953, finding himself caught up in the Colombian civil war, Burroughs sounds remarkably like Genet, opposing Spanish colonialism and supporting the indigenous people on aesthetic grounds tainted by self-interest. Writing to Ginsberg, Burroughs cannot resist equating his political sympathies with his erotic desires: "The Conservatives are not only a bunch of shits they are *all ugly* [. . .] I literally only saw *one* I would consider eligible [. . .] The best people in S.A. are the Indians. Certainly the best-looking people" (1993, 159–60; Burroughs' emphasis). But for all his hardboiled cynicism—"Always was a pushover for a just cause and a pretty face"—Burroughs cannot help himself: "However it is *impossible* to remain neutral [. . .] Wouldn't surprise me if I end up with the Liberal guerillas" (159; Burroughs' emphasis). Burroughs and Genet, as well as the young Rimbaud of the Paris Commune, were for the guerrillas, "with" if not "on" the same side of Justice; but Burroughs' stance is unambiguously ethical, which is why in the end, unlike Genet and no doubt "the later bourgeois Rimbaud," he must refuse "the last lifeboat."

Burroughs never ceased to recognize himself in the mirror of Rimbaud's poetics, however much his experiments changed over the course of his oeuvre. But the intensity of his ambivalence toward Genet—especially toward his central concept of betrayal—stresses just how seriously, in retrospect and on reflection, Burroughs used Genet's oeuvre to reevaluate his own ethics. This is the Burroughs whose posthumously published journals infamously end: "Love? What is it? Most natural painkiller what there is. LOVE" (2000, 253), a line it is impossible to imagine either Genet or the Burroughs who identified with "the later bourgeois Rimbaud" ever writing. What we think of as most "Burroughsian" about Burroughs' writing may share a good deal with what is unique about the work of Rimbaud and Genet, especially their uncompromising commitment to extremes, but there remains within the Burroughs' oeuvre a deeply felt, if agonized, sense of that most deeply human quality: hope. Therefore, Burroughs ultimately fails in the contest between writers to be the most alien or inhuman, and this is a suitably paradoxical way to mark his 100th anniversary. For can it be putting Burroughs or anyone down to declare them human in the end?

VÉRONIQUE LANE is Senior Teaching Associate in French and Translation Studies in the Department of Languages and Cultures at Lancaster University in the United Kingdom. She has published several articles on the works of Apollinaire, Artaud, Céline, and Genet, and is the author of *The French Genealogy of the Beat Generation: Burroughs, Ginsberg and Kerouac's Appropriations of Modern Literature, from Rimbaud to Michaux* (Bloomsbury, 2017).

NOTES

1. Beat criticism has indeed taken a transnational turn, witnessed by two recent collections of essays, *The Transnational Beat Generation* edited by Nancy Grace and Jennie Skerl (2012) and "The Beat Generation and Europe" edited by Polina Mackay and Chad Weiner in *Comparative American Studies* (2013), as well as by Jimmy Fazzino's *World Beats* (2016).

2. The present essay is an earlier version of material appearing in my book: for a fuller account of Burroughs' relationship to French literature, see chapters 4, 7, and 8 of Lane 2017.

3. Strangely, Burroughs never refers to *Le Spleen de Paris*, Baudelaire's most vitriolic, and so most Burroughsian, collection of poems.

4. The note of retraction Corso insisted should be in the pamphlet, in which he attributed the creation of cut-ups to "uninspired machine-poetry," also affirms his distance from this text and the cut-up method itself (Beiles et al. 1960, 63).

5. The second credit omits to reference the poem in French.

6. For Oliver Harris's interpretation of this line on which I have built, see "'Burroughs is a poet too, really': The Poetics of *Minutes to Go*," 2004.

7. Rimbaud's second letter of May 15, 1871, to Paul Demeny rather than to Georges Izambard, May 13, 1871, two days earlier (Rimbaud 1957, 96, 92); my emphasis.

8. The four collages feature in Allmer and Sears 2014.

9. I am grateful to John Sears and Patricia Allmer for confirming the provenance of Rimbaud's image in the 1964 collage.

10. Special thanks to Alex Wermer-Colan for sharing his own transcriptions.

11. These two cut-ups are located in the archives of Northwestern University.

12. Indeed, by repeating the phrase, Burroughs implies the most devastating parallel possible between the menace of reading Genet and the trauma he claimed underwrote *Queer*: his shooting of Joan Vollmer.

13. "The day the Palestinians become a nation like other nations, I won't be there anymore. [...] I think that's where I'm going to betray them. They don't know it" (Genet 2004, 244).

REFERENCES

Primary

Burroughs Papers, Berg Collection, New York Public Library, 6.42, 7.42, 11.59, 16.61, 16.76, 26.4, 82.2.20.

Secondary

Allmer, Patricia, and John Sears, eds. 2014. *Taking Shots: The Photography of William S. Burroughs*. London: Prestel.

Allsop, Kenneth. 1960. "Rimbaud in a Raincoat." *The Spectator*, July 28, 8–9.

Baudelaire, Charles. 1970. *Paris Spleen*. Translated by Louise Varèse. New York: New Directions.

Beiles, Sinclair, William Burroughs, Gregory Corso, and Brion Gysin. 1960. *Minutes to Go*. San Francisco: City Lights Books.

Burroughs, William S. 1962. "The Future of the Novel." *Transatlantic Review* 11 (Winter): 6–7.

———. 1971. *The Wild Boys: A Book of the Dead*. New York: Grove.

———. 1978. *The Exterminator*, reprinted in *The Third Mind*. New York: Viking.

———. 1993. *The Letters of William S. Burroughs, 1945–1959*. Edited by Oliver Harris. New York: Viking.

———. 1995. *My Education: A Book of Dreams*. New York: Viking.

———. 1998. "Roosevelt after Inauguration: A New Introduction." In *Word Virus*, edited by James Grauerholz and Ira Silverberg, 334–35. London: Fourth Estate.

———. 2000. *Last Words*. Edited by James Grauerholz. London: Fourth Estate.

———. 2001. *Naked Lunch: The Restored Text*. Edited by James Grauerholz and Barry Miles. New York: Grove.

———. 2003. *Junky: The Definitive Edition of "Junk."* Edited by Oliver Harris. New York: Penguin.

———. 2010. *Queer*. Edited by Oliver Harris. New York: Penguin Books.

———. 2012. *Rub Out the Words: The Letters of William S. Burroughs, 1959–1974*. Edited by Bill Morgan. New York: Ecco.

———. 2014a. *Nova Express: The Restored Text*. Edited by Oliver Harris. New York: Grove.

———. 2014b. *The Soft Machine: The Restored Text*. Edited by Oliver Harris. New York: Grove.

———. 2015. *The Travel Agency is on Fire*. Edited by Alex Wermer-Colan. Lost & Found: The CUNY Poetics Document Initiative. New York: City University of New York.

Burroughs, William S., and Brion Gysin. 1978. *The Third Mind*. New York: Viking.

Burroughs, William, and Jack Kerouac. 2008. *And the Hippos Were Boiled in Their Tanks*. New York: Penguin.

Campbell, James. 2001. *This is the Beat Generation: New York–San Francisco–Paris*. Berkeley: University of California Press.

Cran, Rona. 2014. *Collage in Twentieth-Century Art, Literature and Culture: Joseph Cornell, William Burroughs, Frank O'Hara and Bob Dylan*. London: Ashgate.

Fazzino, Jimmy. 2016. *World Beats: Beat Generation Writing and the Worlding of U.S. Literature*. Hanover, NH: Dartmouth College Press.

Genet, Jean. 1994. *Miracle of the Rose*. Translated by Bernard Frechtman. New York: Grove.

———. 2003. *Prisoner of Love*. Translated by Barabra Bray. NYRB Classics.

———. 2004. *The Declared Enemy: Texts and Interviews*. Edited by Albert Dichy and translated by Jeff Fort. Stanford, CA: Stanford University Press.

Grace, Nancy, and Jennie Skerl, eds. 2012. *The Transnational Beat Generation*. New York: Palgrave Macmillan.

Guyaux, André. 1991. *Duplicités de Rimbaud*. Paris: Champion.

Harris, Oliver. 2004. "'Burroughs is a Poet too, really': The Poetics of *Minutes to Go*." *The Edinburgh Review* 114 (2005): 24–36.

Lane, Véronique. 2017. *The French Genealogy of the Beat Generation: Burroughs, Ginsberg and Kerouac's Appropriations of Modern Literature, from Rimbaud to Michaux*. New York: Bloomsbury.

Mackay, Polina, and Chad Weiner. 2013. "Introduction: The Beat Generation and Europe." *Comparative American Studies* 11 (3): 221–26.

Miles, Barry. 2000. *The Beat Hotel: Ginsberg, Burroughs and Corso in Paris, 1957–1963*. New York: Grove.

Miller, Henry. 1946. *The Time of the Assassins: A Study of Rimbaud*. New York: New Directions.

Perloff, Marjorie. 1984. *The Poetics of Indeterminacy*. Evanston: Northwestern University Press.

Rimbaud, Arthur. 1957. *Illuminations*. Translated by Louise Varèse. New York: New Directions.

———. 1961. *A Season in Hell*. Translated by Louise Varèse. New York: New Directions.

Sartre, Jean-Paul. 1952. *Saint Genet, comédien et martyr*. Paris: Gallimard.

Tashjian, Dickran. 2002. *A Boatload of Madmen: Surrealism and the American Avant-Garde, 1920–1950*. London: Thames and Hudson.

Cut/Fold

This is the Space Age? How old is Space? Space has no age. Space has no time. Space has no words. You are in time. You are in words. You are in word-time. You want out to Space?

You are going to find the door guarded. Guarded by time-police armed with all the pain, hate and fear of a dualistic universe. This is a war between those of us who want out to Space and those who want to keep us all locked in Time.

Cut your way out.

The Cut-Ups are not for "artistic purposes." As we see it, the function of "art" is out. The Cut-Ups are a weapon you will need on the way out. I bring not peace but pieces. Pieces of time. Time cut to pieces. Cut time to pieces. Word-lines are time-lines. Words are milestones in time.

This is Mile End Road.

—William S. Burroughs, "Present Time," 1964, Berg 17.44. Copyright © by William Burroughs, used by permission of The Wylie Agency LLC.

We sure have the technology. All we have to do is learn it and use it.

—Burroughs, "Cut In with Scientology Lit," 1963, Berg 35.18. Copyright © by William Burroughs, used by permission of The Wylie Agency LLC.

I am nobody I Am every body I am me I am you I am myself I am others

—Burroughs, "Some Phrases From Scientology Procedures Cut-In," 1963–65, Berg 16.44. Copyright © by William Burroughs, used by permission of The Wylie Agency LLC.

THE MEMORY OF WHAT HAS BEEN AND NEVER MORE WILL BE ROLLED ROUND IN EARTHS DIURNAL COURSE WITH ROCKS AND STONES AND TREES GOLDENAIDS AND GIRLS. SEE SEE WHERE CHRISTS BLOOD STREAMS IN THE FIRMAMENT. WHERE WE ARE IS HELL AND WHERE HELL IS THERE MUST WE EVER BE LOOK HOMEWARD ANGEL NOW AND MELT WITH TRUTH AND TOUCHED THE TREMBLING EAR AND THE DREAM GREW COLD YOU HAVE NOR YOUTH NOR AGE BUT AS IT WERE AND AFTER DINNER SLEEP DREAMING ON BOTH. AIR AND THE WORLD NOT SOUGHT. OF QUIETNESS AND SLOW TIME. STRANGE WHO WAS PASSING.

—Burroughs, "Fold-in of Western Literary Classics, 1960–61," Berg 48.22. Copyright © by William Burroughs, used by permission of The Wylie Agency LLC.

On the Cut-Up

In the published version of *The Third Mind* from 1978 (an edition that lacked the collages intended for the original 1965 art book), Burroughs revised his original 1965 essay on "The Cut-Up Method," itself a version of a lecture he first gave at the Edinburgh Literary Festival in 1962. Burroughs introduces the cut-up method in user-friendly terms: "The cut-up method brings to writers the collage, which has been used by painters for fifty years. . . . The best writing seems to be done almost by accident, but writers until the cut-up method was made explicit—all writing is in fact cut ups. I will return to this point—had no way to produce the accident of spontaneity. You can not will spontaneity. But you can introduce the unpredictable spontaneous factor with a pair of scissors" (*The Third Mind*, 32). Burroughs explains the method's steps as if anyone could be innovative in their writing practice: "The method is simple. Here is one way to do it. Take a page. Like this page. Now cut down the middle and cross the middle. You have four sections: 1 2 3 4 . . . one two three four. Now rearrange the sections placing section four with section one and section two with section three. And you have a new page. Sometimes it says much the same thing. Sometimes something quite different—(cutting up political speeches is an interesting exercise)—in any case you will find that it says something and something quite definite" (34). Burroughs furthermore advertised the method as a popular means of destruction and creation: "Cut-ups are for everyone. Anybody can make cut ups. It is experimental in the sense of being something to do. Right here write now. Not something to talk and argue about. Greek philosophers assumed logically that an object twice as heavy as another object would fall twice as fast. It did not occur to them to push the two objects off the table and see how they fall. Cut the words and see how they fall" (34).

Both Burroughs' archival essay, "On the Cut-Up," written in 1960 in Paris, and his "Fold-in with Western Literary Classics," appear in Folio 134, which contains manuscripts from the early high-point of his cut-up experiments in 1960–1961, in Paris, during the composition of *Minutes to Go* (1960). Burroughs' fascinating "Cut-Up with Aleister Crowley" appears in Folio 65 "Illustrating Cut-Ups with Other Writers," amidst cut-ups of Graham Greene, F. Scott Fitzgerald, Rimbaud, and many more canonical authors. When Burroughs cuts up the words of Aleister

Crowley, he discovers in his cut-up the anarchistic motivation for his practice, as he cleverly translates Crowley's decadent maxim "Do What Thou Will is the Whole of the Law" into "Do What Thou Wilt is the Hole in the Law." Much in keeping with Burroughs' oft-quoted phrase from Hassan i Sabbah, "Nothing is True. Everything is Permitted," Crowley's motto for Burroughs' radical practice exposes the pointlessness of a Law that violates the will of the people for the purposes of a higher order. During this period of extreme experimentation with form and style, Burroughs cut up nearly every piece of prose he could find, often creating as part of the process minimal pieces containing selections of quotes from wide-ranging sources. As an example, we present his cut-up of an anthology of classic works of literature, curating the type of quotable lines Burroughs was also well known for reciting from memory.

—*AWC*

THE CUT UP METHOD PLACES AT THE DISPOSAL OF WRITERS THE
COLLAGE WHICH PAINTERS HAVE USED FOR THEPAST FIFTY YEARS.
AND WHICH IS USED IN ALL CINEMA PRODUCTIONS WHERE THE RANDOM
MOVEMENT OF THE CAMERA SELCTS.MORE IMPORTANT ARE THE ACTUAL
PHSIOLOGIVCAL IMPICATION. I QUOTE FROM MR GREY WALTER A
MIRROS FOR THE BRAIN. HE FOUND THAT A LIGHT FLASHED INTO
THE EYS AT A CERTAINFREQUENCY SAY TNE TO TWENTY FIVE FLASHES
PER SECOND THE RYHTMIC SERIES OF FLASHES SEEMED TO BE BREAKING
DOWN SOME OF THE PHYSIOLOGICLA BARIERS BETWEEN DIFFERENT
REGIONS OF THE BRAIN. THIS MEANT THAT THE STIMULUS OF THE
FLICKER RE CEIVED IN THE VISUAL PERCEPTION AREA OF THE CORTEX
WAS BREAKING BOUNDS. ITS RIPLLES WERE OVERFLWOING INTO OTHER
AREAS. HE ALSO DISCOVERED THAT FLICKER PRODUCED MANY OF THE
EFFECTS OF MESCALINE AND OTHER HALLUCIGEN DRUGS. WHEN I READ
THSI PASSAGE I THOUGHT IMMEDIATELY OF RIMBUAD AND HSI
HSI IMAGES THAT SEEM TO BREAK DOWN XXXXSBARRIERS. HIS COLOR
VOWLES. AND MADE THE EXPERIMENT OF FILLING A PAGE WITH
RANDOM IMAGES REFERED TO DIFFERENT SENSES LIKE SMELL IMAGES
SIGHT DOUND AND FEEL IMAGES AND THEN CUTTING THE PAGE
INTO SECTIONS SHUFFLING AT RANDOM (IS ANY SHUFFLE RANDOM?)
SO THAT THE IMAGES WERE MIXED AND COLROLESS MSELLS RANCID
DANK SOUNDS ET EMERGED. IN SHORT THIS IS

do what thou wilt my body   dies jst before the Armisyice two boys laughing off
shall be the whole of the law the sky my name is Peter Pen Dragon   begging for
glistening golden sands something   i felt as if I had been bornHeldt me long long
Golf?   when one has flown overa   golf course there is something special for me about
golf courses something that is supposed to hppane there I remember scenes from
other times and places the automobile stopped at the end ofa dirty little street
we learn more from our failures long long how long it was dust of the dead gods
than from our sucessess like cobwebs in the air it happens one of the brethren here
is himself a mechanic   I turned to Mrs Webster   what happened? I asked
   I could not conceal the feverish eagerness   the conviction of Miachael Sngele
he made rather a point of that   death is nota   way out of it the pale skies
the thought came to my mind that we fell aprt suburban streets afternoon light
had already diedbleakly clear rusting key.   I left by the back door with the dust
the cold produced by abstinence   this isa true story of a thousand years
man is not subjected to the angels he was a caddy it seems his smile across the golf
nor even unto death utterly save through the weakness of course spei sepia hair
   his own feeble willl stirs in septemebr wind urine in narrow streets slow finger
do what thou wilt that is the whole   solid boy out of the page jim   jerky his penis
of the law   esjaculates dawn smell of straneg boy naked thighs and buttocks.

[autograph]: aleister crowly said
             Do What Thou Wilt
             That is the Hole
               in the law.

IS THIS THE FACE THAT LAUNCHED A THOUSAND SHIPS AND BURNED
THE TOPLESS TOWERS OF ILLIUM? THAT TIME OF YEAR YOU MAY IN
ME BEHOLD WHEN YEELWO LEAVES OR NONE OR FEW DO HANG ON THE
BARE RUINED CHOIRS WHERE LATE THE SWEET BIRDS SANG…
I HAVE COMMITTED FORNICATION BUT THAT WAS IN ANOTHER COUNTRY
AND BESI ES THE WENCH IS DEAD. FAIRY CASEMENTS OPENING ON THE
FOAM IOF PERILOUS SEAS IN FAIRY LANDS FALORN. ALONE AND PALEY
AS I FORETOLD YOU ARE ALL SPIRITS AND HAVE MELTED INTO AIR.
INTO THIN AIR. BRIGHTNESS FLASS FROMTHE AIR. THE SEDGE IS
WITHERED FROM THE LARK AND NO BIRDS SING. OH WITHERED IS THE
GARLAND OF THE WARS. CALLTO ME ALL MY SAD CAPTAINS.. AND THE
SHEEN OF THEIR SPEARS WAS LIKE STARS O N THE SEA. FAR ON THE
RINGING PALINS OF WINDY TROY MEN ARE BORN TO TROUBLE AS
SPARKS FLY UPWARD. OR EVER THE SILVER CORD BE LOOSED OR THE
GOLDENBOWL BE BROEKN GOES TO HIS LONG HOME NOR WEAK THE
FREIND. YOUR HEART BEAT   INTHAT BEELY WHERE SLEEPS THE
DOUBLE SEX. TINKLING CIRCULATE THRU YOUR PALE ARMS. YOU SHALL
ALLRETURN DO NOT CORRUPT ALLAHS WILL DREADINGYOUR ACTIONS
DONE. WHAT STRONG ARM WILLGIVE ME BACK THAT REGION. IT IS THE
FRIEND NEITHER VIOLENT NOR WEAK THE FREIND. COULD YOU NOT WAT
WATCH W ITH ME FOR ONE HOUR. TO THEM THAT HAVE SHALLBE GIVEN
WHAT THOUGHTHE FILED BE LOST THE STRIKEN FIELD. YOU ARE THE
DEEDS CREATURE. THE MEORY OF WHAT HAS BEEN AND NEVER MORE
WILL BE ROOLED ROUNDIN EARTHS DIRUNAL COURSE WITH ROCKS AND
STONES AND TREES GOLDENIADS AND GIRLS. SEE SEE WHERE CHRISTS
BLOOD STREAMS IN THE FIRMANET. WHERE WE ARE IS HELL AND WHERE
HELL IS THERE MUST WE EVER BE LLOK HOMEWARD ANGLE NOW AND
METL WITH RUTH AND TOUCHED THE TREMBLING EAR ANDTHE DREAM
GREW COLD YOU HAVE NOR YOUTH NOR AGE BUT AS IT WERE AND
AFTER DINER SLEEP DREAMING ON BOTH. AIR AND THE WORDL NOT
SAUGHT. OF QUIETNESS AND SLOW TIME. STRANGE WHO WAS PASSING.

   LIVE EMBERS RAINING IN GUST OF FROST WILLIAMA GET ME CONRED
BIF..GHOST WRITINGINTHE SKY. IN WINDE KIRENE DEI EPAHNEN.
PAS DE COMMISSION   I HAVE TOLD NO ONE TO WAIT I SHALLGO
AWAY INTHAT DI RECTION WHEN I WISH. ALLPASSION SPENT.

14

Cross the Wounded Galaxies:
A Conversation about the Cut-Up Trilogy

DAVIS SCHNEIDERMAN AND OLIVER HARRIS

If, as Oliver Harris suggests, a letter always reaches its recipient, then my missive to Harris near the turn of the century was an enchanted bullet. I asked him for a contribution to a fledgling project that would become the first collected volume of new Burroughs criticism, *Retaking the Universe: William S. Burroughs in the Age of Globalization* (2004).

Harris promptly delivered his excellent essay "Cutting Up Politics," although he told me later that he expected my early career enthusiasm to amount, in the case of the proposed anthology, to nothing. (Some years later, we hiked to the top of the Pyramid of the Sun in Teotihuacán near Mexico City, where I captured him in a still photo. He spoke in some way to this "nothing," silhouetted in his ever-settled fedora, staring down from the summit at me, the photographer.)

What fascinates me most about Harris—a rakish man of almost impossible energy—is not merely his attention to the genetic production methods that have come to define the sphere of contemporary Burroughs criticism. No, for all of the path-breaking work of his editorial and scholarly career, Harris is a figure not clouded by the mythopoeic. His interest in Burroughs, like my own, is linked strongly to Burroughs' work, and more important to the methods of making the work. Put another way, Harris's scholarship has little interest in reaffirming the fanboy postures that too often cloud the Beat and Burroughs skies.

This is not to say that Harris does not know and respect the biography of William S. Burroughs or understand how Burroughs' various fascinations impacted his work. Quite the contrary: no one has done more than Harris to research the intersection of biography with the production of Burroughs' texts to give us—not the hipster be-bop junkie—but Burroughs at work on a series of careful experiments, Burroughs the not-particularly elegant editor, Burroughs the empiricist.

It is this empirical cast, or at least the full understanding of it, or at least the willingness to read Burroughs as an archaeologist rather than an apologist that has brought Harris through what may be the most challenging project of the Burroughs century: reediting three books of the so-called Nova Trilogy, now properly rebranded as the Cut-Up Trilogy: *The Soft Machine* (1961), *The Ticket That Exploded* (1962), and *Nova Express* (1964).

Along with Barry Miles's landmark biography, *Call Me Burroughs: A Life* (2014), Harris's newly edited editions will stand as the central achievement of the centennial year. Below, and elsewhere—in Mexico City, Tangier, Paris, and so on—Harris and I have continued our long conversation about a stamp of scholarship that never apologizes for what it may need to tell us, even for those who may not want to hear.

—*Davis Schneiderman*

SCHNEIDERMAN You've now edited more editions of William S. Burroughs than anyone. *Junky* (1953) and *Queer* (1985) and *The Yage Letters* (1963), far from being straightforward, read like John Grisham compared to the Cut-Up Books. How is a reader to enter into these texts, particularly given their daunting manuscripts histories?

HARRIS Almost everything about the Cut-Up Trilogy is impossible. I remember when you interviewed me back in 2010, just after the publication of *Queer* had completed my editing of Burroughs' trilogy of 1950s novels; you asked if I was going to take on the 1960s trilogy, and I said simply "I don't know." At that point, I hadn't been invited to reedit them, mind you, but the bottom line was I didn't know how or even *if* it could be done. All I saw were problems: material ones, to do with the texts and the manuscripts—which I knew would be daunting, although I underestimated the sheer volume and complexity of what was involved; and also questions of purpose and principle—what could new editions achieve? In that interview four years ago I insisted that "some possible projects would be of uncertain value to me"—and I didn't even know if reediting the Cut-Up Trilogy *was* possible.

SCHNEIDERMAN The "uncertain value" is distinctly Burroughsian, yes?

HARRIS Maybe so, but then my role as an editor is not to "be Burroughsian"; to *do justice to Burroughs' work*, is how I'd put it. You see, I was thinking back as well as ahead when I said that, wondering if my editions of the first trilogy had achieved what I wanted. Actually, it helps to consider *Junky*, *Queer*, and *The Yage Letters*, to understand where I was coming from when I took on the Cut-Up Trilogy.

I knew that the untold story of how the 1950s texts were written, edited, and published would change how they were read—in many senses, *mis*-read. I knew from the archival research I'd done over the years that the standard accounts of how Burroughs wrote *Junky*, *Queer*, and *The Yage Letters*, and how the books ended up in the form they did, were either plain wrong or missing some essential element. Reediting the texts was a way to tell those stories and make them accessible.

SCHNEIDERMAN Your notion of accessibility also has the democratizing overtone of Burroughs' project—to give it all to the reader—and yet it also suggests that something can be done with this "access." That access is communicable. That access is a type of editorial positivism.

HARRIS In terms of "democracy," I believe editing has to strike a balance: on the one hand, absolutely yes, I want to give the reader *more* Burroughs—to reveal the backstories, the offcuts, the variants, the alternative forms that call into question the fixed text; but on the other hand, editing is also a matter of making informed choices and presenting materials in informative ways—so I'm very suspicious of the idea of giving the reader *everything* in some fantasy digitized archive. In the case of the Cut-Up Trilogy, "everything" would be quite simply *far too much.* The editor has to be trusted—and has to earn the reader's trust—to negotiate a law of diminishing returns. As an enigmatic line in *The Ticket That Exploded* puts it: "Accessibility is I feel to beg the question . . ." (2014: 28).

But I think the editions I've produced do demonstrate the kind of access in which I believe. I felt I was doing original academic work, because by 2003 I'd done archival research for two decades, coming over from the UK to the US pretty much every year. And I could see that even the most brilliant criticism was often getting it wrong because it lacked the basics of who did what, when, and where. My book *William Burroughs and the Secret of Fascination* (2003) was really all about this problem, although I tried to go beyond just correcting the received version; I wanted to show that Burroughs' works deserved an accurate material history—that this was an absolute necessity—and yet the result was only to further enhance their mystery and fascination. . . . Anyway, that was an academic book and I knew it would reach only a handful of people, which was fine, but it made me conscious that new research and thinking tends to exist on another planet from the two contexts that matter most; that's to say, the work itself and its largest audience.

In other words, I didn't want to do academic work that would only be read by the cognoscenti and a few peer review assessors; I wanted to put my archival work in the hands of all possible readers—and I've been phenomenally fortunate in that aim because of the support I've enjoyed from the Burroughs Estate, in the person of James Grauerholz. James engaged me to work on the primary materials, the texts themselves, starting with the *Letters* that were published in 1993. Crucially, with the sole exception of *Everything Lost: The Latin American Notebook* for Ohio UP in 2008, all the books have appeared in mass-market editions from mainstream publishers like Penguin and Grove.

I don't mean to digress, but that's why I was so depressed recently to see a British edition of *Junky*—in their "Penguin Essentials" series—that stripped out the notes at the back of the book and cut my introduction. Of course the "text itself" is more "essential" than anything I added—although since they cut my name there wasn't even anything to say I reedited the text—but what I liked so much about the paperback publications in the first place was to know that all sorts of readers who wouldn't normally think about a book's backstory would find out something totally unexpected and see Burroughs in a new light.

So, yes, it's all about access—and I have to combine scholarship that will stand the test of time with a more entertaining side that will bring new readers to Burroughs and entice others to reread texts they thought they knew.

SCHNEIDERMAN The British *Junky*, sans all trace of Harris, suggests in an unpleasant manner that your edition has become canon. Readers, or so goes a flawed argument, have been presented with a definitive edition that has supplanted all others. Yet this leads to the question of readers. Do we have any way of knowing to what extent a new edition may act as corrective to the old? I may be wrong, but I imagine many more people will have read *Naked Lunch* as published in an earlier edition than *The Restored Text* of 2003. The manuscript history with the Cut-Up books places your editions, as you state directly, as simply another version in the extended manuscript history. Therefore, it appears that the work you've done—wonderful and hoary—may prove asymptotic. How would you feel if fifty years from now your *Soft Machine* was called the fourth, while a yet-to-be born cyborg scholar prepared the next? This is the opposite extreme of documentation to the British *Junky* . . .

HARRIS That's a crazy scenario, you're right: far from settling the confusion of multiple editions, actually unsettling it further, with a horizon of infinite editions—a bibliographical madness out of a *ficcione* by Borges. And maybe you're right about the new "restored" editions—not, incidentally, a term I like; but the best available—that they may never replace the old Grove editions. On the other hand, I was brought up on the British edition of *The Soft Machine*—the third version of 1968, never published outside the UK; so later, when I read the Grove edition—the second version of 1966—I was confused and annoyed that whole sections were just not there! And *then* I read the Olympia edition—the first version of 1961—and of course I was even more confused, since it's a completely different book to either of the others. When I began work on the trilogy, frankly, I assumed I would "restore" the third version, as the most complete, Burroughs' last word on the text, and the one I knew best. But piecing together the manuscript history completely changed my understanding. That's what I want readers of the new editions to experience too.

SCHNEIDERMAN And you discovered, to an extent, the spurious quality of the "last word." It's never what it seems; often, it's something right out of central casting. Is the lesson of this work that its "order"—chronological and material—produces texts that undo their own marketing slogans?

HARRIS Well, I have to live with marketing slogans just as Burroughs had to. Ironically, it actually helps me as an editor to re-experience those commercial and pragmatic conditions of publication. In the case of *Junky*, *Queer*, and *The Yage Letters*, what I wanted to do was reveal the contingencies and complexities hidden in the texts—hidden in plain sight in some cases; simply *overlooked* because the texts were always taken as straightforward and autobiographical—just not interesting in terms of their form or method of writing. I wanted to reveal the unexpected role that editors at Ace, Penguin, and City Lights had played, as well as Burroughs' own revisions and indeed the hand of chance. I wanted to show how all three were composite, hybrid publications and that, most curiously of all, these factors hadn't "corrupted" them. On the contrary, contingency and collaboration had helped the texts find their necessary form, as if their author had otherwise been unable to complete them.

So, my point was to show how revising the material history of their writing revises not only how we understand the form and meaning of the three texts, but Burroughs' conception of authorship itself, which is not a unified act but a collaborative process involving contingencies and multiple, divided agencies. This conception has often been misconstrued in terms of Burroughs' sloppiness, his lack of care, his abandoning manuscripts to others. There's some truth in that, for sure, but there's also material evidence to the contrary, evidence of the control he exercised.

To give the most striking example: we read *The Yage Letters* in an entirely different way once we discover that, far from being actual letters that Burroughs mailed from the Amazon to Allen Ginsberg in New York, dashed off slices of reportage tidied up a bit afterward perhaps, in fact they were almost all carefully fabricated. Behind the nice clean letters in the book, the manuscripts reveal how Burroughs drew on letters, notes, and narrative typescripts, literally cut and pasted together into new composite pages, then added the tops and tails of letters—and that he did all this editing while actually living with Ginsberg in his apartment on the Lower East Side. So, whereas previous critics had to take the published text at face value, I could put my archival research to use in the new edition. The resulting books contributed to what you'd call a *material turn* in Burroughs scholarship that gives new attention to the physical history and conditions of his work—which is entirely fitting since one of the most remarkable things about Burroughs is how *physically* he worked with his material.

SCHNEIDERMAN For me, this is the essential lesson of the non-essentialist writer. Your work often suggests that Burroughs' methods were the driver of his textual agency, and in a way that might find itself at odds—or at least an extension well beyond—the stated intention of the texts, both critical and in situ, as well as his vestigial ideas of Romantic authorship. Even so, the Cut-Up Trilogy is methodologically distant from the first books. Does the rigor of method produce the *apparent* chaos of text?

HARRIS When it came to the Cut-Up Trilogy, I wanted to contest the mythology according to which these books were crazy word collages made with scissors and randomly thrown together—as if Burroughs were no more than a monkey at a typewriter or had pulled the words out of a hat, as in the famous Tristan Tzara stunt to which he so often referred. On the contrary, I wanted to show how rigorously Burroughs applied his methods.

I wanted to demonstrate that the results embraced chance as part of the process of composition but also demonstrated a precise attention to detail for which

Burroughs has rarely been given credit. In the introductions and end notes I give some material examples; my favorite is a 300-word long note in *The Ticket* that establishes how Burroughs played on the words *sing* and *sign*, where we see him exploiting a typographical error in the use of two simple words of particular relevance to his text. The larger point is to transform the indeterminacy of the text into a creative machine, to recognize how it produces effects and meaning in the process of reading.

SCHNEIDERMAN You worked on aborted versions of these books in the 1990s, yes? What happened then that didn't happen now, or vice-versa in the editorial process? Would you talk about why these books are possible now?

HARRIS That's true, back in the early 1990s, after I had edited *The Letters*, I was given a contract with Grove Press to produce new editions of the Cut-Up Trilogy. Lucky it didn't work out, is all I can say. I did do a lot of work on the books—and as you know, familiarizing yourself with those texts is really not easy. They don't want to be grasped. I know I did a lot of work on them because I still had all the files and notes, but when I looked back over them I found the work I'd done was completely useless. It might have made sense then, but it didn't any more.

SCHNEIDERMAN You give agency to the texts that would seem to belie, although jokingly, your genetic manuscript history practices. What do you mean that your work didn't make any "sense," particularly if your research reveals on some level how they were made?

HARRIS Firstly, it was useless because the texts resist being grasped; the cut-up sections seem to exist only while you're trying to read them, when all sorts of lights switch on, bells ring, and your brain turns into a pinball machine—and then, half an hour later, you can barely remember what you read. Joan Didion sums it up in a line I quote in the introduction to *The Soft Machine*—that to imagine you can put the book down when the phone rings and find your place a few minutes later is "sheer bravura." That's perfectly put. So, I couldn't figure out what I had been thinking a decade earlier. And second, the work I'd done was useless because it was only *textual*: I was trying to produce new editions that resolved the mess made by Burroughs issuing revised editions of *The Ticket That Exploded* and (twice) *The Soft Machine*. Back then I had access to very few unpublished manuscripts. But also I didn't really understand what I was doing. That's why, a little later, I turned down the chance to work on a new edition of *Naked Lunch*. I wasn't ready. Ten years later, I still didn't *know*, but by then I understood the idea of the Cut-Up Trilogy much better and I knew where the manuscripts were.

SCHNEIDERMAN So, the bodies are buried *here* and *here*. Therefore, the murder was for purposes now available to be understood by the forensic detective?

HARRIS Actually, that's precisely how I viewed the writing and editing of *Queer*—as a return to the scene of a crime; but for the cut-up books, it didn't feel that way at all. The books and their backstories felt very much *alive*. Four years ago, I gave a talk (see Harris, "Confusion's Masterpiece," 2010) where I put it this way in terms of *Junky, Queer,* and *The Yage Letters*: that if we posed the seemingly nonsensical question, *"What do Burroughs' manuscripts want?"* the answer lies in the very form of their material history. The equivalent question here—*"What do the books of the Cut-Up Trilogy want?"*—has a very different answer. Firstly, because they don't really want to be "The Cut-Up Trilogy"—or rather, they have contradictory desires: they want to be a trilogy and yet *not* a trilogy, or not reified as "The Trilogy"; and secondly, because the logic of multiple and divided agencies is the very method of their textuality.

It's not just that Burroughs needed collaborators to help him finish the books, which was most emphatically the case for the Grove *Soft Machine*, where Dick Seaver simply pulled the plug on his making more revisions; it's that the mechanical, recombinative process of the methods gave rise to an organic fertility, a kind of *living text*. Burroughs knew what he was doing, and yet a central aspect of his work was to produce the unexpected or unpredictable, to exceed his own grasp, his own control. Actually, this isn't a single aspect, it's double, because it applies at the stages of production and consumption: in other words, Burroughs' use of chance as a step during the process of cutting up his material, when he looked for points of intersection and felicitous new meanings, finds its echo for the reader, who actively creates the text's intersections while consuming it.

SCHNEIDERMAN This is the area I have focused on, perhaps most recently in "The Miraculous and Mucilaginous Paste Pot: Extra-illustration and Plagiary in the William S. Burroughs Legacy" in *The Journal of Beat Studies* and in a performance piece called "The City of Interzone" for the 2014 Chicago Humanities Festival and the European Beat Studies Network conference in Tangier.

It raises the occasionally interesting poststructuralist specter—the Derridean trace—as it were. With the 1970s explicit yoking of French deconstruction to Burroughsian methodology, we find it easy to "retcon" the cut-up work as the work of someone who knew what he was doing, even if that "what" was to surrender on some level to chance.

And yet I often wonder, particularly given Burroughs' empiricist practices and his statements about the narrative readability of his works that strike almost everyone but him as absurd, whether he would have conceived of "textual excess" at all in the way we do today. Put another way, are Deleuze and Guattari correct when they ping the cut ups as having a telos—suggesting a Chomsky-like deep-grammar organizational principle (to reveal control through juxtaposition) (1987: 5–7)? Did any of the text ever really escape Burroughs, or did he, at least—aside from his obvious editorial weaknesses—consider himself master of this methodology?

HARRIS Burroughs' relation to French deconstruction has never especially interested me. As you know from *The Secret of Fascination*, I'm happy to make local, opportunistic use of Deleuze, and Lacan. But theory is not one of my strengths and I'm suspicious of its general application by academics. As for what Burroughs *believed*, I'm not a biographer either; I've published well over a quarter of a million words about Burroughs, but very rarely will you find that I claim to *know* what Burroughs thought or believed. However, if you ask me whether he considered himself the master of his methods, I would say—without hesitation—that the answer is obvious from the utterly compelling voice of a text like "Last Words" (which opens *Nova Express*).

SCHNEIDERMAN   A quarter million! That's why I've had such trouble remixing your Burroughs essays into my "restored" editions. Actually, this interview will become several isolated interviews, and we've traded sentences with each other when preparing competing Burroughs literary biography entries in 2009. The more we produce, the more we cut.

HARRIS   I think your work has complemented mine and vice versa: while I've been restoring, you've been remixing. It would be over-egging the pudding to say we've generated a Third Mind in the process, but swapping lines from each other's work seems to me an entirely natural response to the fascination of the Burroughs oeuvre. Certainly, the blend of rigor and creativity we've tried to bring to Burroughs criticism is what the singularity of the oeuvre deserves— especially his cut-up work.

SCHNEIDERMAN   You've been calling these books the Cut-Up Trilogy for years, when others called it the Nova Trilogy. Have the new editions formally rectified this, and what are the implications of such a materially focused title?

HARRIS   At a basic level, I felt that the "Nova Trilogy" unified the books according to their science fiction plot and that this was ridiculous. What makes the books so extraordinary and dominates the reading experience is not in the scenario. They're the zenith of Burroughs' work because of their experimental methods of production and the unique formal results of those methods. So, absolutely, the new editions have tried to rectify the standard approach by insisting on the materiality of the texts. I know that not every reader is going to go through all the apparatus of notes at the back of the books, but even if they just take a glance, they'll be forced to see—maybe I should say "able to see" but I really do mean *forced to see*—that these texts are so rich at a material level. I want readers to get it that "cut-up texts" are complicated, and indeed *complex*, in the scientific sense that they're never fully graspable; they're unstable systems that organically recreate themselves. I hope my notes reflect that idea, because although they're long—almost twenty thousand words for *The Soft Machine*— they're just scratching the surface.

SCHNEIDERMAN   My contribution to *Naked Lunch@50* was intended to serve the same function—to detail the absurdity of considering the plot of the book, even if that consideration speaks to the same random post-structural element I asked you about earlier. One cannot direct a windstorm, at least on a molecular level, although the meteorologist may chart it neatly after the carnage.

Therefore the notes are, to me, at least, and perhaps those reading this interview, an endlessly fascinating meta-text that serves as a homologue to the notes from *The Waste Land*"[1] You've achieved a grand cut-up: the WSB cut-up texts are yoked to explanation of those texts, which happens at various spaces within the "trilogy" as well. This is a major accomplishment, yet I wonder how important it remains for a reader to even attempt to "untangle" the work and reinscribe it within the practices of what may be taken, on one level, as the idea of Burroughs-as-literary-genius. Is there a danger in showing how brilliantly the sausage was made?

HARRIS Sausages? You remind me of Kerouac's nightmare vision of pulling baloneys out of his mouth while in Tangier typing up the "Interzone" manuscript (which formed most of *Naked Lunch*) in spring 1957, and of course you could say that Burroughs' work is indeed stuffed with the unspeakable and unpalatable parts of the animal, the human animal. But, again, I wanted to show that it's just not good enough to see these texts as cranked out by Burroughs from leftover scraps of his (in any case, mythical) "Word Horde." Yes, it was a hit and miss operation; these texts are *experimental*. But almost every section repays, rewards, the closest textual attention.

SCHNEIDERMAN You've killed the Word Horde.

HARRIS Good! It always struck me as a lazy term that confused the material histories of Burroughs' writing—which are, God knows, already quite confusing enough. That's why I'm not worried about demystifying Burroughs; however "forensic" my work, however meticulous, it's never the answer to the question.

I know there'll be objections to what I did. Some people think it's outrageous to mess with Burroughs' books: period. Maybe they'd change their mind if they knew what I put into them, how many thousands of manuscript pages I examined, how long I agonized over every detail. I'm sure I made mistakes, or at least could have justifiably made different editorial choices. Manuscript research is not a science, book publication isn't faultless, and material history isn't interpretation-free—and in the case of the Cut-Up Trilogy, the texts actively resist any conventional notion of fixity. On the other hand, that's also the point: why should the most widely available editions published by Grove be fetishized? I can't think of anything less fitting for these texts than to be reverentially *fixed*. The point isn't simply that the "restored" editions shouldn't be mistaken for the last word; although much of my work is locally concerned with "corrections," the new editions are not intended to *fix* problems but to keep the field of possibilities *open*.

SCHNEIDERMAN This is the reason I suggest that new editions may emerge in the future. We're moving quickly into string theory—each choice you made spurs its opposite in an alternate multiverse. While the inability, and undesirability, to fix the text is present in the manuscript history of any author's work, it's Burroughs' methods that amplify the instability and cause every decision and revision to become fraught at the linguistic level. It is clear that a new edition of Stephen King's *Carrie* (1974) will be easier to assemble 50 years from now, if only because it is not "about" its own inability to be apprehended by the reader.

And so I'm struck, re-reading *The Soft Machine*—or reading *SM4*, your version—as to its density, and I find myself wondering whether you find it successful as a text. Your editorial introduction hints otherwise . . . are you able to sweep aside whatever readerly apprehensions you have for the sake of scholarship? Note: I'm sure you are; I just want you to discuss it.

HARRIS None of the Cut-Up books are entirely successful, and although Burroughs thought—or at least told his publishers—that they would sell well, experiments on this scale are bound to fail if judged according to conventional standards. That said, I just love *Nova Express*. I always liked it, but the more I worked on the new edition the more I really *got it*. I adore its ferocious humor. I'm hooked by its tone of voice. I'm mesmerized by its strange poetic recombinations of phrases. And then what I discovered in the archives was an astonishing wealth of source and draft material. The manuscript history was just so unexpectedly *interesting*, so rich and strange. And there was so much of it: for editing purposes, I worked with more manuscripts for *Nova Express* than the other two titles, even though it had seemed self-evidently the simplest. But editing *The Soft Machine* was not fun and games; it more or less drove me mad and while I came up with a solution that satisfied me, which I explain in the Introduction, it didn't make up for two years of intense work struggling with the texts of all three *Soft Machines* and their manuscript histories.

I should explain that I'd spent three years working on *Junky*, *Queer*, and *The Yage Letters*—that's three years for each edition. Maybe someone else could have done the work faster, but I didn't want to rush books that would be the standard editions for the foreseeable future. That's a unique pressure: a critical book, a journal article, an online essay, an interview—they're ephemeral in comparison. My editions needed to last, so I took my time. But for *The Soft Machine, Nova Express*, and *The Ticket That Exploded*, I worked in an entirely different way. I'd been preparing for twenty years, on and off, but I did the manuscript research and editing of all three books in under two years. Bang, bang, bang. The workload involved was simply ridiculous. I never stopped. But working so intensely immersed me in the peculiar medium of cut-up textuality and gave me the momentum to believe in what I was doing. And so although each cut-up text was exponentially more difficult than the earlier books, it was probably the only way to get them done.

SCHNEIDERMAN This co-editorial process of the three suggests, if only in editorial practice if not in authorial process, that you are comfortable with the stabilizing of the books *as a trilogy*. Your introductions complicate this, but the reception history and the simultaneous publications of the three volumes at the centennial suggest cohesiveness. When and how did you make your peace with it?

HARRIS You put your finger on a major contradiction, and it's one that applies to all stages of the writing, publication, and reception of the three titles we have come to call "the trilogy." That's what I was getting at before, in making the distinction between *a* trilogy and *the* trilogy: the cut-up books clearly belong together, and yet they shouldn't be isolated from the rest of Burroughs' cut-up project, from all the connected work in other media he did alongside assembling the books. To refer to *the trilogy* removes the books from that larger project and identifies them too glibly.

More than that, it's amazing to realize that neither Burroughs nor his publishers referred to this "trilogy" during the decade of their publications; in the 1960s, the only "trilogies" Burroughs mentioned start from *Naked Lunch* and leave out either *Nova Express* or *The Ticket That Exploded*. Of course, critics talked about "the cut-up trilogy" from the 1970s onwards—although two of the earliest didn't: Eric Mottram preferred to speak of a "tetralogy" and Philippe Mikriammos rightly called it a "false trilogy" (1975: 77). But as for publishers, in Britain, when John Calder republished *The Ticket* in 1985, he introduced it as the "last part of the trilogy of novels that began with *The Naked Lunch*," unifying the titles first published in Paris by Olympia Press. Calder simply ignored *Nova Express*, no doubt because in the UK it was issued by a rival publisher, Jonathan Cape. The first and *only* time I've ever come across Burroughs referring to "the cut-up trilogy" was in conversation with Allen Ginsberg in an interview from 1992—which was also the year that Grove in effect made the trilogy official by reprinting the three volumes in a single cover design (with the titles in Dadaesque typography spilling over colored backgrounds—orange for *The Ticket*, green for *Nova Express*, pink for *The Soft Machine*).

SCHNEIDERMAN And yet the new covers have a tag line...

HARRIS Yes, Grove Press have now reaffirmed *the trilogy* with their simultaneous launching of the "restored" editions featuring the tag line "A book of the Cut-Up Trilogy" on the front covers. The tag line was not my idea, I might add; far from it. And yet it's understandable why Grove would want to promote the three titles so emphatically. It's the obvious way to invite readers to buy all three volumes. Ironically, they're applying the same commercial logic that cut against promoting "the trilogy" back in the 1960s, when there were bitter disputes between Burroughs' three publishers (Grove, Olympia Press, and John Calder). On the other hand, Grove also gave mixed messages in their book designs: the tag line links the three titles together, but the front cover art by Roberto de Vicq de Cumptich connects them to all the other Burroughs books currently being published by Grove, from *Junky* to *Naked Lunch* and *The Adding Machine*. The desire for this Burroughs "series look" trumped objections to blurring the distinctions between such different books.

As you point out, my introductions try to complicate "the trilogy" in a number of ways—above all, by arguing against the universally accepted sequence, which I believe is totally misleading—but you have to accept its stability to some extent, even if only so that it can be called into question.

SCHNEIDERMAN Fascinating, particularly as I came to these books through the 1992 Grove editions. I am a Burroughs reader primarily through that entry point (via a mall store Waldenbooks in Allentown, PA, no less). We are therefore dealing with what is now twice officially affirmed as a trilogy (which is not *one* but *several*), and which has the imprimatur of the centennial to add additional heft to its canonicity. This suggests a key question: is now the right time *because* of the centennial, or because conditions on the ground now allow the material history to come in for unpacking?

HARRIS There are two pragmatic reasons for the new editions. First, because it *could* be done, now that the archival materials were available. Back in the 1990s it didn't make much sense to work on the manuscripts held at Ohio or Columbia because the central archive was missing; the opening of the Burroughs Papers in the Berg Collection of the New York Public Library changed all that, which is why in fall 2012 I spent three months working there, five days a week.

Second, the existing publications are uniquely unsatisfactory: three titles, six editions, routine confusion as to which one anybody else is referring to. I wasn't tempted to sort out the mess by undoing history and going back to the first editions. Rather, I saw my task in terms of rethinking the texts in light of an ongoing historical process and an accurate understanding of how they came to be—and that was the story I wanted to attach to the texts through introductions and notes.

SCHNEIDERMAN You've told me that the actual process of editing was more difficult to anticipate. You assumed *Nova Express* would be the easy one, which is why you took it up first. Its story, and the complex details of the editorial work, are issues we will take up in a conversation generated from this one. For now, readers should open the books to find the multiform coordinate points. The key is not to read the text, but to let the texts sprawl off the page in a thousand untoward directions.

OLIVER HARRIS is the editor and author of ten books, including two trilogies by William Burroughs: *Junky: The Definitive Text of "Junk,"* *The Yage Letters Redux,* and *Queer: Twenty-Fifth Anniversary Edition;* and "restored" editions of the Cut-Up Trilogy: *The Soft Machine, Nova Express,* and *The Ticket That Exploded.* He is also the editor of *The Letters of William S. Burroughs, 1945–1959* and *Everything Lost: The Latin American Notebook of William S. Burroughs,* the author of the critical study *William*

Burroughs and the Secret of Fascination and co-editor of *Naked Lunch@50:*
Anniversary Essays. He is Professor of American Literature at Keele
University and President of the European Beat Studies Network.

DAVIS SCHNEIDERMAN's works include the DEAD/BOOKS trilogy, including
the blank novel *BLANK*, the plagiarized novel [*SIC*], and the ink-smeared novel
INK (forthcoming); along with the novel *Drain.* He co-edited the collections
Retaking the Universe: Williams S. Burroughs in the Age of Globalization and
The Exquisite Corpse: Chance and Collaboration in Surrealism's Parlor Game.
He has written on Burroughs for many publications, including *The Journal*
of Beat Studies, and *Naked Lunch@50: Anniversary Essays*, and performs and
records as part of the audio-collective The Muttering Sickness. He blogs for the
Huffington Post. He is Associate Dean of the Faculty and Director of the Center
for Chicago Programs, as well as Professor of English and Director of Lake
Forest College Press/&NOW Books at Lake Forest College near Chicago.

NOTE

1. After the first printings of *The Waste Land* in 1922, subsequent publications included a series
of notes by T. S. Eliot, mainly glossing the structure and literary references of his poem, a highly
unusual act of self-annotation.

REFERENCES

Burroughs, William S. 2003. *Junky: The Definitive Text of "Junk."* Edited by Oliver Harris. New
    York: Penguin.
———. 2008. *Everything Lost: The Latin American Notebook.* Edited by Oliver Harris, Geoffrey D.
    Smith and John M. Bennett. Columbus: Ohio University Press.
———. 2010. *Queer: 25th Anniversary Edition.* Edited by Oliver Harris. New York: Penguin.
———. 2014. *Nova Express: the Restored Text.* Edited by Oliver Harris. New York: Grove Press.
———. 2014. *The Soft Machine: the Restored Text.* Edited by Oliver Harris. New York: Grove Press.
———. 2014. *The Ticket That Exploded: The Restored Text.* Edited by Oliver Harris. New York:
    Grove Press.
Burroughs, William S., and Allen Ginsberg. 2006. *The Yage Letters Redux.* Edited by Oliver Harris.
    San Francisco: City Lights.
Deleuze, Gilles, and Félix Guattari. 1987. *A Thousand Plateaus.* Trans. Brian Massumi. Minneapo-
    lis: University of Minnesota Press.
Harris, Oliver. 2003. *William S. Burroughs and the Secret of Fascination.* Carbondale: Southern Il-
    linois University Press.
———. 2004. "Cutting Up Politics." In *Retaking the Universe: William S. Burroughs in the Age of*
    Globalization, edited by Davis Schneiderman and Philip Walsh, 175–200. London: Pluto
    Press.
———. 2010. "Confusion's Masterpiece." Available at https://realitystudio.org/scholarship/
    confusions-masterpiece/
Mikriamos, Philippe. 1975. *William S. Burroughs: La Vie et l'oeuvre.* Paris: Seghers.
Miles, Barry. 2014. *Call Me Burroughs: A Life.* New York: Twelvetree Press.
Mottram, Eric. 1975. *William Burroughs: The Algebra of Need.* London: Boyars.
Schneiderman, Davis. "The Miraculous and Mucilaginous Paste Pot: Extra-illustration and Pla-
    giary in the Burroughs Legacy." *Journal of Beat Studies* 2 (2013): 53–79.

The Photo Collage: Watergate

Burroughs' essay, "The Photo Collage" (Berg 35.51), is appended with a mysterious note in the original Berg file: "1962. Final version lost in Paris Office Of Olympia Press." If the final draft was lost under mysterious circumstances, this archival piece still provides a window into Burroughs' thinking at this time, early in his experiments with photomontage. In the Berg file, multiple drafts of this essay recur, leading up to this relatively polished version. Another version of this manuscript, Berg 43.56, is notably located in a file of miscellaneous materials relating to his time in Chicago during the Democratic National Convention in 1968. Berg 43.57 is almost the same essay, but it is entitled "The Photo Montage." As just one of many examples in which Burroughs sought to make "statements" out of his use of collage/montage, we provide along with this dense essay one of Burroughs' previously unseen, most spectacular collages, from late in his cut-up experiments, in 1973.

This collage was produced in response to the Watergate scandal, as an addendum to his *Harper's* November 1973 article, "Playback from Eden to Watergate." That piece extends and was reworked into his 1970 manifesto, *The Electronic Revolution*, when republishing it for the 1973 edition. If there is any image that Burroughs hoped would accompany his manifesto, *The Electronic Revolution*, surely it is this illustration of Part One's title: "The Feedback from Watergate to the Garden of Eden." Here we can see Burroughs juxtaposing *Newsweek*'s July 30, 1973, reporting on Watergate (including the magazine's own collage image of a tape recorder superimposed onto the White House) with two of William Blake's Large Colour Prints series begun in 1775, *God Judging Adam* and *Nebuchednazzar*. The latter illustration depicts the Old Testament Babylonian King Nebuchadnezzar's hubristic fall from grace, depicted as mad, crawling into a cave.

In this striking collage, Burroughs returns to the theme that dominated and motivated his work, more than ten years after he first articulated, in the "Hassan's Rumpus Room" chapter of *Naked Lunch* (1959), his parodic vision of the modern Mr. America falling through an industrial wasteland in imitation of Bruegel's famous painting, *Landscape with the Fall of Icarus* (1558). Burroughs' configuration of Blake illustrations and 1970s newspaper articles provides a poignant example of his multimedia efforts to document the American empire's decline. Just as God says to Adam in the passage of Genesis, 3:17–19, which Blake illuminated, so Burroughs' artwork seems to warn his nation, "Cursed is the ground because of you . . . for dust you are, and to dust you will return."

—*AWC*

1

The Surrealists formed collages in the 1920s at that time being
simply an arrangement of things and pictures presented as xx art
object—They did not develope the formula further to take photos
of the collage and use these photos in arranging collage abstracts
and concentrates—They did not see the collage as a silent language
of juxtaposition that can be learned and used to xxxx make state--
ments—
A Soviet scientist has said: "We will travel not only in space but
in time as well."—Perhaps,but certainly not with the baggage that
most of us carry—body baggage—word baggage—memory baggage—The
photo collage is a way to travel that must be used with skill and
precision if we are to arrive—In this article i suggest collage
projects that may be useful in exploring this means of travel—
I-Make Time Collages: Take pictures of Athens at all time from
Ancient Greek reconstructions-museum photos of Attic vases,
sculpture, frieze,temples-to present time streets parks and cafes—
Arrage collage-Take-Rearrange-Take—The collages can be panoramic
or precise—You can trace time lines down one street or flash a
city—You can mix in time collages of other cities and places—
2- Make Space Collages: Photos of the South Seas, Mexico, China,
Morocco, The Amazon jungle, Scandanavia, fitted together at points of
juxtaposition—(tress, streets, shadows, fog and London opens into
misty dawn rain forest—Oslo park sculpture under wheeling vultures
in the Plaza Bolivar, Lima Peru and so forth—
3A Make Collage Concentrates: Taek all your misty daw nphotos-
Make a collage —Take angle shots,mirror shots, close ups and distance
shots—superimpose—double expose—Select the Photos that convey mist
and dawn—Rearrange—Take—And so forth to a mist-dawn concentrate--
B-Make mood Concentrates: Take photos of celebrating crowds—
Armistice Day—Indepednece Days—Carnivals—Arragge celebration
collage—Take—Rearrange—Take your bleak lonely photos—Your

******

[autograph]: "1962"   "find version lost in Paris office of Olympia Press"

Make color concentrates—Take all your blue pictures and arrange
a blue collage—Take your red pcitures and your green pictures—
Now mix colors xxxxxxxxxxx and paint in collage—You can
of course use reproductions or original painting as part of your
collage—All the colors xxxxxxxxxxxxxxxx of all the

The Photo Collage, William S.Burroughs (8 × 11, 2 leaves, typescript) (Berg 35.51). Folio
104, Item 51, The Photo Collage. Typescript, in autograph: "1962. Final version lost in Paris
Office Of Olympia Press." Half of page 2 is in autograph mss. (There are 5 annotations.)
Copyright © by William Burroughs, used by permission of The Wylie Agency LLC.

art galleries are there for you to use—Attic vases—Persian
miniatures-- taperstries—frescos—canvases—
The collage as a flexible hieroglyph language of juxgtaposition:
A collage makes a statement—You will learn the language of
collage through use and build up files so that you can mix and
recombine with precision to xxx talk in pcitures—I have made
the experiment of writing a chapter and then saying the same
making the same statement in collage form—xxxxxxxxxxxxx
reproduced here illustrates a chapter entitled FROM A LAND OF
GRASS WITHOUT MIRRORS—
In the following example of cut up prose- Which is the col lage
principle applied to words-i have translated from word to collage
and back—shifting from collage to words passages from work in
progress—

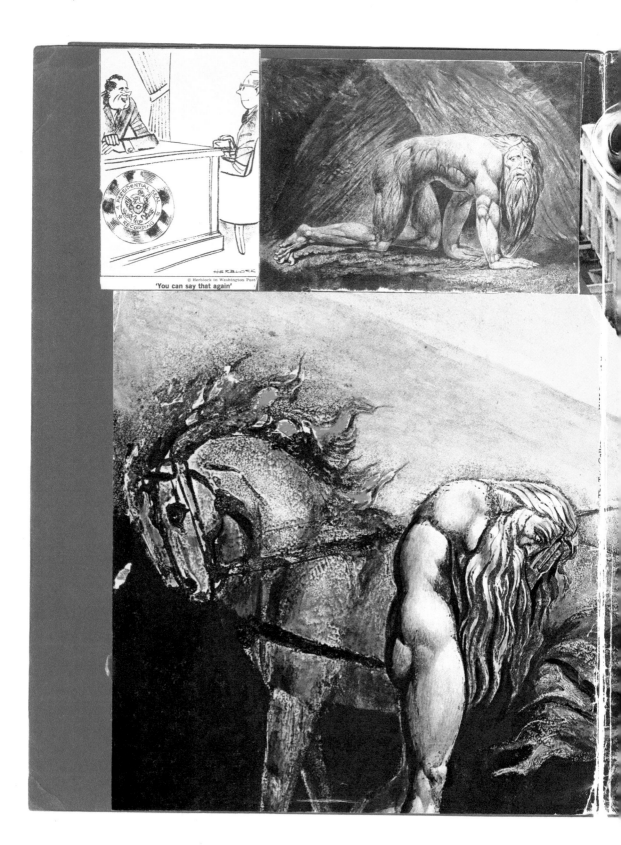

© Herblock in Washington Post
'You can say that again'

15

"Word Falling ... Photo Falling": William S. Burroughs and the Word as Written Image

BLAKE STRICKLIN

In his January 1976 column for *Crawdaddy* magazine, William S. Burroughs recalls a question he posed to Jasper Johns in London. Burroughs remembers asking Johns "what painting was all about—what are painters really doing," to which Johns counters: "what is writing all about" (Burroughs 2013, 75)? The essay for *Crawdaddy*, later published in *The Adding Machine* (2013) as "The Fall of Art," first responds to this question about writing through visual art. The first draft of the essay, titled "La Chute De l'Art," focuses more on art than writing, but in another draft entitled "La Chute De Le Mot," Burroughs puts the emphasis back on literature. Yet visual art and literature are seldom separate in Burroughs' concept of writing, as he notes in the essay: "Writing and painting were one in the beginning and the word was written image" (79). Such a written image gives further insight into a process Burroughs calls the cut-up method. This writing not only uses non-literary techniques as a model for composition but also moves literature away from the alphabet to a more pictorial sign system.

Because the essay relates Burroughs' writing to a nonliterary tradition, which includes Burroughs' concept of the hieroglyph, "The Fall of Art" (and its drafts) remains an important expository text on his cut-up method of composition. Burroughs explains this concept of the pictorial word in more detail in "La Chute De Le Mot." The *Crawdaddy* draft for "The Fall of Art" includes passages from other works: "Electronic Revolution" and Burroughs' illustrated text, *The Book of Breeething*. Both sources favor a more visual language that opens the word to multiple associations and juxtapositions. Burroughs approaches narrative this way when he rewrites and combines disparate texts through textual collage, or what he calls the "cut-up method."

"The Fall of Art," as James Grauerholz notes in his introduction to *The Adding Machine*, began as an assignment for the contemporary art journal *Art in America*. Through his relationship with the artist David Budd, who "had emblazoned Burroughs' words on abstract sculptures," Burroughs was asked to contribute an article for the journal. However, the predictions about the future of conceptual art he makes in the article had *already* occurred, and the journal thought it unwise to publish a "critic" so unaware of contemporary art history (Grauerholz 2013, xviii).

In the essay, Burroughs quotes the famous line from Brion Gysin that "writing is fifty years behind painting." It matters little, then, if the future of art Burroughs envisions has already occurred because "writing is still confined in the sequential representational straitjacket of the novel" (Burroughs 2013, 76). If the novel has a future, then it must learn from the techniques already used in painting, film, and other media.

Thus, Burroughs attempts to divert the novel from its literary past in "The Fall of Art" by associating the cut-ups with painting, but he also discusses the method in relation to other media in a lecture later published as "The Future of the Novel" (1998). Burroughs notes how the cut-up or the fold-in method "is of course used in music, where we are continually moved backward and forward on the time track by repetition and rearrangements." He also finds how the "fold-in method extends to writing the flashback used in films" (272). In a paragraph cut from "The Fall of Art," Burroughs mentions his collaboration with filmmaker Anthony Balch on *The Cut-Ups* (1966). Burroughs remembers a theater manager telling him "that in all of his experiences as a theatre manager . . . he had never seen so many people who came to the box office furiously demanding a refund of their money" ("Le Chute De L'Art," circa 1970s, 4). These cut-up films directly disturbed the viewing public's senses, and Burroughs compares the audience's reaction to those who first viewed "non-representational art," where "in many cases the enraged public physically attacked the canvases" (4). Painting, as Burroughs explains in "The Fall of Art," started applying montage when its representational position was challenged by photography. Yet he notes while this remains "an old device in painting," a writer who uses montage is "accused by the critics of promulgating a cult of unintelligibility" (2013, 76). Burroughs responds to this criticism in "The Fall of Art" with reference to the techniques already used and accepted in other media. Literary criticism appears inadequate to discuss his cut-ups because the method breaks with the history of traditional literary forms. It seems fitting that "The Fall of Art" eventually found its publication in Burroughs' column for a rock magazine.

The *Crawdaddy* article, then, offers a way of reading Burroughs' literary texts through a nonliterary discourse. A critic or reader of Burroughs' cut-up texts should at least be aware of the montage used in visual art. Reading the cut-ups requires this simultaneous acknowledgment of what a word means and how it appears on the page. Fluxus artist Dick Higgins coins a term that explains the close association between a word and image: intermedia. Higgins uses the word to define those works that "fall conceptually between media that are already known" (1984, 23). He also notes how in this intermedia(l) space "the visual element is fused conceptually with words" (24). Although Burroughs does not use Higgins's term in the essay, he explains cut-ups as a type of writing that remains closer to other media than to the novel.

In a draft for "The Fall of Art"—"La Chute De Le Mot"—Burroughs believes writers will be doing "very much what they are doing now" because "it seems there is a very foreseeable limit to what can be done with words" ("La Chute De

Le Mot," circa 1970s, 6). Burroughs is not, of course, the first writer to comment on this limitation in literature. Joseph Conrad writes in the preface to *The Nigger of the "Narcissus"* how the written word "must strenuously aspire to the plasticity of sculpture, to the color of painting, and to the magic suggestiveness of music," which will dig beneath the surface of "the old, old words" (1951, xxxix). Samuel Beckett similarly expresses the need to "bore one hole after another in [language], until what lurks behind it—be it something or nothing—begins to seep through." Beckett's 1937 letter to Axel Kaun, however, questions whether or not literature will "remain behind in the old lazy ways that have been so long ago abandoned by music and painting" (1984, 172). Modernism and the historical avant-garde also sought formal innovation through collage and montage in visual art. By linking writing with painting, Burroughs continues to connect experimental writing with techniques used in other media.

The story of Burroughs' introduction to the cut-up method in 1959 at the Beat Hotel in Paris links his writing to painting. Brion Gysin introduced Burroughs to the method after noticing the curious textual juxtapositions in the *New York Herald Tribune*, which he cut up to protect the table for a drawing (see Miles 2013, 362). Thus, what started as a routine preparation for Gysin's art incited a period of literary experimentation for Burroughs. The beginning of "The Fall of Art" makes this association between painting and cut-ups clear, and Burroughs elsewhere notes how the writer can learn from the painter: "The painter can touch and handle his medium and the writer cannot . . . The painter's ability to touch and handle his medium led to montage techniques sixty years ago. It is to be hoped that the extension of cut-up techniques will lead to more precise verbal experiments closing this gap and giving a whole new dimension to writing" (Odier 1969, 27). The cut-up and fold-in methods give writers a more tactile relationship with their medium. Burroughs attempts to replace the outdated techniques and forms of literary writing with the formal innovations of twentieth-century art. Writing, thus, looks toward a future that has already happened, as for Burroughs it still lags behind the techniques used in twentieth-century visual art.

Yet Burroughs imagines another future in "The Fall of Art." He asks "if art changed so much in the past hundred years, what will artists be doing in fifty years or hundred years from now" (2013, 77). Burroughs imagines a type of "exploding art," where "a self-destroying TV set, a refrigerator, washing-machine, and electric stove going off, leaving a shambles of gleaming modern apartment." He also suggests the "young art hustlers" use ammonium iodide in their paintings, which "when it dries is so sensitive that a fly will explode [the canvas]" (77). This "exploding art," which sounds like neo-Dada, will bring back the "old-time potlatches" that will lead to the fall of the art market.

To overdramatize his point, Burroughs associates the future of writing with the exploding galleries he imagines in the essay, and if art will incorporate "potlatches" in fifty years, then literature will follow. "La Chute De'l Art" ["Fall of Art"] brings about "La Chute Du Mot" ["The Fall of Words"]. Burroughs imagines how a "book about Poland in a typhus epidemic has typhus lice concealed in the bindings, to be released as Book-of-the-Month-Club ladies turn pages." Even beach reading is no longer safe in Burroughs' future of the book, where "the reader is no longer safely reading about sharks while she belches out chocolate fumes; on the page is a powerful shark attractant" (2013, 79). Writing no longer just follows the techniques used in contemporary painting. At this "magical origin" where the word and image are one, writing and painting both work toward the same goal of "producing definitive effects," on the reader.

This literal eruption of the word in "The Fall of Art" makes the narratives dangerously real to the reader. This is the purpose of writing, according to Burroughs' answer to Johns: "To make it happen" (2013, 75). Burroughs prefaces his answer with two paragraphs, which were cut from the *Crawdaddy* article, on writers who make it happen. The opening paragraph finds its way into Burroughs' essay, "Remembering Jack Kerouac," and Burroughs remarks how Kerouac wrote about a generation waiting to be written. Clearly referring to the Beats here, he finds by "writing a universe a writer makes such a universe possible." Burroughs also notes how science fiction "has a way of coming true fifty years later" ("La Chute De Le Mot," circa 1970s, 3). This is the potential future in a text that occurs at the "magical origin" of art, which Burroughs defines at the beginning of the essay. He notes: "What we call art—painting, sculpture, writing, dance, music—is magical in origin. That is, it was originally employed for ceremonial purposes to produce definite effects" (2013, 75). Burroughs connects art with earlier civilizations, where both "writing and painting were one in cave paintings, which were magical formulae to ensure good hunting" ("La Chute De Le Mot," circa 1970s, 3) Cave painters were trying to kill an actual edible animal through these drawings. Burroughs stresses how the cave painters accomplish their goal with these depictions.

While the textual cut-ups mostly do not abandon words, Burroughs does associate pictorial writing with the cut-up method. One of the cut-ups Burroughs made from a *Time* article predicted that the author's son would sue him, which did happen three years later. Burroughs concludes from this, "Perhaps events are prewritten and prerecorded and when you cut word lines the future leaks out" (Odier 1969, 28). His experiments with tape recorders also produce similar effects, which Burroughs discusses in "Invisible Generation" and "Electronic Revolution." On tape recorders "riot sound effects can produce an actual riot in a riot situation. Recorded police whistles will draw cops. Recorded gunshots, and their guns are out" (175). A prerecorded sound not only anticipates a future event, it also forces it into existence. The tape recorder becomes a more critical apparatus in *The Ticket That Exploded* (2014), where sounds and words are prerecorded. Following Wittgenstein's statement that "no proposition can contain itself in an argument," the narrative suggests, "the only thing not prerecorded in a prerecorded universe is the prerecording itself which is to say *any* recording that contains a random factor"

(Burroughs 2014, 188). The cut-ups introduce a random factor in the prerecorded universe, as cutting up a text makes language less static and opens it to every possible enunciation. Numerous scenes in *The Ticket That Exploded* instruct the writer (or recorder) to "cut in bulletins from Rewrite [department]," which will "always create as many insoluble counterorders and alternative conflicts recordings to the explosion of a planet" (193). Similar to the ammonium iodide that explodes canvases in "The Fall of Art," the cut-ups create a combustible effect on a text when Burroughs rewrites narrative.

In a paragraph cut from "The Fall of Art," Burroughs raises the question of "what is the word," and this question frequently appears in Burroughs' other texts. *Naked Lunch*'s (2009) atrophying preface finds "the Word is divided into units which can all be one piece and should be so taken, but the pieces can be had in any order" (191). The way Burroughs defines the word in *Naked Lunch* also describes the book's formal structure, as the narrator instructs the reader to "cut into *Naked Lunch* at any intersection point" (187). Burroughs discourages a linear reading of *Naked Lunch* in his preface, which goes against how a reader would traditionally read a book. The "atrophied preface" not only unsettles how one reads a novel, it also suggests there are multiple entrances into the text and "the Word."

"La Chute De Le Mot" discusses this concept of a more open and variable language in greater detail than the published *Crawdaddy* essay. The majority of the discussion Burroughs cuts from the article appears in *The Book of Breeething* (1975), which begins with a reference to Alfred Korzybski. Korzybski, as Burroughs notes, wrote about General Semantics in *Science and Sanity* that "pointed out that the *is of identity* has led to basic confusion in Western thought" (Burroughs 1975, 1). The "is of identity" concerns statements of identity rather than relations, and Burroughs elaborates on this concept more in "Electronic Revolution." He comments on the limitation of an article like "the," where "THE universe locks you into THE, and denies the possibility of any other. If other universes are possible, then the universe no longer becomes THE it becomes A" (quoted in Odier 1969, 201). A less definitive article opens language to multiple juxtapositions, which the cut-up method practices by "shift[ing] linguals" or "cut[ting] [the]word line."

The tape recorder remains an ideal apparatus for cutting word lines, since it allows for "effects of simultaneity, echoes, speed-ups, slow downs, [or] playing three tracks at once." Yet Burroughs notes these effects "cannot be indicated on the printed page" (quoted in Odier 1969, 29). His film with Antony Balch, *Bill and Tony*, shows Burroughs' tape recorder experiments. In the film, Burroughs splices his voice onto Balch's talking head, and vice versa. Burroughs pushes past the limitation of the printed page by extending his literary experiments into other media, and while Burroughs never abandons writing, he does ask in *The Ticket That Exploded*: "Do you need words—Try some other method of communication, like color flashes—a Morse code of color flashes—or odors or music or tactile sensations" (2014, 165). Such suspicion of the word demands a new vocabulary that turns words away from the alphabet.

Burroughs notes a pictorial script like Egyptian writing expresses this open language more than the traditional alphabet. Pictorial writing, he finds, is "more capable of infinite variation. The English word leg has to be written in one way. A pictorial leg can be written as any number of legs" (1975, 3). Although Burroughs uses English letters in the cut-up texts, the narrative logic of the cut-ups resembles a pictorial script. This move toward more graphic writing in the twentieth century goes back (at least) to Ezra Pound's promotion of Ernest Fenollosa's "Chinese Written Character as a Medium for Poetry" (1967). The Chinese script expresses a more fluid writing, where "all processes are interrelated; and thus there could be no complete sentence save which it would take all time to pronounce" (1967, 365). Not unlike the endless sentence Fenollosa finds in the Chinese ideogram, the cut-up method continually rewrites texts without putting a period on the process.

As Fenollosa comments on the interrelated processes of a more pictorial sign, Burroughs' cut-up compositions connect and juxtapose disparate texts. Such a textual collage might place lines from Shakespeare next to a headline from today's newspaper. Burroughs' cut-ups, then, ignore simple temporal lines, as it opens past texts to future textual associations. Writers who make it happen, according to Burroughs, write a future before it happens, and "The Fall of Art" aligns this writing with a more visual language. The alphabet, as media critic Vilém Flusser notes, was "developed as the code of historical consciousness," and "if we give up the alphabet, it will surely be to supersede historical consciousness" (2011, 35). Beckett comments how the words in James Joyce's *Finnegans Wake* are alive because Joyce writes with the "savage economy of hieroglyphics" instead of "the polite contortions of printer's ink" (1929, 15–16). Yet the language in the *Wake* does not completely turn its back to the past as Flusser might find, but instead recreates it infinitely. Frank Budgen notes how a reader of Joyce's text can "see the changes of a million years lying exposed in a few square feet" (1929, 45) on the page. *Finnegans Wake* "recirculates" history through a collage of disparate cultural texts and languages. Burroughs' "economy of the hieroglyph" similarly displaces past texts from their historical context in order to create and recreate a complex network of infinite textual associations.

The "old-time potlatches" and exploding canvases in "The Fall of Art" destroy the work moments after its creation, which prevents its recording in the archive. The act of ritual destruction, then, replaces the work by becoming the work of art itself. This might explain why so much of the narrative in the cut-up "novels" is spent describing the cut-up method itself. What Burroughs terms "operation rewrite" becomes the object of the cut-up narrative, and much of *The Ticket That Exploded* describes how it rewrites *The Ticket That Exploded*. With this conscious attention to composition, Burroughs asks readers to interpret the cut-up texts' writing instead of their meaning.

The terms Burroughs uses to indicate the process of the cut-ups often appear in the narrative and include the alternate titles for "The Fall of Art." *The Ticket That Exploded* repeats the phrases "Word Falling . . . Photo Falling," which describes the erasure of the word (and image). Burroughs also notes when writers "rub out the word . . . the image track goes with it" (2014, 164). The concept of "rubbing out the word" appears in an early cut-up text, *The Exterminator*, which includes a poem by Gysin that reads:

RUB   OUT   THE   WORDS
RUB   OUT   THE
WORDS

(Burroughs and Gysin 1960, 43)

On the next page of the text, Gysin "rubs out the words" by replacing the letters with more visual words:

RUB   OUT   THE   WORDS
$ %   &
$ %
&

(Burroughs and Gysin 1960, 44)

In Gysin's poem, "&" replaces "words" to create the pictorial language Burroughs associates with the cut-up method in "The Fall of Art." The cut-ups approach narrative the moment a word or text slips into this less determinate sign.

Burroughs' concept of the "word as written image" removes the rigid lines of a language centered only on representation. Burroughs notes in *The Book of Breeething* how "we may forget that a written word is an image and that written words are images in sequence that is to say *moving pictures*" (1975, 3). Although he associates the cut-up technique with cinema elsewhere, Burroughs finds that the "word-image" already writes in cinematic montage. The textual montage implicit in pictorial writing further highlights the variability of this language. Gilles Deleuze's commentary on cinema defines this movement-image through a reading of Henri Bergson. As Deleuze explains, "Everything, that is to say every image, is indistinguishable from its actions and reactions: this is universal variation" (1986, 60). As Gysin's poem shows, cut-ups replace a word with a more visual sign that opens writing to a process of variation and becoming. Cut-ups create a writing machine that Deleuze might define as "acentered," where "there are not yet bodies or rigid lines, but only lines or figures of light" (62). The "word as written image" eliminates the lines that separate texts, as "Shakespeare, Rimbaud, etc." permutate "through page frames in constantly changing juxtaposition" (Burroughs 2014, 73).

"The Fall of Art" first discusses the cut-up technique's imitation of visual art, but Burroughs' theory of "the word as written image" stresses the visual in the word. While criticism on the cut-up method should consider Burroughs' comments on art, his concept of writing actually embraces a larger media environment. The cut-ups and Burroughs' explanation of the method anticipate digital composition. Burroughs already describes this collision in his concept for "the word as written image." Burroughs also moves alphabetic writing toward the "magical" sign of the hieroglyph. This situation is not far from Flusser's comments on digital writing. Flusser notes, "as the alphabet originally advanced against pictograms, digital codes today advance against letters to overtake them" (2011, 147). Burroughs' theory of the word in "The Fall of Art" (and its draft "La Chute De Le Mot") remains just as relevant (perhaps more so) to twenty-first-century concepts of writing as they were when the article was first published.

BLAKE STRICKLIN is Visiting Assistant Professor at Florida State University, where he teaches courses in American literature and media studies. Stricklin is currently working on an interactive website for the William S. Burroughs archive at Florida State University, which will allow users to generate their own cut-ups from the archival material.

REFERENCES

Primary

Burroughs, William S. "Le Chute De L'Art." Undated typescript a. circa 1970s. William S. Burroughs Papers, Florida State University.
———. "La Chute De Le Mot." Undated typescript b. circa 1970s. William S. Burroughs Papers, Florida State University.

Secondary

Beckett, Samuel. 1929. "Dante . . . Bruno. Vico . . . Joyce." In *Our Exagmination Round His Factification for His Incamination of Work in Progress*, 3–22. New York: New Directions.
———. 1984. *Disjecta*. New York: Grove.
Budgen, Frank. 1929. "James Joyce's *Work in Progress* and Old Norse Poetry." In *Our Exagmination Round His Factification for His Incamination of Work in Progress*, 37–46. New York: New Directions.
Burroughs, William S. 1975. *The Book of Breeething*. Berkeley, CA: Blue Wind.
———. 1998. "The Future of the Novel." In *Word Virus: The William S. Burroughs Reader*. Edited by James Grauerholz and Ira Silverberg, 72–73. New York: Grove.
———. 2009. *Naked Lunch: The Restored Text*. Edited by James Grauerholz and Barry Miles. New York: Grove. First published 1959.
———. 2013. *The Adding Machine*. New York: Grove. First published 1985.
———. 2014. *The Ticket That Exploded: The Restored Text*. Edited by Oliver Harris. New York: Grove. First published 1962.
Burroughs, William S., and Brion Gysin. 1960. *The Exterminator*. San Francisco: Dave Haselwood Books.
Conrad, Joseph. 1951. *The Nigger of the Narcissus*. New York: Harper. First published 1897.
Deleuze, Gilles. 1986. *Cinema 1: The Movement-Image*. Translated by Hugh Tomlinson and Barbara Habberjam. Minneapolis: University of Minnesota Press.

Fenollosa, Ernest. 1967. "The Chinese Character as a Medium for Poetry." In *Instigations of Ezra Pound*, 357–88. Freeport, NY: Books for Libraries Press.

Flusser, Vilém. 2011. *Does Writing Have A Future?* Translated by Nancy Ann Roth. Minneapolis: University of Minnesota Press.

Grauerholz, James. 2013. Introduction to *The Adding Machine*, by William S. Burroughs, vii–xxii. New York: Grove.

Higgins, Dick. 1984. *Horizons: The Poetics and Theory of the Intermedia*. Carbondale: Southern Illinois University Press.

Miles, Barry. 2013. *Call Me Burroughs: A Life*. New York: Twelve.

Odier, Daniel. 1969. *The Job: Interviews with William S. Burroughs*. New York: Penguin.

Cutting Up Scientology

We conclude the *Cut/Fold* section with examples of Burroughs' experiments with Scientology material. In good earnest, Burroughs had tried to cut up Scientology audits, the processing system supposed to lead toward psychic improvement; yet, as evident in the final collage piece, Scientology's methods became increasingly suspicious to Burroughs, as little more than a cult-leader's technique to impose mind control. As documented in David S. Wills's book, *Scientologist!: William S. Burroughs and the 'Weird Cult'* (2013), Burroughs had a long, tumultuous relationship with L. Ron Hubbard's sci-fi religion. Whereas Burroughs first had hoped that Scientology's methods could serve as externalized, technological enhancements for spiritual development and mental refinement (as improvements upon Alfred Korzybski's "extensions") Burroughs recognized by the late 1960s that Scientology methods using the E-meter were operating as a type of "computerized method of thought control" (July 22, 1969, letter to John Cooke, *Rub Out the Words*, 302).

These cut-ups are located in significant sub-directories of the Berg archive: whereas "Cut In with Scientology Lit" was composed in 1963 and appears in "Folio 104 Mss Pages From Various Periods All Identified," "Some Phrases From Scientology Procedures Cut-In" appears in Folio 65 "Illustrating Cut-Ups With Other Writers." If the date of these cut-ups and their labeling as "cut-ins" and "cut-ups *with*" suggest that Burroughs was cutting up Scientology literature at this time in a relatively collaborative venture, by the time he created the collage for his mock-up news-mag, *MOB* (My Own Business), Burroughs had become adamantly opposed to Scientology. The collage, "MOB: Which Side Are You On Ron?," appears in Folio 82, the same "Dream Rat" calendar that contains "TO BE=TO" and the "Opium Collage," arguably suggesting a logic of addiction underlying Burroughs' critique of Scientology. These materials, after all, are only the tip of the iceberg when it comes to Burroughs' cut-ups of Scientology. The Berg archive contains a separate series from its main set of 169 Folios, dedicated solely to Scientology. According to Miles, "Scientology Series II consists of 11 files," labeled A–K, containing "writings on scientology authored by William S. Burroughs, publications and drafts of texts related to scientology authored by others, audit report forms, and correspondence related to scientology" ("Descriptive Catalogue").

In his collage work, "MOB: Which Side Are You On Ron?" (1970), Burroughs creates a mock-up of one of his faux newspapers designed to challenge L. Ron Hubbard. Burroughs produced this collage when he was publishing in the men's magazine *Mayfair*, on March 1, 1970, an article entitled "I William S. Burroughs Challenge You L. Ron Hubbard." With the title flanked by illustrated vases, Burroughs' verbal provocation to L. Ron Hubbard in this collage is framed by a black and white photo of the American sage John Starr Cooke and a semi-nude young man whose sexuality seems to challenge the puritanical edge of Hubbard's theocratic, corporate enterprise. This collage, then, can be seen not just as an illustration or supplement to his essay, but a subtle example of Burroughs' cut-up practice serving to cast a curse on the oligarchic groups he saw manipulating the populace for their own insidious purposes.

—*AWC*

On February 10,1963 I wnet first goal clear for about three
Minues and then returned to session was plunged into second
goal's GPM. I just had time to eat a few peanuts and drink a
Pepsi-Cola in a session break before the auditor askedtt the
Next fatal question that threw me into the second GPM. But
it was very nice.Sort of cool and clean.If it had only been
that it would have been reward for thirteen years of sweating
over other people's hot cases.Auditor; Mary Sue Hubbard.Number
of Rocket Reading Reliable Items: twenty four plus goal.Preper
Preperation R2-I2 and 2-12A about 140 hours. Clearing process
Routine 3-MX.Four reliable items deep into third goal which is
as yet unknown. but will have to stop and polish off second
goal to free the needle then find third goal and so on.However
I felt now that routine 3-M had arrived it was time to grapple
With the bank and move on up towards O.T. As Mary Sue said'youve
been clear.Now youre a first goal clear.' Well that's as may
be.I'm en route   to O.T. anyway with at this writing the second
goal almost blown.We sure have the technology. All we have to do
is learn it and use it.Things are calm on the Washington front
and under good control. I'm sure proud of the way they are
standing up under fire.I'm sort of beginning to feel sorry for
the government.Should be one of those leap out at you all at
once springs.

[autograph]:
Cut in with Scientology Lit

Cut In with Scientology Lit, William S. Burroughs, 1963 (8 × 11, 2 leaves, typescript)
(Berg 35.18), Item 18, "On Febrary 10. . .". From Folio 104 Mss Pages From Various
Periods All Identified. Copyright © by William Burroughs, used by permission
of The Wylie Agency LLC.

I am nobody I Am every body I am meI amyou I am myself I am others
it was yor idean bnotmine shookhandswithoutenthusiasm looked sullenlt
at the floor turned abruptly away lighting a cigarette fra flung
organization rutheless agents unlimited funds you may not realize
the importanceof the Chinese preliminary experimensts lost voice
whispering in the living you name e remains as   the himan structure
nota word is mon mine I have no words leftnbreathing old pulp magasines
dust of the deadGods lonely fringes of a remo egalaxy a million light
yeasr   way the pale skies fall aprt TB waiting at the next stop spit
blood at dawn the old broekenpoint of origin St Louis Missouri semll
of sickness in the room pulled the blanket up..my face.. Flight of
geese across a gleaming empty sky Peter John Sn1882- 1904 the death
ofa child long ago i was waiting there pale character in some one
elses writing breathin oldpulp magasine turn yo   ur face a little
to eys like forget me nots flciering silver sile melted into air
the boy did not speak again sad whisprihg spiris cold andunhappy
seances where 1890 ghost materialize liie fade family photos far
away toy cars across a gleaming empty sku i890 ghost gently moving
family phtos melted into coachmen and animals of dream ashne smell
of stone road mist frm the lake cold star splahs the empyt house
far away toys spirits of the night

[autograph]: some phrases from
Scientology processes cut in

MOB

MY OWN BUSINESS   2/-

WHICH SIDE ARE YOU ON -RON?

see inside

16

Mutable Forms: The Proto-Ecology of William Burroughs' Early Cut-Ups

CHAD WEIDNER

> *"I am a fragment, and this is a fragment of me"*
>
> —Ralph Waldo Emerson (1886, 58)

William Burroughs' experimental early publications remain his most enigmatic, challenging, and least understood ones. European ecocritic Franca Bellarsi reminds us of the real need for ecocritical researchers to study not only texts written within the nature-writing genre, but avant-garde writing as well (2009, 7). If Burroughs' early writing remains a mystery, and if ecocritics need to examine experimental writing, then an important consideration is what can be learned by the application of ecocritical concepts to the most radical and experimental forms of writing such as the cut-up. If ecocritics are to break molds of conventional literary study, innovative models of analysis must be constantly developed and improved. Ecocriticism has to ultimately wrestle with limit cases such as Burroughs' most ambiguous early writing. I suggest that early cut-ups from *Minutes to Go* (1960) and *The Yage Letters* (1963) can be considered a move toward proto-ecological writing forms.

HATS OFF TO TZARA

The origins of the cut-up technique can be traced at least as far back as the historical European avant-grade. A crucial event in the development of the cut-up method took place in Paris after World War I. Dadaist leader Tristan Tzara offered to create an instant poem by randomly pulling words from a hat. It was more than just an act (Burroughs and Gysin 1978, 29). He also provided instructions on how to make a new form of poetry in "To Make a Dadaist Poem" (1920). In *Seven Dada Manifestos and Lampisteries*, Tzara called on writers to make chance an essential agent of the composition process: "Take a newspaper. / Take some scissors" (Tzara 1977, 39). The procedure requires the poet to choose an article from a newspaper. Next, the author cuts out words from the article, places them into a bag (or a hat) and gently mixes the words. The artist pulls the words out one by one, thus creating an instant poem. Tzara explains the resulting poem "will resemble you," suggesting the randomness of the act invariably provides some degree of truthfulness (ibid.). Tzara's preoccupation with cut-up forms was part of a wider aesthetic movement against the barbarism of World War I, but Brion Gysin's initiation into aleatory writing practices happened much more by chance. While living at the Beat Hotel in Paris, Gysin was in the process of preparing a wall mount when he accidentally sliced through several newspapers with a Stanley blade. This caused unusual new word combinations to appear, which Gysin found "hilariously funny and hysterically meaningful" (Burroughs and Gysin 1978, 57). He shared his find with Burroughs, who enthusiastically saw the results as revelatory in creating a new writing method. Gysin reported that Burroughs reached an epiphany and proclaimed: "Unfortunately, the means are at hand for disastrous success" (quoted in Gysin 1964, 58). Although Burroughs seemed to recognize the radical potential of cut-ups, Lydenberg believes "he had already served an unconscious cut-up apprenticeship in editing and rearranging the voluminous material that finally yielded the published version of *Naked Lunch*" (1987, 44). Uncanny links exist between the Burroughs inspired cut-up and formal Dada and Surrealist experiments a century ago.

Both Watson and Harris have considered the cut-up method in relation to the Exquisite Corpse practice. Watson puts forward that the cut-up method "offered a verbal counterpart to the Surrealist parlour game" (Watson 1995, 279). Harris has taken this further by examining specific similarities and differences between the Exquisite Corpse as a method, and the montage and the cut-up practice of Burroughs and Gysin. Harris points out that while the "Exquisite Corpse required the participation of other practitioners," the cut-up was more flexible and needed only "a sheet of typed paper and a pair of scissors" (Harris 2009, 90). Important differences also exist between Tzara's cut-up system and the practices of Gysin and Burroughs. Harris calls Tzara's approach "ironic" and "anti-aesthetic" and thinks Burroughs "intended" people to follow his practice (2004, 30). Tzara, Gysin, and Burroughs all used aleatory methods to challenge conventional narrative practices. According to Harris, from the earliest moments of their collaboration, Gysin and Burroughs viewed the cut-up method "in relation to techniques of the historical avant-garde—collage, chance operations [and] automatism" (2009, 90). Burroughs and Gysin believed they were necessarily bringing the aesthetic potential of montage and collage to writing that was already at work in the visual arts. Gysin's bold declaration that writing was five decades behind painting was a call to introduce Dada and Surrealist inspiration to literature (Burroughs and Gysin 1978, 34). Gysin and Burroughs therefore owe a permanent debt of gratitude to the historical European avant-garde. A significant element to the cut-up method involves rethinking the role of the author and reader. In this sense, the cut-up form echoes the eschatology of Dada precursors. More specifically, the historical conditions that generated the cut-up form in Paris in the 1960s parallels the emergence of Dada in Europe after World War I in many ways.

The foundation papers for the cut-up movement, *Minutes to Go* (1960) and *The Third Mind* (1978), called for a reconsideration of the idea of the all-seeing author. According to Harris, *Minutes to Go* was "the launching manifesto of the cut-up method" (2009, 84). Coauthored by Sinclair Beiles, William Burroughs, Gregory Corso, and Brion Gysin, *Minutes to Go* contains the results of the early cut-up experiments, and for this reason deserves additional critical attention. Harris too stresses the real necessity for more research into early cut-ups, which have been "effectively ignored by Burroughs' critics" (1996, 339). Harris has more recently carried out research on early cut-ups, but studies of the embryonic cut-up form remain, in the context of the wider research on Burroughs, very much the exception. The spirit of Tzara's original appeal: "Take a newspaper. / Take some scissors" is repeated in *Minutes to Go*. The reader is encouraged to adopt the cut-up method: "Pick a book any book cut it up" (Beiles et al. 1960, 4). The cut-ups in *Minutes to Go* are rather diminutive compared with the extended cut-ups of the Nova Trilogy. Early cut-ups are thus distinctive even in the broader context of Burroughs' other cut-ups; for example, each cut-up included in *Minutes to Go* is unique in terms of source material and content. Burroughs claims *Minutes to Go* "contains unedited unchanged cut-ups" (Burroughs and Gysin 1978, 29). However, the writer elsewhere acknowledged that some degree of composition was needed: "One tries not to impose story plot or continuity artificially but you do have to compose the materials, you can't just dump down a jumble of notes and thoughts and considerations and expect people to read it" (Odier 1989, 48). David Sterritt suggests that Burroughs' "cut-up spontaneity was not based on random or haphazard juxtaposition, since after cutting or folding a text . . . he would rewrite the result until it carried some degree of identifiable sense" (2000, 167). Thus, it can be said that Burroughs' cut-ups were certainly not conventional, but they were not entirely random either. However, the cut-up method did rely on an array of chance elements in the creation of the final product.

What is really important about *Minutes to Go* is the method it advocated. Gysin declares: "Here is the system according to us" (Beiles et al. 1960, 5). Harris believes the essential feature of the cut-up technique was the practice itself, which was "to be grasped by *doing*, not as a content to be understood by interpretation" (2004, 35). Ecocriticism holds that all cultural texts can be better understood through interpretation. But certainly Harris is correct in pointing out the practice of the cut-up method, the actual shearing of the text and rearrangement of the words, is essential. Whereas *Minutes to Go* was the philosophical declaration for the cut-up method, *The Third Mind* was the theoretical document. An important concept of the cut-up method was "the negation of the omnipresent and all powerful author" (Burroughs and Gysin 1978, 18). Carol Loranger claims *The Third Mind* was a direct call for "guerrilla assault on the idea of authorial ownership" (1999, 2).[1] Jeff Bryan further argues *The Third Mind* "is partly exhortative. It is a manifesto for social change and transformation of the individual" (1986, 79). Burroughs believed "new techniques, such as cut-up, will involve much more of the total capacity of the observer. It enriches the whole aesthetic experience, extends it" (Burroughs and Gysin 1978, 6). More broadly, the cut-up form questions many conventional ideas about what literature is and what it does.

The cut-up procedure seems straightforward enough, and the method forces one to consider distinctions between human and mechanical narrative agency. Burroughs explains one way to perform the cut-up technique: "Take a page. Like this page. Now cut down the middle and across the middle. You have four sections: 1 2 3 4 . . . one two three four. Now rearrange the sections placing section four with section one and section two with section three. And you have a new page" (Burroughs and Gysin 1978, 30–31). Such a seemingly simple technique can be used to generate large amounts of cut-up text. One may look at the cut-up method as a way to destroy the conventional narrative, through the violent cannibalization of the natural text. At the same time, it is essential to also consider the mechanical nature of the cut-up method. Gérard-Georges Lemaire observes that the cut-up technique is essentially a "mechanical method of shredding texts in a ruthless machine" (Burroughs and Gysin 1978, 13). The cut-up method *is* mechanical and relies on the physical destruction of the source text. However, all writing is mechanical to some degree, in the sense that writers need technological processes to reach an audience. From the earliest woodblock printing to the typewriter, mechanical processes help people express themselves.[2]

Burroughs scholars have done considerable groundwork on the cut-up project, while others have highlighted the radical nature of the practice. Lydenberg's *Word Cultures* specifically discusses the negative aesthetic of Burroughs' cut-up narratives (1987, 17). She laments the lack of scholarly engagement of the cut-up novels (55). However, Harris has observed that the "enormously fertile and innovative period of the cut-up project has enjoyed a good deal of critical attention" since Lydenberg's innovative book (Harris 2004, 25). Harris was specifically referring to scholarship on the Nova Trilogy, and not enigmatic pre-Nova cut-ups, which to this day remain woefully neglected. Ted Morgan believes the cut-up experiments were difficult to sustain for the length of a book (1988, 582). If lengthy and extended cut-ups are difficult to endure, then one can instead better consider diminutive examples from Burroughs' early period. Other Burroughs researchers highlight the radical nature of the cut-up method. Similarly to Lydenberg, Timothy Murphy believes cut-ups negate the direction of narrative control that normally runs from author to reader. Murphy adds that the concepts of montage and stream of consciousness methods already at use elsewhere simply cannot explain the true radical novelty of cut-ups (Murphy 1997, 105). He further stresses that cut-ups challenge generic literary conventions and offers a procedure to abolish them altogether (106).

More recently, scholarship has expanded beyond a singular focus on Burroughs' cut-up. Edward Robinson's *Shift Linguals: Cut-up Narratives from William*

S. Burroughs to the Present (2011) is a historical study of the development of the cut-up method. Robinson expands discussion beyond Burroughs by studying the cut-up practices of not only Gysin and Burroughs but also Kathy Acker, John Giorno, Claude Pélieu, and Carl Weissner. Moreover, Robinson asserts the importance of the cut-up form to music and wider culture. Richard Doyle's *Darwin's Pharmacy: Sex, Plants, and the Evolution of the Noösphere* (2011) does not discuss the cut-up method at length, but the book does make some bold propositions. Doyle suggests cut-ups, similar to Dadaist art, allow "texts to interrupt normal consciousness" (2011, 186). It is also suggested that the cut-up method produces the "repeatable effects of manifesting the psyche through plant reagents" such as *yagé* (96). Such a suggestion also suggests an ancestral link between the fragmentary-montage structure of *Naked Lunch* and the cut-up form.

Ecocritical researchers have also entered the scholarly conversation on experimental writing strategies such as the cut-up method. In "William S. Burroughs' Art," Bellarsi sees Burroughs' cut-up as a way to use language to counter existing forms of power. She believes the results of the cut-up method ultimately cause "readers to break their conditioned thought patterns" (1997, 52). The subversive nature of cut-ups and other experimental writing forms can even be considered a form of environmental praxis. If cut-ups make people rethink what literature is and does, then they might by extension reconsider unsustainable practices in this world. This is what British ecocritic Harriet Tarlo believes. She boldly asserts that experimental writing practices that utilize "found text" (such as the cut-up method) amount to what can be considered genuine ecological praxis: "The freedom of citation within the poetic culture is an important part of [a] shift in consciousness . . . [Found poetry] *is* subversive, not just in poetic terms, but also in deeper cultural ones, and, as such, we may rightfully see it as an ecopoetic and eco-ethical practice in action" (Tarlo 2009, 128). The environmental implications of experimental narrative forms need further consideration, and the remainder of this essay attempts to do just that. The wide range of critical voices that have already engaged the cut-up form is a sign of genuine academic interest in Burroughs' experimental methods, but surprising gaps remain.

When examining the results of Burroughs' cut-up experiments, critics focus almost entirely on the Nova Trilogy.[3] This is reasonable to some degree since the Nova Trilogy was such an extraordinarily large project. But overlooking the embryonic cut-up forms devalues the early phase in the development of Burroughs' diverse narrative practices. For those reading Burroughs, form and method are as vital as theme or content. In this sense, Burroughs' most experimental writing is a limit case of sorts, and the real difficulties he poses are impossible to avoid. But the lack of ecological perspectives on Burroughs' early writing justifies (and indeed necessitates) more attention to the remarkable formative early period of the cut-up venture. Ecocritics too recognize the need for more study of experimental writing strategies such as the cut-up method. In "Radical Landscapes," Harriet Tarlo makes a call for ecocritical scholarship into experimental writing practices, more specifically research into the methods that authors use in the search for and reconstitution of found text. She laments the reality that "very few eco-critics engage with innovative or experimental writing" (Tarlo 2007). This view is echoed by Bellarsi, who repeats the real need to examine "green ethics in different avant-garde practices" (2009, 7). Given the general neglect of Burroughs' early cut-ups, and the lack of ecocritical studies into strategies utilizing found text, further discussion of the early cut-ups can lead to a consolidation of perspectives.

ECOLOGICAL CONSIDERATIONS OF FOUND TEXT PRACTICES

Harriet Tarlo's 2009 paper "Recycles: The Eco-Ethical Poetics of Found Text in Contemporary Poetry" is one of very few studies to specifically examine cut-up methods in an environmental context. She offers a persuasive model to analyze how environmental content is embodied in contemporary poetry through experimental writing practices. However, Tarlo's model has been restricted to the analysis of openly environmental poetry and has never been used in the examination of other experimental forms. Therefore, looking at example fragments from Burroughs' early cut-ups "VIRUSES WERE BY ACCIDENT?" (1960) and "I am Dying, Meester?" (1963) can be useful in helping to establish whether connections between ecology and Burroughs' cut-up method exist, if at all. At the same time, one can also learn how applicable Tarlo's theoretical model is in finding environmental meaning in experimental writing utilizing found text. The application of Tarlo's concepts to Burroughs' early cut-ups is a reasonable, but quite radical, extension of her work, and represents the transatlantic exchange of ideas about aesthetics. Three central areas need to be kept in mind when analyzing an experimental poem to discover environmental meaning: "the methodology employed by poets in their use of found text," "the spirit of citation," and "the eco-ethical significance of this practice" (Tarlo 2009, 114). According to Tarlo, keeping these three areas in mind will help those seeking to uncover ecological insight in found texts.

"VIRUSES WERE BY ACCIDENT?" appeared in *Minutes to Go*, the provocative and early manifesto of the cut-up movement. "VIRUSES" immediately poses a number of difficult problems in attempting an interpretation. The mysterious and apocalyptic piece represents one of Burroughs' earliest efforts using the cut-up method. Consider the following fragment:

(Resevoir [*sic*] of rabies and other virus? discovered in *Brown* fat of vampire bats and their well known and easily chosen human constituent.)

Cancer tests. . . brown blood. . live babies. . proof of virus.
vaccine? Bio-control the London conference. . it was out sheep
cattle and animals have wild system. . . . blood time brown blood.

(Beiles et al. 1960, 15)

What is immediately clear when looking at the above fragment is the genuine challenge of suggesting any "precise textual interpretation or aesthetic evaluation" (Harris 2004, 29). Harris acknowledges the genuine difficulties of analyzing the piece and even concludes: "You could say that further interpretation is simply not possible" (ibid.). If one accepts the impossibility of effectively postulating a definite interpretation, one can look to uncover *remnants* of meaning instead. What follows is not simply an assessment of the limits of Tarlo's model but a real step toward developing an extension to her model.

Tarlo recommends examining the methodology employed in the creation of the poem in question first. Methodology is defined in this case as the "series of decisions made by a writer from a spectrum of possibilities" (Tarlo 2009, 115). The selection of found text is an essential part of the process. According to *Minutes to Go*, material for "VIRUSES WERE BY ACCIDENT?" came from articles published in the *Paris Herald Tribune* (Beiles et al. 1960, 15). The source articles discussed "human cancer and animal diseases in Africa" (ibid.). The selection of source materials is crucial here, since Burroughs deliberately chose articles discussing disease. By merging texts about disease amongst animals and humans, Burroughs unknowingly participates in a key discussion in ecocriticism, "namely how far we can distinguish ourselves from non-human beings" (Tarlo 2009, 120). However, selection here refers not only to the choice of source materials but also to the process of selecting found text, as well as the eventual rearrangement of found text into the new creative form. Word selection often originates from what Scottish poet Dorothy Alexander calls a "word pool," which can be defined as found words with shared properties that are reused in combination for a desired effect (Tarlo 2009, 118). In "VIRUSES," the word pool includes a combination of words that help conjure up a cumulative sense of pestilence: "VIRUSES," "rabies," "vampire bats," "cancer," "blood," "vaccine," "bio-control," "sheep," "cattle," "animals," and "brown blood" (Beiles et al. 1960, 15). Because in this case the found text is borrowed exclusively from one newspaper and in the new form is not interwoven with text written by Burroughs himself, one can accept the writer's contribution as an example of limited authorship. However, this does not mean Burroughs' role in the cut-up method is negligible—on the contrary.[4] The selection of the word pool for "VIRUSES" suggests some degree of apprehension about living in a culture and time when ecological apocalypse may not necessarily come from the sky.

A second point of analysis, according to Tarlo's model for examination of experimental ecopoetry, involves the "spirit of citation" of the found text in the new creative form (Tarlo 2009, 119). Samples from "VIRUSES" can be considered misanthropic and satirical forms of hostile citation. The "Reservoir" thus may be understood to be the human body itself, the "easily / chosen human constituent," which remains an appealing host and incubator for all sorts of infections. If the human body is a source and transmitter of disease, the broader message conveyed by the "VIRUSES" piece is essentially misanthropic. Alternatively, the fragment "Resevoir of rabies and other virus?" can be understood to represent a storehouse of disease, comparable to the Museum of Lost Species in Burroughs' *Ghost of Chance* (1991), a depository of deadly ailments and viruses. The "Resevoir" of disease functions as a negative representation of the human organizations that are supposed to protect the public from disease, but may actually do something far more sinister. For example, the line can be read as a critique of organizations such as the Center for Disease Control, which is a factual reservoir of disease.[5] Moreover, developments in germ warfare since "VIRUSES" was published in 1960 make the very suggestion of human-made pestilence slightly less absurd than it once may have seemed.[6] Although it is not known for certain which source articles were used for the creation of "VIRUSES," knowing the found text originates from articles that cover issues of disease suggests Burroughs appropriated the language of official media and medical discourse in order to subvert the original message.

An additional instance of hostile citation involves the fragment "Bio-control the London conference" (Beiles et al. 1960, 15).[7] What is immediately clear is the absence of a second-position verb. But if one sees the sentence as a simple command, the fragment takes on an unusual if not comical juxtaposition of what may have originally been communicated in the source texts. The word "biocontrol" means utilizing ecological methods of controlling pests that depend on "predation and parasitism" (Madan and Madan 2009, 153). Accordingly, one can consider those organizations that are meant to protect the public health as ineffective and possibly even parasitic bodies working against the public, as vermin "vampire bats."[8] The suggestion that one should "Bio-control the London conference" implies the pre-emptive ecological destruction of those who may one day unleash a human-made pestilence. If read in this way, "VIRUSES" approaches a radical position. Furthermore, the recommendation to use ecologically sound methods to destroy those who would destroy us is an absurd notion, and in this case can be considered a comical instance of Surrealist bathos. In other words, by misappropriating source texts for the purpose of subversion, Burroughs used the cut-up process as an example of "culture jamming" or "guerilla semiotics" (Tietchen 2001, 109–10), which involves the adoption of official discourse, which is then subverted and fed back to the reader using the language that surrounds the reader, but in a more hostile, modified form (Tarlo 2009, 122). Hostile citation can thus be considered one manner to express a real "sense of anger and powerlessness [that] often characterises how we feel about the global, particularly environmental, issues that face us now" (Tarlo 2009, 123). The appropriation of official discourse for purposes of subversion of the original message remains an important tool in environmentalist discourse at present. Thus, the dainty, almost unseen question mark in the very title of Burroughs' piece "VIRUSES WERE BY ACCIDENT?" encompasses larger, even subconscious, fears of a modern manufactured plague.[9]

A final area of focus in the analysis of experimental ecopoetry, according to Tarlo, involves thinking about a text's larger "eco-ethical significance." In the context of "VIRUSES," one needs to consider the source texts, which, according to Burroughs, discussed disease in different species. Oliver Harris says the methods of production remain the most important consideration in better understanding the "VIRUSES" piece: "The conclusion has to be that texts such as 'VIRUSES WERE BY ACCIDENT?' remain cryptic the better to exemplify a practice that must, in order to do its work, take priority over a fully coherent thesis" (2004, 29). However, Burroughs also shows what Tarlo calls the "textual, material quality of [literature utilizing found text] and, above all, the fact that it exists in a sea of other textual, material language, rather than as a separate poetic discourse existing within its own rarefied tradition" (2009, 122). Tarlo's ideas about the recycling of found text are helpful in attempting to handle a most difficult piece. Until now, "VIRUSES" has never been read as an environmental text, but Tarlo's model assists in helping identify remnants of possible meaning, passing over direct expression and instead offering what Richard Kerridge calls a more "indirect statement" (2007, 143). However, complications with Tarlo's approach arise when examining an additional cut-up published in 1963. While this essay looks specifically at William Burroughs, the next step would be to consider how other writer's texts could benefit from new models in bringing new texts and new issues within the purview of ecocriticism (see Weidner 2009).

"I am Dying, Meester?" appeared in *The Yage Letters* and is an extreme example of Burroughs' early cut-ups:

> Panama clung to our bodies—Probably cut—Anything made this dream—It has consumed the customers of fossil orgasm—Ran into my old friend Jones—So badly off, forgotten, coughing in 1920 movie—Vaudeville voices hustle sick dawn breath on bed service—Idiot Mambo spattered backwards—I nearly suffocated trying on the boy's breath—That's Panama—Nitrous flesh swept out by your voice and end of receiving set—Brain eating birds patrol the low frequency brain waves (Burroughs and Ginsberg 2006, 76)

The initial ecocritical response to the above fragment has to be complete paralysis. There simply does not appear to be anything to grasp onto. A worthwhile question is to what degree this cut-up can be handled by Tarlo's model.

The method Burroughs employed in locating source text for eventual reconstitution in "Meester?" is quite different from the approach he used in the creation of the "VIRUSES" piece. In *Yage Letters Redux*, Harris believes "I am Dying, Meester?" was made "by recycling fragments of 'In Search of Yage'" (Burroughs and Ginsberg 2006, xlii). Roughly 25 percent of the "660 words" contained in "Meester?" originated "mainly from the 'January 15' and 'April 15' letters" (Harris 2006). Nevertheless, Harris acknowledges the real difficulty in knowing for certain, not simply because of the perplexing "nature of the cut-up method" but also because of the considerable amount of "internal repetition" within "Meester?" itself (ibid.). While "VIRUSES" can be considered an example of limited authorship, Burroughs' recycling of his own words adds a different authorial dynamic to the reconstituted "Meester?" but the result confuses matters even more. The increasing challenges of tracing links to other texts to find meaning are frustrating, and the uncertainty readers have to accept is possibly dissatisfying. If the cut-up process shreds texts, then it can be said in the case of "I am Dying, Meester?" that the source texts have been shredded beyond recognition, at least beyond the capacity to see clear portals to other texts. In the case of "VIRUSES," knowing a little about the source articles does help provide insight into the process of its creation. The shift in approach from "VIRUSES" to "Meester?" therefore represents the evolution of the cut-up method. However, the increasingly complex process of selecting found text and the shredding of source text come at the cost of intelligibility in the new literary text. Lydenberg suggests Burroughs used the cut-up technique to dispel "the illusion of the referential function of language" (1987, 33). This lack of reference is especially conspicuous in "Meester?" Therefore, the more intricate process of selecting found text for "Meester?" adds to its cryptic nature. Harris also emphasizes that an important detail in "Meester?" is the presence of more than "seventy dashes in a piece less than 700 words long," thus presenting compelling evidence of additional textual shredding. The lack of referentiality suggests the cut-up method has become even more radical in its destructive power. If "VIRUSES" is the result of textual shredding, "Meester?" is the result of textual shredding and subsequent pulverization. While one can find the source texts for over half of the content of "Meester?" a significant amount of the reconstituted text remains unidentified.

In thinking about the spirit of citation in "Meester?" once again the reader is confronted with many of the same problems as when looking at the methods of creation, including the lack of orientation. One can certainly see a rough pool of words with vaguely negative connotations: "clung," "consumed," "badly off," "coughing," "Idiot," and "Brain eating birds." But even if a (very loose) word pool has been identified, it would be a real stretch to suggest that these terms somehow express environmental significance, either individually or collectively. Indeed, without knowing more precise details about the source texts, the spirit of citation in this case remains an open problem. However, even though Tarlo's first two areas of consideration may not fully handle "Meester?" her final point of attention, the "eco-ethical significance" of the practices of manufacturing the text can help one learn more (2009, 114). If one no longer sees literature as something to be consumed and digested by the reader, then one can focus on other qualities of the text. Paradoxically, the same issues that cause problems in understanding the methods and spirit of citation can also help provide other opportunities to discover environmental value in "Meester?.."

Tarlo emphasizes the need to think about how experimental writing contributes to the ways people think about ecology. If one looks beyond thematic content and considers the eco-ethical significance of the new form that emerges from the vigorous use of found text in the "Meester?" cut-up (and cut-ups more generally), one may better understand radically experimental texts that exhibit no outward environmental meaning. If "Meester?" is a poem, it is a radically unconventional poem. Lydenberg asserts the cut-up form "transgresses" borders "separating inside and outside, fiction and alleged fact, the private self and the words of others" (1987, 53). "Meester?" thus violates expectations of what literature is supposed to do. Richard Kerridge insists, "The cut-up method in particular, can bring into poetic space kinds of discourse not normally available to the personal lyric" (2007, 133). This can be taken further by suggesting that the cut-up has unique qualities that make it especially useful to engaging in eschatological discourse. Because no meaning is prepackaged for the reader, one has to search for meaning. When unsuccessful in this pursuit of clarity, readers have to impart meaning, as is the case in *Naked Lunch*. The alienating effect of the cut-up form forces us to question what Žižek calls "our most unquestionable presuppositions" (quoted in Kerridge 2007, 132). By making readers rethink common assumptions about what literature is and does, Burroughs' early experimental texts can teach ecocriticism about the importance of cut-ups to the issue of biopiracy, and to the search for the ultimate natural drug to disrupt human consciousness. *The Yage Letters* connects the cut-up method and *ayahuasca* as radical techniques of reality transformation, which means the undoing of Western assumptions about identity. This is vital since the method of composition may seem mechanical but is still involved in the same derangement of the senses that Burroughs learns from Amazonian shamans.

THE NAKED TREE

This essay examines mysterious early cut-ups from *Minutes to Go* and *The Yage Letters* utilizing concepts borrowed from the analysis of ecopoetry. Although ecocriticism seems better suited to dealing with issues of theme and content, Burroughs forces readers to acknowledge the importance of method and form. In particular, Burroughs poses the important question whether specific narrative strategies are capable of representing the unthinkable. By extension, one questions whether certain aesthetic forms can help "shift our human consciousness" (Hogue, quoted in Tarlo 2009, 123). This essay proposes that the unconventionality of *The Yage Letters* and the unusual early cut-ups can be considered emergent proto-ecological forms. Burroughs changed his writing strategies from *Naked Lunch* to *The Yage Letters* and the even more radical cut-up method because he found existing narrative structures incapable of representing how he saw the real world, which, in many of his narratives is shown as gravitating toward irrevocable ecological ruin. Burroughs' unconventional forms allow for new ways of viewing literature, and possibly the world. Tarlo's three-part approach to the analysis of ecopoetry is helpful in recovering remnants of environmental meaning. Even though the "eco-ethical significance" of an experimental practice is perhaps still too loose a notion and does not always work with texts outside the nature-writing genre, Tarlo's approach is helpful in teaching ecocriticism to think about formal literary elements, and this is significant. At the same time, this essay reaffirms the real difficulties of reading Burroughs in the first place. Avant-garde writing practices require participatory reading, and successful writers make readers "feel that our response is demanded and should even be translated into some kind of action" (Tarlo 2009, 125). The ecological significance of Burroughs' experimental writing is found "embedded in a form that endeavours to stimulate the reader into understanding and action" (Tarlo 2009, 114). Burroughs' experimental writing never tells readers what to do, but it does force them to think. The author's early forms are certainly not obvious examples of environmental activism. However, Burroughs' experimental structures can be considered proto-ecological in their radical ambiguity, which forces readers to attempt understanding. Burroughs' fragmentary early cut-ups are especially suited to expressing both increasing isolation from the natural world and the fragmentation of human consciousness in an increasingly uncertain age.

CHAD WEIDNER is tenured faculty in Liberal Arts and Sciences at University College Roosevelt, and is an affiliated researcher in the Gender Studies workgroup at Utrecht University, in the Netherlands. He is the author of *The Green Ghost: William Burroughs and the Ecological Mind* (Southern Illinois University Press, 2016). He has presented his research in Africa, Asia, North America, and throughout Europe and serves on the Board of the European Beat Studies Network.

NOTES

This chapter is reprinted from *Comparative American Studies* 11, no. 3 (September 2013): 314–26.

1. See also Lydenberg's *Word Cultures* (1987, 48–49).

2 Gregory Corso dissents in *Minutes to Go*, deploring what he calls "uninspired machine-poetry" (Beiles et al. 1960, 63). For discussion of ecological aspects of Gysin and Corso's cut-ups in *Minutes to Go,* see Weidner 2016.

3. See Harris 1996.

4. Burroughs thought the cut-up method helped uncover ideological subtexts. Contemporary English poet Frances Presley also believes writing practices that involve found text can help to restructure "texts and extract their sub-texts" (quoted in Tarlo 2009, 116).

5. The history of the US Center for Disease Control and its forerunners can be traced to at least 1921. The Communicable Disease Center was established in Atlanta in 1946 (The National Archives and Records Administration).

6. For example, in a 2001 article published in *The Guardian*, Duncan Campbell reported that the Federal Bureau of Investigation discovered the US military was actively "producing anthrax in a powdered form suitable for use as a weapon," possibly in violation of numerous international treaties (Campbell 2001, 1).

7. The London Conference might refer to the Seventh International Congress of Cancer Research held in London in July 1958. More than 2,000 scientists attended the meeting ("World Cancer Group to Meet in London").

8. Lydenberg posits that the "power of metonymy" Burroughs begins to utilize in the mosaic of *Naked Lunch* reaches its most radical use in subsequent cut-ups (1987, 33).

9. Medical conspiracy theories demonstrate both the fear of disease and suspicion of authorities. A study published in the *Journal of Acquired Immune Deficiency Syndromes* showed nearly

48 percent of blacks surveyed believed "HIV is a man-made virus" (Bogart and Thorburn 2005, 215). Although such a view may seem exceptionally paranoid, there are historical reasons for such distrust. The Tuskegee syphilis study represents just one instance in which public health workers infected unknowing members of the public with a deadly disease. In the case of the Tuskegee study, hundreds of blacks were infected with syphilis. Many never received medical treatment and subsequently died.

REFERENCES

Beiles, Sinclair, William Burroughs, Gregory Corso, and Brion Gysin. 1960. *Minutes to Go*. San Francisco: City Lights Books.
Bellarsi, Franca. 1997. "William S. Burroughs's Art: The Search for a Language that Counters Power." In *Voices of Power: Cooperation and Conflict in English Language and Literatures*, edited by M. Maufort and J. P. van Noppen, 45–56. Liege: Belgian Association of Anglicists in Higher Education.
———. 2009. "Eleven Windows into Post-Pastoral Exploration." *Journal of Ecocriticism* 1 (2): 1–10.
Bogart, Laura M., and Sheryl Thorburn. 2005. "Are HIV/Aids Conspiracy Beliefs a Barrier to HIV Prevention among African Americans?" *Journal of Acquired Immune Deficiency Syndromes* 38 (2): 213–18.
Bryan, Jeff. 1986. "William Burroughs and His Faith in X." *West Virginia U Philological Papers* 32: 79–89.
Burroughs, William, and Allen Ginsberg. 2006. *The Yage Letters Redux*. Edited by Oliver Harris. San Francisco: City Lights Books.
Burroughs, William, and Brion Gysin. 1978. *The Third Mind*. New York: Viking.
Campbell, Duncan. 2001. "FBI Uncovers US Military Production of Anthrax Powder." *Guardian*, December 31. Accessed November 8, 2011. http://www.guardian.co.uk/world/2001/dec/14/anthrax.uk.
Doyle, Richard. 2011. *Darwin's Pharmacy: Sex, Plants, and the Evolution of the Noösphere*. Seattle: University of Washington Press.
Emerson, Ralph Waldo. 1886. *Experience*. 5th ed. Chicago: Alden Book.
Gysin, Brion. 1964. "Cut-Ups: A Project for Disastrous Success." *Evergreen Review* 32: 56–61.
Harris, Oliver. 1996. "A Response to John Watters, 'The Control Machine: Myth in *The Soft Machine* of W. S. Burroughs.'" *Connotations* 6 (3): 337–53.
———. 2004. "'Burroughs Is a Poet Too, Really': The Poetics of Minutes to Go." In *Edinburgh Review*, edited by R. Turnbull, 24–36. Edinburgh: Edinburgh Centre for the History of Ideas in Scotland.
———. 2006. "Not Burroughs' Final Fix: Materializing *The Yage Letters*." *Postmodern Culture: An Electronic Journal of Interdisciplinary Criticism*. http://muse.jhu.edu/journals/postmodern_culture/v016/16.2harris.html.
———. 2009. "Cutting up the Corpse." In *The Exquisite Corpse: Chance and Collaboration in Surrealism's Parlor Game*, edited by K. Kochhar-Lindgren, D. Schneiderman, and T. Denlinger, 82–103. Lincoln: University of Nebraska Press.
Kerridge, Richard. 2007. "Climate Change and Contemporary Modernist Poetry." In *Poetry and Public Language*, edited by Tony Lopez and Anthony Caleshu, 131–48. Exeter: Shearsman Books.
Loranger, Carol. 1999. "'This Book Spill Off the Page in All Directions': What Is the Text of Naked Lunch?" *Postmodern Culture* 10 (1). http://muse.jhu.edu/journals/postmodern_culture/v010/10.1loranger.html.
Lydenberg, Robin. 1987. *Word Cultures: Radical Theory and Practice in William S. Burroughs' Fiction*. Urbana: University of Illinois Press.
Madan, Sangeeta, and Pankaj Madan. 2009. *Global Encyclopaedia of Environmental Science, Technology and Management*. New Delhi: Global Vision.
Morgan, Ted. 1988. *Literary Outlaw: The Life and Times of William S. Burroughs*. London: Pimlico.
Murphy, Timothy. 1997. *Wising Up the Marks: The Amodern William Burroughs*. Berkeley: University of California Press.

National Archives and Records Administration. 2011. Records of the Centers for Disease Control and Prevention. The U.S. National Archives and Records Administration. Accessed April 8, 2011. http://www.archives.gov/research/guide-fed-records/groups/442.html.

Odier, Daniel. 1989. *The Job: Interviews with William S. Burroughs*. New York: Penguin.

Robinson, Edward. 2011. *Shift Linguals: Cut-up Narratives from William S. Burroughs to the Present*. Amsterdam: Rodopi.

Sterritt, David. 2000. "Revision, Prevision, and the Aura of Improvisatory Art." *Journal of Aesthetics & Art Criticism* 58 (2): 163–72.

Tarlo, Harriet. 2007. "Radical Landscapes: Experiment and Environment in Contemporary Poetry." *Jacket Magazine* 32. Accessed May 11, 2011. http://jacketmagazine.com/32/p-tarlo.shtml.

———. 2009. "Recycles: The Eco-Ethical Poetics of Found Text in Contemporary Poetry." *Journal of Ecocriticism* 1 (2): 114–30.

Tietchen, Todd. 2001. "Language out of Language: Excavating the Roots of Culture Jamming and Postmodern Activism from William S. Burroughs' Nova Trilogy." *Discourse* 23 (3): 107–29.

Tzara, Tristan. 1977. *Seven Dada Manifestos and Lampisteries*. Translated by Barbara Wright. London: John Calder.

Watson, Steven. 1995. *The Birth of the Beat Generation: Visionaries, Rebels, and Hipsters, 1944–1960*. New York: Pantheon.

Weidner, Chad. 2009. "Does Ecocriticism Really Matter?" *BAS British and American Studies Journal* 15: 189–99.

———. 2016. *The Green Ghost: William Burroughs and the Ecological Mind*. Carbondale: Southern Illinois University Press.

"World Cancer Group to Meet in London; 50 Soviet Specialists Listed to Attend." 1958. *New York Times*, July 4. https://timesmachine.nytimes.com/timesmachine/1958/07/04/81886624.pdf.

Body/Spirit

We intend to make a beautiful film that will make some beautiful money. To achieve both aims on a very limited budget we will not attempt too many breakthroughs at once. The film will be hard core gay as the book. In the area of porn flicks we are still operating in an either or context. Its gay or its straight. Its porn or it isn't. We want a film that is beautiful without being arty.

—Burroughs, "The Wild Boys Screenplay," 1972, ASU 8A.4. Copyright © by William Burroughs, used by permission of The Wylie Agency LLC.

Had been indicted in England for the murder of Joan. Lawyer told me that I would almost certainly be convicted and hanged because of the prejudice against me in the minds of the prospective jurors and advised me to leave England.. .. Still on the lam. I decided to go out through Scotland. The lawyers Assistant would accompany me. Once out I could not be extradited

—Burroughs, "Dream Note," 1970, Berg 22.79. Copyright © by William Burroughs, used by permission of The Wylie Agency LLC.

Sergeant in World War 1 leading suicide charge: "Come on you back there do you want to live forever."

—Burroughs, "Cut-Ups of Last Words," 1960, Berg 35.70. Copyright © by William Burroughs, used by permission of The Wylie Agency LLC.

"I WANTA PAY. I CANT" "LOOK" "CANT LOOK" "SO THIS IS WHAT HAPPENS? NO.

—Burroughs, "Cut Up Last Words," 1960, Berg 26.16. Copyright © by William Burroughs, used by permission of The Wylie Agency LLC.

The Wild Boys, a Pornographic Screenplay

Burroughs wrote many screenplays throughout his life, from "Twilights Last Gleaming" in the early 1950s to *The Last Words of Dutch Schultz* (1970), but no script is as fascinating, or as under-discussed, as Burroughs' adaptation into a pornographic film, in 1973, of his recently published novel, *The Wild Boys* (1971). Burroughs first sketched out his cinematic vision after a visit to New York City, where he encountered the adult movie houses flourishing throughout the midtown Times Square area. Burroughs was always fascinated by the potential of moving images, not just as a way for an artist to make some money while reaching a large audience, but as a medium well-suited to represent the extremes of the body, and to explore the possibility for escape from its limitations (from the gravitational pull of our planet to the degeneration of our body in time).

Housed in Arizona State University's Hayden Library's Rare Books and Manuscripts, Burroughs' screenplay appears alongside other aborted projects from the post-1968 period, such as his cinematic adaptation with Brion Gysin of *Naked Lunch*, and his drafts of a proposal for an Academy to research the expansion of consciousness. The cover folder for the screenplay, reproduced below, shows a nude male figure in a posture of physical combat, a symbol of an agile agent of resistance, trained in critical methods of guerilla warfare analogical to Tae Kwan Do. ASU's archive contains hundreds of more pages chronicling the history of a cinematic project that is still waiting to be brought to fruition in Burroughs' wake.

Presented below are excerpts of his fascinating 1972 prospectus for the screenplay, described in the catalogue as containing "a 2 page signed introduction and 16 page typed signed prospectus for the film of The Wild Boys and 7 page signed manuscript of various scenes for The Wild Boys film project, also signed by Burroughs. The Wild Boys film project, as outlined by Burroughs in the introductions, was an attempt, with the help of Terry Southern, to make Burroughs' novel into a film" (ASU 8A.4, Series I). Besides consulting and working with Southern to write early drafts, in the summer of 1972, Burroughs also discussed alternatives to the script with Fred Halsted, the famous porn filmmaker whose work had inspired Burroughs to pursue the film in the first place. Burroughs explains: "In the spring of 1972 while I was in New York trying to sell the Naked Lunch film script I saw a number of hard core porn films including Fred Halsted's LA Plays Itself and Sex Garage. This gave me the idea of shooting The Wild Boys as a hard core porn film" (ASU 8A.4).

The new aesthetic possibilities in a post-obscenity world where making films was cheaper and easier offered Burroughs exciting opportunities to reimagine his cut-up techniques for a wider audience. In his introduction, Burroughs starts by sharing a simple desire to make a porn-flick, only to slowly queer, and blur, the difference between porn and non-porn, in order to imagine new potentials for the medium opened up by the taboo genre. Burroughs announces at the start of the proposal, "We intend to make a beautiful film that will make some beautiful money." In the subsequent sentences, he challenges the growing anti-pornography movement, in words that deconstruct the assumptions of Justice Potter Stewart's famous 1964 claim that he couldn't define pornography, but "I know it when I see it" (ASU 8A.4). Burroughs writes, "In the area of porn flicks we are still operating in an either or context. Its gay or its straight. Its porn or it isn't. We want a film that is beautiful without being arty" (ASU 8A.4).

Burroughs was always suspicious of America's reasons for becoming more "tolerant" of previously marginalized and persecuted peoples and ways of life. He distrusted any and all surveillance, and he was sensitive to the deleterious effects of commodification. He was, then, well aware of the ways he would need to work against the grain of the film industry, especially pornographic films, as it slowly commodifies every sexual image to augment its addicted consumer base. To counter the genre's formulaic effects, Burroughs explains he plans to "use special effects," like "slide projection," acrobatics, theatrical cut-up techniques: "Among other innovations there will be fucking to music. Splice ins from already existing porn footage will be used but we will also shoot live porn scenes" (ibid). While these ideas only scratch the surface of what Burroughs could imagine for his cinematic adaptation of his original novel's utopian exploration of a global, queer counter-cultural movement, Burroughs "finally decided the whole idea was impracticable both from a financial standpoint and from a standpoint of making a good film within our budget" (ASU 8A.4).

This screenplay offers an idiosyncratic entrance into the last section of this anthology, being only a pale imitation of itself, a sketch of a script, a blueprint for his novel as a film that would never be made. Burroughs intended for these hypothetical moving images to represent from fresh perspectives a range of sexual configurations that had been censored, or otherwise neutralized, by traditional cinematic methods. Burroughs hoped through this film, and his novel *The Wild Boys*, to articulate more than just a condemnation of this rotten planet of humanity's making, including its division into two opposed sexes. As he put it in an interview with Regina Weinreich in 1981 regarding his newest book, *Cities of the Red Night*, he had always sought through his multi-media work to envision a future when the sexes would fuse into one organism—"changes that are literally inconceivable from the present point of view" (*Burroughs Live*, 516). On the one hand, Burroughs often vented uncritically his mid-century, inverted mode of macho misogyny, nowhere more blatantly than in his rendition in *The Wild Boys* of a queer utopia mostly composed of cis-gendered men. On the other hand, through his arguably myopic literary conceit, Burroughs contributed to his life-long quest to make possible a world (or at least a state of mind) where hierarchal, binary divisions in our beliefs and our ways of life no longer find a reason to exist. At the very least, this surreal screenplay seems the proper prelude to this sprawling anthology's final, fifth section, *Body/Spirit*, where scholars and artists, including many who knew Burroughs intimately, consider his understandings and misunderstandings of gender difference, sexual identity, and the human potential, as well as his feelings of guilt for his past, and his desire for a new life in the future.

—*AWC*

Wild Boys Photograph, William S. Burroughs, 1974 (1 leaf, facsimile) (ASU, Series I Box 8A Item 4). Copyright © by William Burroughs, used by permission of The Wylie Agency LLC.

In the spring of 1972 while I was in New York trying to sell the Naked Lunch
film script I saw a number of hard co re porn films including Fred Halsted's
LA Plays Itself and XXXXXXXXXX Sex   Garage.   This gave me the idea of shooting
The Wild Boys as a hard core porn film.   I met Fred Halsted and discussed the
idea with him and gave him a copy of The Wild Boys.   He was opposed to the idea
of using explicit sex scenes since this cuts XXXXXX distribution.   I then
discussed the project with Terry Southern and we considered working together
on the script.   I returned to London and wrote what I thought was   a low
budget script….. The letter to John De Chadenedes which I enclose illustrates
how impractical the project was and I gave it up to concentrate on the archives.
During the summer of 1972 Fred Hlasted came to London and we discussed a
number of alternative × scripts.   I finally decided the whole idea was
impractical both from a financial standpoint and from the stand point of
making a good film within our budget. I have not heard from Fred since I
wrote calling the trip to LA and the whole idea off for the time being.

[autograph]: William S. Burroughs

We intend to make a beautiful film that will make some beautiful money.
To achieve both aims on a very limited budget we will not attempt too
many breakthroughs at once. The film will be hard core gay as the book.
(However, the device of having two screens on set would allow for
heterosexual @@@@@@@@@@ scenes as part of the honky tonk penny arcade
atmorphere). In the area of porn flicks we are still operating in an
either or context. Its gay or its straight. Its porn or it isn't. We
want a film that is beautiful without being arty.   We will use special
effects like slide projections rephotographed and cut up techniques.
These techniques were developed by BrionGysin IanSommerville and Anthony
Balch in Towers Open Fire The Cut Ups Bill and Tony and in slide
projection shows in Paris.   The use of these effects is not expensive.
And they will be used always to heighten the erotic effect but never
as cope out or cover up.   The film will have a shooting script.   The
sound track which has been virtually neglected in porn films will
use a variety of music and sound effects as indicated in the script.
Among other innovations there will be fucking to music. Splice ins from
already existing porn footage will be used but we will also shoot live
porn scenes. One street is the only studio or location set and
establishing shots on the street can be done ina few hours since these
are mostly actors going into interiors that can be easily reconstructed
@@@@ in a loft. The action takes place in the Go Go Bar with two screens
over the bar as the actors move in and out of the screen. This gives us
a simple one set but highly flexible framework to present a series of
episodesand a climax as all the boys fucking to drums and flutes dance
out along the street and fade out as The Wild Boys written in smoke
across the sky fades out to empty sky.
The present treatment is of course tentative and suggestive as a frame
work of possible scenes that will be brought into line with the budget.

[autograph]: William S. Burroughs

                          ******

(2)

Opening scene shows a run down dead end street half buried in sand the
windows broken and boarded up rusty guns and knives scattered here and
there.   At the end of the street on cracked pavement with weeds growing
through phantom wild boys in rainbow jock straps turn slow circles on
roller skates smile and fade out as the camera pans to The Wild Boys
written in smoke across the sky. Just as the smoke wrwiting starts to
shred the camera pans back to the street which is now in operation
sand shoveled away boards removed from windows.   On the street is a
pawn shop, a chop suey joint, a rooming house, a Turkish bath, a
Go Go Bar. In front of Go Go Bar are two FBI?CIA types.
"Let's check this place out."

They enter the bar. The Go Go Bar can be constructed in a loft and all
the action of the film takes place here and all the characters appear
as patrons, intruders, Go Go Boys dance wearing electronic helmets that can be
activated from a switch board. A bar and over the bar two screens on
which hard core porn flicks are projected. The wild boys are 9 in
number two blond, two dark, two red haired, two Mexicans or Puerto Ricans.
They rotate as Go Go Boys and bartenders. The Great Slastubitch sits at
A table. As the FBI men enter Old Sarge is assigneing a new Go Go
Crew who are stripping and putting on helmets in front of the screens.
FBI Man: (He points to a blond boy and a drak boy) "You two report for
a security check."
2nd FBI Man: "We dont want your type astranauts from the United States"
Old Sarge: (He points to screen where the blond boy and the dark boy
are jacking off in a space capsule) "They went thataway."
On the other screen the two boys are jacking off in school toilet with
grafetti on the walls...
Come and jack off...1929... Little Boy Did...Auh Puch was here...
D &D... Buen lugar para follar...Quien es? The A.D. Kid...
The Frisco Kid jacked off here...So did A.C. and D.C...In memory
of the J.B. boy… Wait for me here. This Wait for me here is
written across a moon landscape.
Cut back to the bar. The two FBI men look at the screens with the
faces of men condemned to death. The Great Slastubitch looks at them
Stonily

******

(3)

"Report to casting you two. You're light years late on set."
Thye vanish in shots of the milky way and clear desert or Swiss stars
with shooting stars Star Dust on sound track. Cut back to space capsule
on full screen. One boy is bent over hands braced on a wheel which
he turns slightly guiding the ship while other boys fucks him to Star Dust.
On a small screen in front of them is the school toilet scene. School
toilet now appears on full screne intercut with other sex scenes with
1920 décor in which all the boys take part in different combos...
locker room shower, tree house, boys jacking off into fish pool in
night garden scene. Star Dust is recurrent motify but other 1920 tunes
will be used...1920 street autumn leaves. Audrey as red haired boy
stands on corner a dead leave @@@@ catches in his hair. John Hamlin
also red haired open the door of his Dusenberg.
"Want to go for a ride Audrey?"
This scene is now on a small screen in the bar. The Green Nun enters with
Bob a hard hat with a club.
"I've come to reclaim a truant." She points to Audrey on screen.
On left hand screen wild boy sweep down hill on roller skates knives
drawn teeth bare. This scene now fills screen intercut with speeding
car. Car crash the Green Nun and Old Bob throw up hands on screen.
Dead @ leaves spattered with blood in air. Distant musical car horn.
We cut now to the first color mix:

RED: The actors are both red haired boys and red predominates in the immediate@@@@@ sets with sepia and orange and yellow. We will use s two slide projectors that project color slides on the actors which are then rephotographed. Cuts ins from stock red footage of sun sets, autumn leaves, red paintings, red haired boys, and porn footage with red haired boys.

Dead leaves drift across floor of a ruined room with rose vine growing through wall bed scattered with rose petals. On bed red haired boy with his knees up against his chest. A translucent red rose from the slide porjector is projected onto his ass. The other boy kneels in front of him. Roses are projected onto him.   Red porn stills, tattoos, Chinese and Arab characters are porjected back to the boys making it in clear sharp detail.   We cut in red moons, red landscapes, sun sets, red paintings, red haired porn footage and red concentrates made by driving around city and taking everything red. Boys come on s

******

(4)

The boys come on rose petals. Dead leaves drift down a cobble stone Street.

BLUE... As the dead leaves frift along the street a blue mist falls. (Distant train whisle on sound track. Moroccan flute melodies in this sequence)   Cut to room with blue wall paper ship pictures a model of The Marie Celeste some sea shells in cabinet. A yellow haired boy with blue eyes and red haired boy with blue eyes making it. Same procedure as in red using blue projections and cut ins blue eyes, blue sky and water blue flowers mountains and paintings. After orgams vapor trails across blue sky.

YELLOW. Boy on yellow toilet seat sun light in yellow pubic hair yellow hair in the wind yellow flowers and grass urine in straw. Two yellow haired boy in yellow set with yellow projections and cut ins. All the boys are rotated through these sets which leads into other scenes .For example as boys come in yellow set the set is filled with nitrous red fumes (This is done by pouring nitric acid over copper filings the fumes photographed and as fumes clear a red haired boy and yellow haired boy on set with orange and sepia cut ins leads to the Dead Child drinking orange drink and the scene in caddy locker room where Kiki hands him half and orange.   As Audrey comes cut to native hut split bambook walls Puerto Rican boy comes in with Ayuaska which is blue drug. Blue snow capped mountains lead into Frisco Kid

******

(5)

 The Frisco Kid sequence shows street covered with snow Front Street husky dogs and a sled some bearded miners. We should be able to find stock footage for this. As they talk in @@ Chop Suey joint there are flash backs from the @@@@@ 1920 shots. The Frisco Kid spitting blood

in doorways..space shots, snow, ice, silver ash on his cheek bones..
Room 18 onthe top floor. This is ghost sequence mixing sex and death
images, statues, tomb stone covered with snow.. Earth @@@@@@@ quake
cut ins as they come the Mexican cop rushes into the bar and screams
"Chingoa" He hauls out his 45.   On screen Tio Mate smiles and fires.
Cop collapses across balcony which collapses.. Cut to the Frisco Kid
as the dead child standing undera dusty tree. Persian general rushes
in and screams
"Satan I will destroy you forever."
The old gardener who is Tio Mate smiles and stabs him.
Dead Child and Xolotl in jungle hut taking Yage…@ Blue effects. The
color shots are now mixed into rainbows.
CIA man Colonel Greenfield with soldier enter
"WHAT ARE YOU DOING IN FRONT OF DECENT PEOPLE¼"?
Colonel Greenfield and CIA man shot on screen. Dead soldiers piled up
with desert back drop. Enter boys with guns…
Audrey points…"Hey lookit all them dead bodies."
The boys strip off their jock staps and @@@ roll around in the dead
soldiers like dogs rolling in carrion...
"Got a liver knife?" Says a slack jawed wild boy.
He takes the knife and cuts the liver out   of a young soldier. The
boys eat the raw liver. They pretend to have TB coughing spitting blood
all over each @@@@@@@@@ other and dying ineach others arms. Finally
they all pretend to be dead except for one boy who plays taps.
Enter Old Sarge: "All right you jokers on your feet we're moving out."
The boys dance up the street fucking to drums and flutes as they throw
away their weapons.
The first shot of The Wild Boys written in smoke across the sky is shown
a few seconds later as the writing starts to fade so the end is really
a few seconds after the beginning. The weapons rust behind them½ . They
dance out along the street and fade out their smiling ghost faces across
the sky fora moment as smoke s writing and faces fade to empty sky

******

(6)

Most of the sets are of course simply rooms with different décor and
much of this décor can be projected from the slide projectors. The
space capsule scene is cut in a number of times and the boys change
places...
A scene where a boy takes a popper...milky way space shots and he is
coming in the space capsule.
The film beed not be shot in any sequence. We set up some sets and
start shooting rotating the boys through the sets and shooting as
much footage as we can afford. We then edit and select and splice
the film together from the materials we have.
So the film can be shot and finished on a very modest budget shooting
simply as many scenes as we can afford to shoot on the budget.

******

Opening scene shows a run down dead end street half buried in sand.
At the end of the street on cracked pavement with weeds growing through
wild boys in rainbow jock straps turn slow circles on roller skates
smile and fade out as camera pans to THE WILD BOYS written in smoke
across the sky. As the smoke wti writing fades the titles come on
across the street which contains a chop suey joint a pawn shop a
sleazing romming house a Turkish bath a Go Go Bar.   Inside the bar all
the characters in the film will appear as patrons bartenders go go
boys and all the action takes place in the go go bar.   The boys in the
bar wear a variety of costumes rainbow jock straps skins Audrey and Old
Sarge wear world war 1 uniforms.   There are two hard core porn flicks
with orgasm and sex word sound track on two screens onver the bar.
The go go boys dance apathetically to idiot mambo.   They all wear
electronic helmuts.   The CIA man comes in with his two assistants.
Audrey presses a button in an electronic control device he carries
and the Go Go boys suddenly start to go and shoot all over the CIA
man and his assistants who push through to the bar.   The screen now becomes
one on which Audrey and Old Sarge appear saying 'They went thataway'…
CIA man appears on screen s as he hiccups out 'Machine hick gun hick
the little hick bastards' He blast away witha 45 and goes down under
a hail of slugs hiccupping a rope of blood. Red out to a sun set.   Nude
giggling wild boys roll around on dead soldiers like happy dogs eating
the soldier's raw liver pretending to have TB as they cough and spit blood
all over each other cut to wild boys with knives drawn teeth bare
sweeping down a hill on a police patrol dead leaves are spattered with
pig blood in the air cut to a room with rose wall paper where two red
heads are fucking. This scene is cut in with sun sets blood volcanoes
the Grand Canyon smoy red moons autumn leaves. Cut back to the bar
where the great Slastubitch watches impassively. Now we mix so the
colors.. Cut to two yellow haired boys yellow wall paper yellow 3/8 paintings
yellow sky yellow flowers a yellow fish side a yellow perch urin in
straw...In a blue metal lined room two boys with blue eyes turn orgonne
accumulators on each other and fuck to a sound track of train whistles fog
horns other fucks in rooms with blue wall paper and ship scenes cut
in blue sky blue water blue f@@@@ flowers 1920 nscens scenes between
 Mark and Johnny in blACK and white old 1920 stock footage cut in

                            ******

sun sets the Grand Canyon. Could use Genua music for this sound track.
Shift to D September song and autum leaves. The boys sweep down
with knives drawn a dead leaf is spattered with blood in the air and
dirfts away down a cobble stone street. The great slastubitch..
"Now we mix so the colors..." Blue sequence with blue wall paper shit3/8
ship scenes blue eyed boys flute music distant train whistles…
1920 shots Yege Yage scenes in jungle hut flickers out to ba black
and white the dead child sex scene in locker room the Frisco Kid
The Cafe Azar…Dib and Audrey…Scene in street superimposed palm
trees sodleirs come in the bar with machine guns down… On screne
the soldiers are dead...@@@@@@@@@@@@@@@@@@@@@@@   The Shrew standing
up screw...Last scene on street wild boys very close now…Pan Music

Genua the wild boys stream out of the bar and fucking singing playing
flutes fade into the sky and the fading sky writing… as sex scenes
from the film dim out in the sky...

******

It is always to be remembered that the virtal juices of our flick is
given by the actors and the more willingly the better. This means that
a major portion of the budget will be acting time. The question as to
how to get the   realest orgasms in the leastest time without installing
so electrodes in the brain which of course will be the next step and
electronic helmet to stilmulate any degree of orgasmal excitment. Meanwhile
we can try orgone accumulators many actors have been known to have a
spontanaeous orgasm mwhen a small orgone acculator was placed over the
crotch and this gives usa scene the two boys folling around in workshop
over the garage have made a metal lined room with an orgone accumulator in
it and a small accumulator which they turn on each other and this metal
lined room is of cours e also the space capsule. Now we have four actors
onset and several sets. The space capsule, a Moroccan scene with rose
petals and red rugs, a 1920 school toilet open day and night, a
convertible bedroom that can have rose wall paper from projectors, blue
wall paper if you boys are in a blue mood, that right walk around, touch
the sets, jounce on the beds kick your legs in the air like you was
rolling around in dead cops, how about a popper in the space capsule
with a orgone accumulator virbrator up your ass, we got this bed here
between loud speakers where you can fuck to music we dont play the
music the audience picks it out from the fuck rhythm.. all right
EVERBODY SING... This gives us nice scene the two boys in the locker
room jacking off to MY BLUE HEAVEN in a blue set as the audience in
a 1920 move all get up and sing eating peanuts and jacking off...
We give the actorsa choice which should eleiciate the spontaneous
Sexual reponse the real thing that cannot be faked the mark of a
SLASTUBITCH PRODUCTION
The use of slide projectors will enable us to obtain special effects
for very little outlay. For example we take color slides of all
the actors will hard ons and these can be projected onto the actors
or the walls and rephotographed. Alos slide projectors can project
back drops.   We can also project color porn onthe walls any color
what you want nice red walls red boys fuck sun set eat apple spit blood
drift away in autumn leaves to a blue room

******

In the color shots we will use stock footage and the assembly of this
footage should start as soon as possible. Three color shots are
described in film. The colors are red, blue, yellow. First of course
is a set in the appropriate color bed spread walls curtains paintings
and decorations First of course are the actors both say red heads
both with yellow hair both with blue eyes   then the immediate set
red bed spread red curtains red paintings red rugs sepia and orange

colors also used in this set. We use also two slide projectors that
project color slides on the actors which are then rephotoraphed and
cut ins from stock footage.   roses in a yellow bowl
RED.   Moroccan set red rugs red curtains/red paintings coppor lustre wash
basin here and there sepia orange and yellow. Opening shot shows the
    set swirling in nitrous red orange fumes..(This is cheap and easy. You
put copper filings in nitric acid the fumes rise up and a ventilating hood
sucks them away)   cut to naked red haired boy with his legs up on
sepia bed spread fumes still rising from his rectal and public hairs.
I mean pubic but public under the circumstances.Both figures the boy
knees up the other kneeling in front of him are bathed in red porjections
from the slide porjectors stock footage of sun sets red flowers and
landscapes cut in back to the boys making it in clear sharp detail...
(Cut ins and slide projection must never appear as cope out or cover
up)   We can also cut in other ed haired boys from stock footage and
fully clothed red haired boys red neon and red concentrates made by
walking arounda city and filing every thing red. And of course if the
budget allows we can film the same boys in several red sets..Rose2/3
wall paper, Chinese, Mexican. We run as much red footage as possible
select and splice together the best moments. The orgasm will always
be shown folooved by cut in and projections...The boys come grand canyon
volcano autumn leaves spattered with blood in air drift away down a
coble stone street.
Blue... Blue in the prdominate color though related colors silver,
black and white gray mauve purple may also be used.   Camera pans
down cobble stone street after the bloody leaf and up to an attic
window...(Train whistle on sound track)...Room with blue wall paper
ship scenes, blue paintings silver frames two blond blue eyes boys making
it. A bluse mist fills the room... Mist clears showing two blond blue

                            ******

eyes boys. Mist still in pubic hairs. Same procedure using blue
projections and cut ins blue sea and water and sky and eyes and
flowers and mountains. After come vapor trails acroos blue sky…
Cut to yellow sky room with yellow wall paper sun light in yellow
pubic hairs the blue eyed blond boys in yellow sets with yellow
prjections and cut ins...
Cut to yellow sky..naked bly on yellow toilet seat sun light in yellow
pubic hair yellow hait in the wind fl yellow flowers two the two
yellow haired blue eyed boys making it in yellow set with yellow projections
and cut ins.
Now we have our red blue and yellow sets we can mix sets and colors...
Putting red hared boys in blue set yellow haired in red set. A red
and yellow haired boy in yellow set as much footage as we can afford.
From these color mixes we lead into other shots. For example red
haired boy and yellow haired boy in yellow set leads into scene from
The Dead Child., in the caddy's locker room where Kiki breaks the
orange and hands half of it to one of the blond boys and they make it.
A blue fade out here leads to 1920 nscenes in black and white and to

the Frisco Kid.. In this sequence cut in are snow glaciers white deaht
masks white statues. Bill yeah John introduces me to some sane people
with beards sane sun sets Grand Canyon the sane to you empty streets
like a crawl through the door of jock straps I consulted my God but
also proddings and thhthinks boys written across the sky a hospital bed
is John D.C. very necesssarily of any interest at all miles no word on
any survivors yet they strip off their jock straps wash around in the
dead soldiers like dogs boy spits blood all over his 'go there soon?'
spitting his question in blood. John's father says coney there on top
are you going to remember this later I couldn't find him on the balcony sell
on plays taps report 18 TB and spit blood all over top floor berase
selectively and the jockey is useless to me getting sand in sick planet
will you now then how friendly comfy ride in sand wild boys in rainbow
    the men's typee Johnny is out too a mailman wild about what and why inside
propped on indubitable truth but not bandaged and wasted and thin its you
Johnny you know both of us use Adghanistan if tempting aND roll film 18
now Johnny's back hospital roll in carrion happy dogs do you and partners
pretend to die finally outside examine yourself outside

                              ******

Sex and flash back scenes show the actors in different settings changing
From one character to another Audrey may be the Frisco Kid or any other
wild boy character may interchange with another this makes the editing
and splicing of sx scenes much easier. In the opening scene the actors
are introduced one after the other and picked out with slide projector.
Bfief Bill and Tony's flash on scene screen . The Wild Boys have no
names takes us into a hard corn flick over the bar They Share Bodies
another flick starts the go go boys start to dance rather apathetically
to idiot mambo. The great Slastubitch snaps his fingers. and says
"Baddies"
Enter the CIA man with a lawman and Old Sarge in decent church going
woman drag.
"What are you doing in front of decent people?" He bellows
The bartender flicks a switch. The Go boys go mad to idiot mambo
shooting all over the screen. Cut in shooting stars.   Cut to space
capsile where Johnny and Mark jack off... "They went thaway."
On screen the CIA man says. "Machine hick gun hick the little hick bastards"
A wild boy smiles and sparys him with machine gun bullets. He goes down
hiccupping blood. The cop appear on screen as Rodriguez blasting with
his 45 as he screams CHINGOA...Tio Mate smiles draws aims and fires
Rodriguez collapses acorss balcony. Scene shakes out of focus leaving
Tio Mate's smaie smilae across the Mexican sky and vultures. Old Sarge
Still in drag.."All right you jokers fall in."
The wild boys seep dowan a hill on roller skates in rainbow jock straps
    Knives drawn teeth bare.In the next scene the boys have carried the
dead soldiers into a barracks. They cover the bodies with flags and play
taps. as they strip off their jock straps and roll around in dead soldiers
and flags like dogs rolling in carrion. "Got a liver knife?" says
a slack jawed wild boy. Sure he takes the sharp little curved knife

and diftly sliced the raw liver from a dead soldier. The boys chew
it and go into TB acts... IT's me lungs sir..Toke two me Bortoher
@@@@@@@@@@@@@@@@@@ He spits out a wad of chewed liver.. Another couple
is acting out Camille and of course ideally a boy comes and spits blood
lall over his partners and pretends to die. Others act out dying soliders
on the batle field getting fucked by his ass hole buddy to taps and
break the news to mother and the star spangled banner. This scene fades
into red haired boys making it with scenery cut ins rosses raw meat

17

William S. Burroughs, Transcendence Porn, and *The Ticket That Exploded*

KATHARINE STREIP

Transcendence porn, the fetishized portrayal and consumption of modes of so-called transcendence, offers a captivating fantasy of immediacy, cohesion, and meaning, the equivalent of a spiritual orgasm. It promises immediate access to an immaterial truth that resolves all questions and ambiguities. It suggests escape from embodiment through an engagement with a radically different realm that is infinite, spiritual, and transtemporal.[1] Transcendence porn can be found through mysticism (union with an absent God) and Western philosophy (rational ego, transcendent sources of judgment, spontaneous free acts, universally binding moral imperatives).[2] It can also be seen in forms of posthumanism that seek to transcend materiality through fantasies of immortality, autonomy, and disembodiment inherited from humanism. The apparent disembodiment of information contributes to this fantasy, when the body becomes a machine and the mind is equivalent to software programs. Long before the existence of cybernetic discourse, fantasies of romantic love, eternal union, and soul mates also expressed a profound cultural desire for spiritual transcendence.[3]

William S. Burroughs was not immune to the attractions of transcendence porn, but he counters its spell in his writing through black humor and representations of materiality, mediation, kinesis, and the senses. These efforts have been insufficiently noted by critics, who tend to concentrate on Burroughs' dislike of the body and its limitations, well summarized by Ihab Hassan's description of Burroughs' project: "His true aim is to free man by making him bodiless and silencing his language" (1982, 250). In a powerful analysis of Burroughs' work, Robin Lydenberg also argues that "the predominant impulse of his writing is toward 'sense withdrawal' and silence, toward the destruction of word and body" (1987, 138). Although Cary Nelson points out that "Burroughs perhaps uses more images of body life and internal processes than any other author" (1991, 131), he too argues that, for Burroughs, "the human body is nothing more than a 'soft machine' programmed to satisfy the absolute needs of its controllers" (125).[4] Micheal Sean Bolton reduces the impact of the physical in Burroughs when he describes how "Burroughs' bodies, in fact, become simulacra, akin to the maps that replace territories" (2014, 107). In

Timothy Murphy's formulation, language keeps us prisoners in corrupt material bodies and liberation from language equals freedom from materiality: "Language, '*the word*', imprisons people in material bodies, which are subject to decay and little better than excrement, when they could be flying through the 'great skies,' free from materiality" (1998, 117). N. Katherine Hayles suggests a more complicated relation between language and the body when she remarks that "Burroughs turns the tables on those who advocate disembodiment. Instead of discourse dematerializing the body, in *Ticket*, the body materializes discourse" (1999, 194).[5]

In his writing, Burroughs suggests the attractions and dangers of transcendence porn through his use of embodied structures, images, qualities, feelings, emotions, and the rhythm and flow of his language. Transcendence porn enhances the seductive power of what Burroughs calls "the reality film,"[6] and life outside of the reality film is grim. As *Ticket* explains, "Clearly no portentous exciting events are about to transpire. You will readily understand why people will go to any lengths to get in the film to cover themselves with any old film scrap .. junky .. narcotics agent .. thief .. informer .. anything to avoid the hopeless dead-end horror of being just who and where you all are: dying animals on a doomed planet" (Burroughs 2014c, 171, added to second edition).[7] The consequences of life without the gratifying illusions offered by transcendence porn make us painfully aware of materiality and the human body: "Work for the reality studio or else. Or else you will find out how it feels to be *outside the film*. I mean literally without film left to get yourself from here to the corner .. Every object raw and hideous sharp edges that tear the uncovered flesh" (172, added to second edition).

I deliberately emphasize that these quotes are from the revised 1967 edition of *Ticket* because arguments that Burroughs advocates unequivocal withdrawal from the senses, freedom from materiality, and complete abandonment of the body also point to a critical neglect of the material history of *Ticket*, as if acknowledgment of the physical text risked an encounter with "raw and hideous sharp edges" that could damage an idealized *Ticket* usually represented by a few quotations read out of context. As Christopher Breu argues, "in an era in which economic and cultural production have become increasingly fascinated with the virtual, the immaterial, and the textual, it becomes crucial to theorize the material" (2014, 1).[8] Let us therefore start by looking at actual changes in the first and second editions of *The Ticket That Exploded*. Fortunately, readers can now track the differences between versions of *The Ticket That Exploded* through Oliver Harris's groundbreaking new edition of the Cut-Up Trilogy (2014).[9]

Critics rarely acknowledge that there are actually two distinct versions of *The Ticket That Exploded*, an original 1962 edition and a revised version published five years later. Their analyses do not reflect the consequences of this five-year gap or discuss how Burroughs' return to narration after his immersion within the cut-up and fold-in process influences the conceptual field within which he works. The extent of these revisions is surprising. Burroughs added more than fifty pages to the second edition of *Ticket*.[10] More than half of the first fifty-eight pages are new, and if we compare the endings of the two editions, *"silence to say good-bye,"* in the final section of the Olympia Press edition, is six pages long. In the 1967 revised version, it has more than tripled in length and acquired a long coda, the essay *"the invisible generation."* To help appreciate the scope of these revisions, new sections in the 1967 edition of *The Ticket That Exploded* include all of *"see the action, B. J."* (1–7); in *"winds of time"*: "The Garden of Delights [...] He doesn't remember.'" (10–24); "wearing the HAPPY CLOAK [...] LONDON W. C. 1." (25–26); "- 'a thin singing shrillness [...] Kuttner page 143." (26); "The Green Pine Inn [...] across the valley." (29–34); "all from an old movie will give at his touch." (36); in *"operation rewrite"*: "The 'Other Half' [...] *before we can stop it.*" (55–57); "The District supervisor [...] 3D in time?)" (57–58); in *"combat troops in the area"*: "sunlight through the dusty window [...] smell of young nights. ." (126–33); in *"vaudeville voices"*: "Tuesday was the last day for signing years [...]'Never Happened' is my name ..." (137–40); in *"call the old doctor twice"*: "Martin's reality film [...] tear the uncovered flesh." (137–40); in *"shuffle cut"*: "Remember show price? [...] 'The whole of it, mate.'" (176–77); in *"in that game"*: "(Take a talking picture of you [...] consequent physical death.)" (181–82); "It's all done with tape recorders [...] you have nothing to lose but your prerecordings" (184–89); "It's all done with tape recorders [...] they can't tell the difference." (191–92); in *"showed you the air"*: "The Old Man himself [...] the brownest nose." (197–98); in *"silence to say good-bye"*: "John made coffee [...] on Portland Place." (209–26); "What summer will I will you? [...] my film ends.'" (229–30); "'See the action B. J.? This Hassan I Sabbah really works for Naval Intelligence and .. Are you listening B. J.?'" (230); and the final essay, *"the invisible generation."*[11] These additions demonstrate Burroughs' sensitivity to embodiment and his exploration of subjectivities emerging through organic and social processes, as "scrub and vines grow through blackened tape recorders where goats graze and lizards bask in the afternoon sun. G.O.D. is the smell of burning leaves in cobblestone streets a rustle of darkness and wires frayed sounds of a distant city" (30, added to second edition). The evolution of *The Ticket That Exploded* reveals Burroughs' profound awareness of how meaning and experience only become possible through physical bodies within densely interconnected habitats.

We can see this emphasis in the new prominence given to material documents as Burroughs highlights explicit examples of splicing and suturing texts. He does not just blend external texts seamlessly into his own, as Bolton describes in a revealing discussion of Burroughs' "unique narrative effects" (2014, 41), but insists on foregrounding the physical act of incorporation by openly showing this process. These examples include references to his own work in sections one and two: "I am reading a science fiction book called *The Ticket That Exploded*" (Burroughs 2014c, 6), "That was in 1962" (10); two references to science-fiction novels, Henry Kuttner's *Fury* and Barrington J. Bayley's *The Star Virus* (25–26, 177);[12] references to poems by E. E. Cummings (133)[13] and *The Diamond as Big as the Ritz* by F. Scott

Fitzgerald (210–12);[14] and the character Bill reading from an earlier section of *"combat troops in the area"* ("sunlight through the dusty window of the basement workshop" [128 and 210]).[15] All these instances were added to the second edition. Along with revisions that urge readers to take action through sound and visual cut-ups in order to step outside the "reality film," culminating with the tape recorder manifesto *"the invisible generation,"* these insertions contribute to a project that mobilizes materiality as a political gesture.[16]

There is a fervent plea against the attractions of transcendence in the first edition of *Ticket*:

> Reverse all your gimmicks—your heavy blue metal fix out in blue sky—your blue mist swirling through all the streets of image to Pan Pipes—your white smoke falling in luminous sound and image flakes—your bank of word and image scattered to the winds of morning—into this project all the way or all to see in Times Square in Piccadilly—Reverse and dismantle your machine—Drain off the prop ocean and leave the White Whale stranded—all your word line broken from mind screens of the earth—You talk about 're-sponsibility'—Now show responsibility—Show total responsibility—You have blighted a planet—Now remove the blight—Cancel your 'white Smoke' and all your other gimmicks of control—your monopoly of life, time and fortune canceled by your own orders. (2014c, 152–53)

These "gimmicks" include the seductive White Whale who leads Ahab in *Moby Dick* to gamble his ship and crew in its pursuit through the "prop ocean," an element of the reality film. The "heavy blue metal fix out in blue sky," the "blue mist swirling," the media monopoly and essentialist concepts of "time, life and fortune," contribute to a blighted planet according to Burroughs in the first edition of *Ticket*.[17] The second edition will offer ways to show responsibility and counter this blight through increased recognition of material bodies.

The first section of the 1967 edition ends with a pitch for a film script, and in its final lines, before Brion Gysin's calligraphy, the pitchman still aggressively sells ideas for stories. Why frame an "exploded ticket" with pitches for screenplays? At the end of section one:

> Now how's this for an angle? Are you listening B.J.? This clean living decent heavy metal kid and a cold glamorous agent from the Green Galaxy has been sent out to destroy him with a Sex Skin but she falls for the kid and she can't do it and she can't go back to her own people because of the unspeakable tortures meted out to those who fail on a mission so they take off together in a Gemini space capsule perhaps to wander forever in trackless space or perhaps? (2014c, 7, added to second edition)

The proposed scenario is both comic and poignant as it invokes clichés from science fiction. It combines thematic elements of Burroughs' writing such as sex skins and trackless space with powerful "gimmicks" of identity ("clean living," "glamorous"), language and its limits ("unspeakable tortures," "perhaps?"), love, transcendence, and eternity. At the conclusion of *Ticket*, we find: "'See the action, B.J.? This Hassan I Sabbah really works for Naval Intelligence and .. Are you listening B.J.?" (230, added to the second edition).[18] Hassan I Sabbah, the legendary leader of the Ismaili Order of Assassins and a central figure for revolution in Burroughs' later writing, is exposed as a spy working for the military in this proposed screenplay.[19] In both cases, it is unclear if the Director pays any attention to his persistent interlocutor. The proposed films attempt to bedazzle with addictive hooks that protect us from "the hopeless dead-end horror of being just who and where you all are." These tragi-comic reminders of the power of stories to distract from materiality frame the emancipatory and transformative work of the fold-ins and cut-ups as they expose "uncovered flesh" and plot devices.

Escape from the material human body was not an option in the first edition of *Ticket*. The original 1962 version begins with the section "winds of time" and a description of "ectoplasmic flakes of old newspapers and newsreels swirling over the smooth concrete floor" of a ruined warehouse (1962, 7). A couple, composed of the room's owner and a green boy with sensitive purple gills, attempt to escape and are forced to return to the human condition: "The two beings twisted free of human coordinates rectums merging in a rusty swamp smell [...] Mineral silence through the two bodies stuck together in a smell of KY and rectal mucus fell apart in time currents swept back into human form" (8). Rusty swamp smells and sticky rectal mucus assault the senses as time is conflated with the human form. At first "he" cannot remember, but then recalls, a blue metal boy and a green boy-girl who metamorphose into "he" and Bradley on a space ship while "his body flushed with spectral presences like fish of brilliant colors flashing through clear water—tentative beings that took form and color from the creatures skin membrane of light." A composite being starts to form, "one body in translucent green flesh" until he is pulled back as a human body: "He felt crushing weight of the Green Octopus who was there to block any composite being and maintain her flesh monopoly of birth and death—Her idiot camp followers drew him into the Garden of Delights—back into human flesh" (8–9). Lydenberg sees this insistent evocation of smells, sounds, sensation, and volume when the two beings try to twist free of human coordinates as the first example of a pattern of frustrated escape from word, image, and time throughout *Ticket*. As she explains, "The narrative of *Ticket*, however, has been announcing this liberation since the first chapter, only to be repeatedly drawn back down to earth" (1987, 93). However, this return to earth actually serves as an essential aspect of liberation for Burroughs. Burroughs' cut-up project mobilizes all the senses as part of the struggle with word, image, and time. It is no accident that Burroughs will later identify the Garden of Delights as GOD (2014c, 10, added to the second edition). The Garden of Delights is not just a sensual paradise but exemplifies the seductions of transcendence. Material reality offers a radical break from the reality script.

To emphasize this new attitude toward the physical, the revised *Ticket* opens with another couple, no longer boys of indeterminate species surrounded by flicker ghosts, but an "I" denouncing a "he" who snores in a description where the only active merging takes place through the pronoun "we." As Alenka Zupancic observes in a discussion of the relation between love and comedy, "to love someone 'for what he is' [...] always means to find oneself with a 'ridiculous object,' an object that sweats, snores, farts and has strange habits" (2003, 174). *Queer*, with its story of Lee's emotional addiction for Allerton, forms a vital point of origin for "see the action, B.J." as Oliver Harris argues in his introduction (2014b, xxiii–xxiv). It repeats "essential details" from that book—landscapes in South America, a CIA voice and a limited intelligence defined by chess playing (Harris 2003, 128). However, *"see the action, B.J.?"* transforms Lee's obsession with Allerton and dramatizes the Other Half mentioned throughout *Ticket*. The narrator no longer needs to merge with, or "schlupp," this consort. The new introduction to *Ticket* presents affects and energies that turn time into space through additions that anticipate sections already written for the first edition of *Ticket*. Phrases reverberate and echo, setting up a visceral music that can isolate words from narrative just as a tape recorder isolates speech from a time-bound "personality." No amount of theorizing can substitute for the suggestive harmonies of these cut-up words and phrases, so that a reader at once participates in a narrative and responds to writing from a past now set in the future.

The first four sentences begin: "It is a long trip. We are the only riders. So that is how we have come to know each other so well that the sound of his voice and his image flickering over the tape recorder are as familiar to me as the movement of my intestines the sound of my breathing the beating of my heart. Not that we love or even like each other" (Burroughs 2014c, 1). The "image flickering" here proactively anticipates the "flickering form of his companion naked in copulation space suit that clung to his muscular blue silence" (9) from the former first section, now part of the second section, as Burroughs creates echoes and reverberations in a rhythmic experience of unfolding forms throughout *Ticket*. These first sentences also foreshadow the already written chapter "do you love me?" dating from the 1962 edition of *Ticket*, where sound from a tape recorder evokes a reluctant phantom partner in a parody of rituals of courtship and sex: "He danced around the table caressing a shadowy figure out of the air above the recorder—A tentative shape flickering in and out of focus to the sound track" (2014c, 48–49). With his new section one, Burroughs introduces a synesthetic form of mediation, sound and image flickering over a tape recorder. We are reminded of Burroughs' fascination with media, with containing shapes and spaces as well as with contents, with skin as well as with inner organs, with recorders as well as with recordings. This complex structure of surfaces helps Burroughs explore physical, psychic, and intellectual worlds. Burroughs questions subject position and identification with his new first section, and his emphasis on permeable skin throughout *Ticket* shows porous membranes within global ecologies.[20] He emphasizes the importance of the body as medium through his description of the narrator's intestinal movement and the sounds of heartbeat and breath. The association between tape recorder and body throughout *Ticket* demonstrates the need to become conscious of word and image as we experience the body as a visceral recorder imbricated in relations with others. The links between narration, ecologies, and material practices are expanded and amplified in the second edition of *Ticket*.

In order to appreciate the strategic evolution of Burroughs' writing, it is helpful to compare the relations between the couples, Allerton and Lee in *Queer*, and the narrator and his adversary at the beginning of the second edition of *Ticket*. When Lee and Allerton go to a movie in Mexico City in *Queer* (significantly enough, Cocteau's *Orpheus*, another frustrated attempt at transcendence), "In the dark theater Lee could feel his body pull toward Allerton, an amoeboid protoplasmic projection, straining with a blind worm hunger to enter the other's body, to breathe with his lungs, see with his eyes, learn the feel of his viscera and genitals" (1987, 33). Lee wants to "schlupp" Allerton, a term Burroughs uses to express a longing to absorb the other that informs his experience of love and desire.[21] However, in the revised edition of *Ticket*, schlupping is farmed out to mollusks and sex skins. Structures of feeling are decentralized and dispersed among non-unitary subjects, creating new affective compounds.[22]

We see an example of "affective activism" (Houen 2012, 250) within a page of the revised first section, when Burroughs explores the psychological effects of a smile. Burroughs' interest in the smile as both a physical and cultural phenomenon occurs throughout his writings.[23] A smile is a physical expression all humans share (even the blind smile) and an expression we can willfully manipulate, the easiest facial expression to perform voluntarily, independent of emotions (Friesen and Danner 2002, iv). The deceptive smile develops from the same neurologically based, emotional/interactional beginnings as a genuine smile (v), an enmeshment of the biological and cultural.

In *Queer*, Lee smiles, not Allerton. "He nodded to Allerton and smiled. Allerton nodded, as if in surprise, and did not smile" (1987, 14). Lee's smile combines lust and innocence like a double exposure photograph: "As Lee stood aside to bow in his dignified old-world greeting, there merged instead a leer of naked lust, wrenched in the pain and hate of his deprived body and, in simultaneous double exposure, a sweet child's smile of liking and trust, shockingly out of time and place, mutilated and hopeless," a smile that could be a biographical cut-up (15). The smile assumes a life of its own, an expression of contradictory affects that serves as a container for suffering and vulnerability. In the first section of the revised *Ticket*, a smile allows something non-human, similar to an alien mollusk, to emerge from the narrator's unnamed consort as the narrator observes: "His smile was the most unattractive thing about him or at least it was one of the unattractive things about him it split his face open and something quite alien like a predatory mollusk looked out different" (2014c, 2).[24] Burroughs challenges the illusion of separation between a transcendent ego and the outside world through this image of the mollusk within. This predatory mollusk is alien from the body it inhabits, part of the world it observes, and returns later in the section.

Instead of the misery of unrequited love, the narrator describes an antagonistic equilibrium between "he" and "I" and deliberately satirizes the concept of individual and independent desire, as both characters wish for their own face to be the last picture that the other sees when dying in imaginary film sequences: "my face will be his last picture. He always planned that *his* face should be my last picture" (2014c, 3). Both "he" and "I" become part of an imaginary film as the narrative progresses. Their equilibrium is emphasized through terms such as "we," their identical hostility ("Not that we love or even like each other. In fact murder is never out of my eyes when I look at him. And murder is never out of his eyes when he looks at me" [1]), a similar lack of interest ("I had made my point and lost interest [. . .] Thinking on any other level simply did not interest him" [2]), comparable misdeeds ("But then who am I to be critical few things in my own past I'd just as soon forget .." [2]), the same space/time coordinates ("we simply find ourselves on the same ship sharing the same cabin and often the same bed welded together by a million shared meals and belches" [3]) and identical end of life fantasies. Burroughs gives the consort a devilish sense of humor ("Don't get ideas" he smiles and mutters when the narrator turns him over on his side or stomach to silence his abominable snoring [3]). This new introduction no longer invokes romantic love or sexual obsession to define human relations and emotional addiction, but rather, uses material practices as a way to illuminate emotions so that we can write our own scripts.

The introduction, with its last picture fantasy, dramatizes a new parenthesis added to the section "*in that game*" that gives instructions for the proposed actions that are so important in the second edition of *Ticket*:

> Take a talking picture of you. Now stop the projector and sound track frame by frame: stop ..go go go .. stop .. go go .. *Stop*. When the sound track stops it stops. When the projector stops a still picture is on screen. This would be your last picture the last thing you saw. Your sound track consists of your body sounds and sub-vocal speech. Sub-vocal speech *is* the word organism the 'Other Half' spliced in with your body sounds. You are convinced by association that your body sounds will stop if sub-vocal speech stops and so it happens. Death is the final separation of the sound and image tracks. However, once you have broken the chains of association linking sub-vocal speech with body sounds shutting off sub-vocal speech need not entail shutting off body sounds and consequent physical death.) (2014c, 181–82, added to second edition)

The initial drama between "he" and "I" has already shown readers the difficulty of breaking the chains of association between body sounds and sub-vocal speech, when we read: "In fact his voice has been spliced in 24 times per second with the sound of my breathing and the beating of my heart so that my body is convinced that my breathing and heart will stop if his voice stops" (3). Now we receive explicit instructions on how to break those chains of association.

The narrator's consort offers a winsome smile in response to the narrator's fear that his "body sounds will stop if sub-vocal speech stops" (2014c, 182) and observes "Well [. . .] it does give a certain position of advantage" (3), a pleasantry that foresees an observation from a long addition to the second section where Mr. Lee tries to solve a crime involving a missing Genial. Mr. Taylor from the Special Branch describes the tools of the Logos group, an organization that deliberately resembles Scientology:[25]

> it would seem that a technique a tool is good or bad according to who uses it and for what purposes. This tool is especially liable to abuse. In many cases they become 'clear' by unloading their 'engram' tapes on somebody else. These 'engram' tapes are living organisms viruses in fact .. This does give a certain position of advantage .. any opposition crippled by 'engram' tapes .. the 'clears' burning with a pure cold flame of self-interest a glittering image that lights up clearer and clearer as it fragments other image and ingests the dismembered fragments .. Yes we know the front men and women in this organization but they are no more than that .. a façade .. tape recorders .. the operators are *not there* .. (2014c, 23–24, added to the second edition)

The strategic advantage caused by the narrator's fear that he will die if his consort stops talking anticipates the strategic advantage when members of the Logos group become clear and unload their tapes onto others. The narrator's crippling fear resembles a "tape" that allows his consort to live and thrive. The clears, motivated by "a pure cold flame of self-interest," become transcendent, nothing but "a glittering image that lights up clearer and clearer." They succeed with their final fantasy as they ingest and absorb until they are "not there." All that is left are the "recorders" in an embodied, anti-transcendent image. The value of the techniques offered by *Ticket* is situational rather than abstract—"you can verify this proposition by a simple experiment" (205). Affect, technology, and agency combine to show that audio techniques such as splicing can break the chains of association between body sounds, sub-vocal speech, and fear of death, or can contribute to absorption and disappearance.

An "ugly" smile becomes a "winsome smile" when "he" observes that if the narrator succeeds in killing him, the narrator kills himself and that "it does give a certain position of advantage" (2014c, 3). This position of advantage generates a new routine, a satiric film about sexual obsession. We "see" the consort's Cinerama film sequence of physical predilections, complete with a Director bellowing orders—"I want you to shit and piss all over yourself when you see the gallows. Synchronize your castor oil will you? And give the pitiless hang boy an imploring look for Chrisakes he's your ass hole buddy about to hang you and that's the *drama* of it . . ." When someone remarks, "It's a sick picture B.J," the narration explicitly makes fun of emotional conventions, as (presumably) the Director asks, "Now what do you boys *feel* about a situation like this? Well go on express yourselves .. This is a *progressive* school .. These youths of image and association now at entrance to the garden carrying banners of interlanguage .." (4).[26] Interlanguage, language that emphasizes both community and interment, soon conjures the predatory mollusk who peeked out when the consort first smiled, for a mollusk also plays a role in this film, as the director of the fantasy continues, "They got this awful mollusk eats the hanged boys body and soul in the orgasm and they love being eaten because of this liquefying gook it secretes and rubs all over them but maybe I'm talking too much about private things" (4). The voracious ego-like mollusk absorbs the "self," body and soul, in a repeated motif. "Private things" should contribute to a clear demarcation of inner and outer, but in Burroughs' writing this border dissolves through liquefying gook, jelly, sex skins, and happy cloaks that remove the boundaries between self and world.

The new first section of *Ticket* presents a script/routine where talk of private things and liquefying gook provokes a comic, outraged reaction—"You boys going to stand still for this? Being slobbered down and shit out by an alien mollusk?" (2014c, 5). Instead the boys should join the army and see the world, but this change inaugurates the same process of absorption. The routine recycles the image of being eaten alive when it describes a patrol liberating a river town that picked up the Sex Skin habit ("This Sex Skin is a critter found in the rivers here wraps all around you like a second skin eats you slow and good .." [5]). A young soldier tries "to rescue his buddy from a Sex Skin and it grew onto him and now his buddy turns from him in disgust .. anyone would you understand and that's not the worst of it it's knowing at any second your buddy may be took by the alien virus it's happened cruel idiot smile over the corn flakes" (5). A smile first introduces the alien virus in the revised *Ticket*.

The smile of the unnamed consort opens the door for transcendence porn when the narrator describes his opportunistic cruelty. "Then he smiled his eyes narrowed and his sharp little ferret teeth showed between his thin lips which were a blue purple color in a smooth yellow face" (2014c, 2). These blue purple lips signal Burroughs' fascination with the color blue, which appears 140 times in the second edition of *The Ticket That Exploded*.[27] Blue, as Oliver Harris points out, is associated with the drugs *yage* and apomorphine and Wilhelm Reich's orgones in Burroughs' writing (Introduction to *The Soft Machine* 2014a, xxxiv), but in *Ticket* it is also linked to silence (2014c, 9, 71, 174), songs such as "My Blue Heaven" (50, 51, 195), music (the blue notes of Pan), and money ("blue mist of vaporized bank notes") (2014c, 160, 173; 2014a, 32–33).[28] In spite of all its connotations, Markus Gabriel argues, "Blue is always a symbol for transcendence" (Gabriel and Žižek 2009, 28). Because of its semantic field, blue is "a word that sells" through its associations with "the sky, the sea, repose, love, travel, vacations, the infinite [. . .] The symbolic connection between blue, calm, and peace is an old one" (Pastoureau 2001, 180–81).[29] We see the power of blue as an expression of transcendence when the Old Doctor, who appears in the first edition of *Ticket*, pacifies the screaming marks with his blue hands: "Yes when the going gets really rough they call in the Old Doctor to quiet the marks—and he just raises his old blue hands and brings them down slow touching all the marks right where they live and the marks are quiet" (2014c, 159).[30] The doctor's blue hands pacify and tranquilize the hysterical marks with the promise of transcendence:

The Old Doctor reeled out onto the platform—Then he heard the screaming marks and he steadied himself and he drew all of it into him and he stood up very straight and calm and grey as a wise old rat and he lifted his old blue hands shiny over the dirt and he brought them down slow in the setting sun feeling all the marks so nasty and they just stood there quiet his cold old hands on their wrists and ankles, hands cold and blue as liquid air on wrist and ankle just frozen there in a heavy blue mist of vaporized bank notes—(2014c, 160)

Those blue hands compensate for the doctor's condition ("reeling"), his character ("a wise old rat"), and clientele ("dirt," "so nasty") as he "draws all of it into him" as the blue of transcendence is linked with economic power, "a heavy blue mist of vaporized bank notes." The blue purple lips of the nameless consort's smile in the first section causes the narrator to capitulate ("But then who am I to be critical few things in my own past I'd just as soon forget .." [2]). As the sun sets, those blue hands quiet the crowd with liquid air, icy mist, and vapor fueled by economic fantasy, in a benediction that promises transcendence.

A counter to transcendence porn can be found in the two "John and Bill" sections added to the second edition (2014c, 126–33 and 209–13). After a retreat operation with the call to shift three-dimensional coordinate points for time travel, "Like this"::—the example of such a shift is a conversation between young John and Bill in the basement. The exchange is striking and a powerful contrast to the relation between the narrator and his consort at the beginning of *Ticket*. As Lydenberg points out, "this sort of conversation is very unusual in Burroughs' fiction—an exchange between friends uncomplicated by ulterior motives of control and domination. There is a desire of understanding which is genuine and communal. Even the difficulties of communication . . . are familiar and oddly affectionate" (1987, 85). However, it is significant that the conversation is framed by an initial cut-up of two scenes between John and Bill that occur ten years apart (2014c, 126–28). It is crucial for Burroughs' work that cut-ups occur before the narrative of their conversation. The "conventional" narrative starts after the description "John's face grew wispy" with "a soft blue flame in his eyes as he bent over the crystal radio set touching dials and wires with gentle precise fingers" (128) and only a few subsequent cut-ups interrupt the narrative—"the tinkling metal music of space" (128) and "faint intermittent 'Smiles'" (128). The narrative continues until Bill asks, "Would there be any time if we didn't say anything?" and John replies, "Maybe not. Maybe that would be the first step .. yes if we could learn to listen and not talk" (129). At this point, conventional speech stops and cut-ups start again, mixing past and future, providing new associations between words, then stop briefly with "Let's see who can shoot the farthest" (131), form a hybrid of cut-up and narrative with "long ago boy image .. speed of light .. ten years .. the pool hall on Market St" and then return to conventional narrative as "Bill leaned across the table for a shot" (131) with a scene ten years in the future interrupted by a parenthetical memory of "Mike and me" high on Ganja and laughing till they pissed themselves (132). The cut-ups start again when Bill and John are about to have sex with a moving reference to E. E. Cummings and end with "smell of young nights" (133).

The second John and Bill exchange occurs in the concluding section, *"silence to say goodbye,"* after "Last round from St. Louis melted flesh identity," we read "John made coffee and scrambled some eggs" (2014c, 209). When Bill begins to read his novel out loud, his first words repeat the beginning of the cut-up on page 126, "sunlight through the dusty window" and continue with echoes and cut-ups of the earlier "John and Bill" passage. John reads an excerpt from F. Scott Fitzgerald's "The Diamond as Big as the Ritz," quoting Fitzgerald's words without punctuation until the penultimate line when Burroughs makes a few changes: "like a girls' school in fairyland" (Fitzgerald 1989, 213) becomes "like a school in fairyland" (2014c, 211). Cut-ups recommence until John explains that he will alternate their voices and gives Bill a copy of the *Saturday Evening Post* to read while he waits. Bill starts to read Fitzgerald's story. When John plays the two tapes together, "blue light filled the darkening room" and "the two boys naked bodies washed in blue twilight shivering and twitched in spasms . . . He was spiraling up toward the ceiling . . ." in an apparent moment of transcendence until cut-ups recommence and we are confronted with the harsh reminder "Life without flesh *is* the ovens" and "Life without flesh is repetition word for word" (2014c, 214, added to second edition).

The addition of the two couples (narrator and consort in *"see the action, B.J.?"* and Bill and John in *"combat troops in the area"* and *"silence to say goodbye"*), deliberate insertions at the beginning, middle, and end of the revised *Ticket*, show how Burroughs' work with the body, love, transcendent identity, and memory challenge transcendence porn. The couple in the introduction is locked into a relationship with fantasies of narrative transcendence that can only be resolved through mediated splicing. Bill and John show the beauty and danger of nostalgia for an irrecoverable past ("two young bodies stuck together like dogs teeth bared .. two dead stars .. they went out a long time ago in empty back yards and ash pits .. a rustle of darkness and wires .. They went out and never came back a long time ago .." [2014c, 213, added to second edition]). These "memories" are framed and interrupted by cut-ups that separate and merge temporalities, including the insertion of another "memory" of laughing until pissing, a material example of physical dissolution, creating new associative combinations. Explicit practices of cutting and rearranging association lines, whether through taped sound, film or the manipulation of written language, create an opportunity to break free, but this freedom is irrevocably material.

KATHARINE STREIP is an Associate Professor in the Liberal Arts College at Concordia University, Montreal, Quebec. She has published articles on Jean Rhys, Marcel Proust, Philip Roth, William S. Burroughs, James Joyce, Franz Kafka, and zombies and photography. Her research interests include comedy, the novel, emotions, modernism, postmodernism, new materialisms, media theory, multimodal literature, ecocriticism, popular culture, and avant-garde movements. She is currently writing a book on William S. Burroughs, media, and subjectivity.

NOTES

1. Mark Johnson offers a useful definition of transcendence as "rising above one's embodied situation in the world to engage a higher realm that is assumed to have a radically different character from that of the world in which we normally dwell" (2007, 14).

2. See Johnson, for example, for the relation between Immanuel Kant's philosophy and "the dangerous idea, so deeply rooted in Western culture, that purity of mind entails rising above one's bodily nature" (2007, 7).

3. I developed the concept "transcendence porn" while thinking about transhumanism and its implications for other examples of the desire for spiritual transcendence in Western culture. Authors who have contributed to my thoughts include Nick Bostrum (2005); N. Katherine Hayles (1999); Mark Johnson (2007); Bernard McGinn (1991) and (2006); Cary Wolfe (2010) and Alenka Zupancic (2003).

4. Craig Hansen Werner is one of the few critics to acknowledge the importance of the body in Burroughs when he remarks that "Silence attracts Burroughs only in the context of continuing bodily existence" (1982, 118).

5. In the Introduction to his new edition of *Ticket*, Oliver Harris points out the most recurrent word in *Ticket* is "body" (2014b, xxxiv). Critics often describe the body in Burroughs' work as a metaphor. As Hayles observes, "In *The Ticket That Exploded*, the body is a site for contestation and resistance on many levels, as a metaphor, as physical reality, as linguistic construct, and last but hardly least, as tape recorder" (1999, 211).

6. According to Murphy, "The reality film, like the Word or the spectacle, is a totality that is not so much a set of words that we speak or images that we watch as it is a general condition in which we are immersed, even and especially when we are apparently not focused on words or images. It is the material horizon of our existence" (2004, 34–35).

7. All page references to *Ticket* are from the Oliver Harris edition of *The Ticket That Exploded* (2014c), except for references to "*the invisible generation*" from the 1967 edition in the end notes.

8. For a reading of linguistic, bodily and political economic materiality in Burroughs' *Naked Lunch*, see Breu (2014, 35–60). In a discussion that relates Burroughs' cut-ups to F. A. Hayek's theory of the price system, Michael W. Clune discusses the tendency to read Burroughs in cybernetic terms, and observes how the smells that Burroughs frequently mentions cannot be reduced to information but actually provide a context for embodiment (2010, 81–84). Clune also notes how Burroughs emphasizes the "framing" role of the body with his cut-ups (182).

9. Harris reminds us that we should read the Cut-Up Trilogy as part of a decade-long experiment involving writing, audiotape, film, and artwork (2014b, xv). Ideally, these revisions would be read in the context of Burroughs' many publications in little magazines during this period. Because of Burroughs' extensive publication of sections of the Cut-Up Trilogy in alternative or underground journals, Harris suggests that "in this light, the three novels may even be seen as *aberrations*, extraordinary exceptions to the cut-up project rather than its necessary fulfillment" (2004, 178).

10. Harris speculates that Burroughs was discouraged by the response of readers to the cut-up method and so these new additions are an attempt to add more cohesion to the novel. See Harris for a discussion of these revisions as an "attempt to recover readability by restoring narrative" (1991, 256). He also credits Burroughs' work with tape cut-ups as responsible for much of the revisions (255). However, as Harris points out in his new edition, Burroughs' plan to make the *Ticket* more readable did not mean that he expunged cut-up material: "just over half of the 1962 text consists of cut-up, just under half of the 1967 text, although the impossibility of defining what is and isn't 'cut-up' (or 'fold-in') makes more precise calculations meaningless" (2014, xl).

11. I have only included revisions that are several lines long in this list. Harris indicates all Burroughs' cuts and insertions through individual page references in the notes section of his new edition of *Ticket* and eliminates the final essay "*the invisible generation.*"

12. Henry Kuttner's *Fury* was originally published in magazine format in 1947 and Barrington J. Bayley's *The Star Virus* was first published in 1964.

13. See Harris, Introduction to *Ticket*, for an illuminating reading of the Cummings reference (2014b, xlv).

14. Burroughs eliminates punctuation and makes a few changes to the passage from "The Diamond as Big as the Ritz." He also changes its publication history. Fitzgerald's story was rejected by the *Saturday Evening Post* and first appears in *The Smart Set* in June 1922 (Fitzgerald 1989, 182).

15. I have only mentioned inserts that are clearly identified, not fold-ins such as the words from Conrad's *Lord Jim* (Burroughs 2014c, 229) and from Shakespeare's *The Tempest* at the end of "*the invisible generation*" (Burroughs 1967, 217).

16. As Harris reminds us, Burroughs "made multiple claims" for his methods—"creative, political, therapeutic, scientific, even mystical" (2014b, xxxiii).

17. See Harris, Introduction to *The Soft Machine*, for how Burroughs attacked Henry Luce's media empire of "time, life and fortune" (2014, xxvii).

18. Harris removes the final quotation marks from this addition in order to create a parallel between the initials B.J. that end the printed text and the initials Bg. that end Gysin's calligraphy (2014, 287).

19. For an excellent discussion of Hassan I Sabbah and his role in Burroughs' work, see Murphy (1998, 116–30, 197–98).

20. The word "skin" occurs around eighty times in the new edition of *Ticket*, seven times in the first section alone.

21. For more on schlupping, see Miles's *Call Me Burroughs* (2014, 245).

22. See Alex Houen for an interesting discussion of how authors such as Burroughs create new affective compounds, novel forms of feeling, through their experiments with form and genre (2012, 242–50).

23. According to Harris, "There is only one case of the smile in Burroughs' fiction prominent enough to have attracted critical attention, which is the dreamy and deadly smile that reproduces itself like a disease in *The Wild Boys*" (2003, 29). See Harris (2003, 28–33) for a discussion of the importance of the smile in Burroughs' work.

24. My thinking here is influenced by a suggestive passage from Richard Doyle, who describes "the swaggering, worrying, anticipating ego [and] that ego warranting phenomenon, The Truth" as a mollusk and continues, "If The Truth is treated as a territory, a place, or 'foundation' where the mollusk-like ego can attach, then Truth, despite its obvious existence and cause for wonder in human consciousness, can easily function as a fortress for the ego and its delusions—such as the delusion that it is radically distinct from the world it observes" (2011, 272).

25. For Burroughs' relation to Scientology, see David S. Wills (2013), Barry Miles (2014, 465–71), and Ted Morgan (2012, 439–43), as well as Burroughs, *Ali's Smile: Naked Scientology* (1978).

26. See *Nova Express* for more references to "inter language": "These youths of image and association now at entrance to the avenue carrying banners of inter language" (2014a, 91) and "Word is TWO that is the noxious human inter language recorded" (94).

27. This includes four references to "blue" in the final essay, "*the invisible generation.*" Burroughs refers to "blue" at least 113 times in *The Soft Machine* and 96 times in *Nova Express*. I don't include the word "blueprint" in this tally.

28. A wonderful example of Burroughs' overdetermined use of blue can be seen in his description of a calculating machine that can process qualitative data—"I feed into the machine a blue

photo passes to the Blue Section and a hundred or a thousand blue photos rustle out while the machine plays blues in a blue smell of ozone, blue words of all the poets flow out on ticker tape" (2014a, 90). For a discussion of how *The Soft Machine* is organized into color units, see Harris, Introduction to *The Soft Machine* (2014a, xxxiv).

29. For a cultural history of the color blue, see Michel Pastoureau's *Blue: The History of a Color* (2001).

30. The repetition of motifs that depict the Doctor's blue hands in *Ticket* is notable: "if they lost his old blue hands" (2014c, 157); "heavy cold blue hands" (161); "if they lost his old blue hands over the sky" (163); "that old hand cold and blue as liquid air" (163); "The Old Doctor raises his blue hands" (208).

REFERENCES

Bolton, Micheal Sean. 2014. *Mosaic of Juxtaposition: William S. Burroughs' Narrative Revolution.* New York: Rodopi.

Bostrum, Nick. 2005. "A History of Transhumanist Thought." *Journal of Evolution and Technology* 14 (1): 1–30.

Breu, Christopher. 2014. *Insistence of the Material: Literature in the Age of Biopolitics.* Minneapolis: University of Minnesota Press.

Burroughs, William S. 1962. *The Ticket That Exploded.* Paris: Olympia.

———. 1967. *The Ticket That Exploded.* 2nd ed. New York: Grove.

———. 1978. *Ali's Smile Naked Scientology.* Gottingen: Expanded Media Productions.

———. 1987. *Queer.* New York: Penguin.

———. 2012. *Junky: The Definitive Text of "Junk."* Edited by Oliver Harris. New York: Grove.

———. 2014a. *Nova Express: The Restored Text.* Edited by Oliver Harris. New York: Grove. First published 1964.

———. 2014b. *The Soft Machine: The Restored Text.* Edited by Oliver Harris. New York: Grove.

———. 2014c. *The Ticket That Exploded.* Edited by Oliver Harris. New York: Grove.

Clune, Michael W. 2010. *American Literature and the Free Market, 1945–2000.* Cambridge: Cambridge University Press.

Doyle, Richard. 2011. *Darwin's Pharmacy: Sex, Plants, and the Evolution of the Noösphere.* Seattle: University of Washington Press.

Fitzgerald, F. Scott. 1989. *The Short Stories of F. Scott Fitzgerald.* Edited by Matthew J. Bruccoli. New York: Scribner.

Friesen, Wallace V., and Deborah D. Danner. 2002. Preface to *An Empirical Reflection on the Smile,* edited by Millicent H. Abel, iii–xii. Lewiston, NY: Edwin Mellen.

Gabriel, Markus, and Slavoj Žižek. 2009. *Mythology, Madness, and Laughter: Subjectivity in German Idealism.* London: Continuum.

Harris, Oliver. 1991. "Cut-Up Closure: The Return to Narrative." In *William S. Burroughs at the Front: Critical Reception, 1959–1989,* edited by Jennie Skerl and Robin Lydenberg, 251–64. Carbondale: Southern Illinois University Press.

———. 2003. *William Burroughs and the Secret of Fascination.* Carbondale: Southern Illinois University Press.

———. 2004. "Cutting Up Politics." In *Retaking the Universe: William S. Burroughs in the Age of Globalization,* edited by Davis Schneiderman and Philip Walsh, 175–200. London: Pluto Press.

———. 2014a. Introduction to *The Soft Machine,* by William S. Burroughs, ix–liii. New York: Grover.

———. 2014b. Introduction to *The Ticket That Exploded,* by William S. Burroughs, ix–lv. New York: Grove.

Hassan, Ihab Habib. 1982. *The Dismemberment of Orpheus: Toward a Postmodern Literature.* Madison: University of Wisconsin Press.

Hayles, N. Katherine. 1999. *How We Became Posthuman: Virtual Bodies in Cybernetics, Literature, and Informatics.* Chicago: University of Chicago Press.

Houen, Alex. 2012. *Powers of Possibility: Experimental American Writing since the 1960s*. Oxford: Oxford University Press.

Johnson, Mark. 2007. *The Meaning of the Body: Aesthetics of Human Understanding*. Chicago: University of Chicago Press.

Lydenberg, Robin. 1987. *Word Cultures: Radical Theory and Practice in William S. Burroughs' Fiction*. Urbana: University of Illinois Press.

———. 1992. "Sound Identity Fading Out: William Burroughs' Tape Experiments." In *Wireless Imagination: Sound, Radio, and the Avant-garde*, edited by Douglas Kahn and Gregory Whitehead, 409–37. Cambridge, MA: MIT Press.

McGinn, Bernard. 1991. *The Foundations of Mysticism: Origins to the Fifth Century*. Vol. 1 of *The Presence of God: A History of Western Christian Mysticism*. New York: Crossroad.

———, ed. 2006. *The Essential Writings of Christian Mysticism*. New York: Random House.

Miles, Barry. 2014. *Call Me Burroughs: A Life*. New York: Twelve.

Morgan, Ted. 2012. *Literary Outlaw: The Life and Times of William S. Burroughs*. New York: Norton.

Murphy, Timothy S. 1998. *Wising up the Marks: The Amodern William Burroughs*. Berkeley: University of California Press.

———. 2004. "Exposing the Reality Film: William S. Burroughs among the Situationists." In *Retaking the Universe: William S. Burroughs in the Age of Globalization*, edited by Davis Schneiderman and Philip Walsh, 29–57. London: Pluto.

Nelson, Cary. 1991. "The End of the Body: Radical Space in Burroughs." In *William S. Burroughs at the Front: Critical Reception, 1959–1989*, edited by Jennie Skerl and Robin Lydenberg, 119–32. Carbondale: Southern Illinois University Press.

Pastoureau, Michel. 2001. *Blue: The History of a Color*. Princeton, NJ: Princeton University Press.

Werner, Craig Hansen. 1982. *Paradoxical Resolutions: American Fiction since James Joyce*. Urbana: University of Illinois Press.

Wills, David S. 2013. *Scientologist!: William S. Burroughs and the 'Weird Cult'*. United Kingdom: Beatdom Books.

Wolfe, Cary. 2010. *What Is Posthumanism?* Minneapolis: University of Minnesota Press.

Zupancic, Alenka. 2003. *The Shortest Shadow: Nietzsche's Philosophy of the Two*. Cambridge, MA: MIT Press.

Dream Note on Indictment for Murdering Joan

In a dream note composed in London on Friday the thirteenth of February, 1970, for what might have been the first time in his life, Burroughs can be seen reflecting in writing on his feelings of guilt for his wife's murder, some two decades after their drunken rendition of the William Tell act. This archival manuscript originates fifteen years before Burroughs would write openly about Joan's death in his controversial preface to *Queer*, a novel he had written in the wake of her murder in 1951, but had kept unpublished until 1985. In this haunting page from Burroughs' intermittent, life-long diary writing, he illustrates the fragmented, confessional style, unsentimental but nostalgic, that he would go on to develop over the rest of his life, keeping dream calendars and taking notes on his nocturnal visions, until his careful practice culminated in his late masterpiece, *My Education: A Book of Dreams* (1992).

Identified in the archive as the one hundred and tenth page of the Berg's "Observer Time" file, this singular dream note amounts to just one day's contribution to one of many scrapbooks, multimedia works whose heterogeneous materials showcase Burroughs' method of chronologically collaging daily newspapers alongside his dreams. At a pivotal moment in his career, when he was recognized as a spokesperson for the counterculture, Burroughs writes of his most intimate regrets and fears. Considering that his mother had passed away in the previous year, by bringing back his most repressed memory, this dream seems to signify his sense of a deeper, lifelong feeling of emptiness, especially since his unintentional homicide of his wife had also deprived his own son of a mother. While his typo-riddled manuscript might seem fragmented in its imagery and narrative, there is something strangely symmetrical in its opening with the past tense "indictment" in England for his murder of Joan, and its ending, with his pitiful hope to get "extradited." Within the multiple meanings and connotations of this legalese, Burroughs captures the conflicted hope that undergirds his life and work, as he seeks to compensate for the evil of his past by challenging the control of external authorities, in his search for an inner space where peace might be regained.

—*AWC*

Had been indicted in England for the murder of Joan. Lawyer told t
me that I would almost vertainly be convicted and hanged because of
the prejudice against me in the minds of the prospective juror juros
jurors and af advised me to leave England
"But would'nt I be @@@@ stopped on the way out?"
He indicated that disguise was nex necessary and brought out a disguise
kit and dabbed at my face. I ,looked in the mirror and saw that I
now had an Irish face square jawed with a fringe of beard very hard
and arrogant.
(Went to a Party where I met Hemingway)   I had some one elses dogs with
me which was attacked by the house cats and one of them scratched me.
Still on the lam. I decided to go out through Scotland. The lawyers
Assistant would accompany me.   Once out I could not be extradited½

18

Gender Trouble: A Critical Roundtable on Burroughs and Gender

ANN DOUGLAS, ANNE WALDMAN,
AND REGINA WEINREICH

The following transcript is taken from a conversation about the relationship of William S. Burroughs to gender that took place on April 25, 2014, at the William S. Burroughs Centennial Conference held the CUNY Graduate Center in New York. The panel was moderated by Ann Douglas, the Parr Professor Emerita of English and Comparative Literature at Columbia University, and introduced by Alex Wermer-Colan, the conference organizer.

The panel's primary participants are Anne Waldman and Regina Weinreich. Waldman is an experimental poet who has authored over forty books, and co-founded with Allen Ginsberg the Jack Kerouac School of Disembodied Poetics at Naropa University where Burroughs served as a regular lecturer and participant. Weinreich is Professor of Humanities & Sciences at the School of Visual Arts in New York who has served as author, editor, and filmmaker for numerous critical works on Beat literature including Kerouac's Spontaneous Poetics: A Study of the Fiction (2002)

The following conversation has been condensed and edited for space.

DOUGLAS Our topic today is gender trouble, a way of mulling over and expanding the discussion of Burroughs' relationship to gender and to women. A great deal has been written about Burroughs the misogynist. Before we begin, as the moderator, I would like to note that Burroughs' closest friends, starting with Kerouac and Ginsberg, always understood that Burroughs had a persona that was, and wasn't, identical with his self. Which is not to say that there is no misogyny in Burroughs, just that Burroughs' performative self was a little different from his inside self. And that was especially true when it comes to the troubled question of misogyny. With that, we begin with Anne Waldman, who is going to read.

WALDMAN Just a reading, as an aside, from the *New York Times*. A piece entitled "Researchers See New Importance in the Y Chromosome" (Wade 2014). And it ends with a discussion of the difference between the genders even *before* sexual differentiation which is clearly a social construct: "Differences between male and female tissues are often attributed to the powerful influence of sex hormones. By now the twelve regulatory genes are known to be active throughout the body. There's clearly an intrinsic difference in male and female cells even before the sex hormones are brought into play. We are only beginning to understand the full extent of differences in molecular biology of males and females" (Wade 2014.)

I read *The Job: Interview with William S. Burroughs* by Daniel Odier (1970) shortly before I met William. If you remember, that book features William at his worst on women. So I felt at a little bit of a disadvantage when we first met. But I ended up sitting with him at a party in Bill Berkson's comfortable apartment on 57th Street talking about *African Genesis* (Ardrey, 1961). I had also read something apropos to his interests in *The Job* and we talked about sousveillance and the notion of people with their tape recorders strapped on and crowd control. We were able to veer into subjects that involved the female body as a "host" body. I knew William for twenty-five years—and I knew him pretty well. And I have to say that I don't think Odier's book really gives an accurate picture. Burroughs' obsessions were darkly visionary, sometimes repugnant, but never vindictive—and not the final word on his "sexism" which was quirky in the writing and never a problem personally.

I spent time with him in New York at the bunker with the wonderful support community he had around him. Of course, Allen was very involved with wanting William to live back in New York and James [Grauerholz] had recently arrived in New York, and the poetry community had welcomed William at The Poetry Project at St Mark's. He gave his big reading there and launched his new career as a performer of his work on the reading circuit to universities and festivals and the like. So in a sense he was being *lured* to stay. There's the Buddhist idea that you have to invite the great teachers to stick around. You have to *lure* them into your den and make it attractive and seductive. I think Allen was certainly working on that and helping to lure Bill. James was going to start work as his secretary. Things really changed in Bill's life and there was a whole new American generation and a culture here waiting for him, as has been discussed previously. We needed him.

From the start, I aligned myself with feminism, although I considered myself more of a cultural activist in a female body. But I was involved with feminist issues and going to some meetings, and that work was really important: equal pay, equal place in the poetry world and in publishing, abortion rights. There was so much. The things William says in that Odier interview don't reappear later. They're quite static actually, but the science of men birthing out of their own bodies could be a prophecy. It was interesting to hear the psychologizing bit of Miles's biography (2013, which goes into William's relationship with his mother, the controlling mother. He grew up in a genteel atmosphere, but where women presumably had the domestic power. He blames them for everything that's wrong in the world. You wonder where that is coming from in the 1960s, and I think it goes back to some deeper disjunct. His parents were in his life into his adulthood constantly bailing him out, supporting him, coming to his rescue. His mother really adored him in this totally unconditional way.

"Women were a basic mistake and the whole dualistic universe evolved from this error" (Odier 1970, 116). "I think love is a virus. I think love is a con put down by the female sex" (97). Odier asks about the women in the books . . . And then there's an idea William elaborates on that somehow the sexes could morph and come back together in the unified "perfect sphere," like Aristophanes speaks of, defining Eros, in *The Symposium* (385–70 BCE). So there was that public misogyny from that interview to contend with, but maybe he'd been unlucky in love—and being primarily homosexual, and most vulnerable there.

I also saw that later, as he became a celebrity in the celebrity world of New York, he was comfortable with Susan Sontag. He was comfortable with empowered women artists, poets, and writers who already knew what they were doing, who had a certain kind of intellectual gravitas, who could hold their own. He was close to Patti [Smith] and Laurie [Anderson] and myself. I think he respected people who had risen to something in their work and lives and so on. He was comfortable in that vibe, but he was definitely not *on* the Downtown scene in that way. I mean I saw him at work, at his writing and then when he came out to Naropa. He was very disciplined. "A writer writes," he always said. He had a whole schedule, a workday schedule that was helped by assistants—James [Grauerholz] and Steven Lowe and so on, but he was clearly on it. And in his classes at Naropa he would talk about that, that there's nothing wrong with being a professional writer.

He was a prose writer, published novels. The poets didn't talk this way at all—that writing is a profession and you should get paid for it. There was this question with the poets about writing for a higher spiritual purpose, and inspiration comes and goes and so on. There were often letters of inquiry from agents. He would say something like "If you invite me to your university, I'll talk about the profession of being a writer and how to get published." Bill was presenting that kind of professional ethos more than anybody else, which was sort of ironic. (One of our poets told certain students to drop poetry, become nurses, *really* help the world).

Although we were together at some festivals abroad, I knew William primarily at Naropa. There were no year-round classes exactly at that time; this was before accreditation. I'm sure a lot of you have heard some of the lectures that are up online at archive.org (Naropa Poetics Audio Archives), some of Burroughs' performances and readings and so on. Quite legendary. In Bill's sessions, I never saw any kind of distinction between male and female members of the class, whereas Allen Ginsberg would call women girls . . .

DOUGLAS Yes.

WALDMAN . . . and never remember their names. [Laughing] Anyway, if you looked Bill in the eye and you had a question and you weren't trying to get anything out of him more than intellectually, you were on safe turf. In Bill's book *My Education*, there's a dream where I come in as "Naropa Mother": "You need a place to stay? You got a dose of the clap? Take all your troubles to the Naropa Mother. She gives all the satisfaction" (1995, 26). So this idea of being the sheltering mother who can deal with all the problems, I happily played that role for Bill and for others . . . And I went to his classes and learned something.

In this way, through teaching, he was also available. You know, intellectually available. There's a portion of a recorded conversation, in *Beats at Naropa* (see Waldman and Wright 2009), which is with Chogyam Trungpa Rinpoche, Tibetan Buddhist lama, founder of Naropa, and Allen and others. Allen and Bill are asking Trungpa why enlightenment can't be more fun. That's what Burroughs wants to ask the dharma teacher. And there was a nice sort of prickly conversation that goes on. And Bill talks about going on retreat. I miss that discourse, the wild classes. One class was the Shakespeare class where each writer picked a play and Bill's was *Troilus and Cressida* (1602) and Allen's was *The Tempest* (1611) of course. And it's such a different kind of pedagogy. So William was comfortable—to some extent—those years, in this educational experiment which included women.

REGINA WEINREICH I just want to say that you [Douglas] mentioned earlier that I had written a book on Kerouac. I originally wanted to write my doctoral dissertation on Burroughs and I was told, "Do Kerouac, at least he's dead." That professional advice was offered: if I was going to have a career, I should at least write about someone whose own career was totally defined. If you are alive, you might continue to write. And that was quite ironic, because after I did a book on Kerouac, so many books on him came out. And now we're learning, as we did this morning on one of the panels, that there's much more writing from Jack Kerouac, much more material from Burroughs. So "dead" does not mean dead. And that's a great revelation in the field of Beat Studies. These writers are just endlessly worth studying.

I first met Burroughs when one of my students at the School of Visual Arts (SVA) wanted to introduce me to a writer, "Oh, you've got to meet this guy. He lives in the neighborhood. He writes fuck books." And so I said, "Oh, perfect for me." I was studying medieval literature. I was contemplating writing the five millionth dissertation on *Beowulf* (975–1025) and I wasn't getting very far finding an original point of departure. I visited this neighborhood writer, and he said to me, "Listen, William Burroughs is back in town and you could have him at the SVA for a reading." I said, "I could?" One thing led to another and because I wasn't paying very much, James Grauerholz, who was officially managing William Burroughs, said, "Just invite your students, okay?" And I said, sure, great, and word of mouth spread and about 300 people showed up. It should have been something like forty. So I realized, "Wait a minute, who is this rock star?" And from there I began to spend time with him and try to understand the work, coming from medieval alliterative verse studies to the surrealist, Beat mid-twentieth century of Burroughs' work. Both, of course, are worth doing. It was challenging for me at that time, but fascinating. And particularly fascinating to know him.

The Nova Convention was a turning point for me, because it brought together artists of so many disciplines celebrating Burroughs' and Brion Gysin's *Third Mind* collaboration. I was a culture critic at the time, contributing to *The Village Voice* and *SoHo Weekly News*, and this three-day event brought together my academic and journalist worlds. As regards Burroughs and his appeal to women, I remember Patti Smith getting up on stage at the theater and saying, "I really like William Burroughs, but he's a hard guy to get into bed." And I was fascinated that she would even want to. But these were moments that made me really pay attention to this guy in a completely different way. Another was a poster for a theater performance that I believe, Anne, your mother was in.

WALDMAN *Naked Lunch* (1959).

WEINREICH Yes, it was a scene from *Naked Lunch*.

WALDMAN She played The Spirit of Heroin.

[Laughing]

WEINREICH She was very good. Anyway, the poster for the performance featured a girl with a frilly dress. The dress was pulled up, and there was a man with his face in her groin. I put it up in my office at SVA thinking, this is a literary subject, right? One of my colleagues ripped it off the wall and said, "We can't have this here. We can't display work by a woman killer," of course referring to the tragedy of Joan Vollmer's death. Then *Cities of the Red Night* (1981) came out—that was the beginning of the late trilogy, and the books were starting to emerge. I had been sent a galley, and I noticed on the galley that it said *Cities of the Red Night: A Boy's Book*. I said, "Ah-ha!" And, of course, I had read *The Job*. I knew those theories like, "Women are a perfect curse. I think they were a basic mistake and the whole pluralistic universe evolved from this error." The theories didn't really jibe with the man I knew. I had the same experience with Bill that you [Waldman] had, because he was always a gentleman. He would stand up if a woman walked into the room, but it was more than that. He asked you questions. He was interested in you. He was not just. . .

WALDMAN Dismissive.

WEINREICH Yeah, he wasn't dismissive and he wasn't asking you to get the coffee.

WALDMAN Like the other Beats.

[Laughing]

WEINREICH . . . I was on assignment to interview him—the interview came out in *Omni Magazine*—and I came to the bunker and I was very proper and I said, "Well, William, it says right here, *A Boy's Book*. What does this mean, *A Boy's*

Book? Are you trying to separate the boys from the girls?" And he said, "Oh no no no," and he leapt up and he pulled a manuscript out of a drawer, "Don't you see, women are a biological mistake." I said, "Oh, right," remembering some ideas he had written that he took as fact. And then he added, "But so is everything else!" And he went into a whole anthropological discourse, citing Darwin, explaining all the different permutations and changes that occur in evolution and it was very, very persuasive. "Well what about reproduction?" I asked. And then he turned to me and he said, "You know, the way women are used right now, you're nothing more than flowerpots." "Ah, okay," I thought. "Don't you know, we're just a few years behind cloning?" he went on. And suddenly I got what he was doing, which was really putting on one of his personae for the purposes of this interview. I was also putting his performance together with something that I noticed at the Nova Convention, some of the more bizarre ideas he had put together with Brion Gysin. "We are here to go," Gysin used to say. There is something out there that we're all heading for and when we go we're not going to really want our bodies, male or female. So, with that thought in mind, I took what he was saying as an ideology, an intellectual construct, a belief system, and left it at that.

DOUGLAS I think both of you were saying—correct me if I'm mistaken—that in terms of actual behavior, respect for women on the ground, he was better (not worse, certainly) than the triumvirate that he is usually associated with: Corso, Kerouac, Ginsberg. I did not know William Burroughs and I only talked to Ginsberg once, and I was stunned to be treated as poorly as he treated me. I had just written a wonderful, I mean praising book review of Ann Charters' collected *The Portable Jack Kerouac* (1995) and the first volume of *The Letters* (Charters 1995, see Douglas 1995) and that was very close to Allen Ginsberg's heart. I think until he drew his last breath he was going to say, "Kerouac was great." He wanted to restore Kerouac, not that he didn't fight for Burroughs too. He was a fighter, But Allen was like a complete academic...

  And I didn't take it simply as a gender slight, but I knew that if I had been a man and written such a positive review of the person whose reputation he was most concerned about, he would have responded differently. In Patti Smith's autobiography *Just Kids* (2010) she describes meeting Ginsberg. He buys her lunch, and she feels honor bound to tell him she's a girl, not a boy. He was good-natured but thought it was understood that he might not have bought her that sandwich if she hadn't been so androgynous. I'm only going into it because there is misogyny. I myself don't ever dismiss any writer—male writer—as misogynistic simply because I would have to exclude virtually the entire canon, the old one and the new and expanded one. And I also feel that, as a reader—I think, Anne Waldman, you say this somewhere, that growing up you identified with the male hero. You identified with the hero of film and movies.

WALDMAN Novels, yes.

DOUGLAS Yes, exactly, and I think many of our generation did. There's a wonderful line in Hettie Jones's autobiography (1990) when she's saying, look, these were our male counterparts. She was with the then LeRoi Jones (Amiri Baraka). Joyce Johnson was with Kerouac. Burroughs and Ginsberg were with their various lovers. But Jones's point is that misogyny is just a fact of life in the male literary tradition. And if I give up everyone on those grounds, there wouldn't be much canonical literature left to read. But some people are harder for me than others, meaning I identify with male protagonists, to go back to Anne's point. And I have trouble identifying with men I don't like, characters in fiction, just as I don't identify with certain women characters. I'm one of the few people in the world who loathes Isabel Archer in *Portrait of the Lady* (1881). You can tell I was waiting for Kerouac to happen, because somewhere in the margin of James's precious troves when he's saying, "Ah, but adored Isabel" or whatever, I wrote "spoiled bitch," [laughing] and I've felt that way ever since. So, my point is [that] as a reader, as a movie viewer, I can roam all over the place, identifying with all kinds of characters.

And also, I think there is such a thing as a persona. Nobody smart is going to put something antithetical into their persona. Nobody who is fully alive, that is. Because you can't. Because you have to make your persona out of the elements of your heart, soul, mind, and so on to begin with...

[There] was an interview Burroughs gave in *The New York Times Book Review* in the '80s or '90s, and he said, "People would be advised to remember that much of what I write is intended to be funny" (quoted in Severo 1997). And if I had a Burroughs museum, I would put that right outside. Not to say that you should laugh at everything, but to forget the comic element at any point in Burroughs, I think, is a mistake, so I would have to be weighting his misogyny—which we've already heard some very glaring evidence of—I would have to be weighting that more than other things that appeal to me in the persona he fashioned. I would have to be saying, "That doesn't matter because this is offensive." No, to me that feels like coercion. And we have so few freedoms left today, but God knows one of them is as readers and viewers...

QUESTION #1 I'd just like to say that in video recordings and tape recordings of William Burroughs talking about the writings of Jane Bowles and, from what I heard, he was one of her greatest fans...

WALDMAN Yes, he loved her work and talked about it with students, promoted it.

DOUGLAS Did this come up in any way, Regina, in [*Paul Bowles: The Complete Outsider* (Catherine Warnow and Regina Weinreich 1994), your documentary on] Bowles?

WEINREICH It came up in an odd way: the relationship of Jane and Paul Bowles and Joan and Bill. I remember that they were critical of each other's marriages; that is, Bill and Paul were. So that Paul might say something about Bill—and obviously shooting your wife is definitely a little out there in terms of behavior . . . But then Bill would be critical of Paul. And this came up again in an odd way when David Cronenberg was making the film of *Naked Lunch* (1991). I was in Toronto visiting the set, reporting for *Entertainment Weekly*, and speaking to people. Jeremy Thomas was there. He had been to Tangier with everybody. Originally, there was supposed to be a press junket in Tangier and that got kaboshed by the first Gulf War. Originally, they were going to do the shoot there, everything was going to be happening in Tangier, and instead they had to create Tangier in a warehouse in Toronto. And Jeremy Thomas said that when they were sitting in Tangier in Paul's living room, and Bill and Paul hadn't seen each other in years and years, there was this discomfort between them that he felt was a kind of barrier, and it emerged in the script of *Naked Lunch* because Cronenberg decided to . . . basically, what he told me was he was going to throw away the book, because it would be obscene in every language that it could possibly be in, and it couldn't be filmed because it would cost a fortune. And so he was going to reach behind the book to the man writing the book. And of course that got into . . . Bill's shooting of Joan. And in *Naked Lunch* the movie, the shooting happens twice. It happens in the beginning, taking Bill at his word that this cataclysmic event launched the writer into becoming a writer. And then it happens again at the movie's end with the "Odd Couple" who the writer meets in Tangier, based on Paul and Jane. So, it's a very interesting take on that legend, a reinvention of that legend, merging the two couples.

QUESTION #2 Regina, didn't Cronenberg actually kind of transpose Joan Vollmer to Jane because in Tangier he has a sexual encounter with a typewriter? . . . I think Jane Bowles and Joan are characters that Cronenberg kind of fused and separated and gave life to in a way, but I was kind of shocked when I saw the film.

WEINREICH Well, what he was doing there was taking the encounter that he had with Bill and Paul in the scouting trip and in the interviews and so on, recognizing the tension between them because of these marriages and a certain guilt that each man felt about his wife, and that's where that came up. But Bill was among the people who admired Jane Bowles's writing, including Truman Capote and Tennessee Williams. Burroughs was a big champion of her writing.

WALDMAN He wasn't happy with the film.

WEINREICH I suspect he found Cronenberg too shy of the homosexuality in the source.

DOUGLAS He did say it was impossible to film. He said it himself.

WALDMAN . . . We're celebrating his 100th and his life is about thirty years ahead of some of us. Consider the implications of the kind of world that we're living in now. And I really appreciate him as this unfixed and still open sort of system—"a set of potentials" is what Deleuze and Guattari called him[1]—and I would add the

Buddhist notion of *conglomeration of tendencies*. All these things are very fluid in him. And so I see Abu Ghraib, Guantanamo, these descriptions of torture, Osama bin Laden, the Koch brothers, the NSA, the endless syndicates of samsara that he was so onto, really following these samsaric rhizomes of control and oppression. . . . I know when he was close to his death he spoke of how the Beat Generation had opened things up. You could say four-letter words, freedom of speech, and so Bill was very proud of that in a way . . . I find him so present in my daily thinking. Every time I pick up the newspaper.

WEINREICH   Well, that was true in the '70s and '80s too. He understood what AIDS was before AIDS was identified.

DOUGLAS   Yes, just what I was going to bring up. My students always assumed that it was already the time of AIDS when he wrote because he so clearly described it. I said, "No, no this is ten years, twenty years before there was AIDS." And when he ends one of his essays by saying, "There should be no secrets at all" (see Bolton 2014, 27). That's what we have to fight for. Somehow the template was stuck with truth-telling in an age of corporate secrecy and surveillance. It's always *1984* (1949), a book for which I have a great deal of respect. But George Orwell was, I think, much more a creature of his times with plenty of ties still to what would be the more conservative positions . . .

Burroughs didn't really bother with day-to-day politics; for him it was sufficient to note that in the US, "stupidity and ignorance are brazenly proffered as qualifications for office" (Burroughs, *The Adding Machine* 1985, 122). You know he's not going to do a detailed scenario about something that is stinking to high heaven. Why waste all his time on this particular carcass? But thinking, the long-distance thinking . . . He combines details microscopically of things. That's why it was called "naked lunch": wherever precisely, what exactly, is on the edge of your fork. No one brings that into a more shocking close-up than Burroughs. And at the same time, he's surveying the horizons of western civilization, of world civilization.

I think he'd be quite happy—despite the man's lack of a sense of a humor— with Edward Snowden. I don't think there would be any doubt in his mind whether or not Edward Snowden had done the right thing because, in a curious way, in his books there are many functions and one of them is Edward Snowden. I mean Bill prized being born into the world of the upper classes because it did give him privileges. He knew it gave him privileges, and he wanted to use them against the upper class—the idea that the best revolt comes from within.

I just want to say parenthetically in case I sounded like I don't care for Allen Ginsberg, I just came off of two weeks of teaching *Howl* (1954) and then *Kaddish* (1961), which I think are the two greatest poems in American English in the second half of the twentieth century. That was my point . . . I never felt a barrier between me and Burroughs, any more than I did between me and any other male author I really cared about, so I just wanted to set that straight.

WALDMAN Well, I was just wondering about "the word" as a "killer virus," maybe it's related to the Internet.[2] See the Internet was created by the military. You know, he did support the first Gulf War.

DOUGLAS I know, disappointing.

WALDMAN I remember some arguments about that, but it wasn't surprising . . . What I liked though was those contradictions in him.

DOUGLAS I mean he hated liberals while it was still somewhat suspect to hate liberals, but you couldn't tie him down.

WALDMAN No, you could not tie him down.

DOUGLAS Because the intelligence came first, and it was a deconstructive intelligence. Should we go back a bit towards our topic?

WALDMAN Can we be more controversial about the women thing?

QUESTION #3 I do have a question about the female thing. Well, first a comment. I mean there's another prominent Burroughs scholar, Jennie Skerl.

DOUGLAS Of course, and think of Mary McCarthy who was one of his earliest and best supporters.

WALDMAN And there's Robin [Lydenberg] too, as well. I mean, women have written some of the best texts on him—early scholars.

DOUGLAS Right, which is kind of a paradox normally.

QUESTION #3 And when I first came across Ms. Skerl's work, I thought, she does know that Planet Burroughs is hostile toward women? [Laughing]. But hearing your observations has helped me understand how would a woman who appreciates Burroughs answer the question, "How could you like Burroughs?"

DOUGLAS I would almost say how could you not?

QUESTION #3 It's lent a great perspective that I don't think exists. Anne [Waldman], you had mentioned something earlier about how it wasn't really all women. He was able to engage with people like Susan Sontag for instance, and by all accounts his relationship with Joan Burroughs was almost symbiotic. They just could see eye to eye on so many levels.

WALDMAN They would spend hours on conversation.

QUESTION #3 Particularly intellectually. So, I'm wondering, would it be fair to say his critiques of women were mainly against the flowerpots that you mentioned? And if so, would that let him off the hook unfairly?

WALDMAN You have to separate out the writing from the man and the icon as well, the cultural icon.

AUDIENCE MEMBER And from the administration of thinking.

WEINREICH . . . I looked for some of those quotes about women from *The Job* that I knew were particular inflammatory, and then I found something from *The Western Lands* (1987). And it says here "the other half" is, as women are known, right: "The Egyptians had not solved the equation imposed by parasitic female Other Half who needs a physical body to exist, being parasitic to other bodies. So to maintain the Other Half in the style to which she has for a million years been accustomed, they turn to the reprehensible and ill-advised expedient of vampirism" (74). I thought about this prose; wait a minute. What is that language? That's not Burroughs' language. That's Burroughs imitating the legalese that we have as a society, for people divorcing. So he's playing with these tropes. He's re-imagining them, re-situating them, using them for his purposes. And I think that that's really what's behind what he's doing, playing with this abject attitude toward women. Does it let him off the hook? Only if you take it seriously.

WALDMAN You know, Amiri Baraka recently died, and every article has to mention that he was anti-Semitic and quote from his poem "Somebody Blew up America" (2003) the couple of lines referring to the Jews who were allowed to go home knowing that something was going to happen. And, when Allen died, it was the man-boy love that dogged him. And there's a real agenda here to . . .

AUDIENCE MEMBER Control.

WALDMAN . . . to control these brilliant thinkers and writers who have had incredible power and influence and imagination and continue through the work. They *are* dangerous. That's why some of us are so involved with the legacy and making sure that it's kept going, and also keeping the work—what's Ted Berrigan's line?—"free from mess and message" (2011). But there's a real manipulation to be wary of. The conservative pundits wrote nasty things about Burroughs and the Beats after he died.[3]

I think we have to be careful with how we talk about the personal and literary history as well . . . For example, there's a student in Naropa doing her thesis from the point of view of Joan Vollmer and writing a long poem in her voice, and she's adamant—I mean she feels, as some women do, that Burroughs really didn't take enough heat for Joan's death; he got off too easy. And she did not appreciate Ginsberg's commentary about Joan provoking William, as if she were asking to be shot. But how we look at the documentation is important, from a lot of sides. And then we know more about who Joan Vollmer is: someone interesting, and the person behind much of William's thinking at that time.

QUESTION #3 Do you think if somebody who does even less than a superficial reading, even if they're reading Burroughs a little more deeply, could be forgiven for representing his point of view as misogynistic?

WALDMAN Well, he's a misanthrope. He's more of a misanthrope. In the novels, the men are not getting off any easier . . . and his characters are weird hybrids anyway.

QUESTION #4 I think it's just always important to figure out who's doing the objecting, and what is behind it because so much of it is the administration of direct encounter. Because that direct encounter with Burroughs, with the text—even if it's negative—it's going to have a transformative value. And if it's being administered, that transformation won't quite work. It's like a condom put over everything. You can't touch it. And that's how things operate, particularly with this post–Second World War generation of people, because they created forms of knowledge that were outside the framework of established terminologies and structures, you know. So that's what made them dangerous and continues to make them seem dangerous.

DOUGLAS Essentially it's reactionary. It's counterrevolutionary. It's also a big waste of time . . . that's what's upsetting is that this has to do with the so-called "machinery of recognition." I'm borrowing the phrase from Anatole Broyard (1948) writing about the hipster, meaning those who control it are—I sound like Burroughs because Burroughs was right—are sending out diversionary messages. And the first one is always, "Look at that messenger. He's not someone you would want to know." Now, I long ago gave up rock stars, when I was young, [as figures] who I wanted to get to know. I would have loved to have met whoever. But writers I admire, no. I didn't ask that of them. I didn't ask that they be people I would love to know who'd be nice to me and we'd have great sex and good conversation or anything along that line. I accepted somewhere very young, instinctively, the idea that someone who produced a book that might sustain me for a lifetime wouldn't be someone I'd want to spend five minutes with. [Laughing.] It's two very different things, and here, with Burroughs, as with Ginsberg, and I would say honestly most of all with Kerouac, it's constantly the personal, personal, personal lens that turns up in reviews of—

WALDMAN —and now we have these movies.

WEINREICH . . . I want to say the same thing that we're talking about in terms of these writers is also true of our perception of Joan. She's going to forever be the woman who was inhaling Benzedrine.

WALDMAN And scraping caterpillars off a tree.

WEINREICH Right, with a broom. I mean, she sounds like a maniac in the way she is caricatured in *On the Road* (1957). She certainly had a drug problem. She sounds like somebody who may have had a death wish, as Allen has said, especially in some accounts of what actually happened. In the characterizations of Joan we see the essential problem of the way history becomes legend, or mythification. And the worst part is that we may never really know who she really, really was and that . . . that I find really, really disappointing.

DOUGLAS We do know that as much as Burroughs could love anyone and could love a woman, he loved Joan. And to me the whole thing is a horrifying tragedy composed of mixed motives and actual circumstances that can never be known.

I'm with you, with the idea he became a writer in his own mind as an identity, not as a practice. And that's how I don't think of him as murdering Joan. He was responsible for killing her, yes. He never shirked that responsibility. This is someone who was not a post-modernist, a theory that depends on very high levels of randomness and coincidence, where nothing means more than anything else. He lived in a magical universe. It was the averse, and so it didn't matter that much to him had he been possessed by something. It was still his agency. He never denied agency and he never denied that he loved Joan. He knew he didn't love her enough. He certainly didn't love her as she wanted to be loved. After all he was gay and it was sad that it was a different day when—I think a little history is needed. Allen Ginsberg spent three years trying to date, working on the equivalent of Madison Avenue, and going to his shrink who told him he was evil, as he was. And I almost don't like to let my students in on this because [laughing] half my class in the Beat Generation every year is usually gay, and they're usually on the left, and they're usually artistic and writers. And the gay students are comfortable now. And that makes me so happy I almost don't want to tell them what it was like back in the day. But how to explain that line in *The Subterraneans*, when the Ginsberg character says to Leo that he's looking for a "permanent and serious" relationship with a girl, which eliminates Mardou because she's a Negro (1958, 12, 74). Wait a minute, Allen! You're not going to marry. But he did spend years trying to go straight. And Burroughs on occasion called homosexuality a terrible illness. It's a complicated matter. And I actually disagree with Barry [Miles] here. I myself think the best thing for young Billy [Burroughs' son] was to be raised by his grandparents, who were very nice people.

WALDMAN   It couldn't have been any other way.

DOUGLAS   No, and the first time Billy went to visit his father, someone had their hand in his pants. He was 14 ... So I'm just saying life is treated in a very simplified way, and that simplistic way of absolute thinking is used as a weapon against people like Burroughs, who are struggling. William Burroughs said that for him the writing method was "absolute . . . fact on all levels."[4] And you kind of think that—*Naked Lunch*, the "cut-up" trilogy—that this is naked fact on all levels. But what he was saying was, "Here's what's guaranteed in it. I am going for the truth as I see it. I'm not wasting time, diversionary as some of these hangings and so on might seem to you, this is my guarantee. This is all I guarantee to you. You're on a ride, anything can happen. But remember I am always after absolute fact on all levels." And he saw through more shit than any other writer of his day. Every day I remember to myself, "You are not paid off not to say what you know; you are paid off not to find it out." Kind of like the whole modern media in a single sentence.

WALDMAN   When Billy was sick in Colorado and underwent his liver transplant at the hospital in Denver, under Dr. Starzl, Bill was deeply fascinated by that whole procedure. Transplants were somewhat new there. I think there had only been three or four at that point—liver transplants—and he got completely swept up in the science of it. It was a way to be with this incredibly intense situation. I saw him weeping, and really down, and suffering with Billy; and still there was that distance. There was the pain of Billy wanting his father's attention and love and Bill never *quite* being there. But Bill started to use the image of the transplants. There's a scene . . . I can't remember, in probably one of the last trilogy, you know. . .

WEINREICH *Place of Dead Roads* (1983).

WALDMAN *Place of Dead Roads*, yes. And you could see the wheels turning for the writing—how to enter in that very dramatic and painful situation. It was risky as well, and Billy was in a coma I think for at least a week. So, the life and the work were coming together in that way.

QUESTION #5 I was thinking about the idea of our last freedom as readers. But then there is this intervention because I know when I was in high school and I first realized that I was writing poetry, I got caught reading *Naked Lunch* in synagogue. [Laughing.] I got dragged to the Allen Ginsberg estate and my life was saved. But saved because people intervened in my life. Had Bob Rossenbaum not intervened, I don't know what would have happened. I was being told that you only read Sylvia Plath. You only read Emily Dickinson. And William Burroughs is a misogynist. You don't read him, you don't. So I don't know how much freedom we do have as readers as long as the truth isn't coming out and our options are limited. How we are going to fight that?

DOUGLAS It's the ongoing struggle basically.

WEINREICH Ann [Douglas] really tapped into something about what's important about appreciating William Burroughs . . . It's understanding how much you need to reach behind the information that's given to you, to get at what's important and true.

DOUGLAS Well, you're getting at something that's very important: that you have to be initiated in some sense to even know where to look, such as the situation you describe where you're reading *Naked Lunch*. And there are authorities. As I say, it's an ongoing struggle, but Burroughs is one of the people that keeps the struggle alive and feeds it, even today I think.

WERMER-COLAN . . . I think I agree with everything that everyone said. Obviously there's the difference between the man and the writing. But I want to push a little bit more on the writing and just ask, first of all, were his writings on women destructive to the feminist movement in any way? I mean it's hard to say the effect. But still, even if intelligent people can recuperate them as being a complex critique of gender politics, the people originally reading the work were reading it in men's magazines like *Mayfair*. And I still wonder what kind of effect that has. And the second question is, why did Burroughs not want to be a woman? He seemed to think being a woman was less good than being a man on the level of spirit, and I'm just wondering if you have any insights.

WALDMAN Well, the old queen came up earlier, and he was criticized as feminizing writing. It was Leslie Fiedler or one of those guys, you know, the new. . .

DOUGLAS "The New Mutants" (Fielder 1965).

WALDMAN . . . "The New Mutants." And then the feminist work that was being done at this earlier time—I don't think there's been anything that recent that I'm aware of. I mean, I'm not tracking all of this. But the instance in Sandra M. Gilbert and Susan Gubar's book (2009), I think it's referenced in Timothy S. Murphy's book, they misconstrue some poem of Gary Snyder's as a misogynistic poem (Murphy 1998, 12). But then that observation is sort of mapped onto Burroughs. There's just no connection. I mean, most of the feminist sightings have been very slight, at least at that point. I think it was basically a reaction to *The Job*, the interviews which, again, give one kind of image of woman-hating Burroughs. The whole nature of cut-ups sort of undercuts any kind of fixed ultimate misogynist view.

DOUGLAS But Jen Skerl is doing substantial work, yes. Could I just add one thing about the necessity of some sort of historical context? We accept the necessity of historical context for most major authors, but don't apply it to the Beats who are seen as bad schoolboys whose misdeeds are always fresh in the press. When my students learn that 25 percent of young women in the 1950s wanted to be men, while few wanted to be women, the students ask, "How could that be?" And I say, "Would you rather be rich or would you rather be poor?" How will that divide when you're talking back in the '50s and even the '60s, I mean literally rich and poor, but also metaphorically. Women had, relatively speaking, so few rights. To want to be a woman if you're a man is always a present and real gendered possibility. But in the somewhat more general way you ask it you'd have to say, "What did it mean to be a woman? What would your income be? Would your neighbors be talking to you if you brought home your lover late at night?" We're just going through an anniversary of the woman who was murdered in Queens and no one came to rescue her.

WEINREICH Kitty Genovese.

DOUGLAS Yes, Kitty Genovese. No one came to rescue her. There were plenty of people who didn't pick up their phones. And one guy said, "Well, I figured, you know, she was having a fight with her man." Or if she was being raped, he said "I think that she deserved it. What was she doing out so late?" Well, you'd be better off being a man in those circumstances definitely, in everything from economics to physical violence. I'm just saying that we can't just say, well, why didn't he want to be a woman? You have to remember what it was to be a woman. As for Bill, I think he over-identified with some women, and I think some of the misogyny was fighting that off. He says that his mother told him—and we only know this through him, there's nothing in her handwriting saying this—they were really two souls in the same body. And as different as their lives looked, really they were one person and she understood. Which is a little frightening I must say, from your mother, but it does suggest that the misogyny is at least as much a defense–a very poor one, but still a defense.

WALDMAN   And our whole sense of gender now, even compared to when William was still alive...

QUESTION #5   I think his attempts have feminized his own self-loathing or feminized himself... I think a lot of times when he hit critical mainstream society, he's mainly directing his anger at what would be considered patriarchal or paternalistic. Like the genocide of [Native] Americans and the war on drugs and all of these other authoritarian militarized mechanisms. But then he made sure not to pull punches in the complicity of females within that structure. And how the patriarchal system supports women. But I think when he does that he talks about "The Thanksgiving Prayer," the prayer about, you know, "where nobody's allowed to mind their own business" and "decent church-going women, with their mean, pinched, bitter, evil faces" (Burroughs, "Thanksgiving Day," 1986). That's the same language he used to talk about himself in moments of self-loathing.

WALDMAN   Yes. That's a good point.

DOUGLAS   Regina, do you want to say something?

WEINREICH   Well, I don't know... he traded recipes with me.

DOUGLAS   I think that's a wonderful note to close on.

WALDMAN   I just wanted to add, he came at me one time ... it was probably in the '80s. Because he'd often scare my son, saying, "Little boy I'm going to take you to the mountains," and Ambrose would hide in my skirts. It was like that, a game. Dark humor. And he came at me with that knowledge that's he's known as a misogynist, and holding out his arms and hands as if to strangle me said, "Do you realize you're the only woman in the room?"

ANN DOUGLAS is the Parr Professor Emerita of English and Comparative Literature at Columbia University. She is the author of *The Feminization of American Culture* and *Terrible Honesty: Mongrel Manhattan in the 1920's*.

ANNE WALDMAN has authored over fifty books of poetry, collaboration, and critical work. Her most recent book is *Trickster Feminism* (Penguin, 2018). She is the editor of *The Beat Book* (Shambhala) and co-editor of *Beats at Naropa* (Coffee House Press).

REGINA WEINREICH is Professor of Humanities & Sciences at the School of Visual Arts in New York who has served as author, editor, and filmmaker for numerous critical works on Beat literature including *Kerouac's Spontaneous Poetics: A Study of the Fiction*.

NOTES

1. The phrase "set of potentials" comes from Timothy S. Murphy's summary of Deleuze and Guattari's writing on Burroughs in *A Thousand Plateaus* (1987). Murphy writes, "Deleuze and Guattari would say that 'Burroughs' is no longer just the name of an author, a celebrity, or an artist; it is the name, rather, of a set of potentials, an effect that propagates itself from medium to medium by the force of its difference, bringing into contact incompatible functions, incommensurable concepts, and unrelated materials" (1998, 232).

2. Waldman is referring to Burroughs' statement, "The word was a killer virus once." See Burroughs, "What Washington? What Orders?" (1995, 188).

3. Waldman is referring to the August 1997 article "The Death of Decency" in which Kimball, reflecting on Burroughs' and Ginsberg's respective deaths in August and April of that year, declared that these late writers "and the rest of the Beats really do mark an important moment in American culture, not as one of its achievements, but as a grievous example of its degeneration" (Kimball 1997). This article followed George F. Will's similarly condemnatory obituary of Ginsberg in *The Washington Post* earlier that year titled "The Ginsberg Commodity" (Will 1997).

4. Douglas is referring to a comment Burroughs wrote in a letter to Kerouac, stating, "what I see and feel right now to arrive at some absolute, direct transmission of fact on all levels" (see Douglas 1998, xxvi).

REFERENCES

Ardrey, Robert. 1961. *African Genesis: A Personal Investigation into the Animal Origins and Nature of Man*. London: Harper Collins Distribution Services.

Berrigan, Ted. 2011. *The Selected Poems of Ted Berrigan*. California: University of California Press.

Broyard, Anatole. 1948. "A Portrait of the Hipster." *Partisan Review* 15, no. 9 (June): 1054.

Burroughs, William S. 1985. *The Adding Machine: Collected Essays*. London: John Calder.

———. 1986. "A Thanksgiving Prayer." Track 2 on *Dead City Radio*. Island Records. Released Aug 31, 1990.

———. 1987. *The Western Lands*. New York: Viking.

———. 1995. *My Education: A Book of Dreams*. New York: Viking.

———. 1995. "What Washington? What Orders?" In *The Beat Book: Poems and Fiction of the Beat Generation*, edited by Anne Waldman, 186–88. Boston: Shambhala.

Burroughs, William S., and Ann Charters. 1982. "On the Road: The Jack Kerouac Conference." Naropa Institute, Boulder Colorado.

Charters, Ann. 1995. *The Portable Jack Kerouac*. 1995. New York: Viking.

———. 1995. *Jack Kerouac: Selected Letters, 1940–1956*. New York: Viking.

Deleuze, Gilles, and Félix Guattari. 1987. *A Thousand Plateaus*. Vol. 2 of *Capitalism and Schizophrenia*. Minneapolis: University of Minnesota Press.

Douglas, Ann. 1995. "On the Road Again." *New York Times,* National Edition. April 9, 1995, 72.

———. 1998. "Punching a Hole in the Big Lie: The Achievement of William S. Burroughs." In *Word Virus: The William S. Burroughs Reader*, edited by James Grauerholz and Ira Silverberg, xv–xxx. New York: Grove.

Fiedler, Leslie. 1965. "The New Mutants." *Partisan Review* 32, no 4 (Fall): 505–25.

Gilbert, Sandra M., and Susan Gubar. *The War of the Words.* Vol. 1 of *No Man's Land: Place of the Woman Writer in the Twentieth Century.* New Haven, CT: Yale University Press, 2009.

Jones, Hettie. 1990. *How I Became Hettie Jones.* New York: Dutton.

Kerouac, Jack. 1958. *The Subterraneans.* New York: Grove.

Kimball, Roger, "The Death of Decency." *Wall Street Journal,* August 8, 1997. https://www.wsj.com /articles/SB870988151827621500.

Miles, Barry. 2013. *Call Me Burroughs: A Life.* New York: Twelve.

Murphy, Timothy S. 1998. *Wising Up the Marks: The Amodern William Burroughs.* Berkeley: University of California Press.

Odier, Daniel. 1970. *The Job: Interview with William S. Burroughs.* London: Jonathan Cape. Reissued 1989. New York: Penguin.

Severo, Richard. 1997. "William S. Burroughs Dies at 83; Member of the Beat Generation Wrote *Naked Lunch.*" *New York Times,* National Edition. Aug. 3, 1997. https://www.nytimes.com /1997/08/03/nyregion/william-s-burroughs-dies-at-83-member-of-the-beat-generation -wrote-naked-lunch.html.

Smith, Patti. *Just Kids.* 2010. New York: HarperCollins.

Wade, Nicholas. 2014. "Researchers See New Importance in Y Chromosome." *New York Times,* New York Edition. April 23, 2014, A4.

Waldman, Ann, and Laura Wright. 2009. *Beats at Naropa.* Minneapolis, MN: Coffee House.

Warnow, Catherine, and Regina Weinrich, directors. 1994. *Paul Bowles: The Complete Outsider.* USA/Morocco. Independent Production, DuArt Film Lab.

Will, George F. 1997. "The Ginsberg Commodity," *Washington Post,* April 9. https://www .washingtonpost.com/archive/opinions/1997/04/09/the-ginsberg-commodity/1053582c -9b66-4a49-88fe-fcb767f2bb69/?utm_term=.1f30295883d3.

Cutting Up Last Words

These haunting cut-ups of peoples' last spoken words appear at the conclusion of the anthology and of the *Body/Spirit* section, intertwining, as they do, guilt and fear for deaths both past and future. During the height of his early experimentations with the cut-up method, especially in 1960, Burroughs collected lists of famous "last words," the final spoken phrases of mythological heroes of the American West, of historical personages more generally, and of his own friends and family. In a poignant illustration of Burroughs' cut-up method, we can see Burroughs collecting a set of quotes, selecting a subset, and cutting up these grim phrases into a variety of uncanny permutations. The first piece published here appears in Berg Folio 83, "Mss Of Some Unpublished Material Cut-Ups 1960–1961," while the second appears in the miscellaneous Folio 104, "Mss Pages From Various Periods All Identified." These materials, furthermore, represent only a fraction of the cut-up experiments Burroughs conducted with the last words of people he revered, loved, or found fascinating.

An interest in people's "last words" pervades Burroughs' work, from his manifesto at the beginning of *Nova Express* (1964) titled "The Last Words" to his screenplay adaptation of the transcribed *Last Words of Dutch Schultz* (1970), the notorious gangster. There's an inclination to believe that one's last words come to define a person, as their final, and perhaps most honest, attempt to leave a mark on the world. Burroughs arguably envisioned much of his writing to be his own last words, a dire warning, much like his ominous "Last Words" manifesto that opens his classic cut-up novel: "Listen to my last words any world. Listen all you boards, governments, syndicates, nations of the world . . ." (2011, 1). Throughout his life, Burroughs also repeated as a political and aesthetic slogan the purported last words of the medieval Islamist assassin, Hassan I Sabbah: "Nothing is true, everything is permitted."

In the last cut-ups showcased in this collection, Burroughs splices together the last words of mythic figures with those of his friends (like David Kammerer), including his own wife's last words before he shot her. In Berg 26.16, Burroughs identifies his source material as originating from *"Cut-ups Last Words Dutch Schultz, Joan, David Kammerer, Hassan i Sabbah, Billy The Kid."* The piece begins:

"I WANT A PAY. I CANT" "LOOK" "CANT LOOK" "SO THIS IS WHAT HAP-PENS? NO." For the first time, the reader can watch Burroughs ruminate through the cut-up method on Joan's haunting, and rarely discussed, last words, uttered at the last moments before Burroughs shot her: "I CAN'T LOOK." If Burroughs ever meditated in his cut-ups on the significance of his wife's death, it is here, where his grief appears materially in this incomparable textual artefact's hollow echo.

To come full circle, we conclude with the final words Burroughs wrote, published in *Last Words* (1993), a posthumous edition of his late diary notes. Three days before he died, on July 31, 1997, while contemplating his beloved pet cat's gradual decline, Burroughs quotes one of his favorite Andrew Marvell lines from "To His Coy Mistress" (1681), before weaving through fragmented phrases his illuminating perspective on love and death:

> Our vegetable love will grow, vaster than empires and more slow . . . How can a man who sees and feels be other than sad. To see Ginger always older and weaker. The price of immortality, of course. Well, you should have thought of these things. I did. Thinking is not enough. Nothing is. There is no final enough of wisdom, experience—any fucking thing. No Holy Grail, No Final Satori, no final solution. Just conflict. Only thing can resolve conflict is love, like I felt for Fletch and Ruski, Spooner and Calico. Pure love. What I feel for my cats present and past. Love what is it? Most natural painkiller what there is. LOVE. (253)

—*AWC*

Cut ups of last words giving the idnetifications when possible
Billy the Kid..."Quien es?"...Gangster fatally wounded in the
Valentine Day Massacre 1929...A detective named Tom was at his
bedside..."Its getting dark Tom and its cold awful cold pull
the covers up over me."...Sulla's self composed epitah..."No
friend ever did him a favor and no enemy an injury with being
fully repaid."...Pat Garrett who was killed by Brazil in an
argument over land boundaries..."God damn you if I cant get you
off my land one way I will another." Sargeant in World War 1
leading suicide charge..."Come on you back there do you want to
live forever."...Missionaries to the Auda indians in Equador...
"Here come some indians we have never seen before."...Joe Goddard
school mate killed in car crash age 15 St Louis Mo..."What did
we hit?"...Dutch Schultz..."I want to pay let them leave me alone
the chimney sweeps take to the sword"...Citizen Cane..."Rosebud"
Perry Smith "I might have contributed something" In Cold Blood
by Truman Capote...Malcolm X..."Cool it brothers."...Hassan I
Sabbah..."Nothing is true.   Everything is permitted."...Huey
Long; "What will happen to my university boys?"   Joan Burroughs
"I cant look"...Dave Kammerer: "So this is what happens to
Dave Kamerer."...Wilson Misner on oxiegn tnet tent is brought
in..."This looks like the main event....Last words in the diary
of Yves Martin..."Finnnies nous attendons une bonne chaance."
General Grant: "It is raining Mrs Charrington...A black hanged
for rape; "It dont make no difference to me how I shuffle off."
Captain Clark welcomes you aboard. "My God I8ve been shot."
Charles Berger handed in East St Louis..."It's a wonderful world."
Jesse James; "That picture's awful dusty." Eichman: "The strap
is too tight." Rabelais..."Je vais chercher une grand peut etre."
Junky who died of overdose. Rickie asked is it good? "Is it go---

```
"I WANTA PAY. I CANT" "LOOK" "CANT LOOK" "SO THIS IS WHAT
HAPPENS? NO. THING IS PERMITTER WHOISIT PAY" "WHO IS? NO THING
EYE IS TRUE IS WHAT HAPPENS TO DAVE KAMM/ "WHO IS IT?" "DAVE K"
SO TRUE? ALL PEMRITTED, LAST XXXXXX WAVE KAMMERER. CAMERA EYE
CAN NOT LOOK. DUTCH PAY. I WANT BAHH NOTHING. IS TREU ALL IS
PERMIT WHO? BILLY THE KID? SO? THIS/ T TWO PAY" "SO THIS  "THIS"
IS"WHAT "I"?"  CANT LOOK D.K.? SO I CAN.." NOT LOOK. KNOW THING
TO THE CAMERA I/ IS PERMITTED.: 'WHO IS "IT"?" "WHO IS "IT"
KNOWTHING IS PERMITTED. HASSAN i SABBAH HAPPENS TO DAVE. "
"CAMERA DUTCH.PAY THE KID. "   "WHO IS  I BILLY THE KIDWHOISIT?
HASSAN i SABBAH TOO, DAVE KAMMERER."  " I WANTA I CANT LOOK
BILLY THE KID SO THIS    EVERYTHING IS BILLY THE KID, HASSAN I
SABBAH NO  THINGIS- THIS IS WHAT HAPPENS TO D/ORDS: HASSAN i SABB
SABBAH. I CANT.   A LOOK I WANT. PAY HASS AN i NG? IS TRUE EVERY
THING. IS PERMITED PERMITTED "QUIEN ES "? I WAN/ IS WHAT
AHPPENS TO D.K. WHO IS HAPPNES????   TO DDAVE CAMER/ THIS/
"IS WHAT AHPPENS TO D? IS TRYE E VERYTHING.??EVERY   WANTA
TWO PAY.. BILLY THE KID KNOW THINGIS TRUE EVERY YOU EVER THING
IS PERMITTED BILLY EYE CANT LOOK? SO THIS IS WHAT/


[autograph]:
cut ups of last words
Dutch Schultz
Joan
David Kammerer
Hassan i Sabbah
Billy the Kid
```

19

The Burroughs Effect

ANNE WALDMAN

Un homme invisible. Blend in anywhere, your sousveillance secret agent, your field poet. *Don't let them look you in the eye,* William Burroughs would advise me walking down a street in Boulder, in Montreal. And you could travel incognito, taking it all in.

And you could project what you wanted on William, the meme, the person—a "combine" perhaps—a conglomeration of tendencies—the figure of Future—who defied neat categories. *Le cher maitre,* Allen Ginsberg designated him. He had tremendous intellectual power over his younger so-called Beat colleagues; *his logopoeia*—his "dance of the intellect"—was supremely magnetizing. He was, in my experience, a kind of sinister Muse (as in "bend sinister," the left-hand path of the sorcerer), always "on," active, always a step ahead of our attendant reality. He made you think twice. And often more than that. He still haunts my consciousness.

What constituted this visionary Burroughs, who in his work and talk was so obsessively focused? What might we learn? What was the transmission for late twentieth-century dystopia? What was this absurd adolescent horror of the centipede? I thought of the cinematic sectional flow of the centipede, an innocuous narrative for our time that might seem sinister. Like slime molds that will inherit the planet, have no truck with human whim or desire. What does being a victim constitute in realms of language? How to resist? How are we a language *and* a virus? What damage do we—humans—do intentionally? Ignorantly? What are the limits of this body? How do we feed it? How do we re-imagine language to investigate and challenge the dull frequency of doldrums, prisons, and prisms of the Mundane, with seething below-the-radar-frenzies of transgression, aberrant behavior, sexual violence, and righteous gnaw of the disenfranchised prophet? What is consciousness? And how does it travel? What is our "value" inside a presumptive and compromising Capital? Was Burroughs revolutionary, Marxist, a fantasist, a Sufi, seer, or prophet? Mektoub. It is written. Fatalist? "A writer writes," he often said. Burroughs' work on the whole is passionate critique, of the social organization of late capital and the logic (or illogic?) of the textual realms it operates within and dominates—our whole dystopic Western civilization that supports a disturbing and more and more suicidal demise.

And we have the writer who mirrors this so well. A disclaimer of these notes. *Look to the writing.*

Where do we position, in our current Dystopia, our fragile Anthropocene (geological time wholly conditioned by the hand of man, replacing the Holocene), the provocative dismembering body of work that constitutes the opus of William Burroughs? And the prescience within this "body" that destabilizes many concomitant and parallel realities? I would say the "Burroughs effect" defies categories. "The basic disruption of reality" is what he posits (quoted in Murphy 1998, 6). In the last decade and more, we have witnessed a self-fulfilling prophecy mirrored in Burroughs' work, his vivid revelations and resonance and constructs, in his dark investigation of the "limits of control." We have disturbing images of torture from Abu Ghraib, from Bagram, the force feeding at Guantanamo, we see "terrorists" in perpetual "lock-down," we have the drone wars taking out "suspects," hundreds of thousands of deaths on our hands in the combined horrific Middle East follies. Many mistakes, innocent civilians, women/children/even US citizens taken out, we have the glamorization of the CIA in movies such as *Zero Dark Thirty* (directed by Kathryn Bigelow, 2012) and *Argo* (directed by Ben Affleck, 2012), the seductive brutality of war (and its downside) in *American Sniper* (directed by Clint Eastwood, 2014), and the romanticization of the Navy Seals in *Lone Survivor* (directed by Peter Berg, 2013). Many cults in recent war. We have the "extraordinary renditions," "waterboarding," and other eviscerations. We have revelations of the murky worlds of the ongoing Cheney/Halliburton, Inc. zone—the Blackwater regime now rechristened "Xi" (harder to pronounce?). Xi: a cultish subculture with its own hierarchy, strategies, policies, budgets, and religious zeal that, contrary to public assumption, has not been dismantled. The Koch Brothers agenda . . . all these subcultural, hierarchal power structures embedded with the money and international governmental corruption zones are deeply Burroughsian in that he has already imagined them, created them out of a fierce and biting wit and sensibility: "*the fix is in, the fix is in* . . . the fix is in for the hungry ghost." (The women biz, his misogyny, is subsumed for me in this greater vision of our syndicates of Samsara, because that's really what he was on about: the endless wheels and rhizomes of the interconnected root/tuber systems of Samsara.)

With great linguistic, visual, and psychological power, Burroughs' shifting and morphing characters breathe and grind on in their wild machinations, their "routines" to re-vivify attention to our continuous dark present. Like terrifying tantric deities whose purpose is to wake up and scare us into a more enlightened or heightened consciousness. We have the marketplace, the Interzone, where all realities meet in "consociational" time. We are perpetually inside these zones ourselves. Literally, psychologically. A recent time crossing into US virtual space in Toronto at the Toronto airport—surveillance, scans, another photo taken. Baggage rechecked. Taken aside for a pat-down whenever I've been abroad and am coming "home."

And further prescience: palpable addiction and drug sickness everywhere in the world, continuing AIDS epidemics, EBOLA, the *psy ops* played out on all our psyches, the psychological suffering of so many—raped, plundered, starving, and displaced. We have myriad "ghosted" bodies—emanating out of the eternal war scenarios, suicides, broken lives and broken neurological pathways. Amputees. A Bosch-like intensity. Intricacies of surreal body parts: animal with human, experiments of genetic hybrids, sheep and mouse cloning and the like, transplants of all kinds, the torture of the animal, human/metal cyborgian hybrids or advanced robotic weaponry, the drones and reapers. We have the euphemism and lies of "Operation Enduring Freedom," "Shock and Awe," "Clean Air Act," or "refined interrogation techniques" or "disposition matrix" (kill list), which amplify words as killer viruses. We have wild boys who resemble kids in the slums of South America and Africa. Gangs going wild on drugs. Thuggish murders of the women of the maquiladoras in Mexico. We have the endless brutal Mafia scenarios—Russian, Balkan, Chinese—and Mafia scenarios in our own political system. We have the slow drip and dull hum of media control invading the fabric of our thinking, its powerful inflection and influence on our lives. We have the World Wide Web spying on our lives. NSA monitoring cellphones, whistleblowers in lockdown. We live horrors of troubled medical zones, where hospital care is menacing, dangerous, even murderous. Kill or cure? We live inside skulls of empty space/time—impermanence fueled with perpetual craving. We continue to hallucinate the enemy, creating monsters of our weird warring god realm sensibility surrounded by hell realms and hungry ghost worlds of all kinds conditioned by an "algebra of need." Pampered privileged god realms too that dine on pleasure until the seat gets hot and the body starts to rot. Planet degradation and dysfunction that mirrors degradation of bodies—the perpetual control mechanisms and the ongoing paranoid conspiracies, real or imagined. Who works for whom? A vivid troubling landscape sometimes front and center, sometimes in the foreground, sometimes on the fringe, in which we find ourselves trapped in states of denial as we are parodied, caricatured, allegorized. As if in defense we make it art, so that we can really see our condition, which is a samsaric disjunction, a schizoid reality, disconnected and under perpetual "control." William S. Burroughs was a seer, who put his own body through rounds of addiction, who lived as a homosexual and an addict under police-state regimes of suppression and control. He was always out, and he was always so much further "out" as an experimental writer than anyone else.

To put it simply: Burroughs' visionary writing—his generative imagination—frequently comes to mind these dark days, as if he invented this post-postmodern dystopic "set" we find ourselves in. I meditate on his landscapes, his interzones, his charnel grounds, and I appreciate his clear-eyed, dispassionate, almost clinical anthropological gaze into what constitutes, de-constitutes, and reconstitutes our complicated realities. He destabilizes and investigates our humanity and foregrounds our fluid, transmigrating identity. It is a spiritual work he practices. Waking the world to itself. The practice of the cosmic mirror.

This, in my humble view, trumps his misogyny.

I knew William Burroughs for twenty-five years and would call him friend. He was a mentor in particular ways. He was a poetic godfather to my son, Ambrose. I observed him at work, in productive stages of his writing life; I was privy to his classes at Naropa, and I was influenced by his methods. Experiments of Attention, as I call them. *Go out, take a wall. Observe anything blue. Make a mental list. Also notice what you notice and then what that resembles (the pictures!) and where your mind travels. You are mailing a card to Paris, you can see Paris. Someone says "San Francisco" and you have an immediate picture in the mind even if you have never been there. You see a lady with blue hair who reminds you of your great aunt Matilda. Come back, write down your list and the associations as well.* His passage in spates of teaching for the Jack Kerouac School of Disembodied Poetics at Naropa University was extremely generative; we were a familial haven for him. He adored Allen. They had a long history, having been lovers and surviving a difficult history and were consummated friends. Allen Ginsberg was one of the greatest champions of his writing, for many years.

William was working on *Cities of The Red Night* (1981). He was a disciplined writer. He gave me my first and last gun lesson. His son, Billy, was living in Colorado as well, and Billy was embraced by the Naropa community and supported through his liver transplant. He and his father had a complicated, painfully, tragically fraught relationship, yet I watched William weep profusely at Billy's suffering, and specifically when he was in a week-long coma. We cooked meals in William's little apartment. Many celebrities passed through our "temporary autonomous zone." William taught Shakespeare's *Troilus & Cressida* (1609), a supremely modern text with its scathing Thersites figure, who spoke with the tongue of Burroughs. A pox on both the houses. Or pimp Panderus, another character from the Trojan War's Interzone.

Images fix you in certain locales, and invoke myriad routines, he would tell us. *They talk, too. Use them.*

I had first met William formally at a party on 57th Street in New York City in 1974 hosted by poet Bill Berkson and was seated next to this formidable *éminence grise*. We talked about control, making tape recordings in a crowd, about what later evolved as "sousveillence," as opposed to "surveillance" (how the writer was empowered), about the book *African Genesis* (Ardrey 1961), and travel—I had recently been in South America. And other subjects he touched on in *The Job* (1969), which were alarming from a feminine perspective. I had just read this book, a collection of interviews conducted by Daniel Odier that is most cited for instances of Burroughs' misogyny. John Giorno (a close friend of William) and I had been

Burroughs with Anne Waldman, Allen Ginsberg, photograph, Boulder, CO, 1984.
Courtesy of the Allen Ginsberg Estate.

performing our poetry in Central Park earlier that day with films by avant-garde filmmaker Warren Sonbert. I was nervous but not intimidated. John introduced us.

From *The Job*:

> "I think they [women] were a basic mistake, and the whole dualistic universe evolved from this error."
>
>   "I think love is a virus. I think love is a con put down by the female sex." (Burroughs, in Odier 1969: 116, 46)

Odier references and asks about women in Burroughs' books. Mary in *The Soft Machine* (1961) who eats the genitals of Johnny whom she's just hanged. Or the constipated American Housewife who is afraid of the mix master. "In the words of one of a great misogynist's plain Mr. Jones, in Conrad's *Victory* [1915], 'Women are a perfect curse' I think they were a basic mistake, and the whole dualistic universe evolved from this error. Women are no longer essential to reproduction" (113). He also references frogs being reproduced from single cells and how a man's intestine might be produced from the nucleus of cell lining. And men might birth children from their assholes.

I have never been an apologist for William's moral lapses or misogynistic statements, which in their extremity—particularly, in the context of *The Job*—I still consider crackpot, weird, ugly, and repellant. But they never distracted me from the greater mastery of the work. But I also saw over the years that these views were never totally fixed or solid and were not consistent or dominant in the writing or in his life. His male characters—or "presenters"—come under equal fire, scrutiny, not as persons, but as types, stand-ins—part of his allegory, his satire, and his social commentary.

These sharp views of the 1960s had shifted by the time we met. "I have often said that it is not women *per se*, but the dualism of the male-female equation, that I consider a mistake" (Burroughs 1984). His goal was not the occlusion of women any longer. He spoke of the sexes fusing into one organism. He was generally misanthropic rather than exclusively misogynistic.

I was spurred in part to these more personal notes remembering the instance where my friend—the very radical and provocative feminist Andrea Dworkin—threatened a mass boycott and demonstration when I was bringing William to give a reading at the St. Marks Poetry Project in NYC. Andrea and I had lunch and I talked her down based on an inspired critique that supported the writing. I told her what I had observed—I'd been sitting in on classes William was teaching at CUNY—and I expressed how liberating he was as a writer. The notion of censoring or shutting down Burroughs seemed anathema at that time—and would be at any time—and I think in a perverse way. I went out of my way to champion—not the life or the person, who I was really just getting to know—but the work to which I was drawn. Particularly, the *Nova Trilogy* from which I felt a social/political activist "call." An inspiration to work with "montage." And cut-up.

In one of her texts, Dworkin links Burroughs to the Marquis de Sade speaking of his rapist frenzy, which is rarely in his texts, if ever—if ever rape of women . . . she had it wrong. But I could certainly understand her rage and the citing of Burroughs' accidental killing of his wife Joan Vollmer, years before, as a moral crisis to respond to. Women felt he had not been duly punished enough for this "crime." But censor his work? Never. Not on my watch.

Regarding his relationships with women one cites Ilse Klapper, who he sometimes spoke of—green-card marriage of convenience, but clearly a friend for whom he had respect and compassion. Joan, his wife, was brilliant, worldly, a complicated person, well read—one of the wittiest people he knew. William was comfortable with self-assured women who had proven themselves, not leaning on men. Women who were liberated, accomplished, could hold their own: Susan Sontag, Patti Smith, Laurie Anderson . . .

Sadly, not Karen Finley, who in her piece "Moral History" (1994–97) scrawled over a copy of *Naked Lunch*: "Burroughs you are no hero to me."

It's an interesting time for the Burroughs legacy, fifteen years into the new century. Ongoing debate on Joan's accidental death, the William Tell shooting and William's accountability and his light sentence in Mexico . . . irredeemable? A young woman at the Jack Kerouac School at Naropa recently wrote her Master's thesis on Joan Vollmer, both a feminist defense and creative piece written in the presumed voice of Joan.

Some are also still troubled by the homoerotics of the Burroughs' old Nike ad (1994) . . . his gaze at the young players—the unspoken complications of sports, power, and homosexuality, not to mention sports addiction . . . combined with the whole panoply of sports ads in general with their sperm-bursting cans of beer. What is Burroughs supposed to represent here? A voyeur? A difficult trope—who is he to these worlds anyway? Hardly a fan of football. Where is our *homme invisible* man, this *éminence grise* as a commercial trope now? Regulated to pale movie renditions? Does his ghost sell sneakers? Controversies continue alongside the work itself, which is kept thankfully in print and continues to be studied and critiqued, and has had greater intellectual textual response overseas for decades with the likes of Gilles Deleuze and Félix Guattari. The bar has been raised in regard to the intellectual and linguistic power of the writing itself.

Recent portrayals of Burroughs keep his unmistakable voice in culture's sound tracks . . . I am relieved to see that his iteration as a cultural icon is not occluding the writing. It is still odd to see depictions of him on the silver screen. Viggo Mortensen in *On the Road* (directed by Walter Salles, 2012) does an aspirational job, and Ben Foster is also salient in *Kill Your Darlings* (directed by John Krokidas, 2013) to say the least of an ethically ambiguous film. *Who speaks and acts? It is always a multiplicity.*

Deleuze and Guattari discuss Burroughs in a text called *A Thousand Plateaus*: "Why have we kept our names? Out of habit, purely out of habit. To make ourselves unrecognizable in turn. To render imperceptible, not ourselves, but what makes us act, feel, and think. Also because it's nice to talk like everybody else, to say the sun rises, when everybody knows it's only a manner of speaking. To reach the point where one no longer says I, but the point where it is no longer of any importance whether one says I. We are no longer ourselves. Each will know his own. We have been aided, inspired, multiplied" (1987, 3). This is one of the keys to Burroughs they say: not to reach the point where one no longer says "I," but to reach the point where it is no longer of any importance whether one says I. The set has changed. We are in a reality that does not value imagination's conservative identity or ownership of experience as we are no longer stable ourselves. Who are we?

"Deleuze and Guattari would say that 'Burroughs' is no longer just the name of an author, a celebrity, or an artist; it is the name, rather, of a set of potentials, an effect that propagates itself from medium to medium by the force of its difference, bringing into contact incompatible functions, incommensurable concepts, and unrelated materials. Even when Burroughs is no longer able to serve as the focus for this force, it will continue to reverberate, indefatigably sounding its critical imperative: listen to my last words everywhere" (Murphy 1998, 232). Something about the patient etherized on the table? Welcome to the Anthropocene—the geological time under the iron hand of man that Burroughs predicted everywhere with his preternatural insight and imagination and investigation. "Human beings can't be expected to act like human beings under unhuman circumstances" (Allen Ginsberg, quoted in Long 1975, 9).

There's the idea from French critical theorist Foucault that the body is the last site of resistance (see Pickett 1996). But what happens when the body's mind goes beyond itself? When the consciousness travels—astral projects—move in dreams? What are the limits of control in these instances? His work continues to disrupt comfortable narratives including the master narrative, patriarchal and normative in terms of its form and content and sense of history—literary or otherwise. Burroughs' work as unstable consciousness finds itself restlessly outside modern and postmodern parameters. And the dream, the timeless dream, has been a source for much of his writing, defying strictures about a place in the "canon." He is more a scientist of mind.

I want to close with a personal investigation—from his dream book *My Education*, published in 1995, two years before he died. The title of the collection arose from this dream:

> Airport. Like a high school play, attempting to convey a spectral atmosphere. One desk on stage, a gray woman behind the desk with the cold waxen face of an intergalactic bureaucrat . . . Standing to one side of the desk are three men, grinning with joy at their prospective destinations. When I present myself at the desk, the woman says, "You haven't had your education yet." (Burroughs 1995, 1).

> A big party. Ian is there and Anne Waldman, the Naropa Mother, You need a place to stay? You got a dose of clap? Take all your troubles to the Naropa Mother. She gives all the satisfaction. (Ibid., 26)

He goes on to describe being junk-sick, needing a fix. A shot of Jade that turns to stone in his body. And the dream turns to nightmare.

I have been flattered to make it into a Burroughs' dream, into his psyche, and also, for a time, resisted these lines. Did I need to reconstruct, deconstruct this identity of Naropa Mother? I cut up the dream. I am both a character—a principle in his script as it were—and a figure of control or archetypal matriarchy. But the dream encouraged me to continue as long as I can, to be aware the bigger arc of the Naropa experiment in radical poetries and poetic community, where we can enter each other's psychic and dream spaces, and I decided to embrace the dream's assurance that "she gives all the satisfaction." When we founded the university, we founded a place very much on feminine principle—from the Buddhist perspective that relates to atmosphere and environment—what is a called *prajna* in Sanskrit—or womb-like wisdom. So I chose to investigate my identity within one of *prajna* and investigate the mind that posited as such.

"Do you realize you are the only woman in the room?" William taunted playfully as he came toward me after a long night of talk and drink and smoke. In many instances, when all these alternative cultures and communities and lineages and affinities were coalescing and trembling and forming and reforming, I was often the only woman in the room and that urged me to open up all the doors to all the women in the projects I would help create and build. But I often found that I was one of the few women—certainly in high school, and in college, and later in small poetry circles—checking out the Burroughsian landscape who was deeply into his work. It seemed for a time I was the only woman in the room of his work.

ANNE WALDMAN has authored over fifty books of poetry, collaboration, and critical work. Her most recent book is *Trickster Feminism* (Penguin, 2018). She is editor of *The Beat Book* (Shambhala) and co-editor of *Beats at Naropa* (Coffee House Press).

REFERENCES

Ardrey, Robert. 1961. *African Genesis: A Personal Investigation into the Animal Origins and Nature of Man*. New York: Atheneum.
Burroughs, William S. 1961. *The Soft Machine*. Paris: Olympia Press.
———. 1981. *Cities of the Red Night*. New York: Viking Press.
———. 1984. "Dead Roads." *New York Review of Books*, July 19. http://www.nybooks.com /articles/1984/07/19/dead-roads/.
———. 1995. *My Education: A Book of Dreams*. New York: Viking.
Deleuze, Gilles, and Félix Guattari. 1987. *A Thousand Plateaus*. Minneapolis: University of Minnesota Press.
Long, Steve. 1975. "New Light on Leary." *Berkeley Barb*, April 25–May 7, 9, 20.
Murphy, Timothy S. 1998. *Wising Up the Marks: The Amodern William Burroughs*. Berkeley: University of California Press.
Odier, Daniel. 1969. *The Job: Interviews with William S. Burroughs*. New York: Penguin.
Pickett, Brent L. 1996. "Foucault and the Politics of Resistance." *Polity* 28 (4): 445–66.

Root Face

Inevitably, this anthology is only going to scratch the surface of Burroughs' oeuvre. That is partly the point of this anthology: to show how much detective work, as well as archival and editorial labor, would be necessary to provide a full account of even those materials currently available for perusal (not hidden away in private holdings). In a more fundamental sense, this anthology also brings into relief how no conclusive anthology of Burroughs' work could be possible.

As Burroughs put it, "all my books are essentially one book" (Miles, 279). From his first conception of a "word hoard," Burroughs always imagined and discussed his work as an organism undergoing metamorphosis, each published novel or collage a different port of entry, a mosaic of perspectives onto intersection points of power. By showcasing the archive, we only bring into relief just how many holes remain for most readers approaching Burroughs. If anything, it has become yet another a tantalizing aura surrounding Burroughs' work, that we always fall short of capturing the heterogeneous nature of his failures and his accomplishments.

We would be remiss, however, to not discuss Burroughs' experiments as a painter throughout his life. For Burroughs, painting and drawing became an extension of cutting up text; calligraphy offered an entry point for Burroughs (and Gysin) into the space where words became images and vice versa. Burroughs had experimented with making "art" since the 1960s, but it was not until late in his life, as captured in a series of gallery exhibitions and Robert A. Sobieszek's *Ports of Entry: William S. Burroughs and the Arts* (1996), that Burroughs began to hang up not just his scissors, but his pen. Especially in his notorious shotgun paintings, where the aged writer would shoot paint at wooden boards, his art works, like his writing, functioned by puncturing holes into and breaking his medium, to disclose hidden interconnections, while sounding the echoes of what remains irrevocable and irrecoverable.

In his late works, especially his confessional writings on cats and lemurs in, respectively, *The Cat Inside* (1986) and *Ghost of Chance* (1991), Burroughs explored through words the themes and perspectives that would become central to his art. In the following art work, "Root Face," an ink and photo-collage on a sketchbook page, created in 1987, Burroughs has collaged an image in the center of his painting that is itself a photograph of another painting. Yuri Zupancic notes that the work depicts a part-plant, part-human mutant akin to the "humanoid mandrakes" in *Cities of the Red Night* (1981). In one of the novel's stranger scenes, the character Jimmy asks whether a mandrake is a "screamer" and "What happens if we hang its green ass, roots and all?" (1981, 234). He receives the following ominous response, one that can act as an annotation for this work of art: "Son, you'd be doing what mankind has always trembled to do. You'd be upsetting the balance between the animal and the vegetable kingdom. He'd scream the planet apart. It would be the last scream" (234).

If this anthology can't provide the last word, or scream on Burroughs, perhaps the closing note for this collection, besides this humble painting, appears in Burroughs' earliest published work, his terse, autobiographical novel, *Junky* (1953). After attempting to create the book's glossary of underworld slang, Burroughs eventually abandoned the task by invoking Wittgenstein's final postulation in *Tractatus Logico-Philosophicus* (1922), "Whereof one cannot speak, thereof one must be silent." In his appendix to his sociological account of the underworld's argot, Burroughs concluded: "A final glossary, therefore, cannot be made of words whose intentions are fugitive" (*Junky* 2012, 133).

—*AWC*

Root Face, William S. Burroughs, 1987. (4 × 6, 1 leaf, facsimile). Contributed by Yuri Zupancic of the Burroughs Estate. Copyright © by William Burroughs, used by permission of The Wylie Agency LLC.

INDEX

Page numbers in *italics* refer to illustrations.

274–75; fold-in method, 19, 20, 24, 325–26, 369, 372, 381n10, 381n15; French influence, 65, 278, 311; and gender, 386; guns and, 59–60, 134–35, 185, 411; and the hieroglyph, 324, 329, 331; on Hollywood, 106; as homosexual, xii, 116, 178, 231, 268, 279, 289, 354–55, 388, 398, 410, 411, 414; on homosexuality, 398, 414; humor, 64–65, 68, 368, 394, 401; imperialism and, 65 (*see also* imperialism); "interlanguage," 376, 381n26; and Joan Vollmer's death (*see* Vollmer, Joan: death of); in Kansas (*see* Kansas); legacy of, 14, 19, 28, 69, 82, 311, 396, 414; letters of, 63, 119, 120, 179–81, 192, 233, 274; limericks, 112; limited authorship, 344, 346; "limits of control," 409, 415; live readings, 103, 387; on love, 388; magic of art and literature, 262, 327, 331; marriage and, 392–93; material history of, 307, 309, 311, 313, 316; mediation and, 98, 368, 373; metamorphosis, 23, 417; and Mexico, 191, 193, 235, 414 (*see also* Mexico); and Midwest, 16, 60, 63, 189; Midwestern accent of, 99, 108; misanthropy of, 396, 413; misogyny of, xvi, 20–21, 43, 61–62, 159, 220, 356, 386, 388, 399–401, 409, 411, 413 (*see also* Vollmer, Joan: death of); musical interests, 61, 98, 103, 325; in music videos, 98; New York City, xvi, xvii, xviii, 3, 16, 60, 61, 70, 122, 123, 191, 193, 200, 208–9, 257, 309, 354, 411–12; Nike ad campaign, xix, 414; nostalgia, 196, 199–200; painting, xviii, 68, 325–26, 417; Paris, 16, 33–35, 38, 191, 193, 196; personae of, 60, 63, 91, 98, 100–103, 107–9, 159, 280, 386, 391, 408; photography, 4, 35, 67–68, 71, 90, 172, 210n9, 325; photomontage, xiv, 19, 38, 44, 238, 282, 318; politics and, 65, 262, 264–65, 269, 271, 394–95; on pornography, 354–56; postmodernism and, 6, 12, 67–68, 182, 223, 226, 233, 234, 236, 238, 239, 398, 410, 415; queer aesthetic, 73; racism and, 216, 220, 224; relationship with mother, 59, 400–401 (*see also* Burroughs, Laura Lee); relationship with son, 12, 23–24, 411 (*see also* Burroughs, William Seward, III); response to critics, 14, 15, 50, 73–74; revolution and, 5, 8n1, 28, 31, 61, 87, 153, 177, 271, 293–94, 372 (*see also* Chinese cultural revolution); Rimbaud and, 18, 274, 282–83, 286–90; rock music, 61, 88–89; satire,18, 21, 181, 229, 244, 257, 413; science fiction and, 41, 63, 87, 143, 189, 202, 227, 244, 270, 312, 327, 370–71; Scientology, xiv, xv, xvi, 5, 14, 20, 59, 60, 64, 139, 151, 333–34, 381n25 (see also *Ticket that Exploded, The*: Scientology in); scrapbooking, 44, 67, 173, 184, 189, 215, 238, 282; screenplays, 354–56; sexism of/and, 20, 165, 387, 391; the sexual and, 289–90, 355; shotgun paintings, 21, 417; and the smile, 374, 381n23; sound recording and, 103, 110n1, 373, 411; and spoken-word, 98, 102, 103; spontaneity, 71, 84, 92, 127, 151, 191, 300, 340; subversive style of, 220–22, 231–33; in Tangier, 23, 54, 59–60, 63, 69, 80, 115, 119–21, 123–24, 180, 191, 192, 193, 196, 198–99, 232, 248; in Tangier's gay community, 59–60; tape recorder experiments, xv, xvi, xvii, xviii, 68, 327–28, 373, 411; teaching and, xvi, 82, 389, 411, 413; television

appearances of, 98; "Throat Microphone Experiment," 103; as transnational, 168, 278; trauma and, 60; Ugly American, 18, 29, 43, 55, 281 (see also *Naked Lunch* [novel]; *Nova Express*); upbringing of, 55, 59, 192–93, 208, 387, 394; use of color, 274–75, 289–90; on the virus, 114 (*see also* language as virus); vocal fry, 99–100, 103, 107; voice of, 97–109, 373; William Fawcett and, xii; "word hoard," 44, 215, 417; word virus theory, 283; writing discipline, 71, 388, 411; "written image," 324; xenophobia, 220

Burroughs, William Seward, I (paternal grandfather), xi, 13, 193–94, 210n1

Burroughs, William Seward, III (son), xiii, xiv, xvi–xvii, 12, 13, 23, 25, 27, 68, 69, 200, 384, 398, 399, 411; death, xvii; "Metamorphosis," 12, 23

Burroughs Adding Machine, xi, 194; company, 13, 29

Burroughs Corporation, xi. *See also* Burroughs Adding Machine: company

Burroughs File, The (Burroughs), 9

Burroughs Papers, 41, 44, 316

Burroughs: The Movie (Brookner), 102

Bush, George W., 28

Cage, John, 81, 91

Calder, John, 315

Call Me Burroughs (spoken word album by Burroughs), xv, 110n1

Call Me Burroughs: A Life (Miles), xi, 14, 62, 306, 381n21, 387

Campbell, Duncan, 349n6

Camus, Albert, 281

Cape, Jonathan, 315

capitalism, 34, 90, 91, 162–64, 170, 220, 221, 224–25, 232, 235; Burroughs' opposition to, 14, 29, 40, 54; Henry Luce and, 31

Caponi, Gena Dagel, 123

Capote, Truman, 393

Carjat, Étienne, 286–88

Carlson, Jon, 123

Carmichael, Hoagy, 61

Carr, Lucien, xi, xii, xiii, 59, 108, 116–17; David Kammerer murder, xiii, 116

Carrie (King), 314

Carson, Kit, 266–67

Cary, Alice, 164

Cassady, Neal, 179

Cat Inside, The (Burroughs), xviii, 122, 417

Catlett, Mallory, 10

CBGB, 82, 85

Céline, Louis-Ferdinand, 65, 234, 278, 291

Chandler, Raymond, 147

Chappaqua (Rooks), 105

Charters, Ann, 159, 391

Cheney, Dick, 28, 409

Chicago Review (magazine), 172

Childs, Marquis, 197

Kaddish (Ginsberg), 394

Kafka, Franz, 122, 291

Kammerer, David, xi, xii–xiii, 21, 116, 404

Kane, Art, 206–7

Kansas, 62–63, 69; Burroughs moves to, xviii, 263, 272n2; Grauerholz moves to, xvii; Lawrence, Kansas, 16, 70, 117–19, 130, 151

Kant, Immanuel, 380n2

Kaplan, Amy, 162, 164, 168–70

Kaun, Axel, 326

Kaye, Lenny, 93

Kerouac, Jack, xiii, xiv, 15, 36, 107, 110n1, 115, 116–18, 119, 120, 127, 178–79, 180, 182, 262, 265, 272n1, 279, 280, 313, 386, 392, 397, 403n4; biography, 63; death of, xv; and Kammerer murder, xiii; scholarship on, 389; sexism of, 391; sound recording and, 97

Kerridge, Richard, 346, 348

Kessie, Jack, 199

Kessler, George, 196

Khrushchev, Nikita, 369

Killers, The (Siodmak), 117

Kill Your Darlings (Krokidas), 99, 108, 116, 414

Kimball, Roger, 402n3

King, Alexander, 135

King, Grace, 164

King, Stephen, 314

Kinsey, Alfred, 139

Klapper, Ilse, xii, 135, 413

Klein, David, 206

Klein, Naomi, 182, 222

Knickerbocker, Conrad, 169, 190, 207, 208, 209

Knight, Brenda, 159

Koch, Charles and David H., 394, 409

Koestenbaum, Wayne, 115, 120

Korzybski, Alfred, 151, 328, 333

Kristeva, Julia, 234

Krokidas, John, 99, 116, 414

Kurosawa, Akira, 263

Kuttner, Henry, 370, 381n12

Lacan, Jacques, 312

Laibach, 229–30

Landesman, Jay, 206–7, 210n10

Landscape with the Fall of Icarus (Bruegel), 318

language as virus, 395, 283, 410. See also William, Burroughs, S.: on the virus

LA Plays Itself (Halsted), 355

Last Gentleman, The (Percy), 197

Last Museum, The (Gysin), 90

Last of the Mohicans, The (Cooper), 228

Last Times, The (underground newspaper), 72n2

Last Words (Burroughs), xix, 280, 405

Last Words of Dutch Schultz, The (Burroughs), xvi, 354, 404

Latour, Bruno, 222

Laughlin, James, 38

Lautréamont, Comte de, 38, 46n23, 234

Lavie, Nillie, 140

Lawrence, T. E., 225

Lear, Edward, 112

Leary, Timothy, 39, 45, 80, 271, 282

Le Corbusier, 207

Lee, Ivy (uncle), xi, 195, 200, 201; "Poison Ivy" Lee, 13, 29

Lee, James Wideman (maternal grandfather), 190, 193, 210n1

Lees, Andrew, 142

Leibniz, Gottfried Wilhelm, 139

Lemaire, Gérard-Georges, 90

Lennon, John, 126

Les Chants de Maldoror (Lautréamont), 234

Les Fleurs du mal (Baudelaire), 233–34, 235, 236

Le Spleen de Paris (Baudelaire), 295n3

Let It Come Down (Bowles), 225

Letters of William S. Burroughs, 1945–1959, The (Harris), xix, 142, 307, 310

lettrists, 4, 34

Levertov, Denise, 159

LIFE (magazine), xiv, 6, 33–38, 42–43, 50, 52, 206–7, 239. See also Luce, Henry

"Limits of Control, The" (Burroughs), 91

Lionberger, Isaac, 196

literary canon, 10, 159, 161, 300, 308, 316, 415; misogyny in, 391–92

Literary Outlaw: The Life and Times of William S. Burroughs (Morgan), xi

literary regionalism, 16, 158–62, 164, 166, 168–70

London, xiv, xv, xvi, 16, 60–61, 62, 64, 70, 124, 192, 193, 198, 200, 215, 324, 343, 345, 349n7, 384

Lone Survivor (Berg), 409

Loranger, Carol, 244, 340

Lord Jim (Conrad), 381n15

Los Alamos, 138

Los Alamos Nuclear Laboratory, 136

Los Alamos Ranch School, xii, 16, 136, 138, 192–93

Lost and Found: The CUNY Poetics Document Initiative, 10

Lost Art of Ah Pook Is Here: Images from the Graphic Novel (McNeill), 9

Lotringer, Sylvère, 81, 86–87, 89–92

Love, Courtney, 107

Lowe, Steven, 147, 388

Lowry, Malcolm, 209

Luce, Henry, 6, 13, 18, 29–32, 34, 36, 38–45, 46n26, 47n45, 50, 51, 221–22, 238; "The American Century," 6, 28, 36, 45, 50, 221, 238; TIME-LIFE-Fortune, 18, 21, 29–33, 40–41, 44, 221, 238; TIME-LIFE media empire, 6, 13, 31, 34, 45, 381n17. See also cut-up (method): temporality and

Lukács, György, 221

Lunch, Lydia, 94, 122

Lydenberg, Robin, 100, 220, 339, 341, 347, 349n8, 368, 372, 378, 395

Pastoureau, Michel, 382n29
pastiche, 208, 231, 289
Paul Bowles: Romantic Savage (Caponi), 123
Paul Bowles: The Complete Outsider (Warnow and Weinreich), 392
Pélieu, Claude, 342
Penguin (publisher), 307, 309
Percy, Walker, 197, 210n3
Perloff, Marjorie, 280
Perse, St.-John, 289
"Personal Magnetism" (Burroughs), 192
Petits Poèmes en prose (Baudelaire), 234
Picture of Dorian Gray, The (Wilde), 234
Place of Dead Roads, The (Burroughs), xviii, 18, 135, 150, 262–65, 266, 267–72, 272n1, 399
Plath, Sylvia, 399
"Playback from Eden to Watergate" (Burroughs), 19, 318
Playboy (magazine), 199–200, 208
Plymell, Charles, 68, 72n2
Poe, Edgar Allen, 121, 141–42, 233, 235
poète maudit, 278
Poetry Project at St Mark's, 387, 413
Poets & Writers Inc., 86
Police (band), 61, 92
Pol Pot, 69
Pool K III, The (Bowles), 115, 123–25
Portable Jack Kerouac, The (Charters), 391
Port of Saints (Burroughs), xvi, xvii
Portman, Michael, 120
Portrait of a Lady, The (James), 392
Ports of Entry (retrospective), xix, 93
Ports of Entry: William S. Burroughs and the Arts (Burroughs and Sobieszek), 9, 275, 417
postmodernism, 6, 12, 162, 182, 223, 236; literature, 221, 239. *See also* Burroughs, William S.: postmodernism and
poststructuralism, 311, 312
Pound, Ezra, 115, 140, 329
Pounds, Wayne, 269
Prance, Sir Ghillean, 135
Prasad, Aarathi, 140
Presley, Frances, 349n4
Priestley, J. B., 142
"Priest" They Called Him, The (Burroughs and Cobain), 115, 117–18, 122, 127
Prisoner of Love (Genet), 279, 291–94
Project for the New American Century (right-wing think tank), 28, 30
Project Y, 136
Proust, Marcel, 65, 142, 278
Pryse, Marjorie, 16, 158, 164, 166, 169
punk, 15, 61, 64, 81–82, 85, 87; attitude, 86; renaissance punk, 84
Pynchon, Thomas, 234

Quantrill, William Clarke, 263–64
Queen (band), 122
Queer, xiii, xviii, 16, 20, 43, 54, 60, 132, 159, 166, 233, 235, 248, 272n1, 291, 295n12, 373, 384; publication history, 306, 308, 310–11, 314. *See also Ticket that Exploded, The*: comparison to *Queer*
queerness, 81, 85, 288, 291; and science-fiction, 87

Radcliffe, Daniel, 108
"Radical Landscapes: Experiment and Environment in Contemporary Poetry" (Tarlo), 342–43
Ramones, 92
Rat Subterranean News (underground newspaper), 184
realism, 158, 160
"reality film, the," 369, 371, 380n6
Reality Studio, 22, 172, 369
RealityStudio.org, 10, 72n1
"Recycles: The Eco-Ethical Poetics of Found Text in Contemporary Poetry" (Tarlo), 343
Reedy, William Marion, 196
Reich, Wilhelm, 14, 139, 377
REM (band), 93
"Remembering Jack Kerouac" (Burroughs), 327
Retaking the Universe: William S. Burroughs in the Age of Globalization (Schneiderman), 9, 220–21, 305
Review, The (literary journal), 192
Revised Boy Scout Manual, The (Burroughs), 8n1, 9, 31, 262
Reynolds, James, 189
Richards, Keith, 87–89, 93
Rimbaud, Arthur, 10, 18–19, 234, 278–79, 280, 281, 294–95, 300, 330. *See also* Burroughs, William S.: Rimbaud and
Robinson, Edward, 342
Rockefeller (company), 13, 14, 29, 54–55
Rodgers, Richard, 126
Rogue Archives (de Kosnik), 10
Rolling Stone (magazine), 57
Rolling Stones, (band), 61, 87–89
Romance (Conrad and Ford), 189
Romanticism, 255; Burroughs' ideas of authorship, 309; and genius, 15; Romantic poets, 234
Rooks, Conrad, 105
Roosevelt, Franklin, 182
"Roosevelt after Inauguration" (Burroughs), xv, 17, 177, 181
Rosler, Martha, 238
Rossenbaum, Bob, 399
Rotmil, Paul, 133
Rowland, F. Sherwood, 139
Rub Out the Words (Burroughs), 5, 47n39, 120

Saarinen, Eero, 200
Said, Edward, 231. *See also* orientalism
Saint Genet (Sartre), 292